The Evolution of Psychotherapy

The Third Conference

The Faculty

FRONT ROW (from left to right): Lynn Hoffman, Albert Ellis, Lenore Walker, Thomas Szasz, Cloé Madanes, Claudia Black, Miriam Polster, Peggy Papp, Mary Goulding, Olga Silverstein, Margaret Singer, and Stella Chess. MIDDLE ROW: Eugene Gendlin, Otto Kernberg, Judd Marmor, Joseph Wolpe, William Glasser, Jeffrey Zeig, Salvador Minuchin, Alexander Lowen, Irvin Yalom, Aaron Beck, and Erving Polster. BACK ROW: Arnold Lazarus, Donald Meichenbaum, James Hillman, James Bugental, Paul Watzlawick, Francine Shapiro, James Masterson, Joseph LoPiccolo, Ernest Rossi, and Jay Haley.

The Evolution of Psychotherapy
The Third Conference

———◆———

Edited by

Jeffrey K. Zeig, Ph.D.

Brunner/Mazel, *Publishers* • New York

Library of Congress Cataloging-in-Publication Data
The Evolution of psychotherapy : the third conference / edited by
  Jeffrey K. Zeig.
    p.   cm.
    Papers from the 1995 Evolution of Psychotherapy Conference
sponsored by the Milton H. Erickson Foundation and held during 1995
at Las Vegas, Nev.
    Includes bibliographical references.
    ISBN 0-87630-813-2 (hardcover : alk. paper)
    1. Psychotherapy—Congresses.   I. Zeig, Jeffrey K.
II. Evolution of Psychotherapy Conference (1995 : Las Vegas, Nev.)
RC475.5.E964   1997
616.89'14—dc20   96-36789
                                                          CIP

Published by
BRUNNER/MAZEL, INC.
19 Union Square West
New York, New York 10003

Manufactured in the United States of America

10 9 8 7 6 5 4 3 2 1

This book is dedicated to

Roxanna Erickson Klein, R.N., M.S.
for years of friendship and
for steadfastly being there from the inception.

Contents

SECTION III.   CONTEMPORARY APPROACHES

SECTION IV.   ERICKSONIAN APPROACHES

SECTION V.   EXPERIENTIAL APPROACHES

SECTION VI.   FAMILY THERAPISTS

SECTION VII.   PHILOSOPHICAL APPROACHES

SECTION VIII.   STATE OF THE ART

About the Milton H. Erickson Foundation

The Milton H. Erickson Foundation, Inc., is a federal nonprofit corporation.

It was formed to promote and advance the contributions made to the health sciences by the late Milton H. Erickson, M.D., during his long and distinguished career. The Foundation is dedicated to training health and mental health professionals. Strict eligibility requirements are maintained for attendance at our training events or to receive our educational materials. The Milton H. Erickson Foundation, Inc., does not discriminate on the basis of race, color, national or ethnic origin, religion, age, sex, or physical challenge. Members of the Board of Directors of The Milton H. Erickson Foundation are Jeffrey K. Zeig, Ph.D.; Roxanna Erickson Klein, R.N., M.S.; Elizabeth M. Erickson, B.A.; and J. Charles Theisen, M.A., M.B.A., J.D.

ELIGIBILITY

Training programs, the newsletter, audiotapes, and videotapes are available to professionals in health-related fields, including physicians, doctoral-level psychologists, podiatrists, and dentists who are qualified for membership in, or are members of, their respective professional organizations (e.g., AMA, APA, ADA). Activities of the Foundation also are open to professionals with graduate degrees from accredited institutions in areas related to mental health (e.g., MA, MS, MSN, MSW). Full-time graduate students in accredited programs in the above fields must supply a letter from their department, certifying their student status, if they wish to attend events, subscribe to the newsletter, or purchase tapes.

TRAINING OPPORTUNITIES

Our premier training event is the Evolution of Psychotherapy Conference, first organized in 1985 in Phoenix. It was hailed as a landmark conference in the history of psychotherapy. More than 7,200 professionals attended, making it the largest meeting ever held solely on the topic of psychotherapy.

Faculty included Aaron T. Beck, the late Bruno Bettelheim, the late Murray Bowen, Albert Ellis, Mary Goulding, the late Robert Goulding, Jay Haley, the late Ronald D. Laing, Arnold Lazarus, Cloé Madanes, Judd Marmor, James Masterson, the late Rollo May, Salvador Minuchin, Zerka Moreno, Erv Polster, Miriam Polster, the late Carl Rogers, Ernest Rossi, the late Virginia Satir, Thomas Szasz, Paul Watzlawick, the late Carl Whitaker, the late Lewis Wolberg, Joseph Wolpe, and Jeffrey Zeig.

In 1990, the Evolution Conference was held in Anaheim, California, with a similar faculty and also included James Bugental, William Glasser, James Hillman, the late Helen Singer Kaplan, Alexander Lowen, Donald Meichenbaum, and Mara Selvini Palazzoli. Keynote addresses were presented by Viktor Frankl and Betty Friedan. Almost 7,000 professionals attended.

The Erickson Foundation cosponsored the European Evolution of Psychotherapy Conference in July 1994 in Hamburg, Germany, with about 6,000 in attendance. The European Evolution Conference offered a faculty similar to previous Evolution meetings with the addition of Frankl, Eugene Gendlin, Klaus Grawe, Otto Kernberg, Adolf E. Meyer, Helm Stierlin, and Irv Yalom.

The 1995 Evolution of Psychotherapy Conference was held in Las Vegas with more than

6,500 registrants and also included on the faculty, a special section of State-of-the-Art contributions by Claudia Black, Stella Chess, Lynn Hoffman, Joseph LoPiccolo, Peggy Papp, Francine Shapiro, Olga Silverstein, Margaret Singer, and Lenore Walker. Gloria Steinem was the keynote speaker.

The Erickson Foundation organizes International Congresses on Ericksonian Approaches to Hypnosis and Psychotherapy. These meetings were held in Phoenix in 1980, 1983, 1986, 1992; in San Francisco in 1988; and in Los Angeles in 1994. The Los Angeles Congress commemorated the 15th Anniversary of The Milton H. Erickson Foundation. Each of the Congresses attracted between 1,000–2,000 attendees.

The Foundation organizes the multidisciplinary Brief Therapy Congresses. The first Brief Therapy Congress was held in 1988 in San Francisco and doubled as an Erickson Congress. In 1993, the Foundation sponsored the Brief Therapy Conference in Orlando, Florida. The 1995 Brief Therapy Conference is slated for December 11–15 in San Francisco. The Brief Therapy Conferences attracts 2,000 or more registrants.

The Foundation also organizes three and four-day national seminars. The four-day seminars are limited to approximately 450 attendees, and they emphasize skill development in Ericksonian hypnotherapy. The 1981, 1982, and 1984 seminars were held in San Francisco, Dallas, and Los Angeles, respectively. In 1989, The Foundation celebrated its 10th Anniversary with a training seminar in Phoenix. In 1995 and 1996, The Foundation sponsored three-day seminars in San Francisco and Dallas, respectively, on the topic of Sex and Intimacy, in which experts addressed the challenges of treating couples.

In addition, the Foundation sponsors five-day Intensive Training Programs, with Fundamental, Intermediate, and Advanced (supervision) levels held throughout the year in Phoenix. In Phoenix, the Foundation office is equipped with observation rooms and audio/video recording capabilities so that supervision can be provided. Also, Regional Workshops are held intermittently in various locations.

The Foundation's scope is international: It has sponsored and co-organized seminars and conferences in Germany, Mexico, and Brazil on brief therapy, family therapy, Ericksonian therapy and the evolution of psychotherapy. Congresses, Conferences, Seminars, Regional Workshops, and the Intensive programs are announced in the Foundation's newsletter.

ERICKSON ARCHIVES

In December 1980, the Foundation began collecting audiotapes, videotapes, and historical material on Dr. Erickson for the Erickson Archives. The goal is to have a central repository of historical material on Erickson. More than 300 hours of videotape and audiotape have been donated to the Foundation.

The Erickson Archives are available to interested and qualified professionals who wish to come to the Foundation to independently study the audiotapes and videotapes that are housed at the Foundation. There is a nominal charge for use of the Archives. Please call or write for further details and to make advance arrangements to view the Archives. Donations of historical materials to the Archives are welcome.

AUDIO AND VIDEO TRAINING TAPES

The Milton H. Erickson Foundation has available for purchase professionally recorded audiotapes from its meetings. Professionally produced videocassettes of one-hour clinical demonstrations by members of the faculty from the 1981, 1982, 1984, 1989, 1995, and 1996 Seminars and the 1983, 1986, 1988, 1992, and 1994 Erickson Congresses also can be purchased from the Foundation. Audiotapes and videocassettes from the 1985, 1990, 1994, and 1995 Evolution of Psychotherapy Conferences and the 1993 Brief Therapy Conference also are available from the Foundation.

AUDIOTAPES OF
MILTON H. ERICKSON, M.D.

The Erickson Foundation distributes tapes of lectures by Milton H. Erickson from the

1950s and 1960s when his voice was strong. Releases in our audiotape series are announced in the Newsletter.

TRAINING VIDEOTAPES FEATURING HYPNOTIC INDUCTIONS CONDUCTED BY MILTON H. ERICKSON, M.D.

The Process of Hypnotic Induction: A Training Videotape Featuring Inductions Conducted by Milton H. Erickson in 1964. Jeffrey K. Zeig, Ph.D., discusses the process of hypnotic induction and describes the microdynamics of techniques that Erickson used in his 1964 inductions. (Available in Japanese.)

Symbolic Hypnotherapy. Jeffrey K. Zeig, Ph.D., presents information on using symbols in psychotherapy and hypnosis. Segments of hypnotherapy conducted by Milton Erickson with the same subject on two consecutive days in 1978 are shown. Zeig discusses the microdynamics of Erickson's symbolic technique. Videotapes are available in all formats, and in American and foreign standards. For information on purchasing tapes, contact the Erickson Foundation.

PUBLICATIONS OF THE MILTON H. ERICKSON FOUNDATION

The following books are published by and can be ordered through Brunner/Mazel Publishers, Inc., 19 Union Square West, New York, NY 10003:

A Teaching Seminar with Milton H. Erickson (J. Zeig, Ed. & Commentary) is a transcript, with commentary, of a one-week teaching seminar held for professionals by Dr. Erickson in his home in August 1979. (Dutch, German, Italian, Japanese, Portuguese, Russian, and Spanish translations available.)

Ericksonian Approaches to Hypnosis and Psychotherapy (J. Zeig, Ed.) contains the edited proceedings of the First International Erickson Congress. (OUT OF PRINT)

Ericksonian Psychotherapy, Volume I: Structures; Volume II: Clinical Applications (J. Zeig, Ed.) contain the edited proceedings of the Second International Erickson Congress. (OUT OF PRINT)

The Evolution of Psychotherapy (J. Zeig, Ed.) contains the edited proceedings of the 1985 Evolution of Psychotherapy Conference. (German and Japanese translations available. Russian translation in progress.)

Developing Ericksonian Therapy: State of the Art (J. Zeig & S. Lankton, Eds.) contains the edited proceedings of the Third International Erickson Congress.

Brief Therapy: Myths, Methods, and Metaphors (J. Zeig & S. Gilligan, Eds.) contains the edited proceedings of the Fourth International Erickson Congress. (Spanish translation available.)

The Evolution of Psychotherapy: The Second Conference (J. Zeig, Ed.) contains the edited proceedings of the 1990 Evolution of Psychotherapy Conference. (Russian translation in progress.)

Ericksonian Methods: The Essence of the Story (J. Zeig, Ed.) contains the edited proceedings of the Fifth International Erickson Congress.

The Evolution of Psychotherapy: The Third Conference (J. Zeig, Ed.) contains the edited proceedings of 1995 Evolution of Psychotherapy Conference.

The Ericksonian Monographs, Vols. 1–10 contain the highest quality articles on Ericksonian hypnosis and psychotherapy, including technique, theory, and research, during Stephen Lankton's tenure as Editor-in-Chief.

The following book is published by and can be ordered through Jossey-Bass Inc., Publishers, 350 Sansome Street, San Francisco, CA 94104:

What Is Psychotherapy?: Contemporary Perspectives (J. Zeig & W.M. Munion, Eds.) contains the commentaries of 81 eminent clinicians.

CURRENT THINKING AND RESEARCH IN BRIEF THERAPY: SOLUTIONS, STRATEGIES, NARRATIVES

Evolving from *The Ericksonian Monographs*, the Foundation recently established *Current Thinking and Research in Brief Therapy: Solutions, Strategies, Narratives,* which will be published annually. Only the highest quality articles on brief therapy theory, practice and research will be published in the Brief Therapy Annual. Contributions are encouraged. Manuscripts should be submitted to William Matthews, Jr., Ph.D., Editor-in-Chief, 22 Fox Glove Lane, Amherst, MA 01002. The Associate Editor is John Edgette, Psy.D. For subscription information, contact Brunner/Mazel Publishers.

NEWSLETTER

The Milton H. Erickson Foundation publishes a newsletter for professionals three times a year to inform its readers of the activities of the Foundation. The newsletter is sent to approximately 13,000 professionals around the world. Subscriptions are free within the United States. There is a charge of $20.00 for two-year foreign subscriptions to cover handling and mailing costs. Articles and notices that relate to Ericksonian approaches to hypnosis and psychotherapy are included and should be sent to Betty Alice Erickson, M.S., L.P.C., Editor-in-Chief, 3516 Euclid, Dallas, TX 75205. The Executive Editor is Dan Short, M.S. Business and subscription matters should be directed to the Erickson Foundation at 3606 North 24th Street, Phoenix, AZ 85016-6500. The *Newsletter* accepts advertising. Interested parties should contact our business office.

MAILING LIST RENTAL

The Foundation rents mailing lists of conference attendees and newsletter subscribers to qualified parties. Inquiries to our business office are welcome.

EXHIBITORS

Exhibitors are welcome at our annual meetings. Contact the business office for information.

MILTON H. ERICKSON INSTITUTES

More than 60 Milton H. Erickson Institutes/Societies in the United States and abroad have applied to the Foundation for permission to use Dr. Erickson's name in the title of their organization. Institutes provide clinical services and professional training in major cities around the world. For information, contact the Erickson Foundation.

THE MILTON H. ERICKSON FOUNDATION LIFETIME ACHIEVEMENT AWARD

The Foundation presents its highest honor to deserving individuals on an irregular basis. Previous recipients are Jay Haley, M.A. (1980), Ernest L. Rossi, Ph.D. (1986), Paul Watzlawick, Ph.D. (1988), Elizabeth M. Erickson, B.A. (1989), Kay Thompson, D.D.S. (1992) and Stephen Lankton, M.S.W. (1994).

Acknowledgments

◆

The success of the Third Evolution of Psychotherapy Conference is due to the assistance of many dedicated persons: Special recognition should be given to Elizabeth M. Erickson, B.A.; Roxanna Erickson Klein, R.N., M.S.; and J. Charles Theisen, M.A., M.B.A., J.D., who comprise the Board of Directors of The Milton H. Erickson Foundation, Inc. They gave generously of their time and energy in making many executive decisions about the conference.

On behalf of the Board of Directors of the Erickson Foundation, I thank the distinguished keynote speaker, Gloria Steinem, as well as faculty and cofaculty of the meeting. The success of the Evolution Conference is a result of their efforts and contributions. The cofaculty included Judith Beck, Ph.D.; Carleen Glasser; Clifford N. Lazarus, Ph.D.; Heiner Steckel, Dipl. Päd.; Molly Sterling, Ph.D.; Janet Wolfe, Ph.D.; and David J. W. Young, Ph.D.

I am grateful to the moderators for the outstanding service they performed at this conference, and for their assistance in serving as an editorial board for these proceedings. The moderators were Ellyn Bader, Ph.D.; Sofia M. F. Bauer, M.D.; Betty Alice Erickson, M.S.; Brent Geary, Ph.D.; Carol Kershaw, Ed.D.; Camillo Loriedo, M.D.; William Matthews, Jr., Ph.D.; W. Michael Munion, M.A.; and Bernhard Trenkle, Dipl. Psych.

A new faculty group who made peerless contributions to the conference were the "State of the Art" faculty, which included Claudia Black, Ph.D.; Stella Chess, M.D.; Lynn Hoffman, ACSW; Joseph LoPiccolo, Ph.D.; Peggy Papp, ACSW; Francine Shapiro, Ph.D.; Olga Silverstein, M.S.W.; Margaret Singer, Ph.D.; and Lenore Walker, Ed.D. Three of the SOA faculty presented papers which are included in this book. The others presented three-hour workshops.

The Executive Director of the Foundation, Linda Carr McThrall, deserves special recognition for her outstanding administration of the conference activities and for coordinating the work of the Erickson Foundation staff. I am grateful to Korrie Brewer, assistant registrar; Theresa Germack, administrative assistant; Sylvia Cowen, bookkeeper; Diane Deniger, volunteer coordinator; Greg Deniger, conference registrar; Jeannine Elder, faculty coordinator; Karen Haviley, receptionist; Alice McAvoy, staff assistant; Susan Velasco, administrative assistant; and Lori Weiers, M.S., editorial assistant.

Also, I commend the graduate student volunteers who assisted the staff prior to the conference and served as monitors at the conference. Additional thanks to Janet S. Edgette, Psy.D. for editing papers; Philip McAvoy, M.S.W. for assisting in mailing of brochures; and Barry Shephard of SHR Communication Planning and Design, who designed the conference logo.

Special thanks to the University of Nevada, Las Vegas—Departments of Psychology, Social Work, Counseling and Educational Psychology and to the University of Nevada, Reno—School of Medicine, Department of Psychiatry and Behavioral Sciences, which cosponsored the conference.

Welcoming, Elizabeth M. Erickson, B.A.

━━━━━━━━◆━━━━━━━━

This meeting was sponsored and organized by The Milton H. Erickson Foundation, which was named in honor of the work of my husband, Milton H. Erickson. In his lifetime, he supported the cooperation and interchange of ideas, the blending of resources and the merging of knowledge that brings about high levels of understanding, advances our abilities professionally and individually, and enriches society.

We are indebted to Jeffrey Zeig, whose exceptional foresight and organizational skills developed the Erickson Foundation, and through that, actualized this phenomenal opportunity of higher learning for all of us. Dr. Zeig is a true genius in this area.

As I look out at this gathering, all of us, with such a peerless faculty, I think back to that time, 22 years ago, when Jeffrey first met my husband. I know no one could have guessed what would evolve from that serendipitous meeting. Erickson always taught: Work hard, learn everything you can, take advantage of every opportunity that is offered, share with others, and follow your dreams. In many ways, this meeting is a metaphor of how he lived and what he taught. So I say to you for him: work, learn, share, live, and dream.

Thank you, Jeff, for letting all this happen.

Convocation

◆

Benjamin Franklin wisely intoned that when a person "empties his purse into his head," no one can take it away. "An investment in knowledge always pays the best interest."

You, the attendees of the Las Vegas Evolution of Psychotherapy Conference, have incurred a considerable expenditure, both in time and money to take part in this meeting. However, I can promise you from experience that you have made an investment that will reap considerable dividends.

This is the fourth Evolution of Psychotherapy Conference. The first meeting was held exactly ten years ago in Phoenix, Arizona, and with 7,200 in attendance, was the largest meeting ever held solely on the topic of psychotherapy. That meeting also celebrated the 100th birthday of psychotherapy. Some historians date the inception of our discipline to 1885 when Freud first became interested in the psychological aspects of medicine. Therefore, today in 1995, we are celebrating psychotherapy's 110th birthday.

The second Evolution of Psychotherapy Conference was held in Anaheim, California, five years ago and attracted 6,800. As a special treat for attendees, we rented Disneyland one evening for a private party. In a similar tradition for the present meeting, we have rented "Starlight Express" for a private show on Friday night. I suppose that represents lateral progress. We have graduated from Mickey Mouse to the Little Engine that Could.

The first two Evolution Conferences were very special events, generating extraordinary interest. Most of the present faculty were at those meetings. Unfortunately, a number of exceptional faculty who presented at the two previous meetings are no longer with us, including Bruno Bettelheim, Murray Bowen, Robert Goulding, Helen Singer Kaplan, R.D.

Laing, Rollo May, Carl Rogers, Virginia Satir, Carl Whitaker, and Lewis Wolberg.

The most recent Evolution Conference was held in Hamburg, Germany, in July 1994, and was organized in conjunction with my friend and colleague, Bernhard Trenkle. Approximately 6,800 attended.

The Evolution Conferences are organized by The Milton H. Erickson Foundation. The Erickson Foundation is a nonprofit educational organization of which I am the founder. Dr. Erickson was a member of the Board of Directors until his death in 1980. Both Mrs. Erickson and I have served on the Board since its inception. Additional Board members are Roxanna Erickson Klein and J. Charles Theisen.

The administration of the Conference is directed by Linda Carr McThrall and her staff. We have a staff of 10 at the Erickson Foundation, and it is through their diligent efforts that this meeting is possible.

The Milton H. Erickson Foundation organizes a number of different types of meetings, including a regional conference on the topic of Sex and Intimacy, set up in collaboration with The Couples Institute in Menlo Park under the direction of Ellyn Bader and Peter Pearson. In addition, we organize the Brief Therapy Conference, which is the only multidisciplinary conference solely on the topic of brief therapy. The previous two meetings, held in 1988 and 1993, each attracted in the neighborhood of 2,000 professionals.

The Erickson Foundation also has organized six International Congresses on Ericksonian Approaches to Hypnosis and Psychotherapy. These are held every three years. Furthermore, we organize small group Intensive Training Programs in Ericksonian psychotherapy, which are customarily held in Phoenix.

I want to say a little bit about the structure of the current Evolution Conference. The meeting has been designed to maximize the opportunity for attendees to achieve their personal educational goals.

After this Convocation, the meeting divides into an academic component of Invited Addresses and an experiential component of Workshops. This afternoon, there will be eight concurrent workshops. The same schedule will be repeated on Thursday. On Friday and Saturday morning, there will be interactive events consisting of conversation hours, panels, demonstrations, and dialogues. On Saturday afternoon and Sunday morning, again there will be workshops and addresses. The keynote address, featuring Gloria Steinem, will be Sunday at Noon.

Each of the previous conferences has had a theme, and this meeting is no exception. We have asked the faculty to emphasize the topic of "The Evolution of the Clinician," as it is such a timely subject.

In the beginning, Freud devised the heavenly conscious and the earthly unconscious. Since then, there has been a virtual myriad of ideas about theory and practice.

Our field has evolved in diverse directions in the last 110 years. Much of this evolution has consisted of the development of disparate schools. However, the era of distinct and separate schools of psychotherapy has, to a large part, ended. Most clinicians adhere to a more eclectic practice, integrating methods from many different approaches.

Regardless of approach, a crucial factor in the success of psychotherapy is the evolution of the clinician. We are the primary tool to foster the therapy. When we step into the consulting room to see patients, we primarily have

our*selves*. Yes, we augment ourselves with techniques and theory, but much of the variance of successful psychotherapy is derived from the personality of the clinician.

The faculty whom we bring to this meeting can offer you unique and valuable perspectives on the evolution of the clinician as well as the Evolution of Psychotherapy. These are the people who have shaped the face of 20th Century practice. It is both my pleasure and my honor to introduce them to you now.

I look at the faculty and program for the meeting and marvel. Were I a registrant, I don't know how I would choose which event to attend. There are so many excellent programs held simultaneously.

We at The Milton H. Erickson Foundation are most grateful to the faculty for their contributions, and we are especially grateful to you for being here.

Before I introduce our next speaker, I want to add parenthetically the reason why this meeting is being held in Las Vegas. To some, it may seem a bit anomalous to hold an austere gathering so proximate to the casino, but I can now tell you the reason that the meeting is located here. It is solely for a self-serving purpose that I can tell you my Las Vegas joke. I have had to wait a long time to tell it.

A patient breathlessly breezes into the office of the Las Vegas therapist and cries out, "Doc. You've got to help me. I've turned into a deck of cards." The clinician responds, "I'm sorry. I'm busy now. Shuffle off to the waiting room. I'll deal with you later."

JEFFREY K. ZEIG, PH.D.
DIRECTOR
The Milton H. Erickson Foundation

SECTION I

Analytic Therapies

Convergences and Divergences in Contemporary Psychoanalytic Technique and Psychoanalytic Psychotherapy

◆

Otto F. Kernberg, M.D.

Otto F. Kernberg, M.D.

Otto F. Kernberg, M.D., F.A.P.A., is Associate Chairman and Medical Director of The New York Hospital-Cornell Medical Center, Westchester Division, and Professor of Psychiatry at the Cornell University Medical College. He is also Training and Supervising Analyst of the Columbia University Center for Psychoanalytic Training and Research. In the past, Dr. Kernberg served as Director of the C.F. Menninger Memorial Hospital. Later, he was Professor of Clinical Psychiatry at the College of Physicians and Surgeons of Columbia University. Dr. Kernberg is President of the International Psychoanalytic Association. He is the recipient of numerous awards for his contributions to psychoanalysis. Dr. Kernberg is the author of six books and the coauthor of four others. He received his medical degree in Chile in 1953.

A broad survey of the psychoanalytic field reveals both convergences and divergences in technique. The major convergences include earlier interpretation of the transference and increased focus on transference analysis, as well as growing attention to countertransference analysis and increasing concern with the risks of "indoctrinating" patients. Greater emphasis is found on character defenses and the unconscious meanings of the "here and now." Also noted are trends toward translating unconscious conflicts into object-relations terminology, as well as toward considering a multiplicity of royal roads to the unconscious.

Regarding divergences, significant controversies continue about the importance of the "real" relationship, and the therapeutic versus the resistance aspect of regression. Divergences also continue regarding reconstruction and recovery of preverbal experience, drawing the lines between psychoanalytic psychotherapy and psychoanalysis, the role of empathy, and the relation of historical to narrative truth.

Note: This presentation is a modified version of the paper titled "Contemporary Psychoanalytic Techniques" published in the *International Journal of Psycho-Analysis* 1993, 74:659–673.

INTRODUCTION

One of the most interesting developments in recent years within psychoanalytic theory and the theory of psychoanalytic technique has been the gradual increase in mutual communication among psychoanalysts from different theoretical approaches, leading, at times, to what might seem a somewhat loose ecclecticism, but, often, to the creative stimulation of new formulations and research (Kernberg, 1993). One major consequence of such non-adversary confrontations in recent times has been the awareness that the same psychoanalytic material may be subject to very different viewpoints and to interpretations along alternative lines, and that even within each particular psychoanalytic orientation, analysts perceive and interpret quite differently from each other.

As a result, there has been a major philosophical shift in the field, a questioning of the traditional assurance in describing facts in the patient's material, an emphasis on the conceptual frame and perceptive sensitivities of the analyst, and the acknowledgement of the unavoidable importance of the analyst's theoretical model in perceiving and organizing his observations. Carried to an extreme, such a questioning attitude may lead to nihilistic denial of the possibility of any objective information and knowledge being available regarding the patient's unconscious motivation and psychic past other than the unconscious meanings derived from the present interpersonal psychoanalytic situation per se. A radical questioning of the professional authority of the psychoanalyst is a natural consequence of these developments.

On the basis of a review of recent writings on psychoanalytic technique in the European, Latin American, and North American literature, I think it is possible to detect certain areas of major convergences of technique affecting Kleinian, ego-psychology, British Independent (what used to be called the "middle group"), French mainstream (non-Lacanian), interpersonal (earlier called "culturalists") and self psychology literature. Growing divergences in other areas of technique continue to separate some of these orientations from others.

The opportunity to discuss clinical material with colleagues from different psychoanalytic societies and orientations in various countries has strengthened my impression of these developments. The recent publication of major texts on technique further reconfirms that impression.

What is equally interesting is that even in texts that clearly announce their author's own bias, viewpoints of alternative schools are included, and one finds a generally more flexible attitude toward other viewpoints, an indication, in short, that older antagonisms have given way to a concern for communicating differences.

In what follows, I attempt to summarize briefly some major areas of both convergences and divergences. In attributing certain approaches to a certain school, I have had to simplify and generalize, sometimes not doing justice to fine distinctions between viewpoints within each approach.

I believe that the first task in psychoanalytic listening is to accept the unavoidability of a theoretical frame of listening, the influence of the psychoanalyst's own unconscious on the listening process, and an ongoing concern to limit or reduce the effects of such an unavoidable frame on the communication with the patient and on the patient himself. I believe that analysts who propose that their listening is intuitive, atheoretical, or simply empathic are operating within schemes of references that may be even more influential on the listening process than is the case when the psychoanalyst's theoretical frame is clear in his mind as well as the risk that this frame may restrict or distort his patient's communications.

This is precisely the paradox: the clearer our frame and our awareness of it, the greater the possibility that we may protect ourselves from imposing this frame on the patient's thinking by means of interpretive communications that are "unsaturated"—that is, wide open in their implications—inviting the patient to a broad range of responses that may confirm or disconfirm our theory of the moment. In short, a first and crucial issue affecting psychoanalytic listening is the relationship between the theoretical frame of the psychoanalyst or the psychotherapist, and the openness and wide spectrum of his capacity to listen to the patient in the context of that frame (Kernberg, 1995).

CONVERGENCES

TRANSFERENCE

There is a general tendency toward earlier interpretation of the transference, and an increased focus on the centrality of transference analysis in all psychoanalytic approaches (except, probably, the Lacanian). The heightened stress and early focus on the transference is moving the technique of ego psychology, for example, closer to that of object relations theories. There seems to be less overall emphasis on the uniqueness of dreams, on the recovery of concrete memories, on external reality, and more on both early and systematic analysis of the unconscious meanings of transference developments.

Gill and Hoffman's (Gill, 1982; Gill & Hoffman, 1982) empirical research on transference initially received a mixed reception, but left an important imprint not only on American ego psychology but on interpersonal psychoanalysis and on Thomä and Kächele's. Much of the early criticism of Gill and Hoffman was directed at their strong focus on the analyst's contribution to the transference and on their stress on the interactional matrix within which transference develops, but their pointing to the importance of defenses against the transference (rather than to the defensive functions of the transference itself) influenced ego-psychology thinking, increasing the attention paid to the subtle, particularly nonverbal, manifestations of the transference from early in the treatment. This general tendency toward heightened alertness and earlier interpretation of the transference within ego psychology has narrowed the gap between American ego psychology and British approaches to the transference. Indeed, a complementary move among the British, particularly the mainstream Kleinians as represented by Spillius' edited volumes, indicates that Kleinian authors are exercising greater caution in their interpretation of the transference.

The recent work of Joseph (1989) and Segal (Levine, 1992), as well as Spillius's (1988) own observations throughout her books, all point to a more systematic attention on the part of Kleinian analysts to the analysis of character resistances and their relation to the transference, to a more gradual analysis of the patient's associative and attitudinal material from surface to depth, and to omitting direct references to genetic material in early stages of transference interpretation, moving, in this regard, in the direction of both the Independents and the ego psychologists. Significant differences nonetheless persist in the interpretive approaches to the transference among the different schools.

CHARACTER ANALYSIS

There is a general tendency to focus on the analysis of the patient's habitual—and often unobtrusive yet rigid—behavior patterns in the psychoanalytic situation: character defenses instead of the unconscious meanings of particular symptoms, experiences, or memories. This approach, however, does not have the qualities of a confrontational (and at times authoritarian) "overcoming" of character resistances as did that of Wilhelm Reich (1933).

In this respect, it is as if Kleinian technique were moving into the direction of ego psychology. This trend was spearheaded by Rosenfeld's (1964) descriptions of the transference resistances of patients with narcissistic personality, his emphasis, in his later contributions (1987), on the clarification of the patient's experiences as well as nonverbal manifestations reflecting persistent, repetitive characterological features, and again, in Joseph's (1989) and Segal's (Levine, 1992; Spillius, 1988) emphasis on chronic, repetitive, subtle, yet significant aspects of the patient–analyst interaction.

Although from an ego-psychology perspective the rigidity of traditional "Reichian" character analysis has long been abandoned, under the impact of treating more seriously ill patients, a renewed focus on character analysis has been evident in practice if not expressed in systematic formulations in this area. The fact that character pathology and severe personality disorders are becoming increasingly prevalent indications for psychoanalytic treatment may be contributing to this trend, but so is the growing awareness that the analysis of verbal contents that bypass character structure often leads to intellectualization and pseudoinsight (Kernberg, 1983, 1987, 1992).

THE HERE AND NOW

The focus on the unconscious meanings in the "here and now" is increasing. A major agreement is evolving regarding what Sandler and Sandler (1984) have described as the "present unconscious" in contrast to the "past unconscious." In a general reaction against the risk of premature genetic reconstructions and particularly an intellectualized reconstruction of the past on the basis of patients' conscious memories that bypass unconscious fantasies and meanings in the transference, there is a general trend to carefully explore such unconscious meanings in the here and now before attempting reconstructions of the past. This trend is linked to the increasing concentration on analyzing the transference in general. Analysis of the here and now does not imply a neglect of the unconscious past. Although certain tendencies to overemphasize the interactional aspects of the psychoanalytic situation (sometimes linked to an existential approach) may neglect dealing with the infantile determinants of the transference, this is not the implication of the growing tendency to carefully explore unconscious meanings in the here and now before linking these with the unconscious past.

The ego-psychology formulations on the metapsychology of interpretation—in particular, the economic, dynamic, and structural criteria of interpretation most cogently formulated by Fenichel (1941)—always stressed the importance of proceeding "from surface to depth"—from the analysis of defense or resistance to the analysis of impulse or content. Kleinian technique, in contrast, used to focus on interpretation at the deepest level of anxiety (Segal, 1973), and tended to move quickly into genetic interpretations (often conveyed with a language referring to body parts and fantasies of the infant assumed to exist in the first year of life), and thus risked fostering intellectualization in the patient if not inducing him into a restrictive translation of his experiences.

In reaction to this trend, contemporary mainstream Kleinians avoid early, premature genetic reconstructions, and attempt to analyze unconscious meanings "in the here and now" at a level more consonant with the patient's current way of formulating his experiences, and, as mentioned before, in the process, increasingly focus on the manifestations of character pathology in the transference. Hanna Segal (personal communication) now stresses interpretation at the most active rather than the deepest level of anxiety, and with the patient's current level of mental functioning. Etchegoyen's (1991) text illustrates a parallel development among the Argentinian Kleinians.

INCREASING FOCUS ON TRANSLATION OF UNCONSCIOUS CONFLICTS INTO OBJECT RELATIONS TERMINOLOGY

It is important to differentiate the technical approach to the clinical material from the ongoing controversy regarding the relationship between object relations theory and drive theory, a controversy that separates neatly those object relations theoreticians who maintain drive theory (Jacobson, Mahler, Klein, Kernberg) from those who consider object relations theory incompatible with Freudian drive theory (Sullivan, Fairbairn, Mitchell, Greenberg). Technically, there is a general tendency to express impulse/defense configurations in terms of corresponding unconscious, internalized identification with self and object representations that carry the corresponding drive derivative or its affective expression.

The British and Interpersonal schools of course have always formulated their interpretations in object relations language, and this also holds true for self psychology (with the significant difference that self psychology disregards the existence of aggressively invested internalized object relations). But the ego-psychology literature on technique also has increasingly been formulated in object relations terms as, for example, in the developmental approach derived from Mahler (Akhtar & Parens, 1991), and in the work of Arlow (1991), Gill (Gill & Hoffman, 1982), and Sandler (Sandler, Dare, & Holder, 1992). It may be argued that psychoanalytic theory has implied an object relations theory from its very beginning, but the increasing linkage of affect dispositions and drive derivatives with self and object representations that are part of ego and superego structures has only become dominant, it seems to me, in the nonobject relations theory approaches in recent years.

COUNTERTRANSFERENCE

Parallel and well-known developments regarding countertransference have taken place within ego psychology and the Kleinian and Independent approaches, typically illustrated by the contributions of Heimann (1950), Little (1951), Racker (1957, 1968), Annie Reich (1951), and Winnicott (1949, 1960). The net effect of these contributions has been to broaden the concept of countertransference from its narrow sense (as the analyst's unconscious reaction to the patient or the transference) into the broader sense of the total emotional reaction of the analyst to the patient. These contributions also signaled a shift from a negative—what one might even call a phobic—attitude toward the countertransference (as an assumed reflection of the analyst's unresolved neurotic conflicts) to an important instrument for investigating the transference and the total patient–analyst interaction.

As we know, interpersonal psychoanalysts started out with such a global definition and technical approach to the countertransference (Fromm-Reichmann, 1950; Searles, 1979). Racker's (1957) pathbreaking clarification of concordant and complementary identifications in the countertransference provided a theoretical frame for countertransference analysis that has been utilized widely in all object relations theory approaches, and has become a centerpiece in Etchegoyen's Kleinian treatise (1991). Jacobs' recent text (1991) illustrates how these concepts have become part of the mainstream of ego-psychology thinking in the United States as well, and Epstein and Feiner's (1979) selection of papers on countertransference points to parallel developments in a broad spectrum of psychoanalytic approaches, including French authors (McDougall, 1979).

Major differences remain, however, on the extent to which transference and countertransference analysis are linked: Interpersonal psychoanalysis gives an almost symmetrical attention to transference and countertransference, a tendency less prevalent among the Independents, and even less so among ego psychologists and Kleinians. I think it is fair to say that all analysts utilize the exploration of their own affective responses to their patients in a consistent and much freer way than earlier clinicians did. By the same token, however, there is also a general tendency to utilize countertransference analysis only in the formulation of interpretations, while carefully avoiding its direct communication to the patient.

From a theoretical viewpoint, the expansion of the concept of countertransference and its utilization in the formulation of transference interpretations implies a gradual acceptance—in varying degrees and with varying limitations—of the concept of projective identification as an important means of defense and unconscious communication in the transference. The actualization or enactment of past conflicts in the transference, particularly with "role reversal" (Kernberg, 1984) of the original pathogenic object relation on the part of the patient, is met by a "role responsiveness" of the analyst (Sandler, 1976). The analyst's trial identification with the patient includes the activation of reciprocal roles in the countertransference.

INCREASING FOCUS ON PATIENT'S AFFECTIVE EXPERIENCE

Psychoanalysts have always focused on the patient's affective experiences. Fenichel (1941) eloquently summarized the risks of two polarities of resistance: an intensity of affect as a defense against cognitive awareness of an unconscious conflict, and a reliance on intellectualization and rationalization as a defense against affective awareness of such a conflict. However, here I am referring to the gradual transformation of the traditional ego psychological focus on intensity of *instinctual* conflicts per se as determining the "economic" criterion of interpretation (Fenichel, 1941) (or throughout the Kleinian school as well as ego psychology, the focus on *libidinal and/or aggressive investments)*, into the detailed study of the *affects* that represent or reflect the dual drives in the clinical situation.

Regardless of one's position regarding the controversy over whether drive theory should be replaced or complemented by other motivational theories, in the clinical situation the dominance of affective investment has come to be accepted almost universally as the most appropriate point for analytic intervention (with perhaps the exception of Lacanians). This point has been stressed most strongly in recent contributions from the Independent group (Bollas, 1987, 1992; Casement, 1991; Ogden, 1989; Stewart, 1992).

To interpret where the dominant affective investment is, however, does not mean simply to address the material that produces more conscious affective display. The ongoing exploration of the relationship between dominant themes in the transference, affective dominance in the total material presented by the patient, and affective dominance in the countertransference, represent, at an operational level, the concrete analysis of transference and countertransference developments in each session. To determine the extent to which external reality, developments in the transference, and the emergence of repressed infantile material contribute to shaping the concrete affective climate of each session is perceived as a major task by most contemporary psychoanalytic approaches.

STRESS ON MULTIPLICITY OF "ROYAL ROADS" TO THE UNCONSCIOUS

As mentioned earlier, the emphasis on dream analysis as the royal road to the unconscious has diminished as our understanding of the multiple channels of communication the unconscious takes in the analytic situation has increased. Brenner (1976) observed that "The traditional emphasis on the importance of dreams in psychoanalytic therapy has been at the expense of attention to the place in analysis of such other mental phenomena as daydreams, slips, metaphors, jokes, reactions to

works of art and even neurotic symptoms. . ." (p. 165). In the context of interpretive interventions, Gray (1986) points to the multiplicity of "surfaces" of the psychoanalytic material, thereby illustrating the potential flexibility of an ego-psychological approach that directs the patient's attention to a broad variety of defensive operations. Other developments within ego psychology include Kris's (1982) renewed focus on the technical utilization of the patient's free association, and Schwaber's (1983) emphasis on the analyst's exploration of the patient's subjective experience of the analyst's interventions, particularly when there are disruptions in the communicative process. It is here, I believe, that a major flexibility of approach to the patient's material has become evident throughout different approaches, a flexibility I attempted in earlier work (Kernberg, 1992) to synthesize as the simultaneous attention to "three channels" of communication, namely (1) communication of verbal content through free association, (2) communication by means of nonverbal behavior and the formal aspect of language, and (3) communication by the total, constant, implicit object relation developed in each analyst–patient pair as contrasted to the moment-to-moment shift in dominant transference–countertransference equilibrium.

With regard to the formal aspects of verbal communication, Liberman's (1983) pioneering work in Argentina on the relationship between psycholinguistic styles and dominant character patterns, crisply highlighted in Etchegoyen's (1991) text, provided a new frame for understanding communication within the psychoanalytic process. Rosenfeld (1987), in describing the relationship between narcissistic character pathology and its transference manifestations, updated the importance of the transformation of narcissistic character defenses into transference resistances within a Kleinian frame, a transformational process independently highlighted by Grunberger (1971) from the French psychoanalytic mainstream, and by Kohut's (1971, 1977) self psychology.

Within ego psychology, Levy and Inderbitzin (1990), in their succinct summary of four different conceptualizations of "analytic surface," describe how: "[Paul] Gray's focus on opportunities for illustrating defensive ego operations, [Merton] Gill's careful attention to here-and-now transference manifestations, [Anton] Kris's search for discontinuities in the patient's free associative process, and [Evelyne] Schwaber's consistent efforts to clarify deficiencies in the analyst's understanding of the patient's subjective experiences all take off from various suggestions inherent in Freud's ideas about technique. They organize the analyst's listening and responding" (p. 386).

Levy and Inderbitzin also criticize, however, the danger of getting lost in any particular "microscopic focus," in that the analyst may lose his awareness of other issues. They stress the importance of flexibility, and the multiplicity of choices of material in each analytic hour. Bion's (1967) caution to interpret "without memory or desire" points to a related concern about exploring afresh the material in each session, without restricting preconceptions.

I believe one may summarize the dynamic and economic criteria of interpretation from a contemporary perspective by stating that interpretation should be guided by the analyst's assessment of dominant affective investment at any particular time, predominantly but not exclusively through the analysis of the transference, and proceeding from surface to depth, with the awareness of the existence of multiple surfaces, and the possibility that the same impulse/defense organization may be approached from alternative surfaces into a common depth.

INCREASING CONCERN WITH "INDOCTRINATION" OF PATIENTS

Widespread concern has been expressed over the risks of involuntarily seducing the analysand into the theory or at least the language of the analyst, the consequent risk of producing "transference cures" rather than transference resolution, and an apparent but false confirmation of the analyst's theories as they are reflected in the patient's reorganization of his subjective experience. This preoccupation has taken different forms within the different approaches: Ego psychology has criticized the concept of "resistance" as poten

tially fostering an adversarial relation between patient and analyst, and imposing the analyst's views on the patient (Schafer, 1976); Kleinians address the problem in Bion's "Notes on Memory and Desire" (1967); Lacanians write of the notion of the analyst as the "subject of supposed knowledge" (see Etchegoyen, 1991, chapter 11). The consistent emphasis on empathy with the patient's subjective experience in self psychology also contains, implicitly, a criticism of authoritative interpretations (Schwaber, 1990). Interpersonal psychoanalysis and the Independents, in stressing the fundamental importance of clarifying disruptions in the patient–analyst communication, always have implicitly focused on the risk of the analyst imposing his views on the patient.

The problem is that the analyst's theoretical orientation will inevitably influence his style of communication, and the patient, given his alertness to the analyst's communications, will necessarily extract a view of the analyst's approach. It is usually not difficult to recognize his theoretical background from any analyst's particular interventions. An analyst's cautious avoidance of any interpretation that might be challenged by the patient as an "imposition" may lead to the acting out of sadomasochistic transferences as much as if the analyst inappropriately imposes his formulations on the patient. It is the awareness of this dialectic that increasingly influences psychoanalytic technique, and leads to a general tendency toward avoidance of formulations that might lend themselves to intellectualized reorganization of the patient's experience, bringing about closure rather than opening a potential space for the unexpected.

INCREASED QUESTIONING OF LINEAR CONCEPTS OF DEVELOPMENT

There is an increasing tendency to question the linear sequence from oral to anal to genital and oedipal conflicts, in contrast to the elaboration, within the psychoanalytic process, of highly individualized sequences of condensed oedipal and preoedipal structures. The current trend is for the analysis of transference paradigms to operate with an oscillation between the analysis of highly condensed, synchronic structures that incorporate disparate aspects of the past, and the analysis of any particular diachronic line of development that temporarily emerges within those condensed structures. This development, perhaps most strongly accentuated among Lacanian but characteristic as well of non-Lacanian French psychoanalysis, also focuses on the structural aspects and developmental consequences of early oedipalization, the archaic Oedipus.

This emerging consensus, in my view, is still being obscured by the older controversy regarding the dominance of oedipal and/or preoedipal issues in psychopathology, which separates self psychology and some radical interpersonal psychoanalysts, on the one side, from ego psychology, the British schools, French mainstream, and Lacanian psychoanalysis, on the other. Careful exploration of the developmental schemata of all these approaches, however, indicates, I believe, that the intimate interrelationship between preoedipal and oedipal conflicts and structures decreases the importance of the more traditional linear models of development.

For example, the original oedipal structuring of reality, the archaic Oedipus situation, proposed both by Lacanian theory and by the French mainstream (Benvenuto & Kennedy, 1986; Chasseguet-Smirgel, 1986; Lacan, 1966; Le Guen, 1974) points to the original function of the father as the third party interfering with the symbiotic relationship between mother and infant, so that the progression from archaic oedipal conflicts to the advanced oedipal conflicts occurs simultaneously with the development of oral and anal conflicts. At the same time, psychoanalytic literature in general that deals with severe character pathology and borderline conditions points to the intimate condensation of oedipal and preoedipal conflicts in these patients (Akhtar, 1992; Kernberg, 1984, 1992; Rosenfeld, 1987).

My own viewpoint is that the more severe the patient's psychopathology, the more do we find condensed manifestations of early and later conflicts, so that only in advanced stages of the treatment do we find transferences that conform to the classical models of predominantly oral or anal unconscious conflict material. From a theoretical viewpoint, the importance of retrospective modification of past experience in the light of later ones (Freud's *Nachträglichkeit*) has changed the nature of our discussion of the emergence of very early, particularly preverbal material in the psychoanalytic situation (more about this later).

DIVERGENT TRENDS IN CONTEMPORARY PSYCHOANALYTIC TECHNIQUE

The previous section, describing convergent trends within the technical approaches of different psychoanalytic schools at this time, included my own ideas. In fact, because my work has focused on efforts to bridge ego psychology and object relations theory, the correspondence should not be surprising. In the section that follows, which examines divergent trends in contemporary psychoanalytic technique, I shall spell out where I stand regarding each of the issues to be explored.

THE "REAL" RELATIONSHIP, AND TRANSFERENCE-COUNTERTRANSFERENCE ISSUES

Here, in spite of a variety of technical approaches rather than a sharp dichotomy, there are significant differences in the conceptualization of the psychoanalytic process, differences that cut across the major schools referred to before. At one extreme is the assumption that everything in the patient–analyst relationship is transference, and that even the "unobjectable" aspects of the transference, related to what Zetzel (1956) described as the therapeutic alliance and Greenson (1965) as the working alliance or working relationship, reflect transference dispositions stemming from a normally achieved trusting relationship between the infant and the mother. In self psychology, for example, the assumption that all during the treatment, the analyst fulfills self–object functions that continue as a normal aspect of human life for all individuals implies such a view. This position, which considers all aspects of the analyst–patient relationship as reflecting transference dispositions, as Thomä and Kächele (1987) point out, makes it difficult to conceptualize how the transference can be analyzed and resolved.

Those who, like most ego psychologists, assume that a "real" relationship exists independently from the transference and that the therapeutic alliance reflects the working relationship between the healthy part of the patient's ego and the analyst in his professional role may unwittingly foster a distortion of the psychoanalytic situation into a direction of conventionality, in which unacknowledged, culturally and socially determined joint biases of patient and analyst contribute to restrict the full investigation of the transference: this is, in effect, a critique that Deserno (1990) in Germany makes of the concept of the therapeutic alliance.

The role of the analyst is related to another factor, namely, whether the therapeutic effect of psychoanalysis derives from interpretation alone, or as a result of a new experience that will permit the compensation of developmental deficits and arrests and facilitate the resumption of growth in the patient by means of a new (we might even say corrective) emotional experience. This latter position often emphasizes as well the particular personality of the analyst in contributing to this new experience. In all fairness, here it is not a matter of the analyst's artificially providing the patient with a "corrective emotional experience," in other words, of manipulating the transference, but of providing a genuine, authentic relationship in which the personality of both participants, and certainly transference and countertransference analysis, participate.

A third factor, which intersects with these two, is represented at one extreme by the position that the transference is an exclusive creation of the patient, the unconscious reproduction in the here and now of pathogenic conflicts and object relations from the past, with the analyst remaining outside these conflicts except to facilitate their clarification by the successive analysis of transference paradigms. This position is often linked with the traditional concept of the transference neurosis; that is, the sequential deployment in the transference of the patient's unconscious conflicts, with a gradual concentration of these conflicts in the transference as opposed to other areas of the patient's life, and with the possibility of their gradual resolution by systematic transference interpretation.

This traditional position, rather strongly maintained by both ego psychologists and Kleinians, was challenged by Gill (Gill & Hoffman, 1982) within ego psychology and developed further by Thomä and Kächele (1987), all of whom emphasize the analyst's contributions to the transference. This point had been stressed earlier by both the Independents and interpersonalists. Thus, paradoxically, traditional ego psychology contrasts the real relationship to the transference relationship, but still deemphasizes the importance of the analyst's personality. By the same token, the interpersonal approach (Greenberg, 1991; Mitchell, 1988) proposes that the analyst's personality unavoidably influences the transference, and that in order for the patient to experience the analyst as a "safe" object, the analyst needs to modify his behavior to maintain himself equidistant from the danger of being "unsafe" and from colluding with the transference. This approach thus stresses at the same time the unavoidability of mutuality in transference-countertransference activation, and, implicitly, what may be considered a manipulative adaptation by the analyst to the patient's transference.

My own view is that the reality of the analyst's personality becomes important only insofar as it serves as an anchoring point for the transference, where it requires ongoing self-scrutiny by the analyst of his own behavior and countertransference reactions. I also view the patient's capacity to use the "real" aspects of the therapeutic relationship in the case of very ill patients; that is, to perceive the analyst realistically in his therapeutic role, as a *consequence* of the analysis of regressive transferences. In contrast, the analyst's regression to his own defensive character patterns as a consequence of severely pathological transference-countertransference developments with chronically regressed patients requires the protection of the treatment frame, and analytic working through of the transference simultaneously with the analyst's work on and attempts to utilize the understanding derived from his own countertransference. In short, I agree with Etchegoyen's (1991) critique of the exaggerated emphasis on the importance of the analyst's personality in the interpersonal approach.

The psychoanalyst, I believe, should behave as naturally as possible, without any self-revelation and without gratifying the patient's curiosity and transference demands, and acting, outside his specific technical function, within ordinary norms of social interaction. The analyst's acting as his natural self, however, must be matched by his specific role, which is a position of technical neutrality that by definition also implies that he may not reveal his own preferences, commitments, desires, and fears, in order to provide maximum freedom for the patient to develop his transference dispositions and his own solutions to his intrapsychic conflicts (Kennedy, 1993). The position of a blank screen from that viewpoint does not imply invisibility of the analyst's personality, but naturalness and authentic respect for the patient's freedom to arrive at his own decisions.

Technical neutrality, in short, does not imply anonymity, and natural behavior does not imply that the analyst is not in a consistent, stable professional role relationship with the patient. Nor does technical neutrality imply that the psychoanalyst's personality will not be influencing the patient, in the same way as the patient necessarily will influence the psychoanalyst by means of the development of countertransference reactions. The reality of the analyst as a professional person concerned with understanding the patient, empathic with the patient's suffering, alert to the patient's destructive and self-destructive temptations, cannot but provide, in the long run, a uniquely helpful human experience. Some patients may not have had any human experience of such a positive nature before in their lives. The positive influence of the analyst's personality, however, will necessarily be undermined by the patient's distortions of the analyst as part of transference developments—under ideal circumstances, the systematic analysis and resolution of the transference will permit a sublimatory internalization of realistic aspects of the analyst's personality as part of the reorganization of the patient's personality throughout the treatment.

THE THERAPEUTIC ASPECTS VERSUS THE RESISTANCE ASPECTS OF REGRESSION

The controversy in this area is related to the preceding one, and refers specifically to the transference regression of patients with severe psychopathology. The Independents, following Balint (1968) and particularly Winnicott (1965), propose the therapeutic value of regression in the transference in patients with severe personality disorders, particularly those who are severely schizoid or antisocial, and those with generally "false self" characteristics. The assumption is that the analyst's capacity to tolerate this regression and to hold the patient during it permits a new encounter, a resumption of normal growth at certain points even without full verbalization of this experience by the analyst. Interpersonal psychoanalysts, especially the earlier work of Sullivan (1953) and Fromm-Reichmann (1950), as well as Searles (1979), also consider the possibilities of the therapeutic effects of severe regression, as long as the therapist analyzes the negative, terrorizing misinterpretations of the treatment situation that interfere with the regressed patient's capacity to resume emotional growth.

The Kleinians, in contrast, particularly as represented in the work of Rosenfeld (1987), stress the importance of a systematic analysis of the positive and negative transference of severely regressed patients, with the analyst remaining in a technically neutral position. The object relations approach that has evolved within ego psychology (Jacobson, 1971; Kernberg, 1975, 1984; Kernberg, Selzer, Koenigsberg, Carr, & Appelbaum, 1989) has proposed a technique that provides structuring of the treatment frame in order to protect the severely regressed patient and the treatment situation and at the same time stresses the importance of an essentially interpretive approach. Etchegoyen (1991) spells out in detail recent contributions from a Kleinian perspective to the analysis of severe regressions in the transference that permit maintaining a consistent psychoanalytic frame and the technical neutrality of the analyst.

My view is that, particularly with those severely regressed patients where a psychoanalytic approach is still warranted, the provision of sufficient structure to be able to maintain an analytic setting and to interpret the primitive defensive operations and object relations of the patient in the transference permits the gradual transformation of regressive transferences into more advanced ones, strengthens the patient's ego, and permits him to collaborate in the analytic exploration. Under these circumstances, the analysis of the reasons for deviations from technical neutrality (when such deviations occurred) permits protecting and reinstating the psychoanalytic frame.

Recently, increasing attention has been paid to severe cases of borderline, narcissistic, and perverse psychopathology. This has highlighted the importance of some patients' efforts to protect themselves from the extremely painful awareness of their primitive hatred by the destruction of the communicative process in the analytic situation, and the very viability of the analytic situation itself. One might say that severe, often life-threatening forms of acting-out, destructive violence in the sessions, or a constant challenge to the boundaries of the psychoanalytic situation symbolically reflect the struggle between love and aggression at deepest levels of regression: Now the psychoanalytic frame stands for the survival of the analytic process geared to resolving this calamity. I believe that when the interpretation of the patient's consistent attacks on the analytic frame does not manage to protect the frame, to "contain" or "hold" the analytic relationship, limit-setting, or structuring of the analytic situation becomes essential. Such limit-setting in itself represents a modified frame that permits the continuation of the interpretive work, and it is eventually to be followed by the interpretive resolution of that limiting structuralization itself.

PSYCHOANALYSIS AND PSYCHOANALYTIC PSYCHOTHERAPY

In this long-standing controversy, two problems are involved: the boundaries of what may be considered standard analysis in contrast to its modification or extension for patients who are not able to undergo such treatment, and the question of the "dilution" of standard technique when a clear distinction between psychoanalysis and psychoanalytic psychotherapy is not maintained. This does not include those who wish to experiment freely with the elements of the psychoanalytic technique and apply it to new fields.

In general, both ego psychology and Kleinians favor a firm distinction between psychoanalysis and other psychotherapies, while the Independents and interpersonalists maintain more flexible boundaries regarding the treatment. Such greater flexibility probably also applies to child psychoanalysis within the French mainstream.

My own view is that because it is helpful to evaluate the specific effects of the technical approach being used, it is preferable to differentiate rather sharply between standard psychoanalysis and psychoanalytic psychotherapy. At the same time, I recognize the enormous value of psychoanalytic psychotherapy, in contrast to the traditional view of it as a "second best" treatment. I have proposed differentiating psychoanalytic psychotherapy from standard psychoanalysis by a modification of three basic tools derived from standard psychoanalytic technique. First, interpretation in psychoanalytic psychotherapy is restricted to clarification, confrontation, and interpretation of the unconscious meanings in the here and now only, while genetic reconstructions are reserved for the advanced stages of treatment. Second, transference analysis in psychoanalytic psychotherapy is modified in each session to incorporate attention to the long-range treatment goals and the dominant, current conflicts in the patient's life outside the sessions. Third, technical neutrality must be modified by the need for structuring or setting limits in the treatment situation, but eventually must be reinstated by the therapist's clarifying to the patient by means of interpretation the reasons for departing from the neutral position in the first place (Kernberg, 1975, 1984; Kernberg et al., 1989).

THE ROLE OF EMPATHY

Here the controversy is particularly between self psychology and all other psychoanalytic orientations. Whereas self psychology stresses the primacy of the analyst's empathy with the patient's subjective experience and the need to focus on such experiences particularly at moments of disruption of the affective relationship between patient and analyst, the other approaches consider the capacity for empathy a general precondition for all psychoanalytic work, and broaden the concept of empathy to include not only the analyst's empathy with the patient's central emotional experience but also with that which the patient cannot tolerate in himself, projects, and/or dissociates.

In this regard, the utilization of the concept of projective identification, originally coined by Klein (1946) but gradually adapted by Independents, interpersonalists, the French mainstream, and significant sectors of object relations and ego psychology approaches, implies the need to empathize not only with the patient's current self-experience, but also with what the patient projects, dissociates, or represses. All psychoanalytic approaches point to the importance of empathy as a precondition for the capacity for countertransference analysis and its utilization in transference interpretation. In contrast to self psychology, the other approaches focus on the importance of the multiplicity of observational data in the psychoanalytic situation.

A related general conceptual issue that separates self psychology from other psychoanalytic techniques is the extent to which negative transference simply reflects the traumatic disruption of a "self–self object relationship" (that is, of a positive transference), or reflects the activation of "negative introjects," of persecutory in contrast to idealized self and object representations activated in the transference, as all nonself psychology approaches affirm.

With severely ill patients, where verbal communication itself may be distorted in the serv-ice of defense, at times, in an effort to remain empathically in touch with the patient, the analyst may adapt himself to the patient's style, thus unwittingly reinforcing the resistance. At other times, the analyst's complete absorption in an effort to understand the patient's confusing communication at the cost of a loss of the analyst's internal freedom to interpret this very process may also paralyze his analytic function; here, one might say, efforts at empathy may become dangerous. An opposite danger, under such circumstances, is for the analyst to fall back defensively on his general theoretical formulation, thus, in effect, disconnecting himself from the disorganizing process in the transference that would have required his understanding.

"HISTORICAL TRUTH" VERSUS "NARRATIVE TRUTH"

Schafer's (1976, 1992) and Spence's (1982) contributions represent a radical proposal that replaces the reconstruction of historical truth and causality by the construction of new narrative "myths," and questions the possibility of reconstruction of the historical past in contrast to the traditional assumption that the reconstruction of the historical past facilitates and signals the resolution of the transference. It may be that this controversy represents a temporary turbulence in psychoanalytic thinking, in the sense of pointing to the problematic nature of many reconstructions, to the fact that most historical reconstructions represent less history than constructions on the basis of the unconscious meanings in the here and now, that the logical fit of the present into the past is often problematic, and that the correlation or correspondence between past and present is open to vastly different views. Klein's (1952) proposal that the transference represents real experiences from the past, fantasied experiences from the past, and defenses against both, probably reflects a widely accepted intermediate position in this controversy, and it is a position with which I agree.

Recent knowledge regarding actual severe physical, mental, or sexual trauma in the early infancy and childhood of patients with regressive psychopathology has not solved this problem. Between the historically documented, severely traumatizing situations in our patients' past and their current unconscious mental structures lie significant transformational processes. The direct interpretation of present transference regression in terms of an assumed repetition of such past trauma may bypass the unconscious meanings of the trauma and its developmental structuralizations. A typical example is neglecting to interpret in victims of physical or sexual abuse not only the affects of their experience as victim but also of their unconscious identification with the aggressor, and of the elaboration of that identification activated in the transference.

TECHNICAL NEUTRALITY AND CULTURAL BIAS

Cremerius (1984) raises the question of whether there is an unconscious collusion between analysts and patients regarding social, cultural, and political issues, ideologies, and power struggles. Here, the approach of some feminist and Marxist psychoanalytic groups converge. In contrast to this viewpoint, the question of whether an excessive concern over hidden ideologies may transform the analytic encounter into a political project has been raised. At the same time, however, in support of the concern over ideological distortions, the avoidance of covert—and overt—political issues, including psychoanalytic politics, may reflect an unconscious collusion between patient and analyst. Efforts to recognize how these hidden ideologies affect the psychoanalytic process may, I believe, enrich it.

THE RECONSTRUCTION AND RECOVERY OF PREVERBAL EXPERIENCES

The traditional criticism by ego psychology of Kleinian analysis has centered on the Kleinian interpretation of the assumed developments in the first year of life, and the related assumption of a degree of sophistication and complexity of unconscious fantasy at that time that does not seem warranted. Paradoxically,

recent infant research has demonstrated a much higher level of complexity of mother–infant interaction in the first year of life than ego psychology traditionally assumed. Further, on the basis of their own experience over the past 30 years, Kleinian analysts have become much more cautious and reluctant in carrying out early genetic reconstructions of the preverbal period.

Simultaneously, the impact of Mahler's investigation of children with symbiotic psychosis and of the separation-individuation process has given a new impetus to the exploration of expression of preverbal material in patients' nonverbal manifestations and relationship to the analytic setting (Akhtar & Parens, 1991). Child observation, Mahler's developmental approach, and the analytic exploration of regressive transferences from many viewpoints all point to the importance of continuing to investigate the preverbal in the analytic setting. The increased emphasis on "retrospective modification" on the part of the Lacanian school, as well as by the French mainstream, has provided an additional impetus to explore condensation of the preverbal with material from later levels of development, a position not far from an ego-psychology viewpoint according to which all aspects of early development can be seen only in the context of their developmental transformation under the impact of advanced oedipal relationships (Arlow, 1991). In short, it may be that this is a controversy that is being laid to rest.

I believe that the sources of information that require the psychoanalyst's attention can be grouped, first, into those stemming from the content of the patient's communications, the nature of his free association, the affective implications with which he is conveying the development of his subjective experience in the hour—what I have called, in earlier work, "channel one" (Kernberg, 1994). Second, or "channel two," is the nonverbal aspects of the patient's communication, his nonverbal behavior as well as the style and structure of his language, in contrast to the content of his verbal communication. Free association thus has a central role not only in indicating the extent of a conscious freedom to communicate, but also in conveying a defensive style in its very structure.

Channel three is the countertransference, conceptualized in a contemporary sense as the total emotional reaction of the analyst toward the patient, with a particular emphasis on concordant and complementary identification as part of it. These various channels of communication operate with different intensity at different times with the same patient, and according to the severity of the patient's psychopathology: The more severe the character pathology, the more channels two and three tend to dominate channel one.

I pay particular attention to where the dominant affect of the patient's experience is, considering that the affectively dominant material first requires attention and usually leads to a natural ordering of the analytic process. Affective dominance does not necessarily mean consciously experienced affect, but a dominant affect as it emerges in the conjoint analysis of all the sources of information to which psychoanalytic listening is open. Most frequently, but not exclusively, affective dominance coincides with transference developments, and so it is important for the analyst to be open to explore unconscious conflicts other than those in the transference, although usually such exploration eventually leads, directly or indirectly, to the transference.

Most importantly, I expect that psychoanalytic listening will facilitate the emergence of ever-clearer representatives of the dynamic unconscious, be that in the form of repressed unconscious conflicts or in the form of dissociated and split off aspects of the unconscious in cases that involve severe psychopathology. I assume that unconscious conflict always involves the conflict between opposing internalized object relations under the impact of peak affect states, so that the sexual and aggressive drives are represented, respectively, by a series of idealized and erotized relations, and of aggressive and persecutory ones.

I assume that the basic units of such internalized object relations under the frame of primitive peak affect states always involve at least a self-representation and an object representation and the affect linking them, and that defensive structures as well as the impulses against which they defend are represented by such respectively defensive or impulsive internalized object relations.

The psychoanalytic setting established by the initial treatment contract constitutes the frame for a potential "normal" object relation derived from the conscious purposes and working arrangements of patient and analyst. This conscious and preconscious normal object relationship will be submerged rapidly by the emerging primitive, repressed or dissociated, projected or split off aspects of primitive object relations that will be reenacted in the transference. Transference analysis is by far the dominant scenario of psychoanalytic understanding, interpretation, and working through, and as I mentioned before the analysis of countertransference occupies an important place in it.

This may be a good place to point out my questioning of a contemporary trend that attributes as much importance to countertransference as to transference analysis, in the sense that it considers them as almost symmetrical. I believe that it is crucial to analyze the patient–analyst interaction and the total interpersonal field that it represents, but with a clear dominance in it of the analysis of the patient's unconscious conflicts in a setting in which the relationship, by definition, is asymmetrical. The analyst's unconscious participates in influencing the countertransference and the transference as well; but the acknowledgement of such unconscious elements in the analyst as influencing analytic work has to be tempered by the awareness that the analyst's unconscious may be both stimulating the transference in "enigmatic" ways (Laplanche, 1992), and yet constitute an ultimate residual and inexplorable rest after the patient's contributions both in the transference and in his evocation of specific countertransference reactions in the analyst have been explored in the context of the interpretation of the transference. Otherwise, there is a risk of an analysis of the interaction in terms of a mutual exposure at a preconscious level that may contribute to draw the interpretation into a conventional surface rather than dealing with the explosive and uncanny aspects of the dynamic unconscious.

REFERENCES

Akhtar, S. (1992). *Broken structures: Severe personality disorders and their treatment*. Northvale, NJ: Aronson.

Akhtar, S., & Parens, H. (Eds.). (1991). *Beyond the symbiotic orbit*. Hillsdale, NJ: Analytic Press.

Arlow, J. A. (1991). *Psychoanalysis: Clinical theory and practice*. Madison, CT: International Universities Press.

Balint, M. (1968). The basic fault. *Therapeutic aspects of regression*. London: Tavistock.

Benvenuto, B., & Kennedy, R. (1986). *The works of Jacques Lacan: An introduction*. London: Free Association Books.

Bion, W. R. (1967). Notes on memory and desire. *Psychoanalytic Forum, 2*, 272–273, 279–80.

Bollas, C. (1987). *The shadow of the object*. New York: Columbia University Press.

Bollas, C. (1992). *Being a character*. New York: Hill and Wang.

Brenner, C. (1976). *Psychoanalytic technique and psychic conflict*. New York: International Universities Press.

Casement, P.J. (1991). *Learning from the patient*. New York: Guilford.

Chasseguet-Smirgel, J. (1986). *Sexuality and mind*. New York: New York University Press.

Cremerius, J. (1984). *Vom Handwerk des Psychoanalytikers: Band 1 and 2*. Stuttgart: Friedrich Frommann Verlag Günther Holzboog.

Deserno, H. (1990). *Die Analyse und das Arbeitsbündnis*. München: Verlag Internationale Psychoanalyse.

Epstein, L., & Feiner, A.H. (1979). *Countertransference*. New York: Aronson.

Etchegoyen, R. H. (1991). *Fundamentals of psychoanalytic technique*. New York: Karnac.

Fenichel, O. (1941). *Problems of psychoanalytic technique*. New York: The Psychoanalytic Quarterly.

Fromm-Reichmann, F. (1950). *Principles of intensive psychotherapy*. Chicago: University of Chicago Press.

Gill, M.M. (1982). *Analysis of Transference, Vol. I*. New York: International Universities Press.

Gill, M.M., & Hoffman, I.Z. (1982). *Analysis of Transference, Vol. II*. New York: International Universities Press.

Gray, P. (1986). On helping analysands observe intrapsychic activity. In A. Richards & M. Willick (Eds.), *Psychoanalysis: The science of mental conflict*. Hillsdale, NJ: Analytic Press.

Greenberg, J. (1991). *Oedipus and beyond*. Cambridge, MA: Harvard University Press.

Greenson, R. (1965). The working alliance and the transference neurosis. *Psychoanalytic Quarterly, 34*, 155–181.

Grunberger, D.B. (1971). *Le Narcissisme*. Paris: Payot.

Heimann, P. (1950). On countertransference. *International Journal of Psychoanalysis, 31*, 81–84.

Israel, P. (1994). *Formulations to the patient*. London: Institute of Psycho-Analysis.

Jacobs, T.J. (1991). *The use of the self*. Madison, CT: International Universities Press.

Jacobson, E. (1971). *Depression*. New York: International Universities Press.

Joseph, B. (1989). *Psychic equilibrium and psychic change*. London: Tavistock/Routledge.

Kennedy, R. (1993). *Freedom to relate psychoanalytic explorations*. London: Free Association Books.

Kernberg, O.F. (1975). *Borderline conditions and pathological narcissism*. New York: Aronson.

Kernberg, O.F. (1983). Object relations theory and character analysis. *Journal of the American Psychoanalytic Association, 31*, 247–271.

Kernberg, O.F. (1984). *Severe personality disorders: Psychotherapeutic strategies*. New Haven, CT: Yale University Press.

Kernberg, O.F. (1987). An ego psychology–object relations theory approach to the transference. *Psychoanalytic Quarterly, 61*, 197–221.

Kernberg, O.F. (1992). *Aggression in personality disorders and perversion*. New Haven, CT: Yale University Press.

Kernberg, O.F. (1993). Convergences and divergences in contemporary psychoanalytic technique. *International Journal of Psycho-Analysis, 74*, 659–673.

Kernberg, O.F. (1994). Reactions contre-transferentielles aigues et chroniques. *Rev. Franc. Psychoanalyse, 5*, 1563–1579.

Kernberg, O.F. (1995). The analyst's authority in the psychoanalytic situation. *Psychoanalytic Quarterly*.

Kernberg, O.F., Selzer, M., Koenigsberg, H.W., Carr, A., & Appelbaum, A. (1989). *Psychodynamic psychotherapy of borderline patients*. New York: Basic Books.

Klein, M. (1946). Notes on some schizoid mechanisms. *International Journal of Psycho-Analysis, 27*, 99–110.

Klein, M. (1952). The origins of transference. *International Journal of Psychoanalysis, 33*, 433–438.

Kohut, H. (1971). *The analysis of the self*. New York: International Universities Press.

Kohut, H. (1977). *The restoration of the self*. New York: International Universities Press.

Kris, A.O. (1982). *Free association*. New Haven: Yale University Press.

Lacan, J. (1966). *Écrits 1*. Paris: Éditions du Seuil.

LaPlanche, J. (1987). *Nouveaux Fondements pour la Psychanalyse: la Seduction Originaire*. Paris: Presses Universitaires de France.

Laplanche, J. (1992). *Seduction, translation, drives*, J. Fletcher & M. Stanton (Eds.). London: Institute of Contemporary Arts.

Le Guen, C. (1974). *L'Oedipe Originaire*. Paris: Payot.

Levine, H.B. (1992). Freudian and Kleinian theory: A dialogue of comparative perspectives. *Journal of the American Psychoanalytic Association, 40*, 801–826.

Levy, S.T., and Interbitzin, L.B. (1990). The analytic surface and the theory of technique. *Journal of the American Psychoanalytic Association, 38*, 371–392.

Liberman, D. (1983). *Lingüística, interacción comunicativa y proceso psicoanalítico*. Tomo I and II. Buenos Aires: Ediciones Kargieman.

Little, M. (1951). "Countertransference and the patient's response to it." *International Journal of Psychoanalysis, 32*, 32–40.

McDougall, J. (1979). Primitive communication and the use of countertransference. In L. Epstein & A.H. Feiner (Eds.), *Countertransference*. New York: Aronson.

Mitchell, S.A. (1988). *Relational concepts in psychoanalysis*. Cambridge, MA: Harvard University Press.

Modell, A.N. (1990). *Other times, other realities*. Cambridge, MA: Harvard University Press.

Ogden, T.H. (1989). *The primitive edge of experience*. Northvale, NJ: Aronson.

Racker, H. (1957). The meaning and uses of countertransference. *Psychoanalytic Quarterly, 26*, 303–357.

Racker, H. (1968). *Transference and countertransference*. New York: International Universities Press.

Reich, A. (1951). On countertransference. *International Journal of Psychoanalysis, 32,* 25–31.

Reich, W. (1933). *Character analysis.* New York: Farrar, Straus, and Giroux.

Rosenfeld, H. (1964). On the psychopathology of narcissism: A clinical approach. *International Journal of Psychoanalysis, 45,* 332–337.

Rosenfeld, H. (1987). *Impasse and interpretation.* London: Tavistock.

Sandler, J. (1976). Countertransference and role responsiveness. *International Review of Psychoanalysis, 3,* 43–47.

Sandler, J., Dare, C., & Holder, A. (1992). *The patient and the analyst.* Madison, CT: International Universities Press.

Sandler, J., & Sandler, A.M. (1984). The past unconscious, the present unconscious, and interpretation of the transference. *Psychoanalytic Inquiry, 4,* 367–399.

Schafer, R. (1976). *A new language for psychoanalysis.* New Haven, CT: Yale University Press.

Schafer, R. (1992). *Retelling a life.* New York: Basic Books.

Schwaber, E. A. (1983). Psychoanalytic listening and psychic reality. *International Review of Psycho-Analysis, 10,* 379–392.

Schwaber, E. (1990). Interpretation and the therapeutic action of psychoanalysis. *The International Journal of Psycho-Analysis, 71,* 229–240.

Searles, H.F. (1979). *Countertransference and related subjects: Selected papers.* New York: International Universities Press.

Segal, H. (1973). *Introduction to the work of Melanie Klein.* London: Hogarth Press.

Spence, D.P. (1982). *Narrative truth and historical truth: Meaning and interpretation in psychoanalysis.* New York: Norton.

Spillius, E.B. (1988). *Melanie Klein today: Developments in theory and practice, Vols. I and II.* London: Routledge.

Stewart, H. (1992). *Psychic experience and problems of technique.* New York: Routledge, Chapman, and Hall.

Sullivan, H.S. (1953). *The interpersonal theory of psychiatry.* New York: Norton.

Thomä, H., & Kächele, H. (1987). *Psychoanalytic practice, Vol. I.* New York: Springer-Verlag.

Winnicott, W.D. (1949). Hate in the countertransference. *International Journal of Psychoanalysis, 30,* 69–75.

Winnicott, W.D. (1960). Countertransference. *British Journal of Medical Psychology, 33,* 17–21.

Winnicott, W.D. (1965). The maturational processes and the facilitating environment. *Studies in the theory of emotional development.* New York: International Universities Press.

Zetzel, E.R. (1956). Current concepts of transference. *International Journal of Psychoanalysis, 37,* 369–376.

Discussion by Thomas Szasz, M.D.

◆

I am very pleased and honored to have been asked to discuss Dr. Kernberg's paper. It is a challenging and interesting assignment.

I assume that I was asked to be the discussant because Dr. Kernberg and l share a deep mutual respect and affection. Or perhaps because there is a kind of professional connection: I am one of the oldest living members of the American Psychoanalytic Association, and he is the most important figure in psychoanalysis in the English-speaking world today.

As a clinician, Dr. Kernberg has long been engaged in two difficult tasks. One is helping patients in a humane and "psychoanalytic" way; the other is trying to save psychoanalysis. Helping gravely troubled people who have difficulty coping with life is surely a noble affair and Dr. Kernberg is deservedly recognized for his efforts. Although psychoanalysis is no longer my cup of tea, I am going to comment on his presentation from a psychoanalytic point of view, which seems to me the only fair way to approach it.

Dr. Kernberg's other task—trying to save psychoanalysis as a profession—is more problematic. His efforts in that direction as well have been valiant. He has certainly saved psychoanalysis from at least one prominent but misguided practitioner, Heinz Kohut, who tried to redefine psychoanalysis as a kind of neo-Ferenczian, touchy-feely enterprise. Dr. Kernberg's intellectual rigor was an important counterweight against offering a sort of indiscriminate approval of patients as a cure-all for people who felt unappreciated as children.

Now let me say some things about his paper. It is, as you witnessed, a thorough and scholarly exposition of the present state of psychoanalysis, especially in the English-speaking world. It is a complicated essay—a kind of mini-encyclopedia, really—that does not lend itself to critical discussion, especially in an oral presentation. Instead of formally discussing it, then, I shall react to it from a frame of reference that was dear to my heart in the past, in my earlier incarnation as a psychoanalyst.

I should like to begin by pointing out something that Dr. Kernberg did not mention, but which to me is one of the most distinguishing features of psychoanalysis—that it is a situation of exceptional intimacy. Two people are alone in a room, often many times a week, over a prolonged period of time. One of them, sometimes both of them, speak about the most intimate aspects of their lives. Intimacies they don't speak about they communicate inadvertently, by virtue of the nature of the analytic situation.

It seems to me that a confidential verbal relationship may be more intimate than a sexual relationship, which we tend to regard as the epitome of intimacy. Films and novels are full of depictions of young people who barely know each other, falling into bed and engaging in satisfying sexual intercourse. Yet neither has the faintest idea about who the other one is. Verbal intimacy cannot be generated so effortlessly or so quickly. It takes a lot more effort—and existential commitment and trust—to have a significant and satisfying verbal intercourse than to have sexual intercourse.

Now I would like to say a few words about transference and countertransference. A long time ago I wrote a paper titled "The Concept of Transference." It was two-part paper. The second part, if I remember correctly, was titled "Transference as a Defense of the Analyst." That was the gist of it. As an illustration, I cited Freud's account of his experience with one of his female patients who, not surprisingly, fell in love with him. Freud mentioned this to his young wife. She was not happy to hear it. To reassure her, and perhaps himself, and perhaps because he himself believed it, Freud added: "Of course, she can't be in love with me. For that one has to be a Breuer." Nothing could be further from the truth.

Transference, especially in the context of interpersonal intimacy, is a challenging phenomenon, construct, or however we want to conceptualize it. The psychoanalytic situation, if it works, generates great intimacy. Unless age or gender or other factors work against it, the patient is likely to develop some erotic and personal feelings towards the therapist, and vice versa. What is reality and what is transference? Who is to say? It is a question about how we construct reality; how we interpret or understand what is going on; how we conceive of therapy; and so forth. Let me add that I don't believe that we construct reality out of a vacuum. There is something real out there. But what *that* is, is not a fact to which we have access, and the patient doesn't.

When transference is deemed to be negative, the possibilities for mistake and mischief are even greater than when it is thought to be positive. The patient may be angry with the analyst, possibly with good reason, but the analyst may dismiss this by saying: "The patient is not really angry with me. She is angry with her father (mother). I gave her no reason to be angry." This is a particular construction. Is it accurate? Appropriate? Useful? I think the best way to deal with such issues is by discussing them calmly, not by some kind of autocratic interpretation.

I know I repeat myself in saying that the analytic situation is one of great intimacy. I am using the word intimacy in a wholly positive sense. Most people crave intimacy. Humanly, morally, intimacy is a good thing. Still, there is something wrong, perverse as it were, with the intimacy of the analytic situation. Unlike intimacy in real life, analytic intimacy doesn't go anywhere. It is a dead end and must be accepted as such. This is why the relationship between the patient and the analyst after the end of therapy is somewhat problematic. It isn't like the relationship between a patient and a dermatologist or a client and a lawyer. In analysis, there is a never-ending barrier, like the incest barrier in the family.

Before concluding, I should like to pose some questions to Dr. Kernberg, especially as they pertain to treating so-called borderline patients. It seems to me that such people have, in everyday language, one or another of two problems or both. One is that they have poor impulse control. They want what they want and they want it now. They don't like to ponder options. They want action. The other is that they are spoiled adults. Some were perhaps spoiled children. Others were deprived children. The result is often the same. They want things from the therapist other than the relative deprivations of a purely analytic contact; they want things that fall outside the scope of therapy, even therapy elastically defined. How do you structure the therapeutic situation in such cases? Do you expect the patient to lie on the couch or do you want him to sit up and look at you or do you leave these things up to him? How much physical distance should there be between the patient and the therapist? How much handshaking?

How do you deal with missed appointments? With lateness? With silence? With the patient wanting to leave before the end of the hour? How do you deal with money, not just of payment and nonpayment, but also of excuses, such as "I am waiting for my insurance claim to come through," or whatever?

How do you deal with the patient who wants drugs? Who says, "I am anxious, give me a tranquilizer," or "I can't sleep, give me some sleeping pills."

One more question: How do you determine the indications for psychoanalysis? How much input does the patient have into that decision? Prominent therapists, like Dr. Kernberg, often get patients who are familiar with their work, who want what the therapists want to offer. Alternatively the patients are often themselves sophisticated therapists who know what they want. How do you deal with these contingencies?

Dr. Kernberg, I don't know if you had anything to do with choosing me as a discussant. But I appreciate the opportunity. Thank you.

Response by Dr. Kernberg

I usually don't talk about myself at conferences, but I would like to say something personal here. Unfortunately, I was not involved in selecting Dr. Szasz as my discussant, but I was happy when it occurred. I saw it as an indication of the sensitivity of Jeffrey Zeig, who knows all of the faculty and knows who to pair and who not. So, my first tribute is to Dr. Zeig.

I think I can mention here that my relationship to Dr. Szasz has been a complicated one. It started out at a conference many years ago when I was director of the Menninger Hospital. We were on a panel and he was rather tough with me. He didn't even remember the conflict the second time we met.

Over the years, I've grown increasingly respectful of Dr. Szasz and come to admire him very much. He has been extremely courageous to go against the currents; to talk about the responsibility of people, the responsibility of therapists, the responsibility of patients; to talk against the corruption of treatment, the misuse of treatment, the misuse of psychiatry. He has been a very important voice of our conscience.

But I only had the opportunity of establishing a more personal relationship with him recently, at the July 1994 Evolution of Psychotherapy conference in Hamburg. It was the best experience I had in Hamburg, which was a very good experience, all in all. So, it's a source of real pleasure to be sitting here with Dr. Szasz, whom I very much admire. I wish we had more like him in the psychoanalytic establishment.

There are some easy questions that he raised, and some difficult ones. Let me respond to the easy ones first.

Use of the couch: I still think it's helpful for standard analysis with healthier patients, but I don't have time to go into reasons. I don't use the couch in psychoanalytic psychotherapy. Face-to-face interviews are better because you observe what the patient is doing. Also, I'm less concerned with what I'm showing. I don't "go into hiding" because the analysis of the countertransference permits a much more natural attitude toward the patient.

What about handshaking? Dr. Szasz and I come from European traditions. I was brought up in Latin America, in Chile, where my analyst would shake my hand before and at the end of each session. I think they used to do the same in Europe. In this country it's not done and I don't do it. I maintain myself within ordinary social norms, and when society changes, I'm cautious how much I go with the trend.

For example, there's a tendency now to call people by their first names. I tend to call my patients by their last names. You could analyze whether I'm square or old-fashioned or whether or not there's a theory behind it.

How do I deal with late and missed appointments? Money? I treat my sick patients as responsible individuals. I treat every patient as if he has a nucleus of normality, a square millimeter of normality. I talk to that aspect even if the rest is chaos and craziness. This is what I mean by "technical neutrality." I establish strict limits. If the patient misses appointments, I start out analyzing it as much as I can. If the behavior doesn't change, I tell the patient that obviously my understanding is not sufficient to analyze an action that is destroying the treatment: If the aberrant behavior doesn't change, I'll end the treatment. I provide a limited amount of time, and then I'll analyze what the patient does in the limited amount of time that he still has.

I tell the patient what treatment I think he needs. This, I think, represents my authority. I don't think it's authoritarian. I don't negotiate with the patient, but I tell patients my opinion; they can go see other therapists and make their own decisions. Here's a medical analogy: If a patient comes to me, I might opine, "You need a gall bladder operation." He says, "I don't want a gall bladder operation, I want my appendix out." I tell him, "You are going against my judgment, you need a gall bladder operation." I see how that settles. Maybe he will agree.

Indication for psychoanalysis. Neurotic personality organization sufficiently severe to warrant the treatment because for mild things, I don't use psychoanalysis if a patient doesn't need it. If a person needs no treatment, I am happy to tell him that. But I don't use only psychoanalysis. For example, a woman came to see me. She was a group therapist, and she was married. She couldn't reach orgasm with her husband. She had an affair with her co-therapist, with whom she could reach orgasm. But she felt that she loved her husband, and she came to see me because she wanted to be able to have a satisfactory sexual relation with him. I diagnosed an inhibition of the orgastic phase and an hysterical personality. I told her I recommend sex therapy and then psychoanalysis. She was very surprised. I sent her to Helen Kaplan, who saw her for three or four months and resolved the sexual inhibition with her husband. Then the patient came back and said, "Thank you, now can you refer me to a psychotherapist?

I said, "I'm not going to refer you for psychotherapy. It will be psychoanalysis or nothing. You are a therapist, intelligent, well trained. You can run circles around any psychotherapist. You have significant personality problems, and I am afraid you will run into trouble in the relationship with your husband again. This is why I recommended psychoanalysis."

She said, "Well I'm not for that recommendation."

I said, "Fine, come back to see me whenever you want to. You know professionals in New York. If you want psychotherapy, you don't need my recommendation. I just don't recommend things in which I don't believe."

She came back a year later. There were problems with her husband, again sexual inhibition. I referred her to a colleague. She went through psychoanalysis and changed significantly. I had a follow-up in five years, and she did very well. This illustrates my approach.

Okay, those are the easy questions. Now the tough ones. Dr. Szasz pointed to some crucial issues I didn't mention in my paper—first of all, transference and countertransference.

What is transference in contrast to a realistic reaction to the therapist? There has been sharp critique in psychoanalysis that psychoanalysts really call transference what they don't like. Merton Gill made this point and I very much agree with him. I think that when the patient reacts realistically to the analyst's quirks, that's not transference. Transference begins where there are irrational or absurd reactions to the therapist. It's a dangerous situation in which analysts can become arbitrary. Dr. Szasz is absolutely right.

There are some people who say that transference is a compromise formation between analyst and patient. This is the opinion of the intersubjectivists and also of German analysts such as Thomä. I disagree with that. I reserve the term "transference" for that part which comes from the patient because if I do not, I get too much into an intersubjective mess theoretically.

Now, here comes the *most* difficult part. When Dr. Szasz said, "It's normal that a person should develop erotic feeling in such an intimate relation," he was absolutely right. Freud indicated that all love contains a transference element. There is repetition of the erotic intimacy with somebody who was very intimate—in other words, an early caretaker. In the case of "seduction," Jean Laplanche, the French analyst whose work I admire, says that the mother in the relationship commits the original "seduction." That original seduction transforms the erotic potential of the infant's body into the erotic drive. That's a fantastic formulation with which I fully agree. I don't have time to go into it. So yes, intimacy is a temptation and it is perverse if it's been misused. If it is used to understand what is normal and reasonable and what is distorted and conflictual, it becomes therapeutic.

Also there is a teasing element in the treatment, and that teasing element is one of the basic ingredients of the erotic relationship. I cannot go into more detail about it, but in my book *Love Relations* I discuss that situation in some detail. It is a concept that comes from French psychoanalysts.

So, in short, transference is to be handled like radioactive material, very responsibly, and with an awareness of how easy it can be misused.

Now about countertransference. The traditional concept of countertransference ignored the realistic relation to the person's behavior. The modern concept has overcome that. It also has overcome a "phobic" attitude toward countertransference. We react to the patient, and that is perfectly normal. The patient is angry, he provokes us, and we get angry. If the patient is sexually seductive, and we get sexually aroused, that's fine as long as we register it and use it for interpretive purposes rather than acting on it. There, then, is the moral boundary of the psychoanalytic situation that dictates the total moral responsibility of the therapist toward the patient.

The Evolution of an Analytic Psychotherapist:
A Sixty-Year Search for Conceptual Clarity
in the Tower of Babel

◆

Judd Marmor, M.D.

Judd Marmor, M.D.

Judd Marmor, M.D., is Adjunct Professor of Psychiatry at the University of California, Los Angeles, and was Franz Alexander Professor (now Emeritus) of Psychiatry at the University of Southern California School of Medicine in Los Angeles. Prior to that he was Director of the Divisions of Psychiatry at Cedars-Sinai Medical Center, Los Angeles and held numerous other academic appointments.

Dr. Marmor is Life Fellow and Past President of the American Psychiatric Association, and Past President of the American Academy of Psychoanalysis and of the Group for the Advancement of Psychiatry. He is a Fellow of the American College of Psychiatrists, a Founding Fellow of the American College of Psychoanalysts, and an Honorary Fellow of the Royal Australian and New Zealand College of Psychiatrists.

Dr. Marmor graduated from Columbia University College of Physicians and Surgeons in 1933. He has received numerous awards, including the Founders' Award from the American Psychiatric Association, the Ittleson Award from the American Orthopsychiatric Association and the Pawlowski Peace Prize. Dr. Marmor is the author of eight books and coauthor of one. He has written or collaborated on more than 300 scientific papers, primarily on psychoanalysis and human sexuality.

FORMATIVE EXPERIENCES

When I graduated from medical school over sixty years ago, at the tender age of 23, I already knew that I wanted to be a psychiatrist. It was not that I found other aspects of my medical education uninteresting. Quite the contrary! I found them all intriguing. However, when I first encountered people with serious mental disorders, I found the mystery of what lay behind their behavior particularly compelling. The intense distress and manifest irrationalities that many of them displayed, the "sickness of the soul" for which no obvious explanation seemed to exist, stirred my emotions and my empathy as had none of my other medical experiences. From that time to the present the twin challenges of psychiatric theory on the one hand and psychiatric treatment on the other have continued to be at the center of my professional efforts and concerns.

Most psychiatric theories of the late 19th and early 20th century revolved essentially around the concept of human beings as biological machines: Disturbances are attributed either to an hereditary defect or weakness, or to some external noxious agent such as a germ, toxin, or injury. I still recall making rounds on the wards of St. Elizabeth's Hospital in Washington, D. C., in late 1933 with a senior psychiatrist who kept pointing out various "stigmata" in the patients, such as the high arching of their palates, irregularities of their teeth, and webbing of their fingers, that presumably indicated their genetic weaknesses. The major shift away from this kind of approach occurred with the emergence of Freud's contributions. Without negating the importance of organic factors, he was the first to lay major emphasis on developmental experiences in childhood as the basis of most functional psychopathology. Because that made sense to me, I entered upon psychoanalytic training soon after completing my psychiatric and neurological residencies. (In the 1930s psychiatry was still the junior sibling of a specialty called neuropsychiatry!)

AN INITIAL CRITIQUE

As time went on and my knowledge and experience grew, however, I found myself beginning to question various aspects of Freudian theory. For one thing, the semantics of Freudian metapsychology, with its concepts of cathexes, countercathexes, and fused and defused libidinal instincts, appeared too far removed from the realities with which my patients were struggling. For another, Freud's focus on early sexual conflicts and the Oedipus complex as the primary source of psychopathology, with its obvious roots in the historical and social context of the sexually repressed, strongly patriarchal, middle-class culture of the 19th century Vienna in which he had grown up, seemed to me to be too narrowly based. Thus, Freud attributed the development of conscience and ego-ideal values (the so-called "superego") to "castration-anxiety" secondary to repression of the male child's incestuous desire for his mother. Castration anxiety, Freud asserted, then led to the child's

defensive identification with the father and the father's values. It was on this basis that Freud concluded that women could not have as adequate a superego as men, because they did not go through that kind of developmental crisis! This just didn't make sense to me even as a young analytic student. On the contrary, the women I knew had as fully developed or even more highly developed consciences and moral values than most of the men I knew! As my experience broadened, it seemed quite clear to me that what Freud called the superego actually began to develop in *both* boys and girls well before the Oedipal years, through the accrued, learned acquisition of values from both parents, and that it developed most healthily in children who had parents whom they admired and wanted to emulate, rather than whom they feared. Incidentally, this simple shift in conceptualization, which seemed almost self-evident to me even in my early years of training, did not take place officially within the ranks of psychoanalysis until many years later and not without a major internal struggle. The resistance of classical analysts to object-relations theory and self psychology arose precisely from the fact that the latter two movements were breaking away from the conflict-driven concept of the Oedipus complex and shifting the emphasis towards pre-Oedipal developmental deficiencies in the relationships between the young child and the mother. This did not mean that sexual conflict was no longer considered relevant in mental illness, but that deficiencies in pre-Oedipal nurturing experiences were viewed as equally important and probably even more basic.

ADDITIONAL INFLUENCES

By the late 1930s and early 1940s, as I came into contact with the writings of Harry Stack Sullivan, Abram Kardiner, Karen Horney, and Erich Fromm, my theoretical views began to broaden in other areas. These authors emphasized the importance of the broader social context in the shaping of personality—something that Freud had tended to minimize except insofar as he saw civilization as suppressing the free expression of sexuality. Another influential figure in those years was Sandor Rado, who emphasized that the major strivings of human beings were adaptive rather than libidinal in nature; this too seemed more congruent with the clinical realities that I was observing.

Other authors expanded my perspectives further. The meticulous observations by Piaget (1952) of how children learn to perceive their universe and how their capacity to form concepts develops were extremely enlightening to me, as was Lawrence Kohlberg's (1963) description of how the capacity for mature moral values evolved. Piaget saw the process of adaptation as a continuous one, with each period building on the information and models acquired in the earlier ones, rather than due to developmental shifts of libidinal energy from one erogenous zone to another, as Freud had taught. I was also impressed by John Bowlby's (1969) clarification of how certain fundamental patterns of adaptation were rooted in evolutionarily acquired brain structures, and that one of the most important of these patterns was the built-in need of all human infants, like the infants of other mammals, for attachment to a nurturing and protective parent figure. Margaret Mahler (1969) described this pattern clinically in her important studies; subsequently Stella Chess and Alexander Thomas (1977) demonstrated how genetic differences of temperament contributed significantly to the nature of the interaction between infants and their mothers.

AN EVOLUTION TO SYSTEMS

Thus, over time a shift gradually took place in my thinking about psychiatric etiology from the predominantly intrapsychic conflictual psychoanalytic model to an open-system model in which the behavior and thoughts of my patients were evaluated in the context of their total field situation. I no longer looked for the locus of psychopathology only within their individual psyches and nuclear family experiences, but rather in their total system of relationships, not only within the family but also in the community, in addition to possible biological and genetic contributory factors. This did not in any way minimize my appreciation of the importance of my patients' emotional and spiritual strivings or their search for meaning in life, but I was aware at all times that these strivings were shaped by the *total system* in which each of them had developed. That, of course, is why patterns of human sexual, spiritual, and religious behavior take so many different forms, each of which may seem natural or even innate to people who have developed within those particular systems.

ON PRACTICE

So much about the way in which I reached my current theoretical stance about a systems approach to an understanding of how personality and psychopathology develop. I realize that I have given you a very brief and sketchy account of what took me many years of reading and clinical experience to discover. But to deal with it in greater detail would take me too far afield, and I would like, therefore, to turn now to my parallel odyssey in the field of psychotherapy with which this Evolution of Psychotherapy conference is primarily concerned.

If I was perplexed by the plethora of theories about mental illness, my confusion was compounded as I strove to find my way through the veritable jungle of advocated therapies in our field, each asserting that it alone was the best (or the only!) road to mental health, and each with its own unique jargon—a veritable Tower of Babel!

The problem was even more complicated for me as a budding psychoanalyst because throughout the 1950s, the 60s and the 70s, and indeed to the present time, apart from the diverse schools of psychoanalytic therapy, there were literally scores of totally different approaches to psychotherapy, each with positive results reported by its practitioners. There were behavioral therapies rooted in theories of learning that totally rejected the psychoanalytic focus on the patient's unconscious conflicts, and that developed a wide spectrum of innovative techniques involving rewards, aversive stimuli, desensitization, implosion, social reinforcement, assertiveness training, role playing, and rehearsals—to mention only a few. Another group of therapies were part of what became known as the human potential movement and focused on ways of achieving peak emotional experiences, expanding consciousness, getting in touch with the true self, releasing repressed feelings, and even merging with the cosmos by way of transcendental experiences. Still other therapies, such as Rolfing or bioenergetics, which was originated by one of the faculty members of this conference, Alexander Lowen, placed a major emphasis on body manipulation. Then there were emotional control and relaxation therapies such as Zen and transcendental meditation, and also a variety of religious and inspirational therapies, some of the roots of which went back to prescientific times. In addition, there were numerous therapies that went beyond the pattern of individual psychotherapy, such as conjoint therapy of couples, family therapies, group therapies, marathon therapies, bibliotherapies, poetry therapies, art therapies, dance therapies ... all proclaiming the unique virtues of their particular variation.

Although it would take me too far afield to try to deal fully with this vast melange of therapies, I will return to comment on some of them later on in this chapter. What I would like to do at this point is to come back to the theme of my search for clarity within the framework of my chosen field, psychoanalytically oriented psychotherapy, and to indicate how and why it evolved as it did over the past five decades.

AN EVOLVING ANALYTIC
PERSPECTIVE

At the time that I completed my psychoanalytic training, I was still under the influence of the belief that the psychoanalytic cure depended on the insights that patients received by way of the therapist's specific interpretations, which, in turn, were based on the patient's free associations, memories, and dreams. With the help of these insights, patients were expected to revive old (usually infantile) conflicts and relive them in the transference to the analyst as an important part of the curative process. Freud himself later abandoned his early assumptions about the curative value of the recovery of infantile memo-

ries (although I might mention, as an aside, that it still lives on in the widespread assumption of some practitioners that remembering childhood sexual abuse can be curative in itself). Despite the fact that at that point in my development I still did not question these fundamental assumptions, I *had* already begun to have doubts about the kind of behavior that was expected of the analyst in the interaction with the patient. In accordance with the rules set out by Freud, analysts in the 1930s and 1940s were expected to preserve an austere neutrality and to present themselves as a kind of blank screen on which the patient's free associations could be played out without being influenced by the analyst's real persona.

Thus, analysts were taught to remain relatively passive and silent behind the couch even when their patients asked them specific questions. Although I could understand this technique as a meaningful *research* posture, I could not, even then, see it as being a *therapeutic* way of relating to patients, who often felt understandably alienated or frustrated by it. Moreover, as I delved into the early psychoanalytic literature, I found that Sandor Ferenczi (1920), one of Freud's earliest followers, had argued that a more human approach to patients was more effective. Many of you may know that in an effort to be a remedial parent-surrogate, he experimented with an occasional touch, or hug, or even kiss, for which Freud soundly berated him. In a prophetic letter, Freud wrote to him: "Picture what will be the result of publishing your techniques. ... A number of independent thinkers in matters of technique will say to themselves: Why stop at a kiss? ... Bolder ones will come along who will go further. ... The younger of our colleagues will find it hard to stop at the point they originally intended, and God the Father Ferenczi, gazing at the lively scene he has created, will perhaps say to himself: Maybe after all I should have halted in my technique of motherly affection before the kiss." (Jones, 1957, pp. 163–164).

Freud was right about this of course, and Ferenczi drew back from these more extreme expressions of affection; but he continued to insist on the therapeutic value of a more humane and emotionally interactive relationship with patients. My own personal contacts during my training years with Clara Thompson (who had been analyzed by Ferenczi), and with Karen Horney and Frieda Fromm-Reichmann reinforced my conviction that the impersonal Freudian model was not optimally therapeutic. Indeed, Fromm-Reichmann was one of the first psychoanalysts to challenge the traditional assumption that for psychoanalytic therapy to proceed smoothly, the patient *must* lie on the couch. This rule, she pointed out, grew historically not only out of Freud's original work with the hypnotic techniques of his time, but also because it was much more difficult and embarrassing in Freud's day to discuss sex and other intimate personal topics face to face than it is today. As for Freud's confession that also it was a hardship for the analyst to be looked at directly by patients for eight hours a day, Fromm-Reichmann (1950) pointed out that this followed from the requirement that the analyst must not react outwardly in any way to what the patient might say. If, however, the therapist could interact spontaneously and with objective human warmth with the patient, being looked at would become less of a strain. But, in any event, as she indicated, the fact that use of the couch makes the *analyst* feel more comfortable does not necessarily mean that it is better for the *patient*!

The landmark publication in 1946 of Alexander and French's seminal volume (1946) on psychoanalytic therapy also exerted a major influence on my thinking. The point that Alexander made that resonated strongly with me was that the *rituals* of psychoanalytic therapy should not dominate the *process* of trying to understand and help the patient. This encouraged me and other young analysts of that day to begin to experiment with flexibility—working with patients *off* the couch and seeing them less frequently than the mandated four or five times a week.

But there was another issue in those years that concerned me greatly. My instructors and supervisors, in accord with the then-prevailing assumptions of psychoanalytic therapy, all placed great importance on making the correct interpretation to the patient. However, I was aware of the fact that within the psychoanalytic movement itself there was a great deal

of theoretical diversity and conflict. Indeed, New York City in the late 1930s and 40s was a veritable cauldron of conflicting psychoanalytic theories and schools. There were classical Freudians, Adlerians, Jungians, Rankians, and followers of Horney, Fromm, and Sullivan, each group with its own points of view and theoretical interpretations. Inasmuch as I had friends who were members of these diverse analytic schools, I was fascinated to observe that they were all reporting equally good results, and that *their* patients were equally as enthusiastic about their experiences with their analysts as our patients were with *ours*!

As a result, I began to ask myself, how, if "cure" was dependent on the "specific" and "correct" interpretations made by the analyst, was it possible for psychoanalysts of diverse theoretical orientations to achieve comparable therapeutic results? It seemed obvious to me that if interpretations within one theoretical framework were just as effective as those within another, it *could* not be the precision of the varying intepretations that was responsible. There *had* to be some common denominator present that was cutting across all of these different psychotherapeutic approaches to account for such results.

COMMON DENOMINATORS: A COLLABORATIVE STORY

A few years later, in the early 1950s, an opportunity presented itself for me to study common denominators more intensively. I became a participant in a collaborative research study into the nature of the psychotherapeutic process, undertaken with Franz Alexander and a number of other analytic colleagues. In the course of this three-year study the psychotherapeutic transactions between several experienced psychoanalysts and their patients were meticulously recorded by trained observers through one-way mirrors in every session. A basic premise of this research was that no therapist, or patient, for that matter, could adequately describe what went on in the psychotherapeutic process, because they were both an intrinsic part of the process itself, and only outside observers could perceive the *totality* of the transactional experience between them. Prior to that time, it had generally been assumed that such external observation would drastically affect or modify the psychotherapeutic process, but we found (as is now generally recognized) that except for some initial self-consciousness on the part of both therapist and patient, the psychotherapeutic process went on as usual.

What did we discover? The most important single awareness that emerged from this long and meticulous study, which was published under the title of *The Dyadic Transaction* (Eisenstein, Levy, & Marmor, 1994), was a recognition of the subtle *complexity* and *multiplicity* of the interacting variables, *both verbal and nonverbal*, that entered into the psychotherapeutic process. Where we had previously thought psychotherapy was something a therapist did *to* or *for* a patient, we now clearly saw it as something that took place *between* them, with the therapist's particular interpretations being only one of many factors involved.

Let me give you some idea of what these factors are, and later I will try to demonstrate how they also play a role in nonanalytic forms of psychotherapy.

As I have indicated, we found that the nature of the relationship between the patient and the therapist was a much more complicated matter than was generally recognized. Patients enter into psychotherapy because of distress, maladjustment, or confusion, seeking help from therapists who are endowed, by virtue of their social role, with a help-giving potential. Thus, patients bring with them not only varying degrees of motivation, but also a measure of expectancy and hope that the therapist will be able to help them. The *real* attributes that patients also bring to the therapy—their intelligence, their social and vocational competence, their value systems, their life situations, and their ability to verbalize—all play a part in the therapeutic transaction, as well as do the nature of their disorders and the quality and quantity of their unconscious defenses, resistances, and transference distortions.

The therapists in our study also brought both conscious and unconscious attributes into the psychotherapeutic interaction. Therapists, we now know, are not interchangeable units, like razor blades. We found that their real attributes—their warmth, genuineness, empathy, knowledge, appearance, emotional maturity, and personal style—all played a significant role in each patient–therapist reaction. Add to these the therapist's own conscious and unconscious emotional needs, ambitions, and value systems, as well as any countertransference distortions that might be present, and you begin to get a faint inkling of the multiplicity of variables involved in the patient–therapist relationship. Our research strongly indicated that the way in which this matrix evolves and is shaped in any individual encounter is the basic foundation upon which a positive or negative therapeutic outcome depend; and this, I submit, is also the common denominator that underlies the success or failure of diverse psychotherapeutic approaches.

Although the importance of the therapist's personality was recognized almost 100 years ago by Dejerine (1913), the famous professor of psychiatry at the Salpetriere, who asserted that psychotherapy depends "wholly and exclusively upon the beneficial influences of one person on another," Dejerine saw it essentially as a one-way street, with the personality of the therapist exerting an influence upon the patient. Our modern view about this relationship has become a more sophisticated one. Harry Stack Sullivan in the 1950s described it as an "interpersonal" one, with the therapist functioning as a "participant observer." Grinker (1961) enriched this concept a decade later by emphasizing the two-way nature of the relationship, calling it a transactional process rather than an interactional one, with therapists and patients influencing one another. This is now generally recognized in the psychoanalytic literature, although most contemporary psychoanalysts discuss it in terms of transference and countertransference. The newest term in this area is the intersubjectivity of the patient–therapist relationship, but it deals with the same phenomenon. As you can see, at least in the past 20 or 30 years, we are dealing with a fine old wine being presented in a variety of bottles!

Returning to our research findings, within this basic matrix of the therapist–patient transaction we uncovered a number of other important elements. The ability of patients to confide and express their deepest feelings to a person whom they trusted and counted on to be supportive, understanding, and ultimately helpful, was an important factor, particularly initially, in reducing emotional tension. This factor often goes by the name of abreaction, or catharsis.

Then we found that the therapists, by virtue of their questions, confrontations, and interpretations, by what they chose to focus on or ignore, and by their nonverbal as well as their verbal reactions, began to convey to the patient a certain cognitive framework upon which their therapy was based. There are some schools of therapy, such as the Gestalt and the behavioral schools, that deny that any cognitive teaching is involved in their methods. Yet I submit that *cognitive teaching, whether explicit or implicit, is an inevitable part of every psychotherapeutic process*, because once you begin to explain the rationale of your approach to a patient you are setting up a cognitive framework. Psychodynamic therapists in effect say to patients, "You have developed these problems in the course of your personal development in relationships to significant people in your past. This has created certain distortions in the way you look at life and the way you perceive yourself, and we are going to try to uncover the sources of these problems and as you understand their origins you will begin to feel better." Gestalt therapists tell their patients that their problems are due to a failure to be sufficiently aware of their repressed feelings, and that by uncovering and expressing them more freely, they will begin to feel better. This, too, is a cognitive framework. Behaviorists who tell their patients that they have acquired certain inappropriate habits and perceptions as a result of faulty conditioning are also setting up a cognitive framework upon which their psychotherapeutic approach depends. In all of these diverse therapies, the purpose of this cognitive explanation is to give patients a meaningful context for understanding why and how their problems have developed.

OTHER COMMON FACTORS

Therapists also convey their *value systems* to patients in the course of their interpretations. Some psychoanalysts assume that a meticulously neutral stance avoids such communication of values, but this is a myth. Therapists of all schools *inevitably* purvey their values to their patients, wittingly or unwittingly, by what they react to as "healthy" or "neurotic." Actually, the therapeutic objectives of most psychotherapists in our culture reflect our culture's normative ideals, in that they all aim at enabling their patients to have more meaningful and satisfying social and sexual relationships, to work and love effectively, and to become productive and responsible human beings.

Moreover, in the course of pursuing these objectives, a certain amount of operant conditioning takes place in all therapies. This occurs via the responses that therapists of all schools make to the patient's verbal or behavioral expressions. Certain "healthy" behaviors are approved of, other "unhealthy" ones are disapproved of. This is not necessarily explicit. The response may just be in the shrug of a shoulder or a facial expression. Even behind the couch, when and how analysts express their "uh-huhs" are subtle cues to which patients are very sensitive. A number of research studies have demonstrated experimentally that these minimal signals of interest or disinterest, approval or disapproval, not only influence the content of the patient's communication, but also act as a subtle operant conditioning system by means of which approved thought and behavior is reinforced and that which is disapproved is discouraged. Another kind of operant conditioning that takes place is what Franz Alexander called "the corrective emotional experience." The fact that therapists generally respond more objectively, more empathically, or more realistically to the patients' emotional or behavioral expressions than did the significant authority figures in their past lives becomes an additional operant conditioning factor within the relationship.

Still another factor that we observed was the way in which patients, consciously or unconsciously, tended to model themselves after the therapist, and gradually to incorporate some of the explicit or implicit values to which they were being exposed. This kind of modeling is called "identification" or "introjection" by analytic psychotheraplsts, while learning therapists call it "social learning." Regardless of what name we attach to it, there is no doubt that it is one of the most important ways in which human beings learn from one another.

Another important element that occurs in all therapies, even though there are schools that would tend to deny it, is the element of suggestion and persuasion. *Whenever therapists present the rationale for their particular technique and imply or explicitly state that the patient will feel better as a result of following that therapeutic model, an element of suggestion is inevitably present.* The patient's expectation of being helped, the implicit assumption that this help will be forthcoming if he or she complies with the therapeutic program, and indications received in therapy that certain patterns of behavior are more desirable or healthy than others, all involve implicit, if not explicit, elements of suggestion and persuasion. And, as we know, the greater the faith of the patient in the therapist, the greater the degree of idealization or positive transference, the greater the impact of these suggestions on the patient.

Finally, for therapeutic change to really become consolidated, the new patterns that are being worked on need to be reinforced by a certain amount of rehearsal and repetition. This rehearsal can be explicit, as in certain behavioral therapies; it can be implicit, as occurs in the "working-through" process of analytic psychotherapy; or it can be in the form of homework assignments, as in cognitive therapies. But regardless of how it is done, patients must be enabled to apply the new adaptive techniques that they have learned in the course of therapy to other aspects of their lives, in work, with friends and peers, and within their family relationships.

COMMON FACTORS ACROSS THERAPIES

After compiling these research findings I became interested in whether these factors were also present in other therapeutic approaches, and I spent a number of years during the 1960s and 70s observing (using either personal observation or videotapes) the ways in which therapists from other schools operated. It is characteristic of all psychotherapeutic schools to try to explain the success of their approaches on the basis of a single or unique principle that differentiates their technique from all others, and presumably makes it superior. Analytically oriented psychiatrists attribute their success to their particular cognitive insights and transference interpretations; Rogerians believe that their technique uniquely releases the patient's own self-actualizing mechanisms; behavior therapists are convinced that the specific conditioning technique that they employ is the essential factor in their achieved therapeutic results; Gestalt therapists place their emphasis on the release of repressed emotions; Transactional Analysts, on the bringing into awareness the "game patterns" employed by patients in their interpersonal relationships, and so on. As a result of my studies, I became convinced that, as Hans Strupp (1973) has also pointed out, in no instance are the therapeutic results of these various schools ever due only to any such unitary factor. The substantial weight of the evidence was that the same factors that I outlined as common denominators in various forms of dynamic psychotherapy were operative in these other approaches also, although diverse therapies did differ in the emphasis they put on one or another of these factors.

Let me illustrate briefly how this operates in some of the different approaches that I studied. The Rogerian client-centered approach places its emphasis on creating a good client–counselor relationship, and assumes that no interpretive interventions are involved. Instead of making interpretations, Rogerian counselors empathically reflect back to patients their own statements from time to time, and within the context of this benign relationship they assume that patients begin to reconstitute themselves by virtue of their own innate self-actualizing tendencies. However, when one observes Rogerian therapy, one notes that Rogerian therapists encourage and reinforce certain patterns of communication and behavior in preference to others, if only by the tone of their voices, the expressions on their faces, the material that they choose to reflect back in contrast to that about which they make no comment at all. Thus they implicitly communicate to the patients their values and therapeutic objectives. Rogerian therapists, no less than others, become models for identification, and implicit suggestion and persuasion is inevitably involved. Cognitive insight is deemphasized, it is true, and whatever cognitive learning takes place is more apt to result from implicit rather than explicit communication. Thus, most if not all of the psychotherapeutic variables that I have listed for dynamic psychotherapy also are present, albeit in modified form, in Rogerian therapy, together always with the overriding importance of the therapist–client relationship.

What about behavior therapy? Joseph Wolpe's technique of "reciprocal inhibition" is an excellent paradigm of this approach. If you observe the way he works, either directly or in his videotapes, it is quite clear that a great deal more is going on in his therapeutic process than simply his technique of reciprocal inhibition. His relationship with the patients is warm and empathic; he takes a careful history; he makes interpretations; he communicates values; he uses suggestion and persuasion by telling patients that if they go through his series of hierarchical relaxations, they will begin to feel better. This is not only suggestion, it is also cognitive interpretation, because in effect it says, "Your problem started as a result of faulty conditioning and faulty habit-formation, and in the process of deconditioning these habits by our technique, you will begin to feel better." Here too, the quality of the relationship, the cognitive learning, the corrective emotional experiences, the empathic nature of the therapist–patient relationship, modeling, and rehearsal are all present.

In the Gestalt approach, which places great emphasis on emotional release and purports to downgrade cognitive awareness, the emphasis is on uncompromising emotional honesty and expressiveness—an important emphasis that is shared by most psychodynamic schools. But there *is* also a cognitive element, because patients are taught, either explicitly or implicitly, that their difficulties are the result of a failure to properly recognize and express their true feelings, and that the path to cure lies in being able to do so. Here, too, we see the same variables in operation, albeit in a different mix. The basic matrix of the patient–therapist relationship, the initial discharge of emotional tension in a setting of hope and expectancy, the powerful operation of suggestion by the assurance that if the therapist's program is followed improvement will ensue, operant conditioning by covert or overt indications of approval or disapproval from the therapist, the therapist's implicit or explicit offer of him or herself as an identification model, and explicit techniques of rehearsal are all present and demonstrable in Gestalt therapy.

Incidentally, Gestalt therapies, as you know, are often held in group settings, where the impact of suggestion and persuasion is powerfully enhanced by the group process itself. Group therapies fall into just as many different kinds of schools as do individual therapies, but in groups, too, the particular ideology that is employed lends support to the relationship and the process. Groups offer a wider variety of transactional possibilities than occur in one-to-one therapies, and a potential for multiple corrective experiences. Also, new adaptive techniques more often are openly rehearsed in the group situation than in individual one-to-one therapy.

The fact is that although psychotherapy takes numerous forms, I have yet to observe any psychotherapeutic technique in which the basic elements of a trusting and empathic patient–therapist relationship, suggestion, persuasion, identification, emotional support, cognitive learning, emotional release, and reality testing were not important factors in the therapeutic process and in the progress that the patient made.

INTEGRATING METHODS

Nevertheless, despite all that we have learned, there is no room for complacency in the field of psychotherapy. There are numerous unsolved research questions, and I beg you to be cautious when someone implies that all of the answers are in. One of the important challenges with which we are faced is to try to decide with some degree of assurance what specific form of psychotherapy is best suited for any particular patient. Although there are many patients who can be helped equally by diverse approaches, it is also true that some forms of psychotherapy are probably more suitable for some patients and some disturbances than others. Just as there is no single best way of teaching all subjects to all people, there is almost certainly no single best way of treating all patients and all conditions.

Incidentally, important recent advances in our knowledge about neurotransmitters and psychopharmacology have added a useful dimension to our ability to alleviate major psychotic disorders and even some refractory nonpsychotic ones, but I must emphasize that I have yet to see any of these disorders in which adjunctive psycho- or sociotherapy was not also indicated and helpful.

In my own work, because of my systems-theory orientation I try to focus therapeutically on wherever I feel the systemic disturbances are most operative. Thus, although I may prescribe medication when appropriate, I also do conjoint marital therapy when the problem lies in the conjugal relationship, family therapy when there are relevant problems in the dynamics of the family, recommend group therapy when I perceive that a regulated social interaction would be helpful, and also have used hypnosis, particularly in post-traumatic dissociative disorders. In all instances, I try to avoid putting every patient on a Procrustean bed of a singular therapeutic method but rather adapt my approach to the patient's own unique needs. This also includes varying the frequency of visits, and doing brief dynamic psychotherapy when feasible.

CONCLUSION

In closing, I hope I have succeeded in giving you some insight into the way my concepts on the nature of the psychotherapeutic process have evolved, and how they have shaped my therapeutic methods. It is probably too much to hope that we shall ever see an end to the partisan proclamations of the superiority of one particular technique over all others, but if we learn to live with and respect our differences, and recognize that the temple of truth may be reached by different routes, perhaps we members of the mental health professions can set an example from which the rest of our troubled world could greatly benefit!

REFERENCES

Alexander, F., & French, T. (1946). *Psychoanalytic therapy.* New York: Ronald Press.

Bowlby, J. (1969). *Attachment.* New York: Basic Books.

Chess, S., & Thomas, A. (1977). *Temperament and development.* New York: Brunner/Mazel.

Dejerine, J. (1913). *The psychoneuroses and their treatment by psychotherapy* (S. E. Jelleffe, Trans.) (pp. vii–viii). Philadelphia: Lippincott.

Eisenstein, S., Levy, N. A., & Marmor, J. (1994). *The dyadic transaction: An investigation into the nature of the psychotherapeutic process.* New Brunswick, NJ: Transaction.

Ferenczi, S. (1950). The further development of an active therapy in psychoanalysis. In *Further contributions to the therapy and technique of psychoanalysis.* London: Hogarth.

Fromm, E. (1941). *Escape from freedom.* New York: Farrar & Rinehart.

Fromm-Reichmann, F. (1950). *Principles of intensive psychotherapy* (pp. 10–12). Chicago: University of Chicago Press.

Grinker, R. (1961). Transactional model for psychotherapy. In M. Stein (Ed.), *Contemporary psychotherapies.* New York: Free Press.

Horney, K. (1937). *The neurotic personality of our time.* New York: Norton.

Jones, E. (1957). *The Life and Work of Sigmund Freud, Vol. 3.* New York: Basic Books.

Kardiner, A. (1939). *The individual and his society.* New York: Columbia University Press.

Kohlberg, L. (1963). The development of children's orientations toward a moral order. I: Sequence in the development of moral thought. *Vita Humana, 6,* 11–33.

Mahler, M. (1969). *On human symbiosis and the vicissitudes of individuation.* New York: International Universities Press.

Piaget, J. (1952). *The language and thought of the child.* London: Routledge & Kegan Paul.

Rado, S. (1956). *Psychoanalysis of behavior.* New York: Grune & Stratton.

Strupp, H. (1973). Toward a reformulation of the psycho-therapeutic influence. *International Journal of Psychiatry, 11*, 263–265.

Sullivan, H. S. (1945). *Conceptions of Modern Psychiatry.*

RELEVANT MARMOR REFERENCES

(1962) Psychoanalytic therapy as an educational process: Common denominators in the therapeutic approaches of different psychoanalytic schools. In J. Marmor, *Psy-chiatry in Transition*, 2nd Ed., 1994. New Brunswick, NJ: Transaction Publishers, pp. 195–209.

(1964) The nature of the psychotherapeutic process. In *Psychiatry in Transition*, 2nd Ed., 1994, pp. 296–309.

(1968) New directions in psychoanalytic theory and therapy. In *Psychiatry in Transition*, 2nd Ed., 1994, pp. 251–264.

(1971) Dynamic psychotherapy and behavior therapy: Are they irreconcilable? In *Psychiatry in Transition*, 2nd Ed., 1994, pp. 310–326.

(1982) Psychoanalysis, psychiatry and systems thinking. *Journal of the American Academy of Psychoanalysis, 10*, 337–350.

Discussion by Jay Haley, M.A.

◆

Dr. Marmor's paper is so comprehensive and so rich, it's very difficult to comment on it. I tend to choose something to disagree with in my comments, and it's very difficult to find something to disagree with in what he says.

What especially interested me are the steps Dr. Marmor took from the method of psychoanalysis to a broader view—in fact to the recommendation that you should design a therapy for each patient. That's a tremendous voyage to have taken over the years.

I was, of course, too young to know when psychoanalysis was a rebellious force against the organic psychiatrists. I know it was for a period, and then it became successful and became a conservative force and had a considerable influence. You couldn't talk about therapy except within a framework of psychoanalysis, and you had to differ with it or go along with it.

For example, the 1960s. I was talking to a training analyst who said he was very disappointed with the new crop of psychoanalysts. He said that when he was young and became an analyst, analysts were rebelling and they were original. They were the deviants in the field. Now, they were the conservative force. He said that all the young people just wanted to be told where to sit, and what to say, and what they should wear in the way of a suit. They were a very conservative crowd.

It's within that framework that I came into therapy. For me analysts were a force making it difficult to think in any broader way.

It's hard to remember how conservative they were and what an influence they had. I remember a personal example—and what I can do here is just free associate to various situations brought up by this paper.

I went to a psychoanalytic institute in San Francisco because there was a psychiatrist from India who was going to talk on the Oedipal complex. I was curious about what he'd say. He gave a very interesting talk. He said that there was a population in India whose rule was that a mother and a father could never quarrel about anything except their oldest son. Anything they had to quarrel about they had to put in terms of the oldest son. That was just the rule of the culture.

He said that this made a very different Oedipal problem for the oldest son in that culture compared with the Oedipal problem for people in Vienna. I thought that it was interesting to reflect on the culture relativity of a basic idea like the Oedipal complex. But the head of the institute stood up and said, "I don't think this man knows anything about the Oedipal complex or about psychoanalysis and he shouldn't be imposing his views upon us."

Everybody in the room was embarrassed, and yet that's the kind of force that psychoanalysis was becoming in those days, a very limiting one.

One of the influences on me was Sullivan, and I remember the reaction to Sullivan. Sullivan proposed that there were two people in the room while therapy was going on who were undergoing analysis. This aroused great indignation among many analysts, who thought they were a neutral screen to be projected upon. They weren't doing anything that influenced the patient.

The way Sullivan supervised would be to say, "What were you doing when the patient said that?" Or, "What had you just said?" That is, he assumed that the patient, particularly the schizophrenic, was responding to the therapist.

I was supervised by Don Jackson, who was personally supervised by Sullivan. So Jackson passed on that emphasis on therapy being a transaction of the two people in the room. It's been accepted pretty well in analytic circles now, but at that time that idea was heresy.

You know, one of the curious things is that most family therapists, or many of them, have had some contact with Sullivan. I was a consultant with the Group for Advancement of Psychiatry and we did a survey of family therapists in the 1960s. The vast majority of them had some contact with Sullivan, either personal or in therapy, or in some way.

Sullivan didn't start family therapy. Some people argue that it was because he didn't like women. Therefore, he didn't sit down with mothers and their kids. He wouldn't, in fact. He made a ward in a hospital in which there were only men; there weren't any women who worked there or were patients there. It was a prejudice he had that kept him from founding the family therapy field. But he had a great influence by propounding the idea that in therapy there is more than one person involved.

At that time there was an attempt to loosen up the thinking of psychoanalysis. They created the Academy of Psychoanalysis, with which Dr. Marmor was involved. They would bring in people with different views, trying to break up the conservative force of the analytic movement.

I remember how it struck me that people hang on to certain ideas even though they give up the ideology. For example, psychoanalysis was a method and the important thing was to do the method correctly. Other issues were not as important as that, and that idea was transmitted to a variety of schools of therapy that were then developing.

I remember at the Academy of Psychoanalysis, Don Jackson and I gave a paper, I think it was 1959 or 1960. For the first time a number of people there heard about the possibility of interviewing a whole family. They had never heard of that and some people thought it was interesting. There was a group from Philadelphia there and they decided to start using this procedure.

So, they went back to Philadelphia and they began to see families and they invited me to visit them. They had been going for about three months, and I went and watched a session in which they had a one-way mirror set up, like we did, and they had two therapists in the room, and they had a family with an 18-year-old daughter. The daughter had been sexually abused by the father, and she was put in the hospital, which was the tradition in those days.

This interview occurred before the first time she was going home for the weekend. There was a question: What was going to happen when she got home? But nobody discussed it. So, when the therapists came out of the room at the end of the interview and we talked about it, they said they wished the family had brought up the issue of what's going to happen this weekend. Would there be the possibility of any sexual activity?

I said, "Well, why didn't you bring it up?"

They said, "Well, you don't initiate what is said in family therapy."

I said, "Well, you do initiate. You don't wait for the patient to initiate. You can say something yourself in family therapy."

They said, "That's not the way it's done."

So I said, "Well, if you didn't do that, you could have come behind the mirror and left the family in there." Many families would go right to a major concern if the therapist would get out of the way.

They said to me, "You don't go behind the mirror in family therapy."

I said, "What do you mean, you don't go behind the mirror? One of the major family therapists, Charles Fullwieller, who probably introduced the mirror in therapy, spent most of his time behind the mirror. He would start a family talking and then he would go behind the mirror and watch them. Then he'd go in and make a comment and go back out again." I said this was a legitimate procedure.

They said, "That isn't what you do in family therapy." Now, they had been doing it three months, and they already had the methods established: You had two therapists. You never left the room; you didn't initiate what was to be said. They began to contend that their therapy was better than any other family therapy because it was so deep and intense.

What I'm getting at is that they could give up some ideology that bound them to see individuals, but they kept some of the processes that they couldn't get rid of. "Method" is one of those things that hangs on. People make an issue of doing the method right rather than doing what's appropriate for the therapeutic situation.

But one of the things, too, that interested me was Dr. Marmor's comment about the study of psychoanalysis with observation by Franz Alexander and others. I was on Gregory Bateson's research project for ten years. We were investigating a variety of issues, including the nature of therapy.

We filmed or observed whichever therapists we could. We wanted to get some idea of what therapy was all about. We had great trouble getting psychoanalysts to be filmed or observed. When we found out that Franz Alexander also had trouble getting analysts filmed, we felt it wasn't just us: We weren't just a deviant group.

At the time I thought analysts didn't want to be filmed because they were concerned about showing their competence. I began to think, as I talked to them and interviewed them, that they didn't want to be filmed because they didn't do what they were supposed to do. There was a way you were supposed to behave in analysis and they didn't behave that way. But when an issue was made of it, then they had to say, "Yes, that's how we behave."

I recall finding this out. Bernie Gorton, a therapist who was an Ericksonian in Philadelphia, shared an office with an orthodox analyst. I was over at Bernie's house one night and he invited the analyst for dinner. The analyst gave me a lecture on how you should be absolutely neutral. You shouldn't give any kind of a directive. You should just be a screen to be projected upon and that was what analysis was.

So, I said, "That's very interesting," or words to that effect.

After he left, Bernie said, "You know, that isn't the way he does analysis at all."

I said, "How could that possibly be?"

He said, "Well, I share this office and we come out and have coffee between patients and he tells me sometimes what he does with patients. It isn't that." He said, "Like today he was saying at lunch. 'I have this woman, and I don't think she'd be improving at all if I hadn't told her I'd spank her if she didn't improve.' "

Now, he would never admit that for any public presentation. I realized that even if you could corner an analyst and get him to be observed or on film, he wouldn't behave the way he claimed he behaved ordinarily. When you're investigating therapy and trying to find out what causes change, you want what they do, not what they're supposed to do. So, it was a difficult and interesting problem to research therapy.

One of the issues to me is that many people went through a psychoanalytic period and then tried to recover from it. It's not easy to do because it has a comprehensive ideology as well as ways of interpreting anything that happens. In many ways it was like a religion and it's difficult to kick a religion.

You know, it reminds me of a priest I know who quit the priesthood and was still working as a social worker. One day he told me that he was in the Bronx in his usual street clothes, and he went into a tenement, went down a hallway in a slum, and a woman passed him and said, "Hello, Father."

He realized that she knew he had been a priest. I remember him saying that you can take the priest out of the religion but you can't take the religion out of the priest. I think many people trying to recover from psychoanalysis have this problem. They see everything within the framework of psychoanalysis and then they have to interpret it while denying psychoanalysis. It's a difficult and interesting problem.

If you listen from that point of view to Dr. Marmor's history, starting with psychoanalysis and going through the variety of therapies he mentioned at the end, there is a tendency for him to see these therapies from an analytic point of view. That is, I think one could hear his talk as a struggle to recover from psychoanalysis.

I hope that he has many years ahead to complete that task.

The Disorders of the Self and Intimacy: A Developmental Self and Object Relations Approach

James F. Masterson, M.D.

James F. Masterson, M.D.

James F. Masterson, M.D. (Jefferson Medical School, 1951) is Director of the Masterson Group and the Masterson Institute. He pioneered the developmental, object relations approach to the psychotherapy of the Personality Disorders. Dr. Masterson is a Fellow of the American College of Psychoanalysts, the American College of Psychiatrists, and the American Psychiatric Association. He is on the editorial board of numerous journals and is the author of nine books and the editor of five. Among his honors, he received the Schonfeld Award for Outstanding Achievement from the American Society of Adolescent Psychiatry. He is an Adjunct Clinical Professor of Psychiatry at the Cornell University Medical College. Dr. Masterson is one of the most influential practitioners and teachers of contemporary psychoanalytic approaches.

INTRODUCTION

Therapists' concern with intimacy probably began with Freud's idea that the goal of treatment was to enable the patient to love and to work. The dramatic social changes we have undergone since the sixties have heightened the issue of intimacy for the population in general and particularly for patients with a disorder of the self.

The revolution of the 1960s against authoritarianism, racism, and sexism moved our society towards more individualism, female liberation, and the importance of an independent autonomous self. The female liberation movement reevaluated and redefined the mutual role expectations of men and women in intimate relationships towards greater equality and sharing.

The post–World War II generation who led this revolution applied it to child rearing. Their children, now adults, are carrying these standards out in their lives. The profound effects of these changes on our views of intimacy are seen in the statistics: both parents working, later marriages, 50 percent of marriages ending in divorce. They are also reflected in the popular literature, in such titles as *Women Who Love Too Much*, *How to Get the Right Man*, *Intimate Partners*, *Cold Feet*, and *Peter Pan*.

Notions are bruited about that the new social model will be serial marriages—the first

to have a child, and the second for an enduring relationship, or no marriage at all. This is
despite the work of Wallerstein (Wallerstein &
Kelly, 1990) and others on the profound emotional effect of divorce on children's development.

The ambiguity of these ideas is illustrated
further by the prenuptial contract, which
seems to be a contradiction in terms—two
people who are getting together because they
love and trust each other require a document
based on mistrust. These social whirlpools
complicate the issue of intimacy for everyone
but they most strongly reinforce the problem
for people with disorders of the self, because
difficulties with intimacy have always been a
key feature of the disorder.

DEFINITIONS—THE SELF AND INTIMACY

Webster defines intimacy as "a state marked
by very close association, contact familiarity
engaging one's deepest nature."

The developmental self and object relations
definition is the capacity to commit the real
self to an object through feelings of love and
sexual attraction, to see that object as a whole,
both good and bad, to support the object's real
self in a close, ongoing, enduring relationship
with minimal impairment from fears of engulfment or abandonment, and to sustain that commitment despite feelings of disappointment or
frustration.

The capacities of the real self, which emerge
as the self becomes autonomous, make a vital
contribution to the capacity for intimacy. They
include such capacities as self activation,
soothing, spontaneity, sense of self-entitle-
ment, acknowledgement of self-activation, continuity of self, capacity to see the object as
whole, capacity to be alone, to tolerate anxiety and depression, and to commit to the object
and to mourn loss of the object. One has to
have an autonomous, whole self to more or
less freely commit to the object.

THE DEVELOPMENT AND FUNCTION OF THE SELF'S CAPACITY FOR INTIMACY

The self's capacity for intimacy emerges
and evolves through the stages of separation-
individuation or through the stages of subjective self and verbal self to the Oedipal stage,
and is then tested and refined during adolescence and adulthood.

In the separation-individuation stage the
self emerges and develops to take on its full
capacities. A successful separation-individuation stage leads to the emergence of a whole
self representation with a relationship of
mutual trust between the self and the object—
the self having a realistic sense of entitlement
of support and realistic sense of life's difficulties and frustrations.

There are differing views of how the emergence of the self occurs. Mahler (Mahler, Pine,
and Bergman, 1975) considered the chief issue
to be separation of the image of the self from
that of the mother, and described the child as
going through four stages. Stern (1985), on the
other hand, who thinks that the child is able
to perceive the mother as separate from birth,
sees the key issue as the self's capacity to
become autonomous, whole and take on its
functions. Stern described the self as going
through four stages: core self, emerging self,
intersubjective self, and verbal self. Both of
these researchers, however, agree on one fundamental consideration: In order for the self to
emerge and become whole there has to be, as
Mahler reported, "a mother providing supplies
and support for individuation and for self activation" and as Stern put it, "mother providing
empathic attunement to the child's emerging
self." Since there are no perfect mothers and
no perfect children there may be scars emerging from these stages that do not necessarily
represent a diagnostic disorder but rather
minor difficulties with capacities for autonomy,
creativity, and intimacy. And what person does
not have a problem with one or another of
those capacities?

Completion of the separation-individuation
stage, which happens at roughly between 0 to

3 years of age, leads to the Oedipal stage. The child enters this stage with an autonomous self and the capacity to see the object as a whole. The child then invests the parent of the opposite sex with sexual and affectionate feelings, which take precedence over the formerly one-dimensional view of the parent as care-taker—in other words, the relationship becomes sexualized and competition arises with the same-sex parent.

These conflicts submerge under the force of repression during the latency period, roughly from five to twelve years of age.

Due to the onset of the sexual drive in adolescence, these conflicts reemerge. Then, guided by the incest taboo, the residues of unconscious Oedipal conflicts are worked through by turning from the parental objects to peer objects during sexual emancipation. Adolescent experimentation in the external environment then takes place to achieve two goals: to establish an inner sexual identity for the self and to identify the intrapsychic sexual object that fits that identity.

In early adulthood, with sexual identity identified and the intrapsychic sexual object defined, the last task is to experiment in the environment in order to find a fit between the external object and the internal object—as Freud emphasized, the finding of the object is really a refinding. The individual tests the waters with the object and evaluates the object's response. As the object's response is positive—supportive of the individual's self—interaction of mutually supportive real selves occurs, leading to physical intimacy. Physical intimacy leads to fulfillment of the search and completion of the cycle. The romantic and sexual idealization that accompanies "falling in love," although strongly based on fantasy, facilitates the process and eventually gives way to a more realistic and enduring relationship based on the gratifying interaction of the two selves. Of course, this includes both the sexual and the romantic interaction.

This pathway to intimacy is gradual, based on the mutual need to test the other and to protect one's own healthy narcissistic vulnerability. Sex is such a powerful drive to emotional intimacy that it can cement a close relationship, and used prematurely it can often

make closeness impossible by aborting the essential testing aspect of the relationship necessary to establish a real relationship based on knowledge and interaction.

THE ILLUSION OF INTIMACY IN DISORDERS OF THE SELF

For a patient with a disorder of the self, intimacy is a demand for real self-activation, which evokes separation anxiety, which evokes defense. These patients' impaired real selves, lacking autonomy and also lacking trust in the object, cannot tolerate or manage a real intimate relationship because it evokes their fears of being engulfed and/or abandoned. In order to be able to experience feelings of closeness and sexual gratification they have to devise a defensive system, which on the one hand protects them from the fears and on the other hand allows feelings of closeness. They always titrate the one against the other—not so close as to stir up fear, and not so far as to lose the feeling of closeness.

This appears in the clinical evidence as follows: the borderline by clinging and/or distancing defenses against these fears, the narcissistic disorders by the need for mirroring defense of the exhibitionistic or the idealizing defense of the closet narcissistic disorder, the schizoid disorder by the need for a master–slave or self-in-exile defense. Each produces its own distorted illusion of intimacy: The borderline patient defines intimacy as a relationship with a partner who will take over responsibility and offer approval for regressive behavior. The narcissistic patient defines intimacy as being admired or adored or "basking in the glow" of the idealized other. The schizoid defines it as being in perfect compliance with the object in prison, but connected. The illusion is created by these patients that the relationship "works."

What they mean is not that there is a more or less harmonious mutual sharing of real selves but that their defense has been put in place, which allays their fears and thereby enables them to feel affection and sexual excitement as long as they continue to deny the maladaptive defensive aspect of the relationship. This can be seen clinically by the following types of relationships.

THE ILLUSIONS OF INTIMACY

Partial Relationship: The patient establishes a relationship with a significant other who is not in reality available for a number of reasons. The other may be married, or a workaholic, or a traveler, and so on. The advantage of this relationship is that because the other is not available in reality it does not evoke the patient's fears of engulfment or abandonment and then it is possible to experience feelings of love, sex, and romance without being impeded by these fears. For example: two couples are on a cruise together, and the man in one couple starts an affair with the woman in the other couple. At the end of the cruise the man of the one couple has fallen in love with the woman and tells her he is about to divorce his wife. The woman in the other couple says that's fine for you, but if you ever get married again look me up.

Instant Intimacy: The testing and the trial period essential to the establishment of a real relationship evokes such enormous separation anxiety with these patients that in order to relieve that anxiety they abort the testing process and jump prematurely into a relationship. It's a common experience to start treatment with a borderline patient who is not in a relationship and shortly thereafter the new patient meets somebody at a bar, has a sexual encounter, and they're living together. The function of this particular kind of intimacy is a defense against the anxiety evoked by the therapeutic relationship. The patient then titrates the one relationship against the other. As increasing therapeutic involvement evokes separation anxiety the patient moves closer to the other relationship. Fortunately, the instant intimacy has made the patient deny the destructiveness of the partner, which eventually emerges and can be dealt with by the therapist.

The Clinging Relationship (marriage or the relationship established to avoid individuation): This commonly occurs when individuals pass through modal stages in the life cycle that require more individuation—for example, leaving high school, graduating from college. It is at this point, when they will have to function on their own, that they reach out for a partner to defend against the anxiety that having to function on their own evokes.

Distancing Relationships: This occurs in a variety of ways, from no relationship at all to relationships that are distant. For example, one partner is away a good deal of the time. A good clinical example is of a couple—one lived in New York, the other lived in London—who began dating across the Atlantic Ocean and then made the mistake of deciding to get married. The man left London, came to New York to live, and once the distancing defense was overcome, in a very short time the couple were at each other's throats.

Sex Without Emotional Involvement: One example is sexual promiscuity with the rapid progression of sexual partners without any emotional investment, or sex without emotion with the same partner.

Emotional Involvement Without Sex: Relationships formed on the basis of mutual clinging that do not involve sex.

Narcissistic Patients: The patient who is unable to find the perfect mate, or the couple who get together on the basis of mutual idealizing that leads to mutual disappointment.

Sadomasochistic Relationships: Where the partner is used for the reinforcement and discharge of sexual anxiety and tension.

The Couples Who Fight but Stay Together: The question often arises—when a couple fights so much why do they stay together? The answer, of course, is that they stay together because they fight so much. The message is that it is preferable to have an external negative object to project the internal negative object on rather than have to contain and feel the depression and negative feelings associated with one's own internal object. The relationship suffers but the patient maintains more intrapsychic comfort.

There seems to be a relationship between the degree of negativity of the internal object and the need for an external object on which to project it. The more negative the internal object the more the need to pick an external negative object.

What is illustrated here is how the need to reenact distorted internalized object relationships takes precedence and erodes the capacity to have a mutually satisfying intimate relationship.

The normal pathway to a relationship of experimenting and testing and evaluation of feedback does not occur. In the rosy glow of the idealization of sex and romance which occurs in the early stage of any relationship, the patient throws caution to the winds in order to act out and ofter to reenact their internalized object relations. It is only later when the realities that were denied begin to impinge that difficulty arises. Incidentally, can you imagine what this normal idealizing process that occurs early in the relationship does to the already present clinging and idealizing defenses in patients with disorders of the self?

In working with these difficulties with intimacy I found certain comments helpful. For example, I will say to a patient who distances: "You could walk through a room with twenty people, nineteen of whom were available and pass them all up and pick the one unavailable person." Secondly, to those who are using extreme denial of their significant other's negative aspects I will often cite the movie "Some Like It Hot" where Joe E. Brown is taking Jack Lemmon, who is dressed as a woman, in a motorboat to meet his mother. Jack Lemmon does everything he can to discourage Joe E. Brown from this endeavor, and finally, when Brown is not hearing and not responding to these efforts, Lemmon flips off his wig and says, "Besides, I am a man." Joe E. Brown looks over calmly and says, "Well, you can't have everything."

One reliable method to determine whether a new relationship for a patient in treatment is adaptive and progressive or regressive and defensive is as follows: If the patient reports that the new person makes him feel so comfortable and so at ease the answer is the negative. This is an object that provides defense. However, if the patient talks about being so attracted to the other, but also so nervous he can hardly sit still, this is a positive sign. This person is presenting the challenge of a real relationship, which evokes the patient's separation anxiety.

THE PROBLEM OF LOSS WITH DISORDERS OF THE SELF

A whole self representation is necessary in order to be able to separate from a relationship and repair the loss through grieving. This takes time and frees the self to form a new relationship and can often produce emotional growth. For people with a disorder of the self, the end of a relationship is a crisis which reinforces their innermost fears of abandonment, and unable to grieve because of the lack of a whole self representation, they are forced to resort to their characteristic defenses—denial, detachment, acting out. These, however, do not free the sense of self, so they are left to continue reenacting the same scenario in future relationships. It is often astonishing to note how hard they strive to pick a partner who is different than the last, and who indeed on the surface seems to be different, but who inevitably turns out to be the same.

THE THERAPEUTIC TASK

The therapist's task is to decode these defensive illusions and bring to the patient's attention that what he or she had felt was an expression of an intimate relationship was in reality an illusion consisting of defenses against abandonment or engulfment coupled with denial of the maladaptive part of the relationship.

BORDERLINE DISORDERS OF THE SELF—PROBLEMS WITH INTIMACY

In the case of the borderline patient, relationships are dominated by the need to defend against the fear of abandonment or depression; they will be unreliable, vulnerable to frustrations, and heavily dependent on the mood or feeling at the moment. The borderline lover will have trouble sustaining relationships because the loved one will be seen as two entities, one rewarding and satisfying, the other withholding and frustrating.

There may be no continuity in the way the borderline views his or her partner. It shifts moment to moment and is either totally good or totally bad. In any event, the loved one is never perceived as a complex, richly ambiguous person embodying faults and virtues simultaneously.

A WOMAN ACTING OUT THROUGH CLINGING:

This was a 33-year-old attractive single woman who lived alone in an apartment close to her parents, did not work, and led a jetset life with neither goals nor direction.

Chief Complaint: Depressed, with no self-esteem and destructive relationships with men. She could not seem to find an appropriate man and the men she did find eventually rejected her and she felt devastated. At age 27 she was married to a man who later became addicted to drugs and was arrested. Six months prior to coming for treatment she had been pregnant and engaged, but the man broke the engagement, she was again crushed, had an abortion, and became depressed and suicidal.

Family History: Her father virtually ignored the patient as a child but when she became an adolescent he idealized her verbally without giving any support to her real self. Her mother demanded overtly and covertly that the patient give up her real self and take care of her. Any expression of the real self was devalued, attacked, and extinguished. The patient managed through high school, went away to college, got depressed, began drinking and sexual acting out. Came

home after one year and went to work in a job in sales where she was fairly effective for several years.

Psychodynamics: The mother's lack of acknowledgement and attacks on the patient's real self led to an abandonment depression characterized by feelings of being smothered. She was engulfed as well by fears of being abandoned, and a profound feeling of hopelessness about her wishes for support of the real self. The feeling of hopelessness about support was reflected back on her impaired real self; in other words, she was unloveable, and it was hopeless to try. Her only viable existence was through clinging to mother and to unavailable men. The awareness of the hopelessness was defended against by acting out, and so she would pick inappropriate men and act out intense romantic fantasies through immediate clinging, denying the man's inappropriateness or unavailability.

She created an illusion of a real relationship and because it was an illusion it enabled her to experience feelings of romance, love, and sexual pleasure, and renew a sense of hope of being loved. Unfortunately, the inevitable, inexorable end of these misadventures—the man rejecting her—actually replayed in reality and thereby reinforced her deepest most buried and defended-against fear—that she truly was unloveable and so there was no point in trying to be loved.

The central dynamic was to externalize, reenact, and replay the devastating loss she experienced in her early relationship with her mother in order not to feel and remember it.

As she controls her acting out, she says "I have been trying to make a silk purse out of a sow's ear, don't I deserve more in a man? I used to feel if I stood up for myself a man would disappear. I'm now defining the kind of man I want for the first time."

To illustrate the success of the internal realignment she reported another blind date—"he was an attractive man, wealthy but there's no chemistry between us—I'm not attracted to him—he's not up to my speed—not where I want to go in life—does not seem to have any life of his own and just because he is nice and attractive and has money is not enough." This control of the acting out leads to the depression and her negative self image: "I feel like I'm a paraplegic from a car accident, lonely, depressed, hopeless. I hear mother's voice saying I can't make it on my own, I'll fail and be rejected."

A MAN ACTING OUT THROUGH CLINGING:

This was a 50-year-old businessman married to his third wife.

Chief Complaint: "Although I'm successful at work my depression is getting worse for the last three years with suicidal thoughts—great conflict with my wife whom I find demanding but boring, and I've lost sexual desire for her." Within the context of this depression there had been an upsurge of life-long character problems: difficulties with self-activation, passivity and self-destructive behavior in general—either clinging or withdrawing and provoking the object.

Past History: Mother was borderline, very depressed, clung to the patient, and after his birth had several miscarriages. The father from his behavior seemed to have been either a narcissistic disorder or a psychopath. He was an alcoholic, had recurrent failures in business, ignored the mother and the patient, and had blatant sexual acting out.

The mother viewed the father's narcissism and sexual acting out as expressions of masculinity, and while she tolerated it in the father she vigorously attacked the patient's efforts at self-activation, masculine and otherwise, which reinforced his clinging. The mutual clinging, reinforced Oedipal conflict. Although he was chronically depressed he got through the developmental years without clinical episodes but functioning way below his capacity. He barely made it through the last year of college and graduate school due to an avoidance of self-activation and work to defend against depression. Since that time his work has been moderately successful. The first of his two wives left him, and he had two prior tries at psychotherapy without much improvement.

He described the intimacy problem as follows: His wife of five years was 40, a dietician. He described her as self-centered, demanding, attacking his self-expression, sexu-

ally unresponsive and refusing to have treatment. He tended to cling to her, acting out his wish for reunion, and the more he clung the angrier his wife got and the angrier she got the more she withdrew and the more he clung. His not setting limits encouraged her acting out of rage and shaped her behavior to be more and more like his intrapsychic object—making her a more suitable object for his projection and reenacting rather than relating.

Psychotherapy: The confrontation of his avoidance promoted self-activation. He attempted to do better at work and in social relationships but continued to avoid dealing with his relationship with his wife.

His depression increased as he activated himself but did not continue to deepen and memories did not emerge—he was individuating without separating. Confrontation then turned more rigorously toward his clinging to his wife and his denial of her attacks on him.

He began to curb his clinging to her and take responsibility for himself as a husband in the marriage, setting limits to her narcissistic demands. This led for a while to an increase in her attacks, more conflict, and even less sex.

It also led, on his part, to guilt about assertiveness because he saw it as narcissistic or psychopathic. He could not decide whether his disappointment in his wife was due to his perceiving that she was narcissistic or maybe his perceiving that she was not narcissistic enough to serve his need to project an Amazon on her. At the same time he dreamed of the need for an Amazon and a monster attacking him. He questioned, "What will I do without the Amazon? I need her to control and intimidate me."

He finally behaved more appropriately as a husband, stuck to his guns, and eventually stopped his projections. His wife, free from this stimulus to resonate with his negative projection, settled down. The attacks stopped, and the relationship improved. Next, combined pre-Oedipal and Oedipal sexual conflict came to center stage.

The patient complained of his lack of sexual response, trying to force his wife into treatment. She refused. I asked him why he didn't discuss problems with her in detail and tell her what he wanted. I mentioned that every time he asserted himself she had more or less responded. She did respond to his discussion, and then his guilt about sexual assertion with a woman surfaced and he was impotent.

His potency, however, returned in a short period, and later on in the course of working with the sexual problem he started a sexual affair, the details of which illustrate the need for him to defend against his guilt. He found someone he saw once a week for one hour solely for sexual relations. He was neither particularly attracted to her nor did he particularly like her. In questioning his motive for such an affair I pointed out that what motivates most people to have an affair is attraction and sexual excitement, but he goes from a wife who is not exciting enough to a mistress who is not exciting enough, so I couldn't see what he gained from this move. This led to further exploration of his guilt about sexual assertiveness, which he defended against by avoiding opportunities for excitement with either his wife or the other woman.

A BORDERLINE PATIENT WITH DISTANCING DEFENSES:

A 40-year-old woman with a borderline disorder of the self who was working at a job below her capacity described her love relationships as follows: She would get a telegram from Johannesburg, South Africa, from a man who was planning to visit New York for a week. He would arrive, they would engage in an intense round of romantic dinners, shows, drinking, and sex, and she would feel that he was in love with her. He would disappear and after an interval another man would come under similar circumstances and the same process would be repeated. In the meantime, no man ever appeared on the streets of New York. I finally asked her to clarify this for me by saying: "I wonder if you could help me clarify this? It seems to me for a man to qualify for your bed he has to come by plane. I wonder why this is?" This led the patient to control the distancing defense and a man appeared on the streets of New York attempting to establish a relationship and she almost dissolved in separation anxiety.

NARCISSISTIC DISORDERS OF THE SELF—PROBLEMS WITH INTIMACY

The inflated false self causes enormous problems with intimacy. In fact, narcissism and intimacy problems are practically synonymous. The exhibitionistic narcissist is unable to relate to other people except in terms of his own inflated self-image and his unrealistic projections of himself onto others. Every relationship involving a narcissistic personality requires adulation and perfect responsiveness from the partner or an idealization of the partner so that the narcissist can bask in the other's glow. Whenever these requirements are frustrated, or appear to be lacking from the narcissist's point of view, he experiences a lack of empathy and projects this onto the partner. And he or she devalues the partner, since she is not living up to the narcissist's wishes. The narcissist's overblown sense of entitlement makes it almost impossible for him to see what he is doing in these situations because he cannot imagine that his own projections onto the partner are causing him such severe dissatisfaction in the relationship. He feels entitled to the narcissistic supplies and automatically responds with rage and devaluation of others when he doesn't get them. The narcissist's ability to appear charming and sensitive to others acts like a Venus flytrap for the unsuspecting lover who can often be at a loss as to how to extricate herself or himself from the tangle of rage and blame that results from narcissistic disappointment.

The more reinforcement that life provides the narcissist in terms of success, money, power, or prestige, the more the narcissistic personality feels entitled to a mate who will provide the same. This may be one of the reasons that the divorce rate runs exceptionally high among people with wealth and power; they grow so accustomed to getting what they want from others in life that they expect the same in their close relationships.

The most common arrangement is the narcissistic husband whose clinging borderline wife idealizes him and uses his sense of superiority to shore up her own inadequate self. She is usually very compliant, subservient, and eager to give him what he wants, but she always fails to meet his standards. Then her husband turns on her, attacks her for her inadequacies, and in so doing reinforces her negative feelings about herself. It is often only in treatment that she realizes how little she is getting out of the relationship.

A MAN WITH CLOSET NARCISSISTIC DEFENSES:

A 33-year-old single, successful, professional man.

Chief Complaint: "I have no sense of self-worth—I'm not able to be as assertive as I would like to be—too ready to please others—don't do what I want—am not my own person—no passion for anything—tend to be tired and depressed—I'm afraid to commit myself to a relationship with a woman—I maintain a number of relationships and when intimacy threatens I back off."

He has two women friends. He lived with a 27-year-old woman for seven years while having affairs on the side. He described her as warm and loving but very passive, childlike, and boring. The second, 33, a fellow professional, he has seen for one year. In contrast he finds her exciting—more of a peer—but she is insisting on marriage. He reported: "I have no room left to maneuver—I've got to be more honest—I find marriage extremely frightening—the woman might change and I would be stuck—I have no confidence that a woman would change her life and if she does it makes me very anxious—I tend to be attracted to hangers-on because they are easier to acquire, and it takes less energy to get what you want."

Past History: Father was an alcoholic who took little interest but nevertheless seemed to enjoy life without responsibility. His mother, on the other hand was bitter, depressed, with no sense of self, demanding, intrusive, lived an extremely isolated and alienated life. He felt totally enclosed by her and he had to comply with her completely. Within the frame of this compliance until age nine he had felt a tremendous sense of self—special and unique—better than anyone—a superstar—precocious in school. He wanted to be a part of everything. However, around this time "I realized I wasn't

the superstar that others were. There were better students, better athletes and I retreated from engagement to protect the image of myself as superstar. Then as a teenager I rebelled—started to take drugs and left home."

A MAN WITH EXHIBITIONISTIC DEFENSES:

A 53-year-old professional man, married with three children, the last of whom is a 13-year-old daughter.

Chief Complaint: A family problem with the daughter.

History of Present Illness: Both wife and daughter report the father's angry outbursts and irritability at home that tend to focus on the daughter. "She's the problem." On closer examination it seems both the father and the mother are using the daughter as a vehicle to act out their conflict.

In the last two years the father's business has been in great turmoil, with much loss of long-standing status and structure. He battled that out fairly successfully but got more angry, depressed, and disappointed in both his wife's and his daughter's ostensible lack of support. He attacked them, denying any depression. Nevertheless he had great difficulty sleeping and was fifty pounds overweight.

The problem with intimacy was revealed by the wife reporting that on the surface both partners are active, with productive and busy lives, but underneath the relationship has deteriorated as she gradually withdrew from his lack of sexual interest and his constant need to be special and admired. Five years ago she had begun resuming professional work to take her out of the home.

The patient finally reported his lack of sexual interest for many years and emphasized his difficulty with intimacy as follows: "I was an only child—my mother was overwhelming and intrusive but it didn't seem to bother me, and I confided only in her and was quite open as a child. Throughout childhood and early adolescence I felt quite special, unique, and admired so I didn't make much effort in school.

"When I was around fifteen or sixteen I could no longer stand my relationship with mother. She couldn't accommodate my getting older—I had to separate and cut off. I did so and at the same time I threw myself into school in order to become an outstanding student and then an outstanding professional. I have felt distant in relationships ever since.

"I hold back—I expect people to come to me but I am not welcoming when they do. With my mother I was a super child, I did not have to work for it, and I relied on my wife to fill the gap. I am disappointed, hurt, and angry that she's withdrawn from me. She's busier than ever and seems more interested in our daughter. I can't tell her. My daughter is the problem because she is demanding closeness at a time when I need distance."

A WOMAN WITH A CLOSET NARCISSISTIC DISORDER FUSES WITH AND DISTANCES FROM AN IDEALIZED OBJECT TO MAINTAIN SENSE OF SELF:

A 29-year-old woman, a painter.

Chief Complaint: Conflict in the marriage and inability to let go. She has been married for six years after living together for one year, but two years ago she began having an affair with a coworker. Two months prior to coming to see me she told her husband that she was going to leave him.

The husband, a businessman, 32, she described as having two sides. The side of him that reinforced her fusion fantasies was as follows: "We are too close, like Siamese twins, I felt like a baby, warm and safe and comfortable, I felt wrapped in cotton wool, but on the other hand alienated from reality. I confused his body with my own—was more concerned about his psyche than my own."

She described his other side as follows: "He was self-absorbed, obsessed with money, stingy, could not communicate emotion, had sexual difficulties—but she was terrified that he would leave her."

She described her fragmented self as follows: "feeling hurt, wounded, exquisitely hypersensitive, almost having no skin, permeable to everybody and everything, terrified that my husband would disappear."

She described her lover as an artist in his mid-forties, who was also having a relationship with another woman at the same time.

Past History: Her mother had an exhibitionistic narcissistic disorder and turned her over to a governess at birth. Mother was hostile, sadistic, attacked all self-expression and required her to mirror and comply with her expectations. Father was an alcoholic who died when she was three. The principal saving grace was a close relationship with a governess who was a mother surrogate until age six. She managed in school and college, spending much of her time alone and absorbed in her painting. However, when she went off to college she had a severe depression for four years until she met her husband.

Diagnostic impression was a patient with a closet narcissistic disorder who required fusion and distancing defenses to maintain a sense of self. I began psychotherapy once a week to slowly evaluate her capacity to manage and deal with the inevitable disappointment, vulnerability, and exposure that would be associated with the frustration of her fusion fantasies in treatment.

I made a mirroring interpretation of her narcissistic vulnerability: It was so painful for her to focus on herself that she soothed that pain by focusing on her husband and others. She internalized these interpretations, began to activate her real self. She left the lover. She was activating her real self in her daily life, managing the recurrent narcissistic disappointment in the interviews, and was now being seen three times a week.

At this point, she decided that she must divorce her husband. She told him but then had a panic dream about being abandoned with the loss of self, which she then defended against by emotional distancing and detachment. She reported about the husband, "I'm either terrified or cut off at separating—I'm strangled by being with him."

At this point I was going on vacation. She reported, "I had a fantasy of you dying on the trip and I shut off all feelings, but I'm now beginning to sense a pattern where before I felt the victim of chaos. I'm amazed how I have to cut off all feelings with people, but I am still able to paint." She elaborated on her narcissistic vulnerability of self by saying, "I have no feelings with you or anyone else unless they totally endorse me; otherwise I'm hurt. I panic and cut off. I can't handle closeness without distance but also can't stand to be distant."

During the course of this working through she managed to do a substantial amount of successful painting. She reported her transference fantasies: "I have fantasies of merging with you, of being taken care of, of disappearing into your body like a wave of suction I'd float in and disappear. At the same time, I realize I can play this out here where I am safe."

These fantasies were interpreted as defenses against her narcissistic vulnerability but she then turned to acting out these defenses. At this point a man entered the scene—fifteen years older, vastly successful, physically huge—with an enormous charisma and social position. He had been married once in his twenties and then divorced, and had no enduring relationships since. He was a workaholic who was extremely socially isolated. He pursued her avidly—told her how much he loved her—wanted to marry her—but the relationship was conditioned by several elements: First, distance. His work took him away for twelve weeks at a time, several times a year. Second, she was required to forego herself and cater to him. He was powerfully verbal and seductive. He promoted her symbiotic fantasies and she wished to disappear inside him so her self-activation was minimized.

This lasted about a year. Typical of the distancing defense, they kept their two apartments, which required her to commute back and forth. He avoided her efforts to get him to make a permanent commitment till she finally stood her ground. She couldn't go on this way. Overnight, literally overnight, as his fear of engulfment emerged he told her he could not go on—he could not handle the closeness. She dealt with the feeling of loss by detaching and withdrawing. Interpretation and confrontation of her acting out fell on deaf ears.

About nine months later a fourth man entered the scene. He was four or five years older—a professional, single, extremely affectionate, responsible, and very supportive of her. There was no distance in the relationship, because he worked in New York City. She liked him, was attracted to him, but felt there was something missing—that he was not a strong enough person. However, she wondered if his being around constantly was what was really bothering her, because she needed distance in order to be able to maintain a sense of self. "I'm either trembling with anxiety that he will reject me or I am constantly monitoring him or I am mad at him for not being more—continuity with him bothers me because I have a need to withdraw, to be alone and detached. Don't know which of these states is real or if either is real. Is he not right for me or does his being right for me frustrate my symbiotic wishes and stimulate my fear of loss of self so that I can't see him as he is? He acknowledges and supports my self so I can't bury and lose it in him and it makes merger fantasies unworkable. I can't seem to sustain my self with another person."

A CLOSET NARCISSISTIC DISORDER OF THE SELF:

Ms. A., tall, slender, blond, a 40-year-old homosexual woman, was a successful interior decorator and the divorced mother of two children. She complained of difficulties in interpersonal relationships.

History of Present Illness: The patient had had her first homosexual relationship while in college. Later, she fell in love with a man, married, and in so doing lost her sense of self. She became "all things to her husband and children." She was married for ten years, during which time there were no homosexual relationships.

She reported: "After ten years, I realized I had no self, nor did I have any intimacy with my husband. I started to drink; I had a low tolerance for alcohol and became an alcoholic. I had blackouts. I drank for three years until last year, when I joined AA and started an affair with a woman. During the three years that I was drinking, I had three relationships: two with women and one with a man. All of the relationships were difficult and conflictual. I tended to sell out to women who were attracted to me."

"I then met another woman, an older woman who reminds me somewhat of my mother, and I have been having a relationship with her for the past year. I find her very distant. I find myself giving and then pulling back, and we have a lot of conflict."

"I have great difficulty acknowledging myself. I feel I have no self. I have trouble asserting myself. On the other hand, I have this idea that I can get away with anything. At one point I took Prozac but put on 35 pounds."

Personal History: "Mother was domineering, paranoid, with a will of iron, angry, attacking, stingy, a monster who never let me alone. Mother was also a very successful career woman. Father was a rather inadequate, kind, and distant man who was never available and who did not help me with my mother."

The patient was the oldest of three children, with sisters five years younger and seven years younger. She had to take care of the sisters, who also had serious problems in relationships.

"I was a latchkey kid, and at one point my mother took me to a psychologist, although I don't remember why."

SCHIZOID DISORDERS OF THE SELF

THE CASE OF GEORGE S.

A 47-year-old businessman, currently separated from his wife of twenty years. The relationship has been on and off over all those years with many separations, one lasting for almost five years.

Marriage: About his marriage, George S. said, "I need a certain distance, and Ann [his wife] needs a certain closeness. The closeness makes me feel unsafe and I distance. She says that the distance makes her feel unsafe, and so she clings." (I think this is a beautiful description in one sentence of the differing relational conflicts between the schizoid and the borderline patient.)

Reflecting on this pattern, the patient commented, "It sure as hell is difficult to cut the cord. On the one hand, I feel like I want a connection, a family. But this always feels suffocating, as if I must accommodate totally. And

I feel trapped. On the other hand, when I am by myself there are none of these bad feelings. But being unconnected can feel bad, as if I am worthless, devoid of a function. I guess that my dilemma is that I have a deep need for a connection and an equally deep need for separation and privacy." The patient felt that these themes have been present all his life.

"I have always had a problem committing to people." But not to things. He was always quite independent and successful in his professional life. His responsibility and obligation to his work, whether in school, college, or his profession were never at issue. He could be as involved as needed, without ever feeling unsafe. However, "in most relationships I require a certain distance."

Early History: He wondered whether it went back to his relationships growing up. He reflected that his parents were good people, yet they were always "at wits end." He felt that they just could not be bothered with him. "I knew I really couldn't count on them emotionally. Home was never a safe harbor, and I had to distance myself. I want a connection, but I don't want to be in prison. I have a connection thing, I want a feeling of being connected, but not at the cost of enslavement. There is a signal when I get too close. I stop wanting to have sex. It becomes dangerous. I don't trust easily about my feelings. When I get close I begin to feel that you are trying to manipulate me for your own purposes. It feels like you are trying to pry me open and in order to feel safe I must stay apart."

THE CASE OF MARGARET C.

A 36-year-old woman.

Family History: "My mother was selfish; there was no bonding experience." Her father had been gone a great deal and, after the patient was born, the mother gave up her work resentfully and stayed home to raise the two children. Therefore, the patient always felt that it was her fault that her mother was unhappy because her birth had changed her mother's life. Despite the mother's scornful rejection, the patient felt that it was the mother who was really strange and different. Though she told herself that she did not want to be like her mother when she grew up, she was always terrified that she would be.

Chief Complaint: She maintained a distance from friends, feeling cold and uninvolved. Rather than deep friendships, she felt that she needed someone "out there" to whom she could feel connected when she felt especially alone. These experiences of desperate aloneness came as acute, overwhelming feelings of anxiety. She described this as a sense of being totally isolated. "This is what I fear it must be like to be dead; a sense of being totally disconnected from the world. Like being buried alive. Like being paralyzed, unable to speak or communicate. Alone forever." This profound experience of alienation (the self-in-exile) felt like an acute anxiety attack, for which she had been treated with a variety of medications, to no avail.

The patient had finally dealt with these feelings by marrying an acquaintance from work two years before I first saw her. The relationship had been her first sexual relationship, which gave her little pleasure: "It's something you have to do if you are married." Her husband, though not abusive, seemed content to live parallel lives, speaking and interacting infrequently. Their relationship seemed more one of cordial albeit sexually intimate roommates.

In recent months, however, a crisis had arisen. Her husband had been offered an important promotion, which required him to move to another state. The patient had two choices: move with the husband, or stay in New York and see the husband every several weeks. She described her struggle with intimacy through the projection of her schizoid dilemma and the split object relations units of the schizoid in the following fashion:

"I wish I wanted to move with him, to be with him, but I don't know how I feel. I never really thought about how I felt when I married him. It is as if I must decide for the first time

whether I want to be with him or not. If I go I know that I don't want to settle for what we have now. I know that I want more. But I am so scared to be close to him, to open up to him. I am so afraid that he will try to control me or, as bad, that he just will not care. And if the marriage fails I know he will make it my fault. I will be the bad one, the crazy one, the one who couldn't make it work. I know it would be more comfortable being by myself. I would feel safer. But I am tired of being alone, and sometimes I am scared of being alone. I know the panic will get worse. Is that a reason to stay in the relationship? It seems that any way I turn I will be settling again."

The schizoid dilemma leaves her with only two possible experiences of relatedness: close but in danger of control, scorn or neglect; or distant and self-sufficient but in danger of feeling "different" and of falling into a bottomless pit of alienation and void. Neither "solution" to her schizoid dilemma has anything to do with intimacy. She really "knows" this for the first time in her life, which brings her to treatment to see if there is any other pathway out of her dilemma.

CONCLUSION

These examples illustrate the need for the therapist to decode the patient's illusions that the relationship works, identify the patient's defenses against abandonment or engulfment and bring them to the patient's attention through confrontation or interpretation so they can be worked through in therapy.

BIBLIOGRAPHY

Mahler, M., Pine, F., & Bergman, A. (1975). *The psychological birth of the human infant: Symbiosis and individuation.* London: Hutchinson.

Stern, D. N. (1985). *The interpersonal world of the infant.* New York: Basic Books.

Wallerstein, J., & Kelly, J.B. (1990). *Surviving the breakup: How children and parents cope with a divorce.* New York: Basic Books.

Discussion by Cloé Madanes

◆

First, I would like to thank Dr. Masterson for a very thoughtful paper on a universal problem in human relationships.

Second, even though I come from a very different approach, I spent six years in a very poignant analysis when I was a student in my twenties. So, as I hear Dr. Masterson, I immediately regress to that time. I identify with the problems that he describes.

Parenthetically, I want to mention one thing that hasn't really been discussed in this conference: There is an important difference between reading Dr. Masterson's paper and hearing him give it. This distinction stems from the personality of the therapist.

The warmth that comes through a clinician, the clinician's interest in patients, is difficult to reflect in the writing even of a very good writer. I really admire the respect and concern Dr. Masterson has for his patients. I can see it reflected in his work, especially when he talks about it.

Therefore, even coming from very different approaches, we probably do many similar things because we share a basic warmth and interest in human beings—in the people with whom we work. Hearing some of the remarks that Dr. Masterson makes to patients, I thought that maybe I would have said much the same.

Let me make some comments here about marriage and its problems. Yesterday I had the opportunity to attend Dr. Glasser's workshop on relationships. He asked the audience to provide information on how many people there had been divorced and how many times.

We discovered that out of 750 people, 500 had been divorced at least once. This is the norm now; it obviously is not the exception. It's interesting to speculate about why so many first marriages fail. Since I come from an interactional point of view, when I think of marriage I don't think of two people: I think of two families getting together.

Especially in first marriages, I think about the problems of leaving home, and I think that many people marry for the first time as part of the process of separating from their parents. One of the paradoxes of marriage is that you marry to leave home, and you establish yourself away from your parents' home. As soon as you have done it, one purpose of the marriage no longer exists. You've left, so why then do you have to stay with your new spouse?

I don't know how to solve this issue in therapy; therefore perhaps if we could just hold together second marriages, it would be a big success for therapists. I don't think that we have done so well as marital therapists, given the rising number of divorces.

Another interesting issue is the tendency for those of us who have been married several times to marry the same personality. We start off with somebody completely different and slowly they become like the previous spouse. And, of course, this is because we are the same person.

When we interact with someone, we elicit the same type of behavior. But in fact this is not always true, because in choosing the next partner some people look for the opposite person from what the first partner was. For example, if in your first marriage you were the one who always decided what movie to go to see, and what restaurant to go to, and so on, and you complained because the other one was so passive and you had to make all these arrangements, then the second spouse that you would look for would be one who would know absolutely what movie he or she wanted to see and would decide on the restaurant, and so on. And at the beginning you think this is wonderful: I don't have to make decisions. After a while you get tired of going to bad movies and eating bad food and you begin to miss the first spouse. So, it's a difficult problem.

Another issue that interests me in Dr. Masterson's address is the issue of the Oedipus complex, which is at the basis of psycho-analysis and which he mentions in the beginning of his paper. I have a serious question about the idea that children are sexually inclined towards the parent of the opposite sex. Therefore, I went back to Freud and I looked at how this idea developed. As it happened, Freud had several patients, all women, who told him about sexual abuse situations with their fathers or brothers. And he believed them. In fact, he gave a paper in front of the medical association, for which he was severely criticized, in which he proposed there was tremendous incidence of sexual abuse and incest that was being covered up and denied in the society of his day.

For several years he didn't write or comment on this issue again, until he finally came up with a paper in which he took the whole problem to the realm of fantasy. Apparently he discovered that some of his patients had lied to him; the abuse had not really happened. From this he generalized that all his patients had lied to him and decided that it was the patients' secret desire to have a sexual rela-

tionship with the parent that had led them to fantasize that they actually had been molested.

Well, today we know that it's true that there is a high incidence of sexual abuse of children: Those patients of Freud's probably were really sexually abused.

In taking the problem to the realm of fantasy, Freud took us away from real relationships into fantasized relationships, into internal objects. But even worse than that, he added insult to injury because not only had those patients been victimized, but on top of it they were told that they fantasized and wanted the victimization. It's like saying to a woman who was raped, "You were looking for it. You wanted it."

I think this is a major problem. We are going to have to do something about our conceptualization of the basis of psychoanalysis because now we know that sexual abuse does exist, and that the chances are that it's the parents that eroticized the relationship with the children, not the children that eroticized the relationship with the parents. I would be very interested in Dr. Masterson's comments about that.

Response by Dr. Masterson

I think you made some very good points about Freud's experience in these cases. He first thought these were actual occurrences. At that time, he was with Janet in Paris and he used to go to the morgue to see autopsies of children who had been abused. Then he did turn around. But I see it a little bit differently than you do.

It's not that Freud set up a notion of the Oedipal complex that was false, although he did lead away from the reality of sexual abuse that is now being addressed so many years later.

If you want to find out about whether or not children have sexual feelings about their par-

ents, Freud is not the place to go. Margaret Mahler did child observation studies of normal children going through the first three years of development. Other researchers continued the study after the age of three. They conducted naturalistic observational studies of little boys and girls, and they described these kids expressing their feelings. They all expressed sexual feelings about their parents.

Now, it could be, as you say, that it's the parents who sexualize the kids. For years now the analysts have tried to treat personality disorders as an Oedipal complex. Of course, it didn't work. Then they blamed the patient: This patient is untreatable. Then we finally found out personality disorders have nothing do with the Oedipal complex: They derive from pre-Oedipal developmental arrests.

As you will notice in the cases that I describe, the Oedipal complex is a secondary feature. When patients are talking about the sense of self in relationships, they are not describing Oedipal problems. They are describing problems in development that have to do with what I call disorders of the self.

Also, I was intrigued by your comment that people marry a new person, and over time they always turn out to be the same type. This is a pattern that goes way beyond disorders of the self, but it's certainly what we see.

All of us have had the experience of a patient reporting that they are with a new man (or a new woman) and saying, "He thinks I'm so and so. He doesn't realize that underneath it I'm just like his last wife (husband)."

And I think that the process of ending up the "same" is what I tried to illustrate in my paper. It is because these patterns are determined by inner object representations. That's what you look for out there, something that fits inner object representations. And, of course, when the one you pick fits that pattern, the relationship runs into trouble. Then you realize you don't want to get into that again, so you pick someone whose surface is different, but underneath it's the same. So it's a constant reenactment of what I call internalized object relations. Those internalized object relations need to be changed for you to get a new partner and to have the sense of self that can allow you to live with a new partner.

As I've indicated, heaven forbid that you get somebody who is terribly healthy because all that's going to do is make you more and more anxious, and then probably you will devalue yourself in order to deal with your anxiety.

I reflected about Cloé's comments about first marriages as a way of separating from home. Of course, in disorders of the self there is separating without separating. What they do is substitute a dependence on a spouse for dependence on the parents. And, at least in my clinical experience, they don't come to us when they are making that decision; they come when it fails and then it's too late.

SECTION II

◆

Cognitive-Behavioral Approaches

Cognitive Therapy: Reflections

Aaron T. Beck, M.D.

Aaron T. Beck, M.D., D.M.S.
Aaron T. Beck is a University Professor Emeritus of Psychiatry at the School of Medicine of the University of Pennsylvania. Dr. Beck is the author of ten professional books and 300 articles published in professional and scientific journals. He received his M.D. in 1946 from the Yale School of Medicine. Dr. Beck is the recipient of numerous professional honors and serves on many editorial boards. He has received a number of research grants and his areas of special research interests are the psychopathology of psychiatric disorders, prediction of suicide, and the cognitive therapy of depression and other disorders. Dr. Beck is one of the originators of cognitive therapy.

INTRODUCTION

There was a time in my life when I was really alone in thinking about cognitive therapy, or some type of short-term therapy, as a new approach to depression and some of the other psychiatric disorders. There was really nobody I could speak to, nobody who was really interested, except my wife, Phyllis, and my teenage daughter, Judith. And when I told Judy about it, she said: "Dad, that does make sense to me." Thus reassured, I persevered and ultimately was rewarded by Judy's own evolution as a cognitive therapist, researcher, and author. I have previously described the evolution of cognitive therapy (Beck, 1967). In this chapter, I will present an overview of psychotherapy and cognitive therapy. Then, I will review some of the myths about cognitive therapy. Finally, I will present some of the newer formulations of cognitive therapy.

AN OVERVIEW OF PSYCHOTHERAPY

Turning to the field of psychotherapy in general, we note that very often a particular technique is elevated to the status of a psychotherapy in itself. Somebody in the 1950s counted up 200 psychotherapies; by the 1960s it was up to 300; and the last count that I heard of, it was up to 450 psychotherapies! Every time a clinician comes out with a new technique it is likely to be labeled a "psychotherapy."

In the past, I have outlined what I consider are the basic requirements for a system of psychotherapy to be considered a "system" rather than simply a "technique." This does not mean, of course, that some of the novel techniques cannot be useful, but these cannot be regarded as fully developed psychotherapies.

As indicated in Table 1, the first requirement for a system of psychotherapy is a *theory*

TABLE 1
Standards for a System of Psychotherapy

1. A theory of personality and psychopathology.

2. Empirical data to support the theory.

3. Operationalized therapy that interlocks with the theory.

4. Empirical data to support the therapy.

of personality and psychopathology. Theory is critical in terms of understanding patients. If you were an especially skilled surgeon, you would need a knowledge of anatomy, pathology, and physiology in order to operate. If you did not have a knowledge of anatomy, you might start working on the liver but end up in the aorta! In other words, you have to know where you are going, and how to get there.

The second requirement is *empirical data* to support the appropriate theory of personality and psychopathology. Investigators have spent years, if not decades, working in the vineyards trying to devise experiments to test various cognitive concepts, whether directly related to cognitive therapy or to cognitive psychology (which is probably the basic science of cognitive therapy).

The third requirement for a system of psychotherapy is an *operationalized therapy* that interlocks with the theory. You should be able to derive the therapy readily from the theory. There should be a congruence between what you are thinking and what you are doing. There have been many theories of therapies through the ages in which there was no congruence between theory and therapy. A historical example is Mesmer's technique and theory of "animal magnetism." In such a case you might as well discard the theory and just stick to the therapy. There also should be *empirical data* to support the therapy itself, a point that I will return to subsequently.

Finally, a complete system of psychotherapy should stipulate the mechanisms of improvement. Symptomatic improvement, for example, may result from the modification of dysfunctional thinking, but durable improvement comes from modification of the underlying *beliefs*, or, as we say technically, from sche-

matic change, from actual modification of the schemas themselves.

MYTHS ABOUT COGNITIVE THERAPY

Many times people talk about a "revision of standard cognitive therapy." In one sense, there is no such thing as *standard* cognitive therapy; that is a myth. There is a *specific* cognitive configuration for every specific disorder, and within each specific disorder there is a specific therapeutic application for the specific patient. While there are general broad principles of cognitive therapy across all conditions and a large set of strategies to choose from, there is no one cognitive therapy. Our 1979 book on cognitive therapy for depression outlines in detail what happens in depression (Beck, Rush, Shaw, and Emery, 1979), but it doesn't tell us how you treat drug addiction, sex offenders, panic disorder, or multiple personality disorder. You need a specific cognitive model and specialized techniques for each of those conditions.

Another myth is that cognitive therapy is simply a set of techniques aimed at identifying and correcting "irrational thinking." This is wrong on two counts. First, as shown in Table 2, cognitive therapy is defined in terms of the cognitive model (or theory) of psychiatric disorders. This model then serves as a kind of map to guide the therapist in selecting the kind of interventions that seem most appropriate at a particular time for a particular patient with a particular set of problems. While the specific cognitive techniques provide a powerful vehicle for effecting cognitive change, they are not the only—or always the best—methods for

TABLE 2
Definition of Cognitive Therapy

1. Cognitive therapy is defined in terms of the cognitive model rather than the specific techniques employed.

2. The model stipulates that psychological disorders are characterized by dysfunctional thinking derived from dysfunctional beliefs.

3. Improvement results from modification of the dysfunctional thinking and durable improvement from modification of beliefs.

a particular patient at a particular time. We also use experiential, dramatic, and conversational strategies, depending on the patient's needs at a particular time. A popular but naive and simplistic definition asserts that cognitive therapy is simply a technology aimed at changing people's thoughts. But the model, rather than the specific technique employed, is the hallmark of cognitive therapy.

I can illustrate this definition with a specific example. I once was consulted by a college professor, with whom I simply had a conversation for 45 or 50 minutes. He came in highly suicidal and wanted to carry out what he considered a "rational suicide" based on his supposed intellectual deterioration, presumably the result of "brain damage" due to a tranquilizer he had taken. I simply engaged him in a conversation regarding the kind of projects he was engaged in and asked him to critique the work of other investigators. Although his thinking was retarded at first (due to depression, not brain damage) he became quite animated in his exposition of his work. After he was able to give me a comprehensive and lucid description of his work for 30 minutes, he was no longer suicidal. Without my having to point it out, it became obvious to him that his mind was still functioning very well and it was consequently not "necessary" to end his life. At the start, I had an idea of his problem—his erroneous belief that he was deteriorating—and I used a kind of cognitive map to guide me in questioning him and drawing him out. There was nothing in what I did that a novice would call "standard cognitive therapy." Yet, through this experiential exercise, the patient's fundamental erroneous belief about himself was corrected, and he could view himself and his future more realistically.

To address another myth, we do not consider the thinking associated with particular disorders as "irrational." In their present circumstances, the patients' idiosyncratic thinking may be problematic, dysfunctional, or maladaptive—but not irrational. Under other circumstances (in the face of imminent danger), the exaggerated thinking of the anxious patient, for example, could be adaptive, even life saving.

Another myth is that "cognitions cause psychopathology" or "cognitions cause depres-

sion." In reality, cognitions do not *cause* depression, nor do they cause any other disorder. However, as an expression of information processing, they are centrally involved in psychopathology just as they are in normal functioning. The cognitive model stipulates that dysfunctional thinking is the essence, is the core, not the cause of psychological disorders. You might ask "If cognitions do not cause depression, what does cause depression?" We don't really know exactly what causes depression. Part of the answer depends upon what you mean by "cause"—whether you are thinking at a molecular level, an interpersonal level, or a strictly intrapsychic psychological level. I think the best way of looking at this issue is that there are many possible determinants of depression and they vary enormously from one person to another. Some are continuously cycling bipolar patients who have an overriding endogenous component. You would think that because their disorders are so biological and they do respond to some degree to the appropriate cocktail of drugs, psychological interventions would not help. In fact, psychological interventions in conjunction with drug treatment do help; the drugs tend to produce a ceiling on the highs and also floors under the lows, but they are not perfect. We find rich cognitive material, just as rich as in the reactive depressions, and are then able to utilize cognitive therapy to help the patients along. However, even though cognitive events are instrumental in fluctuations of the disorder—and cognitive interventions may help—there is no justification for concluding that the psychopathology is "caused" by cognitive factors.

Long ago (Beck, 1967) I discussed the negative cognitive triad in depression and showed the relationship between patients' perception of themselves, their future, and their own personal world on the one hand, and the various symptoms of depression. What is new in my latest version is the notion that when a person is experiencing a wide variety of motivational, behavioral, and somatic symptoms, these particular experiences in themselves are processed cognitively (so there is a continuous feedback loop). If the patient is inclined to stay in bed and to neglect her family and work, for example, her observations of these behaviors and somatic symptoms are then "translated" by her information processing into: "I am lazy; I am an irresponsible person; I deserve to be punished" and a vicious cycle is established. The dysfunctional thinking involves not only cognitive distortions but an uncontrolled fixation upon some topic of concern (for example, danger).

Dysfunctional thinking in the specific disorders is derived from specific dysfunctional beliefs, and we cannot overemphasize their importance. It is possible to modify people's distorted thinking, for example, without ever touching their basic belief structure. As a consequence, they may improve symptomatically but within a few weeks or months they relapse and return to therapy. Patients with panic disorders, for example, may recover from their panic attacks but they still have agoraphobia, because a basic belief, such as "If I go into a supermarket or subway, I may have a heart attack and die," has never been dealt with adequately. All that has been affecting these cases has been the catastrophic thinking during the time of the panic attack itself, but not the avoidance-producing beliefs. You have to be able to elicit the related beliefs and test them out.

We may not know that dysfunctional beliefs exist in these various psychopathologies until we start to explore them. For example, at one time I thought that eating disorders were simply problems with eating and I did get some pretty good symptomatic relief from cognitive therapy with some of these patients. But then it turned out that many relapsed after a period of time, because I had not been aware that these patients generally had a negative self-image—a negative core belief about themselves. To get a sustained improvement and prevent the development of anorexia nervosa in bulemic adolescents, we had to explore the beliefs about the self.

Another fallacy is that the cognitive model asserts that individuals operate on cognition alone. This is the myth of "exclusive cognitivism." In cognitive therapy we think of the total personality. We emphasize the word "cognitive" because the theory and therapy are based on an information processing model. The first bit of information that comes into the human apparatus has to pass through the information processing system. Irrespective of whether the stimulus appears internally, as, say, a pain in the stomach, or externally as, say, a menacing animal approaching us, a stimulus first has to go through the information processing system if it is to affect the organism. But the model also stipulates that when there is something wrong with information processing, whether it is due to drugs like the bromides or LSD, it is going to cause a disturbance in the other components of the personality, in the affective, the motivational, and the behavioral domains. So when you are working with an individual patient you have to look at him or her as a totality, not simply in terms of his or her "distorted cognitions."

Another problem that has posed difficulties is the "contextual vacuum" fallacy. You may read or hear that cognitive therapy deals just with cognitive distortions, whereas interpersonal therapy, say, deals with the interpersonal context, to which I respond: "What do you think we talk about in cognitive therapy, if not personal issues?" Cognitive therapy certainly deals with interpersonal issues and in this sense encompasses interpersonal therapy. The cognitive model (Albert Ellis also emphasized this many decades ago) is based on the notion that there are situations, particular stimuli, which impinge on the individual, the data of these situations are processed, and then the processing ends up in affect, behavior, motivation, and so on. In most conditions, relations with people contribute to the patient's problems and need to be dealt with.

The next fallacy has to do with "superficiality." In recent years we have become more aware that it is not sufficient simply to look at the provocative situation and the cognitive distortions. We have to look at the basic beliefs, because these basic beliefs (or schemas) are what really mold the individual's interpretation of situations. If you do not have a knowledge of a person's basic beliefs, you are not really going to understand what is going on in the individual's reaction to various situations. So it is really important in dealing with your patients to try to find out their various concepts about themselves, their future, and their outside world.

The next fallacy is what I call the "tool-box fallacy." This is the notion that cognitive therapy consists merely of cognitive tools or techniques. However, cognitive therapy is based on certain principles that go beyond simple techniques or strategies. One of these principles is *collaborative empiricism*, cultivating a good working alliance with the patient. Where we may differ from some therapies is in our emphasis on empiricism. We try to test out our own beliefs about the patients and the patients' beliefs about themselves. *Guided discovery* is derived from Socratic questioning—you have in mind where you want the patient to go, and through very clever questioning you get the patient to go there, or to go somewhere else if it turns out that your original idea was wrong!

The cognitive techniques that people are familiar with do not constitute the whole of cognitive therapy: examining conclusions, testing hypothesis, using guided imagery. We also use so-called "behavioral techniques." In fact, in depression, particularly in more severely depressed people, we generally start off with behavioral techniques, such as graded task assignment, and, of course, homework. In the personality disorders (for example, in avoidant personality disorder) we use experiential methods, such as role-playing, recreating past traumatic events, and revivifying childhood memories.

When we were working with depression originally, individuals came in already in a state of high arousal. And so it was possible to get them to look at their interpretation of reality and to evaluate them right on the spot. They had what we would call "hot cognitions." When we treat personality disorders, however, we have to correct deeply embedded beliefs, or schemas. Therefore, we have to use powerful experiential techniques in order target these strongly held schemas. To do this I had to go back into the patient's childhood experiences, a return to my earlier work in psychoanalysis—a development that some of my colleagues have called "the return of the repressed." We review the pathogenic childhood situations and induce the patient to reevaluate these experiences in order to obtain the schematic change.

This new addition to our therapeutic tool-box, thus, has to do with recreating traumatic events from the past. When the traumatic events have occurred in the recent past, it often turns out that it may be counterproductive to reproduce the event. David M. Clark (Clark, Salkovskis, Hackman, Middleton, Anastasiades, & Gelder, 1994) brought to my attention some work that he had done with rape victims at Oxford. He found that it may not be necessary to put the victim through a painful recreation of the actual traumatic event to obtain an improvement in the posttraumatic stress disorder. It is possible to deal with the *meaning* of the event, which is not so disturbing as reliving the event itself. One patient, for example, believed that she was an "object" as a consequence of being exposed to date rape, that her boyfriend must have regarded her as an object otherwise he wouldn't have treated her in that way. In response, David used Socratic questioning: "Were you an object before you dated this guy? How long have you been an object? And how would I recognize an object when she's walking down the street?" Through the questioning she was able to recognize the problem—the *meaning* and the *significance* of the event—without having to go through recreating all of the traumatic aspects. Of course, this observation has to be tested out in a systematic study, but it represents an innovative cognitive approach to such problems. With childhood events such as incest, and physical or verbal abuse, however, it generally is necessary to reproduce the event itself and to have the person reexperience it (in fantasy, of course.)

COGNITIVE SCHEMAS

I would now like to consider the dysfunctional beliefs in various disorders. An illustrative case is a director of a large research organization, who presented with a plethora of psychopathological symptoms. He was very successful—and in his mind at least he was of Nobel Prize caliber. Despite his performance, which was very good over the years, he had a wide area of psychopathology. Among his diagnoses were major depressive disorder (which may have been, to some degree, a bipolar disorder); panic disorder; generalized anxiety disorder; and multiple phobias. He also had a compulsive personality disorder and a narcissistic personality disorder, which in a way "goes with the territory." During his depression, he perceived himself as worthless and inadequate, useless, unproductive, and a fraud, and therefore I couldn't use reassurance with him and say, "Look at all you have done. I really admire you greatly." That attempt at reassurance immediately could have destroyed the relationship because the patient would have thought: "Boy, he's a real jerk to see me this way." Or he would have felt bad, thinking "I have deceived him too." This patient had an extremely negative self-image, and any inputs that I would make would be filtered through this negative image. He was sure his personal world was shrinking. There was some reduction in the funding that was available to him— his federal grants *were* shrinking—and a number of his postdoctoral fellows were leaving.

In addition, the new president of the corporation was arrogant, controlling, and authoritarian, so that for the first time in his professional life my patient was not a free agent, able to do whatever he wanted. He imagined that all of his researchers were going to leave, that he wouldn't receive any grants, that he'd have financial disaster, that he would end up on skid row, and that he wouldn't be able to support his wife and two children. As he looked back on the past all he could see were serious mistakes; he attributed his "success" to the fact that he had deceived other people. ·

My patient was very much driven, placed a great emphasis on achievement, productivity, systems, efficiency, perfectionism, and responsibility. That was his personality. Now, what were his fears? He was anxious all the time in addition to being depressed, and when he wasn't depressed he was still anxious because he feared he would lose his resources, his staff, his funding, and his creativity, which of course did decline when he was depressed. He thought this was an irreversible process. In addition, his continuous anxiety was reflected in gastrointestinal symptoms. He would periodically think that he had cancer of the bowel, which then added to his anxiety. Occasionally he would get sharp pains in his belly and so he

got panic attacks, at which time he thought he was having a heart attack.

Now, in helping this patient, it wasn't sufficient simply to focus on the relief of symptoms. It is of course possible to deactivate the depression program through a wide variety of methods; we can do it through classical behavior therapy, through insight therapy, through cognitive therapy, through any of the targeted drugs. All of these methods do tend to discharge the highly charged schemas that you find in the depressed person. But they do not prevent the patient from having relapses, so it was necessary to delineate the patient's beliefs. One of his beliefs was, "If I don't succeed, then I am a failure." Another of his beliefs linked with depression was, "If I am rejected, I'm unlovable." He also had a hypomanic belief: "If I succeed, I will be proclaimed as a genius." Even with all his accomplishments, he was always afraid that the next step would be fatal. And so he had the belief, "Even if I succeed all the time, I can always slip and fail, and that would be disastrous."

The belief behind his panic was: "Any inexplicable physical or mental experience means an imminent physical, mental, or behavioral disaster." In other words, he would make catastrophic misinterpretations of his various internal experiences. What about suicidal wishes? He believed, "Since I cannot succeed, I would be better off dead. " If he were sociotropic, he might have the belief, "Since I am unlovable, I might as well kill myself."

SCHEMAS FOR OTHER CLINICAL PROBLEMS

We have been able to pinpoint specific beliefs for all of the other syndromes that we deal with. The patient with anorexia nervosa has beliefs such as "If I am fat, I am unattractive. On the other hand, if I can control my weight, my appearance, and so on, I have some control over my life." The patient with addictions has a belief such as "If I am feeling low, anxious, and so on, it is best to have a snort, a smoke, or a shot." In our study of cocaine abuse, we find that almost all abusers have these kinds of self-medication beliefs. Just focusing on the behavior and getting them to be abstinent does not ensure that they are going to stay abstinent. The only insurance is to modify the basic schemas (or beliefs) that are motivating their craving and consequently their drug taking.

Sex offenders, similarly, have a whole medley of beliefs, such as "Sex with my child is good for her or him. Sex will bring us closer. It's better if he/she has sex with somebody who cares than with some stranger."

In marital relationships there are beliefs such as "My partner should know what I want without my having to ask," and "If I have to ask for something, then it spoils it."

We have been able to list about 15 specific beliefs for each personality disorder (Beck, Freeman, et al., 1990). Once you know what these beliefs are, then they serve as a guide for treating the personality disorders.

- The dependent personality believes that "I am helpless." This belief is reflected in attachment behaviors.
- The avoidant personality believes that "I might get hurt," and thus avoids situations of vulnerability.
- The passive-aggressive personality believes that "I might get stepped on," and thus is resistant to authority.
- In the paranoid personality, the belief that "people are out to get me" leads to hypervigilance.
- In the narcissistic personality, the belief that "I am special" leads to self-aggrandizement.
- The histrionic personality believes that "I need to impress."
- The compulsive believes that "Errors are bad" and is overly demanding of him or herself and of others.
- The antisocial believes that "People are there to be taken."
- The schizoid believes that "I need plenty of space."

LOVE BELIEFS

I would like to return to the research scientist, the patient whom I described earlier, in order to expand on my theory of "core beliefs." For several years now I have thought that although patients had a very wide variety of beliefs, there was some *general unifying principle* that could be the basis of all of these beliefs. I narrowed these diverse beliefs down to two major sets. The first dimension has to do with *autonomy*. These beliefs are, for example, "I am either effective or I am ineffective"; "I am either productive or I am helpless." The other set of beliefs are the *sociotropic* beliefs. The basic belief here is "I am either lovable or I am unlovable."

Now, this scientist believed at a deep level that "I am helpless and ineffective." This core belief was based on a range of traumatic childhood experiences, which were expressed in his current reactions to people. When he worked with other people in his organization, he perceived them as unreliable and uncooperative; his conditional belief then was "If I am not in control, things will collapse." Because he had this belief, we would expect his chronic state to be anxiety. In order to compensate for what he feared might happen, he developed a set of imperatives such as "I must control myself at all times, otherwise I might fall apart. And I must control others." When his control was not totally effective, he would become very upset because it meant *he* was ineffective ("either–or" thinking).

In addition to this compulsive personality characterization, he also had the features of a narcissistic personality disorder. At the basic core level he had the belief: "I am inferior." This belief was translated into a formula according to which he would interpret situations: "If I don't succeed at something, then it means that I am inferior." Thus whenever he fell short of his goals, it meant he was inferior. To compensate, he was very ambitious and driven *not* to fail. So he developed another formula: "If I succeed, then I am superior." He went through life succeeding practically all the time because he was very talented and hardworking. But underneath it all there was this nagging belief that he might fail, because he continued to believe at a deep level that he was inferior to other people. The result was that he never had a really happy day. Even though he kept achieving, he was on a treadmill and he never could get the kind of contentment that he was seeking.

Since the rules that governed his behavior were "I must be the best at everything. People must regard me as the best," his strategy was to succeed at everything and demonstrate his superiority. This set of beliefs did not prepare him well to react appropriately to adverse situations, such as a famine of research grants; he found that he could not do as much as he did before. He found that he had to extend himself more, but the more he extended himself into administrative duties, the less time he had for creative work. Because he wasn't creating as much, he did not get invited to serve on governmental boards or speak at international meetings. And when he saw that happening, his cognitive processing delivered up a conclusion such as "Because all the heavy hitters were invited to speak in Zurich and I wasn't, I must really be considered inferior." The cumulative weight of situations like that gradually drove him into depression.

It is important for the patient to recognize the formulas that drive his depression. After we have established proper rapport with our patients and we are sure of our ground, we generally share this type of conceptualization with them, try to get them to see the way that they are operating, and to formulate some more functional or realistic goals and more realistic ways of viewing reality.

EMPIRICAL STATUS OF COGNITIVE THERAPY

I indicated earlier that there must be empirical support for cognitive models if we are going to be happy with them. There now have been a number of review papers, some of which have come to the conclusion that there is strong empirical support for the cognitive model of depression. The most recent critical review on this subject in the *Psychological Bulletin* by Haaga, Dyck, and Ernst (1991) summarized a good deal of empirical support for some concepts, such as the negative cognitive triad in depression. When he was a graduate student at the University of Pennsylvania, Don Ernst reviewed all the papers up to 1987 relevant to the cognitive model of depression. As indicated in Table 3 he located 180 studies with more than 200 comparisons. He found that the closer the experiments were to the actual clinical phenomena, the more extensive was support for the cognitive model, whereas the further away that the experiments were from the clinical phenomena, the less likely there was to be support. Nonetheless, the support was very strong, all in all.

There were 150 analyses that were supportive of the cognitive triad and 14 that were either nonsupportive or rejected the cognitive

TABLE 3
Review of 180 Studies of Cognitive Model of Depression
(Don Ernst, 1987)

	SUPPORT	NON SUPPORT OR REJECT
	N OF ANALYSES	N OF ANALYSES
COGNITIVE TRIAD	*150*	*14*
SELF	55	3
EXPERIENCE	61	6
FUTURE	34	5
SCHEMAS	*31*	*6*
VULNERABILITY ACTIVATION		
PRIMING		
INFORMATION PROCESSING	*19*	*0*
BIAS		
PERCEPTION		
RECALL		
	200	20

triad. For the schema theory, there were 31 supportive and 6 nonsupportive. In terms of cognitive processing, using various types of experimental techniques borrowed from cognitive psychology, there were 19 studies that were supportive of the cognitive model and none that were nonsupportive. These studies had to do with bias, perception, and recall.

Of course, clinical trials are crucial to evaluate the effectiveness of therapy. A review of outcome studies by Keith Dobson (1989), in which 28 sites carried out outcome studies on cognitive therapy with unipolar depression, indicated that by and large the results favored cognitive therapy. There also have been many studies, almost all in the United Kingdom, on generalized anxiety disorders. Among the most recent were investigations by Butler, Fennell, Robson, and Gelder (1991) at Oxford, and Durham, Murphy, Allan, Richard, Treliving, and Fenton (1994) at Edinburgh, in which cognitive therapy turned out to be more effective than the comparison groups (which used behavior therapy and analytic therapy).

Panic disorders treated with cognitive therapy have been studied at many sites and they all have come out with consistently positive results. In a controlled study done at the University of Pennsylvania, cognitive therapy was found to be superior to supportive therapy (Beck, et al, 1992). A far more elegant study by D. M. Clark et al (1994) at Oxford reported that cognitive therapy turned out to be superior at the end of treatment and also at one-year follow-up to imipramine and applied relaxation. For whatever reason, panic patients seem exquisitely sensitive to this type of therapeutic intervention.

A study of heroin dependence carried out in the 1970s by Woody and associates (1983) reported that the psychotherapeutic techniques, including cognitive therapy, worked well in comparison to counseling for addicts who were dependent on heroin.

A crucial clinical question is: What value is it if you get patients better in 10 or 12 weeks and they relapse as soon as they leave therapy? It is necessary, therefore, to look at the one, two, and three-year follow-ups. There have been follow-ups done from one to three years, comparing cognitive therapy with antidepressant medication for unipolar depression. In four of the studies cognitive therapy was more successful at one, two, and three-year follow-ups. These studies were done at diverse locations in the United States and in Britain.

In the National Institute of Mental Health Collaborative Study of the treatment of depression, the results of the follow-up study were not significantly different between cognitive therapy and antidepressant medication. Out of eleven comparisons between cognitive therapy and imipramine, cognitive therapy came out superior (although not significantly so) in eleven out of eleven comparisons. In terms of the percentage that recovered, 49 percent of cognitive therapy patients were listed as recovered, compared to 38 percent of the imipramine; for patients who recovered and who did not relapse, 30 percent, as compared to 19 percent. Only three cognitive therapy patients (14 percent) had to return to treatment, as compared to 43 percent in IPT and 44 percent in imipramine. The people who returned to treatment were treated for varying lengths of time. The cognitive therapy patients who returned to treatment had the shortest period of re-treatment, 4.2 weeks as compared to 11, 20.3 and 7.8 for the other treatments.

We can only look at that 28 percent or 30 percent of recovery without relapse and realize that there is still much to be done. Perhaps that is the challenge of increasing our sophistication theoretically and technically. In an unpublished study, Brian Shaw has shown that there was a very strong relationship between the quality of the therapy and the outcome: Better therapists really get better outcomes. Therefore, there is no substitute for training.

In summary, as shown in Table 4, there are at least 20 different applications of cognitive therapy. Not only has it been applied to the usual Axis I diagnoses, but it has been found to be helpful in schizophrenia, sexual disorders, marital problems, suicidal behavior, sexual offenders, substance abuse, and so on. In addition, there is the recent application of cognitive therapy to various medical disorders, such as HIV positive cases who were anxious or depressed, poststroke cases, patients with colitis, cardiac problems, hypertension, and chronic fatigue. So, whenever I am at a

TABLE 4

Cognitive Therapy of Various Disorders

1. Depression
   (a) Unipolar
   (b) Bipolar
   (c) Rapid Cycling
   (d) Dysthymia

2. Anxiety
   (a) G.A.D.
   (b) Phobias

3. Panic
   (a) With Agoraphobia

4. Obsessive-Compulsive

5. Dissociative Disorder
   (a) Multiple personality

6. Posttraumatic Stress Disorder
   (a) Disaster
   (b) Rape

7. Suicidal behaviors

8. Schizophrenia

9. Marital/family problems

10. Sexual Disorders

11. Substance abuse

12. Sexual offenders

13. Medical
    (a) HIV
    (b) Post-stroke
    (c) Colitis
    (d) Cardiac
    (e) Hypertension
    (f) Chronic back pain

14. Psychosomatic
    (a) Chronic fatigue
    (b) Headache
    (c) Premenstrual distress

15. Personality disorders

conference and people say "Well, what has cognitive therapy *not* worked for?" nowadays I have to say "I don't know, because it hasn't been tried yet."

REFERENCES

Beck, A.T. (1967). *Depression: Clinical, experimental, and theoretical aspects.* New York: Harper and Row.

Beck, A.T., Freeman, A., & Associates. (1990). *Cognitive therapy of personality disorders.* New York: Guilford.

Beck, A.T., Rush, A.J., Shaw, B.F., & Emery, G. (1980). *Cognitive therapy of depression.* New York: Guilford. [Also published in Sussex, England: John Wiley & Sons Ltd.]

Beck, A.T., Sokol, L., Clark, D.A., Berchick, R.J., & Wright, F.D. (1992). A crossover study of focused cognitive therapy for panic disorder. *The American Journal of Psychiatry, 149*(6), 778–783.

Butler, G., Fennell, M., Robson, P., & Gelder, M. (1991). Comparison of behavior therapy and cognitive behavior therapy in the treatment of generalized anxiety disorder. *Journal of Consulting and Clinical Psychology, 59*(1), 167–175.

Clark, D.M., Salkovskis, P.M., Hackman, A., Middleton, H., Anastasiades, P., & Gelder, M. (1994). A comparison of cognitive therapy, applied relaxation and imipramine in the treatment of panic disorder. *British Journal of Psychiatry, 164,* 759–769.

Dobson, K. (1989). A meta-analysis of the efficacy of cognitive therapy for depression. *Journal of Consulting and Clinical Psychology, 57*(3), 414–419.

Durham, R.C., Murphy, T., Allan, T., Richard, K., Treliving, L.R., & Fenton, G.W. (1994). Cognitive therapy, analytic psychotherapy and anxiety management training for generalised anxiety disorder. *British Journal of Psychiatry, 165,* 315–323.

Haaga, D.A.F., Dyck, M.J., & Ernst, D. (1991). Empirical status of cognitive theory of depression. *Psychological Buletin, 110*(2), 215–236.

Sokol, L., Beck, A.T., Greenberg, R.L., Berchick, R.J., & Wright, F.D. (1989). Cognitive therapy of panic disorder: A nonpharmacological alternative. *Journal of Nervous and Mental Diseases, 177*(12), 711–716.

Woody, G.E., Luborsky, L., McClellan, A.T., O'Brien, C.P., Beck, A.T., Blaine, J., Herman, I., & Hole, A. (1983). Psychotherapy for opiate addicts: Does it help? *Archives of General Psychiatry, 40*(6), 639–645.

Discussion by Salvador Minuchin, M.D.

◆

Okay, I want people to know that I now live in Boston. I moved from New York where I lived for thirteen years. Before that I lived in Philadelphia for fifteen years. During the years I was in Philadelphia I was in the same department as Aaron Beck, but we had few dialogues. So, it is interesting that today after twenty-five years, I have the opportunity of listening to Aaron and enjoying his presentation, which is very lucid. I am in agreement with a lot of things he said.

However, I am much less optimistic than Aaron. I feel envious that after fifty years as a psychiatrist he still is as optimistic about psychotherapy as he is. As I get older, and I have more and more failures, I start to question many things about psychotherapy.

It's also interesting that under the Erickson Foundation umbrella, we can learn about different approaches to therapy. It's wonderful to hear the important concepts that Dr. Beck has presented to us. We can think, "Okay, how do they jibe with the thinking of systemic therapists," "How do they jibe with the thinking of dynamic therapists," "How do they jibe with the thinking of social constructionists?" There are representatives here of different points of view. I am not a cognitive therapist—I am a systems therapist, I am a family therapist, and therefore the things that are unsaid about the individual are partial to me because I always see the individual in a social context. I do not see the anorexic patient. I do not see the phobic or the depressed patient. I don't see the psychosomatic patient. I see the psychosomatic family. I see the anorexic's family. It is a very different experience from individual treatment.

Aaron talks about systems of belief and changing systems of belief. I know that systems of belief do not exist in a decontextualized person. Systems of belief are shared; they are part of the generic culture. For instance, if I am working with a depressed low socioeconomic Hispanic woman in her family I would think that the hypochondriac and depressed responses are culturally determined. In the Hispanic culture there is a tremendous amount of depressive responses that are normal in a woman. My response changes when I see the context.

Where I see an anorexic girl, I see her with her family. It is an interesting phenomenon that anorexia is, for the most part, a female rather than a male disturbance. Many years ago Mara Selvini Pallazoli wrote about the significance of the culture inducing anorexia in females and not in males. Therefore, my response to the presentation of Aaron Beck is: It's interesting. I like it. He presented studies, one cannot argue with studies. He presented studies that indicate: This is the way of treating certain phenomena.

The phenomena that he describes are a problem to me. In the fifteen years that we worked together at the University of Pennsylvania I was a marginal person in the psychiatric department, because I was not a "good" psychiatrist. I investigated families and patients in the context of their families; therefore, the diagnostic manual was not important to me.

I do not, for instance, describe the patient's characteristics in the way in which Dr. Beck describes them. I do not describe characteristics that are very much part of the psychiatric literature. He describes psychiatric phenomena.

I describe assessments of families. I am concerned with the way in which the maintenance of a symptom is part of the family organization. If I have a depressed woman, first, I would think, "How does her husband treat her?" It is very possible that the negative sense that the woman has of herself is very much a part of a daily encounter with a demeaning husband. Therefore, if I change her system of belief and her husband continues being critical and demeaning, I have a problem. Moreover, how can I change her system of belief in my office and not address the cultural context of the family that maintains her symptom?

So I have a kind of thinking that had caused a lot of difficulty at the University of Pennsylvania because I would say, "If you are a drunkard, how is your spouse, or your father, or your mother, codependent? How do they hold your glass?" "If you are anorexic, how do your parents ensure that you should not eat?"

One of the things that I want to ask Aaron is, How do you respond from a cognitive therapy perspective to that kind of challenge that comes from a systems therapy? Okay?

Response by Dr. Beck

◆

I'm glad that after so many years we finally get a chance to get together. The questions that you raised are very valid. I'd like to spend a lot of time on them, but I know the audience would like to ask questions too, so I'll be briefer than deserved about the very cogent points that you have made.

There are various levels of analysis. I wouldn't quarrel with a psychopharmacologist about the level of biological disturbance, for example, in depression. Nor would I quarrel with the systems theory theorist. We look at different levels and so our interventions are going to be somewhat different. Yet, in my opinion, it's very likely that interventions at different levels may be quite equivalent.

Nonetheless, Dr. Minuchin raises a good point that relates to another myth, which I called the contextualistic fallacy and says that the cognitive therapist doesn't take the context into account.

Now, if you're a good cognitive therapist, you have to be aware of different levels. You can't just go in blindly and look for hard cognitions; you have to be aware of the biological part, which may have a lot to do with the origin and the maintenance of the depression. You also have to know the context.

Take an anorexic patient. Dr. Minuchin, as you all know, really pioneered the treatment of anorexia. One can analyze the anorexic patient on many levels, including the family level and the individual level. At the family level, Dr. Minuchin would work with the family dynamics and how they impinge on the patient. He will examine all the interactions of patient and family.

I would summarily be aware of the interactions of the patient. Indeed, if it's a couple's problem we would bring the spouse in. But if we're just working individually with the patient, I would look at issues of control. Instead of modifying the relationship with the family in terms of control, I would get to the basic beliefs of the anorexic patient. The anorexic patient might come out with the belief: "The only part of my life that I can control is my eating. Everything else is controlled by other people. But one thing I can do is control my eating. Now, another reason I have to control my eating is because I have an image of myself as being undesirable to other people. I think that I'm useless, I'm bad, I'm wicked and rejectable" and so on. "By controlling my eating I can emphasize beauty even though other people say that I'm not fat. I really do think I'm fat," and so on and so forth.

Cognitive therapists would then work at that level. We don't just want symptomatic change; gaining weight in itself is not a great desideratum: Sometimes anorexics will gain weight, but because the therapy has devastated their whole idea of control they'll go out and commit suicide. That's happened with some of the behavioral approaches to anorexia.

Instead it is important to work with the patient's self-image so that she learns things. I think this is an advantage of cognitive therapy. The patient learns how to solve intrapsychic and interpersonal problems. We would coach this patient on how to deal with the members of the family so that she would not respond in a negative way to whatever intrusions the family makes.

Then, when she grows up, assuming she's over the anorexia, she's learned enough about herself and how to deal with the outside world that she will be able to cope with problems later on when the family is no longer in existence.

That's where we diverge in terms of where the emphasis is. But I would like to emphasize that we're not ignorant of the family problems, and indeed a number of cognitively trained people do deal with families, but they emphasize the family's beliefs. I once gave an example to Dr. Minuchin, and he said that he agreed with the example of the beliefs but not necessarily with the intervention.

Also, in the family, the anorexic child has parents who have different beliefs. One parent may believe that children should be disciplined; the other parent may believe the child has to be cultivated very properly. If they disagree about child rearing, their conflict gets played out on the child. Then the child is confused. "Do I go this way? Do I go the other way?" Then the sense of control is undermined because the child is so traumatized. Then she reestablishes her control with the idea that, "The only way I can protect myself against my parents is to control my eating." Then that gets both the parents to react, and so on and so forth.

So, we are conscious of what goes on in the system; we have a different way of doing it. I would say that the reason Dr. Minuchin didn't have more to do with us is his location. I do believe that geography determines history, and his location was apart from the rest of the department. If he had had a proximate office, we'd have been in contact every day and we would have worked this out thirty years ago.

The Evolution of Albert Ellis and Rational Emotive Behavior Therapy

◆——————◆——————◆

Albert Ellis, Ph.D.

Albert Ellis, Ph.D.

Albert Ellis is the President of the Institute for Rational Emotive Behavior Therapy in New York. He has practiced psychotherapy, marriage and family counseling, and sex therapy for more than 45 years. Dr. Ellis has received the Humanist of the Year Award from the American Humanist Association; the Distinguished Professional Contribution to Knowledge Award from the American Psychological Association; and the Personal Development Award from the American Association for Counseling and Development. He has written or edited more than 50 books and monographs, and he has published more than 600 papers in psychological, psychiatric, and sociological journals and anthologies. A Fellow of six professional organizations and a Diplomate of three professional boards, he received his Ph.D. degree in Clinical Psychology from Columbia University in 1947.

I have picked quite a topic for myself! "The Evolution of Albert Ellis and Rational Emotive Behavior Therapy." Even if I stick to only the first part of this topic—"The Evolution of Albert Ellis"—I could easily take the whole fifty hours of this conference to partly summarize that glorious and noble process. That, alas, would leave no time for the other main presenters to show how they magnificently evolved—and they may not like that.

Fortunately, as I shall soon show, I don't give too much of a shit about other presenters disliking me. Most of them already do! They hate my telling them that I am—of course!—right and that they are—indubitably!—wrong. In my youth, I would have stupidly bothered myself about that, would have shown a dire need for their approval, and would have told them that they were great guys or gals and scholars. Instead, of course, the real turds I thought they were. What, me be honest and impolite? Never!

It took me almost my first two decades to talk myself out of that crap of being ingratiating. I was born and reared to be shy and scared. Throughout my childhood and teens I had a real social phobia. I viewed public speaking as a fate worse than public masturbation. I opened my physically large mouth only among a group of my close friends. I avoided telling jokes for fear of flubbing the punch lines. I said nothing—literally nothing—about my feelings for the pretty young girls that I kept falling madly—in fact, obsessively-compulsively—in love with. As for approaching any of the young women I immoderately lusted after from the age of twelve onward, forget it! I heard and saw nothing but "evil" and "horrible" rejection—so I kept my big trap shut. In spite of my deranged passion for everything in skirts, up to the age of twenty my dating amounted to zero. Yes, nothing, nil, none, zero.

As you can imagine, I was highly unenthusiastic about my extreme social inhibitions. I knew I was scared witless and from my reading and my observations of my more popular male friends, I even knew what to do about it—take risks. I didn't. I decided to—and didn't. I almost began to—and froze.

Naturally, I beat myself for all this evasion. I knew what I wanted—and I knew that I was copping out. So I castigated myself for, first, avoiding "dangerous" social situations. For, second, feeling desperately anxious about them. For, third, knowing how to lick my anxiety and stubbornly refusing to go through the pain of overcoming it.

I even put myself down for the efforts I made to overcome my social phobias. I read many articles and books on psychology and philosophy, particularly from the age of 16 onward. I became interested in the philosophy of human happiness and made myself much less miserable about some of my other problems. How? Mainly by reading Confucius, Gautama Buddha, Epicurus, Epictetus, Marcus Aurelius, and other ancient philosophers. Also, from studying modern thinkers like Spinoza, Kant, Hume, Emerson, Thoreau, Santayana, Dewey, and Russell.

I gained a lot in these self-help ventures. In my early teens, I was plagued with insomnia, and often was able to sleep only a few restless hours a night. But I learned that I was worrying about sleeping itself and was able to stop that kind of worrying and to use monotony-focusing techniques. As a result, I soon was sleeping much better.

I began my writing career at the age of twelve and soon had scores of rejection slips for the stories, essays, and comic poems that I kept sending out. But I strongly convinced myself that I was not a rotten writer—nor even a *rotten person* (RP)—when I was not getting published.

At the age of sixteen, I thought I was addicted to masturbation and was guilty about that. No, not because of the sex aspect, but because at first I wrongly thought I was overdoing it and was lacking in self-control. But I soon saw that I was not a worm for acting wormily. I managed to accept myself as a happy masturbator, and never to put myself down when my penis went up.

Like most young students, I was also a miserable procrastinator. In high school, I never took a textbook home, did my homework in the 10 minute periods between classes, and studied for my exams the night before I had to take them. In college, I did the same for my freshman year but then realized how stupid and self-defeating this was. So I taught myself to finish my term papers within a few weeks after the beginning of the term—which amazed all my professors!—and to leave a few weeks before my exams to study for them. I thus became—or made myself—into an elegant nonprocrastinator.

As you can see—especially if you are peering behind lenses of your own neurotic self-defeatism—I did very well with several of my own neuroses in my early and late adolescence. Not—as Carl Rogers might have foolishly claimed—because I had a close, trusting, open, congruent relationship with a therapist or with anyone else. I didn't. At that time, I had no close relationships with anyone, except my younger brother, Paul. Not with my family, or with any of my good number of male acquaintances. Certainly not with any of the women I madly loved and would have given my all to be close to.

My main influences—and they were profound—were philosophers, psychologists, essayists, novelists, dramatists, poets, and other writers—all of whom I voluminously ingested. And digested. For I never was a true believer. I *thought* about what I read—and critically ripped most of it up. I could fairly easily see that Socrates was something of a sophist. That Plato was often a silly idealist. That Kant courageously threw out God and then cravenly brought him in the back door. That Freud was an arrant overgeneralizer. That Jung was a brilliant but sloppily mystical thinker. That Wilhelm Reich was pretty psychotic. That Carl Rogers was a nice fellow but an FFB—a fearful fucking baby. Et cetera!

So I *thought* about what I read. I experimentally *used it* on myself. Later, I *tried it out* with many of my clients. I did very well—except, at first, with my social phobia. I could speak one to one or in small groups of my friends. I had school and political associates. But, aside from my brother, Paul—who was younger than I, and almost always followed my teachings—no really close friends. And no lovers! Hell, as noted above, I had no damned dates.

So at the age of nineteen, mainly for political reasons, I decided to work at overcoming my terror of public speaking. I was appointed the leader of a radical youth group, but never spoke for it in public. So I used my philosophical teachings to strongly convince myself that nothing terrible would happen if I spoke for my group; and that, however uncomfortable I would be the process, I would hardly die of this discomfort (Ellis, 1990a, 1990b).

In other words, I started to convince myself of the two main philosophies that I later incorporated in Rational Emotive Behavior Therapy (REBT):

1. *Unconditional Self-Acceptance (USA)*. People—including me—can always decide to accept themselves *un*conditionally—just because they *choose* to do so. You, I, and everyone can resolve and agree to accept ourselves *whether or not* we perform well and *whether or not* other people approve of us or love us. Better yet, according to REBT, we can *decide* to only rate our thoughts, feelings, and actions, in accordance with how they fulfill our chosen goals and purposes—but not to rate or evaluate our *self*, our *being*, our *essence*, or our *personhood* at all. No, not *at all* (Bernard, 1991, 1993; Ellis, 1962, 1972, 1994, 1996; Ellis & Harper, 1975; Hauck, 1991).

2. *High Frustration Tolerance*. We are born and then raised with tendencies to feel highly frustrated and annoyed about many things that happen to us and about many of our unfulfilled desires. This is fine and healthy, because frustration motivates us to improve our lives. But we often also whine and needlessly upset ourselves when bad things happen to us and good things don't.

Therefore, in addition to teaching people unconditional self-acceptance, REBT encourages them to have high—though not too high!—frustration tolerance (HFT) (Dryden, 1995; Ellis, 1979a, 1980, 1985, 1988, 1994, 1996; Yankura & Dryden, 1990, 1994).

Applying these two philosophies to myself in my late teens, I decided to overcome my public speaking phobia. I read that John B. Watson, the first behaviorist, and his assistant, Mary Cover Jones, did in vivo desensitization with young children. They deconditioned them to their fear of mice or rabbits, which they at first placed ten feet away from the children, by distracting them, and by gradually moving the animals closer to them. In a short time, most of their subjects were joyfully petting these previously terrifying animals.

"Shit," I said to myself. "If in vivo desensitization is good enough for little children, it's good enough for me. I'll try it with my terror of public speaking. If I fail, I fail. If I die of discomfort, I die! Too damned bad!"

REBT was practically born during the next three months. For after anxiously and painfully giving political talks during that time, I discovered several important things. First, I didn't die. Second, I did reasonably well at my talks, in spite of my great discomfort. Third, my anxiety soon began to wear off. Fourth, I got better and better at speaking. In fact, I later discovered, as my friends and listeners pointed out, that peculiarly enough, I had a talent for public speaking that had been totally obscured by my horrified avoidance of risking even a single speech.

This was all somewhat unsuspected. But the real surprise was that within several months I started to greatly enjoy public presentations, was practically never anxious in the course of them, and made them a large part of my life. I made what amounted to a 180-degree turn in this respect and effected what is still fairly rare in psychotherapy—a complete cure.

"Great!" I said to myself. "But what is more important to me than public speaking? What do I *really* want to do that I'm completely avoiding doing? Obviously: approaching the

101% of women that I lust after and want to mate with. I'd even like to marry a few of them! What the hell am I going to do about that?"

I soon made plans to right the grievous wrong that I had been inflicting on myself and the women of the world. I lived near the Bronx Botanical Gardens, one of the loveliest places in New York. About 150 days a year I went there to smell the flowers, lie on the grass, read, and silently flirt with innumerable women. Flirt, but never, never encounter. Typically, I would sit on a bench on the Bronx River Parkway, a few feet away from a seemingly suitable woman seated on another bench. I'd look at her and often she would look back at me; and I could sense that some of these women were interested. But no matter how much I told myself that the time was ripe to approach, I soon copped out and walked away, cursing myself for my abysmal cowardice. I knew, of course, especially after my overcoming my public speaking panic, that I wouldn't die of rejection. But I still felt much too uncomfortable to try even a single approach.

During the summer of 1933, when I was on vacation from college and about to go back for my final year, I gave myself a historic homework assignment that greatly changed my own life—and in some ways changed the history of psychotherapy. I spoke to myself very strongly. "Look!" I said, "You forced yourself to get over the horror of making public speeches and now you're goddamned good at doing that. You actually enjoy it! So why not do the same with your silly terror of picking up women? No nonsense! Do, don't stew!"

My assignment to myself was simple. I would go to the Bronx Botanical Gardens every day when it wasn't raining in the month of July; would look for women sitting alone on park benches; and, instead of sitting a bench away, as I always anxiously did, would sit on the same bench with them. Not in their lap—but on the same goddamned bench. I would then give myself one minute—one lousy minute!—to talk to each one of them. No debate, no caviling, no nonsense!! If they bit me, they bit me! One lousy minute!

That was a very wise homework assignment that I gave myself. For I was knowingly risking failure and rejection; and I was doing what was most *un*comfortable for me to do. Moreover, I was giving myself no time to procrastinate about trying, no time to ruminate and thereby to build up my worrying.

Well, I forthrightly did it. I went to the park every day in July and found—count 'em!—130 women sitting alone on a park bench: All manners, shapes and sizes. Certainly enough to provide me with reasonable excuses—that they were too young, too old, too short, or too tall to talk to. But I allowed myself no excuse whatsoever—none! I sat next to all of them—the entire 130.

I found that 30 of them immediately waltzed away. They rejected me before I even got going! But, I said to myself, strongly, "That's okay. That leaves me a sample of an even hundred— good for research purposes!"

So I continued my research. I spoke to the entire hundred of these women, and within one lousy minute! About the birds, the bees, the flowers, the trees, their knitting, their reading—about anything and everything. Mind you, I had never done this a single time before. But I was determined! On to the fray!

If Fred Skinner, who was at that time a young psychologist at Indiana University, had known about my experiment, he would have probably concluded that I would have got extinguished. For out of the hundred women I talked to, I was finally able to make only one date—and she didn't show up! But I found, empirically, that nothing terrible happened. No one took a butcher knife and cut my balls off. They only do that to men these days! No one vomited and ran away. No one called a cop. In fact, I had a hundred pleasant conversations, and began to get quite good at talking to strange women in strange places. So good, in fact, that for my second hundred subjects I became more persuasive, and was able to make three different dates with women. None of whom, fortunately, I married.

Once again, as happened with my public speaking, I was able to make a 180-degree change. For the rest of my life I have been able to talk to women whenever I wish to do so—on planes, trains, elevators, park benches, and you name it. And with one of these pickups I actually did live for awhile! (Ellis, 1988, 1990a, 1990b).

How does all this relate to my finally creating Rational Emotive Behavior Therapy, using it successfully on myself and with thousands of my clients, and promulgating its principles and practices throughout the world? In several important ways. Let me recount just a few of them.

1. I discovered the great value of cognition, philosophy, reasoning, and self-persuasion in changing one's dysfunctional feelings and actions. I had been mildly devoted to the ideas of novelists, dramatists, and poets since the age of twelve, and got some great ideas from writers like Byron, Shelley, Dostoyevsky, H.G. Wells, George Bernard Shaw, Upton Sinclair, Theodore Dreiser, Edgar Lee Masters, and others. I had been even more deeply devoted to card-carrying philosophers, such as those mentioned above, since the age of sixteen. I thought about what the philosophers I read said, tried out some of their suggestions, and never would have forced myself to speak uncomfortably in public and to encounter new women without first changing some of my ideas about absolutely *needing* to succeed and *having* to be approved without help from these sources. So with the aid of these thinkers, I made the understanding of cognitive processes one of the main elements of my prepsychoanalytic therapy from 1947 to 1953, and after I practiced psychoanalysis and found it to be just about the least efficient form of therapy ever invented, I returned to active-directive therapy in 1953, and emphasized cognition again—and again and again! (Ellis, 1962, 1985, 1988, 1994, 1996).

2. I was always skeptical of orthodox psychoanalysis, mainly because I read all the major works of Freud, Jung, and other leading analysts between my sixteenth and twentieth years, and found them interesting but unhelpful. Their sexual ideas helped make me into a sex liberal, but I could easily see that psychodynamic understanding, in itself, led to little personality change. Later on, when I read Fromm, Horney, Sullivan, and other neo-analysts—almost all of whom were actually neo-Adlerians—I became more attached to psychoanalytic inquiry and planned change. But I still saw that it was not sufficiently philosophical and active-directive. Its deficiencies in these respects encouraged me to originate a form of therapy, REBT, that was as active as I had been with myself while I was overcoming my panic about public speaking and socializing (Ellis, 1957, 1968).

3. My early self-training in cognitive and behavioral therapy fortunately turned me off from Carl Rogers, whose therapy was notably deficient in both areas. Carl—who from my personal contact with him always seemed to be somewhat shy and diffident himself—took from the existentialists, such as Martin Heidegger and Paul Tillich, the same philosophy of unconditional self-acceptance (USA) that I also derived from them. But he unfortunately thought that USA could mainly be conveyed to people by modeling and by giving them, personally, unconditional positive regard. He signally failed to see that it usually has to be actively taught and encouraged, as well as given. After working hard to give USA to myself, I realized how passive Rogers was, and therefore incorporated the energetic *teaching* of USA into REBT (Ellis, 1972, 1985, 1988, 1994, 1996).

4. I learned from writers, and particularly from novelists and dramatists, the value of unconditional other acceptance (UOA). I practiced this one myself when I was sixteen, and decided that my hostility toward my sister, Janet, wasn't doing me, her, or anyone else any good, and was in fact sabotaging some of my own desires. So, although Janet at that time was a royal pain in the ass to me, to our family, and to most other people, I decided to forgive her and permit her to use my large collection of popular and semiclassical songs. My brother, Paul, who still hated Janet, was startled to see the change in me and never went along with it until many years later. But I saw that I felt immensely better and relieved, stopped obsessing myself with negative thoughts about her, and actually benefited from several nice things that she did for me thereafter. So I kept working at forgiving my enemies, and incorporated unconditional acceptance of others, along with many anti-hostility techniques, into REBT.

5. I particularly noted, when I discovered that my anxiety *about* my sleeping was interfering with my sleeping, that I had both primary and secondary symptoms of my neurosis. I may have been aided in this respect by philosophers, some of whom noted the same thing. Thus, Seneca, over two thousand years ago, was perhaps the first to note what Franklin D. Roosevelt's ghostwriter later cribbed from him: "We have nothing to fear but fear itself." So I may have been impressed with that. I was especially helped by a book I read on insomnia when I was seventeen, which pointed out that first insomniacs worry about some problem or possible failure, and thereby keep themselves awake. But once they produce their symptom, insomnia, they worry about having this symptom—and they then create a secondary symptom that may be worse than their primary one in keeping them from sleeping. So, as noted above, I worked at stopping my worrying about my possible failures, as well as at stopping my worrying about losing sleep, and did very well at improving my insomnia.

When I started to do therapy, and especially when I stopped doing psychoanalysis, I saw clearly that a large percentage of my clients had both primary and secondary symptoms—especially anxiety about anxiety and depression about depression—and I incorporated into REBT the techniques of therapists' assuming that this kind of disturbance often exists, pointing it out to clients, and showing these clients how to minimize it.

6. Perhaps the most distinctive aspect of REBT that is somewhat different than the theories of the other cognitive behavior therapies (CBTs)—such as those of A. T. Beck (1976, 1991; Beck & Emery, 1985), J. S. Beck (1995), Lazarus (1989), Mahoney (1991), Maultsby (1984), Meichenbaum (1977) and Raimy (1975)—is its assumption that the basic philosophies, schemas, or core irrational beliefs that people usually follow to make themselves neurotic largely involve their adopting and creating absolutistic musts. Virtually all the popular CBTs include these musts but do not hold, as does REBT, how basic and underlying they are, and how they lead to most of the other profound irrationalities—such as awfulizing, I-can't-stand-it-itis, and self-denigration—with which people often plague themselves. I saw this fairly clearly when I read Karen Horney's

Neurosis and Human Growth in 1950, because she emphasized the "tyranny of the shoulds."

Actually, however, I had largely figured out this exceptionally important trigger of emotional disturbance from reading several philosophers—especially Epictetus—and from my personal experience in 1936, when I was 23 years of age. I was madly in love, at this time, with Florence, the woman who was to become my first wife, and I was getting nowhere with her because of her indecision about how much she loved me in return. On the one hand, she would say her love for me would put Heloise's passion for Abelard to shame. On the other hand, a few days later, she would say I was too esthetic for her, would show interest in other men, and would neglect me considerably. Several talks with her and 30-page letters to her about her inconsistency got me and her nowhere. She rigidly stuck to her indecisiveness.

One midnight, when I had spent a wonderfully conflicting evening with Florence and was on my way home to my apartment in the Bronx, I was sorely troubled about our still see-sawing relationship and decided to go for a walk by the lake in Bronx Botanical Gardens and to reconsider our on-and-off affair. In walking around the deserted lake, I thoughtfully decided that my love for Florence was stupendous but that it had too much pain attached to it—especially when she continued her stark ambivalence. Maybe, I thought, I should quit the whole affair and find someone who would love me steadily instead of with startling intermittency.

Suddenly I saw the way out of my—not to mention Florence's—dilemma. It was not my strong *desire* for her that gave me so much trouble when it was not thoroughly fulfilled. No, it was my *dire need* for her love. I foolishly believed that she *absolutely had* to return my feelings in kind; and that and only that would solve our problem. Well, that was horseshit! I saw that I could, if I wished, keep my powerful desire, urge, and love for Florence—and I could simultaneously give up my *need, demand*, and *insistence* that she feel exactly the same way as I did.

That was really an astonishing thought: I could love without needing! Indeed, I now started to see, all those other girls with whom I kept obsessively falling in love with since the age of five, whom I couldn't get out of my mind, and whom I was terribly anxious about their loving me back, were in the same category as Florence. I foolishly thought that I *needed* them—that I couldn't live happily *without them*, and *had to* cement a stupendous relationship with them forever. Yes, even though I was too damned shy to let any of them know my feelings.

Need, not love, was the issue! That, I saw as I went for my walk in the woods, was my and everyone else's real problem when we were anxious, depressed, and enraged. We needed—or foolishly *thought* we needed— something that we importantly wanted. We asininely insisted that we absolutely *must*, under all conditions and at all times, *must* be loved, *should* get what we wanted, and ought *never* suffer serious frustration. What quaint ideas! How pernicious! How could we possibly be happy—really and persistently happy— when we rigidly held to these unrealistic notions? We couldn't.

So, believe it or not, in that one twenty-minute walk by the lake, I gave up most of my neediness—especially my dire need for Florence's love. I still desired very much to be with her, and would still try to win her love. But I definitely didn't *need* it. Just as soon as I could, I would tell her this, tell her that I had stopped insisting that she *had to* return my strong feelings, and then see what kind of a relationship, if any, we could work out. If, at worst, she wanted to break up, I could accept that. If she wanted to go on with the relationship and still be ambivalent, I could accept that, too. But, if so, I would eventually find another woman who would be more constant. Not that I *needed* to, but just that I *wanted* to find one.

I got together with Florence the very next night, told her how I had propelled myself out of my need for her, and asked her what she wanted to do now. To my surprise, she was very impressed with my newly found non-neediness, wished that she could have it herself whenever she was madly in love—and suggested that we should have an experimental, nonneedy marriage. We would secretly marry—because we didn't yet have the income to live together—would maintain an open relationship, and would see how it all worked out. As long as we were both nonneedy, maybe it would. But if it didn't, too bad. Neither of us would have to feel hurt, angry, or depressed.

How Florence and I actually began and later ended our marriage is another story. The main point of this one is that I really did make a startling change in myself during my walk around the lake in Bronx Botanical Gardens. For the rest of my life I have had very strong desires— many of them!—which I have striven to fulfill. But I have rarely thereafter thought that I *absolutely needed* what I wanted, nor *strongly needed* to avoid what I abhorred. And later I put anti-neediness, anti-awfulizing and anti-musturbation solidly into REBT.

I did so in 1955, at the start of Rational Emotive Behavior Therapy. The dozen irrational beliefs that I originally postulated as a main source of human neurosis all include explicit or implicit musts and needs. Later on, when I had used REBT for a few years with hundreds of clients and done a few research studies on it, I more clearly stated that when people are classically neurotic, they seem to have one, two, or three basic or core musts and needs: (1) "I *absolutely must* do well or I am no good!" (2) "You *decidedly must* treat me fairly and considerately, or you are a rotten person!" (3) "My life conditions *absolutely have to be* the way I want them to be, or I *can't stand* it and can't have any real happiness at all!" Many other irrational or self-defeating beliefs exist, as I and other cognitive-behavior therapists have pointed out. But underlying them and basic to them seem to be implicit or explicitly musts, shoulds, demands, and commands. Whether I would have ever seen this so clearly without my getting over my own neediness during my walk around the lake in 1936, I'll never of course know. But that walk and the thinking I did in the course of it certainly helped! (Ellis, 1962, 1985, 1988, 1994, 1996; Walen, DiGiuseppe & Dryden, 1992; Wolfe, 1992).

7. Another distinctive aspect of REBT is its notion, which most other psychotherapies still resist accepting, that there are two basic, and somewhat distinct, kinds of negative feelings:

healthy ones, such as sorrow, regret, frustration, and annoyance, when something goes against your personal interests and tastes; and unhealthy negative feelings, such as depression, despair, rage, panic, and self-hatred, when similar unfortunate events occur. In other words, REBT quarrels with Wolpe's (1990) Subjective Units of Discomfort (SUDS) Scale, which puts negative feelings from zero to 100, but has only one scale that includes what REBT calls healthy and unhealthy negative emotions. I hold, instead, that when you experience failure, rejection, and discomfort you can healthily feel mild to strong negative feelings of regret and frustration, or you can add to these healthy negative feelings mild to strong feelings of depression, horror, and panic (Ellis, 1985, 1988). Thus, REBT gives you two continua of negative feelings for the price of one!

I partly worked out this distinction for myself when I was in the children's ward of the old Presbyterian Hospital in New York for ten months during my seventh year, suffering from nephritis. My father, who was a businessman who neglected his three young children, rarely came to visit me, and my mother, who had my younger brother and sister to care for, only visited me once a week. Meanwhile other mothers, fathers, and family members visited their children twice a week regularly.

Especially on Sundays, when all the other children in my ward had a number of visitors and I usually had none, I was at first angry, and sometimes depressed, about my great deprivation. But as I saw that this deprivation was definitely going to continue, I worked at making myself feel quite sorrowful and regretful, but rarely seriously upset, about my lack of visitors. This experience seemed to teach me that whenever something went wrong in my life I had the choice of *how* badly I would let myself feel about it; I continued to use this knowledge, and created healthy instead of unhealthy negative feelings when I was deprived. So when I started to do REBT in 1955 I clearly distinguished positive feelings from negative feelings: healthy ones from unhealthy ones. The belief that REBT neglects or downplays people's feelings is quite incorrect. It even encourages them to feel *strongly*

displeased, sorry, frustrated, regretful, and annoyed when things go wrong in their lives. This is what I managed to make myself feel when I was a seven-year-old patient in New York's Presbyterian Hospital.

8. I hadn't really thought about this until I began writing the present paper. But REBT's concept of helping people to make themselves less disturbed and also less disturb*able* also probably originated in my personal anti-neurosis campaign when I was a youngster. For I started to get this idea when, as I have described, I worked on making myself unneedy, as well as on getting over my terror of public speaking and of approaching strange women. In both these instances, I made a 180-degree turn and went from serious disturbance to just about complete nondisturbance.

In making this radical change, I discovered several things: (a) I was no longer greatly disturbed about failing and being rejected as I had often previously been, though I was still sorry and displeased about these happenings. (b) I still did not *want* to do badly but I entirely lost my *terror* of failing. I was no longer uncomfortable about trying to speak in public and to approach women; and when I did poorly, I accepted this with equanimity and didn't in any way put myself down for my failures. (c) I began to actually *look forward* to taking the risks that I previously had been phobic about taking. I actually *enjoyed* taking them. (d) I *knew* that my panic about trying to speak and to encounter new women was gone, and that in all probability it would not return. (e) My fear of failing at other pursuits—like interviewing for a job or taking an important test—also almost totally vanished. (f) I had much greater self-efficacy, and looked forward to success at ventures at which I previously predicted I would dismally fail. (g) I began to see that practically *nothing* bad that might happen to me, including important failures and rejections of *any* kind, would set me on the downward path to anxiety and avoidance of risk-taking. (h) I became much more adventurous and actually sought out new pursuits that I had previously seen as dangerous but now saw as exciting and inviting.

Because I achieved this *elegant* solution to my emotional problems, and because I was pretty certain that they would not reoccur even if serious failures and deprivations happened to me, I began to see that the methods that I used to help myself—especially radically changing my philosophy and repetitively doing what I was afraid to do no matter how uncomfortable I at first was in doing it—would most probably work with other neurotic individuals. I also began to believe that in some cases, where people strongly and actively adopted my anxiety-attacking methods, they could make themselves both less disturbed and eventually less disturb*able*. So when I began practicing REBT in 1955, I included in it what I call the elegant solution to emotional problems—that is, clients quickly and deeply undisturbing themselves; and, if they continue to strongly do so, ultimately bringing themselves to the point where they are much less disturbable than they previously were. Yes, even though humanity as a whole continues to be highly upsettable! (Ellis, 1979b, 1985, 1988, 1994).

9. Although I seem to have been born and reared with a strong propensity to make myself anxious rather than depressed, I have some normal neurotic tendencies to depress myself when things are going unusually badly. Thus, I depressed myself for a while when I was 33 years of age and I broke up with a woman, Gertrude, whom I had passionately loved for five years, and still loved when we parted, because we had radically different ideas about living together. She was much more sociable than I, and wanted to be sure, when we were planning to marry, that we lived in a totally open apartment, with no closed doors between the rooms so that neither of us could arrange for any privacy. And she was planning on our having fairly big dinner parties, not to mention other kinds of parties, twice a week. With my own emphasis on seeing many clients and doing quite a bit of reading and writing, this kind of chit-chatty life simply wasn't for me. So we agreed to only be friends, and shortly thereafter she got engaged to marry a man who was more social than I.

I felt depressed for a short while, but quickly started to use the methods I had previously used to overcome my feelings of anxiety, and was pleased to see that they worked very well.

I strongly convinced myself that I didn't *need* to live with Gertrude, though I very much wanted to do so. I made myself see that she wasn't the only possible mate for me; that I could have a good life without her; that I wasn't a loser for not living up to her highly social standards; and that I would in all probability soon find a more suitable partner. That was pretty good, cognitively. But I also threw myself into more studying and writing; I started building my psychological practice; and I began actively dating, which soon led to my having another steady love relationship.

This experience tended to show me that feelings of depression, like those of severe anxiety, are usually related to demands that I (and other people) *absolutely must* perform well and *must not* be deprived of their important wants. Although I agree with Aaron Beck (1976; Beck & Emery, 1985) that specific automatic thoughts that people frequently use to make themselves anxious are somewhat different from those that they use to make themselves depressed, I still think that their underlyingly *musts* and *demands* are similar. Thus, I have said for years—and I still do—suppose that I, you, or anyone else thoroughly believes, "I *prefer* very much to do well and be loved by significant others, but I never, never *have to* fulfill these preferences. Too damned bad if I do not achieve them! I greatly *desire* to get what I want when I want it and to avoid severe pain and discomfort, but I never *need* what I desire and I can always find other enjoyable things. Tough shit if I am deprived! Now let me work like hell to try to get what I want!" If anyone really thinks this way and consistently carries these thoughts into action, would he or she ever become and remain severely anxious or depressed? Yes, perhaps, if their body chemistry was severely awry and they had endogenous anxiety or depression. Otherwise, I doubt it.

Anyway, my belief that both anxiety and depression usually stem from strong absolutistic musts, needs, and demands, and that they can mainly be relieved by thoroughly giving up these commands and changing them back into *only* the preferences from which they originate, this theory and practice of REBT once again largely stems from my own emotional growth and development. And my use of REBT on myself has, I think, led to further growth and development.

Time is running out, so let me end before I get going on another book. Having presented this lovely paper, I strongly *prefer* that all you listeners see what a brilliant person I am, acknowledge how I have beautifully evolved over the years, and realize that REBT is a marvelous form of therapy that is backed by my personal experience as well as by convincing clinical and research findings.

Alas, many of you, for whatever reasons, will not go along with my preferences. Well you obviously don't *have to* do so. My wish may well *not* be your command. You are entitled to be as stupid as you wish to be about this. Too damned bad! Tough shit! By stubbornly refusing to take your objections *too* seriously, and by refraining from unhealthily upsetting myself about them, I shall once again show how REBT clearly works. At least for a sensible, sane, and of course completely rational person like me!

REFERENCES

Beck, A. T. (1976). *Cognitive therapy and the emotional disorders*. New York: International Universities Press.

Beck, A. T. (1991). Cognitive therapy: A 30-year retrospective. *American Psychologist, 46,* 382–389.

Beck, A. T., & Emery, G. (1985). *Anxiety disorders and phobias*. New York: Basic Books.

Beck, J. S. (1995). *Cognitive therapy: Basics and beyond*. New York: Guilford.

Bernard, M. E. (Ed.). (1991). *Using rational-emotive therapy effectively: A practitioner's guide*. New York: Plenum.

Bernard, M. E. (1993). *Staying rational in an irrational world*. New York: Carol Publishing.

Dryden, W. (1995). *Brief rational emotive behaviour therapy*. London: Wiley.

Ellis, A. (1957). Outcome of employing three techniques of psychotherapy. *Journal of Clinical Psychology, 13,* 344–350.

Ellis, A. (1962). *Reason and emotion in psychotherapy*. Secaucus, NJ: Citadel.

Ellis, A. (1968). Is psychoanalysis harmful? *Psychiatric Opinion, 5*(1), 16–25. Reprinted. New York: Institute for Rational-Emotive Therapy.

Ellis, A. (1972). *Psychotherapy and the value of a human being*. New York: Institute for Rational-Emotive Therapy.

Ellis, A. (1979a). Discomfort anxiety: A new cognitive behavioral construct. Part 1. *Rational Living, 14*(2), 3–8.

Ellis, A. (1979b). Rejoinder: Elegant and inelegant RET. In A. E. Ellis & J. M. Whiteley, *Theoretical and empirical foundations of rational-emotive therapy* (pp. 240–267). Monterey, CA: Brooks/Cole Publishing.

Ellis, A. (1980). Discomfort anxiety: A new cognitive behavioral construct. Part 2. *Rational Living, 15*(1), 25–30.

Ellis, A. (1985). *Overcoming resistance: Rational-emotive therapy with difficult clients*. New York: Springer.

Ellis, A. (1988). *How to stubbornly refuse to make yourself miserable about anything—yes, anything!* New York: Carol Publishing.

Ellis, A. (Speaker). (1990a). *Albert Ellis live at the Learning Annex*. 2 cassettes. New York: Institute for Rational-Emotive Therapy.

Ellis, A. (1990b). My life in clinical psychology. In C. E. Walker (Ed.), *History of clinical psychology in autobiography*. Homewood, IL: Dorsey.

Ellis, A. (1994). *Reason and emotion in psychotherapy*. Revised and updated. New York: Birch Lane Press.

Ellis, A. (1996). *Better, deeper and more enduring brief therapy*. New York: Brunner/Mazel.

Ellis, A., & Harper, R. A. (1975). *A new guide to rational living*. North Hollywood, CA: Wilshire.

Hauck, P. A. (1991). *Overcoming the rating game*. Louisville, KY: Westminster.

Horney, K. (1950). *Neurosis and human growth*. New York: Norton.

Lazarus, A. A. (1989). *The practice of multimodal therapy*. Baltimore, MD: Johns Hopkins.

Mahoney, M. J. (1991). *Human change processes*. New York: Basic Books.

Maultsby, M. C., Jr. (1984). *Rational behavior therapy*. Englewood Cliffs, NJ: Prentice-Hall.

Meichenbaum, D. (1977). *Cognitive-behavior modification*. New York: Plenum.

Raimy, V. (1975). *Misunderstandings of the self*. San Francisco: Jossey-Bass.

Walen, S., DiGiuseppe, R., & Dryden, W. (1992). *A practitioner's guide to rational-emotive therapy*. New York: Oxford University Press.

Wolfe, J. L. (1992). *What to do when he has a headache*. New York: Hyperion.

Wolpe, J. (1990). *The practice of behavior therapy* (4th ed.). Needham Heights, MA: Allyn and Bacon.

Yankura, J., & Dryden, W. (1990). *Doing RET: Albert Ellis in action*. New York: Springer.

Yankura, J., & Dryden, W. (1994). *Albert Ellis*. Thousand Oaks, CA: Sage.

Discussion by Aaron Beck, M.D.

Well, I certainly enjoyed this full disclosure. Right from the shoulder. Uncompromising statements from Dr. Ellis. I think the whole audience participated in this enjoyment. I thought you might want to retitle your talk, Al, "The Walk Around the Lake." I'm sorry that we didn't have a similar lake in Philadelphia. It might have done me a lot of good.

I'd like to take this opportunity to express my own personal indebtedness to Al, which has been probably overlooked as Al has, in his unvarnished way, pointed out several times.

Many years ago, when I was emerging from my own transformation as a psychoanalyst, I hit upon some new ideas. One of the observations I made had to do with the following phenomenon. When people were experiencing some unpleasant affect, whether it was anxiety or sadness or depression, they often had a quick silent thought that occurred just before then. It took many years for me to discover this, and this was something that I realized that people used to communicate to themselves, but not to the outside world, and so they would not actually report these in their analytic sessions.

I also made some other interesting observations, but these were so out of keeping with the dogma of the time that I wondered if this was just a self-delusion or whether I might be on to something. And I did have the temerity to publish some of this. I did it in the guise of research findings to make it more acceptable. And then, at one point, I believe Al actually read one of my pieces and he got in touch with me. I found that somebody else was walking along the same path that I was, and this was really a great confirmation for me; maybe there was something there. And actually we have gone along the same path ever since then except my path has been much wider, obviously, and much closer to the truth than his. But if he wants to believe that he has the exclu-

sive hold on knowledge, so be it. Al, be my guest.

In any event, there's no question that he was the pioneer, I believe, in modern-day psychotherapy. He really cleared the road for the rest of us who followed behind, and he really took the brunt of all of the criticism and the humiliating attacks that were launched on him. I think he actually enjoyed it, frankly. However, he has been wrong on a few things, and I'm going to take the liberty to mention some of them.

First of all, let me mention things about which he has been right on: He's absolutely right about the shoulds and the musts. However, just as he mentioned, these affects themselves have a normal, aspecting factor that is just as critical to human function as the experience of pain when we injure ourselves. It's just as important to have these signals of sadness or anxiety when we are exposed to real-life situations, because they tend to mobilize us to do something about a situation. So I do believe, that most experts, including Wolpe, will find a place for the normal affects and the normal emotions, but because we primarily deal with people who are distressed in some way, we tend to focus on the unnecessary distress that people have, rather than on the normal mechanisms that help to keep us alive. And these affects, the ones that Al has been talking about, actually are survival mechanisms.

Now, similarly, the shoulds and the musts, and the needs, and so on, have a normal component to them. In our own work with patients, we use what we call a normalizing rationale. We will say, for example, "While it is important for self-survival to have the 'shoulds' to a particular extent, in your particular case they're overdone and therefore you fall into the trap (as Al mentioned) of the tyranny of the shoulds." First, I would like to point out where the shoulds have value in human functioning, and then I will show where the shoulds go wrong.

All this has to do with what you might call the birth of the shoulds. What actually drives human behavior? In my opinion there are two major forces that drive us to do what we do. We do things because we like to do them, because we get pleasure out of it. In the same vein, we do things with the anticipation of pleasure, whether it's sex, going to conferences, enjoying a good book, watching television, and so on.

Now, those are things that are easy to do because we anticipate pleasure and, to some degree, we get pleasure. But, there's a whole set of other things that we don't necessarily enjoy at all, but that we should do, such as stopping at red lights when we're in a hurry to get some place. You don't do it because you want to, necessarily, or because you're rewarded for it, but you do it because it's ingrained. And many of the imperatives, I believe, can be found all through the animal kingdom. We have our shoulds and musts, and I-should-nots and I-must-nots, because they serve an adaptive purpose.

Among the adaptive purposes that they serve, the injunctions for example, help us to do things that will keep us alive, such as the proper hygiene, brushing our teeth in the morning, and so on, and following certain social rules that will allow us to get along in society instead of being massacred by being too much of a rebel, or being thrown into jail.

We have various prohibitions that allow us to avoid certain dangers. Now, there are certain social dangers that of course are exaggerated in the neurotic. If somebody started to try to frighten an audience by yelling "Fire!" that person would get a severe punishment. It wouldn't be just a fantasy punishment, but it could be something that could have an enduring effect on them. So, in that sense, the prohibitions are important.

The observation of moral rules is also very important. If everybody did their own thing, society soon would cave in and we would have anarchy. That's another valuable part of the shoulds and musts.

Also, we are social animals and we have to put shoulds and musts and expectations on other people. If we don't to some degree, then we're going to be stepped on. So, you can't walk through life as an innocent, expecting people to treat you just right. In some way you have to be able to recognize when your own rights are not being observed and to force yourself or force other people at least to treat you decently. I don't think that Al would necessarily disagree with any of these things, but where we possibly would come to a disagreement is with the excessive shoulds.

This is where the tyranny of the shoulds comes in. I certainly agree with Al's notion of the three categories of shoulds. The first has to do with the beliefs, the shoulds that we level against ourselves—"I should be perfect, I should try to impress you all, I should tell Al where he's wrong . . ." and all of these things become like vises that actually restrict our behavior.

The second set of shoulds has to do with what we expect from other people—You people in the audience should believe everything that I say, and if you don't, then there's something really radically wrong with you, somehow you're really very bad.

The third set of shoulds has to do with life in general—life should treat me very well and should not frustrate me.

For the problematic types of individuals whom we see in our practices, the shoulds are an extremely important part of their neuroses. However, the shoulds are not disembodied, or autonomous; rather there's something that's driving the shoulds.

Now, what is driving the shoulds? Let me give you an example of a patient whom I saw recently. She was a journalist who was really very successful in her job. But she was always anxious, and when we looked at her anxiety we saw that the anxiety was driving her to do things that were really unnecessary, and which, in themselves, created more anxiety.

When she was going out on an assignment, she felt that she should do a good job. Why did she feel she had to do a good job? Because underneath the should was a kind of "catastrophizing." She was afraid that if she didn't do a good job the public would ridicule her, her editor would discharge her, and her husband would leave her. So what was driving the should in her case was a kind of "catastroph-izing" (incidently that is an Ellis word for which, Al, I am indebted). So, she was driven by this fearfulness. The fearfulness then drove her to become a perfectionist, and the perfec-tionism then drove her crazy.

Her husband was a professional. When she had a dinner party for her husband, she felt everything had to be just so. She had to make sure that the seating arrangement was per-fect, the menu was perfect, food was cooked perfectly, and everybody had a good time. And she felt that this absolutely had to be, and if it did not occur that way she would become anx-ious. But what was driving this was the fear that unless she did a perfect job, the guests would dislike her and then the dislike would carry over to her husband and would hurt her husband.

And so in my own work with her it was nec-essary to work not only with the shoulds, but with the fears that were underneath the shoulds.

Now, this is kind of the paradigm that I believe gets you to anxiety. People kind of "should" themselves into anxiety, but the anxi-ety also pushes the people into the shoulds. What you have here is a vicious cycle.

In our therapy we like to look at both parts. Why not put your money across the board rather than put everything just on one of those squares? In my opinion, the wider the net you have, the more fish you're going to catch, and the more money you're likely to make. So, you spread the risk around by looking at both.

I think that some people respond very well to the shoulds and the musts because they say, "Gosh, doc, I never thought of that before, it never occurred to me," and they'll start to see it. Other people, who are more anxiety-ridden, really do have to have the therapist help them with looking more objectively at what their basic fears are.

In depression, the problem is not that I should "do something," the problem is that I should "have." People are depressed because of things that they believe occurred in the past over which they had some control. The whole idea of control is very important.

The shoulds often give people a spurious sense of control. We think things should be better because we have the myth that if only we would do things in a certain way we could make them better. It's very difficult for many people to accept the fact of life, which is that we don't have maximum control over what happens to us and what happens to other people. However, we do have *more* control over what happens to us.

Depressed people have this to the nth degree, and so they think, "If only I had done such and such, then this would not have hap-pened." And it can be levied against them-selves like, "I should have written a better paper. I should have done a better job with the patient. If I had, she wouldn't have committed suicide and since I did not do a good job, as is evidenced by the appearance. . . ." I am then self-critical.

Now the anger paradigm is similar to this, and that is levied against other people: "You should have done such and such, and since you did not do such and such, you are a worm in Dr. Ellis' words. I am angry and since I am angry, *ipso facto*, I am entitled to punish you in some particular way."

Now, again to borrow one of Dr. Ellis' words, I think this more elegant paradigm is a better road map than the one that Dr. Ellis has provided for you.

In any event, I do want to thank Dr. Ellis again for a very stimulating and extremely entertaining review of how Albert Ellis evolved, and again, to personally thank him for what he's done in helping me to develop my own therapeutic techniques. Thank you.

Response by Dr. Ellis

◆

Let me briefly respond to Tim Beck's discussion. I agree with just about everything he said because there are two different kinds of shoulds. One is a preferable should, and the human race really probably couldn't exist without that, and as he indicated neither could animals. They preferably should do this—should be moral, should get along with others, should come early to their jobs, and so on and they get realistic, social, and self penalties if they don't. So you can't get rid of the preferable shoulds.

But, as I pointed out, the fact seems to be that humans, when they are neurotic, just about invariably also have absolutistic shoulds. In Rational Emotive Behavior Therapy, we separate their absolutistic from their preferential shoulds. Consequently, we have taught for many years that clients by all means had better consider, think about, and act on their preferable shoulds. But when they are neurotic—which really means self-defeating and socially defeating—and they get in trouble in the group in which they live, then they had better face the fact that they are not sticking to the preferable shoulds, the good ones that Tim Beck just outlined. Neurotics make a magical jump from "Because it's good to meet a partner, to come early to my job, to perform well, to refrain from murder and stealing, therefore, I *absolutely have* to do so, and I'm a worthless person if I don't do as I *absolutely* should!"

I hypothesize that every single human, all over the world, has the innate propensity to frequently change their *preferable* to *absolu-*

tistic shoulds. They foolishly convince themselves that because it is so *desirable* to act in many ways (and as Tim Beck rightly said, to not act against human social interests), therefore they absolutely *have to* do so and are total nogoodniks when they don't.

As you can read in my writings, in REBT we teach clients, "By all means have goals, desires, preferences, and values. If not, you won't last as a human, and even if you survive, you won't be happy. But when you are depressed, when you are panicked, when you are enraged, when you have low frustration tolerance (otherwise known as whining about the un-niceties of the world), then you'd better face it: you are sneaking in a *should*. If you stay with, 'I'd *like* to do 'X' but I *never* have to. Too bad if I don't.' Or if you believe, 'I hate to do 'Y' and if I do, I am wrong, but I am never a worm for being wrong,' then you would *not* awfulize about your errors and would not damn yourself, your whole person, for making them."

So if people really got rid of "I *absolutely must* do well," and replaced it with "I'd really *like to*, but I don't always *have to*," they'd be much less neurotic. And if they changed, "You *absolutely must* treat me kindly," into "It would be very delightful if you treated me kindly but I can still lead a happy life if you don't," and if they also gave up insisting, "Conditions *must absolutely* be the way I want them to be," then they would have one difficult time catastrophizing, awfulizing, running away from things, and making themselves seriously anxious, depressed, enraged, and self-hating.

Can Psychotherapy Be Brief, Focused, Solution-Oriented, and Yet Comprehensive? A Personal Evolutionary Perspective

◆

Arnold A. Lazarus, Ph.D.

Arnold A. Lazarus, Ph.D.
Arnold Lazarus is Distinguished Professor at the Graduate School of Applied and Professional Psychology at Rutgers University. Dr. Lazarus serves on the editorial boards of nine professional journals. He also has served as president of the Association for Advancement of Behavior Therapy; he is a recipient of the Distinguished Service to the Profession of Psychology Award from the American Board of Professional Psychology, and the Distinguished Psychologist Award from the Division of Psychotherapy of the American Psychological Association. He received a Ph.D. degree in 1960 from the University of the Witwatersrand, Johannesburg, South Africa. Dr. Lazarus has written, coauthored, edited, or coedited 14 books, and has written and been the coauthor of more than 200 professional papers and chapters. He has had 24 editorial appointments from professional journals.

INTRODUCTION

We all have certain experiences that can be described as "epiphanous"—a critical incident that forever alters a perception or understanding of an event. One such circumstance occurred during the third year of my undergraduate curriculum. In class, I was making various assertions, whereupon the professor inquired "How do you know that?" I replied: "Well, Freud said it; I was merely quoting the master." What stands out most vividly was the professor's exhortation: "*Never bow to authority.*" He pointed out that Freud may well have been a genius, but even geniuses make mistakes. He stressed that one must *always look*

to the data. This understanding freed me to challenge anyone and everyone, which made me a royal pain in the neck, but also got me thinking and enabled me to ask questions and find answers that eluded my more timorous and respectful peers.

Over the years, this admonition—*Never bow to authority but always look to the data*—has served me well. It showed me how, as the saying goes, to cut to the chase. By now, I must have asked the questions—"How do you know that?" or "Where are the data?"—thousands of times. Nevertheless, I have observed an alarming tendency among many attendees at the Evolution of Psychotherapy Conferences to date: People were apt to bow to authority in

Phoenix, Anaheim, and Hamburg. Most seemed extremely reluctant to challenge or question the speakers. They appeared to say, in effect, "Who am I to dispute or query the likes of Minuchin, Ellis, Beck, Meichenbaum, or Kernberg? If the Masters say something, it must be so." I hope by imploring you to ask questions, inquire about the data, and feel free to challenge anyone and everyone, some members of this audience will undergo an epiphanous experience of their own.

THE IMPORTANCE OF FOLLOW-UP INQUIRIES

The foregoing remarks lead to an obvious question: Why listen to anything I have to say? Upon what have I based my conclusions? Perhaps follow-ups have been the single most important course of action from which I have derived my assumptions and inferences about the enterprise of therapy. During the 1960s, which was the heyday of my behavioristic zeal, my follow-ups showed that many treatment gains were short-lived. The dreaded "symptom substitution" was rarely a factor, but after receiving the usual range of "behavior therapy" techniques, clients tended to relapse more often than my colleagues seemed to admit. Careful scrutiny of those cases who failed to maintain their gains persuaded me that they had learned an insufficiently wide range of coping responses. Thus, I advocated "broad-spectrum behavior therapy" in place of the more circumscribed methods that were in vogue, and in 1970 I began writing *Behavior Therapy and Beyond* (Lazarus, 1971), arguably one of the first books on what has come to be called cognitive-behavior therapy.

A pivotal case described therein concerned a panic-stricken and severely agoraphobic woman who responded very well to the usual sequence of behavioral methods—imaginal and in vivo desensitization, assertiveness training, calming self-statements, and other ancillary self-control procedures. After some five months of behavior therapy, she felt confident enough to travel around freely and with minimal anxiety. Nevertheless, although she was delighted by her newfound ability to remain relatively anxiety-free while moving about and engaging in the niceties of social interaction, she continued to view herself as a worthless person who was contributing nothing of value to society. Consequently, we launched into a discussion of values, and focused on various issues that my esteemed discussant, Donald Meichenbaum, would probably classify as "a constructive narrative perspective." The logic of these discussions led the client to conclude that, "If you want to *feel* useful, you have to *be* useful." Accordingly, she founded an organization that distributed basic essentials such as food and clothing to the needy, and she subsequently opened centers in other communities. In a follow-up interview one year later, she stated that she viewed herself as "eminently worthwhile," and added "thanks to the fact that I exist and care, thousands of people now derive benefit."

I referred to the foregoing case as pivotal because it raised two trenchant issues for me at the time:

1. Is it likely that her treatment gains would have been maintained if the therapy had ended after the formal behavioral procedures had enabled her to travel about with minimal anxiety? (My one-word answer to that question is "No!")
2. Was it necessary to formulate a specific raison d'être to give value and meaning to her life? (Here my one-word answer is "Yes!")

It was this case that led me to hypothesize that unless both specific behaviors and particular cognitions were addressed, outcomes probably would be transient rather than durable. Thereafter, careful follow-ups of several additional cases suggested that relapse is highly likely unless, at the very least, a two-pronged or bimodal treatment result revealed both clear evidence of behavioral gains and distinct changes in cognition. (I might mention that upon publishing these views, I was expelled by H. J. Eysenck from the editorial board of *Behaviour Research and Therapy* and scorned by certain members of the behavior therapy community. They accused me of being a closet analyst who was bringing "mentalism" back into the fold!)

Subsequently, I conducted additional follow-ups that added more to the picture and eventuated in the multimodal view that *seven* discrete but interactive modalities call for scrutiny if treatment is be truly thorough or comprehensive. For those who are unfamiliar with my multimodal orientation I will quickly touch on a few of the main issues.

THE ESSENCE OF THE MULTIMODAL VIEWPOINT

Every patient–therapist interaction involves *behavior* (be it lying down on a couch and free associating or actively role-playing a significant encounter), *affect* (whether the silent joy of nonjudgmental acceptance or the sobbing release of pent-up anger), *sensation* (ranging from the spontaneous awareness of tension or bodily discomfort to the deliberate cultivation of specific sensual delights), *imagery* (such as the fleeting glimpse of a childhood event or the contrived perception of a calm-producing scene), and *cognition* (the insights, values, ideas, attitudes and narratives that constitute our fundamental beliefs about ourselves and the world at large). All of these take place within a network of *interpersonal relationships*. An added dimension with many clients is their need for medication or *drug* treatment. The first letters of Behavior, Affect, Sensation, Imagery, Cognition, Interpersonal and Drug provide the acronym BASIC ID or the preferred BASIC I.D. This is not a linear description of human temperament and personality but one that emphasizes the interactive nature of these modalities that exist in a state of reciprocal transaction and flux, connected by complex chains of behavior and other psychophysiological processes (Lazarus, 1989, 1992).

This somewhat discursive introduction will now allow me to set the stage to provide an affirmative answer to the question, "Can psychotherapy be brief, focused, solution-oriented, and yet comprehensive?" and to demonstrate how effective brief treatment can be achieved.

THE IMPORTANCE OF BREADTH

In this era, brief or short-term therapy is very much in vogue. Virtually anyone can be brief, but can they also be effective and achieve durable results? As I have been stressing, my follow-ups suggest that if a therapist focuses narrowly on only one dimension, treatment gains probably will not endure. Those who emphasize depth are apt to probe specific elements of their patients' unconscious processes. Thus, some short-term psychodynamic therapists focus exclusively on pre-Oedipal or Oedipal conflicts; others address their clients' separation anxiety, or dwell solely on interpersonal role disputes. Certain cognitive therapists attend only to cognitive distortions or irrational beliefs. Such tactics will, from my point of view, overlook significant aspects that call for remediation. I have seen many clients who claimed to have attained profound insights after spending many years in insight-oriented therapy, but who still embraced dysfunctional philosophies of life (probably because nobody had specifically disputed their irrational ideas), who were still very tense (partly because they had never learned how to apply deep muscle relaxation), and who suffered as a result of (sometimes extreme) interpersonal ineptitude (because they had never acquired the necessary social skills).

I submit that if a therapist wants to be effective, retain a constructive focus, arrive at creative solutions, and be both short-term and comprehensive, the following eight issues must be ruled out or adequately dealt with if necessary:

1. Conflicting or ambivalent feelings or reactions;
2. Maladaptive behaviors;
3. Misinformation (especially dysfunctional beliefs);
4. Missing information (for example, skill deficits, ignorance, or naiveté);
5. Interpersonal pressures and demands;
6. External stressors outside the immediate interpersonal network (such as poor living conditions or unsafe environment);

7. Severe traumatic experiences (including sexual abuse or gross neglect in childhood); and

8. Biological dysfunctions.

I have rarely treated anyone who did not manifest the first five issues. Everyone is conflicted about something and has at least one or two unfortunate habits. Few things are cut and dried, and ambivalence is ubiquitous. Likewise, we are all misinformed about certain subjects or factors, and to a greater or lesser extent everybody lacks certain skills and significant pieces of information. As for interpersonal pressures and demands, only a hermit can escape these realities, but complete and total social withdrawal is not exactly a healthy solution. If biological dysfunctions are present or suspected, the necessary medical attention becomes a high priority. In my experience, when external stressors and severe traumatic experiences are part of the variance, it is usually necessary to consult outside resources and agencies, and effective or meaningful short-term interventions become less likely. Thus, poverty stricken individuals will benefit more from social agencies that can help them with welfare and food stamps, and the survivors of the Oklahoma bombing need social and community support systems beyond any formal psychotherapy.

THE BASIC PROCEDURES

Typically, with most outpatient referrals, a careful initial interview and the use of the Multimodal Life History Inventory (Lazarus & Lazarus, 1991) provide the bulk of the material for treatment planning and the selection of appropriate techniques and procedures. In the hands of competent clinicians, the initial interview provides answers to most of the following questions:

1. What were the presenting complaints and their main precipitating events?
2. What seemed to be some significant antecedent factors?
3. Who or what appeared to be maintaining the client's maladaptive behaviors?

4. Was it fairly evident what the client wished to derive from therapy?
5. What are some of the client's strengths or positive attributes?
6. Why is the client seeking therapy at this particular time?
7. What was the client's appearance with respect to physical characteristics, grooming, manner of speaking, and attitude?
8. Were there any signs of "psychosis" (thought disorders, delusions, incongruity of affect, bizarre or inappropriate behaviors)?
9. Was there evidence of self-recrimination, depression, homicidal or suicidal tendencies?
10. Did it seem that a mutually satisfying relationship could be established, or should the client be referred elsewhere?
11. Were there any indications or contraindications for the adoption of a particular therapeutic pace and style (cold, warm, formal, informal, supportive, confrontational, tough, or tender)?
12. Did the client emerge with legitimate grounds for hope?

Obviously, an initial interview with someone who is seriously deranged, nonverbal, or extremely withdrawn will not shed light on all the foregoing issues. The implication of the twelve points is that the initial interview not only identifies significant trends, problems, and functional connections, but also provides a framework for assessing the timing and cadence of each interaction. The initial interview, supplemented by information derived from the detailed 15-page Multimodal Life History Inventory (which cooperative clients usually complete after the first session, and if possible mail in before the second meeting) permits the therapist to draw up a Modality Profile (a list of salient problems across the client's BASIC I.D.).

A CASE IN POINT

By describing the short-term and focused treatment of an actual client, I hope that most of the foregoing assertions will fall into perspective.

The client I have selected was a 40-year-old, twice divorced, childless woman who held a well-paid executive position in a large organization, and complained that she had felt extremely depressed during the previous five to six months. As C. N. Lazarus (1991) has underscored, DSM labels shed little light on diagnostic precision and do not point a clear way to clinical decision making, whereas a BASIC I.D. formulation immediately highlights a trajectory towards lucid problem identification and remediation. Thus, after the initial meeting and upon the completion of the Multimodal Life History Inventory, the following Modality Profile was constructed:

Behavior: Decreased activity; frequent crying; insomnia or fitful sleep pattern; somewhat unkempt; negative self-statements; too much solitary time; gets no exercise.

Affect: Depressed; lack of enthusiasm and joy; often experiences frustration and anxiety, especially when work demands escalate.

Sensation: Chronic abdominal discomfort; tension in jaw and neck; constant fatigue; pains in lumbar spine; intermittent chest pains; no enjoyment of food.

Imagery: Unpleasant dreams, which she cannot recall; poor self-image; father's angry face shouting "You're stupid!"; flashbacks to memories of abuse from her first husband; pictures herself failing; sees herself being fired from work.

Cognition: Categorical imperatives; dichotomous thinking; perfectionistic; sees virtue in suppressing her emotions; catastrophizes; concentration difficulties; hopes to remarry "eventually"; wishes she were not an only child but had a younger sister.

Interpersonal relationships: Unassertive and easily exploited; has no friends; tends to regress in parents' company; hypersensitive to criticism; fears rejection.

Drugs/Biology: Weight loss; poor appetite; no libido; indigestion; early morning awakening; concerned about her physical health; takes antacids daily; had taken Valium 5 mg at bedtime but stopped because it made her feel worse; family history of depression (two maternal aunts had received courses of ECT).

Those who are familiar with the DSM IV will agree that she satisfied most of the criteria of a Major Depressive Episode. However, the interactive network of problems across her BASIC I.D. opened many doors for further consideration. The initial interview and life history inventory translated her "depression" into about 40 particular but mutually related issues or problems. Clearly, the first step is to prioritize one's recommendations or interventions. I believe that my initial move was one that virtually any clinician would have made—I recommended that she undergo a thorough medical examination. She did not have a family doctor, so I recommended two internists whom I respect. The physician she chose suspected a gastric ulcer that was confirmed by radiological examination. An antibiotic was prescribed and she was given an acid blocker. An elevated cholesterol level and arthritic changes in her lumbar spine rounded out the medical findings. She was referred to an orthopedic surgeon who, in turn, recommended a physiotherapist and gave her a regimen of specific lower back exercises for home use.

The pattern of her depression and allied symptoms, as well as her family history, led me to assume that antidepressant medication might prove useful. Because the internist had recommended Prozac and was willing to prescribe it, there seemed no need to involve the services of a psychiatrist. Not surprisingly, the acid blocker and the SSRI had her feeling significantly better a month after her first visit to me. Some organically oriented practitioners might have been content to leave it at that, but as I emphasized at the beginning of this paper, follow-ups suggest that narrowly focused treatments tend to be associated with relapse. While the goal of therapy is not the elimination of every single problem, we nevertheless must inquire about what still needs to be treated, and in which particular order? If this happened to be a class in multimodal assessment and therapy at Rutgers University rather than a distinguished audience in Las Vegas, I would call for suggestions from each student. Given the present circumstances and format, let's get down to the main point of this invited address.

It is my contention that when therapy has to be brief, short-term, or time-limited, clients' needs are often best served by addressing at least one issue from six of the modalities.

Because affect cannot be directly modified but has to be accessed through one or more of the other six modalities (see Lazarus & Lazarus, 1990), if you achieve even one behavioral change, one shift in sensation, one alteration in imagery, one difference in cognition, one modification in the interpersonal modality, and one biological alteration, you will have set a reciprocal transaction of six positive events into motion. This is what I mean by brief, focused, solution-oriented yet comprehensive psychotherapy.

Returning to the client in question, in her D modality, the specific interventions (taking an antibiotic, an acid-blocker, and Prozac, and receiving physiotherapy) proved extremely effective and opened her to a broader health-minded outlook (she changed her diet and took to walking several miles a week). What should be modified in her B, S, I, C, and I modalities?

B: She elected to engage in systematic exercise (walking several miles a week) and was strongly supported in that endeavor. The rest of the entries in this area seemed to disappear after she went on medication (decreased activity, frequent crying, insomnia, being unkempt, making negative self-statements, and spending too much time alone).

S: Here, tension stood out, and specific relaxation training was recommended.

I: As a homework assignment, she practiced shrinking her father and her abusive former husband down to the size of tiny ants and stepping on them (a method I learned from Neurolinguistic Programming).

C: I gave her a copy of my co-authored book *Don't Believe It For A Minute!* (Lazarus, Lazarus, & Fay, 1993) and asked her to read selected items for discussion in our next session. (Although I have heard Dr. Meichenbaum denounce the value of self-help books, I will argue that if a picture is worth a thousand words, certain books, or sections thereof, are not worth a thousand sessions, but they can be as valuable as a dozen or so).

I: A few sessions of social skills and assertiveness training seemed strongly indicated.

In the majority of instances, I draw on methods that have been empirically validated (Chambless, 1995), but if an unproven method seems to hold promise, I may apply it in selected instances (such as the NLP technique of shrinking adversaries down to the size of ants) and observe its impact. If a majority of clients report favorable results, I may add it to my arsenal (see Davison & Lazarus, 1994). [For a thorough exposition, see Lazarus, A.A. (1997). *Brief But Comprehensive Psychotherapy: The Multimodal Way.* New York: Springer.]

OUTCOME AND FOLLOW-UP

The client received a total of 14 sessions over the span of seven months. By then, she was no longer depressed, did not require the acid blocker, had reduced her Prozac from 40 mg to 20 mg a day, was dating two men and had become sexually involved with one of them, and stated, "All in all, I feel pretty healthy." About 16 months later she was contacted for follow-up information and reported that she had maintained her gains, although when she had stopped taking the Prozac completely (about four months previously) she started feeling "not quite right" and was therefore still taking 20 mg daily. In her case, many of the specific problems that were not directly addressed were all tied to her depression (unkempt appearance, negative self-statements, no libido, no pleasure from food, failure images, and concentration difficulties) and they all improved as soon as her depression abated. In other cases, such as clients who present with anxiety rather than depression, a similar positive generalization seems to ensue. There seems to be a ripple effect wherein a change in one modality has an impact on many of the others. Nevertheless, some tenacious problems require direct intervention and in these instances one cannot rely on generalization effects. This usually becomes self-evident as therapy proceeds.

In the shortest and simplest of terms, whenever time is limited I strongly recommend that clinicians make a point of modifying at least one element in Behavior, Sensation, Imagery, Cognition, Interpersonal relationships and Drugs/Biology. It is my contention that these focused interventions will set in motion a most salubrious chain of events and achieve a comprehensive range of constructive changes.

REFERENCES

Chambless, D. (1995). Training in and dissemination of empirically validated psychological treatments: Report and recommendations. *The Clinical Psychologist, 48,* 3–23.

Davison, G. C., & Lazarus, A. A. (1994). Clinical innovation and evaluation: Integrating practice with inquiry. *Clinical Psychology: Science and Practice, 1,* 157–168.

Lazarus, A. A. (1971). *Behavior therapy and beyond.* New York: McGraw-Hill.

Lazarus, A. A. (1989). *The practice of multimodal therapy.* Baltimore: Johns Hopkins University Press.

Lazarus, A. A. (1992). Multimodal therapy: Technical eclecticism with minimal integration. In J. C. Norcross & M. R. Goldfried (Eds.), *Handbook of psychotherapy integration.* (pp. 231–263) New York: Basic Books.

Lazarus, A. A., & Lazarus, C. N. (1990). Emotions: A multimodal perspective. In R. Plutchik & H. Kellerman (Eds.), *Emotion: Theory, research & experience. Vol.*

5. Emotion, psychopathology and psychotherapy. (pp. 195–208) San Diego: Academic Press.

Lazarus, A. A., & Lazarus, C. N. (1991). *Multimodal life history inventory.* Champaign, IL: Research Press.

Lazarus, A. A., Lazarus, C. N., & Fay, A. (1993). *Don't believe it for a minute! Forty toxic ideas that are driving you crazy.* San Luis Obispo, CA: Impact.

Lazarus, C. N. (1991). Conventional diagnostic nomenclature versus multimodal assessment. *Psychological Reports, 68,* 1363–1367.

ACKNOWLEDGMENT

I am most grateful to Allen Fay, M.D., and Clifford N. Lazarus, Ph.D., for their incisive criticisms of my initial draft.

Discussion by Donald Meichenbaum, Ph.D.

◆

Thank you very much. It is a pleasure for me to respond to Dr. Lazarus' thoughtful and provocative presentation. My response is entitled, "In Homage to a Royal Pain in the Neck." I am personally indebted to Dr. Lazarus, as is the field of psychotherapy. Let me begin with my own personal indebtedness. Apropos of our current setting of Las Vegas, I am reminded that Dr. Lazarus taught me how to play blackjack in a gambling casino in Atlantic City, New Jersey. He took me under his wing and taught me the finer points of 21. Gambling is only one area where I have turned to Dr. Lazarus for mentoring.

Another form of kindness that Dr. Lazarus provided was offered in my formative years as a clinical researcher. I recall at a meeting of the Association for Advancement of Behavior Therapy (AABT) I was walking in the hallway when a somewhat chagrined colleague came up to me and said, "You made it. You made the list!" "What list?" I asked somewhat perplexed. He answered, "Oh, Dr. Wolpe's article just came out listing the 'malcontents' in behavior therapy." I asked, "Who else was on the list?"

He said, "Arnold Lazarus." My immediate thought was that I was in good company.

Because of his views, as Dr. Lazarus noted, he was removed from the editorial board of the journal *Behaviour Research and Therapy.* At the same time I had been writing a column in the *Behavior Therapy Newsletter* highlighting the potential role of cognition and emotion in behavior therapy. In their desire to have a clean sweep of malcontents, I was asked to discontinue my column, which I did. Similar pressure was brought on the program chairmen of AABT meetings not to include cognitive-behavior therapy papers in the conference and a letter was circulated to have so-called "cognitive" types kicked out of AABT. For someone new to the profession, this challenged my confidence. I could, however, turn to Arnold Lazarus for reassurance as a mentor.

His book *Behavior Therapy and Beyond* highlighted the potential role of cognition and emotion in psychotherapy and became a landmark in the development of a cognitive-behavioral treatment approach. The book reflected the combination of clinical creativity and a commitment to accountability. We see this in Dr. Lazarus' presentation today, as well. Listen to the terms that punctuate his presentation. "Look to the data." "Conduct a follow-up." "Cut to the chase." "Inquire about the data." "Don't bow to authority." "Question me."

Lazarus also practices what he preaches. How many psychotherapists call their clients 16 months following treatment in order to see how they are doing? How routine are short-term and long-term follow-up assessments in your therapy practice?

But my task as a commentator would not be complete if I only paid homage to the speaker. There is another side to our relationship that also goes back some time. Arnold wrote a book on multimodal therapy. I was asked to review this book for the journal *Contemporary Psychology*. In my review I noted its clinical creativity, but on the other hand I expressed concern about whether the field of psychotherapy would advance by embracing the "technical eclecticism" that Dr. Lazarus was advocating. I still have these concerns today.

The journal *Contemporary Psychology* has an interesting editorial policy concerning book reviews. When you do a review of a book, the book's author can write a rebuttal, and then the reviewer can, in turn, rebut. Then the author, once again. And finally, the reviewer. In order to keep such exchanges manageable, each rebuttal has to use one half of the number of words as the one before. By the third go-around, the *essence* of what I wrote was, "And the same to you, fella!" I am glad that our relationship has survived that exchange.

Before I enumerate my concerns about Dr. Lazarus' approach, there is one other item that I only learned today that I should mention. I owe Dr. Lazarus an apology. In his presentation he used the mnemonic BASIC I.D. to summarize his assessment and treatment approach. He spoke about it as BASIC I (period) D (period). I always thought his mnemonic referred to BASIC *ID*, with its psychoanalytical roots. If I wrote this mnemonic on the blackboard almost any clinician would read it as BASIC *ID*, disregarding the periods. One might wonder why Dr. Lazarus refuses to say the natural "ID," instead of I (period) D (period)? But, that is a question for another day.

Is the BASIC I.D. model (no matter how you pronounce it) a useful way to advance the field of psychotherapy? As an organizing mnemonic, it is helpful as a mental checklist for clinicians and their clients. But shall the field of psychotherapy advance from such an atheoretical approach that is unlikely to explicate the mechanisms of change and unlikely to elucidate the decision rules used by artful clinicians?

If a clinician samples treatment approaches from each modality subsumed under the BASIC I.D. (behavior, affect, sensation, imagery, cognition, interpersonal and drugs), then envision the challenge for a researcher. For instance, we once wrote a chapter on all of the different ways clinicians have used imagery in psychotherapy. We came up with well over 100 different ways. Then consider all of the diverse ways clinicians have used behavioral, cognitive, interpersonal, and pharmacological treatment approaches.

How shall the clinician choose among the various imagery techniques? Should the therapist follow the suggestion offered by Dr. Lazarus when he asks a client who was abused or criticized to reduce the image of the perpetrator or critic to that of an ant and then step on him or her? Should we use this imagery approach or sample from the hundreds of other alternatives? How should the clinician decide? Should we conduct parametric outcome studies concerning different imagery approaches with clients with different disorders? Then should we do the same for the diverse behavioral and cognitive approaches? The therapist would wait forever to learn how best to proceed.

Perhaps we should clone (if not computerize) Dr. Lazarus, so he can explicate the rules he uses when formulating his decision tree. Moreover, how much of this decision tree should be collaboratively developed with the client and not arbitrarily imposed by the therapist? For example, imagine the therapist saying to the client: "As I listen to you describe your situation, I get the impression, and correct me if I am wrong, see if I have picked up on what you are experiencing, that there are a number of problems that you are having in various areas."

At this point, the therapist could spell out the client's difficulties in the interpersonal domain with regard to connecting with others and how these difficulties have roots in the past. The therapist can also note issues in other areas involving the client's physical condition and affective reactions, beliefs, and the like. The client and therapist could collaborate in generating a case conceptualization and "negotiate" how the therapy process might proceed. Along the way, the client and therapist could take stock of how the treatment goals have, or have not, been achieved and take corrective actions.

It is likely that in the process of identifying treatment goals, targeting behaviors, formulating a treatment rationale and a case conceptualization, conducting self-assessment ("homework"), and developing a therapeutic alliance, a great deal of "hopeful" change occurs. Perhaps it is in these so-called "nonspecifics" of therapy, where the client is learning to become his or her own therapist, that a great deal of change occurs. To support this argument consider research findings that in the cognitive treatment of unipolar depression, 60 to 80 percent of the reduction in depressed symptomatology occurs within the first four sessions, well before specific cognitive restructuring procedures are introduced (see Ilardi and Craighead, 1994). Are the therapeutic changes that Dr. Lazarus achieves due to the specific techniques he employs under the heading of BASIC I.D., or are they due to his modeling and engaging clients in a thoughtful and clinically sensitive collaborative problem-solving approach? Perhaps Dr. Lazarus could come up with a mnemonic for these nonspecific features.

Moreover, I think that the field of psychotherapy needs to struggle with developing a theory of behavior change. The field of psychotherapy needs to move beyond an atheoretical technical eclecticism where each therapist can selectively weave a tapestry of diverse interventions. Where should such theory come from?

One possibility is from research on specific disorders. For example, the recent research on panic disorders by Dave Barlow, David Clark, and others indicates specific ways to conceptualize the disorder of panic attacks and what can be done to help them. From such research efforts, a theory of behavior change will likely emerge (see Meichenbaum, 1995).

A second promising source for a theory of behavior change derives from a constructive narrative perspective. We have been exploring how clients change their stories over the course of therapy. If we had had an opportunity to listen to the therapy sessions of Dr. Lazarus' client over the 16 months, how would her story change? To what degree do certain themes and concepts emerge? Does her narrative or story-telling convey a shift from seeing herself as a victim to becoming a survivor, if not a thriver? Does her narrative reflect features of control as evident in the choice of her language? Does she now use expressions reflecting metacognitive (executive) control such as "notice," "catch," "interrupt," "game plan," "have choices," and the like? Does her narrative account reflect the ability to become an observer of her own behavior? Does she cast herself as being more heroic in meeting and overcoming challenges? Does her narrative reflect hope?

We are exploring whether these narrative changes reflect active mechanisms or an epiphenomenon that accompanies other change influences. At this point, we don't know the answer. I believe that such research efforts will move the field out of a quagmire of eclecticism that represents a banner and rationale (excuse) for giving clinicians permission to do anything they want to do, and instead move the field toward a more theoretically testable position. We should never forget that one of our goals should be to develop a theory of behavior change. Can we identify the common tasks of psychotherapy (as I discussed in my address) and then explicate the mechanisms that account for how the client changes, let alone generalizes and maintains such change? (I have summarized our work on constructive narrative change in Meichenbaum, 1994).

I have one final observation that was stimulated by Dr. Lazarus' presentation. It has to do with the use of self-help books that are given to clients. As Dr. Lazarus notes, we should be cautious when giving clients self-help books. We need to ask:

1. Is the conceptualization being offered by the author simplistic, and if so does it have the potential to make the problem worse?
2. Is the self-help book written at too high of a level for my clients (with too much jargon)?
3. What are the data that using such self-help books is actually helpful?

Dr. Lazarus' critical concerns about accountability need to be extended to self-help books. It is because of his long-term commitment to data and because of his creative contributions to the field of psychotherapy that I wish to pay homage to Arnold Lazarus.

One of my childhood heroes was an iconoclastic, somewhat pugnacious journalist named I. F. Stone. Stone was committed to scholarship and honesty, integrity and creativity, beauty and passion, accountability and conscience. In my paper, I cited a number of clinical researchers who would be deserving of what I called the "Izzy" award, named after I. F. Stone.

I cannot think of a clinician living today who is more deserving of an Izzy than Arnold Lazarus. I would have you join me in saluting him. "And the same to you, fella!"

REFERENCES

Ilardi, S. S., & Craighead, W. E. (1994). The role of nonspecific factors in cognitive behavior therapy for depression. *Clinical Psychotherapy: Science and Practice, 1,* 138–156.

Meichenbaum, D. (1994). *Clinical handbook and practical therapist manual for assessing and treating adults with PTSD.* Waterloo, Ontario: Institute Press.

Meichenbaum, D. (1995). *Treatment of mixed anxiety and depression.* New York: Newbridge Communications.

Response by Dr. Lazarus

◆

I would like to thank this splendid audience and express my genuine gratitude to Dr. Meichenbaum for his very flattering, witty, and poignant comments. Let me address a few specific issues.

Don always raises highly significant themes and underscores crucial considerations. He correctly states that out of hundreds or perhaps thousands of imagery techniques at our disposal, clinicians need guidelines on deciding how and why to select a particular scenario. How can this be achieved? First, it seems to me that the mind-boggling variety of available imagery methods can be pared down to perhaps a dozen or two that are of true merit. Many imaginal scenes strike me as absurd and I would never use them unless and until I can be presented with data regarding their efficacy. For example, telling a client to picture a dragon and chase it up a mountain, or presenting a scene in which a client tries to trace the source of a river, are very different from applying coping and success images that a client rehearses on a daily basis. Some imagery procedures are based on esoteric theories and extremely chimerical notions about human functioning. "Picture a scene in which you are sitting on your own lap and kissing yourself." Some of them are even a lot weirder than that!

Most of the images that I employ involve empowering scenes that people can rehearse over and over in their mind's eye. The assumption is that before we can attain something in reality, we usually first need to be able to see ourselves achieving it in fantasy.

It seems to me that Dr. Meichenbaum was questioning the way in which therapists select appropriate response couplets. "What led you to ask the client to picture standing up to his boss?" "Why did you elect to recommend to the client that a physical checkup seemed necessary?" Effective therapists do not fly by the seat of their pants—their clinical choices and responses are predicated on implicit and explicit rules and assumptions. In training my students, I make extensive use of response couplets. A client inquires, "Do you think I should visit my mother over Christmas?" The therapist now *must* respond. He or she may respond by saying nothing, by reflecting on the client's question, by insinuating that the very question smacks of dependency, by taking a position for or against such a visit, by suggesting an alternative course of action, and so forth. In my supervision groups, we listen to tape recordings of sessions, and at judicious points the recorder is turned off and we discuss a range of responses that might be deemed positive, neutral, or negative. In this way, trainees get a feel for what to do and what to avoid under specific circumstances. Dr. Meichenbaum's questions about clinical decision making are extremely important and compelling.

Allow me to correct a false impression. My technically eclectic, multimodal approach is not atheoretical. It rests on a broad-based social and cognitive learning theory to which elements from a general systems theory perspective are also included. I am opposed to theoretical integration and draw only on theories that can be verified or disproved. The foregoing theories seem to blend harmoniously into a broad-based range of factors that seem to account quite adequately for most vagaries of human conduct and personality. There's obviously no time for me to elaborate at this juncture.

Again, my grateful thanks to my excellent and erudite discussant and to this very supportive audience.

The Evolution of a Cognitive-Behavior Therapist

Donald Meichenbaum, Ph.D.

Donald Meichenbaum, Ph.D.
Donald Meichenbaum (Ph.D., University of Illinois, 1966) is a Professor of Psychology at the University of Waterloo, Canada. He was the associate editor of Cognitive Therapy and Research *and the editor of the Plenum Series on Stress and Coping. Dr. Meichenbaum serves on the editorial board for a dozen journals. He is Fellow of the American Psychological Association and the Canadian Psychological Association and a recipient of the Izaak Killam Fellowship Award from the Canada Council. He has published six books and numerous articles, mostly on cognitive behavior modification and coping with stress.*

INTRODUCTION

The presenters at this conference have been asked to tell the story of how their approach to psychotherapy has evolved. This question is not that different from the types of questions that psychotherapists ask their clients. Perhaps therapists do not use these exact words, but their intent is pretty much the same. Psychotherapists are interested in soliciting their clients' stories to know: "What led you to seek therapy, especially now?"; "Who is most bothered by this problem?"; "How would you like to change?"; "What seems to be getting in the way?"; "What in your life is going right?"; "How can I be of help?"; and the like. In response to such queries, clients tell their stories. (In fact, in a recent *Clinical Handbook*, I have summarized the best questions that therapists can use

to solicit their clients' accounts. See Meichenbaum, 1994).

Like my clients, I too have a story to tell. Now, there are many ways to tell the story of how I evolved as a psychotherapist. I could tell this story in scholarly terms, noting the philosophical, theoretical, and empirical underpinnings of a cognitive-behavioral treatment approach. But I have already done so in my last paper at the Evolution of Psychotherapy conference (Meichenbaum, 1992). In that paper, I noted that cognitive-behavioral therapy emerged from:

1. the growing dissatisfaction with a behavioral conditioning model of human behavior;
2. the development of social learning theories, appraisal theories of emotion, and the

cognitive revolution in psychotherapy (Dember, 1974)

3. the contributions of semantic psychotherapists as reflected in the writings of Dubois, Adler, Horney, Kelly, Ellis, Beck, and Arnold Lazarus, among others (Raimy, 1975).

It is now time for a different version of my story of how cognitive-behavior therapy developed, perhaps one that is more personal in nature. The present invitation has provided me with an opportunity to reflect on what I consider to be the origins of my approach to psychotherapy. Questions about origins tend to pull for a developmental account. If I were pressed to note the major influence on my development as a psychotherapist, I would have to nominate my mother.

ORIGINS

My mother is an interesting woman. Even though she is now in her late seventies, she is active, vibrant, and continues to work full-time in New York City. On occasion she visits me in Ontario, Canada. Whenever she visits, she comes bearing stories. Often these anecdotal accounts involve her work experience. For instance, on a recent visit she related an incident when a coworker, Sadie, asked my mother to help her move some boxes.

"So you moved boxes, with your back?" I asked, with some trepidation.

"That's not the worst," she announced.

"Not the worst? What happened?"

"Don't ask," she replied.

Which obviously, means ask. Now my mother has a unique way of telling stories. She not only tells what happened to her, but she also includes in her storytelling a detailed description of each accompanying thought and feeling she had, and a running evaluative commentary of which thoughts and feelings were helpful and which thoughts and feelings were maladaptive. She also tells why.

"So you moved boxes?" I asked.

"Yes, Sadie asked me to help her with first one small box and before I knew it there were several more larger boxes to move. Then, I realized I shouldn't be lifting this. I remember

what happened the last time I did something like that. Then I started to get down on myself, getting more and more upset about how I readily comply with these types of requests. Then I noticed I was working myself up. I caught myself and thought, 'You don't have to get upset.' I realized I had choices. What was done was done! Next time, when Sadie, or anyone else, asks me to do something that I know I shouldn't do, I won't. . . ."

As my mother was telling me her story, I had an insight. I realized that I had listened to such tales throughout my entire formative years. Every evening at dinnertime we each shared stories of what had happened to us that day, how we handled or failed to handle events, and what we had learned. Our thoughts and feelings were part of the dinner menu. In addition, free of charge, my mother initially provided, and later solicited from me and my two sisters, a commentary about our behavior, thoughts and feelings. She conveyed how we each could notice, catch, interrupt, and choose different thoughts and feelings. My mother was an indefatigable storyteller, and more importantly, a story-maker. She helped each of us mold and author our own stories.

It dawned on me that my entire research career and my psychotherapeutic approach has been spent trying to validate my childhood experience. How do people talk to themselves (think), feel, and behave, and how does this internal dialogue influence and guide how they perceive events and appraise their ability to handle such events? In turn, how do peoples' feelings and behaviors influence their automatic thoughts (cognitive events); how they process information (cognitive processes); and how they implicitly follow tacit core beliefs (cognitive structures)?

Moreover, I wondered just how *similar* my psychotherapy sessions were to what I had experienced around my dinner table. Could I use the art of questioning, cognitive modeling, the process of fading supports (technically called "scaffolding"), the conveyance of hope and optimism, the bolstering of my client's sense of self-confidence, the anticipation of possible problems and setbacks, as my mother had done during dinner?

But was my mother's style unique to her or do people in general use similar processes to cope with the perturbations and predicaments of life? If you look at the people who live in New York City, they all seem to be talking to themselves. If you live in a large urban crime area, with high risks around each corner, you quickly learn to talk to yourself. For example, when you are leaving a subway station at night, a potential victim, you are prone to talk to yourself (silently, so you do *not* attract undue attention).

"It's okay, I can make it to my apartment without getting mugged ... Only two more blocks. Look at those guys at the corner. This could be a high risk situation.... Hold on. I'll cross the street. I'll walk by those people. There is more light over there.... Wow, I made it!"

In New York City, this is called a survival skill. You get to Ontario, and they call this cognitive behavior modification.

In order to further appreciate the pervasiveness of this phenomenon in New York, consider that I grew up close to where the moviemaker Woody Allen was raised. Anyone who has seen his classic films, including *Annie Hall, Hannah and Her Sisters*, and *Crimes and Misdemeanors*, will recognize the frequent occasions when his characters talk to themselves. In fact, I was convinced that somewhere along the way Woody Allen must have had dinner with my mother. How else could I explain his success? But given the recent turn of events in his life, I am now convinced he never ate dinner with mother. She was too good at instilling guilt. He would never have behaved in such a fashion if he had eaten dinner with my mother.

OTHER INFLUENCES

But my mother was only one influence in my development as a therapist. There were two other people who shaped my approach to psychotherapy, my father and the journalist I. F. Stone. My father always impressed upon me the need for reverence and genuine admiration for those who seek truth, but a healthy skepticism to the point of disdain for those who find truth.

But this adage was best personified by my teenage hero. For most teenagers, heroes come in the form of athletes and musicians, perhaps authors and film stars. My hero was a short, somewhat cherubic but pugnacious iconoclastic journalist named I. F. Stone, Izzy to those who read his independent weekly newsletter on a regular basis. It is likely that you don't know who Izzy was. He was an influential journalist who wrote nine books and who, with his wife, published a weekly newsletter in which he would expose governmental duplicities and pompous authoritarian accounts of daily events. He would pore over governmental reports and data (particularly during the Korean and Vietnam wars) and with muckraking brilliance scathingly question and unmask deceit, dishonesty, and fraud, while challenging basic assumptions and puncturing myths. He stood up to McCarthyism in his book *The Haunted Fifties* and was the conscience of America during the sixties in his analysis of the Vietnam era (Stone, 1967). I. F. Stone was called the "essential journalist." He was brilliant in his intolerance for bullshit. When Izzy retired in his seventies, he taught himself Greek and translated original Greek philosophers. What more could one want from a hero?

I had a dream. I wanted to become the I. F. Stone of psychotherapy—the essential psychotherapist—and I have worked hard at it. When cognitive-behavior therapy (CBT) first emerged, I independently wrote and published an annual newsletter that critiqued the field of CBT so it would *not* become another passing therapy fad, but would be built on a sound empirical basis. I wanted to help create and nurture a community of cognitive-behavioral clinical researchers and influence a generation of graduate students in what they studied. The newsletter started small, initially with a few hundred clinical researchers, and by the time I discontinued it four years later the subscription list consisted of 3,000 members in some 20 countries. In the newsletter, I would critique each aspect of CBT and note what critical questions needed to be examined. I was able to track which research ideas that I had suggested in the newsletter subsequently would appear in *Dissertation Abstracts* two, three, and four years later.

CRITICAL INQUIRY

On several occasions I have been invited to present keynote addresses at conferences, to engage in debates with luminary figures, or to review landmark books. In the best tradition of Izzy, I have taken these opportunities to question and challenge the field to reconsider their basic assumptions and to critique what we know and don't know. Perhaps the best signs of respect and admiration are to ask those you read carefully to question what they have written or said. In the same way that psychotherapists want to teach their clients to self-monitor and self-interrogate, I wanted to encourage my colleagues to adopt a similar inquiring attitude about their work. Consider the following examples:

1. I presented at a biofeedback conference and highlighted data that false feedback for treating clients with certain medical disorders was just as effective as targeted feedback. In fact, positive treatment results have been reported even when the biofeedback machine was not plugged in. Less expensive forms of relaxation were just as effective as elaborate biofeedback interventions (Turk, Meichenbaum, & Berman, 1979).
2. I debated behaviorists such as Hans Eysenck and questioned whether there was any evidence for classical or operant conditioning with adult humans (Brewer, 1974).
3. I have reviewed books by Albert Ellis (Meichenbaum, 1977), Arnold Lazarus, (Meichenbaum, 1977), and Al Bandura (Meichenbaum, 1990), and have questioned the basis of their approaches. For instance, when it came to self-efficacy theory, I wondered whether the jargon of social learning theory was disguising a simple form of "bubba psychology." Does self-efficacy theory simply boil down to the fact that if you ask someone to do something on a 0 percent to 100 percent scale and they say they can do it, then there is a high likelihood that they will do it? Was there more to this major theoretical perspective than just a set of commonsense theorems? In this same vein, see Smedslund (1978), a Scandinavian psychologist, who has translated social learning theory into English. Could such critiques by Meichenbaum and Smedslund cause the field to pause and wonder what psychologists are really saying when they strip away the veneer of psychological jargon?
4. At a recent meeting of the International Society for the Study of Trauma, I was invited to give a keynote address on the status of psychotherapy with victimized individuals. Although the field is in its infancy, I had much to praise. I also had serious concerns, as illustrated by two popular forms of interventions, namely, Eye Movement Desensitization and Reprocessing, (EMDR) (Shapiro, 1989) and Critical Incident Stress Debriefing (CISD) (Mitchell, 1983). Each intervention has received much attention in both the professional and the popular media. One can find remarkable claims offered in support of each intervention.

What would I. F. Stone have to say about each treatment approach? He would be puzzled why some 13,000 clinicians would pay $300 each to be trained in EMDR. He would point out that EMDR had its origins in an anecdotal account by Dr. Francine Shapiro. She reported that as she was taking a walk in the woods, she noticed that when she engaged in saccadic eye movements her disturbing thoughts would lose their distressing impact. Perhaps this was an insight upon which a therapy approach could be based? Then Stone, the essential journalist, would note that Gerald Rosen (1995) found that individuals are unable to be aware of such saccadic eye movements.

Do eye movements actually play a critical role in contributing to the reported treatment outcome, or was Shapiro responding to an illusory correlation? A recent critique of EMDR by Lohr and his colleagues (Lohr, Kleinknecht, Conley, Dal Cerro, Schmidt, & Sonntag, 1992) has questioned the efficacy of EMDR and noted that eye movements play little or no role in the outcome.

Now, I don't know whether EMDR works or not, but that is not the point of this exposition. The question is how Rosen's and Lohr's conclusions are reported and addressed by advocates of EMDR. A similar concern emerges in the case of CISD. There is now evidence that debriefing following disasters may make some individuals worse (Meichenbaum, 1994). How are these findings highlighted by those who advocate CISD?

My concerns can be turned as readily to cognitive-behavioral interventions as to other forms of psychotherapy. Consider the most successfully documented form of psychotherapeutic intervention that is available today, the cognitive-behavioral treatment of panic attacks. Consider the evaluation of the treatment of clients with panic disorders offered by Magraf and his colleagues (Magraf, Barlow, Clark, & Telch, 1993). They observed: "We are no longer dealing with experimental treatments that still have to prove themselves. Instead, cognitive-behavioral treatments rest on firm experimental evidence that justifies their application in everyday practice" (p. 6).

Indeed, the data that Magraf and colleagues cite by Barlow, Beck, Clark, Ost and others are impressive. But what would I. F. Stone say about this resounding endorsement? He would surely commend these researchers for their search for effective interventions, but he would want to ensure that the promoters of a cognitive-behavioral approach were also courageous enough to note:

1. Hornsveld, Garssen, and Van Spiegel's 1995 observation that the hyperventilation challenge task that is central to the intereoceptive exposure treatment of panic patients may not be as critical as initially proposed. It may be the general exposure to stressful tests and not the specific breathing retraining that is essential.
2. Shear, Pilkonis, Cloitre, & Leon (1994) recently reported findings that providing panic patients with education plus nondirective supportive psychotherapy was just as effective as cognitive-behavioral interventions.
3. J. Gayle Beck and Zebb's (1994) observations that: "Panic control therapy is *not a panacea*. For example, despite research emphasis on panic-free status at the end of treatment, *many patients continue to report anxiety-related restrictions* indexed by secondary measures such as social fear

and specific phobias. Additionally, although significant pre-post changes are noted in most investigations of panic control therapy, comparisons with community norms often reveals *continuing treatment needs* (pp. 600-601, emphasis added).

Thus, consumers of the psychotherapy outcome literature therapists are torn between the enthusiastic endorsement of Magraf and colleagues and the sober evaluation of Beck and Zebb. You can anticipate where I. F. Stone would lean.

Every area of intervention, psychological or pharmacological, is in need of clinical researchers who have adopted an I. F. Stone critical-minded approach. Advocates of psychotherapy need to ask hard questions and not oversell their approach. Those who adopt this approach would be worthy recipients of an Izzy award, if one were available. Here is an illustrative list of potential candidates. You, the reader, can send me your own nominations.

1. Hans Strupp, who found that caring compassionate university professors did as well as psychotherapists in treating university students (Strupp, 1989).
2. Kazdin and Wilcoxon (1976), who found that credible control groups did just as well as systematic desensitization groups, thus questioning the desensitization paradigm.
3. Weisz and Weiss (1993), whose metaanalysis of psychotherapy outcome studies with children and adolescents yielded strong positive effect sizes (.71–.84). However, this effect was only evident in research-based interventions with homogeneous clinical populations and with therapists who received extensive training and who followed manualized treatments. These positive effects were significantly diminished when treatments were applied in clinical settings.
4. Buckalew and Sallis (1986), who found that the size, form, and color of psychotropic medication were critical to their efficacy (although pharmacologically equivalent, large pills are more effective than small pills, capsules better than pills, and colored pills better than white pills).

5. Fisher, who found that double-blind studies are usually not really double blind. (See Munoz, Hollon, McGrath, Rehm, & van den Bos, 1994, for a summary of this research.)

From my perspective, each of these investigators deserve an Izzy award for their courage, scholarship, and creativity in challenging the field of psychotherapy. Who will earn an Izzy award at this Evolution Conference? Where are the essential psychotherapists when we need them most, especially now when managed care is calling for brief efficient validated therapies? Where is the truth in advertising when it comes to psychotherapy?

REFLECTIONS ON PERSONAL EVOLUTION

My story does not end in my paying homage to those who shaped my development. As my father taught me, it is easy to critique others. The real skill is whether you can turn that criticism to your own efforts. I have been doing clinical research for 30 years. I would be deeply depressed if the position I now hold was the same one I held when I began. Not only would that be boring, but it would also be unresponsive to empirical findings and to changing conceptual theoretical frameworks.

Elsewhere (Meichenbaum, 1993), I have traced the changing conceptions of cognitive-behavioral interventions. To summarize this change briefly, the *initial conception* of a cognitive-behavioral perspective was to view the client's cognitions as covert behaviors, similar in nature to overt behaviors, subjected to the so-called laws of learning (whatever they may be). This theoretical perspective gave rise to a number of specific behavioral interventions in the form of covert conditioning, aversive modeling (see Meichenbaum, 1977 for a discussion of the inadequacies of this behavioral perspective).

The second conception of cognitive behavior modification viewed the clients' cognitions through the theoretical prism of information processing and decision-making research. Now the central metaphor of the computer-guided cognitive-behavioral interventions is reflected

in the development of self-instructional training, stress inoculation training and cognitive restructuring procedures. The catechism of CBT now embraces such concepts as automatic thoughts, internal dialogue, cognitive events, processes and structures, confirmatory bias, mental heuristics, decisional balance sheet, and relapse prevention. The Piagetian concepts of schema, assimilation, and accommodation found a new home in the discourse of cognitive-behavioral therapy.

And now, I am into my third conceptualization of cognitive-behavioral therapy. While the results from cognitive-behavioral centers are quite encouraging, as noted by Hollon and Beck (1993) and as illustrated in the research by Wilson on eating disorders, Beck and Hollon on depression, Barlow, Clark and others on panic disorders, Heimberg on social phobias, Turk on chronic pain, Novaco and Deffenbacher on anger control, Kendall on impulsive children, and many others, there is still much room for improvement (as the quote from G. C. Beck and Zebb has highlighted). Perhaps the information-processing perspective that challenged clients' so-called irrational beliefs and educated them about their cognitive errors and distortions was not adequate to their clinical needs.

The third conceptualization of cognitive-behavioral therapy, the one in which I am now immersed, can best be described as a *constructivist narrative perspective* (CNP). A CNP focuses on the accounts or stories that individuals offer themselves and others about the important events in their lives. The CNP views humans as meaning-making agents who proactively create their own personal realities or meanings (Mahoney, 1993; Meichenbaum, 1993; Neimeyer, 1993). Constructivists do not believe that people are disturbed because they distort reality. Rather, a constructive psychotherapist proposes that there are multiple realities and one of the tasks of psychotherapy is to help clients appreciate how they construct their realities; how they author their own stories.

The important feature of a meaning system is not its veridicality or its validity, but its viability. The constructivist form of cognitive-behavioral therapy is less structured, more exploratory, and more discovery-oriented than is standard cognitive therapy. In contrast to standard forms of cognitive therapy, the constructivist approach places greater emphasis on past development, tends to target deeper core beliefs and processes, and explores the behavioral impact, emotional toll, and personal price of the client holding certain root metaphors. Constructivist therapists help their clients explore how they create their realities and the consequences that follow from such constructions. This is quite different from challenging the so-called irrationality of the clients' thoughts and beliefs. In fact, research indicates that if the therapist challenges the client's thoughts directly, then this tends to freeze the clients' beliefs (Kruglanski, 1980). Instead, how can the therapist engage clients in a collaborative therapeutic alliance whereby they can feel sufficiently secure and confident in order to perform personal experiments, whereby they can collect data that are incompatible with their prior expectations? How can the therapist insure that clients take such data as evidence to unfreeze their beliefs about themselves and the world?

THE BASIC TASKS OF THERAPY

In order to accomplish the therapeutic objectives I have identified seven basic tasks of psychotherapy. It is proposed that these seven tasks are common to all forms of psychotherapy. The impetus for establishing this list of basic tasks came from my putting together a Clinical Handbook on the Treatment of Clients with PTSD and from an invitation to make a movie for Newbridge Communications on the short-term treatment of a client with mixed anxiety and depression.

In preparation for this film I immersed myself in the literature on the common factors in psychotherapy and on the integration of various forms of psychotherapy. If you, the reader, only had approximately 75 minutes to demonstrate 12 sessions of psychotherapy, what would you choose to include in the film? What do you think are the essential, critical tasks of psychotherapy? The following list represents my best hunch. Although these tasks are enumerated sequentially, they take place

over the full course of therapy and are addressed as the client and the therapist sample from them as needed.

1. Develop a therapeutic alliance and help clients tell their stories.

Next to client characteristics, the quality and nature of the therapeutic alliance accounts for more variance in treatment outcome studies than do any other set of variables. The development of a therapeutic alliance and working collaborative client–therapist relationship is critical to all forms of psychotherapy. The relationship provides the glue for all other therapeutic tasks.

The therapist needs to encourage clients to tell their stories at their own pace. A genuine, compassionate, empathic, emotionally attuned, nonjudgmental stance by the therapist facilitates clients telling their stories about what brought them into therapy. But clients should be encouraged to tell their whole story, highlighting what they did to cope, to survive, and even to thrive in spite of any developmental and ongoing stressors.

2. Educate the client about the clinical problem.

Inherent in every form of psychotherapy is some form of education. This education may be didactic or Socratic, deductively presented or inductively codiscovered with clients. This educational process takes place during the course of treatment. The types of questions the therapist asks, the tests that are administered and reviewed with clients, the self-monitoring procedures used by clients, the information conveyed to clients about their presenting problems and about relapse prevention (warning signs, high-risk situations, coping techniques) are each elements of the educational process.

The educational style that I have adopted to achieve these objectives simulates the popular television detective Colombo, as portrayed by Peter Falk. This Socratic approach is designed to guide and coach the clients' discovery, not to change their minds, not to correct their thinking. The questions are designed to coach and guide clients to discover and invent solutions to problems. The questions also provide a framework for inviting clients to examine their experiences in a new way that can nurture hope and trigger change.

3. Help clients reconceptualize their problems in a more hopeful fashion.

A central feature of cognitive-behavioral interventions is the attempt to help clients reconceptualize their predicaments into problem-oriented terms that will lend themselves to solutions. Clients often describe their presenting situations in vague, global, metaphoric terms ("My life is like a glob of misery, a total personal tragedy"). One major task of psychotherapy is to help clients to transpose these vague negative accounts into specific problem-oriented statements. Instead of viewing events as personal threats and provocations, one goal of therapy is to help clients view them as problems-to-be-solved and to chunk them in ways that lead to more hopeful solutions. In this manner, the clients can come to see:

1. that their presenting problems have a beginning, a middle, and an end;
2. that problems consist of different components (feelings, thoughts, sensations, behaviors) that vary across situations;
3. that their reactions make sense given their developmental history;
4. that their symptoms reflect that they are in touch with their feelings and do not mean that they are going crazy or losing control;
5. that they have a variety of strengths;
6. and that they can develop their own voices, taking pride in what they have accomplished and ownership of the changes they are bringing about.

The constructivist therapy is designed to help clients develop a more hopeful voice.

4. Ensure that the clients have coping skills.

One of the central features of a cognitive-behavioral treatment approach is to ensure that clients have a variety of intrapersonal and interpersonal coping skills. These skills may include self-monitoring, relaxation and breathing retraining, self-instructional training, imaginal and behavioral rehearsal, cognitive restructuring, assertiveness training, relapse prevention skills, and others depending upon the clients' specific needs. These specific skills-oriented interventions are embedded within a constructivist framework that is designed to bolster the clients' self-esteem and sense of self-worth.

5. Encourage clients to perform personal experiments.

It is not enough to have clients learn coping skills within the clinic setting. There is a need to ensure that the clients practice their coping skills *in vivo*. The therapist and clients need to carefully consider any possible barriers or obstacles that might get in the way of clients practicing their coping skills. As noted, the clients are encouraged to adopt a personal scientist stance so they can view their coping efforts as personal experiments that are designed to provide them with an opportunity to collect data (that is, the results of their personal experiments) that can be taken as evidence to unfreeze their beliefs about themselves and the world. The therapist works with the clients so they will view their automatic thoughts as hypotheses worthy of testing, rather than as God-given assertions.

6. Ensure that the clients take credit for changes they have brought about.

Like scientists, our clients do *not* readily accept data as evidence. Clients may dismiss, discount, and reframe the outcomes of their personal experiments. Thus, it is critical for the therapist to insure that clients take credit for the observed results. The therapist should not leave to chance the possibility that the clients will attribute change to their own instrumental efforts. It is important for the clients to appropriate responsibility for and ownership of the changes that they have brought about. The research on maintenance and generalization of treatment effects indicates that it is critical for the clients to take credit for change and also to provide self-explanations of how they brought them about (Meichenbaum, 1994).

7. Conduct relapse prevention.

It is likely that clients will reexperience lapses and setbacks given the episodic nature of affective disorders and the often long-standing nature of their problems. The final task of all psychotherapies should be a discussion and educational exchange about such possible lapses and setbacks. The therapist needs to work with clients to ensure that the reexperience of symptoms (lapses) does not escalate to the point of relapse, so the clients go back to their pretreatment levels of adjustment. Possible setbacks should be expected and anticipated. They should be viewed by clients as opportunities to practice their coping skills, rather than as occasions to catastrophize. In addition, relapse prevention training is designed to help clients learn how to anticipate high-risk situations (that is, when they are getting stressed out), to recognize warning signs, especially low-intensity anticipatory cues, and to develop coping techniques.

It is not that clients have lapses but rather what they say to themselves and to others about the lapses that is critical in determining the treatment outcome. The therapist cannot leave the clients' internal dialogue following lapses to chance.

The recent movement toward the integration of psychotherapy may benefit from a careful consideration of the common tasks that cut across diverse therapy approaches. As conferees attend various sessions of this impressive gathering of psychotherapists, they can listen for how therapists incorporate (or fail to incorporate) these various common tasks into their interventions.

CONCLUSION

What is the story that the psychotherapist is telling and what has the therapist done to help their clients change their stories? As a result of therapy, do clients offer different accounts? Do the clients now begin to use active transitive verbs—notice, catch, plan—as part of their stories? Do the clients now use more positive metaphors to describe themselves? Are the clients able to anticipate high-risk situations and describe possible coping techniques, as well as take credit for the changes they have been able to bring about? Do the clients begin to tell a new story about themselves and the world?

If the answer to these questions is no, then perhaps the client should have dinner with my mother.

REFERENCES

Beck, J. G., & Zebb, B. J. (1994). Behavioral assessment and treatment of panic disorder: Current status, future directions. *Behavior Therapy, 25*, 581–611.

Brewer, W. (1974). There is no convincing evidence for operant and classical conditioning in adult humans. In W. Weimar & D. Palermo (Eds.), *Cognition and the symbolic processes*. New York: Halsted Press.

Buckalew, L. W., & Sallis, R. E. (1980). Patient compliance and medication perception. *Journal of Clinical Psychology, 42*, 49–53.

Dember, W. (1974). Motivation and the cognitive revolution. *American Psychologist, 29*, 161–168.

Hollon, S., & Beck, A. T. (1993). Cognitive and cognitive-behavioral therapies. In S. L. Garfield & A. E. Bergin (Eds.), *Handbook of psychotherapy and behavior change* (4th ed.). New York: Wiley.

Hornsveld, H., Garssen, B., & Van Spiegel, P. (1995). Voluntary hyperventilation. *Biological Psychiatry, 40*, 299–312.

Kazdin, A. E., & Wilcoxon, L. A. (1976). Systematic desensitization and nonspecific treatment effect: A methodological evolution. *Psychological Bulletin, 83*, 729–758.

Kruglanski, A. W. (1980). Lay epistemology process and contents. *Psychological Review, 87*, 70–87.

Lohr, J. M., Kleinknecht, R. A., Conley, A. T., Dal Cerro, S., Schmidt, J., & Sonntag, M. E. (1992). A methodological critique of the current status of eye movement desensitization. *Journal of Behavior Therapy and Experimental Psychiatry, 23*, 159–167.

Magraf, J., Barlow, J. H., Clark, D. M., & Telch, M. J. (1993). Psychological treatment of panic: Work in progress on outcome, active ingredients and follow-up. *Behavior Research and Therapy, 25*, 315–328.

Mahoney, M. J. (1993). Theoretical developments in the cognitive psychotherapies. *Journal of Consulting and Clinical Psychology, 61*, 187–193.

Meichenbaum, D. (1977). *Cognitive behavior modification: An integrative approach*. New York: Plenum.

Meichenbaum, D. (1977). Acronym therapy: A real or sensible selection. *Contemporary Psychology, 22*, 202–201.

Meichenbaum, D. (1977). Dr. Ellis please stand up. *The Counseling Psychologist, 7*, 43–45.

Meichenbaum, D., & Turk, D. (1987). *Facilitating treatment adherence: A practitioner's guidebook*. New York: Plenum.

Meichenbaum, D. (1990). Paying homage: Providing challenges. *Psychological Inquiry, 1*, 96–100.

Meichenbaum, D. (1992). Evolution of cognitive behavior therapy: Origins, tenets and clinical examples. In J. K. Zeig (Ed.), *The evolution of psychotherapy: The second conference*. New York: Brunner/Mazel.

Meichenbaum, D. (1993). Changing conceptions of cognitive behavior modification: Retrospects and prospects. *Journal of Consulting and Clinical Psychology, 61*, 202–204.

Meichenbaum, D. (1994). *Clinical handbook of treatment of post traumatic stress disorder*. Waterloo, Ontario: Institute Press.

Mitchell, J. T. (1983). When disaster strikes: The critical incident stress debriefing process. *Journal of Emergency Medical Services, 8*, 36–39.

Munoz, R. F., Hollon, S. D., McGrath, E., Rehm, L., & van den Bos, G. R. (1994). On the AHCPR Depression in Primary Care Guidelines. *American Psychologist, 149*, 42–61.

Neimeyer, R. A. (1993). An appraisal of constructivist psychotherapies. *Journal of Consulting and Clinical Psychology, 61*, 221–234.

Raimy, V. (1975). *Misunderstanding of self: Cognitive psychotherapy and the misconception hypothesis*. San Francisco: Jossey-Bass.

Rosen, G. M. (1995). On the origin of eye movement desensitization. *Journal of Behavior Therapy and Experimental Psychiatry, 26*, 121–122.

Shapiro, F. (1989). Eye movement desensitization: A new treatment of post-traumatic stress disorder. *Journal of Behavior Therapy and Experimental Psychiatry, 20*, 211–217.

Shear, M. K., Pilkonis, P. A., Cloitre, M., & Leon, A. C. (1994). Cognitive-behavioral treatment compared with nonprescriptive treatment of panic disorder. *Archives of General Psychiatry, 51*, 395–401.

Smedslund, J. (1978). Bandura's theory of self-efficacy: A set of common sense theorems. *Scandinavian Journal of Psychology, 19*, 1–14.

Stone, I.F. (1967). *In time of torment*. New York: Random House.

Strupp, H. H. (1989). Psychotherapy: Can the practitioner learn from the researcher? *American Psychologist, 44*, 717–724.

Turk, D., Meichenbaum, D., & Berman, W. (1979). The application of biofeedback for the regulation of pain: A critical review. *Psychological Bulletin, 86*, 1322–1338.

Weisz, J., & Weiss, B. (1993). *Efficacy of psychotherapy with children and adolescents*. New York: Sage.

Discussion by William Glasser, M.D.

◆

I feel sorry for myself. Donald is a very hard man to follow. Also, I have no quarrel with anything he said. I've been my own I.F. Stone all my life, starting when I was a psychiatric resident when I opened my mouth and lost all chance of ever becoming a member of the psychiatric staff at the University of California at Los Angeles. I said things like, "I don't know what insight is. Explain it to me." They tried but they couldn't. I kept saying, "It's not clear."

They tried by saying, "It's emotional insight."

I said, "Fine, I don't have trouble with the word emotional, but what is it?"

They never did explain what insight is in a way that would help a client.

What also got me into trouble as I sat in staff meetings where they would present a patient was that someone would talk *about* the patient. No one would actually work *with* the patient; they just kind of looked at the patient and talked about him or her.

The question was always, "Is this patient a good candidate for psychotherapy?" And we were in West Los Angeles, near Brentwood. The patients who came to our clinic were not poor people. I started my whole private practice with people I took from that clinic. They could afford to pay me. And we had great results with these people who were good candidates for psychotherapy. Many candidates

for psychotherapy at UCLA were young, beautiful, charming women who could converse easily. Many were bored; they had no serious problems.

I said, "There's no such thing as a good candidate." I was trying to do what Meichenbaum is suggesting. Treat them all. If they are difficult, it's our problem. I asked one of my great teachers, Dr. Harrington, what does a patient have to bring to psychotherapy?

He said, "The only thing the patient has to do is *be there*. You can't do psychotherapy with someone who never comes. If they are in the office, all the responsibility is upon you as a psychotherapist."

For example, I had a client who was a big strapping 19-year-old man. I started to try to talk a little bit to him to get his story, and all of a sudden, after about maybe 30 to 40 seconds, I noticed that he was not talking. Now, if I'd call one of my old teachers at UCLA and told him, "I got a guy here who won't talk," they'd have told me, "He's not a good candidate for psychotherapy." But life was difficult when you don't have many referrals, so when this patient came to me, he was a good candidate for psychotherapy. I wasn't going to lose him.

He was a student who had gone crazy up at the University of California at Berkeley, had a psychotic episode, and came home. His dad was a plumber, not a rich man.

I said to him, "You don't talk, do you?" I kind of got that insight; he hadn't said anything for 40 to 50 seconds. He just shook his head. I said, "Is this part of your problem, that you don't talk?"

He nodded his head "yes."

"Well, are you going to come and see me?"

He nodded again.

I said, "Well, in psychotherapy, I've got to explain that the patient comes in and talks. And I work with that speech. If you don't talk, this is going to be very difficult."

And he smiled as if, tough luck, Doc.

And so I said, "Well, I wonder how I should deal with this?" In psychiatry school, they didn't cover this particular thing. Maybe it was the day I cut class; I don't know.

Anyway, I called on something which, if you are familiar with my writing on control theory, is always working with all of us, called our "reorganization system." When you don't know what to say, things pop into your mind. You can depend on it if you don't get all panicked and shut it off. Well, I was relaxed. What the hell! I mean he was a patient, he was sitting there, and I was going to treat him.

So I said to him, "Well, if you don't want to talk, that's okay. I'll talk for you." I said, "I'll ask a question, and I'll answer for you. I'll say, "Now I am talking—blah, blah, blah, blah," and then you are answering, blah, blah, blah." I started in. I just talked about anything that came to my mind. What was the difference anyway?

And so he started getting kind of uncomfortable. He finally started showing extreme discomfort, because I was saying things like, "Jim, How come you don't talk? I'm so stupid, I'm going to a psychiatrist and not talking. I've decided not to talk. That's kind of stupid, but that's what I am choosing to do."

Finally, he started to talk. He said, "I don't like this."

I said, "Well, I'm willing to go back to regular psychotherapy." But, I said, "I'm willing to talk for you if you won't. I can do it for an hour; hell, I can do it for a day if I had to. I don't have that many patients anyway. There's nobody knocking at the door, I have plenty of time."

So he said, "I'll talk."

I said, "Fine. Now, let's not stretch things. I realize that not talking is very important to you; I don't want to take this away from you because that would be something you obviously have figured out and really enjoy. Just talk to me. Don't talk to another soul."

Oh, he was real happy about that.

But then my therapy began to take hold. We were talking here about making an alliance, educating, giving hope, just as Dr. Meichenbaum explained. I said, "Your father is a plumber, right?"

"Right."

"And I know he doesn't make much money." I think at that time I was charging maybe $35 an hour. I said, "Thirty-five bucks an hour. Can your dad afford it?"

He said, "Well, it's hard for him."

I said, "Well, you are a big, strong young man; why don't you go to work and then pay for your own therapy?" I said, "I've read a lot of studies that say that when the patient pays for his own therapy, it's more effective."

And he said, "Well, who would hire me if I don't talk?"

Well, I make alliances with all my clients. I didn't have many, but the ones I had, I had good alliances with, and so I called one up. . . . I said, "You'd be surprised who would hire you." I had a patient who was in kind of a shady business and was always hiring people. I called him up and I said, "I got a real nice young man. He is a very good, very smart, Berkeley person; he's out of Berkeley but he'll go back in a little while after he gets over this thing. Will you hire him?"

And he said, "Yeah, yeah, send him over."

I said, "But he doesn't talk."

He said, "That'll be no problem at all. I want him just to deliver the stuff, keep his mouth shut, and leave. That's all I want."

And so I sent him there, and a couple of weeks later the patient reports to me, "You know, I like working for Dave, but he doesn't pay me."

I knew Dave was not a hundred percent square guy but mostly he paid people if they worked for him, and I couldn't figure this out.

So I called him up and I said, "Dave, you haven't paid Jim; he's been working hard for two weeks, and you pay every week."

He said, "Yeah, every Saturday I pay."

I said, "Well, how come you haven't paid him?"

Dave says, "On Saturday all the people who work line up and I'm sitting there with my checkbook. When they come up to me, they say, 'Dave, give me my check.' He comes up, doesn't say a word, so I pass."

So I said, "Jim, you better say just a few words on Saturday morning, like 'Dave, give me my check.' " He said it, and he got a lot bet-ter. The problem came later: We couldn't shut him up, but he got a doctorate in mathematics at the University of California at Berkeley. He is head of the math department in some university and doing quite well, with a family and everything else.

The point of the story is that psychotherapy requires an understanding of how people function, I think a very deep understanding of how people function, which I explain through a theory called *control theory*. And, like Dr. Meichenbaum, I like to say, "Don't believe a word I am saying, unless you try this in your life, evaluate it, and find it works for you."

From Psychoanalytic to Behavioral Methods in Anxiety Disorders: A Continuing Evolution

◆

Joseph Wolpe, M.D.

Joseph Wolpe, M.D.

Joseph Wolpe, M.D., D.Sc., received his medical degree in 1939 from the University of Whitwatersrand in Johannesburg, South Africa. He is Distinguished Professor, Pepperdine University, Graduate School of Education and Psychology, and Visiting Professor at the University of California, Los Angeles. A recipient of the Distinguished Scientific Award for Applications of Psychology from the American Psychological Association and the Lifetime Achievement Award from the Phobia Society, he is a James McKeen Cattell Fellow of the American Psychological Society and a Distinguished Member of Psi Chi. Dr. Wolpe is one of the leading practitioners of behavior therapy. He has written seven books and coedited two, has more than 500 professional publications to his credit, and is the cofounder of the Journal of Behavior Therapy and Experimental Psychiatry.

INTRODUCTION

The influence of Freud's writings upon two generations of psychiatrists and psychologists attests to his remarkable power to instill belief without offering anything in the way of supporting evidence. It is the same as a population's acceptance of the pronouncements of a charismatic purveyor of religious doctrines. Freud's persuasiveness derived partly from the startling originality of his ideas and partly from the way in which he framed them. I myself was swept away by his writings in the early 1940s. I was firmly convinced that I was imbibing unshakeable truths. It was only much later that I realized that I was in part a victim of what would today be recognized as subtle salesmanship. Here is an actual example that influenced me: Halfway through his *Introductory Lectures on Psychoanalysis,* Freud makes the declaration that anybody who has not gone along with him up to this point should drop out of the course. The implication is that an unpersuaded person lacks the intellectual and emotional grasp to deserve participation in Freud's revelations. I clearly recall at the time thinking that this was perfectly reasonable, and being only too happy to be persuaded in order not to merit exclusion.

THE CASE OF LITTLE HANS

Freud's high-handed treatment of his audiences was extremely successful. An assumption of infallibility is uniformly manifest in his celebrated case of Little Hans, published in 1909 under the title *The Analysis of a Phobia in a Five-year-old Boy*, and reverently endorsed by his disciples. Ernest Jones, in his biography of Freud, states that "the brilliant success of child analysis was inaugurated by the study of this very case" (1955, p.292). The case had special significance in the development of psychoanalytic theory because Freud believed himself to have found in it "a more direct and less roundabout proof" of some fundamental psychoanalytic theorems. In particular, he thought that it provided a direct demonstration of the essential role of sexual urges in the development of phobias. For decades, psychoanalysts have quoted Freud's disquisition on Little Hans as a basic substantiation of psychoanalytic theories. Edward Glover (1956) stated: "In its time the analysis of Little Hans was a remarkable achievement and constitutes one of the most valued records in psychoanalytical archives. Our concepts of phobia formation, of the positive Oedipus complex, of ambivalence, castration anxiety and repression, to mention but a few, were greatly reinforced and amplified as the result of this analysis."

In January 1908, Hans' father wrote to Freud that the boy had developed "a nervous disorder." His symptoms were fear of going into the street, depression in the evening, and fear that a horse would bite him. The first signs were observed on January 7, when Hans was being taken to the park by his nursemaid as usual. He started crying and said that he wanted to caress his mother. The following day, he went out with his mother, and when he returned home he said, "I was afraid a horse would bite me." As on the previous day, Hans showed fear in the evening and said, "I know I shall have to go for a walk again tomorrow," and "The horse'll come into the room."

At this point, Freud made an assessment of Hans' behavior, on the basis of which he arranged with the boy's father "that he should tell the boy that all this nonsense about horses was a piece of nonsense and nothing more." The truth was, his father was to say, that he was very fond of his mother and wanted to be taken into her bed. The reason he was afraid of horses now was that he had taken so much interest in their "widdlers." Freud also sug-

gested giving Hans some sexual enlightenment and telling him that females "had no widdler at all."

On a visit to the zoo early in March Hans expressed fear of the giraffe, the elephant, and all other large animals. His father said to him, "Do you know why you're afraid of big animals? Big animals have big widdlers and you're really afraid of big widdlers." This was denied by the boy.

On March 30, the boy had his only meeting with Freud, a short consultation, after which Freud stated that despite all the enlightenment given to Hans, the fear of horses continued undiminished. Hans explained that he was especially bothered "by what horses wear in front of their eyes and the black around their mouths." This latter detail Freud interpreted as meaning a moustache.

In the next few days the details of the origin of Hans' fear emerged. For the first time he told his father that he was most scared of horses with "a thing on their mouths," that he was scared lest the horses fall, and that he was most scared of horse-drawn buses.

Hans: "I'm most afraid too when a bus comes along."

Father: "Why? Because it's so big?"

Hans: "No. Because once a horse in a bus fell."

Father: "When?"

Hans then recounted such an incident, which was later confirmed by his mother.

Father: "What did you think when the horse fell down?"

Hans: "Now it will always be like this. All horses in buses'll fall down."

The father adds that "all of this was confirmed by my wife, as well as the fact the anxiety broke immediately afterwards."

It is an appalling fact that this crucial causal information was totally ignored by Freud, who continued to insist, without providing any factual grounds, that Hans' fear of horses stemmed from a sexual desire for his mother.

That Hans derived satisfaction from his mother and enjoyed her presence is not in dispute, but nowhere is there any evidence that he wished to copulate with her. Similarly, though he never expressed fear or hatred for his father, Hans was told he possessed these emotions. On several occasions Hans directly denied the existence of such feelings when questioned by his father. Freud claimed that Hans' desire for his mother was transferred anxiety, which he inferred from "theoretical considerations that require that what is today the object of a phobia has at one time in the past been the source of a high degree of pleasure." However, not only is there no evidence that Hans sexually desired his mother, but there was also no change in his attitude towards his mother just before the onset of the phobia, as Freud believed there should have been. As regards the assertion that the purpose of Hans' phobia was to keep him near his mother, not only is there no evidence to support it, but it is contradicted by the fact that Hans experienced anxiety even when he was out walking with his mother. If one is infallible, one does not need facts!

No systematic follow-up of the case is provided. However, fourteen years after the completion of the analysis, Freud interviewed Hans, who "declared that he was perfectly well and suffered from no troubles or inhibitions." Hans also said that he had successfully undergone the ordeal of his parents' divorce. Hans reported that he could not remember anything about his childhood phobia. Freud remarked that this is "particularly remarkable." The analysis itself "had been overtaken by amnesia"!

In sum, the facts of the case of Little Hans provide no support for any of Freud's theories. In noteworthy contrast, the phobia is easily seen as a matter of fear conditioning. The great fear that was provoked in Hans when he witnessed a horse that had been drawing a bus falling right in front of him was conditioned to the horse that was in focus at the time (Wolpe, 1990). The facts of the case and a critical analysis of Freud's arguments were presented in detail in an article entitled "Psychoanalytic Evidence: A Critique Based on Freud's Case of Little Hans" (Wolpe & Rachman, 1960). But such is the strength of psychoanalytic indoctrination that although this article was widely read, as indicated by our receiving several hundred requests for reprints, we never encountered either personally or in print any rebuttals or commentaries, and never heard of a single psychoanalyst having had his or her faith shaken by it in the slightest degree.

The case of Little Hans has been presented in some detail not because it is unique, but because it represents a manner of thinking that is widely manifest in all of Freud's writings. In his book *The Myth of Paradigm Shift*, Scharnberg (1984) gives a broad compendium of the illogicalities and sleight of hand displayed in Freud's literary contributions. Because their foundations are flawed, Freud's theories do not deserve the solemn respect that has been so widely accorded them to this day.

PSYCHOANALYTIC THERAPY

However, the flaws of a theory do not negate the possibility that success may attend the methods it generates. A theory full of holes may yet yield a highly successful therapy. Psychoanalytic psychotherapy is in fact usually presented as a success story with a great deal of braggadocio. However, no satisfactory evidence of its special success has ever been provided.

A recent survey of the literature (Wolpe, Craske, & Reyna, 1994) assembled the results of psychoanalytic studies published between 1962 and 1988 and evaluated them on the five criteria proposed by the eminent psychoanalyst Robert P. Knight (1941): symptomatic recovery (relative freedom from or significant diminution of disabling fears, distress, inhibition and dysfunction); increased productiveness at work; improved adjustment to and pleasure in sex; improved interpersonal relationships; and increased ability to handle ordinary psychological conflicts and reasonable reality stresses. Following Knight, we indicated change in the "usual medical groupings" (a) no change or worse, (b) slightly to moderately improved, and (c) much improved. The "much improved" group ranged from patients who no longer had symptoms and who functioned well in all areas, to those who had marked symptomatic improvement and who functioned well, but perhaps suboptimally in some respects. *We counted as successes only patients evaluated as "much improved,"* our rationale being that only these patients could be said to have benefitted in a major way from therapy.

Our survey encompassed four studies—by Brody (1962), Kernberg, et. al (1972), Mintz (1977), and Luborsky et. al (1988), and comprised a total of 1103 patients. Of these, 22 percent were rated much improved. This is not impressive. Even the most mundane methods do better. For example, Hamilton & Wall (1941) reported a 53 percent recovery rate for neurotic patients treated in a general hospital. With respect to the Brody study, Masserman (1943) reported that the average patient was seen three or four times a week for three or four years, which amounts to a mean of at least 600 sessions per patient.

THE ADVENT OF BEHAVIOR THERAPY

The 1950s saw the rise of behavior therapy as the modern successor and the current alternative to psychoanalytic theory. It rests on the experimentally based theory that neuroses consist of learned maladaptive anxiety responses. The strategy that logically emerged from this theory was that to overcome neuroses one must set in motion the unlearning of maladaptive anxiety response habits. This strategy remains the essence of behavior therapy.

HOW THE TREATMENT OF
EXPERIMENTAL NEUROSES YIELDED A
THERAPEUTIC PARADIGM

The realization that neuroses are maladaptive learned anxiety responses emerged from studies of experimental neuroses. These are long-lasting anxiety response habits of high intensity that develop when anxiety is repeatedly evoked in an animal in a constant environment. The effect of the repetition is that a rising level of anxiety is progressively conditioned to the stimuli present in that situation.

The first method of inducing anxiety to generate experimental neuroses that was devised by Pavlov (1927) involved the generation of increasingly severe conflict by means of difficult discrimination. A circle was made a conditioned stimulus to feeding, while an oval was made a food-negative stimulus. Gradually the shape of the oval was then changed to look more and more like a circle. When it became indistinguishable from the circle, the conflict between impulses to eat and not to eat became severe. High anxiety ensued, which was conditioned to the experimental environment.

It was later found more convenient to induce high levels of anxiety by means of a painful but physically harmless electrical stimulation applied to an animal's feet (Masserman, 1943; Pavlov, 1927; Wolpe, 1952). Stimuli in contiguity with the evoked anxiety (e.g., the experimental cage) became conditioned stimuli to anxiety, and with repetition of the electrical stimulation were enabled to elicit it at high intensity. The animal then avoided easily available food in the experimental cage even when it was left there alone with it for a day or more, even though the electrical stimulation was not administered again. The anxiety response elicited by the cage and the consequent eating inhibition were found not to be diminished by repeated and prolonged visits to the cage.

A curious fact about experimental neuroses is that although Pavlov was their innovator, he was to the end of his life convinced that they had nothing to do with conditioning! Their rapid onset and sometimes bizarre manifestations appeared to him to point unquestionably to cerebral pathology. This conclusion of Pavlov's was accepted without question by the many experimenters who followed him in the study of animal neuroses from Krasnogorski (1925) to Masserman (1943). For more information, see Wolpe (1952).

Masserman's experiments were the template for my own work on experimental neuroses, which generated successful therapeutic methods. In a cage 40″ long, 20″ wide, and 20″ high, Masserman used food reinforcement to train cats to open the lid of a food-box in response to a light-and-bell signal. One day, either at the feeding signal or at the moment of food-taking, a grid on the floor of the cage would be electrically charged. The usual reaction to a grid shock was a startled jump as the impulse arrived, followed by a slow dignified stalking away from the food after the shock ended. After several repetitions, neurotic behavior was unremittingly present in the experimental cage, characterized by agitation or immobility, vocalization, sensitivity to extraneous stimuli, trembling, marked pupillary dilation, and invariable refusal of food in the cage even after prolonged food deprivation. Despite great ingenuity in experiments on more than 100 cats, with many variations, Masserman elicited no usable information, for he habitually gave psychoanalytic interpretations to the behavior of his cats instead of learning from his observations. However, he did essay a quasi-behavioral mode of therapy that he called "the forced solution" that had some beneficial effects but did not lend itself to human application.

In experiments patterned on those of Masserman, I studied experimental neuroses in twelve cats between June 1947 and July 1948 at the University of the Witwatersrand in Johannesburg (Wolpe, 1952). A critical control observation that I then made was that grid shocks could produce the neuroses without in any way involving feeding responses. Thus, conflict was not the indispensable causal factor that it had been assumed to be. In addition, I noted that the experimental room and the experimenter himself had become conditioned stimuli to anxiety, but weaker ones. Anxiety responses of still lower intensity were observed in four other rooms, depending in magnitude on the degree of resemblance of each room to the experimental room. I called the experimental room A, and the other rooms B, C, D and E, in decreasing order both of resemblance to Room A and in magnitude of manifest anxiety.

My neurotic cats, like Masserman's, displayed continuous pupillary dilation, trembling, sensitivity to extraneous stimuli, and absolute refusal to eat in the experimental cage. The last indicated that the strength of the anxiety response was overwhelmingly greater than that of the food-seeking drive. Because there was no apparent way to increase that drive any further (it begins to decline after

three days' starvation), I decided to try the effect of decreasing the level of anxiety when food was presented. I made use of the series of rooms noted above. A neurotic animal would first be offered pellets of meat on the floor of Room A, and if he did not eat there the offer was renewed in the other rooms until one was found, often Room E, where the anxiety was weak enough not to inhibit eating. The animal would usually snatch fearfully at the first meat pellet and then take subsequent ones with increasing alacrity, while signs of anxiety progressively faded. The next day he would be offered meat pellets in Room D, and again would eat at first hesitantly and then with increasing ease. Going up the hierarchy of rooms, the animal would eventually eat in Room A, and finally in the experimental cage within it. There, the eating of numerous pellets, widely distributed, achieved the elimination of all anxiety.

This therapeutic program was successful in all twelve animals. It seemed strongly to support the potency of response competition as a way of overcoming maladaptive anxiety response habits. Apparently, the greater the relative strength of the eating response, the more markedly anxiety was inhibited, and the greater was the ensuing measure of conditioned (that is, learned) inhibition of anxiety. It was a logical endpoint that the anxiety response was entirely eliminated.

At this point, a challenging question arose. Had we truly achieved an *extinction* of the anxiety habit, or had we merely overwhelmed the evocation of anxiety by a kind of distraction resulting from the repeatedly reinforced feeding? The following supplementary experiment was undertaken to test this question. At the induction of the experimental neurosis a buzzer had routinely preceded each shock, so that an anxiety response had been conditioned to it as well as to the visual situation. This auditory conditioning was eliminated in each animal by using feeding in a competitive way that paralleled its use with the visual stimuli. A consequence of this procedure was to make food-seeking a conditioned response to the buzzer. Here, too, it was conceivable that it was not a deconditioning of anxiety but a suppression of anxiety due to the distractive effect of food-seeking. If that were the case, the anxiety would reappear if we extinguished the food-seeking response to the buzzer. To achieve this, each animal was given 30 irregularly massed unreinforced presentations of the buzzer on each of three successive days—a total of 90 extinction trials. After this, no trace of the food-seeking response to the buzzer was discernible. A day or two later, the following critical test was performed on each animal. A meat pellet was dropped on the floor about two feet away from the animal, and as he began to approach it the buzzer was sounded repeatedly. In no instance did inhibition of eating or any other sign of resurgence of anxiety appear, although such behavior would have been observed before the extinction. Clearly, the anxiety had truly been extinguished, and not just suppressed.

RECIPROCAL INHIBITION IN HUMAN NEUROSES

Some time after concluding my experiments, I completed a dissertation based on them and went into clinical practice in the hope of applying the findings to human anxiety disorders. The possibility that feeding might be an effective agent for deconditioning in human subjects was suggested by the animal experiments, and I was encouraged by the successful use of feeding that Mary Cover Jones (1924) had reported in the treatment of children's fears. In their discussion of Little Albert, in whom they had conditioned a fear of white rats, Watson and Rayner (1920) had proposed four possible strategies for overcoming the fear, one of which was "reconditioning by having the child eat candy in the presence of the feared object." Jones, who had been a student of Watson's, would place the fearful child in a high chair and give him his favorite candy. The feared object was then brought closer and closer until the child stopped eating. The object was then moved back until the child's eating resumed. With careful manipulation, the object was gradually brought closer without eliciting fear. Jones (1924) gave a detailed example of her method in the case of Peter, a three-year-old boy with a fear of rabbits. Peter had sessions over a period

of two months, at the end of which he was able to handle rabbits fearlessly.

But although the successful treatment of maladaptive fears in animals and children made it natural to entertain the idea of using feeding for treating the fears of human adults, this turned out to be impracticable. A major reason for this was the practical difficulty of arranging for eating to coincide with the arousal of social anxiety, the usual adult problem. Therefore, I began to look for alternatives. Anger gave the impression of being inherently opposed to anxiety. Where it was feasible, therefore, I began to instruct its use for practice in imaginary situations when a person had inappropriate anxiety, for example, at being rejected by an unimportant person. A few months later, I read Salter's *Conditioned Reflex Therapy* (1949), and was impressed and delighted by the author's wide success in overcoming interpersonal anxiety by fostering the outward expression of anger and whatever other appropriate feelings happen to be available. I learned a great deal from this book.

The procedures central to Salter's method, which is now called assertiveness training, are very effective for overcoming timidity. The person is shown how to express, in all reasonable circumstances, legitimate anger, affection, and any other appropriate feelings. Two kinds of behavior change ensue. The fear is inhibited and weakened by the simultaneous expression of the anger, and new habits of motor expression are learned and then reinforced by social success.

While assertiveness training is very effective for overcoming timidity—the unadaptive anxiety that lies behind the inappropriate handling of interpersonal situations—it has little relevance to such social anxieties as are caused by being the center of attention, public speaking, or being the unjustified target of disapproval. It is also ineffective in the treatment of fears of impersonal situations such as those that make up the phobias. A major resource for treating such fears is the calmness produced by muscle relaxation (Jacobson, 1938). But Jacobson's mode of practice was cumbersome. A hundred or more training sessions and long periods of daily practice were the rule with him. Even after all that, beneficial change was uncertain, because the unpredictability of fear in the course of daily life often finds the person unready to counter it when it arises; and in any case even very good relaxation may not suffice when fear is great.

A more practical procedure is to pit the calmness of relaxation against imagined anxiety situations (Wolpe, 1954, 1990). Relaxation training is given beforehand during part of each of several sessions, along with ten to twenty minutes of practice at home each day. At the same sessions, situations from an area of unadaptive fear are listed and then arranged in rank order of their fear-evoking power. The ranked list is called a hierarchy. An individual case may have one or several hierarchies. In the main procedure, called *systematic desensitization*, the patient is made to relax deeply, then asked to imagine a hierarchy's weakest item, and to indicate on the Subjective Anxiety Scale (Wolpe, 1990) the level of anxiety evoked. After a few seconds, the scene is terminated and followed by renewed relaxation. The sequence is repeated until the imagined item no longer evokes any anxiety. More stressful hierarchy items are similarly handled until fear is eliminated from the whole constellation. Almost invariably, the deconditioning of anxiety is found to have transferred to the corresponding real situation.

Desensitization also can be conducted in vivo, using real instead of imagined hierarchical stimuli. The groundbreaking therapeutic experiments of Mary Cover Jones (1924) described earlier technically were desensitization in vivo. An agoraphobic woman I treated, whose anxiety level was related to her distance from a reliable person, was repeatedly brought by her husband to meet me in a public park in the quiet of the morning, and she was instructed to relax at these times. In about ten meetings, exposed in this way to increasingly distant and prolonged separations, she overcame her maladaptive anxiety.

In some patients, perhaps 15 percent, imagined scenes lack "reality" and therefore cannot be used in therapy. This is a major disadvantage. In contrast with the limitless availability of imagined stimuli, appropriate in vivo stimuli are not always ready to hand. Artifices often have to be devised. For example, in

treating patients with a fear of humiliation, I have had them intentionally give wrong answers to simple arithmetical problems. The anxiety this produces fades away with repetition. I then introduce more difficult problems and eventually some that are beyond their capacity, and then I increasingly criticize them. By this sequence of exposures they become less and less vulnerable to humiliation.

OTHER CLINICALLY EFFECTIVE ANXIETY INHIBITORS

1. Sexual Arousal:

The long-known fact that anxiety is a common cause of male sexual inadequacy, and especially of premature ejaculation, suggested to me at an early stage that sexual arousal might, reciprocally, inhibit relatively weak anxiety in sexual situations and in consequence diminish its evocation, as feeding had done in the neurotic cats. Thus, a man's sexual response might be the vehicle for a kind of in vivo desensitization for the anxiety evoked by the sexual encounter, leading to recovery in cases in which anxiety was the reason for inadequacy of performance. This turned out to be a very successful basic strategy, though adjuvants were profitably used in some cases. A survey of eighteen cases showed fourteen to have recovered and three others to be much improved after treatment that usually spanned a few weeks (Wolpe, 1990, p. 305).

The success of this procedure, which I first reported in 1954, was the largely unacknowledged starting point for the development that came to be known as the "new sex therapy," whose main early protagonists were Masters and Johnson (1970) and Kaplan (1974). Though many of their procedures obtained improvement in sexual function through diminishing anxiety on the basis of gradually increasing exposure, they were apparently unaware of the fact that response competition was the basis of change.

2. Verbally Induced Inhibition of Anxiety

Anxiety-eliciting stimuli are presented to the subject's imagination against a verbally evoked competing emotion. An example of this is emotive imagery (Lazarus & Abramovitz, 1962). In the case of a twelve-year-old boy who feared darkness, they made use of the fact that he was emotionally turned on by Superman and Captain Silver. He was asked to imagine that these characters had made him their agent, and that he was traversing dark passages of increasing length at their behest. By careful coordination of darkness stimuli with the boy's counteractive emotional responses, the authors overcame the fear in three sessions, a recovery that endured at an eleven-month follow-up.

3. Eye Movement Desensitization

Eye movement desensitization (EMD) (Shapiro, 1989) is a recently discovered, often very effective use of motor responses for overcoming maladaptive anxiety-response habits. Its most impressive results have been in the treatment of posttraumatic stress disorder. After preliminary analysis has defined the anxiety situations, the patient is asked to maintain a disturbing image while visually tracking the side-to-side movements of the clinician's finger. It usually takes a few sessions for the procedure to decrease the anxiety elicited by the image, with characteristically correlated diminution of such secondary symptoms as nightmares and flashbacks.

4. Nonspecific Inhibition of Anxiety

This term refers to the very important fact, widely ignored in psychotherapy research, that in many cases anxiety is inhibited by the competition of the patient's emotional response to the therapist, and may consequently diminish this anxiety response habit. This process is the apparent basis for most of the therapeutic successes that occur in nonbehavioral therapies. Outcome research should take this phenomena into account, but usually fails to do so.

OVERCOMING ANXIETY BY COGNITIVE CORRECTION

During the last two decades it became increasingly evident to behavior therapists whose treatments are predominantly designed within a conditioning framework that a substantial number of cases of anxiety disorders are based not on classical conditioning but on misconceptions, most of which derive from misinformation. This realization gave credence at least in part to the hypothesis of cognitively based fears that had been put forward by Ellis (1962) and Beck (1976) among others.

How behavior therapists came to give recognition to cognitive etiologies can be understood easily in the context of a common anxiety problem, fear of elevators. The analysis of the case, a vital operation in all behavior therapy, may point in one person to a cognitive causation, and in another person to a conditioning causation. A key question that is put to every elevator phobic is, "Why are you afraid of elevators? Do they pose any danger?" One person might answer, "Yes, there is danger." In elucidation he might say, "If the elevator were to get stuck between floors I would exhaust the air and die of suffocation." Given his mistaken belief, it is logical for him to have this fear, which can be overcome by convincing him that all elevators are ventilated. Conviction might require the help of an elevator technician. The acceptance of the facts usually results in a rapid resolution of this kind of fear in such cases.

A second elevator phobic might respond differently to the question, "What are you afraid of?" He might say, "I'm afraid of the anxiety I experience in the elevator," and will not admit to awareness of any danger. This person has no wrong belief and therefore requires no corrective information. His is a classically conditioned phobia, which indicates the use of such a technique as systematic desensitization. In studies by Hugdal (1981) and Wolpe (1981) it was found that about two-thirds of maladaptive fears are classically conditioned and one-third cognitively based. However, Ellis and even more so Beck believe that *all* fears are cognitively based. Beck insists that thoughts of danger lie behind every fear, though it is in many cases impossible to see how danger can be read into a particular fear. Take, for example, a person in whom fear is elicited by seeing a bloody bandage around somebody's finger. He does not see it as dangerous; therefore, there is no misconception to correct. Of course a cognitivist would probably be able to dredge up a danger, much as Freud manufactured facts to support his theories.

Beck (1976) has argued that systematic desensitization is effective because it leads to a *realization* that fear—for example, of the elevator—is receding. But in taking this position he ignores the sequence of events. What first happened was that the subject in a relaxation-induced state of calmness imagined an elevator-related scene. He was given no new information, yet the repeated imagining of elevator-related scenes led to the elimination of fear upon exposure to an elevator, both in imagination and in reality. Secondarily, there was a realization of the change the desensitization procedure had wrought. There is a very clear contrast between this and the removal of the fear by information in the case described above, where misinformation was appropriately replaced by truthful information to remove a fear.

THE CONTINUING EVOLUTION

Despite its inadequate conceptual foundation and low therapeutic efficacy, psychodynamic therapy has maintained a reputation during most of this century as the most fundamental and therefore the "best" treatment for anxiety disorders. It is only in the last few years that its status has shown signs of declining, and there has been some movement in the direction of its replacement by behavior therapy. In a few countries, most notably Spain and Germany, behavior therapy has come to dominate psychotherapeutic practice and to occupy center stage in the teaching of psychotherapy in departments of both psychiatry and psychology. Nothing like this has happened in the United States, which continues to be an impregnable bastion of psychodynamics. My personal impression of Los Angeles, where I have worked for the past six years, is that psychodynamics is the primary treatment of at least 90 percent of cases of anxiety disorders. The publication of data regarding the comparative superiority of behavior therapy has been effectively blocked. For example, a paper showing that about 80 percent of anxiety disorders are much improved by behavior therapy in between 5 and 31 sessions according to the syndrome (Wolpe, Craske, & Reyna, 1994) was, despite accommodating revisions, rejected by the *American Journal of Psychiatry* with the statement, "Although you have demonstrated the efficacy of behavior therapy, there was no need to do so at the cost of denigrating psychoanalysis." A revision of the paper, submitted to the *New England Journal of Medicine*, was again rejected by psychodynamically oriented reviewers on the flimsiest of grounds. And recently, a paper entitled "The Results of Behavior Therapy in Five Anxiety Disorder Syndromes," which we submitted for delivery at the 1996 American Psychiatric Convention and included data on more than 1000 cases, was turned down on the plea that selection is competitive. So there is an uphill struggle. But recently, for the first time ever, *The Psychiatric Newsletter* has made mention of behavior therapy in four consecutive issues. So, there is hope that evolution will continue.

REFERENCES

Beck, A. T. (1976). *Cognitive therapy and the emotional disorders.* New York: International Universities Press.

Ellis, A. (1962). *Reason and emotion in psychotherapy.* New York: Lyle Stuart.

Glover, E., (1956). *On the early development of the mind.* New York: International Universities Press.

Hamilton, D. M., & Wall, J. H. (1941). Hospital treatment of patients with psychosomatic disorders. *American Journal of Psychiatry,* 551. (1955).

Jones, E. (1955) *Sigmund Freud: Life and work.* London: Hogarth Press.

Jones, M.C. (1924). Elimination of children's fears. *Journal of Experimental Psychology, 7,* 382.

Kaplan,H. S., (1974). *The new sex therapy.* New York: Brunner/Mazel.

Kernberg, O., Burnstein, E., Coyle, L. et al. (1972). Psychotherapy and psychoanalysis: Final report of the Menninger Foundation Psychotherapy Research Project. *Bulletin of the Menninger Clinic, 36,* 89.

Knight, R. P. (1941). Evaluation of the results of psychoanalytic therapy. *American Journal of Psychiatry, 98,* 434.

Krasnogorski, N. I. (1925). The conditioned reflexes and children's neuroses. *American Journal of Disabled Children, 30,* 754.

Masserman, J. H. (1943). *Behavior and neuroses.* Chicago: University of Chicago Press.

Salter, A. (1949). *Conditioned reflex therapy.* New York: Creative Age.

Scharnberg, M. (1984). *The myth of paradigm shift.* Stockholm: Almquist & Wiksel International.

Shapiro, F. (1989). Eye movement desensitization: A new treatment for post-traumatic stress disorder. *Journal of Behavior Therapy and Experimental Psychiatry, 20,* 211.

Watson, J. B., & Rayner, P. (1920). Conditioned emotional reactions. *Journal of Experimental Psychology, 3,* 1.

Wolpe, J. (1952). Experimental neurosis as learned behavior. *British Journal of Psychology, 43,* 243.

Wolpe, J. (1954). Reciprocal inhibition as the main basis of psychotherapeutic effects. *Archives of Neurological Psychiatry, 118,* 35.

Wolpe, J. (1990). *The Practice of Behavior Therapy* (4th ed.). New York: Pergamon Press.

Wolpe, J., Craske, M.G., & Reyna, L. J. (1994). The comparative efficacy of behavior therapy and psychodynamic methods in the anxiety disorders. Unpublished manuscript.

Wolpe, J., & Rachman, S. (1960). *Journal of Nervous and Mental Diseases.* Psychoanalytic evidence: A critique based on Freud's case of Little Hans. 131, 135.

Discussion by Albert Ellis, Ph.D.

◆

Joseph Wolpe's paper makes some interesting and important points, several of which I strongly agree with and several of which, as I shall say below, I have distinct reservations about.

The first point Wolpe makes is that Freud and most of his followers have been inefficient clinicians and marvelous propagandists. As he notes, psychoanalysis has a poor record of effectiveness. I quite agree, because, unlike Wolpe, I was trained as an analyst, practiced classical psychoanalysis and psychoanalytically oriented therapy from 1947 to 1953, and then stopped doing so when I discovered that practically all analytic methods are woefully inefficient.

As I often humorously say, Freud had several important genes for *in*efficiency and mostly attracted followers who were similarly prone to arrant overgeneralization and highly unscientific thinking. I, on the other hand, hopefully have some genes for efficiency and therefore became allergic to psychoanalysis in 1953. I then began experimenting with nonanalytic methods, including both philosophical and behavioral modes. As a result of this experimentation with scores of my clients, during 1953 and 1954 as well as the many other therapeutic methods I researched during this period, I originated the first of the major cognitive-behavior therapies—Rational Emotive Behavior Therapy—in January 1955.

As Wolpe correctly indicates, most forms of behavior therapy are sometimes highly cognitive in that they show anxious clients that they sometimes have misperceptions about supposed dangers. What he fails to note is that anxious people have other important thinking processes that strongly contribute to their neuroses. Therefore, therapy that is behavioral *and* cognitive invariably considers these cognitive processes, too. Consequently, cognitive-behavior therapy, I believe, is *more* effective with *more* anxious clients than the relatively limited aspects of cognitive therapy that Wolpe and his main followers use.

Let me stop for a moment to shoot down one statement in Wolpe's paper that states that "people like Ellis and Beck have a rooted belief that *all* fears are cognitively based." No. Speaking for myself, I believe that some states of anxiety are mainly physiologically or neurologically based; and that some very anxious people are born as well as reared to be anxiety-prone. Therefore, I have for many years recommended medication, biofeedback, relaxation methods, physical exercise, a dietary regimen, and other kinds of physically oriented methods for such individuals—and also, at times, for anxious individuals who have a large cognitive aspect to their affliction. As we realize more and more these days, the mind–body connection goes both ways: crooked thinking often leads to psychosomatic ailments. But unsound bodies also frequently help lead to disordered minds. It's not either/or but both/and.

The main point that I want to make is that Wolpe, like many behaviorists, uses the term *conditioning* too lightly and loosely, and assumes that anxious people are mainly conditioned by their traumatic experiences in a dangerous, hostile, or noxious environment. This is of course partly true. But Wolpe seems to forget that what we call conditioning includes a number of crucial cognitive elements.

Let us, for example, take a case of a strong conditioned fear of humiliation. Wolpe rightly says that this disorder can be deconditioned by having anxious people "intentionally give wrong answers to simple arithmetic problems." Wolpe may not realize it but this is the technique that I invented in the 1960s and that I call a "shame-attacking exercise" (Ellis, 1969, 1971). If Wolpe independently invented it too, that is fine.

It is important to understand that the people who are conditioned to greatly fear being soundly criticized for their mistakes in simple arithmetical problems have several important cognitions included in such so-called conditioning. Thus, they *listen* to people's criticisms and *make themselves* feel ashamed when they experience them. They *discriminate* between certain kinds of criticism that are harmful—such as mean and vicious criticism—and other kinds that are benign—such as well-intentioned humorous criticism. They *decide* that harsh criticism really *is* shameful and humiliating. By their learning and their decision processes, they bring on healthy feelings of frustration and unhealthy feelings of anxiety and shame when they are strongly criticized—and even when they *imagine* that they will be chastised.

Once these "conditioned" anxious people actually get criticized and feel humiliated, they *remember* their previous feeling of humiliation. They often *interpret* and *define* it as awful and horrible—instead of defining it as merely somewhat uncomfortable—and they thereby often *make it* even more fearful and humiliating than they first felt it to be.

In addition, these "conditioned" individuals often *generalize* and *overgeneralize* to other humiliating conditions. Thus, if they once failed at, say, talking to a teacher, being laughed at for failing an arithmetic problem, and then feeling very humiliated, they may then later develop a phobia about making a mistake of almost *any* kind in front of almost *any* person. No matter what the initial stimulus is that leads to anxieties and phobias, these disor-

ders are largely kept alive by one of our most cognitive processes—*overgeneralizing*.

As you can see from some of the words I have just stressed, what we call being conditioned to feel humiliated about arithmetic failures involves a good number of cognitive formulations. And so does the process of deconditioning.

Thus, when Wolpe uses behavior therapy to help people who are very anxious and humiliated about making arithmetical mistakes he often persuades them to use several cognitive procedures. For example (a) *Listen* to his behaviorist explanations of their phobia. (b) *Accept* his explanations. (c) *Follow* his therapy instructions. (d) Make themselves *intentionally* give wrong answers to simple arithmetic problems. (e) *See* that they can carry out Wolpe's instructions in spite of their anxiety. (f) *Observe* that as they force themselves to make mistakes they can also discover some of the *correct* answers to the arithmetic problems they are working on. (g) *Note* that even when they are laughed at for giving wrong answers, nothing terrible *really* happens and the world hardly comes to an end. (h) *Realize* that their feelings of anxiety and shame are *only* uncomfortable and are hardly deadly. (i) *Conclude* that if they can cope with this anxiety-provoking situation, they can most probably *also* cope with other horribly fearful situations. (j) *Congratulate* themselves about dealing so nicely with the difficult homework assignment that Wolpe has given them and *evaluate themselves* as being highly efficacious. (k) Favorably rate their entire self or personhood as being good or outstanding because of their conquering their phobia.

Isn't it fascinating how this simple behavioral disorder—severe anxiety—that Wolpe has presented to us really includes a large number of cognitive processes? And isn't it remarkable that his main behavioral solution to this anxiety disorder—that is, his use of a shame-attacking in vivo homework exercise—also involves many important cognitive processes? Isn't it interesting that he ignores *almost all* the cognitive processes involved in vague terms like conditioning and deconditioning?

My time is running out. So let me repeat that all the behavioral techniques for reducing anxiety disorders that Wolpe mentions include important cognitive elements. In Rational Emotive Behavior Therapy (REBT) with severely anxious people we use all the methods that he mentions—especially in vivo desensitization or exposure. But we also use a large number of cognitive-emotive methods that add to our behavioral orientation. So we get at the cognitive distortions and irrational beliefs that are *also* a significant part of the so-called conditioning and deconditioning process. Wolpe and the behavior therapists are, I think, definitely on the right track. But they would probably be more comprehensive theorists and therapists if they added a number of cognitive and emotive techniques to their behavioral procedures.

REFERENCES

Ellis, A. (1969). A weekend of rational encounter. *Rational Living*, 4(2), 1–8.
Ellis, A. (Speaker). (1971). *How to stubbornly refuse to be ashamed of anything*. Cassette recording. New York: Institute for Rational-Emotive Therapy.

Response by Joseph Wolpe and Dr. Ellis' Retorts

◆

I am very pleased with Albert Ellis' change of heart. Recently, he has started calling himself a rational-emotive behavior therapist, which seems to mean that he is at last recognizing that conditioning processes are involved in some psychotherapy, which he has today confirmed.

But I want to contest his suggestion that behavior therapy neglects certain aspects of people, so that they are left incompletely treated. The fact is that a behavior therapist will routinely survey the total range of sources of maladapted anxiety, whether the anxiety has been conditioned by tragic experience or based on misinformation, and the therapist will treat each anxiety. Also his life and background will be broadly screened. The patient will usually be very well served if he gets a good behavior therapist.

There is an important point that Al Ellis made about cognitive events in therapy. Yes, cognition enters into everything that we do. When we have a conversation, there is cognition on both sides. When Al Ellis and I are talking to you now, we are thinking and you are thinking, and all this is cognitive. When I am telling a person to assert himself in certain situations, I am using his intellect, and he is taking in what I say, cognitively, and will later be using his judgment in carrying out assertive action.

The real point in the dispute relates to the locus of therapy. I am saying that there is a class of anxiety disorders that is classically conditioned. In these, the fear is aroused immediately and automatically by a stimulus—for example, a bloodstained bandage in a doctor's office—without there being any thought of danger. Then you have to use conditioning methods to overcome the fear. The treatment weakens the conditioned fear response. It does not act by providing new information. But after the deconditioning has removed the fear, the person no longer sees himself as feeling fear.

My final point is this: Ellis says that his form of cognitive therapy is more effective—has better results—than behavior therapy. I would be very interested to know where these results have been published. There was, however, a study about two years ago done at Hofstra University that surveyed rational emotive therapy outcomes, both those in print and those in student theses, and found that it did not do very well. It certainly did not do as well as behavior therapy is shown to do in published articles. I don't think that Al Ellis should say that his therapy does better unless he can document it with data.

ELLIS: Let me just add briefly to the points that Joe Wolpe just made.

First, every behavior therapist explores cognitive modalities. They now do so because practically every effective behavior therapist today is a cognitive-behavior therapist. Practically every single one of them has come over to the fold.

Yes, I now call our method Rational-Emotive *Behavior* Therapy. This was not done because the therapy changed, because I always used behavioral methods right from the start, perhaps more than Aaron Beck—probably more than Joe Wolpe. Joe Wolpe's main thing is systematic *imaginal* desensitization. But we have advocated *in vivo* desensitization in REBT since 1960 or so. And my Shame Attacking Exercise, which he mentioned in his original paper, is *in vivo*. Ray Corsini has been after me for about twenty years to change the name from RET to REBT, and I finally acknowledged that he was right so I changed the name.

But it always was Rational-Emotive *Behavior* Therapy.

Then Joe Wolpe says, "Are there examples or studies where cognitive-behavior therapy excels?" The article that he published in his journal was a biased article that covered only a few of the studies of Rational-Emotive Behavior Therapy, and every other journal refused it because they could see that it was obviously biased. We have hundreds of other studies. Aaron Beck, who is more cognitive and less behavioral than we are in REBT, has a thousand studies that show that cognitive therapy is quite effective.

Now, whether or not REBT is more effective than behavior therapy without the use of cognition is still in doubt. I personally think it definitely is, but that's just an opinion. One of these days I hope that the research will show that cognitive-behavior therapy or Rational-Emotive Behavior Therapy is more effective than pure cognitive therapy without behavioral methods and more effective than pure behavioral therapy with very few cognitive techniques added to it.

SECTION III

Contemporary Approaches

Teaching and Learning Reality Therapy

◆

William Glasser, M.D.

William Glasser, M.D.
William Glasser received his M.D. degree in 1953 from Case Western Reserve Medical School. He has worked in every aspect of psychiatry with emphasis on the use of his ideas in public education, drug abuse, physical trauma and corrections. He has published 13 books, including Reality Therapy, Control Theory, Control Theory in the Practice of Reality Therapy, *and* Staying Together.

INTRODUCTION

Reality Therapy is completely based on control theory psychology. This psychology explains that: (a) We all are driven by five genetic needs—survival, love, power, freedom, and fun; (b) All significant behavior is an attempt to satisfy our quality world, a world based on these needs that we continually create and build into our memory; (c) All we do from birth to death is behave; (d) All behavior discussed in therapy is chosen; (e) All behavior is total behavior and is made up of four closely related components—acting, thinking, feeling, and physiology; (f) Problems may originate in the past but they all occur in the present and must be either solved in the present or through a plan for the future; (g) When problems are solved, it is because clients are taught to make better thinking and acting choices than they were making when they began therapy; and (h) An attempt is made to teach clients control theory so that they can apply it in their lives, and in doing so avoid the kinds of problems that brought them into therapy.

ABOUT REALITY THERAPY

Reality therapy, like most psychotherapies, is a conversation between the therapist and the client or clients. Clients judge the therapy to be effective when they both feel and function better. If someone who knows the client well confirms that judgment, it is likely that therapy has been effective. A skilled reality therapist should be able to help any client *who wants help* toward significant improvement in 12 sessions. Clients who are forced into counseling may take longer.

To teach reality therapy, the teacher must demonstrate his or her skills with a real or simulated client. To attempt to teach without demonstrating is like inviting Isaac Stern to explain how he plays the violin but never asking him to play. It is impossible to teach counseling by writing or explaining. Students must see the teacher in action, role playing both as client and as therapist, and they must discuss what they saw and what they did with the teacher.

Real clients can be used but role plays are by far the best because they are more exciting and more techniques can be safely shown. Role players, who should be working with the clients they are playing, usually play tough, interesting clients. Too many real clients are boring to watch because so little happens or it happens so slowly. Also, with a real client you can only go as fast as the client is willing to go. With a role player you can go faster; it can't hurt the role player. When I role play, I feel free to show many more techniques than usually is possible with a real client.

The one advantage to using real clients is that they almost always want help. In contrast, some role players try to play "stump the expert" games but this is far from bad. It gives the expert a chance to show his or her expertise and, personally, I like it. The role player knows that he or she is being watched and often gets quite theatrical (as do many real clients), which takes nothing away and enhances the pleasure of this excellent teaching technique. To teach reality therapy, in the beginning it is best if the role play starts with the first counseling session because then the role is not influenced by what someone else has done. Later it does not make any difference.

Even though role playing is necessary to learn the technique of reality therapy, there are some basics that can be explained. In this short chapter, however, it is impossible to do justice to the complex ideas of control theory. The first book on this theory was written by William Powers (1973), and I did not understand it when I first read it. Powers invited me to Chicago, in 1977, and he explained it to me himself. What Powers (who is not a psychotherapist) taught me was highly theoretical and not usable in counseling. What I have done is to expand and clarify these ideas so that they can be easily understood and used by most people in both their personal lives and in their work as counselors. For an explanation of what I have done, I strongly suggest that you start by reading my 1984 book, *Control Theory*. To use the theory in counseling, I suggest that you read *Control Theory in the Practice of Reality Therapy* (N. Glasser, 1988) as well as my most recent book, *Staying Together* (1995). This book updates the theory significantly and explains how we can all apply it in our own marriages, and as counselors use it with people with relationship problems.

Using my knowledge of control theory, I can usually figure out a great deal of what's going on in the client's mind, and knowing this I often know what to do minute by minute as the therapy proceeds. To confirm these impressions, of course, I check them out with the client, but I am continually surprised at how accurate they are.

When I see patients I use mostly standard English with very little jargon, but I do describe behavior as it should be described through the use of verbs, as I will shortly explain. I do not require that clients know anything about what I teach before they begin, but if they have read one or more of my books so much the better. Once they come for therapy, I attempt to teach them the control theory I use so they can use it for the rest of their lives and so avoid the problems that brought them into therapy. I also try to inject as much humor into the sessions as I can, no matter how upset clients are when they present themselves. What we do is not funeral counseling, and so the lighter the better. If the session gets too heavy, clients tend to think they are in worse shape than they actually are, or they take themselves more seriously than is good for anyone.

If the client starts by asking me if I can help him or her, I always say yes, as long as it is apparent that the client wants help and is willing to converse. When I asked my great teacher, G.L. Harrington, "What does the client need to do in therapy?" he answered, "All the client has to do is be there, all the rest you have to do." In the cases where the client is forced to see me and does not want help, I don't promise help until it is clear that he or she wants it. In cases when clients did not show up, I have gone to their houses to see them there. This did not happen often but it did happen on four or five occasions. Every time, the person came to my office regularly after that home call.

By this time, I think you can see that reality therapy is an active ongoing process where the counselor will do anything within reason to help the client. I have helped people get lodging, buy cars, look for jobs, and get into grad schools if these things were judged to be related to the client gaining more effective control of his or her life, which is the goal of reality therapy. I am always willing to see other members of the family if they want to see me, but I never do so without the client's permission.

To explain what I do, I will use a straightforward case in which the client, a man in his early thirties, saw me for about four months regularly once a week and then, by his choice—I told him it was unnecessary—four or five times during the next year. We had gotten close and it was hard for him to break off abruptly when it became obvious he was functioning well enough to no longer need me. After that follow-up year there was no problem breaking off.

I will call him Jim; he called me Doctor. I don't mind if if a client calls me Bill but most call me Doctor or Doc. What we call each other is not important in reality therapy—it is whatever both of us seem comfortable with, because my purpose is to create a warm, comfortable, supportive environment. To do this, I try to make friends with my clients. Like other faculty at this conference, Stella Chess for example, I do not believe in transference. To help the client I must be a real person, and I do all I can to convince him or her, as quickly as possible, to enjoy talking to the real person I am.

Jim called me to make the first appointment and I did not ask any questions on the phone. I don't want to find out anything that would lead me to prejudge a case. If clients wants to describe the problem I will listen, but I try to shorten the phone conversation by telling them to come in, we'll talk then. I usually see clients for an hour, sometimes a little

more or less, and if it seems necessary I will run over. I tell the next client that I needed more time and I would do the same for her if it were warranted. I'm not a machine; I vary according to what I perceive my clients need, and this assures them that I am a caring person, not a clock watcher. I also will give them extra sessions when they need them, and if money is short we work it out. I always discuss money and work out a fee that is acceptable, and I have never had money problems. (As reality therapy was not popular in West Los Angeles in 1956 when I started out I had to be effective, because my only clients were the few who came to me from the UCLA clinic. I was willing to see them for the clinic rate, which was as low as five dollars a session. Referrals from these first seven clients led to a good practice, which got larger in 1965 when my book, *Reality Therapy*, was published. My advice to therapists who are starting out is to depend on satisfied clients (or in today's climate satisfied third parties) for referrals.)

Jim didn't say much on the phone except that he had to see me as soon as possible. He came in the next day. I blocked out some extra time because he sounded like he might need it, but he didn't. We were able to get a good start in that first hour. To begin, I always look my clients over carefully and try, based on control theory, to guess why they are there even before they tell me. It isn't necessary but it is a game I like to play with myself and it keeps me alert.

I know from control theory that he, like all clients, is struggling with how to satisfy one or more of his *basic needs* and in his case I guessed correctly that it was his need for love. I also guessed, again correctly, that the problem was his wife. It had to be someone from his *quality world*, and it was most likely that this would be his wife. I based these guesses on the fact that he was very well dressed and looked as if he had a good job, so it was not a work problem, a common problem with young men. The tone of his voice, too, from what I had learned from my long experience listening to clients, seemed to indicate a personal problem.

I know from control theory that all we do from birth to death is *behave*, that all behaviors are total behaviors, and *that any behavior that clients talk about in therapy is chosen.* Jim looked to me as if he was choosing the total behavior of "depressing." And he confirmed my observation by telling me almost before he sat down that he was very, very depressed. Unless you are a control theorist, and Jim certainly was not, he would call what he was feeling "depressed" (an adjective) or tell me he was suffering from "depression" (a noun). But because he is choosing this behavior, all reality therapists use the grammatically correct infinitive or gerund to describe this and all behavior.

Because the behavior is chosen, I knew my task was to help him to make a better choice. To do this, first, I would try to help him understand that he was making a choice, and, second, that he had to make better choices than to choose to continue to depress (or any other psychological suffering). Some people misconstrue what I am saying to mean that we choose what happens to us. This, of course, we cannot do. What we almost always choose are all the ways we behave to deal with whatever happens to us. This follows the control theory axiom: The only person's behavior we can control is our own.

Why some people choose behaviors such as homosexuality that are statistically deviant is not yet known. I make no claim that control theory can explain all the reasons why we choose what we do. I do, however, claim that there are usually enough behavioral choices that can be learned in therapy so I can usually can help clients deal better with their problem even if it is not clear why they are choosing it. If, for example, a homosexual person came to me for help, I would not claim that I could help him choose to become heterosexual or nonsexual. I would, however, tell him that given that choice, a choice that no one yet understands, it is very likely I could help him to make better choices—for example, safer sex—than he might be making now to deal with this situation.

To begin a reality therapy session, after the client tells me how he feels—which is how most clients start—I always say one of two things. I say either "Tell me the story" or "What's happening?" I don't ask "What's the problem?" or ever refer to any problem, and I never mention other people or talk about other people unless the client does. If the client starts to talk before I say anything, I listen and only interrupt to get him focused on what is going on now in his life, because I always work in the present. The reason I avoid mentioning the problem is because there is something about the word "problem" that implies that someone else—mother, father, husband, wife, child or boss—may be responsible for what clients are choosing to do with their lives. Because this is never the case, I never want to imply that it may be the case.

The basis of reality therapy was, and still is, that we are all responsible for what we choose to do no matter what has happened in our lives. My whole approach to counseling is that the only person who can do anything about any problem he or she brings into the office is the person sitting opposite me. So I don't want that person to even begin to think that I believe someone else has to do something to solve this problem because this may never happen.

Control theory is called control theory (a more accurate name would be self-control theory but I didn't name it) because it is the theory of how we attempt to control our own behavior at all times. If Jim was choosing to depress, only he could make a better choice. From the start, I know that there are only two aspects of our behavior we can control and counseling focuses completely on these: (a) what we choose to put into our quality world and (b) what behaviors we choose. I asked Jim to tell me what he wanted right now, which I knew was in his quality world, and and if what he was choosing to do had a good chance of getting him what he wanted. If not, he would have to change his behavior. If it turns out, as it did in this case, that he could not get what he wanted, then I help him to want something else that might satisfy the same need. This is what happened in this case. It was obvious that he could not change his wife, and if he wanted love and marriage, which he did, he would have to find someone else.

Because he did not know control theory, Jim, like almost everyone, was following the "commonsense" psychology of the world, stimulus-response psychology. Because of his belief in this theory, it has been my experience that he would tell me that his "depression" was caused by the behavior of someone else, and that person or people had to change. My job was to help him to learn that to get what he wanted, he, not someone else, had to change, and in fact the only person over whom he had control was himself. This is almost always a complete surprise to most clients, so I must not confront them immediately. I must work slowly and carefully to lead them to this new knowledge.

To help accomplish this, I taught him a new control theory definition of behavior called total behavior. Through the use of this behavioral concept, he would learn what parts of his total behavior he could choose and what parts he could not. Total behavior explains that all behavior is made up of four components— acting, thinking, feeling, and physiology. Two of these components, acting and thinking, are voluntary. The other two, feeling and physiology, are not. When I say "All behavior is chosen," I now have to change this to "All total behavior is chosen." Also, as stated, when I talk or write about total behavior I will always use verbs to describe it. I will say choosing *to depress* (an infinitive) or *depressing* (a gerund).

So when I say that Jim was choosing to depress, I mean that he was choosing the acting and thinking parts of that total behavior. He was not choosing the depressing feelings or the physiology. Those feelings are what must accompany the particular acting and thinking that are the voluntary components of the total behavior of depressing. Total behaviors, however, are usually labeled by the component that is most obvious. Some are labeled by the acting component, as when I walk; some by the thinking component, as when I see you playing chess and say that you are deep in thought. Many are described by the feeling component, as when I say I am depressing, anxieting or guilting; and some by the physiologic component, as when I see you throwing up and say you are puking.

In therapy, I focus almost completely on actions and thoughts because these are all Jim—or any client—can change. As much as he may have wanted to talk about the miserable feelings that must accompany the voluntary actions and thoughts of the total behavior of depressing, I tried to get him to focus now on what he could change. He could only change how he felt and/or on his physiology indirectly by choosing a different thought and/or action. For example, we cannot choose to perspire (physiology) unless we choose to exercise or to sit in a very hot room. And we cannot choose joy if a wife we love leaves us. However, we can choose the total behavior of depressing; in fact, most of us would make this choice in this situation.

In the same sense, we cannot choose to depress when we look at our dirty, messy house unless at the same time we very much want the house to be clean. To stop depressing, we must make a successful effort to clean it up or to get someone else to clean it up, or we must stop wanting it to be clean. As long as all we do is look at it (our chosen action) and wish it were clean (our chosen thought), it is almost certain that we will continue to choose the feeling of depressing. And as we do nothing about cleaning it up, our serotonin level also will tend to drop (part of the complicated physiology that is always an involuntary component of this common total behavior). Depressing, therefore, is the feeling component of the total behavior of looking at a messy house and doing nothing when we want so much for it to be clean.

So I listened to Jim for a while as he talked about what he was feeling and maybe what his wife had "done to him" that he doesn't like. But as soon as I judged it was time to make a move, which might have been within minutes after he had come to see me for the first time, I focused and continued to focus by asking both "What do you want?" and "What are you choosing to do to get what you want?" Doing is a good word to describe the combination of acting and thinking that we use to get what we want, which is always in our quality world.

As I said, he soon confirmed my initial impression by telling me that his wife of four years had abruptly left him. He had come home from work to a very brief note from her —"So long"—and found that her things had been cleaned out of their apartment during the day. He also confirmed that she was in his quality world by telling me that he loved her, he *wanted* her back and he was (to use his term) very "depressed" since she left.

This had all happened about a week before the appointment, and since that time he had been so "depressed" that he had not even gone to work. He had been sitting home alone all week. Some concerned friends had come from work, one told him to call me, and here he was. We talked a little bit about his marriage and I asked him why his wife left. Jim had a hard time telling me this but I persisted, and he admitted that he had been, in her words, too domineering. She had been threatening to leave for the past six months.

Jim said that he did not realize that she was this dissatisfied and he was surprised when she left. She had always followed his lead and most of the time it worked out well "for him" and he "thought" for her. I asked him what he wanted now and he said for her to come back, that he would be less domineering if she would return. I asked him what he was doing to get her back and he said, "Nothing really." He had just been sitting home for a week, miserable, and he didn't know what to do. He had thought of finding her and trying to get her to come back but he didn't know how to do it without an argument that he knew would make things worse. I was pleased he had that much understanding. We talked a little more about what he had done that she was not satisfied with and he told me some more details. However, he kept telling me how much he loved her and how much he wanted her back, and he asked again if I could help him.

I then asked him the key reality therapy question, "Since she left you have chosen to sit home and not go to work" (I didn't mention his feelings, only his thoughts and actions), "Could you do anything better?" As I expected, he immediately jumped on the word "chosen," and said that he had not chosen to sit home, he sat home because he was too upset to go out. This is a good example of what most people believe: *that they are not responsible for what they feel, and that because of these feelings (for which are not responsible), they cannot act or think differently.*

My job was to teach Jim that he did have some indirect control over his feelings through choosing to act and think differently. No matter how badly he felt, he could always choose to act and think differently, as he had done when he chose to come here and see me that day. He continued to protest my use of the word "chosen" by saying, "Doctor, I was so upset, what else could I do?" My answer was, "That's what you are here to learn. If you can't learn to act and think differently, you may be unhappy [I did not use the word depressed] the rest of your life." There was a long pause while this sank in. He continued to protest but it was with less conviction. Then he agreed that indeed he had chosen to sit home but he did not know what else to do.

I told him that this was what he had to work out, to find a better choice of acting and thinking than to continue to sit home. I told him that I had frequently worked with people who were doing what he was doing and I had a suggestion. (My practice, when I know what might work, is to make a suggestion.) I told him that he might write his wife a letter and tell her that he saw the error of his ways and that he loved her. He could ask if she would give him another chance. And because he was getting help, he could ask if she would come in and work with him to try to solve the problem.

Jim thought that this was a good suggestion. He went home and wrote a very loving letter, and as I suggested he brought it for me to read. I did not want him to send a pushy letter and I did not know how blind he might be to his pushy self. The letter was good. I told him to give it to his wife's mother, she'd get it to his wife. He had told me that her mother liked him. Before he left, for the first time I mentioned feelings by asking him, "How do you feel now?" As I expected—it was obvious—he said that he felt better. I asked him why and he said, "I think this letter may present a side of me that she wants to find out about. She may reconsider her decision to leave."

I used this opportunity to point out that when he wrote the letter he had direct control over his actions and thoughts and when he did choose to write the letter he felt better. We again talked about the fact that his feelings, good or bad, were directly related to what he was doing or planning to do, actions and thoughts that might or might not get him what he wanted. For reality therapy to be successful, this is a lesson we believe our clients have to learn. The reality therapist's job is to teach it as soon as he or she can. We talk very little about feelings because we know there is no direct way to change them. We focus on what all clients can change, which is their acting and thinking. It takes time, but our clients almost always learn that they only have control over what they feel indirectly through changing what they do. This follows the old geometry corollary: If you change a part you change the whole. The behavioral parts we have control over are our actions and thoughts.

You may be asking yourself why so many of us choose the total behavior of depressing when we are frustrated as Jim was. As I explain in great detail in the book *Control Theory*, there are three logical reasons why most of us choose to depress when the world, as we perceive it, is far different from what we want, which is on our quality world. The reasons are as follows:

1. When we are frustrated, we have to have a quick, sure way to restrain the anger. If the anger were not restrained, we might do something destructive. For instance, Jim could have found his wife and hurt or killed her. Impulsive anger and destructive behavior is the choice of some frustrated men. Women also choose to anger but do so much less than men. Depressing for a while when we are severely frustrated is a necessary behavior until we figure something better to do. Without it, societies break down. We see some evidence of this breakdown in parts of our big cities now.

2. Depressing is a powerful way to ask for help. When we choose to depress—and depressing is the most common of all the miserable behaviors we choose—friends and family members pay attention to our problem and tend to offer help. And it is also a way to justify seeking help from strangers such as counselors. If he weren't depressing, what reason would Jim have to see me? Also, painful as this choice is, it is a way to ask for help that avoids begging. For most of us begging is more painful than depressing because it is directly frustrating to our need for power, which I will explain shortly.

3. We choose to depress to serve as an excuse so that we can avoid doing something we know we should do but we do not want to do or are afraid to do. For example, suppose you've just lost a good job and I come over and ask, "Why are you so upset?" You tell me you've just been laid off. It wasn't your fault; the company was downsizing. I tell you not to sit around but to get going: Get out your resumés and look for work. But it's easy for me to say. You're afraid that there are no good jobs locally and you don't want to move. So you tell me, "That's a good idea, I'll look next week. I'm just too depressed to start this week." And I understand, I have done this myself when I was afraid. You're afraid to look because you fear, and rightly so in many cases, that you will be rejected. But it's too painful even to face that possibility so you say, truthfully, "I'm too upset to look right now," which is socially acceptable. It takes you off the hook for a while.

About a week later, Jim's wife came in and he presented a good case for her to give him another chance. But she didn't buy it. She said that she owed him this much but his argument did not impress her. She said that she was going to leave for good, and she left. This was a dramatic moment and Jim began to choose to depress again strongly. He told me that he couldn't live without his wife. In my judgment he wasn't suicidal, so I used the all-purpose statement taught to me by Dr. Harrington: "What's your plan?" When you are stuck for something to say to a client, this short phrase is most useful.

Jim said, "What do you mean?" And I said, "For example, do you plan to kill yourself?" If I had the slightest fear that he was actually suicidal I would not have said this, but it did serve to lighten the mood. He laughed and said, "No." But again he told me how upset he was. I told him that he could choose to depress as long he wished, but unless he did something more to get what he wanted or chose to want something else he might have a better chance of getting, he would continue to choose to depress. By this time I had taught him enough about total behavior so that he knew he was choosing all his actions and thoughts. He knew, too, that he was continuing to choose to want his wife. I said that I didn't think that she was coming back and he agreed. I told him that if a loving relationship was what he wanted, he would have to choose to find someone else. It took a while but he agreed.

Jim started to look for someone else, and we talked extensively about the fact that he needed to treat the new woman better than he had treated his wife. I was sure that he would find someone, and in a little while he did. He treated her well, they took awhile to make sure, and then they got married. Things were still going well when I lost track of him.

This is a good example of reality therapy and its use of control theory that guides all my counseling. Almost 5000 people all over the world have taken the basic training that is offered by the Institute.* The training is centered on learning the theory through discussion and practice by doing role plays as both the counselor and the client, watching the teacher do them, and then discussing what was done.

I believe that all reality therapy is basically what I have described here no matter what the client's problem. What varies are the techniques you will learn for the rest of your life as you grow more skilled.

REFERENCES

Glasser, N. (1988). *Control Theory in the practice of reality therapy.* New York: HarperCollins.

Glasser, W. (1965). *Reality therapy.* New York: HarperCollins.

Glasser, W. (1984). *Control theory.* New York: HarperCollins.

Glasser, W. (1995). *Staying together.* New York: HarperCollins.

Powers, W. (1973). *Behavior in the control of perception.* Chicago: Aldine Press.

---

*The Institute for Control Theory, Reality Therapy and Quality Management, 22024 Lassen Street, Chatsworth, California 91311. Phone (818) 700-8000, fax (818) 700-0555.

Discussion by Arnold A. Lazarus, Ph.D.

◆

REALITIES AND SOME FANTASIES: A RESPONSE TO DR. GLASSER

Let's begin with the good news.

Many facets of Dr. William Glasser's accounts of reality therapy have always struck me as extremely similar to behavior therapy. He emphasizes that behavior is important in its own right and challenges the value of dwelling on putative complexes and intrapsychic phenomena. The perspectives of learning and teaching as therapeutic mainstays are also in keeping with basic behavioral formulations. Although reality therapy is not as systematic, as data-driven, or as precise as behavior therapy, both approaches are action-oriented and pragmatic, both tend to focus on the here-and-now, and both examine the consequences of behavior instead of dwelling on antecedent or historical events.

I applaud Dr. Glasser's approach to clients—his flexibility, the fact that he is not a clock watcher but may allow sessions to exceed 60 minutes when necessary, his willingness to make home visits on occasion, his avoidance of jargon in favor of standard English, his openness to doing "anything within reason to help the client," and the fact that his approach is fundamentally solution-oriented. Nevertheless, although Dr. Glasser has some excellent ideas, reality therapy and control theory are not the be all and end all, as one might imagine when reading his materials or listening to him talk.

In Las Vegas at the Evolution of Psychotherapy Conference I presented a critique of Dr. Glasser's invited address based on the initial draft of his talk. Subsequently, heeding some of my criticisms, he revised his manuscript. Nevertheless, his second draft still has several of the same matters that concerned me originally.

Here is Dr. Glasser speaking. "Reality therapy, like most psychotherapies, is a *conversation* between the therapist and a client or clients" (italics added). There have been trenchant criticisms of what Peterson (1995) called "conversational counseling" (see Dawes, 1994). As Peterson expressed it, "The modal therapeutic transaction has one person, socially defined as a 'therapist,' talking with another person, socially defined as a 'client,' about the client's psychosocial condition, with the primary aim of relieving the client's distress. In this situation, it is not surprising to find that anybody who has a good brain, a kind heart, and the psychological knowledge that has become part of the popular culture and who is, if nothing else, someone other than the client and presumably an expert, can help most people feel better about themselves" (p. 976). A viable science of psychotherapy needs more than "conversation" and often demands specific techniques that have empirical backing. Also needed are treatment outcomes that supply precise specifications beyond a vague allusion to something called "helpfulness." In terms of general helpfulness, trained and untrained therapists fare equally well, and professionals are no more effective than paraprofessionals (Berman & Norton, 1985; Lambert, Shapiro & Bergin, 1986).

Thus, Dr. Glasser asserts that he is "able to help any client *who wants* help toward significant improvement in twelve sessions" (italics in original). Herein lies a major problem with

Dr. Glasser and Reality Therapy—this use of ambiguous statements in place of lucid and precise referents. What does he mean by help? The need for operational definitions in our field has been emphasized for many years. Without them we may think that we are communicating, but in truth we merely get lost in verbiage. I assume that if a client at the end of a session says "I feel much better now," this may be construed as his or her having been helped. As already stated, in this sense, virtually anyone can be helpful some of the time, but when we are talking in terms of viable therapeutic outcome criteria, vague allusions to generalized helpfulness are entirely insufficient. For instance, just how helpful in twelve sessions (or in dozens of sessions) will Glasser's reality therapy be with clients diagnosed with borderline personality disorders, obsessive-compulsive disorders, or those suffering from extreme post-traumatic stress disorders? The simple case of unipolar depression he elected to present seemed rather prosaic.

One of my main concerns is that Dr. Glasser makes a significant observation and then magnifies it into what I regard as a counterproductive overgeneralization. I am referring to the way he embroiders the fact that in many instances we exercise choice. Everyone from the Greek philosopher Epictetus in the second century A.D., to William Shakespeare, Alfred Adler, and especially Albert Ellis has underscored that events do not upset us as much as the fact that we tend to upset ourselves over them. Thus, there is evidence that we may allow ourselves to feel a certain way, and rather than construing ourselves as entirely governed by our moods and feelings, it is often crucial to realize that we frequently orchestrate our emotional reactions, be they anxiety, depression, guilt, anger or elation. To assert, however, as Glasser does, that we *always* choose our feelings, overlooks many factors, not the least of which is that organic processes including neoplastic, infectious, and metabolic afflictions may be primary causes of depression and/or anxiety. The overstated claim that anyone who is depressed is "choosing to depress" or is "depressing" him or herself, makes a *reductio ad absurdum* out of an important reality. As for Dr. Glasser's statement that "some people choose behaviors such as homosexuality," I find this utterly preposterous.

There seems to be an inherent contradiction in Dr. Glasser's formulation. He states that "all behavior is made up of four components, acting, thinking, feeling, and physiology" and goes on to say that acting and thinking are voluntary, but that feeling and physiology are not. Leaving aside the fact that much of the disordered thinking in schizophrenia and other psychotic disorders is anything but voluntary, if feeling and physiology are involuntary, one might inquire how Dr. Glasser can claim that any feeling of depression is voluntarily chosen—that the person is "choosing to depress." Dr. Glasser's answer is that we choose "the acting and thinking parts of that total behavior." But how does that account for the fundamental underlying feelings? Certainly, we know from cognitive-behavior therapy studies that changes in thought and/or action often can modify untoward feelings or emotions, but that does not prove Dr. Glasser's thesis that the dysphoric moods are *chosen*.

I am not disagreeing that we are often responsible for what we think and do and that, in turn, affects what we feel. The aphorism "As you think and act so shall you feel" is nothing new and did not originate with Dr. Glasser or what he calls control theory, but it is only part of the story, particularly when physiological factors are heavily involved. In Dr. Glasser's insistence on the use of infinitives and gerunds, there appears to be an element of *blaming the victim*— "you are choosing to depress; you are not anxious but are 'anxieting.' " I think that what Dr. Glasser is really trying to emphasize is that we are not helpless victims of circumstance, and that our lives are not basically controlled by outside forces (Lazarus & Fay, 1992). He seems to be saying that the manner in which we react to our feelings, the way in which we behave when we feel depressed, anxious, or angry will strengthen or weaken untoward emotions. As Zilbergeld and I have underscored, "Most of us assume there's not much that can be done about the mind. If it shows us lots of depressing pictures, we go around feeling depressed. . . . It doesn't occur to us that we can change the images and

thoughts. It seems natural to accept what our minds provide. 'That's just the way I am,' we say. We don't understand that it has nothing to do with what's natural. It has to do only with who's in charge" (Zilbergeld & Lazarus, 1988, p. 1). This view seems in accord with Glasser's control theory, but instead of saying to a client, "You are depressing yourself," he might consider making it clear that the client is perhaps choosing to respond in a nonconstructive way to the emotion—such as by staying at home and dwelling on his depression as in the case he outlined. This is far less pejorative and is not so readily open to misinterpretation.

Today, therapists have to face the emphasis on accountability, and the weight that is attached to empirically validated treatments of choice for specified conditions. Chambless (1995) published a range of empirically validated methods (reality therapy is not on that list!) that included the interpersonal psychotherapy of depression (Klerman, Weissman, Rounsaville & Chevron, 1984). Yet Dr. Glasser states that "I never mention other people or talk about other people unless the client does." Before engaging a client in any procedure or process, or when eschewing a particular tactic, the major question to ask is if there is any empirical warrant for the efficacy of that particular psychotherapeutic decision. Of the three dozen or so presenters at this Conference, I think there are only six or seven who think in these terms. This, ladies and gentlemen, does not augur well for the future of our profession.

REFERENCES

Berman, J. S., & Norton, N. C. (1985). Does professional training make a therapist more effective? *Psychological Bulletin, 98*, 401–407.

Chambless, D. (1995). Training in and dissemination of empirically-validated psychological treatments: Report and recommendations. *The Clinical Psychologist, 48*, 3–23.

Dawes, R. M. (1994). *House of cards: Psychology and psychotherapy built on myth.* New York: Free Press.

Klerman, G. L., Weissman, M. M., Rounsaville, B. J., & Chevron, E. S. (1984). *Interpersonal psychotherapy of depression.* New York: Basic Books.

Lambert, M. J., Shapiro, D. A., & Bergin, A. E. (1986). *The effectiveness of psychotherapy.* In S. L. Garfield & A. E. Bergin (Eds.), *Handbook of psychotherapy and behavior change*, 3rd ed. (pp. 157–212). New York: Wiley.

Lazarus, A. A., & Fay, A. (1992). *I can if I want to*. New York: Morrow.

Peterson, D. R. (1995). The reflective educator. *American Psychologist, 50*, 975–983.

Zilbergeld, B., & Lazarus, A. A. (1988). *Mind power*. New York: Ivy Books.

My Evolution as a Body–Mind Therapist: Healing the Split in the Modern Personality

◆

Alexander Lowen, M.D.

Alexander Lowen, M.D.
Alexander Lowen, M.D., received his medical degree from the University of Geneva in 1951. He received degrees in law from the Brooklyn Law School. Dr. Lowen studied with Wilhelm Reich from 1940 through 1952, and has been a practicing psychiatrist from 1952 to the present. He founded the Institute for Bioenergetic Analysis in 1956. Dr. Lowen has published 12 books on his bioenergetic approach and is the founder and Executive Director of The International Institute for Bioenergetic Studies.

INTRODUCTION: A PERSONAL EVOLUTION

Bioenergetic analysis, which is the therapeutic modality that I created in 1954, developed out of the ideas and techniques of Wilhelm Reich, who was my teacher and analyst. I met Reich in 1940 when I attended his course at the New School for Social Research in New York. I was attracted to Reich by his understanding of the relationship between body and mind. At that time I held two degrees in law, a bachelor's and a doctor's degree, and I worked as a teacher in the New York City school system and as an athletic director at various adult summer camps. I felt lost and confused about my life. My pleasure was in physical activity but ambition drove me to succeed on an intellectual level in some profession. I was a victim of the split in this culture between the body and the mind, although I had no awareness of being split. It took me almost three years of therapy with Reich and many years of subsequent work with myself to realize the depth of that split. Although my split had its roots in the culture—that is, in the split between culture and nature—I learned later that it stemmed directly from my family situation. My mother and father had been in conflict ever since I could remember. My mother was a tight, small woman, ambitious and controlling, while my father was pleasure loving and unaggressive. She was asexual in temperament while he was a sexual man. In their struggle for power she withheld sex from him while he withheld money from her. I, of course, was caught in the middle. I had feelings for both and identified on two different levels with each.

MY WORK WITH REICH

I began my therapy with Reich in 1942. His approach at that time was called character-analytic vegetotherapy. Character analysis was his great contribution to psychoanalytic theory. Vegetotherapy referred to a process of working with the autonomic or vegetative functions of the body—those that are innervated by the autonomic nervous system and are not under the control of the conscious mind. The important function he focused on was breathing. He had found that all neurotic individuals unconsciously restrict their respiratory activity as a defense against frightening or painful feelings. That defense also included a pattern of chronic muscular tension that Reich called "armoring" to denote that its function was to protect an individual against injury or insult. It also served to isolate the individual from the pain of emotional injuries suffered in childhood. The chronic muscular tension was part of the mechanism that limited and restricted free and full respiration.

When I was in therapy with Reich, several significant breakthroughs of feeling occurred as a direct result of my gaining the ability to allow my breathing to become freer and deeper. Reich's focus was on the surrender to the involuntary movements of the body. Strong vibrations, tremors, and clonic movements developed in my body, and I could accept and enjoy them with Reich's support. These vibrations were the direct result of freeing my muscles from the unconscious restraint they had been under for many years. Reich pointed out many areas where I was holding against some spontaneous movement and encouraged me to let go. He even put some pressure with his hands on tight areas. When I let go of the tension in my jaw muscles and reached out with my lips, pleasurable tingling sensations developed in them. I have described these experiences in *Bioenergetics* (1994) and again in my newest book, *Joy: The Surrender to the Body and to Life* (1995).

Surrender involves the conscious and unconscious letting go of the ego defenses represented by the body's chronic tension. It means allowing breathing to occur as freely and fully as possible. It is manifested in a wave-like movement that flows through the body downward with respiration. This is the kind of breathing one sees in animals and young children who have not yet been frightened by their parents. It is deep abdominal breathing. One can observe the wave in the spontaneous movements of the body. In respiration, as the abdomen expands to allow the diaphragm to descend, the pelvis moves backward. In expiration the pelvis moves forward as the diaphragm relaxes. When these movements occur freely and fully one has a clear feeling of freedom and pleasure in the body. Since this movement occurs spontaneously in the climax of the sexual act when the individual surrenders fully to the feeling of love, Reich called this movement the "orgasm reflex." After three years of therapy with Reich, with sessions three times a week but with breaks for the summer and a year's absence from therapy, I found that my pelvic orgasm reflex movements occurred regularly during the sessions and occasionally outside of therapy. On one occasion, when my surrender to love during sex was total, I experienced an orgasm that reached the height of ecstacy. When my therapy with Reich ended in 1945 I had a strong sense of ease and freedom in my body, which translated into a feeling of joy I had not known since childhood. I left convinced of the validity of Reich's ideas and committed to becoming a Reichian therapist.

EVOLVING AS A CLINICIAN

I saw my first patient in 1945. I was enthusiastic but it was naive to think that I could do effective therapy without many years of experience. My training with Reich did not prepare me for the depth of the disturbance in the average individual. I had learned a powerful technique, which in Reich's hands could be very effective. He had a strong personality and I had transferred to him a deep longing for a father who could support my growth to manhood.

Others had made a similar transference to him and many had broken through to a feeling of joy as I had. Unfortunately, that feeling of joy did not hold up over time, and the ability to surrender to my deepest sexual feelings did not extend to my sexual activities except on one rare and beautiful occasion. In the next two years I was consulted by two people who had also experienced a breakthrough to a feeling of joy in a short period of therapy with Reich but who could not sustain that feeling after their therapy with him ended. This did not dismay me. I felt strongly that Reich's understanding and approach through the body to emotional conflicts and problems was valid. To prepare myself more fully to function as Reich's disciple I went to medical school in 1947 and did not resume my practice until I became a licensed physician in 1953.

I now realized the reason that Reich's therapy with me failed to hold up was that it didn't go deep enough analytically into my character to resolve the deep conflicts in my personality that were at the base of the split between my mind and body. Further, I was aware that I still had too many muscular tensions in my body that had not been worked through in my therapy with him. I sensed that the release of these tensions needed a more active and intense physical approach. At this time Reich had shifted his main interest from therapy to his research into what he called orgone energy and its use as a therapeutic agent. For this and other reasons I decided to sever my relationship with the group of Reichian doctors and to develop a more effective therapeutic approach based on a deeper understanding of the neurotic character and its physical manifestations in the body. To promote this work I organized the Institute for Bioenergetic Analysis. The term *bioenergetic* was used to emphasize that my new approach was centered upon an understanding of the energy dynamics underlying the living process in both its physical and its psychological manifestations. Years earlier I had been impressed by Reich's declaration at a seminar that only an energetic understanding would enable a doctor or therapist to comprehend the forces in the human personality that promote health or lead to illness. Reich had always talked in terms of energy which he called *orgone* to identify it as a specific life energy. To avoid confusion I called this force simply bioenergy and the work I called bioenergetics.

GROUNDING

One of the most important concepts that I developed in my early work was the principle of *grounding*. That term denoted the degree to which an individual is connected to the ground or earth energetically and with feeling. Since the earth is a person's fundamental reality, the term denotes the degree to which he is connected to his legs, to his body, and to the reality about him. The person who is in touch with the reality of his life and being is said to "have his feet on the ground." This is not just a symbolic observation. It denotes that the person has a feeling of contact with the ground, which is an energetic process as well as a feeling. Of course, when a person stands he has his feet on the ground, but if he doesn't feel the connection he is not emotionally connected to that reality. His connection is more mechanical than vital. Many people walk without any consciousness of their feet touching the ground with each step. Such individuals live largely in their heads, as opposed to living fully and consciously in their bodies. In such people there is a split between the head and the body, and necessarily, therefore, between thinking and feeling.

The concept of grounding gives the therapist an objective criterion to determine an individual's contact with reality. When one studies the feet and legs of patients one can observe how alive the foot is from the quality of the tissue, the skin tone and motility. Flat, pale-looking feet that are relatively immobile indicate a lack of feeling and denote an absence of real contact with the ground. That lack of feeling is due to a diminution in the feet's energetic charge. The opposite condition, strong-looking but tense feet, indicates that while the feet are charged, their immobility prevents any feeling from developing. When a person's feet become more alive through grounding exercises this translates into a greater aliveness in the whole body and a noticeable increase in the brightness of the eyes. This aspect of therapy was never considered by Reich, because his therapy was done with patients lying prone on a bed. It was a position that furthered regression. Working with a patient in the standing position enables the therapist to gauge his independence and maturity. But the ability to judge body expression cannot be fully taught. It has to be gained through the observation of many patients and through working with one's own body. I had been aware that I lacked the sense of security that being solidly grounded provides and I have worked with myself over many years to increase the feeling in the lower part of my body and especially in my feet and legs.

One of the basic splits in the civilized human's personality is between the upper half of the body and the lower. That split can be so pronounced that one has a sense that the two halves do not go together. The lower half of the body represents man's animal nature, while the upper half is linked more directly to his conscious sense of self. We are more animal-like in the functions of the lower half of the body than in those of the upper half. Obviously, it is the conscious mind that distinguishes us from the other animals, not the functions of sexuality, reproduction, and excretion. This split translates into a loss of the connection between love and sexuality. It also undermines the ability to surrender fully to the passion that is sexual love and robs a person of the joy that only the full surrender to the body can offer.

THEORETICAL DEVELOPMENTS

In 1958 I published my first book, *The Language of the Body*. This book was designed to present a comprehensive view of the different character types based upon the energy dynamics of the body correlated with the libidinal development of the individual. The character types discussed in this book are the oral character, the masochistic character, the hysterical character, the phallic-narcissistic character, the passive-feminine character, and the schizophrenic character. Freud earlier had described a basic character type that he called

anal and that he believed corresponded with the anal stage in libidinal development. In 1933 Reich published his brilliant study *Character Analysis*, in which he showed that the failure of psychoanalytic treatment to focus attention upon the character in the analysis led to a chaotic situation in the therapy that defeated its aim. His book contained a wonderful analysis of a masochistic patient that documented his underlying character disturbance. When I met with Reich in 1946, he no longer regarded himself as a psychoanalyst.

As noted earlier Reich called his method character-analytic vegetotherapy. I was greatly impressed with his concept of character analysis and followed his suggestion that a comprehensive study of character types should be made. In 1942, when I began my therapy with him, he was more focused upon the body problem (vegetotherapy) than upon character, which may have been the reason why my own character problems were not worked through. Another reason for that lack, as I discovered later, was that my character problems were too similar to his own.

In *The Language of the Body* I introduced some new energetic concepts. I discussed the flow of excitation in the body longitudinally in two pathways, one along the front of the body and one along the back. The emotional feeling of the flow along the front of the body is experienced as love or longing, while the one along the back is related to aggression, the impulse to move towards an object (person) with feelings of love or of anger. I subsequently learned that these two pathways corresponded with the two basic channels of energy flow in acupuncture. Blocks to the flow of energy or excitation in these channels can be seen as bands of muscular tension that circle the body at the junction of the various segments, most notably at the base of the skull where it relates to the split of the head segment from the thorax and at the pelvic rim where it represents an energetic split between the pelvis and the upper body. For Reich the movements of energy flow were associated mainly with the pulsations of the whole organism in expansion and contraction. In this book I could correlate disturbances in the energy processes of the body directly with character types. This book made it possible to determine an individual's character structure directly by an observation of the form and motility of the body. The energetic ideas expressed in *The Language of the Body* still pervade my thinking about the characterological disturbances that afflict people in our culture and that become conversely manifested in physical illness when the stress of the tensions in the body eventually break down its resistance to disease.

My next book, *Love and Orgasm* (1965), is a study of sexuality in relation to its role in the life of the individual as the main expression of love, the erotic impulse. Reich's concept of orgastic potency as a criterion of emotional health made it clear to me that sexuality is the keystone of the personality. Actually the pelvic bones are fused in the shape of a keystone. As such the pelvis affects and influences all personality functions. Disturbances in personality can be linked directly with sexual issues. To understand this connection, it must be recognized that sexuality is not limited to the genital apparatus but is an expression of the whole body and the total personality. I had originally entitled the manuscript "Sex and Personality" but the publisher wanted the word orgasm in the title. He suggested "The Mature Orgasm" as the title, but because that did not make sense to me I changed it to "Love and Orgasm." This title denotes that in my opinion sexuality is an expression of love and that only to the degree that sexual actions are connected to feelings of love is the sexual act joyful and fulfilling. Unfortunately, negative feelings such as sadism can infiltrate the act of sex, reducing it to a physiological process satisfying only to the degree that it has a cathartic effect.

My next book was an in-depth study of the schizoid personality, a character type that I had examined briefly in my first book. This book, *The Betrayal of the Body* (1967), met with a strong, positive response and established bioenergetics as an important modality of treatment. It explored in detail the split between the body and the mind that is the schizophrenic condition. In the schizoid personality the split is not the complete rupture that occurs in schizophrenia but more like a hairline fracture. The schizoid individual retains a grip on reality but at great cost. Many

of these people are now classified as borderline personalities—in fact, that is what they are, because their functioning is on the border between sanity and insanity. The term borderline belongs to ego psychology and denotes a weakness in the individual's ego structure, but it overlooks the underlying energy dynamics of this personality type.

As part of my quest to deepen my understanding of the human personality and its problems, I did an in-depth study of feelings and emotions that I entitled *Pleasure: A Creative Approach to Life*. Although feelings, particularly the emotions, are a basic aspect of life, we take little time to examine or understand them. One reason for this is that they are not fit subjects for scientific analysis. They are purely subjective states and cannot be quantified. Behavior, on the other hand, is objective, and can therefore be objectively verified and controlled. Nevertheless, feelings are the most important aspect of our lives. When we emphasize doing rather than feeling we reduce the person to an inanimate level, a machine. Of all feelings, pleasure is the basic feeling that denotes a positive life function. It stems from the free rhythmic activity of the body in harmony with its basic pulsating rhythms of breathing, sleeping, eating, and so on. Emotional health means that we are in a state of pleasure all the time; that is, we *feel* good in our bodies. If the pleasurable excitement becomes stronger, the good feeling becomes one of joy. Only these feelings can supply life with its true meaning.

In my work as a bioenergetic therapist I use a number of active physical techniques and exercises to help patients breathe more deeply, release the chronic muscular tension in their bodies, and get in touch with their feelings. Some of these exercises are described in my book *Pleasure*; others are described in *Fear of Life*, a later book; and they are described again in my latest book, *Joy: The Surrender to the Body and to Life*.

In the absence of pleasure, people get depressed. But depression is not the opposite of pleasure. Pain is. Both pleasure and pain are feeling states, which means that the body is alive and feeling, positive or negative. Depression is the lack or loss of feeling. It denotes that the energetic state of the individual is decreased. All bodily functions are depressed, including appetite, desire, movement, and breathing. Depression is a body phenomenon as well as a psychological state. It is best treated on both levels simultaneously. To the degree that a therapist can help a patient sense and express feelings again, the depressive reaction is diminished. Getting a patient to cry, to sob, is the best way to help him rise from his depressed state. Because the depressed person is also energetically depressed—that is, lacking the energy to feel—one must also help him mobilize his body through movement and breathing. My book *Depression and the Body* shows that the aliveness of the body is the biological basis for the sense of reality and the feeling of faith.

In my next book, *Bioenergetics*, I summarized the energetic principles that underlie character structure, both positive and negative. Because character denotes one's consistent pattern of behavior, a person with "good" character would operate on principles that are adaptable to the situation, as opposed to the rigid and unconscious motivation of the neurotic character. In *Bioenergetics* I also summarized the energetic principles that underlay the different character structures, relating them to each other and to the dynamics of the individual's childhood situation. But after having written this book, I began to move away from the use of character types in my work with patients. Getting a patient to understand his character type did not help him to change it. Character is based on an energetic structure in the personality that is beyond the reach of the conscious mind. It operates like a fate that the individual cannot counter. The concept of fate was a turning point in my thinking. I realized that the more one tries to avoid fate the more one ensures its fulfillment. That theme is explicitly set forth and analyzed in my book *Fear of Life*. All neurotic behavior stems from a fear of life and represents the individual's unconscious effort to overcome his fear. But one can't overcome a feeling. One can only suppress the feeling, which means to bury it in the unconscious. One's behavior, then, is not motivated by positive feelings such as pleasure and love but by an ego drive to succeed,

to gain power and security, for these are seen as the antidote to fear.

Since one cannot escape one's fate, the effort to achieve success, power, and security is wasted. It is not only wasteful but it robs life of the energy that is necessary for a secure mind and healthy body. We are all running from life in the mistaken belief that running is the way to protect our health. We are trying to build our bodies into a stronghold that will protect us from illness but in reality this stronghold only protects us from life. In a culture that is largely head oriented we need to work with our bodies to restore their aliveness and gracefulness. The body is not a physicochemical mechanism like a high performance automobile but a pulsating organism whose very existence depends on its inherent pulsating activities such as the beating of the heart, breathing, the peristaltic waves of the intestines, and so on. Fear is a paralyzing emotion. All chronic tension is a direct manifestation of fear. We only can become free of fear to the degree that we release the body from its chronic muscular tensions. I increased my focus upon the body, introducing many new exercises to help a patient feel the tensions in the different parts of his body and to release them. The release of tension is always manifested in spontaneous involuntary movements. Muscles begin to vibrate like springs when the tension is released. Clonic movements develop, associated with the waves of breathing. Some patients become frightened when this first happens, but as they learn to accept this new aliveness feelings of pleasure emerge. My wife started exercise classes for patients based on these principles to further their awareness of their bodies. Patients were encouraged to do these exercises at home as well. My wife and I wrote a manual of bioenergetic exercises that we called *The Way to Vibrant Health*. It is still the standard exercise book for this work.

THE NARCISSISTIC AND BORDERLINE PERSONALITIES

In the 50 years that I have been doing therapy I have witnessed a significant change in the problems that I see in my patients. The splits have deepened. People are more out of touch with their bodies on a feeling level and more into their heads. Bodies look and are deader and, in many cases, more distorted than I had seen earlier. But this change in the aliveness of bodies is not limited to my patients. The general public shows a similar loss of aliveness in their bodies, manifested in the massive overweight condition of so many people, in the loss of gracefulness in their movements, and in the lack of brightness in their facial expressions. People are more active, do more things, travel more, but this hyperactivity is in most cases the antidote to depression. In therapy the dominant complaint is that something is missing that would give their lives meaning. Patients have no sense of being fulfilled in love, in their relationships, or in their work. They survive, and this is about the only meaning their lives have.

In itself survival doesn't give life meaning, and so many individuals constantly search for meaning in different esoteric activities. Others look for meaning in the achievement of success or the acquisition of power and wealth. But these are narcissistic pursuits and do not affect the deep, inner feelings of emptiness. Those who fail in these narcissistic pursuits may be better off, for they are forced to look inward to find the cause of their dissatisfaction. But that inner search is frightening and painful. It requires the guidance of an experienced and competent psychotherapist to venture into the depths of the modern soul where death and despair lie. We avoid feeling our despair and facing the fear of death by living on the surface. This is the narcissistic pattern. Those who come to therapy hope that the therapist can help them improve their conscious behavior so that it will be more successful. Few are prepared to deal with the underlying cause of their distress.

The other side of this picture are individuals with a borderline personality who are in touch with their feelings of death and despair but cannot dissociate from those feelings to function effectively on the surface. They are borderline because their egos have not gained the strength to suppress their pain and distress. In their case, as I see it, the traumatic events that split the unity of their personality occurred before they were three years old. In the true narcissistic personality the damaging traumas occurred later, between the ages of three and six. This is the Oedipal period, when sexual identity becomes established. It is in contrast with the earlier period, which is predominantly oral. Thus the borderline personality struggles with the feelings of need and helplessness, and the narcissistic individual denies his need and compensates for his helplessness through seduction and manipulation. Broadly speaking, I would describe the narcissistic group as those who act effectively but without feeling, in contrast to the borderline group who are in touch with their feelings but cannot integrate them into effective action. In both cases the split is between the ego, with its control of the voluntary muscular system, and the deep feelings of the inner body, which we could describe as heart feelings or gut feelings.

THE BODY SPLITS

To understand how splits develop we need to look at the body's basic anatomy. The human body, like that of other mammals and of reptiles and birds, is constructed on the principle of a tube within a tube. The inner tube functions to ingest, digest, and metabolize food to provide energy. In human beings the lungs develop from the inner tube, which means that the respiratory activity belongs to the body's involuntary processes. The outer tube, which includes the large, voluntary or striated musculature, is concerned with moving the organism. In contrast to the voluntary or striated muscles, the muscles of the inner tube are smooth, smaller, and have no striations. These smooth muscles that surround the bronchi, the arteries, and the tubes of the digestive system are activated by the autonomic nervous system, which is not subject to conscious control. In contrast, the larger, striated muscles are activated and controlled by the central nervous system of which the ego is the conscious part.

Deep feelings and emotions are largely associated with the activity of the inner tube. I refer to what are commonly called "gut" feelings. Such feelings and emotions are experienced in the whole body although they are centered in the inner tube. We speak of a belly cry or a belly laugh to denote the deeper feelings of sadness or pleasure. When what we feel is largely on the surface it does not qualify as a deep feeling. It is more sentimental than emotional. For the Japanese the center of the personality is located two inches below the navel in the belly. A person in touch with this center is said to have "hara" or to be centered. This concept is fully explained by Karl Durkheim in *Hara* (1962). True love is connected to feeling in the heart, as I pointed out in my book, *Love, Sex and Your Heart*. However, it cannot be felt unless the excitation in the heart is strong enough to reach the surface where perception and expression occur. While we cannot produce a feeling, we can block it from expression through the conscious mind. Of course, no one would deliberately block the feeling of love unless he or she had experienced a loss or betrayal of love that was so painful as to amount to a sense of heartbreak.

In a child the pain of heartbreak is frightening because it is experienced as life-threatening. A child who has experienced rejection by a parent will close him or herself off to love in self-defense. Children will bury their desire for love as they bury the pain of the rejection. They do this by suppressing the impulse to cry, which is the primary expression of a child who is hurt. Suppressing the pain of the rejection and the crying that would release the hurt isolates and imprisons the soul of the child to protect him or her against the possibility of another such disaster. Suppression creates the deep-seated despair that one will never find true love and the joy of fulfillment. The split in the modern personality also can be described as the loss of connection between the sophisticated adult who lives on the surface dominated by his thinking, and the buried child within who has the deep feelings and the potential for a rich and fulfilling life. John Bradshaw talks about the need of the modern individual to get in touch with the child within.

What is needed to treat the split is a surrender of the narcissistic ego and the courage to feel the despair, the pain, and the deep longing for love. This is not a matter of words, which are the language of the ego, but of deep body feelings, which are the language of the soul. The patient needs to cry, to sob deeply, to feel what happened to him, and to scream his protest. Sound is the mode of expression of our inner tube as movement and action are the mode of expression of the outer tube. Few people in our culture can cry deeply enough— that is, from their guts—or long enough to release the pain and free them from their despair. Generally, it will take at least several years of working with the body to reduce its chronic tensions and increase its energy so that the person will have the strength and ability to descend into the depths of his being to find his soul.

I would like to finish by describing the case of a man who entered into therapy with me this year. He even came to this conference so I could demonstrate how I work to heal this split in the modern personality.* Then I will close with a second case.

CASE I

Jack Marshal is a 43-year-old man who consulted me because he felt that his life was empty. He had never married and had had only one relatively short-lived love affair. He made a living playing the stock market and was moderately successful in this activity. Physically he was of average height but markedly overweight. Apart from his weight he had no complaints about his physical condition. He seemed affable and generally wore a smile on his face. Jack had come to see me because he felt that his problem was connected with the deadness of his body. He was aware that he had little feeling in his body and that he lived largely in his head. Over the years he had tried psychotherapy with several different analysts without any effect upon his emotional state. Reading my books, he was convinced that his problem needed a physical approach grounded in psychoanalytic understanding.

Jack had been overweight as a child and young adult, but not as overweight as he was when he consulted me. He told me that about ten years ago he had had a very intense sexual

---

*The videotape of Dr. Lowen's session with Jack can be procured through the Erickson Foundation.

love affair, which broke up after several months when his lover left him. He described that time as the most painful in his life and said that he had cried every night when going to sleep. When I asked him if there was any connection between the loss of love and his increased weight, he smiled and said "Yes." Putting on weight was his way to deaden his body not to feel the terrible pain of his loss. In effect, he had survived this terrible experience by embalming it in his heavy body. It would take courage to restore the life to his body, for that meant that he would have to reexperience the pain of his lost love, but Jack felt that he had no alternative.

Not every person who suffers the pain of lost love deadens his body by putting on weight as a survival mechanism. Jack was conditioned to this defense by the events of his childhood. He was an only child whose father was largely absent emotionally while his mother was overinvolved with him. Jack was the recipient when his mother acted out her frustration and need for contact that stemmed from her frustrating relationship with his father. As Jack put it, "She was constantly at me, continually talking to me, at times haranguing me to the point that I couldn't stand it." Because he couldn't get away from her it was driving him crazy. I pointed out to him that he avoided this fate by "armoring"; that is, deadening the outer layer of the body so that she couldn't get at him. This armoring involves tensing the muscles of the outer tube so as not to react and thereby not to feel. For Jack to work through this problem, his body had to become more alive and develop more feeling. It was not enough for him to understand why he developed his problem; it was necessary for his body to become more alive.

I use two basic exercises to accomplish this. One is for the patient to breathe while lying on his back over the bioenergetic stool. This exercise is stressful and somewhat painful, but it forces the patient to breathe. As more oxygen is introduced into the body its energy is increased. In this position, using the voice by making a sustained sound deepens the breathing. It may lead to crying, which is a releasing emotion. When the patient reverses the position by bending forward in the grounding position, vibrations develop in the legs as waves of energy or excitement flow into them. The vibratory activity of the body is a direct manifestation of its aliveness. A healthy person is vibrantly alive. To the degree that the body vibrates the patient feels his body. It is a very positive experience and patients report that they feel themselves differently. They actually feel more of themselves. I used this exercise regularly with Jack, and each time Jack reported feeling more alive. Of course, at the same time we talked about his life and his problem.

The other exercise is kicking. The patient lies on a bed and kicks it with extended legs. To kick is to protest, and Jack has much to kick about in terms of the harmful effects of his childhood. In the therapy I combine the kicking with verbal expressions of protest, such as, "Why?" "Leave me alone!" "You are driving me crazy!" and so on. Using the voice while doing the kicking mobilizes the inner tube and integrates the movements with the sound. This helps overcome the split between the inner and outer aspects of the personality. When Jack first described how he felt tormented when his mother constantly talked at him, I had him do the following exercise. Taking a face towel into his two hands, he twisted it strongly, crying out "Shut up! You're driving me crazy!" The exercise had a positive effect upon Jack, although he did not reach an intense feeling. It made sense to him, and he felt more alive afterwards.

The most important emotion that this therapy works with is crying. It was very difficult for Jack to cry with sobs. That difficulty stemmed from two sources. On an ego level crying meant failure, helplessness, and the surrender to his mother. Deep within himself he was still the child needing to resist her. Having gained independence and adulthood he was not going to surrender his position of strength. Physically he couldn't cry. The tension of holding in his tears since infancy was too great. He had lost control of his body. In his therapy with me he did want to cry but he could not. That situation slowly ameliorated through the work with his body.

Mobilizing Jack's ability to express anger was another big challenge. I had him beat the bed regularly in his sessions and I encouraged him to do the same exercise at home. He needed to feel his anger so he could experience his potency as a man. His impotence as a male emotionally and sexually was the underlying reason that his relationships with women failed. It was slow work, but Jack was well aware that he had no choice. He recognized that there was no other way. It would take a long time, but Jack sensed through the glimpses of good feeling that the reward was sure.

CASE II

Gretl had no defense against her pain and her despair. She felt it, although at times she could dissociate from it and let herself go with her friends to some feelings of pleasure. Gretl could let herself cry but never deeply enough, for at that deep level she wanted to die and felt afraid that she would die. The split in Gretl's personality was more severe than in Jack's. It was manifested physically by a contraction about the waist that separated the upper half of Gretl's body from the lower. The upper half of Gretl's body was soft and not rigid, but it was weak because it did not have a strong base upon which to rest. She had been married and had had several love relations, but none of them gave her the feeling of security that was lacking in herself.

Gretl was a psychotherapist. Because she knew all the answers she could set up a facade of competence and strength—on the head level, of course, not on the body level. On that level she felt weak, and as she got more in touch with her body, she felt that she had been devastated. She had a history of sexual abuse on an emotional level that she had never worked through in previous therapies. None of her previous therapists, whose approaches were purely verbal, were aware of the depth of her misery, but it was clearly evident to me when I looked at her body. This meant that her body had to change if she was to fulfill her being and find her joy.

Gretl was in therapy with me for five years, during which time she went deeply into her despair and pain. She needed my support and encouragement to do this but she very strongly sensed that there was no other way for her. She cried almost every session as her breath-

ing deepened and she felt the fear and the pain in her belly. The pain was tied to her fear, which was that she would be destroyed if she allowed herself to feel sexual. When she began to feel sexual sensations in her pelvis she panicked, but she also welcomed them. When the waves of excitation passed into the lower part of her body it vibrated strongly with convulsive movements due to the severe tensions in that area. Gradually the movements became softer and more harmonic as she surrendered to them and she began to feel the pleasure of being a woman.

I have described Gretl's case more fully in my new book, *Joy: The Surrender to the Body and to Life* (1995). Her body changed dramatically. It filled out, and the split between the upper and lower halves was hardly noticeable. She still had some problems in her life, as we all do, but she had no feelings of fear or despair. She felt a growing confidence that she could handle her life as a mature woman, for Gretl was now in her early forties. She was committed to the life of the body, and to the bioenergetic exercises that she did regularly to maintain her contact with that life. She was keenly aware that the culture in which she lived had a strong antilife bias, based as it was on power and money. She also found that she functioned much better in her work as a therapist, which increased her sense of well-being.

CONCLUSION

My evolution has brought me to where I understand that the body will heal itself if one surrenders to it. The surrender to the body means feeling it fully from head to feet. It means sensing all the chronic muscular tensions in the body, understanding their history and their function in the present. It means feeling one's pain and sorrow and crying. It means being able to protest the loss of one's innocence and one's joy. And it means the ability to be angry about that loss. Finally, it means an acceptance of the failure of all one's efforts to overcome one's problems, "to make it," to succeed. It means to have faith in the body, for it is the abode of God, and to trust its feelings because they express your truth. I had to learn this before I could teach it to my patients. And I have to learn it again and again, because my narcissistic ego still thinks that it knows best.

REFERENCES

Dürkheim, K. (1962). *Hara*. London: George Allen & Unwin, Ltd., 1962.

Freud, S. (1908/1953). *Character and anal eroticism*. In *Collected Papers*, *II*. London: Hogarth Press.

Lowen, A. (1958). *The language of the body*. New York: Macmillan.

Lowen, A. (1965). *Love and orgasm*. New York: Macmillan.

Lowen, A. (1967). *The betrayal of the body*. New York: Macmillan.

Lowen, A. (1980). *Fear of life*. New York: Macmillan.

Lowen, A. (1994). *Pleasure: A creative approach to life*. New York: Penguin/Arkana.

Lowen, A. (1994). *Depression and the body*. New York: Penguin/Arkana.

Lowen, A. (1994). *Bioenergetics*. New York: Penguin/Arkana. Coward, McCann & Geoghegan.

Lowen, A. (1994). *Love, sex and your heart*. New York: Penguin/Arkana.

Lowen, A. (1995). *Joy: The surrender to the body and to life*. New York: Penguin/Arkana.

Lowen, A., & Lowen, L. R. (1992). *The way to vibrant health: A manual of bioenergetic exercises*. New York: The International Institute for Bioenergetic Analysis, 1992.

Reich, W. (1945). *Character analysis*. New York: Orgone Institute Press.

Discussion by Judd Marmor, M.D.

◆

I have been engaged in the practice of psychotherapy now for almost 60 years. Almost from the beginning of my career, I became intrigued by the fact that different therapists, operating under different theories and utilizing different techniques, all seemed to report comparable favorable results. The recognition of this fact had two important consequences for my subsequent career development. First, it made me recognize that the therapeutic success of a method could not in itself be taken as proof of the scientific correctness of its underlying theory or methodology. Second, it stimulated in me a powerful interest in exploring the nature of the psychotherapeutic process and in trying to root out the common denominator that enabled so many diverse approaches to achieve comparable results. Over the years, I wrote a number of papers on what I thought these common denominators were, and in the late 1950s I became involved in an intensive three-year research study of the psychotherapeutic process, the results of which were published in a volume called *The Dyadic Transaction: An Investigation of the Nature of the Psychotherapeutic Process*, which I co-authored with two of my co-observers, Dr. Samuel Eisenstein and Dr. Norman A. Levy.

All of this is by way of introduction to my comments about Dr. Lowen's fascinating presentation. Let me say at the very outset that although I shall be taking issue with a number of his concepts, I hope that neither you nor he will misunderstand my remarks as implying that his therapy is without value. Quite the contrary! I have no doubt that Dr. Lowen is an excellent psychotherapist. I see him, as I'm sure most of you do after hearing his presentation, as a warm, caring, passionate man with powerful convictions who unquestionably inspires strong feelings of positive transference in most of his patients. However, I do question his *explanation* of why his patients respond positively to his therapeutic method. Dr. Lowen places a primary emphasis on the relief of their muscular tensions as the core factor in his therapeutic results, a conviction that he acquired originally from his own analyst and teacher, Wilhelm Reich. Now I do not dispute his observation that many, if not most, people with neurotic disorders suffer from muscular tensions. There are a wide variety of therapies that address themselves to this problem in one way or another, among them transcendental meditation, biofeedback, Joseph Wolpe's technique of reciprocal inhibition, and various other forms of direct or indirect relaxation therapy. We know, too, that the technique of hypnosis also rests heavily on inducing the patient to achieve complete muscular relaxation accompanied by deep breathing.

However, I find myself diverging from Dr. Lowen's viewpoint where he appears to regard the muscular tension of his patients as if it is in itself the primary cause of their emotional problems rather than an interactive consequence of those problems. Thus, he seems to place his therapeutic emphasis in getting his patients to achieve deep muscular relaxation, to breathe slowly and deeply, and he tries to help them achieve emotional abreaction through weeping, screaming, kicking and pounding the bed, and acting out their anger by role playing with imagined traumatic figures in their past.

Many of you, I am sure, will recognize that similar techniques are employed in Gestalt therapy, where Fritz Perls' rallying cry was, "Don't think, feel!" Others of you will be reminded of the emphasis on loud screaming in Irving Janov's "Primal Scream" technique. These abreactive techniques all hark back to the early history of psychoanalysis when Freud believed that such emotional catharsis experiences were in themselves curative. As his experience grew, however, he learned that the relief that they produced was transitory, and he then developed the more difficult technique of working through his patients' resistances and dreams by the method of psychoanalysis.

It is interesting to note that Dr. Lowen also talks of the process of working through when in describing the partial failure of his own therapy with Wilhelm Reich he states, "I still had too many muscular tensions in my body which had not been worked through," as though the primary task of therapy is to achieve muscular relaxation rather than to change patients' perceptions of themselves and of others.

In a curious kind of way Dr. Lowen seems to separate mind and body, although I am sure he believes that there is an essential unity between mind and body. However, in his comments he tends to discuss the central nervous system as if it is primarily a conscious, intellectual organ, and he differentiates it from the body's muscular tensions and energies, which he sees as unconscious and under the control of the autonomic nervous system. Let us not forget, however, that the central nervous system encompasses more than the cortex. It is intimately interconnected with the subcortex, the thalamic and hypothalmic nuclei that control various aspects of our emotional life including our autonomic reactions. Thus the dichotomy between a conscious central nervous system and an unconscious muscular system is a false one.

Now I am not implying that stimulating or relaxing the body musculature cannot have an effect on how we feel, but I am questioning the primacy of that as the *source* of our feelings rather than our experiences in life, in childhood and throughout our subsequent development. It is as if we are talking about a dog and its tail, and Dr. Lowen tends to see the tail wagging the dog! Clearly it never does. The dog is always the one that wags the tail even though we all know that the tail can be a very *expressive indicator* of how the dog is feeling inwardly as well as outwardly to other people.

I am sure that Dr. Lowen would assert that he does more than merely focus on his patients' muscular tensions, and *I have no doubt that he does*. My criticism is that he presents his material *as if* achieving muscular relaxation were the *core* of his patients' problems, and he tends to leave out much, if not all, of the contributory conscious and unconscious cognitive, emotional, and experiential factors that are relevant to their muscular tensions and their psychopathology.

The point that I am making is that I am inclined to question whether the primary basis for the ability of Dr. Lowen's patients to respond positively to his techniques rests on the various exercises that he emphasizes. Rather I am convinced that much more is going on between Dr. Lowen and his patients, that in fact it is the profound *interaction* that takes place between them at a deep emotional level that is the primary source of the success of his technique. To put it more succinctly, it is not what he does to or with his patients but what takes place between them in their relationship that helps them to make progress.

The basic matrix of every successful therapeutic encounter—and this has emerged from both my own research and that of others—consists of a good patient–therapist relationship, resting on the patient's need and expectations of being helped and on the trust engendered by the therapist's genuine interest, respect, and empathy for the patient. There is no doubt in my mind that Dr. Lowen's warmth, sincerity, and genuine interest in his patients engender a profound trust and positive transference. Within this matrix a number of other elements also operate. For one thing, as we have seen, there is a great deal of emotional *catharsis* that Dr. Lowen encourages and that contributes to a relief of emotional tension. But he also presents to his patients a *cognitive framework* in which he emphatically attributes much of their difficulties to bioenergetic muscular tensions, and he strongly implies that the relaxation of those tensions will relieve their difficulties. I am sure that you will recognize that there is a powerful element of *suggestion* operating here, and the more powerful the positive transference the greater the impact of these suggestions will be. Dr. Lowen is a passionate and eloquent advocate of his theories and there is no doubt in my mind that most of his patients form strong positive transferences to him. He also makes use of simple but skillful metaphors to drive his points home, such as the metaphor about grounding, or of the split between the upper half of the body and the lower half, or of a similar split between an inner tube of the body and an outer tube, or of flows of excitation in the body, one along the front dealing with love and one along the back dealing with aggression. He works all of these metaphorical concepts into his therapeutic interaction with his patients, although as a matter of fact no verifiable neurophysiological basis for them exists. However, in the context of the powerful positive transference that he inspires in his patients these metaphors reinforce a conceptual framework that they are able to use in moving toward greater adaptive effectiveness in their lives. Indeed there is a powerful inspirational quality to Dr. Lowen's approach that comes through when you listen to him. He talks

with enormous sincerity and passion about love being connected to the heart, about feelings reflecting the language of the soul, and on having faith in the body because it is the abode of God. These are powerful inspirational messages, and if the patient believes strongly in the messenger such messages will be useful in motivating the patient on the road to recovery.

I wish to make it clear that in emphasizing the role of suggestion and persuasion in Dr. Lowen's method it is not my intention to denigrate it. My research over the years has clearly indicated that suggestion and persuasion are part of every psychotherapeutic technique, including that of psychoanalysis itself. Other factors that take place in Dr. Lowen's therapy, as I believe they do in other forms of therapy too, are *operant reconditioning* of the patient by means of explicit or implicit approval–disapproval cues and also by a corrective emotional relationship with the therapist. Another important factor is *identification with the therapist*, just as Dr. Lowen developed with Wilhelm Reich. By incorporating part of the therapist into themselves, patients acquire the strength to move forward and function more adaptively.

It is characteristic of all psychotherapeutic schools to try to explain the success of their techniques in terms of a single and unique principle that differentiates their own approach from all others and presumably makes it superior. Thus, analytically oriented psychiatrists attribute their success to their special cognitive insights and transference interpretations; Rogerians believe that their technique uniquely releases the patient's own self-actualizing mechanisms (you will recognize a similar belief in Dr. Lowen's presentation also); behavior therapists are convinced that the specific conditioning technique that they employ, whether it be reciprocal inhibition, desensitization, implosion, or something else, is the essential unitary factor in their achieved therapeutic results; Gestalt therapists place their emphasis on the release of repressed emotions; transactional analysts on bringing into awareness the script patterns employed by patients in their interpersonal relationships, and so on. I am strongly of the opinion that in no instance can the therapeutic results of these different schools of therapy be attributed to such presumptive unitary factors. As Strupp has cogently put it, "There is not, and it is doubtful that there ever will be, a pure technical intervention in psychotherapy analogous to a particular surgical procedure or the injection of a specific drug. Instead, any psychotherapeutic technique is firmly imbedded and thoroughly entwined with the therapist's personality and the total history of a particular patient-therapist interaction, including its current context." I think that sums it up as well as anything I can say and I will not add further to it. It was a privilege for me to hear Dr. Lowen; I thank him for that privilege, and I congratulate him most bioenergetically!

SECTION IV

Ericksonian Approaches

Self-Organizational Dynamics in Ericksonian Hypnotherapy: A Nonlinear Evolution for the Psychotherapist of the Future

♦

Ernest L. Rossi, Ph.D.

Ernest L. Rossi, Ph.D.

Ernest Rossi (Ph.D., 1962, Temple University) is in private practice in Malibu, Calif. Rossi has extensive experience as a Jungian Analyst; he is affiliated with the C.G. Jung Institute in Los Angeles and served as chairman of its certifying board. He is a recipient of a Lifetime Achievement Award from The Milton W. Erickson Foundation.

Dr. Rossi, the editor of Psychological Perspectives: A Semi-Annual Review of Jungian Thought, *is a prolific author, having published books on dreams and on the psychobiology of mind–body healing. He also has written extensively on the hypnotic approach of Milton H. Erickson, and is the coauthor, with Erickson, of four books, the editor of four volumes of Erickson's collected papers, and the coeditor of four volumes of Erickson's early lectures, seminars, and workshops. His most recent book is* The Symptom Path to Enlightenment: The New Dynamics of Self-Organization in Hypnotherapy *(Palisades Gateway Publishing, 1996. Fax 310 230-1067).*

INTRODUCTION

The current impoverishment of the linear academic approach to hypnosis is well described in a recent issue of *The American Psychologist*, the official journal of the American Psychological Association. I summarize this conceptual impasse of academically oriented hypnosis research with a series of quotations from its leaders in the first portion of this chapter. The second half of this chapter is devoted to exploring an alternative nonlinear approach to hypnotherapy based on the new Science of Self-Organization, an approach that is becoming known by many other names, including Synergetics, Nonlinear Dynamics, Adaptive Complexity, and Chaos Theory. It is proposed that research in Ericksonian hypnotherapy and the evolution of the therapist in general will make profound progress by reformulating their foundations on this new nonlinear approach to the dynamics of naturalistic self-organization in hypnosis and psychotherapy.

PART I:
THE SELF-ACKNOWLEDGED IMPASSE OF LINEAR ACADEMIC HYPNOSIS

The detailed descriptions of the *state transitions* through many different levels of hypnotic experience by Bernheim (1886/1957) and others led to many early qualitative descriptions of "hypnotic depth" (Davis & Husband, 1931). These early qualitative scales eventually inspired the pioneering psychologists of our era, such as Clark Hull, Ernest Hilgard, and Eysenck, who investigated the dynamics of hypnosis experimentally. They all began by trying to define the domain of suggestion with behavioral tests and observable responses that could be easily measured in a more quantitative linear manner. This led to the creation of the well-known hypnotic susceptibility scales, which were presumed to be the new instruments for measuring the essence of therapeutic suggestion as a behavioral and psychosocial process with little, if any, connection to the psychophysiological views of the fathers of hypnosis. After three generations of research with these behavioral scales of hypnotic susceptibility, however, we seem to have reached an impasse and a series of paradoxes (Balthazard & Woody, 1985). Naish, for example, has recently summarized the situation as follows: "As [hypnotic] susceptibility is normally assessed, a high scorer is one who *produces* the behavior, the *reason* for its production remains unknown . . . The claim was frequently made that cognitive processes are involved in the production of 'hypnotic' effects. However, the exact nature of these processes generally remained obscure" (Naish, 1986, p. 165–166).

The basic impasse and emerging paradox of current-day hypnosis is that a remarkable number of the highly respected researchers who developed and utilized these scales of hypnotic susceptibility are now reporting that whatever hypnosis may be, its domain cannot be limited to the behavioral or psychosocial processes as defined by these scales. Ernest Hilgard, for example, recently summarized the domain of hypnosis with these words, "The first point is that hypnotic behavior cannot be defined simply as a response to suggestion . . . Although hypnotic-like behaviors are commonly responses to suggestion, the domain of suggestion includes responses that do not belong within hypnosis, and the phenomena of hypnosis cover more than specific responses to suggestion" (Hilgard, 1991, pp. 45–46). Hilgard seems to be saying that the domain of hypnotic suggestion and the behavioral

responses to it as currently defined are not adequate or complete. So, what is missing?

From our historical perspective, we propose that what is missing from the domain of current suggestion theory as it has been developed by behaviorally oriented researchers like Hilgard is precisely the *psychophysiological phase transitions* that the fathers of hypnosis described with their many outlines of the degrees of hypnotic depth (Lloyd & Rossi, 1992; Rossi & Nimmons, 1991). A major goal of this chapter is to reconnect with the psychophysiological foundations of hypnosis that have been lost to most modern researchers (Rossi, 1996). In one recent volume, for example, the editor (Schumaker, 1991, p. 19) asks, "Are we progressing toward a biology of suggestion?" Aye, back to the future! Braid defined the domain of hypnosis as "psychophysiology" back in 1855 (Rossi, 1986/1993). Having lost its psychobiological roots it is no wonder that much current research in hypnosis seems to be impoverished in its understanding of the role and potency of suggestion. Having cut suggestion from its biological roots, current psychological research apparently has lost it altogether in the "statistical byways of unreliability."

H. J. Eysenck summarizes this loss of the reality and role of suggestion most pungently as follows: "There is no single, unitary trait of suggestibility, no one uniform type of reaction to different kinds of suggestion in human subjects. There are several, or possibly many different suggestibilities which bear no relation to each other. These are uncorrelated and, in turn, correlate differentially with other cognitive and emotional variables. This finding is of considerable interest and importance . . . It does make books containing in their title the word 'suggestibility' of rather doubtful value!" (Eysenck, 1991, p. 87). Once again, we seem to have an admission by a leading behaviorally oriented researcher that the domain of therapeutic suggestion has fallen into a muddle of correlated and uncorrelated "cognitive and emotional variables" when it is limited to these domains defined in a linear manner. Eysenck apparently does not have a clue to the fact that nonlinear relationships could well account for data indicating there are many suggestibilities "that are uncorrelated and, in turn, correlate differentially with other cognitive and emotional variables." Such situations are highly characteristic of nonlinear dynamics.

The paradox of our leading researchers beginning their careers by defining hypnosis as behavioral responsiveness to suggestion and then, after a lifetime of research, turning around and saying, in effect, that hypnosis cannot be operationally defined simply as responsiveness to suggestion, and that there is no unitary human trait of suggestibility, must give all thoughtful students and clinicians pause. Kirsch and Lynn (1995), for example, have recently summarized the current status of opinion in this area among academic researchers as follows.

Is there a uniquely hypnotic state that serves as a background or gives rise to the altered subjective experiences produced by suggestion? Having failed to find reliable markers of trance after 50 years of careful research, most researchers have concluded that this hypothesis has outlived its usefulness. Nevertheless, most clinicians still believe that hypnosis is a unique state with causal properties; as do some influential theorists. Because the state hypothesis is an existential rather than a universal proposition, it cannot be disproved, but can, in principle, be verified. As E. R. Hilgard noted, 'The fact that no signs are now present, or that none are likely to be found, does not deny the possibility that some subtle indicators will be eventually uncovered' (p. 978). (Kirsch & Lynn, 1995, p. 854).

The presence of paradoxes in science usually is taken as an important clue that there is something wrong with current theory and practice; an important transition and expansion is usually required before further progress can be made. Paradoxes frequently point to places where theory and practice need to be revised in some fundamental way. Paradox usually inspires investigators to plan and execute new directions in research to resolve it. Elsewhere I present detailed evidence that the source of the current impasse in the traditional academic approach to hypnosis is its inappropriate use of oversimplified *linear* models to study complex human experience (Rossi, 1996). As an alternative, I discuss the possibilities of new *nonlinear* approaches to the ever-shifting existential states that we call "Ericksonian hypno-

therapy." In particular, I explore the recent findings of the Synergetics school, which is now developing new conceptual and experimental nonlinear approaches to the classical phenomena of hypnosis and suggestion. But for now let us focus on a creative alternative to direct suggestion as the essential dynamic of hypnotherapy in the clinical work of Milton H. Erickson and others.

PART II:
THE NEW NONLINEAR DYNAMICS OF ERICKSONIAN HYPNOTHERAPY

SELF-ORGANIZED CRITICALITY

A child playing on a sunny beach lets a handful of sand slowly trickle through her fingers to make a sweet little pile that forms all by itself. She does not realize that her little sand pile, with a critical slope of about 34 degrees, is a simple example of spontaneous self-organization in nature. If she carefully lets another handful trickle down on top of the first, the sand pile will grow a little higher but the slope will remain the same, because a tiny series of little avalanches will follow a power law to maintain the developing sand pile in a precise three-dimensional cone pattern of self-organization.

To see the world in a few grains of sand is more than a poetic metaphor. Per Bak and Kan Chen (1991) suggest that sand piles illustrate *self-organized criticality*, a kind of generic domino effect that accounts for the cascade of avalanches that continually sculpts the sand pile. If the sides of the cone momentarily grow too steep or too shallow, the number and size of the avalanches will spontaneously adjust themselves. The child made the sand pile, to be sure, but it was nature's dynamics that shaped it just so. Bak and his colleagues carefully study the dynamics of composite systems of sand piles as a simple model of more complex systems such as earthquakes, ecosystems, economic market data, and the human brain, with its approximately 10^{12} neurons. These are all examples of self-organized criticality that require no programming or master organization chart from the outside to tell them how to work. They are simply following nature's laws from within. Bak and Chen describe their ideas as follows.

We propose the theory of self-organized criticality: many composite systems *naturally evolve to a critical state* in which a minor event starts a chain reaction that can affect any number of elements in the system. Although composite systems produce more minor events than catastrophes, chain reactions of all sizes are an integral part of the dynamics. According to the theory, the mechanism that leads to minor events is the same one that leads to major events. *Furthermore, composite systems never reach equilibrium but instead evolve from one metastable state to the next* (Bak & Chen, 1991, p. 46, italics added.)

One might think of more exotic examples of self-organized criticality. Throughout history, wars and peaceful interactions might have left the world in a critical state in which conflicts and social unrest spread like avalanches. Self-organized criticality might even explain how information propagates through neural networks in the brain. It is no surprise the brainstorms can be triggered by small events. (ibid, p. 53)

CRITICAL STATES

But what has all this analysis of sand piles to do with psychotherapy in general and hypnotherapy in particular? *Critical states!* There has been a great deal of controversy about defining hypnosis as an "altered state" or "relaxed state" or "somnambulistic state," or, as I have proposed, "hypnosis is the relative entrainment of any of the normal variations of our natural circadian (~ daily) or ultradian (~ hourly) states of consciousness and being" (Lloyd & Rossi, 1992; Rossi & Nimmons, 1991). What Bak and his colleagues contribute with their theory of self-organized criticality is the implication that all complex systems such as the human brain never really reach "stable equilibrium." Instead our brain is in continual evolution from one metastable state to the next. Further, I would propose that a flexible Ericksonian approach to psychotherapy is an optimal route to optimizing the evolution of self-organization and identity in hypnotherapy (Erickson & Rossi, 1989).

We have all been misguided a bit about the traditional idea of stable equilibrium and the concept of homeostasis—the view that the physiological ideal of life is to remain in a "normal," stable, unchanging state (Rossi, 1996). The new view of life as perpetually balanced on the edge of self-organized criticality has important implications for hypnosis. It means that our 200-year-long hypnotic fascination with changing mental states—however we wish to conceptualize them—is not a perverse pursuit of the strange and bizarre in human nature. Our interest is as normal as apple pie. Only now is mainstream science beginning to catch up with us. The new science of self-organization now proposes to explain with numbers, maps, graphs, and computer models how we were right all along: Human nature is an ever-shifting dynamic of metastable states in self-organized criticality on the edge of creative adaptation (Peak & Frame, 1994).

SELF-ORGANIZED CRITICALITY IN ERICKSON'S WORK

There are many other profound implications in Bak's concept of self-organized criticality for hypnosis and psychotherapy. The late Milton H. Erickson, M.D., continually reminded us of the domino effect in life as well as in psychotherapy. Seemingly small, insignificant events in everyday life—a little inspiration here, a discouraging word there—sometimes can be amplified into profoundly important changes in the course of a person's life, particularly when he or she is teetering on a critical edge of some change or other. During these periods a casually administered hypnotherapeutic suggestion that can initiate even the smallest behavioral change, a mere grain of sand in the cascade of typical daily activity, can set off a domino effect of greater and greater changes that eventually become an avalanche of life transformation and self-reorganization.

As we shall see, the domino effect is a general and essential feature of the nonlinear dynamics of the self-organization in human experience. We can experience extraordinary sensitivity to initial conditions where tiny differences in the beginning of a relationship, for example, can lead to vastly different outcomes, while paradoxically enough the exact reverse could also be true: Apparently catastrophic outside events, such as the loss of family and fortune, can sometimes leave us unmoved within the core of our character. It is precisely these disproportionate cause-and-effect relations in human affairs that the traditional type of linear thinking in psychology has been unable to cope with. As folk wisdom would have it, "With some people, you just never know!"

Dr. Erickson liked to explore disproportionate effects of what he called a "yo-yo-ing of consciousness" (Erickson & Rossi, 1979). From our new perspective we would now call this a subjective experience of a "critical phase transition in consciousness" as patients go into or out of hypnotherapeutic trance. Erickson would induce a deepening of trance during the initial hypnotic induction, for example, by counting from one to twenty and suggesting that patients would go deeper with each number so a very deep trance would be experienced by the time they heard "twenty." Later, to awaken patients from trance, Erickson would count backwards from twenty to one, with the trance "lightening" with each count. The critical phase transition in consciousness was experienced when Erickson mischievously reversed the count when he came about halfway from twenty to one. Erickson would solemnly intone, "20, 19, 18, 17, 16, 15, 14, 13, 12, 11," with his voice going from a deep bass to a lighter and lighter tone as the numbers got smaller and smaller. During this countdown the patient presumably moved from trance closer and closer to normal waking consciousness. When he reached 10, however, Erickson would pause for an extra second or two and then, instead of going down to nine as the patient expected, Erickson suddenly switched back upward by continuing with "11, 12, 13, 14 . . ." with a correspondingly deeper tone to reinducing trance depth. Sure enough, most patients would later report they experienced "a jerk and turn about" as they suddenly felt themselves unexpectedly falling back into a deeper trance with a mild sense of confusion.

When questioned about it later, many patients did not even know why they suddenly felt themselves propelled back into a deeper trance. Why did Erickson do this, quite apart from his own obvious interest in the clinical exploration of the trance experience? He explained that many patients who experienced hypnotherapy for the first time did not believe that they really were in trance. Somehow their consciousness did not recognize its own altered state, Erickson claimed, until he "jerked it around a bit" to convince the patient that an altered state was indeed being experienced. As far as I am aware, this simple and elegant approach to altering consciousness has never been documented scientifically. There could be no better documentation of the nonlinear thesis that the essence of hypnotherapy is a utilization of the creative instability of the brain and mind precariously poised on the edge of chaos between the "attractors" we label as "altered states, attitudes, emotions, images, obsessions, compulsions, symptoms, or habits" and the possibilities of new and better states of "self-organization" and "identity."

NONLINEAR MODELS

There is a shadow that falls between the clinical complexity of nonlinear reality and the simple linear models that are used in linear academic research. Often using literary metaphors, clinical psychodynamics attempts to formulate the nonlinear twists and turns of the mind and behavior. Most of the academic researcher's traditional methods, however, have been oversimplified with linear models. The linear net with a large regular mesh of statistical holes usually fails to capture the slippery nonlinear eels of human psychodynamics (Prigogine, 1980). It is easier for researchers to deal with linear systems, where one and one make two, nothing more and nothing less. In nonlinear mathematics, however, the same equation or system of equations can have two or more solutions. Thus we say that nonlinearity is the source of multiple possibilities (Hall, 1991; Poincaré, 1905/1952).

The traditional classical approach of linear science, where natural aspects of the world are isolated and reduced to fragments that can be portrayed in simple models, breaks down when we study the emergence or synthesis of wholes on whatever level: a whole society, person, brain, neuron, or energy flux, or the genetic matrix of a whole cell. The naturally nonlinear nature of the world consists of many layers of systems where everything seems to be related to everything else. It is precisely this nonlinear interrelatedness and interdependence of everything that leads to the emergence of the new, so that we say, "The whole is more than the sum of its parts." Sally Goerner expresses this well in the context of outlining the current nonlinear revolution from classical reductionism to an understanding of the emergence of the new in the nonlinear dynamics of chaos theory:

But there is another concept that is also critical to the nonlinear revolution: inter-dependence. Popular chaos literature often confounds inter-dependence and nonlinearity, but actually they are not related. Nonlinearity has to do with proportionality. Inter-dependence has to do with whether or not two things mutually affect each other (or, in mathematical terms, whether or not the two are functions of one another). A conversation is an inter-dependent (also called interactive) communication between two people—both people are affected, and the exchange becomes a reciprocating mutual effect system. . . . *Independent systems like linear systems are actually just useful idealizations. In the real world there are no truly linear systems and there are not truly independent systems—not even soliloquies. The notion of truly independent systems has also tended to create erroneous assumptions about how the world (vs. our models) works.* . . .

How does this relate to a new vision of things? Classical approaches such as calculus and linear approximations first broke down when people tried to make their models more realistic, which meant including nonlinear inter-dependent aspects that had been there all along. The classic example of this is the three-body problem. Newton established the classical vision of precise prediction by applying equations of motion to the solar system. He did this using a simple two-body model; he looked at the effects of a massive body, the sun, on individual smaller bodies, the planets, taken one at a time. Chaos was first discovered when people tried to increase the precision of the model by adding the

effects of just one more body (say, a moon or another planet). This model of the solar system is a three-body problem. The problem was that this minutely more sophisticated model could not be solved by approximation methods and had unexpected behaviors that did not appear in the two-body model. The three-body problem exhibits chaos. *Newtonian predictability is an illusion of the simpler model.* (Goerner, 1995, pp. 20–21, italics added.)

There is something so profoundly different in this shift to the nonlinear world view in all fields from mathematics and physics to psyche that we expect it will continue to shatter many of our previous conceptions of nature as we get a better grasp of the new dynamics of self-organization. Above all is the concept of mind and human experience perpetually in transition on the creative edge between stability and chaos.

CONCLUSION

A detailed study of Erickson's approaches to hypnotherapy reveals that he intuitively understood the nonlinear dynamics of human experience even though he probably never knew anything about nonlinear concepts that originally came from mathematics (Rossi, 1996). In Europe there is a school of research called Synergetics that is already making considerable progress in exploring and applying nonlinear dynamics to hypnosis as well as to clinical psychology and psychotherapy (Tschacher, Schiepek, & Brunner, 1992). Several recent research volumes published here in America are developing these insights in a manner that has profound implications for a renewal of academic research with nonlinear dynamics (Kelso, 1995; Kruse & Stadler, 1994, 1995; Smith & Thelen, 1993). If we can follow their lead, I believe that we will see a new nonlinear dynamics in our approach to research on Ericksonian hypnotherapy in the future. It will be an exciting new chapter in the evolution of the psychotherapist from the rather lean linear conception of reality to the nonlinear world view of adaptive complexity and a naturalistic approach to self-organization.

REFERENCES

Bak, P., & Chen, K. (1991). Self organized critically. *Scientific America, 264* (1), 46–63.

Balthazard, C., & Woody, E. (1985). The "stuff" of hypnotic performance: A review of psychometric approaches. *Psychological Bulletin, 98*(2), 283–296.

Bernheim, H. (1886/1957). *Suggestive therapeutics: A treatise on the nature and uses of hypnotism*. Westport, CT: Associated Booksellers.

Davis, L., & Husband, R. (1931). A study of hypnotic susceptibility in relation to personality traits. *Journal of Abnormal Social Psychology, 26*, 175–182.

Erickson, M., & Rossi, E. (1979). *Hypnotherapy: An exploratory casebook*. New York: Irvington.

Erickson, M., & Rossi, E. (1989). *The February man: Evolving consciousness and identity in hypnotherapy*. New York: Brunner/Mazel.

Eysenck, H. (1991). Is suggestibility? In J. Schumaker (Ed.), *Human suggestibility: Advances in theory, research and application*. New York: Routledge.

Goerner, S. (1995). Chaos, evolution and deep ecology. In R. Robertson & A. Combs (Eds.), *Chaos theory in psychology and the life sciences*. Northvale, New Jersey: Lawrence Erlbaum.

Hall, N. (Ed.). (1991). *Exploring chaos: A guide to the new science of disorder*. New York: W. W. Norton

Hilgard, E. (1991). Suggestibility and suggestions as related to hypnosis. In J. Schumaker (Ed.), *Human suggestibility: Advances in theory, research and application*. New York: Routledge.

Kelso, J.A.S. (1995). *Dynamic patterns: The self-organization of brain and behavior*. Cambridge, MA: MIT Press.

Kirsch, I., & Lynn, S. (1995). The altered state of hypnosis: Changes in the theoretical landscape. *American Psychologist, 50*:10, 846–858.

Kruse, P., & Stadler, M. (Eds). (1994). *Multistability in cognition*. Berlin: Springer-Verlag.

Kruse, P., & Stadler, M. (Eds.). (1995). *Ambiguity in mind and nature: Multistable cognitive phenomena*. New York: Springer-Verlag.

Lloyd, D., & Rossi, E. (Eds.). (1992). *Ultradian rhythms in life processes: A fundamental inquiry into chronobiology and psychobiology*, New York: Springer-Verlag.

Naish, P. (Ed.). (1986). *What is hypnosis? Current theories and research*. Milton Keynes, Open University Press: Philadelphia.

Peak, D., & Frame, M. (1994). *Chaos under control: The art and science of complexity*.

Poincaré, H. (1905/1952). *Science and hypothesis*. New York: Dover.

Prigogine, I. (1980). *From being to becoming: Time and complexity in the physical sciences*. San Francisco: Freeman.

Rossi, E. (1986/1993) *The psychobiology of mind-body healing*, second Ed. New York: Norton.

Rossi, E. (1996). *The symptom path to enlightenment: Self-organization in non-directive hypnotherapy*, Pacific Palisades, CA: Palisades Gateway Publishing.

Rossi, E., & Nimmons, D. (1991). *The 20 minute break: Using the new science of ultradian rhythms*. Los Angeles: Tarcher.

Schumaker, J. (Ed.). (1991). *Human suggestibility: Advances in theory, research and application*. New York: Routledge.

Smith, L., & Thelen, E. (1993). *A dynamical systems approach to the development: Applications*. Boston: MIT Press.

Tschacher, W., Schiepek, G., & Brunner, E. (1992). *Self-organization and clinical psychology*. New York: Springer-Verlag.

Discussion by Eugene Gendlin, Ph.D.

◆

First, I want to tell Dr. Rossi that he doesn't have to worry about some of the research studies that he mentioned. They are not good research. There is a fundamental law of all research that says that you cannot prove the null hypothesis. If you do not find something, that does not mean it isn't there. If you use poor methods, you cannot find the most obvious things. I did not originate this law. It is basic to the very idea of research. For example, if you choose the wrong measures, you can "prove" that there is no such thing as gender. You can test a very large number of subjects, and count their toes. Then you will find that there is no such thing as gender. Or if you want to prove that it is not raining when it is pouring, use a thermometer. That would "disprove" the rain. But we all know that in research, although we do the best we can to measure something, we still might use the wrong measures and methods. If we don't find anything, it does not mean that what we looked for is not there. Rather, the result is neutral. It just means that we didn't find it.

But hypnosis is special in the sense that it was always known to be there, and hypnosis tended to crack the prevailing official academic ideology. We prize hypnosis for that. In the days when experience couldn't be talked about at all, there was hypnosis. In public places it can be shown that there is such a thing as experience and bodily process and hypnosis.

It is not just hypnosis that is nonlinear; all experiencing is nonlinear. Any moment is a mesh of thousands of aspects that have never been separate. It is even wrong to call them "aspects." If you pay attention to what "experiencing" does in your body, you find that much of your whole life is implicit in most any small thing. Of course you need not attend in this way all the time. In fact, you couldn't get around if you did. But when it matters, it is a great principle to know. On anything large or small, even a little detail, you can stop and say, "How does that make me feel right here in the middle of my body?" You won't get just that little detail because nothing exists just by itself. It is always part of a mesh of experiencing. It is never just *this* situation; it is also how you got into it, and that you are the kind of person who would get into that kind of situation. Your bodily sense of that situation (if you attend and let such a sense come) implicitly includes all that, and also other similar times and your whole history with that sort of situation and what you were trying to achieve or avoid.

Such a bodily sense is at first vague, but then turns out to be more specific and more differentiated than ordinary phrases and notions. But we are trained to be "objective," which also means that if we can't define it, it doesn't exist. And that is not so.

I support Dr. Rossi also in his emphasis on the physiological, except that I would maintain that everything human has all of those dimensions. Only our ways of studying things divides them. Everything human is physiological and psychological, and also economic and spiritual and electrical and chemical.

I deny that something is either psychological or physiological. I think that is a tremendous trap for people in our culture, because our technology is so good on the physiological side. We need to catch up on the psychological, social, political, and economic sides.

The physiological technology is now so good that it can mislead people. Let me tell a story:

I called a client yesterday before I arrived at the conference. I was afraid for her, because while I am out of town her little girl is getting tests on some medical variable. I called my client and said, "Look, you already know something is wrong, and you have been working psychologically with the child for months on it. The condition is in the process of getting better. So, now if they find something 'physiological,' some physical index that goes with it, don't freak out; that wouldn't be surprising. It won't mean that the trouble *is* physiological. There is always something physiological that goes with anything psychological, so just wait six months and have her tested again."

People think that if a psychological condition shows up on a physiological measure, then it is real and threatening. But I argue that anything psychological has physiological correlates; we may or may not have measures to find them. And on the psychological side, we can probably do more to heal something, and with less danger, than intervening on its physiological side.

So Rossi and I largely agree in all these respects. Let me now respond to the differences. I want to pick up where Rossi ended and asked: "Is this focusing?" No, not quite, although we have a lot in common, and it is very important.

Therapists have employed hypnosis, put it down, always rediscovered it, but therapists could not use it as it stood. Recently there has been a great development that has changed the drawbacks hypnosis always had for therapy. No longer does it necessarily make the client passive and dependent. Self-hypnosis also has been greatly expanded, and ways have been found to ask rather than to command the client's body. This line of development makes hypnosis closer to focusing.

With regard to relaxation and altered states, there is a law (this one is well known, but I may be the one to state it this way) that there is an inverse relationship between the amount of content that can be elicited in you, and the degree of full responding with which you can react to that content. When you are asleep and your body is paralyzed, a great deal of content can come, but you have very little capacity to respond to it actively, and your perspective and sense of its meaning is limited. The use of chemicals, illicit as well as legal, demonstrates the same law: Much more than the normal content can emerge, but far less than normal can be done with it.

The old-fashioned and ineffective way of dealing with this was first to flood a person with great amounts of content in an altered state, then later to have so-called "integration sessions" that consisted of old-fashioned therapy, and could make only a little use of the content that had come. The new and much more effective way is to do most of the therapeutic work in extremely light trance, close to the normal state.

The inverse relation also applies in a single moment. If you relax, a lot more can come, but if it was only for a moment, at the next moment you can be fully responsive to what came.

Still another similarity I notice is that Rossi is not mainly interested in content as such, but with the kinds of processes that usually happen in clients. He also wants to show them better modes. There is similar emphasis in focusing. The manner of the process matters much more than the content, and eventually it determines the content.

With so much in common, even with the differences, there is a lot we can learn from each other, and adapt in our own ways.

Since I do not know the recent work with hypnosis well enough, and I want to be precise, let me define the focusing side where I think we differ. In focusing, one relaxes enough to sense what comes in one's body. One deliberately lets the body-sense come without engineering it or editing it. But at the next moment one is fully and normally able to respond to what came. Focusing is a kind of zigzag, a conversation between the two states. If a person relaxes too deeply, this zigzag becomes impossible.

Focusing does not employ hypnosis or trance. I know that one might argue that it does. I have been in trance so light that it differed in no detectable way from not being in trance at all, and still I could do relatively amazing things. Let me describe focusing more precisely: Suppose you go into trance and come

back immediately. Suppose someone takes you to a nice place, and then immediately all the way out again, and then back, and out again, in and out, and in and out. I think you will agree that you cannot do that, and would not want to. You might go in and out once, or even twice, but not rapidly back and forth many times. It would feel painful and make you angry. From this oscillation you can evaluate the level of relaxation at which focusing takes place.

Here is another way to define precisely what degree of relaxation focusing employs. One of the fastest ways we have to let the bodily felt sense of a problem come is to say to ourselves, "I feel just fine about this problem." Instantly the body responds with the opposite, the body sense, which is very definitely not "fine." In hypnosis the body would be likely to accept the suggestion.

Also at each step of focusing, we depend on the body-sense *not* going along, unless something is just right. For example, we ask: "What is the quality of this body sense? Is it heavy, jumpy, all pasted up?" The body-sense doesn't budge; that means none of those words speak for it. At last a word comes that does speak for it; we can tell because the body-sense eases slightly but very distinctly. Then it also feels more open, and soon shows that it really is, because new steps come from it that change the whole problem.

When a word or a step seems to have come from the body-sense, we check it with the body-sense. If there is no directly sensed response, we know we have as yet no step. So you see that we depend on the body-sense to talk back in this way to what we say.

Rossi uses another way to let the body talk back. There are ideomotor signals. I appreciate those. I think we might want to learn them, and adapt them in focusing.

In focusing, when something comes, you would typically respond first with a reception, "Oh, that's how it is; that makes a lot of sense [breath, relief], sure. . . ." You also might actively hold off other responses that you might have, superego attacks, anger, or impatience. You would actively protect the coming, and not let those other reactions close it off. When you have fully received what came, you might then respond further with a question, "Oh, well, if *that's* how it is, well then, how about such and so? Hmmm. . . . No. . . . OK. Well, how about such and such?" Nothing moves. "All right. Well, what does *it* want? . . ." And if still nothing comes, perhaps, "Well, let me stay with it more."

Focusing is a conversation between the body-sense and the conscious person. The two of them have understood that they cannot do without each other. That understanding is a great thing, because people argue so much on either side of these two.

Of course, in these brief comments on Dr. Rossi, I cannot show you focusing. It takes a few days of futzing to find it. Each person encounters certain difficulties, and these have to be worked with individually. Focusing involves going by a certain sense of bodily comfort and discomfort. At first it seems no more than just discomfort, but that is precisely where the opening comes, and new steps of resolution appear. These steps come from inside, and they have a characteristic intricacy and uniqueness that differs very much from anything that the conscious person or a therapist could invent or suggest.

The novelty and progression of steps is central to focusing. It is not the case that what we need is all already formed and waiting, nor is it the case that we have to import it into the person. There is a process of further forming, I call it "carrying forward," in which new steps arise and move beyond a problem.

Another way of talking about my agreement and disagreement is to say, as Rossi indicated, that hypnosis accesses capacities of the human organism that we normally don't have, immense capacities for creative modes of healing. We want those. We surely want to learn those from each other, if we know different ones. There is a mystery also about the fact that we are capable of so much that we cannot have unless another person is present. But if the other person takes control, then we also cannot have our full capacities. They come while that person is there and then we don't have them again. This factor is also being taken into account in the newer ways of working.

I am not opposed to the fact that there is a hypnotist there. But not every hypnotist knows how to remain present as a human being with me in a primary sense. I do not think about my tone of voice or my gestures or breathing, because these things come naturally if I attend to the person. If my mind is *primarily* on those things, then I am not present with the other person. Hypnotists may stand off over there, counseling with themselves, so to speak, but I know from experience that they need not do that. They can return their attention to the person. As a therapist, I also think and consider many things I might say and do, but I do not leave clients for long. The client feels my attention even with closed eyes or gazing forward.

Another difference: I relate to the client's body only through the client. I don't elicit things directly from the client's body without consulting the client. I am like a lawyer, not like a doctor, if you follow me. A lawyer would not go to court and sue someone in my name without my approval or my knowledge. That's why Rogers switched from using "patient" to "client."

I wasn't here yesterday, but the person with whom Rossi demonstrated in his workshop said she felt totally safe, and totally in control with herself, and our focusing people who observed Rossi's work all told me that it felt very good to them.

At the end, just now, you asked my body if it would want to close its eyes. It did, but I would have liked it better if you had told *me* to ask my body. Or, I might have liked it if you had turned to us and asked: "Would you like me to take control of your eyes?" Then I would have said, "Yes." I didn't like you relating to my body directly without me, perhaps because I am not used to it and didn't know to expect it. As it was, I just had to wait until you gave me back my eyes. I like hypnosis a lot, and I know it has an irreplaceable role as part of what we need in therapy. But I think therapy needs to consist chiefly of the client being the active one.

In conclusion, I see a great convergence in the last ten years, and Ernie, I look forward to more exchanges with you.

Experiential Approaches to Clinician Development

Jeffrey K. Zeig, Ph.D.

Jeffrey K. Zeig, Ph.D.
Jeffrey K. Zeig (Ph.D., 1977, Georgia State University) is the Founder and Director of The Milton H. Erickson Foundation in Phoenix, Ariz. He organized the International Congresses on Ericksonian Approaches to Hypnosis and Psychotherapy held in 1980, 1983, 1986, 1992, and 1994, as well as the Brief Therapy Conferences held in 1988, 1993 and 1996. Dr. Zeig is the architect of The Evolution of Psychotherapy Conferences.
Dr. Zeig received the Milton H. Erickson Award for Outstanding Contributions to the Field of Hypnosis from The Netherlands Society of Clinical Hypnosis and the Milton H. Erickson Award of Excellence in Scientific Writing from the American Journal of Clinical Hypnosis. *He has written one book and edited or coedited ten books and five monographs on Ericksonian therapy, brief therapy, and eclectic approaches to psychotherapy that appear in eight foreign languages. Additionally, one book about his work appears in Italian, and another in Spanish. He has taught psychotherapy in more than 30 foreign countries on six continents.*

INTRODUCTION

In psychotherapy we struggle endlessly with the fact that most people live fragmented lives. They are preoccupied with the horrors and the glories of the past or they are preoccupied with the horrors and the glories of the future. They don't live; they just use their left brain to endlessly think about living. This kind of meta-living is just like meta-communication—the disease that all psychotherapists are suffering from. We spend our lives talking about talking, and many times never say anything. . . .

What is the essential objective of psychotherapy? . . . maybe it's to get rid of the past (good and bad) and the future (good and bad) and just be. That is, develop your personhood or your capacity to be

who you are, wherever you are. (Whitaker, 1982, pp. 495–96)

Broaching the distance from the head to the heart is a problem that concerns therapists of all persuasions. Patients commonly understand their difficulties but fail to take effective countermeasures. However, if clinicians can systematically distinguish between technical or theoretical *understanding* and experiential *postures* or *states*, they more easily can modify the distance between the head and the heart. Moreover, the same distinction can help clinicians develop their own personhood.

I have a number of goals for my chapter, each of which concerns the distinction between technical understanding and experiential realization:

Editor's Note: I am grateful to Brent Geary, Ph.D., for suggestions that were incorporated into the final draft.

1. I want to reflect on my own evolution as a clinician, with special emphasis on my evolution as a teacher.
2. I want to outline an experiential method of training that I am developing, which is still in its infancy.
3. I want to stimulate clinicians to apply the method both for their own growth and development and as a tool for clinical practice.

Before proceeding I will make three preliminary provisos: One, talking about experiential methods is difficult at best, and deadly at worst. There is too much of a tendency to metacomment, consequently squeezing the life out of vibrant experiences by talking about them. Therefore, I will intersperse some experiential methods into this presentation, realizing that this particular format, print, is more suited to didactic offerings than experiences.

Two, I am going to rely heavily on Milton Erickson as a model. This is not a case of transference; well, maybe there is a little transference. But I have been a student of therapy approaches for quite a while, and I have closely examined the work of masters from many disciplines. However, in the final analysis, Erickson unquestionably has proven to be the most interesting, the most complex, the best clinician I have ever seen, bar none. He had the most extraordinary range in his ability to therapeutically reach diverse types of patients. I am not the only one who has come to this conclusion. Many notable therapists and practitioners have been profoundly influenced by Erickson and his work.

Three, my interest in hypnosis naturally leads me to view things in terms of states. A more recently acquired interest in drama leads me to a perspective on postures. There is overlap between hypnotic states and dramatic postures: they both are inherently experiential. The world of experience, as you will see, is of primary interest.

As an entrée to the world of experiences, let's consider two cases.

CASE I

A couple came to Erickson with the wife's alcoholism as the presenting problem. Her pattern of drinking was covert; for example, she would garden on the weekends and drink from a carefully hidden bottle. The husband counseled, confronted, criticized, and coerced his wife, all to no avail. The wife continued drinking, to her own detriment and to the detriment of the relationship.

It seemed that the husband also had a "little hobby." All weekend long, he sat in the living room reading "dusty old books, dusty old newspapers, and dusty old magazines." The wife counseled, confronted, criticized, and coerced her husband, all to no avail. The husband continued his hobby, to his own detriment and to the detriment of the relationship.

In the interview, Erickson discovered two seemingly inconsequential details: The couple had a camping bus they had not used in years, and the couple passionately hated fishing.

Erickson's first intervention was to suggest to the wife that she buy a bottle of whiskey and bring it home. She was to hide it in the house. On returning home from work, the husband was to try to find the hidden bottle within an hour. If he didn't, she could drink with impunity in the house.

The wife found great delight in finding a place to hide the bottle that no man could find in one hour. But after a few days of this routine, she became disconcerted and her delight grew thin; the couple returned to Erickson.

To the couple's dismay, Erickson directed them to go fishing. When they declined, reminding him of their distaste, he insisted. Ignoring their mounting protests, he became adamant about his directive. Finally they asked why it was so important to go fishing. "Well," he said, "it's the only correct therapy for you. Wife, if you are in a boat in the middle of a lake, there is no place to hide whiskey. Husband, if you are in the boat in the middle of a lake, there is no place to bring books, magazines, and newspapers. Go fishing!"

The couple rebelled. Instead, they went camping. In doing so, they rediscovered a mutual hobby. They also rediscovered an interest in their relationship. He voluntarily relinquished his isolation. She voluntarily gave up alcohol. They changed on their own initiative; Erickson merely established a climate in which they could examine and alter their behavior.

CASE II

A businessman, caught up in a large deal, came to me complaining of anxiety. When I asked him to specify the feeling, he reported it as "a stone-like sensation" in his chest. When I asked for the internal dialogue that preceded the stone-like feeling, he couldn't identify it. And this was an articulate, psychologically aware man who previously had been excellent at describing his psychodynamics.

I initiated discussion of the topic of reassurance. I asked what kind of reassurance would help him, what kind he needed to hear. He remembered his father, a central figure in his life. His father would tell him that he had done the proper amount of work, "not too little, not too much," therefore, he could "rely on his intuition." The patient was a little older than I, but I straightened up and said, softly but commandingly, "You have done the proper amount of work on your deal. I know it. You've discussed it with me. You can rely on your cunning [something he valued] and your intuition." He started to blink and then closed his eyes.

I told him the story about a dream I had in 1980, prior to the First International Congress on Ericksonian Approaches to Hypnosis and Psychotherapy, which was held as a tribute to Erickson. I was the organizer of the Congress. It was the biggest event that I had undertaken; I was only 33 years old, anxious and inexperienced.

In the dream, which occurred the night before the Congress, Erickson, who was confined to a wheelchair when I knew him, walked up to me and hugged me. In the dream, he said, "I love you." I memorized the phrase. I memorized the feeling of Erickson's body against mine. I awoke, proud of my unconscious mind for supplying the image. On subsequent days, when I proceeded into meeting rooms and when I encountered anxiety, I would bring back the dream, including its words and the feeling it produced.

Then I offered another story about how I would ask a friend to hug me before a big presentation. I would remember the hug on stage.

After I finished my stories, the patient opened his eyes and segued to the idea that he was going to see his father's grave because the ten-year anniversary of his father's death was approaching. I suggested that he could take something from his yard, perhaps a stone, to the cemetery with him. He could hold the stone against his chest and then place it on the gravesite.

Accordingly, I talked with the patient about the importance of symbolism. I described some of the symbols in my office, a number of which were from Erickson. I indicated how I had incorporated Erickson as a symbolic father in many respects.

All along I was directing my clinical intervention at the following questions: How could I help this man modify the sensation in his chest? How could I help alter its meaning, form, substance, and so on? How could I help him change the associations underlying the difficulty?

As the man left my office, he talked about his girlfriend, someone I knew to be important to him. I also knew that he highly valued her supportive hugs. His girlfriend had decided that the picture of his father that had hung in his office should be moved to their home, where all the other family pictures were. As he was walking out of my office at the end of the session, he mused, "I don't think she is right in this case. It would be better if I took the picture back to my office." I took his comment as symbolic confirmation of the effectiveness of the therapy.

For a moment let's suspend customary thinking, which in these cases would examine the dynamics of theory, practice, or even the therapist. Instead, let's consider the posture of the therapist and pose two questions: (a) What position does a clinician take to intervene thusly?, and (b) Can a clinician systematically develop the perspective, power, and social role to offer such treatment? If so, how? Let's answer these questions by using Erickson as a model.

ERICKSONIAN POSTURES

To consider the therapist's posture, I will briefly describe four clinical postures of Erickson: *creating experiences, utilization, orienting toward,* and *communicating for effect.*

One posture that is a hallmark of Erickson's work is the concept of *creating experiences.*

Erickson engineered therapeutic encounters whereby a patient would experientially realize previously unrecognized abilities to cope and change. The case of the couple is a good example. Erickson knew that they had the inherent (but not fully recognized) power to live more effectively. He merely set up circumstances in which they could access that power, readily recognizing that insight was not a precursor of change. Erickson's therapy (and teaching) eschewed insight in favor of experiential methods.

A second posture is *utilization*, which dictates that whatever exists in the therapeutic situation can be harnessed to achieve therapeutic goals. Utilization is the therapist's posture of readiness to respond strategically to any and all aspects of the patient or the patient's environment. In the case of the non-fishing couple, Erickson used the wife's pattern of hiding, the couple's rebellious nature, and their dislike of fishing.

To give such a cursory explanation of the concept of utilization, as I am doing now, is a travesty, because this undermines its place as a defining signature of the Ericksonian method. During the last twenty years, I have strived to master the utilization approach. Moreover, most of my writing on Ericksonian methods in the last ten years has consisted of explications of the utilization method. I have maintained that utilization is to Ericksonian therapy as interpretation is to psychoanalysis, as desensitization is to behavior therapy. It is true that many great clinicians utilize what the patient brings; however, the extent to which Erickson developed his utilization orientation was unparalleled. (For further information on utilization, see Zeig, 1992.)

For a moment, let's accept utilization as a central and defining characteristic of the Ericksonian method, and accede that it has clinical effectiveness. Even so, why is it intrinsically important for clinicians to develop a utilization posture? One reason is that it speaks to an essential aspect of psychological problems. *Psychological problems can be conceived as believed-in limitations*. That is, patients act as if they cannot change or adequately cope. In contradistinction, utilization is a philosophy of sufficiency: The therapist models a proactive

stance of alchemy, creating practical, therapeutic gold out of leaden situations. The patient consequently is encouraged to behave similarly.

Utilization is an approach I use in every hypnotic induction: I will take things out of the immediate reality situation and harness them to accomplish trance goals, such as internal absorption and promoting constructive dissociation. For example, in beginning a group induction one might suggest: You're seated here and you can realize that there may be papers and books in front of you. For a moment you don't need to ... really focus intently on what is in front of you. You can allow something in back of your mind to develop, now. And I don't know if your unconscious mind can vividly remember a time in school when you were reading, a pleasant time reading at the beach, at home now. But you continue to enjoy the developing comfort that can be a part of the evolving experience ...

A third posture characteristic of Erickson's method is the emphasis on indirection, a philosophy of *orienting toward* goals. Orienting toward is similar to the manner in which a religious master uses parables rather than stating options directly.

Many texts provide elucidation of the techniques of indirection. For present purposes, let's presume that the technique of indirection and the posture of orienting toward can be remarkably effective on many therapeutic occasions.

One constituent of the orienting toward posture, guiding associations, is illustrated in the aforementioned Case Two. My method was geared to changing my patient's association to his anxiety. While it is true that effective therapy can proceed by analyzing associations, one also can view therapy as the reassociation of internal life (Erickson, 1948) and guide preconscious associations to create effective treatment.

A fourth posture intrinsically bound to Erickson's method is the idea of *communicating for effect*. Of course, all therapists communicate for directed effect, but Erickson, as a hypnotherapist, was keenly oriented to the intended outcome of his suggestions. In contradistinction, many models of therapy are predicated on uncovering the understructure of the pathology in the individual or family.

Erickson, on the other hand, was more of a pilot than an archeologist or oceanographer.

In his years of studying hypnosis, Erickson investigated how people responded to nuance in communication. He was an explorer of human social responsiveness. For example, he used words surgically to elicit responses; he used verbal implication, gesture, the implication of gestures, and so on. Especially important to Erickson was the way in which people responded to innuendo without full realization of the response or the stimulus that elicited it. A cousin of this important but insufficiently understood phenomenon is the way one person will cough in an auditorium and others will echo, the way strangers sitting side by side will unconsciously synchronize their breathing rate and/or posture. Again, communicating for effect is an area to which I cannot give deserved attention in this chapter; still, it is of essential importance in Ericksonian methods.

So many experts discuss their work vertically, describing the depth of dynamics in the presenting pathology, history, or family pattern. Conversely, as an expert in hypnosis, Erickson set sights on the horizon; he demonstrated people's ability to respond specifically to nuance such as the locus of voice, intonation change, and alterations in tempo.

These four postures—creating experiences, utilization, orienting toward, and communicating for effect—are core concepts in my therapy. To understand why I refer to them as postures and even "states," let's examine their essential nature.

ON EXPERIENCE

Consider the four postures: They could be seen merely as techniques, and in some sense they are. In fact, they, or related methods, are described as techniques in a number of effective approaches to therapy. At present, however, I would like to think of them as experiential postures that a clinician can maintain. This is an important distinction that reflects on training: Techniques can be taught didactically; experiential postures cannot. Therefore, a method is needed to train experiential postures; they are important for both clinicians and clients.

Experiential postures are essential for patients because some concepts can be mastered intellectually; others, such as being happy, cannot. Happiness is an experiential reality; one cannot *do* happiness intentionally. Happiness must be realized, not learned; there are few rational lessons that one can be taught overtly to promote happiness.

Some of the seeming obscurity of Erickson's clinical methods might arise from the distinction between lessons that can be learned didactically and those that must be realized experientially. More often than not, Erickson resided in the experiential latitudes. This was true in both his clinical work and his teaching.

ON TRAINING

I will diverge for a moment to describe Erickson as a mentor. My instruction under Erickson's tutelage was as uncommon as his therapy. He never saw me do hypnosis or therapy, although he sought out reports on some of the cases he referred to me. He rarely provided didactic input; rather he taught as he conducted therapy, by using experiential methods. He offered hypnosis, stories, tasks, allusions, and so on. Not only did he eschew cognitive learning, he opined that it often was more of a hindrance than a benefit. Of course, one could and should read to learn content. For example, Erickson was well aware of the psychoanalytic approaches of his day, having collaborated with Lawrence Kubie and having worked with analysts, including Spurgeon English and Ives Hendricks. However, in interpersonal situations Erickson did not teach content; more commonly, he oriented to the development of the clinician's experiential posture and referred students to books for learning content.

There is an implication in Erickson's teaching method that has influenced my training of clinicians: Training must develop the self of the clinician, not just his or her technical ability. This does not mean personal therapy for the clinician. There are many aspects of self that can be evolved in the clinician in addition to those that can be developed through personal therapy.

As I will demonstrate, systematic methods can be used for overall clinician development.

Before discussing clinical development, I will outline my training model so that the clinician development section can be understood in perspective. (An elaboration appears in Zeig, 1992.)

MY DIDACTIC APPROACH

My teaching model is based on five intervention choice points; namely, *goals, gift wrapping, tailoring, processing,* and *the position of the clinician.* I use some experiential exercises in each of the components to help students master principles and practice. To teach the position of the clinician, I use experiential exercises almost exclusively. Let's briefly examine the first four aspects of the model and then address the fifth in its unique role as an axis on which the other four revolve. Each choice point has a primary question.

The *goal* question is, "What do I want to communicate to the patient?" The goal component that I teach consists of information on data gathering, and instruction on refining the problem and its definition.

The *gift-wrapping* question is, "How do I want to communicate the goal?" The didactic component concerning gift wrapping is one of the most extensive and consists of information on techniques, including the structure of hypnosis; the use of anecdotes; the interspersal method; symptom prescription; and reframing. Techniques of therapy are seen as ways of presenting gift-wrapped ideas to patients; they are not curative in and of themselves.

The third component, *tailoring,* asks, "What position does the patient take?" This component focuses on assessment of the patient's intrapsychic and interpersonal style. It gathers information, which is useful both in modifying the gift wrapping to fit the style of the individual and on using the patient's position to establish treatment goals. An example of altering gift wrapping to fit the uniqueness of the individual would be to alter a hypnotic induction to an intellectual person as compared with an artistic person.

The fourth question is, "How can a dramatic *process* be created to make the gift-wrapped and tailored goal come alive?" There are three stages in the process: the setup, intervention, and follow-through.

Attending to these four intervention points can enhance the power of inventions. One of the obvious merits of this model of intervention is its immediate clinical utility. For example, by using it, the therapist has more choices when encountering resistance: One can change the goal, gift wrapping, tailoring, or process as needed. Moreover, and perhaps most influential in improving therapy outcome, is the last choice point, the position of the therapist. If resistance occurs the therapist can also be changed. No, I don't mean referral. I mean accessing a previously dormant ability within the clinician. As we will later see, systematic experiential methods can be valuable in training the ability of the clinician to be flexible in bringing forth therapeutic abilities.

Figure 1 illustrates the model.

THE THERAPIST'S POSTURE

To consider the *therapist's position* one can ponder "What position does the clinician take?"

The position of the therapist can be divided into four subcategories, *lenses, muscles, heart,*

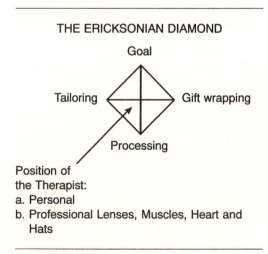

Figure 1. Intervention model

and *hats*, each of which has a professional and personal aspect, modified by experience. First, *lenses* represent the ways of viewing. On a professional level, lenses learned when studying family therapy diverge from those learned in behavior therapy. On a personal level, the lenses learned growing up in one's family of origin differ from those learned in the neighbor's family. Second, *muscles* are the way of doing. Psychoanalysts, for example, often hypertrophy their interpretation muscles, while Ericksonians develop their orienting-toward abilities. Third, compassion is manifested in the *heart*. And fourth, the *hats* symbolize the therapist's social roles.

ON THERAPIST EVOLUTION

Aspects of the therapist's posture continue to evolve through training and experience. Traditional professional sources of growth and development include graduate school, postgraduate training programs, supervision, and experience with a variety of patients. Also contributing are lectures, modeling by experts, personal therapy, supervision, books, tapes, cotherapy, and supervision through a one-way mirror in which a teacher speaks through a trainee. Although these are effective methods in improving the therapist's abilities, they are not especially cohesive or experiential.

I suspect most therapists, regardless of their theoretical persuasion, would ascribe their professional evolution to some combination of the aforementioned sources. A reflexive response to querying clinicians about the primary source of their growth and development is, "I have learned the most from my patients." However, I am suspect of the unspecified nature of this proclamation. Learned what? Learned how to suffer unduly? Learned how to be inflexible, resistant, rebellious? Okay, I should not be such a smart aleck, but I am pushing for a point: Why should an important issue like professional growth and development be left to chance? Can we have a systematic method?

For instance, can one conceive of therapy training as sports training, which requires exercise, practice and discipline? If so, therapists

could regularly train (and crosstrain) to improve their development. Thereby, techniques would not predominate; rather emphasis would be placed on training therapeutic postures, on growth, and on development. In an attempt to advance the growth and development of the therapist, I have developed a systematic experiential training system that I will outline shortly. First I will describe how the model derived from Erickson's work.

ERICKSON'S SELF-TRAINING

A model of the self-training of postures is suggested in Erickson's work. He reported a number of exercises that he used to train himself. To compensate for omissions in his medical school education, internship, and residency, he said that in one of his early jobs, he would get a social history from the social work service, and then intuit and write a mental status examination based on the written history. Then he would take a mental status examination and compare the intuited with the actual mental status examination. Subsequently, he would reverse the process; he would get a mental status examination, write an intuited social history, and compare it with the actual social history. He said that he did that exercise with hundreds of patients. His attempt was not to learn content, but to master a posture, a style of understanding human circumstances.

Also, Erickson reported that he attended to nuances in human social behavior and wrote his extrapolation of what they meant. Working like Sherlock Holmes, he would see a clue and venture a written prediction. He then deposited it with his secretary to await confirmation. For example, perhaps he noticed telltale behaviors and ventured, "This man is having an affair." Again, he seemed to avidly work to develop a posture of extrapolating from minimal cues. He was not focused merely on increasing his base of cognitive knowledge.

Erickson was dedicated to his growth and development throughout his life. Just before his death, I asked him a simple administrative question. He responded, but answered by using an indirect technique; he told a story. I had to "unwrap" the answer. His failure to reply directly interested me: I had the sense that he was playing—even more than that, that he was exercising his orienting toward "muscles," wanting to maintain tonus.

Moreover, Erickson gave me personal development assignments, although not systematically. For example, he told me to go to a schoolyard and watch children. (If you do this, remember, *do not* wear a trenchcoat!). I should predict which child would go to which toy next. Which would leave the group first? The idea of extrapolating and projecting future patterns from small bits of behavior was near and dear to Erickson, and he promoted this posture in his students.

Preserving this tradition, I often adopt a theme of the month, something I work to develop on a professional or personal level. For example, I might dedicate time to being more visually perceptive. I might work on a technical issue, such as developing mastery of the use of hypnotic amnesia or the applications of symptom prescription.

To promote the philosophy of self-training, I provide pragmatic guidelines for students to do the same. In workshops I give students problems for monthly therapist development. For example, here are twelve challenges from recent workshops:

1. For each client, consider the question: What does the patient value? Be specific and write out two or three adjectives per patient.
2. For each client, indicate a specific answer to the following question: How do you, the clinician, know the patient can change or cope better?
3. In each session, use the method of utilization once.
4. Smile when offering hypnotic inductions; gesture freely and congruently while the hypnotized patient's eyes are closed.
5. When you see a new patient, after the first five minutes, predict which hypnotic phenomenon you believe he or she will accomplish best.
6. Collect separate stories about human rigidity and flexibility. When appropriate, tell them to patients.

7. For each patient you see, write a sentence summarizing the patient's unique style of responding.
8. Take away your primary strength for a month. Don't use the method that you most overuse. For example, if you are Ericksonian, don't tell stories. If you are analytic, do not make interpretations. See what you develop in its place.
9. Make a specific prediction about how the patient will resist your assignment or therapeutic directives.
10. For two weeks, write out how patients confuse you. For the next two weeks, write out how you confuse them. Be specific.
11. Make a list of how you desire to evolve as a clinician. Say it silently to yourself before each session as an affirmation.
12. Think in terms of analogies. Take the patient's problem and describe it as a color, a tool, a plant, and a vessel to contain water. See how this influences your treatment.

Don't miss an extended application of this training method: Specific weekly or monthly challenges can be given to patients for their growth and development. This makes good sense. The therapy becomes a game of hot potato. The patient offers problems to the therapist and the clinician presents a problem back to the patient.

I have a reflection on such assignments, and it is a personal reflection. A Native American saying goes, "Tell me and I'll forget. Show me and I may not remember. Involve me and I'll understand."

CLINICAL EXAMPLE

Let's extend the method and think about experiential interventions for issues of transference, remembering that it is a topic about which I am naive. (Is that transference itself?) and in which I am not classically trained.

In a recent Ericksonian supervision group in Brazil, I worked with a woman who suffered from perfectionism. She indicated that her father was a primary source of her striving. Modifying a technique I learned from the Gouldings, I asked her to look successively at each group member and to hallucinate her father's face and hear the words, "You must succeed perfectly." Subsequently, I asked her to conduct the same exercise, using Erickson's face (someone she admired) and hearing in her native language the message, "Dealing adequately with the good and bad alike is the real joy of living." She was quite moved by this simple experiment. My sense is that dreams are not the royal road to the unconscious; experiences are.

Yes, there is a strong experiential tradition in psychodynamic methods, dating at least to Franz Alexander and the corrective emotional experience, but it seems to me that in dynamic methods, experiences are the by-products of understandings. To me, experiences should be the main course, understanding the dessert. Dynamic experiences can precede dynamic understandings.

It is a problem—perhaps with an Oedipal imprint—to reflect on the nature of therapy and training and look back on the development of therapy, which has a history of a little more than a hundred years.

HISTORICAL REFLECTIONS ON TRAINING

In psychotherapy's early days, there wasn't much to learn regarding technique. Inquiry in those days focused on theoretical and conceptual issues. Training emphasized the development of the therapist. Consequently, individuals who elected to become psychoanalysts spent years undergoing a training analysis, thereby learning to rid themselves of their own distortions and transference. The purpose was to develop the analysand as a tool of therapy.

After World War II, however, with the burgeoning number of divergent schools of psychotherapy, attention focused on the methods of psychotherapy, and the development of the therapist receded into the background.

Yet when one conceives of therapy as an art more than a science, it behooves us to train ourselves as artists. That requires an entirely different approach to learning therapy. If we want to learn how to do physics, we can learn the rules of physics by going to a classroom

and listening to scholarly lectures about physics. But if we want to learn how to do drama, theater, or art, then we are not going to be able to learn it in the lecture hall. Rather, we are going to learn it from the inside out, by discovering something inside ourselves rather than learning a specific set of rules.

THEATER AS A MODEL

A couple of years ago, I became preoccupied with the idea of therapy as art, and I began to wonder, "Are we using the wrong model for training therapists? If so, what would be a better model?" I decided to study theater—more specifically, improvisation. Whenever we interact with another human being, we are doing improvisation. Similarly, in psychotherapy, communication is more improvisation than science. So I took a class to learn how theater experts teach improvisation.

Interestingly, many important contributors to psychotherapy had backgrounds in acting and drama. Fritz Perls, Peggy Papp, Jacob Moreno, and Virginia Satir had various amounts of experience in acting, which they used as a tool in the craft of clinical influence.

I joined a small group of 20-year-olds for a six-week adult education class that was led by a woman who had a Ph.D. in drama. I eventually took two more six-week courses in acting and improvisation. We began the initial session by introducing ourselves and saying a word about why we had come. The first student gave his name and said, "I'm here because I want to do theater." Next person: "I'm here because I want to be in the movies." Next person: "I want to do commercials." Next, "Dr. Zeig, why are you here?" "I'm a spy. I want to learn how a dramatist teaches improvisation."

After the introductions, we all stood in a circle to do our first acting lesson: la-las. The task was to repeat a vocal pattern—la-la-la-la-la-la-*la*, la-la-la-la-la-la-*la*, la-la-la, la-la-la, la-la-la, la-la-la-la-la-la-*la*—while adding a body motion such as handclapping.

At first, the teacher led the exercise and we were to copy what she did. After a bit, the teacher turned to me and said, "You be the leader. Pick a different sound. Use the same rhythm. Choose a different motion." So I went, "Pa-pa-pa-pa-pa-pa-*pa*," and made a cradling motion. Everyone copied me. The next student selected "ga-ga," and a new movement. During this, the teacher stepped outside the circle and gave us feedback. "No, Jeff. Your movements aren't sweeping enough. Watch the leader closely and copy her. Not ga-ga. GAH-GAH." Then the exercise was over, and to my astonishment we simply went on to the next exercise. No discussion. No processing of what had just happened. No analysis. No sharing.

When my expectations for follow-up were not fulfilled, I entered a state of confusion. "Wait a second," I protested in my head: "Aren't we going to analyze this? Pick apart the meaning of this experience? I can be a shredder. Give me something, and I will dissect it, shred the chaff from the kernel. Patients tell me things. I dissect them. They tell me their histories, and I dissect them. They describe relationship problems, and I dissect them. Reduce them to little pieces and feed the components back to them. I'm very skilled at this regurgitation process, chewing up a story, digesting it, and returning it to the patient in a more palatable form."

But in this class, we were not dissecting. I couldn't just mindlessly digest and regurgitate. Suddenly, I had to think, "What is this about? What am I learning? What skills are being taught here? What skills are necessary to do drama?" One necessary skill, of course, is articulation. To do any kind of stage work, the actor must have good articulation. I recalled the teacher's observation, "No, Jeff. Not ga-ga. GAH-GAH." I was learning articulation.

A stage actor also needs big gestures. As a psychotherapist, this element was most foreign of all to me. I sit when I work, restraining my body motions as much as possible. Now suddenly I was being asked to use gestures for effect.

The final lesson I learned from this exercise was the importance of modeling. To act you must model. If you are going to become a character, a taxi driver, let's say, you had better be able to observe taxi drivers and model what they do. Maybe you need to be a streetperson. If so, then you had better be able to look around, find a streetperson, and see what it is that a streetperson does.

I concluded from the exercise that these three skills—articulation, big gestures, and modeling—are important in acting, but no one said that. The teacher didn't begin class with a lecture: "The first three rules of acting are articulation, big gestures, and modeling." Rather we did an exercise, and it was understood that somehow we would realize and appreciate that once we got on stage we would access the postures of articulation, big gestures, and modeling. Subsequent improvisational training proceeded one exercise after another.

This was not the kind of learning to which I was accustomed. This was on par with wheeling a bicycle out to the end of the drive for the first time, straddling the top tube, and pushing off.

Learning to ride a bicycle is a visceral learning. You don't learn to ride a bicycle in your left hemisphere. You don't learn the physics of riding a bicycle. It wouldn't help you. You learn to ride *in your body*. To learn about momentum, you have to be on the bike, try to keep your balance, develop awareness of all the ways your body movement affects the direction and stability of the bicycle. You try it and you fall and you try again. And after a while, suddenly you are doing it. Your body learns, and you've got it.

Remember the breathless "Aha!" feeling you got when you suddenly learned how to ride a bicycle? I think psychotherapy training should be like that. In fact, psychotherapy should not only foster that breathless "Aha!" in patients, but psychotherapy training should also foster a similar feeling in students.

PSYCHOAEROBICS_SM

I am about to present my model of training that derives from improvisational training. First, let's take a moment to condense and review what has been covered so far: There is a basic subjectivity about offering psychotherapy that cannot be broached. For one thing, the experiential posture of the clinician is too idiosyncratic. It is projected into the therapy situation and forms part of its core. Therapists whose postures are didactic expound teaching methods and use them effectively. Charismatic practitioners will have that attribute as a therapeutic core, and so on.

There can be alternatives to training by didactics, supervision, modeling, clinical experience, books, tapes, cotherapy, and the one-way mirror. Clinical training should develop the clinician's posture/style/selfhood/orientation/ways-of-being/states. Moreover, a systematic experiential program is desirable. As I have evolved as a teacher, I have added a core component to my teaching. I developed a method to teach experiential postures. Yes, they are Ericksonian methods, but I hope the scope and implications are wider. All therapies should expand training to elicit and evolve core postures. Therefore, after the extended prologue, I will get to the point. I have developed an experiential training system that I call *Psychoaerobics*$_{SM}$.

Let's examine a few of the 70 existent psychoaerobic exercises. There are two classes of exercises: One set of exercises warms up skills that will be later developed and accesses positions that are generic across therapies; the second set consists of more elaborate exercises that develop postures specific to Ericksonian practice.

WARMUP EXERCISE THREE

Warmup Exercise Three can be conducted in a group. One member becomes the Pitcher. It is his or her job to tell an emotionally revealing personal secret to the group. However, rather than saying it verbally, the Pitcher communicates the emotional secret in one of three ways: (1) by mouthing the words but not allowing sounds to emerge; (2) by writing out the secret in the air in complete sentences while experiencing the emotion; or (3) by telling the secret verbally, using a single syllable to mimic words, such as "bah." The other members of the group become Receivers.

In one variation, the Receivers guess the underlying emotion, naming it in one word. (Isn't it convenient that all emotions can be named in one word?) That is not the variation that I commonly use because I am not focused on training skills in diagnostic empathy: Most clinicians have developed this skill prior to

attending one of my workshops. In the variation I commonly use, I train what I call "experiential assessment." In response to the Pitcher's communication, the receiver must move continuously, allowing his or her body to *resonate* with the perceived emotion.

Consider two resonant tuning forks placed on a conductive surface. If one of them is struck, the other vibrates, albeit to a lesser degree. Similarly, the Receiver allows his or her body to mold itself into a posture that reflects the emotion/meaning underlying the Pitcher's secret. When the Pitcher is finished, the Receiver holds the posture so that the Pitcher can examine and discern whether or not the message sent is approximately the message received. Group discussion may or may not follow.

Therapists can experientially assess patients' emotional state by monitoring themselves during the session, including their *own* physical posture. If the clinician notices herself slumping in the chair, perhaps she is responding to the patient's underlying depression. Most therapists cognitively learn verbal empathy at an early stage of their career. Experiential assessment also can be valuable.

Warmup Exercise Three is designed to stimulate openness, cooperation, and playfulness. Moreover, this exercise accesses and primes a skill that, as we will see, is subsequently developed in the second set of exercises, Psychoaerobic$_{SM}$ Exercises One and Two. Before presenting those exercises, I want to reflect on the way in which this warmup exercise can be generalized into the treatment session to add an experiential component to the therapy.

OPTIONS FOR WARMUP THREE:

Clinical options are only limited by the inventiveness of the user. For example, Warmup Three could be used experientially in the therapy of a regressed patient who lacks the ability to discern others' feelings. Practice could occur in individual, group, or family therapy. The patient could access and verbally identify communicated feelings. The assignment could be homework: A rigid family, for

WARMUP EXERCISE THREE

Clinician Posture to Develop: Resource states for participating in **PSYCHOAEROBIC**$_{SM}$ exercises—disclosure and experiential assessment (empathy).

Format: Dyads or group

Roles: One person is the Pitcher; the other is the Receiver.

Method: The Pitcher tells an emotionally and personally revealing secret, but speaks subvocally—using normal gestures, the Pitcher mouths the words, speaking in complete sentences, but does not let sounds come out. The Receiver attends empathetically and allows his/her body to intuitively discern the Pitcher's emotion. The Receiver should stay kinetic, moving constantly in response to his/her perception of the Pitcher's emotion. When the Pitcher completes the secret, then and only then the Receiver becomes a statue and holds his/her final pose so that the Pitcher can see the Receiver's physical portrayal of empathy. The Receivers should *not* openly guess the emotion behind the secret.

    The pair switches roles. The new Pitcher tells a secret and the new Receiver tries to "resonate" with the Pitcher's emotion.

Variations:
1. Conduct the exercise in a group of five or six. Circulate so each member has a turn as Pitcher.
2. Tell the secret in gibberish, rather than subvocally.
3. Pantomime writing out the secret.
4. Tell the secret using one syllable only such as "Bah," "Ru," or "Lee."
5. The Receiver can guess the emotion, naming it in one word.
6. The Receiver(s) can mirror the Pitcher as a technique to discern the underlying emotion.
7. Do not look directly at the secret-teller. Watch with peripheral vision only.
8. Discuss the exercise after completing the task.

Extensions:
1. Practice in therapy sessions (individual, group, or family) with patients who have difficulty with empathy.
2. Practice as a homework assignment within the patient's family.
3. Practice as a game with children to teach empathy.

Attitude: The ideal state for **PSYCHOAEROBIC**$_{SM}$ exercises is playful, cooperative, open, and nonjudgmental.

Note: As with any experiential exercise, only do those that are comfortable to you.

Figure 2. Example Exercise

example, could take turns playing the exercise at dinner.

Furthermore, the exercise could be used fruitfully with children, either in individual treatment or in a group. It could help them develop their skills at verbal empathy. It could be used similarly as a supervision task with novice therapists.

Please understand the underlying philosophy. Empathy cannot be learned didactically anymore than one can learn to swim on a piano bench, or learn to be a chef by being handed recipes. Empathy must be learned experientially, and only practice will lead to improvement. Figure 2 shows the text of Warmup Exercise Three to provide an idea of the actual design of the Psychoaerobic$_{SM}$ Exercises.

WARMUP EXERCISE NINE

Warmup Exercise Nine also warms up the first two Psychoaerobic$_{SM}$ Exercises. Whereas experiential assessment is primed in Warmup One, Warmup Nine primes the ability to change states.

Warmup Exercise Nine is presented in dyads with a Pitcher and a Receiver. The Pitcher offers a series of compliments to the Receiver, who mentally discounts them and physically enters a defensive state. When the defensive state has been achieved, the Pitcher asks the Receiver, "How specifically do you know that you are defensive?" Responses are sequentially eliminated until the Receiver can no longer maintain the defensive state. For example, if the Receiver says, "I know that I am defensive because my arms are folded," the Pitcher requests, "Unfold your arms." If the Receiver says, "I know I am defensive because I am saying negative things inside my head," the Pitcher requires, "Stop saying negative things."

Eventually the exercise reaches a point where the defensive state no longer can be maintained. Upon completion the roles are reversed, and the new Pitcher provides compliments. The new Receiver enters a state of self-esteem, which then is similarly broken down.

Accessing and changing states facilely can be quite valuable for therapists. The exercise also can be extended to patients. Try asking a savvy depressed patient, "How specifically do you know that you are depressed?" After the patient responds, subsequently suggest that the patient make appropriate reversals.

After priming with Warmup Exercises, the formal Psychoaerobic$_{SM}$ Exercises are offered. In the next section I will describe exercises to develop professional "muscles" and "lenses."

PSYCHOAEROBIC$_{SM}$ EXERCISE ONE

Exercise One is designed to develop the Ericksonian skill of *orienting toward*. Orienting torward could be considered a "muscle," a way of *doing*. For present purposes, orienting toward is considered an experiential posture or "state" of the clinician, not merely the technique of using indirection.

The exercise is conducted in a dyad with a Pitcher and Receiver. Prior to commencing the exercise, the Receiver studies the Pitcher for a minute or two and writes five yes or no questions that are relevant and not obvious. For example, asking a meticulous person, "Do you like to play in the mud?" would not be productive because the answer would be obvious. Asking the same person, "Do you like to dress neatly?" would be relevant, but again too obvious. Perhaps a meticulous person could be asked, "Do you like classic movies?"

The five questions are asked and answered sequentially. The Pitcher is to reply truthfully to the questions, but is placed under severe restrictions that make treasured and effective methods unavailable. That is, the answer must be gift wrapped in a story that is to be told in a slow measured monotone. Moreover, no obvious gestures can be made by the Pitcher. The story should be simple and of limited duration. For example, the Pitcher could talk a few minutes about walking to grade school as a child. The content of the story does not have to be relevant, but the *meaning* of the story must be shaded to indicate yes, no, or sometimes. Nonverbal cues cannot be used.

The Receiver is to attend via experiential assessment (a posture primed in Warmup Three), rather than conscious deliberation. One way to attend experientially is for the Receiver to monitor his or her own physical responses. If the Receiver's head nods (or shakes), that answer can be accepted. Similarly, a beginning smile or opening gesture on the part of the Receiver can be taken as a yes, while a tilt of the head or a slight wavering of the hands could indicate sometimes.

At the end of the exercise, answers are *not* compared. Being correct is *not* the goal of the exercise. Rather, at the conclusion, the participants strive to define their respective states when they were at their optimum. Here the talent of entering and exiting states is accessed and harnessed from Warmup Exercise Nine. The Pitcher is to describe the accessed state of orienting toward, answering the question "When I was *best* at orienting toward what *specifically* was I like?" The Receiver is to describe the gift unwrapping state. Each can provide feedback to assist the other in this difficult task.

Exercise One is a typical Psychoaerobic_{SM} Exercise, meant to develop core "postures" (in this case *orienting toward* and *gift unwrapping*) in a core manner; namely, experientially by relinquishing overused and well-developed skills. *Orienting toward* and *gift wrapping* are treated as talents that must be learned experientially in the way bicycle riding must be learned viscerally. *Indirection* may be a technique. *Orienting toward* is considered a state that the therapist can access, similar to compassion or concern. It is posited that through continued practice, the state can be accessed and developed more fully.

The Psychoaerobic_{SM} process is somewhat like physical exercise through circuit training, in which muscle groups are isolated and developed. Moreover, in Exercise One, a talent, communicating directly with words and gestures, is restricted so that latent abilities can emerge. It is a bit similar to the treatment of amblyopia (lazy eye) in which the ophthalmologist patches the good eye to foster development of an inferior function. Also, in Exercise One, the function of "being right" is restrained. Participants cannot compare answers. Thereby, they can focus more fully on accessing states; in this case, orienting toward and gift unwrapping.

PSYCHOAEROBIC_{SM} EXERCISE TWO

Exercise Two immediately follows Exercise One, but in Exercise Two the roles are reversed. This time there are two conditions,

not five questions. In the first condition, the new Pitcher describes an object, such as a tennis racket. (Stories are *not* told.) The description must *mean* a negative emotion; for example, guilt or fear. The emotion is to be fixed prior to the description and cannot be changed during the description. It is technically best if the Pitcher eases into the emotion gradually and orients toward it progressively. Again, gestures and tone are restrained.

The Receiver accesses a state of experiential assessment and discerns the projected feeling through the self-monitoring of minimal cues: A beginning frown might indicate displeasure; a curl of the mouth, frustration; a welling in the eye, sadness. The Pitcher continues the description until he or she can discern an overt behavior indicating an emotional response in the Receiver.

In the second condition, a new object is described; for example, a half-filled glass of water. A positive emotion is pitched, for example, joy, excitement, or confidence.

At the end of the exercise, participants are restrained from comparing answers. Again, the goal is to define the respective states, *orienting toward* and *gift unwrapping*. The exercise is not a competition to be correct. Describing a state is hard but valuable. It is also highly individual. For example, how could we describe the state of curiosity? Could you say, "I know I'm curious because I'm sitting forward, my head is cocked to the side, one eyebrow is higher than the other, there's a feeling of excitement and anticipation in my stomach. I'm waiting to know what comes next. I'm thinking, 'This is interesting!' "

To further elucidate the purpose of Exercises One and Two, let's consider a technical method that Erickson used, called the "interspersal technique." Two outstanding examples come to mind. In working with a pain patient who was a florist, Erickson talked about the growth of tomato plants, interspersing suggestions of comfort into the description. In another case, he told stories to an anorexic and interspersed suggestions of hunger while also stimulating a range of emotions. Although it is interesting to speculate about the techniques and theory of this approach, for present purposes I will limit my discussion to training clinicians.

Let's assume the interspersal technique is valuable. To train therapists to use it, I could take an approach of breaking it down into technical components and, for example, describe and teach indirect forms of communication, such as truisms and presuppositions. Alternately, I could say that the technique of indirection is part of a larger experiential method, an experiential state of *orienting toward*, based upon a posture of the clinician. Then it would be beneficial to conduct Exercises One and Two to garner the posture of orienting toward.

Consider Exercise One. The object of the exercise for the Pitcher is to *orient toward* a thought (yes, no, or sometimes). In Exercise Two, the Pitcher orients toward a feeling. Much of the interspersal technique is based on these processes: One orients toward a thought; one orients toward a feeling; one orients toward a behavior. Eventually preconscious associations elicit constructive action by virtue of what is called the ideodynamic effect, which has to do with the ways in which ideas and associations stimulate action. Essentially, in the interspersal method, the patient is induced into a state of experiential assessment of the clinician's method.

Experiential assessment can be considered integral to hypnosis. Hypnosis does not have to be considered trance, it could be defined as a state of experiential assessment. Hypnotic suggestions could be conceived as ways of guiding associations. In Ericksonian therapy, associations are not analyzed; they are elicited and utilized.

Realize that Exercises One and Two, like physical exercises, should be repeated regularly. These techniques are best developed through regular practice.

Of course, in the training that I conduct, I train both technical methods and experiential postures, but in recent years I have been more inclined to the latter. I even use group hypnosis before and after the exercises to further experientially consolidate learning.

Orienting toward is one of the essential postures in the Psychoaerobic$_{SM}$ system. It is a therapeutic muscle. I arbitrarily chose it as the first to be developed. Other postures specific to Ericksonian practice include developing *acuity, communicating for effect*, and *utilization*.

I will discuss these briefly and provide examples of exercises to develop each of them. Again, keep in mind that I am describing them as postures, not techniques—which they also may be.

The point: After practicing the exercises and accessing postures, when the clinician gets onto his or her therapeutic stage the Psychoaerobic$_{SM}$ states will be available.

ACUITY EXERCISES

The largest number of exercises in the Psychoaerobic$_{SM}$ system are those that elicit acuity and develop therapists' lenses. There are a number of subdivisions of acuity, each of which has specific exercises, including visual attention, auditory attention, concentration, detection of pattern, extrapolating from minimal cues, noticing conspicuous absences, and perceiving expectations (rather than realities). As a warmup for acuity exercises, I might offer students a group induction because hypnosis itself focuses perception.

Due to space limitations, I will only outline a few acuity exercises and present them as simply as possible. An exercise to access *visual perception for details* is as follows: Two participants, one Pitcher and one Receiver, face each other. The Receiver "memorizes" the Pitcher and then closes his or her eyes. The Pitcher then makes three physical changes; for example, removes a watch, changes the location of jewelry, unfastens a button. The Receiver then opens his or her eyes and discerns the changes.

In an exercise designed to enhance *perception of pattern*, one member of the group, who is a native speaker of a foreign language, tells two brief stories, one of which is true, and the other of which contains an emotionally significant lie. The group works at discerning the speaker's pattern of lying.

In an exercise on *extrapolation*, working in dyads members make predictions about each other, based on minimal cues.

After each of the exercises, discussion centers on accessing and developing a robust acuity *state*. Clinical extensions are offered: Similar exercises could be given to depressed patients to stimulate an external awareness that is antithetical to the inward pressures of depression, thereby disrupting the depressed state and eliciting a more helpful externally oriented state. For example, such patients could be given the task of noticing patterns in the clouds as they did as children. They could be given the assignment Erickson gave to me, to go to a schoolyard and examine specified patterns in children.

Likewise, exercises could be practiced in families. My 11-year-old daughter and I play a game at restaurants. We sit down at a new table and I close my eyes. She makes three changes, and I open my eyes and try to discern the things that she modified. Then we switch roles.

In fact, I once asked a researcher in neuro-anatomy if before and after practicing such exercises for an extended period of time, by using state-of-the-art equipment, could changes be noticed in brain functions. He replied, "Most definitely."

COMMUNICATING FOR EFFECT

There are a number of exercises to develop the posture of *communicating for effect*. In one exercise, I have participants conduct hypnosis using gibberish. In the next, I have them induce hypnosis by repetitiously using only one word. In a subsequent exercise, they can only repeat one sentence. Repetitions cannot be monotonous. Each must contain a novel variation in tone, tempo, gesture, voice locus, and so on. Clinicians who have done this exercise often appreciate the experiential learning of how nonverbal methods can elicit targeted responses. Again, the focus is on developing posture, not competence in technique. Competence in methods should stem from posture, rather than vice versa. This is the reverse of customary training, in which one first learns the technique and posture follows.

UTILIZATION

Exercises on *utilization* are based in hypnosis because the method is so integral to Ericksonian hypnotherapy. One exercise is conducted in triads, with a hypnotist, a sub-

ject, and a coach. After the hypnotist elicits a trance, the coach calls out items at regular intervals from a list of provided categories that includes sounds, objects in the room, and emotions. Subsequently, the hypnotist must incorporate the called-out items into the ongoing trance patter, utilizing them to advance trance goals such as absorption and deepening. Again, technical mastery is not sought. The purpose of the procedure is to provide moments in which the clinician experientially accesses the utilization state. Once the state is secured, it can be accessed in future therapy as needed.

PRELIMINARY CONCLUSIONS

At this stage of my evolution as a therapist and trainer, I distinguish between technical methods and clinician postures. In the forms of psychotherapy with which I am familiar, it is possible to teach theory and practice didactically, and that almost always is the starting point. In contradistinction, I maintain that providing therapy is more a matter of posture than technique. Therefore, in contemporary training, state can precede method.

Therapeutic practice is composed of techniques and postures. Consider the fact that light can be considered a wave and a particle. In studying light, sometimes it is best to think of it as a wave; at other times as a particle. Similarly, when considering the therapist, we can emphasize postures sometimes, and techniques at others.

There is a considerable corpus of knowledge of theory and practice in each school of therapy, and technical adequacy can be garnered through cognitive study. That is all well and good. However, the emphasis in training on didactics may inadvertently lead clinicians into counterproductive directions. The primary goals of therapy are helping people cope, change, activate, realize self-esteem, assume responsibility, and so on. These results are achieved through postures that must be learned experientially. If treatment is to be experiential, the training of therapists should stress systematic experiential methods.

The concept is a bit Zen. There is a distinction between what we study and what we live.

Psychotherapy training and practice, like Zen, can stress living experience first.

Using Erickson as a model, I have tried to separate experiential postures from technique. I have attempted to develop a systematic program for the experiential learning of experiential postures, although it is still in its preliminary stages.

I hope the model has greater applicability than just teaching Ericksonian concepts. I would hope that one could invent a Psycho-aerobic$_{SM}$ program to model any master clinician. If one were modeling Aaron Beck, one could ascertain the therapeutic postures of this master cognitive therapist and create experiential exercises for each. One could model Kernberg or Masterson for psychodynamic methods. One could model Minuchin for family therapy, and so on. Moreover, the model could be extended to other fields such as teaching or parenting. What are the experiential postures of a great parent? What exercises could help teach these postures?

Certainly the method could be applied to patients. Clinicians could help a depressed patient develop postures of being externally aware, positive in outlook, and oriented to a goal, by means of experiential methods to help access these states. Of course, techniques also could be used, but my predilection would be to access postures first. A similar model could be used for developing self-esteem in patients. Divide the goal into postures and devise appropriate experiential exercises for each.

My only proviso would be to encourage a systematic excursion into experiential territory, using experiential methods. One also should promote recursive techniques of learning:

There is the old joke about the man who is lost in the downtown area of a city. He is in a new territory and cannot find his bearings. Finally, he sees a man walking toward him, carrying a violin case. He approaches the musician avidly and says, "Sir, please excuse me. I am a bit bereft; I am in a new territory. I don't know how to find my way. Can you please tell me, sir, How do you get to symphony hall?"

The violinist replies, "Practice, practice, practice."

I suggest that we consider both the technical and the experiential, but let's start with the experiential. We can consider that in lessening the distance from the head to the heart it is more important to start first from the heart.

REFERENCES

Erickson, M. H. (1948). Hypnotic psychotherapy. *The Medical Clinics of North America*, May. Also cited in E.L. Rossi (Ed.), *Collected papers of Milton H. Erickson, Vol. IV: Innovative hypnotherapy*, pp. 35–48. New York: Irvington.

Whitaker, C. (1982). Keynote address: Hypnosis and family depth therapy. In J. K. Zeig (Ed.), *Ericksonian approaches to hypnosis and psychotherapy* (pp 491–504). New York: Brunner/Mazel.

Zeig, J. K. (1992). The virtues of our faults: A key concept of Ericksonian therapy. In J. K. Zeig (Ed.), *The evolution of psychotherapy: The second conference* (pp 252–66). New York: Brunner/Mazel.

Discussion by Otto F. Kernberg, M.D.

———————◆———————

I consider this not only as a great pleasure, but really a privilege and an honor to be able to discuss Dr. Zeig's paper. Dr. Zeig is our "big father" here at the Conference and permits all of us to learn and to teach and to exchange

ideas. It is his broad vision that I think is more important than anything else in this Conference to help all of us in learning and teaching.

It is a difficult position for me to discuss training in an Ericksonian technique, given the fact that I am not an Ericksonian therapist. How can I say whether this is a good method of training when I come from a completely different field? It is a great challenge, but of course I assume that Dr. Zeig would not expect that I act as a very knowledgeable expert, criticizing his views on methods and experiential aspects of training, but to relate his approach, as well as the teaching of that approach, to my approach and the way I teach it. It so happens that I am not only a psychoanalyst and a psychoanalytic psychotherapist, but I am also engaged in research on the psychoanalytic psychotherapy of patients with severe personality disorders. I am engaged in a research program that involves systematic training of therapists. Therefore, my group and I have experience in training psychotherapists and in being successful at times and not successful at other times.

One thing I was missing was Dr. Zeig talking about the variable success of the training, because we do wonderfully with some people; with others we do terribly.

It is, of course, very difficult in the course of a brief discussion to compare our methods of training and of treatment, coming from different theories and approaches, but I would like to start with what seems to me a striking similarity, and, I think, a basic theme that I have seen emerging in many presentations in this conference, namely the stress on the *experiential* aspects of psychotherapy in contrast to purely *cognitive* ones. This implies no critique of cognitive approaches to treatment. On the contrary, I think (and I'm sure that Dr. Zeig would agree) that we need precise, sharp, cognitive models because if we have fuzzy thinking that is going to affect everything else. But once we are clear in our thinking, then we have to accept that when people are in trouble, when things fall apart, it is because they have conflicts and disasters in their *emotional* lives. And that psychotherapy is, in essence, dealing with normal and pathological emotional reactions. What we have to diagnose in the psychotherapy situation is the dominant emotional situation of the patient.

Now in Erickson's example—do you remember the case of the couple where she loved drinking and he hated it? He just wanted her to stop and she hated it, and they were fighting with each other. Erickson intuitively gathered in the first session that the dominant issue was mutual attack, revenge, and mutual blaming. And on the basis of diagnosing that situation he immediately took an action that made him the joint enemy of the couple and permitted them to get together. "Go fishing," he suggested. And they were united against this "crazy therapist." And in defying him, paradoxically, they gave each other a chance to get together again.

Erickson dealt with the dominant emotional conflict that he had diagnosed in the first session. That is not easy. Then he used what I would call a paradoxical intervention.

Now, I think that as a psychoanalytic psychotherapist I would have done the same in terms of trying to diagnose what was the dominant issue going on. I was fascinated by Erickson's exercise in recreating the personal history on the basis of a mental status examination, and, at other times, to create a mental status examination of the patient on the basis of the history. That is a wonderful focus on the patient's present personality—the key issue for treatment. There is an image of psychoanalysis as it was in 1950, when the patient would tell what happened when he was three years old and six years old, and so on. Nowadays we consider the remote past secondary in comparison to a full knowledge of the patient's present reality. In psychoanalytic psychotherapy, I try to obtain that information, and I think that Dr. Zeig is doing the same thing with his approach.

I try to find out what the patient's dominant present emotional experiences are.

Now I am coming to the four components of the therapist's posture that Dr. Zeig recommended: creative experiences, utilization, orienting toward goals, and communication for effect. I think that "creative experiences" really means to activate a present affective experience that can be utilized for changing the patient; and utilization, in Dr. Zeig's approach, is making use of that which the patient brings to the session to bring about change in the patient's external reality. And, of course, orienting by indirection is a way of moving the patient, not by telling him what to do, but by telling a story, creating a situation that derives, to some extent, I am sure, from Zen Buddhism, in the sense that the story forces the patient to search for a meaning in himself. It also intensifies the patient's dependence on the therapist. The patient has to recreate what the intended meaning was. But at the same time, it respects the autonomy of the patient, who develops his own meaning. The combination of fostering dependency and autonomy, by means of telling the story, I think, is the essential therapeutic ingredient. And, of course, to this comes Number Four, "communication for effect," which I interpret as the therapist's commitment to what he is doing, his passionate—I would use that term, yes, passionate—conviction that what he is doing is what he needs to communicate, and that creates a new reality for the patient.

Now, if I am reading Dr. Zeig correctly, let me say that in psychoanalytic psychotherapy we use some similar techniques, but not others. First, we try to diagnose the situation, and by diagnosing I don't mean trying to find out whether the patient had an Oedipal conflict at age three. What we try to diagnose is the presently dominant conflict on the basis of what I call "channels of information," on the basis of what the patient tells us: Channel One, verbal communication of the patient's subjective experience; Channel Two, the patient's nonverbal behavior; Channel Three, our own emotional reaction to a patient or to the transference, that is to say, our countertransference. On that basis, we diagnose the dominant present emotional situation, an emotional situation activated in the relationship with us. This relationship with us, we think, is dominated by the transference; that is, a pathogenic unconscious relationship from the past that the patient is repeating again, and again, and again, in an unconscious effort to resolve it without being able to do so.

This past relationship repeated unconsciously by what the patient is enacting with us is what we call "dominant transference relationship." This relationship consists of a component of self, or self representation; a component of the other, or object representation; and a dominant affect linking them. We try to do two things with that relationship: either to

analyze it and permit the patient to understand the meaning of that unconscious relationship in order to resolve it, or to utilize it for a better adaptive effort. The first strategy is psychoanalytic psychotherapy in a strict sense; the second strategy is supportive psychotherapy based on psychoanalytic principles. The main point I want to make is that I think that Dr. Zeig's method represents, from my analytical standpoint, a sophisticated and effective supportive psychotherapy that uses dynamic understanding. It attempts to change the patient's behavior into the direction of better adaptation, making use of the patient's resources, the immediate situation, and the therapist's interaction with the patient, using the methods that Dr. Zeig expressed and that have cognitive (storytelling) and suggestive aspects. Dr. Zeig also used the patient's father transference in a supportive and suggestive way: "Take the stone from your father's grave, put it to your breast and put it back . . . your father will help you to stand up to the situations that made you pretty anxious."

So I see Dr. Zeig's approach as an excellent supportive psychotherapy, and when I say supportive psychotherapy I don't mean "pat on the shoulder" but a highly sophisticated approach that provides the needed help for the patient.

There are other cases in which I think that an alternative psychoanalytic approach might be helpful. For example, the couple referred to by Dr. Zeig did very well with the two sessions. I feel quite envious: the couples I see, in contrast, are a disaster! It takes me months to lead them into any direction, and I am sure that Dr. Zeig also sees couples who are much more complicated, and that he is familiar with couples united against outsiders who try to shift them from their total commitment to mutual destruction. There are some couples who are very good at that.

The exercises that Dr. Zeig described are geared to understanding affects in self and others, and to understanding the relationship between bodily posture, emotional attitude, and cognitive interpretation of the situation. This brings me to the contemporary theory of affect. We are all under the impact of the new understanding that affects are recent psychophysiological systems that emerge in mammals and get maximized in human beings. Affects are massive signals that link the helpless infants with their mothers in the mammal species that need long-term protection before they are mature. Affects are the basic inborn systems of communication that we are wired to read in the other and wired to express without having to think about it. Affectively invested significant relations with others are sources of happiness, of conflicts, and of pathology. The more we can learn about the physical, expressive, subjective, and cognitive aspects of affects, the better we can understand patients' conflicts and our own response to them, and move patients into one or another direction.

Let me go back to how I train therapists. We are also interested in their understanding of affective experience, but we train them differently. We have a basic manual—and by the way, that manual is called *Psychodynamic Psychotherapy with Borderline Patients*. It gives in a nutshell the psychodynamic treatment approach. Our trainees have to learn it by heart, and then they must *free* themselves from it. They call it the Bible and they get rid of it. Then we show them videotapes of therapies in which we can criticize right and wrong interventions from the viewpoint of the theory, and we use their own videotapes. And finally we provide ongoing supervision of cases they treat.

Now, I would like to say something about psychodynamic supervision, because I think it is a counterpart to Dr. Zeig's training. When a therapist presents a case that he is treating to me, I invite the therapist to talk rather freely about the case. I don't need details—I just get the therapist to tell me what went on in the sessions. And I try to reconstruct what went on between the patient and the therapist, while at the same time looking at the kind of relationship that is established between the therapist and me. And I find out that when the therapist understands well, and everything goes well, I get a marvelous feeling as if I had been there while he saw the patient.

In contrast, when everything is a mess, then usually I don't understand what is going on from what the therapist is telling me. At the same time, there evolves an affective situation in the relationship between the therapist and

me as I try to analyze it in the same way as if the therapist were a patient. I try to analyze what the dominant emotional relationship in our interaction is. And in pointing out to the therapist what is going on here, I invite the therapist to examine how he experiences what is happening in his relationship with me, and whether this development may be a reflection of the problem he has with his patient.

This is called parallel process, and it means that an unresolved transference-countertransference bind fixates the relationship between the patient and therapist, who repeats it with me precisely because this bind is unresolved, like a traumatic situation that has to be worked through in the relationship between the therapist and the supervisor. And in analyzing that, I help the therapist to go back and analyze what he didn't understand before with the patient. It is a risky situation, in which it is important to protect the therapist's self-esteem, and in which I always stay away from anything that has to do with the therapist's past. I try to deal with the here and now, respecting the therapist's privacy. As an example, a therapist who sees a narcissistic patient, an aggressive, sexually promiscuous man, tells me that she is afraid of him because she has the fantasy that if she met him at night in a bar, she wouldn't resist his approaches and would end up in bed with him. The fact that she can tell me that means that she trusts me enough to say something very personal.

I wouldn't touch anything about her past or her history, but I would raise the question, "What is it in him that creates this reaction in you?" And that leads us to his aggressive seductive control, which she could not dare to fully verbalize to herself, as well as to her fascination with this danger that she thought was under control but excited her fantasy about the possibility of an enactment in her countertransference. The immediate effect of this exploration in the supervision was the possibility of analyzing the aggressive aspects of the seduction, and the threats to the treatment that this transference implied.

Is there any basic difference between Dr. Zeig's approach and my own? As I said, Dr. Zeig operates in the direction of what I would call a supportive psychotherapy, in that he is willing to use cognitive support, affective support, and environmental intervention to move the patient in a certain direction. I would do that also in supportive psychotherapy, but *not* in psychoanalytic psychotherapy. So that is one difference, that I would use his approach for certain cases and under certain circumstances, and not in others.

Perhaps another difference in the training is that I would try to train the therapists to become aware of their own and their patients' affective responses by analyzing the kind of disturbances that are illustrated in the example that I gave you, rather than with exercises trying to directly influence the cognitive or communicative aspects of affective expression. There is a certain risk that we artificially change the situation in order to get away from what spontaneously would be the dominant affective conflict of the patient. From this viewpoint, I prefer to be on the receptive side, and to let the affective experience emerge from the patient, rather than actively contributing to create it. I prefer to use my countertransference as a radar to diagnose what is going on, rather than relying on an intuitive reaction about what I should do.

I also would like to say that the two examples that Dr. Zeig gave—I don't know whether he did it knowingly or not—beautifully illustrate the two most important aspects of countertransference; namely, concordant identification and complementary identification in the countertransference. By concordant identification, I mean that the therapist identifies himself with the patient's dominant internal experience. In the example in which Dr. Zeig worked with the patient who had anxiety, he felt that the patient needed a good father who was supporting him, and not one who was asking for perfection. And Dr. Zeig became the good father supporting him. And his own fantasies—Dr. Zeig's fantasies—replicated the needs of the patient. So he intuitively felt what the patient needed; that's concordant identification in the countertransference.

In Erickson's example, in contrast, he immediately felt what the couple whom he sent "fishing" were up against. Both of them, husband and wife, were fighting, while somebody else was trying to pull something they both didn't want. Erickson identified himself with that which they were projecting onto each other. Dr. Erickson, from a position of complementary identification in the countertransference, identified himself with a "dominant intruder" that the couple had been mutually projecting. He ordered them to do something that he knew they were going to oppose. In contrast, Dr. Zeig suggested something that he knew was going to be of help to the patient because it corresponded to an internal wish.

How would a psychoanalyst have operated in the first situation? I think the average psychoanalyst would take ten times longer than Dr. Erickson to diagnose the situation and to feel certain enough that some intervention might be of help—so he has my respect!

Regarding the second situation, the psychoanalyst might act exactly like Dr. Zeig if he thought that such a supportive intervention might help. If an analyst had decided that this case was too complex, that a supportive intervention was not going to help, he might have gone into an interpretive mode and reached the conclusion that Dr. Zeig also reached, that this patient was anxious because his wife or girlfriend was trying to move him away from his dependency on his father. She wanted to get that photograph out of the office, and he was in an unconscious conflict between loyalty to father and loyalty to his girlfriend, and this could have been interpreted, and that might have reduced his anxiety. In any case, in these few comments I hope that you have seen in which ways we move in the same direction, in which ways there are differences, and in which ways there are commonalities in our focus on affects that are crucial in our training of therapists.

SECTION V

Experiential Approaches

There is a Fundamental Division in How Psychotherapy is Conceived

$\blacklozenge$

James F. T. Bugental, Ph.D.

James F. T. Bugental, Ph.D.

James F. T. Bugental is semi-retired and devotes himself to teaching and writing; he is also Rockefeller Scholar, California Institute of Integral Studies and an Emeritus Clinical Lecturer (formerly Associate Clinical Professor), Department of Psychiatry, Stanford University Medical School. He received his Ph.D. degreee (1948) from Ohio University. In 1996, he was the recipient of the first annual Rollo May Award of the Division of Humanistic Psychology of the American Psychological Association "for contributions to literary pursuit," and in 1986, he received a certificate "in recognition of the distinguished contribution to the discipline of Clinical Psychology" from the Division of Clinical Psychology, American Psychological Association. He is a past president of the Association of Humanistic Psychology and of the California Psychological Association, a Fellow of the American Psychological Association, and serves on or has served on the editorial boards of eight professional journals. Dr. Bugental has written six books and edited another, and is the author of approximately 150 articles, reviews, comments, and chapters in books.

Last spring, I was asked to submit a title for my presentation and I chose one that represented my thinking at that time, "Is Psychotherapy Evolving into Multiple New Disciplines?" This is a question that concerned me at the time and concerns me now.

However, in the interim I've engaged in a process that has replaced that question with a statement, "There is a Fundamental Split in How Psychotherapy is Conceived." I will still address the earlier topic, but the changed wording demonstrates a process that is central to what I want to say now—the process that we call *searching*.

THE PRESENT CONDITION OF PSYCHOTHERAPY

Psychotherapy as a cultural phenomenon is splintering into many competing—even antagonistic—conceptual-and-practice systems. This trend is likely to continue, even accelerate, in the immediate future. For confirmation of that one need only take note of the current proliferation of theories and applications, many of which are in stark contrast with one another.

For the most part this chapter will examine, briefly and from a partisan stance, what I take to be the state of our field and what I see as a fundamental schism in that field. This division is a too-little-recognized conflict in views of the nature of human beings. However, before launching into that discussion it is useful to remind ourselves of the astonishing burgeoning of what we think of as the realm of counseling and psychotherapy.

A personal view may serve here: When I joined the American Psychological Association as a masters level professional in 1942 there were approximately 3000 members. Currently there are around 142,000. When I joined, few if any members were in private practice and even fewer were clinicians. Now the largest division of APA is the one representing independent practice.

But all is far from harmonious in the house of psychotherapy, whether we look to clinical psychology, psychiatry, social work, or counseling. To name but a few of the competing forces will suggest the stresses accumulating now: certification at various levels; an upswing in malpractice suits; the enforcement of partisan and unduly constricting standards of practice; prescription privileges; and choosing among competing perspectives. These are compounded by the growing menace of managed care, manualized treatment, and the for-profit industrialization of what has heretofore been to some degree a healing *art*.

In our field today, these and other forces are grinding against each other like tectonic plates and producing seismic shocks. Although the big one has not hit yet, it is only a matter of time until our comfortable homes of familiar practice are imperiled or destroyed outright.

In over a half-century as a psychologist, I have seen, accepted or resisted, and learned again and again just how much the human condition is one of constant flux. Despite many efforts to announce the discovery of ultimate parameters, the gravitational force of time repeatedly overcomes those who make such attempts. The program in which we are taking part, well set, in Las Vegas is wisely called "The Evolution of Psychotherapy," not "The Nature of Psychotherapy." It might even better be named "Evolving Psychotherapy" because our work is constantly growing and manifestly and subtly changing.

And what is "psychotherapy," this word that we use so readily and frequently? Its etymology, while interesting, will do no more than reemphasize the changefulness of our language as well as of our field. My own experience is probably typical for those of my generation.

When I became a psychologist in 1941, I doubt I had heard the word psychotherapy, although we did know of "psychoanalysis" as something European emigres did to wealthy people in New York. Working as a psychologist in an army hospital during World War II, I somehow came upon a used copy of Carl Rogers' *Counseling and Psychotherapy*. It was an epiphany!

Discovering that there was something we psychologists could do other than give and report on tests opened vistas that I've been exploring ever since. Remember, this was at a time when "group psychotherapy" in our hospital consisted of assembling 50 or 60 patients in the theater at the post and lecturing them on mental health principles. They were, of course, told to be quiet during this talk. When it was over they were allowed to direct questions to the lecturer, but patients were instructed to avoid talking to each other during the therapy session.

It is my impression that in the years up through the late fifties, most psychiatrists, psychologists, and social workers generally practiced very similar forms of psychotherapy. (At that time the counseling profession had not yet arrived on the scene.) Of course there were some differences, the two most notable being that some were devout psychoanalysts and others could call on pharmaceuticals as they deemed necessary. In the latter regard, however, psychologists and social workers often had cordial relations with a medical person who would prescribe when it seemed indicated. But for the most part what we all did was take personal histories, try to explain to patients the futility of repeating patterns learned in childhood, and give humane, commonsensical advice.

Since those days psychotherapy has become an immense tent under which an astonishing array of activities has been offered: the many forms of psychoanalysis, including Jungian and Adlerian versions, reality therapy, existential-humanistic, control mastery, psychosynthesis, cognitive-behaviorism, transactional analysis, redecision therapy, self-psychology, primal scream, nude marathons, group therapy, couples and family counseling, geriatric, adolescent, and midlife work, dance, art, music, and imagery therapy, and on and on and on.

Today we have begun to ask, "What is therapy?" How shall we decide what is and what is not entitled to bear that name? Should we include those activities that spurn the name but clearly are engaged in similar efforts?

A symptom of the divisive forces at work is the proliferation of specialty therapies. (One is tempted to speak of "boutique therapies.") A member of one of my consultation groups discovered that a client currently had separate therapists for individual work, group sessions, body work, spiritual practice guidance, and EMDR. All five of these were being pursued toward nominally therapeutic goals.

It is my conviction that this array of therapists was unwittingly colluding with the client's resistances. Even so, that is not the issue here. The point is that there are continually more practitioners in the field, and that they are engaged in a widening range of activities that were unheard of, for the most part, 20 years ago. What we have thought of as *psychotherapy* is being affected in a way that is, perhaps, too little recognized.

The apparent core of similarity among psychotherapists has long since become history. What does that tell us about today? About our field with the earthquaking forces now at work?

The simplest point of all this is that change and variation are the essence of being human—indeed, of life in any form. It is this reality that seems to be overlooked in the efforts to depersonalize psychotherapy and to further the machine image of human beings.

And that recognition brings us to . . .

THE CHIEF ISSUE UNDERLYING THE SPLITTING OF PSYCHOTHERAPY

The division between those who see human beings as basically machines and those who regard human beings as something more or other than machines—that is, as a different

order of nature—is the most fundamental contrast in psychology and psychotherapy today. Another way of conceiving that division is in terms of the split between therapies that give primary attention to what is objective and those that focus on the subjective.

Be warned: I am not neutral about this matter. I believe the human being to be a great deal more than a machine and is only to be truly understood when we have some notion of the inner life, the subjectivity of the person with whom we are engaged in a therapeutic effort.

Waters called those holding to the machine model "mechanomorphs." That perspective focuses professional attention on the overt and explicit and advances the notion that what is clinically important about a client is reducible to the standard phrases of the fourth edition of the *Diagnostic and Statistical Manual of Mental Disorders* of the American Psychiatric Association.

Believing in the reality of DSM makes possible manualized treatment programs. It implies that all forms of client distress can be cataloged. It insists that the particular therapist matched with the particular client is unimportant so long as that therapist follows the prescribed treatment manual for the diagnosed condition and that case management can be carried out by someone who never actually sees the person receiving the therapy. It also implies that someone may need only limited professional preparation for the work.

The contrasting view insists on the ultimate uniqueness of each individual. In this perspective, the subjective is the focus of professional attention, and the implicit is as important, if not more so, as the explicit.

A point sometimes misunderstood: To say that each person is unique is not to deny that there are commonalities among all people. It is simply to affirm that how each person shapes his or her way of expressing those shared characteristics is a primary and particular datum for the psychotherapist's attention.

While every person experiences motivations toward certain acts, relations, bodily states, and much else that make up the human experience, the manner or content of how each sets about satisfying those motivations is unique to each individual. For example, while all are born with the potential for relationships, some make a great many acquaintances, friends, lovers, and companions of all kinds; meanwhile, most of us enjoy some relationships and only limitedly engage with others; and there are still others who invert this impulse and become isolated, with minimal human contact.

Of course, our diagnostic categories attempt to deal with these differences and to highlight commonalities within identified groupings. Yet but a little clinical experience soon makes evident how often it is the differences, not the commonalities that are central to the work.

It is no surprise, then, that engagements in the consulting room are as varied as the weather. A significant parallel! Chaos theory teaches us that the only way to *describe* (not to *predict*) weather patterns is by repeatedly including the actual data for one period in the computations for the next, thus ensuring continual variations in the derived patterns. I am far from being qualified to speak at any length about this exciting new conceptual system, but the little I do grasp seems remarkably appropriate to the understanding of human actions and experience.

Before thinking further about the implications of that reality, it is well to pause to recognize that it is not only our clients or patients who are continually different, but that we, the therapists, present a broad spectrum of differences as well. Even graduates of the same training program who profess adherence to the same values and postulates are far from identical in manner, relating, dependence on formal learning, or ways of working with patients.

And still we have only sketched the broad outlines of the continually shifting human situation in which we have chosen to work. When we focus on a particular client, we see that she or he is very different on different days or in different circumstances. Jane Smith at intake impressed the interviewer with her reserve, her balanced way of describing her life, and her lack of urgency for treatment. Jane Smith in her first actual therapeutic interview became acutely depressed and the therapist was concerned to get a no-suicide contract before allowing Jane to leave his office. On her third

interview, Jane became mute and hospitalization was required. At the hospital, Jane . . .

And so the story goes. Change, constant change. The unfinished sentence, "At the hospital, Jane . . ." Jane what? Suicided? Made a remarkably prompt recovery? Became overtly paranoid?

And again we must recognize that we therapists are ourselves continually changing. Dr. Allen has been a steadying influence in the department because of his good humor and years of experience. Today, in a fury, he abruptly shouted at an intern who had made a careless mistake in presenting a difficult patient. Later in the day he apologized, but a little later still, he abruptly told the receptionist to cancel his appointments and he left the clinic. To do what? Get drunk, make love to his secretary, explode in a violent rage at his wife, or . . . ?

But change is even more pervasive when we let ourselves be aware of its omnipresence. Therapist Norma, after seeing Patient A, is subtly different when seeing Patient B than she would have been had she seen Patient B first. Sometimes we recognize this when the first session is markedly different in some way, but mostly we don't recognize it until, perhaps, we hear an audiotape of an interview from six months ago. Then we're apt to be startled, "Did I really do that? . . . Well, I've certainly gotten better since then!"

To be sure, there *may be* those who never vary the way they do their work (I don't say "conduct therapy," you will notice). Making themselves into machines they see only other machines, of course. But those so sadly blinded are not our concern here today.

What does this mean in practical, clinical terms?

Here is the crucial point that I want to advance: We can never learn enough about a client-as-a-machine to fix her or him. Psychotherapy founded on past knowledge about the client—even past knowledge from a minute before—is out of phase with the living person who seeks to change her or his life.

To make this point more vividly, let us venture into a kind of temporal maze that seems to have no possible solution. Here is a snapshot of that maze:

To assess and forecast about a human being and her or his weather-like changeability, we have to take into account the effects of consciousness—and particularly consciousness of one's self. Thus, when planning a therapeutic program or predicting a client's response to treatment, we can use her or his history. But we must not ignore today's experience of providing that history (although that is exactly what often happens). The response we use to plan or forecast may be significantly (or trivially—and we cannot tell which) affected by the client's awareness of this experience.

But, if we start trying to include that, then we need to make a new observation tomorrow, or perhaps this afternoon and again tonight, or perhaps every hour, or half-hour, or continually, at all times. For the client's awareness, no matter how clouded, is also continually influencing the client's being.

Planning a psychotherapy regime or making a diagnosis is akin to writing the formula for a curve. It describes that person or that curve at a given instant. But if we want to write the formula for the weather front moving into our area tonight, we have to have a continual set of operations in which each succeeding formula is affected by the one just before it and affects the one following it. So our diagnosis may be accurate at moment X but we need to make a new observation at Y and factor that in to our computations for Z.

I will leave this objectivity-baffling situation at this point to turn our attention to the present state of our field.

THE PRESENT STATE OF PSYCHOTHERAPY

How shall we define what we mean by "psychotherapy" today? How frequently do therapist and client meet? Who takes the initiative for what they discuss? When and about what does the therapist instruct the client? What use is made of such elements as role playing, physical movement, manipulation of the client's body, emotional enactments, dreams, direct challenges to the client's views, emotions, actions, hypnosis, pharmaceuticals, and so on?

Or suppose we ask what is the principal therapeutic agency, what brings about changes in the client's life and experience. Here are some candidates: insight into earlier events and how they affect present life, catharsis and release, demonstration to the client of the unreality of his or her expectations, restoration of a healthy chemical balance, recognition of a higher power to which an appeal can be made to change one's life, pointed and helpful advice, the quality of the relation established with the therapist (that is, a corrective emotional experience), and so on.

The point is that our field has been burgeoning in all directions. New therapies, new therapeutic doctrines and practices, and new therapists are so numerous that were it not for our cannibalism—for our being clients as well as therapists—we would soon outnumber all other people.

Into this lush jungle now comes the march of industrialization in the form of oil wells of narrow theory, deforestation by overly narrow licensing requirements, and the nationalism of the established traditions—psychoanalysis, control-mastery, cognitive-behaviorism, existential-humanism, transactional analysis, and similar faiths. But all those pale in contrast to the Godzilla of managed care.

The mad scientist who created that monster is objectification, forcing human beings and human concerns into strictly and limitedly objective forms. Long ago Paul Tillich wrote, "[The human] resists objectification, and if [the human's] resistance is broken, the [human, itself] is broken." We live in a time of broken being. Broken because, seeing people only in external terms, it lacks respect for the inner life. J. J. Gibson said, "Psychology, or at least American psychology, is a second-rate discipline. The chief reason is that it does not stand in awe of its subject matter. Psychologists have too little respect for psychology."

Psychotherapy as the "nurturing of the soul" is an expression of respect that impels one to stand in awe of what it proposes and of those who seek its aid. Psychotherapy as the repair of flawed machines prompts no such feelings.

Standardization of treatment, the use of a "template" that requires following preset procedures specified by *DSM-IV*, is the epitome of objectification. It is no distortion to see this as primarily an effort to reduce the human factor—that is, the *human*ness of psychotherapy.

Ironically, this represents a step backward in cultural evolution. Freud sought to create a human science that would be as impersonal and rigorous as the vigorous physical sciences were becoming 100 years ago. Thus he invented the notion of a "blank screen" to eliminate the therapist's personality as a significant datum. Today's most eager exponents of manualized care have the same goal.

This irony is in contrast to what every experienced therapist comes to recognize: It is often the case that we need to pay more attention to the ways in which our client is not like everyone else than to the ways in which she or he is indistinguishable from the usual, the norm, the diagnostic model. (In contrast, mechanomorphic psychology works with the average, the typical, the expected, the generalized image. It often ignores the individual, the special, and the particular.)

A SUBJECTIVIST PERSPECTIVE

What then is a view of psychotherapy from a stance that is respectful of psychology, that is an outlook in awe of human beings, and that is directed toward the subjective?

As we noted above, when we hold to an appreciation for the uniqueness of each individual person—and, indeed, of each individual minute in each person's life—we are confronted with a radically different conception of our enterprise.

Instead of trying to "fix" the ailing machine that is our client, we are engaged in helping this person become more fully self-knowing and self-directing. *Only in this way can that person have the continual self-observations that are required by both chaos theory and the observations that are the results of thousands of hours of working with clients.*

This is the crucial point: We do not seek to gather information about a client in order to somehow repair what is wrong and to help that client have a better life in the future. Such data are constantly being outmoded, and once therapy is over they become increasingly dated

and of limited value. In some cases they may even breed new problems as new situations do not yield to such therapy-based "insights."

Only the person, him or herself, can continually incorporate experience in preparing for the next moment's needs. That preparation is a matter of the subjective, of course. It is an attitude of self-respect, of openness to one's own past, of recognition of how one is in a present situation, and thus of readiness to respond wholistically and effectively. That is, of course, an idealized portrait, but it is one that is approached in varying degrees by most clients who have been helped to develop skills in inward searching. It is in contrast to those who have acquired extensive autobiographical information.

Central to the humanistic image of the person is the phenomenon we call *subjectivity*. Ask someone, "Are you live or on tape?" and when the response is "Live," ask "How do you know?" In one way or another the answer will point to the person's subjectivity. Ignored by those who concentrate on the overt and explicit, this is, to my mind, *the very life of the person*.

The central element of consciousness is the capacity to have *intentionality*, directedness in consciousness, life orientation. Ranging from lassitude and no aware intent to the intense focus of someone fighting for life, intention is always, at least implicitly, a characteristic of life.

The process through which intentionality is expressed we call "searching." It is the questing, seeking, exploring, trying, thrusting of life. Sometimes it is obscured, suppressed, or withheld. When that is so, the life force is diminished and the person is truly ill—emotionally ill, intellectually ill, and, very often, physically ill.

When we recognize that life, itself, is manifested through searching, we are brought to a new understanding of the inevitability of change. Each moment is, in a very real sense, new. Each time we seriously attend to some issue in our lives there is the likelihood that it will be different. That difference may be miniscule, or it may be major.

I introduced this chapter by telling of the change in what I intended to call this chapter between the time when I first thought of the title and today. Searching was implicit as well as explicit, and today's talk is different than what I would have said before, and—and here is the point to recognize—it is different than it will be if I give it again tomorrow or next month or next year. Of course, I froze it in written words last month, so I can read those words now. But we must not be fooled—were I to toss this manuscript aside and pick up the thread now, differences—small and large—would be present.

Indeed, this talk you are hearing kept evolving so that I was quite late in getting it in and to my hapless but patient discussant, Dr. Polster.

Recognizing that the life force is expressed through searching leads us to the conviction that all life is constantly evolving and is in one way or another *searching*. It may be a whale surfacing to spout, a lioness pursuing a gazelle, an ant carrying a single grain of wheat, or a blade of grass pushing through the cement to find the sun. Searching, intention, life. Whether it be the dedicated scientist devoting her or his talents to a project, the gifted artist focusing her or his gifts on a masterwork, a first-string quarterback diving for a touchdown, a junior high girl practicing putting on make-up, a kindergarten boy whispering a secret to a pal, or whatever—each is seeking something, trying to attain something, endeavoring to change something, is devoting his or her life to something beyond the mere fact of immediate being.

WHAT IS THERAPY FROM A SUBJECTIVIST PERSPECTIVE?

Having made a case for thinking about psychotherapy from a perspective that makes the client's subjectivity the primary scene of therapeutic action, I will now use a series of declarative statements to sketch the broad outlines of such work.

1. Human life is ultimately manifested through *awareness* (broadly conceived to include conscious, preconscious, and unconscious zones). The *subjectivity* (the realm of awareness) of the client is the site of whatever changes are effected through psychotherapy.

Whatever changes are accomplished by psychotherapy will be manifested in the client's having a different inner experience of her or his life. This is not the same as the client making a different explicit report of his or her experience. That may or may not occur. Because the phenomenal seat of the client's being is the subjective, changes may be manifested in many ways in addition to the verbal (for example, in relationships, working effectiveness, mood, and affect).

2. The subjective (and the person's life force) is expressed through the *searching* process. This is a constantly present thrust into the future, having the goal of bringing about changes in inner experience.

Searching is the life force in action, seeking the fulfillment of intention, evoking the experiences of life, and mediating its satisfactions and dissatisfactions. The capacity to search is innate, but the ability to use it effectively is dependent upon experience and in many instances on training (although this may not be recognized at the time).

3. The client's experience of feeling genuine *concern* about his or her own life is the chief dynamic or energy source and the only appropriate guidance for the therapeutic work of searching.

Living is searching. The impetus to search arises from intention or concern. It is a useful convention to speak of *concern* as the subjective experience motivating a particular instance of engaging in searching. As such it may be recognized as an energy source for the process and, most importantly, as a source of guidance.

It is here that the particular significance of the subjective stance is most evident. No amount of therapist wisdom nor client motivation can substitute for the guidance function of client concern. When a client is fully experiencing a life concern, he or she will concurrently have an impulse toward what needs to be explored. This is a natural product of the fact that the experienced concern is identical with the impulse that gives rise to the searching effort.

4. The chief function of the psychotherapist is to display to the client the ways in which the client constricts her or his awareness (the *resistances*) and the costs of such constrictions.

As a client endeavors to search within as fully and openly (to the therapist) as possible, it is inevitable that obstacles and distractions will be encountered. These are of many types: embarrassment, shame, guilt, apparent memory loss, and efforts to impress or please the therapist are among the most frequent. Helping the client to become aware of these with as much candor as possible is a step to recognizing how they have interfered with the client's living and satisfaction.

This is an equation crucial to the therapeutic effort: *That which interferes with the free-ranging expression of the client's consciousness in the therapeutic setting is isomorphic with that which interferes with the client's life in general.*

For example, the client who has trouble bringing out his or her anger in the therapeutic hour is likely to be overly meek or excessively rageful in her or his life outside therapy. The client who cannot search freely because of a need to please the therapist is generally someone who is docile and overly agreeable in her or his home and working situations.

But a word of caution: To accept these rough generalizations as ways of interpreting client participation is to totally miss the very point I am making here. Only as the client discovers her or his own meanings is any therapeutic value to be had.

5. The main task of psychotherapy is to increase the range and depth of the client's awareness. Awareness of the main elements of one's *self-and-world construct system* is important to full living and potency in life.

Many of the resistances to free searching that are disclosed in this process will be found to derive from the ways in which the client has defined her or himself and her or his world—the answers to questions such as "Who and what am I? What are my strengths and my weaknesses? What is this world? What are the good things to be sought out? What should be avoided? What powers have I?" and similar issues for which all of us need to have answers all through our lives. As one answers these questions, so will one live out life.

6. The psychotherapist needs to give primary attention to *client process* and to attend to client content only as it is pertinent to *client presence* and *process*.

It is not the therapist's job to give answers to the questions exemplified above; it is his or her job to help the client discover and reevaluate her or his own existing answers. Many times, these are unrecognized consciously or may even be denied or distorted when first brought to light.

7. Therapist interventions need to be timed and phrased so as to take account of the client's *current subjective state* (that is, the context into which the intervention will enter) and the current state of the therapeutic *alliance*.

A therapist operating in a subjective perspective must always be mindful of these two critically important variables: the current state of her or his alliance with the client and how any intervention (or nonintervention) will accord with the current context of the work.

Saying this is not saying that therapist actions should always be smoothly in accord with either or both. Although not frequent, there are times when the best course may be deliberately at odds with those patterns.

8. Therapist and client inevitably collude out of their own subjective needs (*transference* and *countertransference*). Such times provide especially productive areas for discovery and working through.

Psychotherapy consists of two subjectivities mutually engaged in the service of opening and expanding the subjective awareness of one of them (the client). This requires some degree of parallel expansion for the other (the therapist). While, as we have seen, change is constant in each human being, necessarily our subjectivity also tends to maintain a generally stable condition. Being responsive to the particular circumstances of the therapy, we need to maintain a degree of openness to the changes being evoked in both participants.

As we have seen above, working with each client—and, indeed, each session—is in some measure a new experience. The therapist's opening to that evolution may well be growthful for her or him as well as for the client.

9. Therapeutic change comes as the client perceives familiar situations in enlarged contexts (*reframing*) and is more aware of his or her own patterns of participation (*character traits*) in such situations.

Clients often protest that because they have thought of everything about the life issue that is troubling them, they cannot understand how they could come up with anything fresh and helpful from within themselves. This is a superficially logical but ill-founded argument. It is based on the faulty notion that clients have certain containers of information inside themselves and that when those have been exhausted, any further ideas must come from the outside.

What therapy must do is to help the client recognize that in their very natures, they are dynamic processes that endlessly process, create, and store material, and that the limits that seem so firm to them derive from their way of thinking about themselves, not from some predetermined maximum capacity.

When a familiar but troubling situation in the client's life is described repeatedly with a desire to discover (*not simply to report*) new awarenesses will continually appear. Some are pointless, some are partially helpful and beginnings for change, and some may prove truly liberating.

10. The principal outcome of this kind of psychotherapy is an *enlarged sense of one's own being and powers*.

The previous point demonstrates how the client's sense of her or his own capacity is often shrunken and distorted. As the therapeu-

tic work goes forward and the client discovers and resolves some of his or her self-limiting ways of perceiving her or himself, there is a renewed and expanded sense of power and hope.

CONCLUSION

I leave this quick summary of a subjectivist perspective now to make a few concluding comments.

It is unlikely that a new Freud will come to the field of psychotherapy as we know it today. This is so despite the fact that this meeting is replete with gifted candidates for that position.

Yet, in the nature of such things, a new Freud—or Jung or Rogers or whomever you would nominate as a seminal force in our history—is more likely to be among the audience than the presenters at this Evolution of Psychotherapy Conference.

To make a significant and determining impact on human understanding about human beings one must offer a perspective at some contrast—even, perhaps, at odds—with the prevailing views. Simply extending or deepening the familiar outlook may be an important contribution, but it will not open truly new possibilities.

So don't look for the new Freud on the faculty list, but she may be sitting beside you right now.

Discussion by Erving Polster, Ph.D.

◆

Jim and I go back a long way. We first met in 1961 and we have traveled parallel paths. I have much admired his writings, which have been prodigious, clarifying, deep, and sensitive. Many of the things he is saying are things that percolate in my mind as well. The issues

are important to me, although they come out of me very differently from the way they come out of him.

Among the things that Jim is talking about, the one that catches my mind the most is the issue of what psychotherapy *is*. What form would psychotherapy have taken if Freud had been a clergyman instead of a doctor? What form would psychotherapy have taken if Freud had been a politician? Or an economist, as was Marx? We don't know because the phenomena that he dealt with as a physician were brought in by the people he worked with—they were his patients' particular pathologies—and now we who apply the principles he introduced have to be careful not to get stuck with the phenomena he was dealing with in his patients.

So what is psychotherapy and what is its range? When I was in Cleveland in the late sixties, I got pretty satiated with working only in my office. I wanted my work to be more directly imbedded in the community. I had a clergyman friend who knew something of my work and I asked him whether he had any place for my work in his church; anything I could do on a volunteer basis?

He said, "Well, we have a coffeehouse."

I said, "I'd like to come down and sit around the coffeehouse and talk to the people there and see what happens."

He said, "Fantastic."

So I went to the coffeehouse, and I sat at a table and people would gather around the table. They had not come there to see me; they went there for the coffeehouse and had no presenting problems. There would be seven or eight people around the table; a couple of people would leave, a couple more would come. We talked all night long and I began to wonder: What's the difference between this conversation and what they would have said if I had not been there?

I thought the primary difference is that I called attention to their awareness of the feelings, effects, and implications of what they were saying. This is very similar to what Jim is saying in his chapter. But still, it was a strange phenomenon to be talking to people who were not patients, mining for depth although I might never see them again. And they were not expecting the things from me that you would expect a patient to seek.

That experience was interesting to me in itself, but after a couple of weeks these church leaders bought a larger place for a larger coffeehouse. So we moved over there, and

because it was larger, I worked from the stage. There I worked with a community of people; a room filled with 100 to 150 people. These were young folks. Half of them were on drugs; half of them weren't. Half were black; half were white. It was near a university area. We dealt with the issues they were concerned about, like the relationship of hippies to policemen, the relation of education to freedom. There was a wide number of such issues that would come up. Sometimes we would role-play a scene with audience participation; at other times I would lead a discussion given over to the audience at large; always there was an electric enthusiasm. What I am trying to point out is the range of forms psychotherapy might take, going beyond what we now see as psychotherapy. How do we expand our sensibilities to include such things as the communal experience?

I've been talking with a particular hospital regarding their need for psychological work with their people. We are talking about designing meetings for large groups of patients. We would design sessions inviting interpersonal explorations, building in the ordinary human concerns that people deal with in everyday life. They would be called "life-focus groups" rather than "psychotherapy groups." These groups would run on a continuing basis, rather than be limited in the number of sessions.

I bring this up with particular relevance to what Jim was saying about the managed-care problem. The monstrosity of somebody in a distant office telling a therapist who has been working intimately with a patient what he or she should do with this patient is beyond thinking. But much as I dislike it, I must also say, "We created it." We psychotherapists have neglected dealing with the problem that is faced by our society, a system that can't handle long-term therapy by individual psychotherapists, partly because of the huge number of people in need and partly because of prohibitive financial requirements. The society is taking care of this problem in many ways. Managed care is one of them; another one is through self-help groups, including the 12-step groups. The number of people involved is astonishing.

The San Diego Self-Help Directory, in a recent report put out by the county, named some 500 self-help groups in San Diego alone. In his study of self-help groups in America, Alfred Katz reported 750,000 groups in the United States. In 1990, Richard Higgins reported that there were 200 types of 12-step recovery groups and that each week they attracted 15 million Americans to half a million meetings.

This is a seething undercurrent that is a suggestive adjunct to the managed care system, and we therapists have largely disregarded it. Let them go off on their own. It's a nice thing they are doing, we imply, but we don't do much with it.

Take another kind of group, est, for one example. You all probably know something of est, which I don't think is operating anymore. They held many principles in common with gestalt therapy. Yet a gestalt therapist would never do the autocratic things they did. I never attended one of their sessions, but I have read Adelaide Bry's book and I've talked to people who have been there. To me, there seemed a fascistic flavor, one that has given that kind of process a bad name. But why can't one conduct groups like that with kindness, and with more open-minded attention to people's needs, with personal freedom, with inspiration? Many people in psychotherapy circles think inspiration is intrusive or gilds the lily. We behave as though we shouldn't inspire anybody. We often think that if we inspire somebody this implies that they are not doing things independently. Who cares about independence if they get to do what they want to do?

So the question Jim's paper moves me to ask is, "How can we therapists deal with the creation of freshness in the society at large with a novelty, with inspiration, with a sense of the human condition, without having to constrict ourselves to the office situation?" Don't misunderstand me. I am not diminishing the importance of the office situation. I personally love working in my office. The things that happen widely in people's psychotherapy offices are magnificent. But private therapy in its highly individualized orientation must expand the application of its principles to offer communal opportunities as it furthers its own broader relevance.

Response by Dr. Bugental

♦

I am particularly appreciative of two parts of what Erving has told us today. The first is his reminding us that there are many forms of work in psychology—psychology with a lower-case p. The human experience is not summarized in all such efforts as are represented here at this meeting, comprehensive as it is. It is good to be reminded of that fact from time to time. Too easily we slide into thinking that if it isn't psychotherapy or counseling or something similar, it just doesn't exist.

The second point which Erv so wisely puts before us is the reminder that we have not reached the apex in knowledge about humans or even in knowledge about how to do our kind of work we call psychotherapy. To be sure, we're on the road, but new forms, new vehicles, new patterns for our work are continually emerging. Efforts to regiment the whole enterprise will have unwanted effects as well as some that might be creative.

This point of how our field continually changes is illustrated by my recollection of the first group psychotherapy session in which I had any part. This was in an army hospital in 1948, and group therapy was a new concept to all of us on the staff. But, undaunted, we gathered 50 or 60 patients in the hospital theater and gave them a lecture on mental health principles. They were instructed, "Please do not interrupt the speaker. Please do not talk among yourselves. If you have questions, the speaker will take them at the end of this therapy session."

So much for group therapy. Changes have occurred.

The Use of Focusing in Therapy

◆

Eugene Gendlin, Ph.D.

Eugene Gendlin, Ph.D.
Eugene Gendlin is Associate Professor at the Department of Behavioral Sciences at the University of Chicago. He received his Ph.D. in Philosophy from The University of Chicago in 1958. Dr. Gendlin was founder and editor of Psychotherapy, Theory, Research, and Practice *and was winner of the first Distinguished Professional Psychologist Award from the Psychotherapy Division of the American Psychological Association. He has numerous publications including his books on focusing, the approach to psychotherapy that he pioneered.*

INTRODUCTION

I will begin very broadly, and then zero in more and more.

Before I discuss focusing, I want to assert a general principle, in fact the most important one. What is more important than anything else in therapy is *the person*. We need to question all values, all cultures, all assumptions, and all objective truth. Some people say that there is nothing left after such questioning, but that is not so. There is something you don't need to question.

THE RELATIONSHIP

When you look at a human being you can see that someone is in there looking out at you. What is quite arguable is the metaphysical status. A "someone" may be considered a cosmic essence or a bit of floating absurdity. But either way there is somebody there, struggling to lead a life. (When I look at you, I know that *you* are there, trying to lead a life, and you are up against quite a lot.) I am sure of this, and knowing it I can leave everything else in doubt. In fact, I find it best to leave everything else open. I think that every theory about *what* a person is mostly is wrong and destructive if taken seriously.

When I work, I work with the person who is in there looking out at me. Of course a blind person is also someone in there, and so is a mute patient staring at the floor.

As obvious as this is, I find that most of what we are taught makes us lose hold of it. Western science gives us a picture of reality in which people are not possible. The Eastern religions evaporate the person into nonduality. There is much to say for both. We would

197

not want to lose all that science gives us, nor the gifts of the East.

Someone gave me a booklet about Tao, which I put in my pocket with some happiness. It will help me to a big space. I do not think that everything is within the individual; on the contrary, we live within a much vaster universe. But I am here to say, "Don't fall for the omission of the person. I know you are there struggling, and if I can help you with that, then what I am doing is real." Once we have the person, then yes; there is great deal more. There is music, art, the universe, and all the cultures. But the cultures care about how you behave and what you believe; cultures do not care about the person. They seem not to know about people. That may not matter, but anything that makes you deny the person should be rejected.

Processes double when two of us are in contact. The therapy process is larger than either of us can think or predict. It takes us both along with it. That huge process would scare me off, if I had to manage it. If it required certain qualifications, I know I would not have them. But the process requires only *a person*, and that is fortunate because I am a person. I don't know how I made this status; I must have snuck into the wrong line somewhere. But I am sure that I am a person. And that is all that is required.

If I sit down in this chair opposite the person, then the large process will happen. Knowing this, I can sit down there. In the years when many students took drugs, a person often was needed simply to sit for some hours, while someone "came down" from a drug trip. You didn't have to know anything; you just had to be company and see to it that the person didn't jump out the window. All it took was *a person*.

The medical origin of the therapist role imposes an illusion, a false demand that we should know what is wrong and what to do. Because we don't, we become tense. Tension is what we substitute for knowing! My advice is: don't do it. In fact, don't let *anything* come between you and the other person.

When I sit down now, I take all my personal stuff and I put it over here, to one side. Then I take all the techniques and the knowl-

edge that I have, and I put it on the other side. I keep it all close, because I might need it. When my personal stuff registers, it may be information about what is happening. It is a kind of an instrument with which to understand what is going on. I will need the techniques. Sometimes, they help. But the main thing I want to do is to be here.

If you look at me and you happen to see me, you may see that I am shaky, but that is all right, because I am somebody, and I am here, and that is what is required. The process will happen, unless I leave, or my attention wanders and my eyes glaze over, or if I hide and put a well-working technique in between. So I don't do that anymore.

EFFECTIVE LISTENING

The next most important thing I know is to stay constantly in touch with what the client wishes to communicate. I want to stay constantly in touch with that. If I lose track, I have to say, "Wait a minute, I lost you." The minute I don't know what is being said, I have to say, "Wait, tell me that again, I haven't understood it yet." My main vehicle for staying constantly in touch is reflecting back the crux, or the touchy part, of what the person is saying. But saying back is not a method that is supposed to take care of me. I do it so that we stay constantly in touch. Therefore I don't repeat everything. I say the touchy things back, or anything that is hard to grasp.

For example, suppose you tell me a long story. This happened, and then that, and then someone said such and so on. You say that this made you feel ashamed, and then you tell me all the rest of the story. I will just say back to you: "That made you feel ashamed."

It would be easier to say back some of the other parts of the story. "You felt ashamed" is emotionally charged and therefore hard to say back. Anything that is hard to say back needs to be said back. If I were to dodge this, I would be leaving you alone with it. If I come out and voice your charged things, then I am there with you.

This moment-by-moment responding makes for a continuous contact. The minute it is lost, we both feel the difference. The thick connection breaks and I am alone. Then I know that the client is alone as well.

A moment of broken contact happens also when I say too many of my own things one after the other, so that clients must let go of their inner experiencing and strain to attend to me instead. It happens also when I misunderstand. I am articulating the client's experience, but the client is staring at me as if to say "Where did he get that?"At such moments I quickly say, "I can see that that wasn't right; throw that out; tell me again." My clients are used to me saying, "Throw that out." I shove it out of the way with a motion of my hand. After a week or two they know that I don't mean to push anything on them that fails to connect with what arises from inside them. Once they know this, I am free to say anything, try anything. I need not only reflect. I can use every theory and technique I know. If it gets in the way we throw it out. Many therapists don't know how powerful a method "saying back" is. If you do not already use it, try it, especially when clients are stuck and repetitive, or at any difficult juncture in therapy.

When I hear tape recordings of therapy, I hear therapists trying everything else first, taking the client away from just the spots where clients need to enter further, so that something new can emerge. I tell the therapist "First try leaving her there for a minute, and keep her company so she can be with it. If you say it back, she can stay with it a little. It might open up there, where she was speaking from."

Saying back the sensitive places slows the process down so that something new can come. Many clients move quickly, always on the same emotional track. But when they hear back what they have expressed, it provides a few moments during which they can live there, in that felt "place."

Saying back has a kind of rhythm. The client says something; you say it back; the client says, "Well, that's almost it, but it's more like this." You say, "Oh, I see, it is more like this." The client says, "Yes, but you didn't get this little wrinkle yet." You say that back as well, and then there is a very characteristic bit of silence. What was ready to say has been said, and taken in. Now there is nothing ready to say, and so there is room for the next thing to come. Since there is nothing to say, the *non-verbal edge* of the trouble is directly felt.

The process deepens in that characteristic bit of silence at the edge of what can be said. But the client comes to that edge only if we receive what the client is already saying. It is as if the client stood there, holding a tray with a full coffee cup, a sugar bowl, and a little pitcher of cream, and wants to hand it you. As long as you won't take the tray, the client cannot hear what you say very well. The client is still standing there saying, "Take this. This is what I am trying to bring you." As a therapist, when what I say has no effect and I also repeat it without effect, I may notice: Oh! The client is still standing there, trying to hand me what I have been refusing to hear. As soon as I notice this, I say, *"You were trying to say* thus and so," and the client says with relief "Uh-huh." Then, it becomes possible for the client to receive whatever I am trying to say.

FOCUSING INSTRUCTIONS

Within these two overarching principles, the relationship and effective listening, there is the third—focusing instructions. Focusing is not all of therapy. It is a specific process that can be combined with any therapy. You will see why it is so important. It opens a central spot that was long left in a kind of twilight. Every method of therapy depends on it, and yet there has been no way to speak of it, to open it for clients. But it is there to be found by anyone, and some people already have found it. I have specified it, so that it can be found easily, taught, and used.

Focusing is a special kind of bodily experience. Today there is much attention given to the body, but it is mostly the body observed from the outside. Or it is the peripheral body, the body of the muscles and the arms and legs. But there is also the body *felt* from the inside. You already know that one too. But the special kind of inward bodily experience that happens in focusing is not well known. It is still largely a secret. This bodily experiencing is the bodily *sense-of*. It may be *of* a situation, of a problem, of something you said. If you attend in your body, you can let the bodily sense *of* anything come there. This "of" is the key difference to which I am pointing.

THE "SENSE-OF"

For example, right now, can you sense that little strain that you are probably exerting to try to understand what I just said? I have not yet really made it clear. You are prepared to grasp it but probably you haven't quite yet. Can you feel that? That's a bodily discomfort, a bodily sense of effort, but it isn't merely like straining a muscle. Rather, it has a great deal implied in it. It involves straining forward and perhaps some doubt: "Am I going to understand this thing?" and a kind of warning signal: "I don't yet know what he means." It also involves a great deal of knowledge about what a person in this situation could be saying, which lets you know what I could not possibly mean. Even just your not knowing involves your knowledge of people and psychology. Such a lot is implicitly involved in a small discomfort in one's body when it is the bodily sense-*of* a situation. If you attend in the middle of your body just now, you will find this little physical sense of what is actually going on for you just now.

This one might be easy to have, but when it comes to the bodily sense of major problems and life issues, then it may be harder to bear the body sense-*of* them.

The body sense-of even a simple situation turns out to be complex, intricate, and interesting. The thing itself may be trivial, but the body sense-*of* it will not be trivial. It will be a whole complexity. Here, for example, it has to do with your attempts to understand things, perhaps your conflicts about whether you are smart or not, perhaps that you are tired of having to take in information while someone lectures at you. It probably involves all kinds of things about men, teachers, and who knows what else, perhaps whether or not you have always been free to think, or whether or not this material is new for you. Each person here will find a different intricacy behind the simple effort to understand.

Implicitly your bodily sense-*of* anything brings with it an immense part of your life. For example: "What impression is my jacket making on you?" This is totally trivial, but if you can get a little bit of a bodily sense-*of* it, that will be a vast implicit texture of things. It cannot turn out to be trivial.

The bodily sense-of is our crucial connection to so much. Without it we may still sometimes live spontaneously in a whole-bodied way, but when we cannot, when there is trouble, when something cuts us off from the deeper parts of us, then it becomes crucial to find this bodily-sensed edge and to attend directly to it. Only there, in this bodily sense-*of*, can we find directly whatever the trouble is. And when we have worked the trouble through, it is also there, at that edge, that the resolution opens out into a deeper and wider sense of being whole and inwardly connected and continuous.

Such implicitly complex bodily experiencing is always ongoing. It is not yet cut and formed into one thing or another. It goes on at the center. Out of it arise all the familiar kinds of experiences, and they also go back into it. From it arise the familiar cut and shaped kinds of experiences: perceptions, emotions, ideas, words, images, memories, movements, and so on. Therefore this bodily sense-*of* is at the center of psychotherapy, whether we are talking in the vocabulary of psychodynamic analysis or existentialism, whether we work behaviorally, or with dreams, images, or gestures, or in terms of any other specific kind of experience.

In the center is a bodily experiencing that has not yet been divided into any of these different contents and modes. It is not an image, not a thought, not a feeling, and it is not a perception, but it is also not exactly *not* those, because a great many of those are always implicit in it.

AN EXPERIMENT

For example, let me ask you to think of a friend, the first one who comes to your mind. I don't care if you know the person well. Have you got one? Just pick one. Okay, now pick one more. Now we have two different people.

Please take the first one. Put your attention in the middle of your body and think of that person. Then wait a bit and see what physical *sense-of* comes in your body.

Perhaps a physical quality came, which goes with that person. The person gives you a certain bodily sense. You might say you can taste it. It doesn't have a word to name it. If you have a word for it, notice that it is only a handle; it does not tell all your history with the person. You cannot think of it all, but you can feel it all. Can you taste the quality that this person gives you? What it is might surprise you. You might discover something there.

Now switch to the other person. Sense how different your body becomes. *That* is how your body carries the other person. It's a different body sense-*of.* You can invite a body sense-of anything. It will always be intricate, always many things, an "*all that.*" It has all the events, your troubles and future plans and hopes with it. Everything is like that; nothing is just itself.

THE BODILY SENSE

The bodily sense is not an emotion—not just fear, not just anger, not *just* any of those things. You are angry, perhaps, but the body sense-of the situation is wider. If at first you are *only* angry, it can widen out into an *all that.* Perhaps the first edge you find in addition to anger, is for example: "Leave me alone; I *want* to be angry." That is already wider than anger. But more may come, perhaps, "It's partly my fault and I don't want to know that, but I know that." It might widen more, into: "I *hate* knowing it!" Then it might widen further: "What gets me the worst is that I don't know what to do about it, now." It might be, "I always get stuck not knowing what to do about this kind of thing." Those are just words, but in the body what comes is not just this and that which the words say, but the bodily discomfort with the whole situation, *all that,* more than you can think.

So far I have said that one can have a bodily sense-*of* anything, including what you are talking about in therapy. I also want to have brought home that the bodily sense-of is intricate. It is like a Persian rug. And it can surprise you because how our bodies carry a problem is different from the way we have mapped it out. The most important thing on your map usually is not what arises if you ask for the most important thing in the bodily sense. If I had first asked you, "What stands out about your friend?" you would have said this and that, or you might have said that the friend is different from you in this way and that way. But the bodily sense will turn out to have a different main thing. And even if it is the same, surprising aspects will emerge from inside it.

Now I want to point out that a bodily sense-of is not a static thing, not a bunch of facts. It moves. It makes steps. Even if it remains a wordless blank, it implies, pushes for; it is in advance, the feel of the needed further step. It wants to move forward. It's a living being. It wants to live. It wants to heal. It wants to move. It wants to grow. It wants, it wants . . . That's all I am going to say; it wants . . .

A body sense-of is an implying of further living. Further steps come from it. Usually at first very little steps like, "Oh yeah, that." And then it feels a little different. Or, "Oh, another thing about it is . . ." and again the whole thing feels a little different. Cognitively these steps may not amount to much, but physically they are a large change. *When the bodily sense-of opens into a little step, it changes the whole way in which the body has the problem.*

After a few such changes, you would ask: "Well, is it *all* fixed?" You do not answer such a question; rather, it is asked down into the body. Typically, what comes is a changed but still troubling bodily sense, which says in effect: "No." "What is still in the way of its being all right?" The answer speaks up from the bodily sense. Just *this*, this specific uncomfortable edge, is what's not yet all right.

But what is this? We are inclined to infer or guess, but the sense doesn't have to guess; it knows; it is. The discomfort is not just a discomfort; it makes implicit sense. It knows why it is here. So of course, we direct our question to it: "What does it need to be all right?

It may take some effort to bring your attention back to the felt sense, so that the question can be asked there. You must return to the middle of the body, perhaps asking again: "Is it all all right now? . . ." Ah, there is that edge again!! Now it can be asked: "What does it need to be all right?" There is usually a slight shift when the question actually reaches the bodily sense. Then, often, something specific also comes: "Oh yeah, that." At first it may be only a wordless, physical sense of meaning. Soon it opens and more steps come.

CASE EXAMPLE

She has health worries. This cough doesn't go away. Could it be some terminal illness?

She wonders about her relationship to her body.

As she wonders about her relationship to her body, she attends to what comes in her body. It is tension.

She knows focusing and has done it for years. So she hovers around the tension.

What is this tension? What is all that, about this tension? This brings the felt sense, the body sense-of this tension.

Now: *What is in this body sense-of (the tension)?* A first step comes: She finds that this tension has always been there. It was there when she was a little child.

Some tears well up, tears about how that tension has always been there, about how she had always to be tense.

There is some loosening in the body sense-of this tension. Then there is another round of focusing:

Well, why was my body like that when I was so little? What is *all that* about that? Freshly the body sense-of forms in response to that question. Then it opens into another step: It was so tense in my house, and everybody in it was so tense. And my mother was that way in her body. And I absorbed that in *my* body.

After a while of being with that, and crying some, then what she later called "this amazing thing" happened. The felt sense opened and suddenly she had the sure sense that "it did not need to have been this way."

It takes her a longer explanation, later, to say what she means. This is because a step comes as a shift in the body, with its meaning at first only *implicit*. One knows, although it

may take time to find words and phrases. Those are also important. Without saying it, one can easily lose what has come. The words and phrases carry it forward. But it comes as an *implicit* meaning texture all at once. What she sensed, was:

"It would have been OK not to be tense, because nobody was sending me anything bad—that was just their tenseness. But I was too little to know that I didn't have to take that tension in. I didn't make that differentiation, that boundary."

"But this amazing thing happened. I could feel my little girl body being able to open then, *now*."

And more:

"After I could let it open a little, I could feel that they cared about me. There was room in which to feel it. There wasn't room before, so I didn't feel it before. All the room was taken up with tenseness. All my life I couldn't feel that people cared about me!"

The example comes from someone who knows how to focus and has done it for many years. Her steps come of their own accord from the felt sense.

I choose this example because it shows the difference between the type of body sense that is not an implicit meaningfulness, and the type that is. Cough and tension seem not to be internally complex and meaningful. In contrast, an implicit texture of meaning can come. It is the bodily sense-*of*, or about, the sense of *all that* which comes with—anything. In this instance, it is the bodily sense that comes with the tension. *That* one opens into steps.

WORKING WITH
CHILDHOOD EXPERIENCE

Now I need to point to another difference. I want to be very specific, because here we have a sensitive interface between our different ways of working, and each group may know some important factors that other groups lack. Many therapists know very well that attending in the body can swiftly elicit a childhood experience, but they only know about reenacting the experience. Clients repeat those over and over, without actually changing.

I want to emphasize that when a childhood experience comes from a felt sense, it is *not a repetition*, not a re-enactment, not the childhood experience just as it actually was then. In focusing the felt sense is always the person's whole present bodily sense-*of* . . . whatever is being worked on. Our bodies do also preserve a record of past experiences as they were, but in our example here this is not the original experience as such. Rather, the past experience arises from—and is part of—the felt sense that freshly forms *now. At each step she lets the felt sense come freshly, now*. She asks: What is all that, which goes with this, now? That is why new steps come.

For clients who know focusing, childhood experiences come in this way, without searching specifically for them, and as part of a present felt sense. But clients who don't know focusing also tend to have the past as part of the present, if the connection with the therapist is palpable, and if they are not artificially regressed and told to re-enact the past just as it was. They may *be* very much in the past, with very little present perspective, but the ongoing therapy process is thickly *present*, so that they feel the past as part of the wider present. I think that is how new steps come.

FOCUSING QUESTIONS

Steps like these are familiar to us from therapy when it is successful. But they happen over months. My example is from an experienced focuser, but focusing often moves rapidly far down, where otherwise change would take years. Or, when done quickly, the steps happen only upstairs, and the client's body stays the same. But when the body sense gives those little steps, they can go far down in a short time, certainly not always, but often. And one can feel the physical change that comes with them. At first such a bodily sense-of is confusing and murky. We called the process "focusing" because this fuzzy sense then *comes into focus*. So I must warn you that the bodily sense-of a situation is very fuzzy, and seems quite unpromising. It can seem so worthless that you might pass right by it when it does come. We are trained to override our bodies all

day, and of course we need to be able to do that. But this very unpromising body sense-of not only knows a lot of the answers, it also moves into further steps. One way to let it come is to ask in one's body: "Am I comfortable about that?" The question can seem silly. For example, say the client is weeping and expressing terrible feelings. How can we ask the client: "Yeah, but are you comfortable?" And yet it is true that underneath the intense emotions a more global, bodily discomfort may come, which will lead deeper and will generate new steps.

So we respond first to what the client is trying to convey, and then, when it is time to move on, and there is no way to move on, we can ask: "How does it feel here?" Or "How is it in your body?" If nothing comes, we can say: "Don't answer right away. Wait and see what comes if we ask: Are you comfortable *in there*, about this?"

Some clients are able to focus in this way as soon as we ask them to attend in their bodies. You will find that therapy deepens immediately with some proportion of your clients, if you simply ask: "How does that make you feel in your body?" With others it takes longer. Over a period of months, most clients learn to find the bodily sense-of what they are working on. We ask small questions such as: "How does it affect your body?" or "What comes here when you say that?" This can be asked briefly. If the client cannot use it, we drop it and go back to what the client had been saying, without ever derailing a client's own process.

A CRITIQUE OF THEORY

If you examine this theoretically, you will see that it brings us to a very different vantage point. Most theories begin with perception. The organism is supposed to perceive situations through the five senses and then interpret them. Everything is talked about in terms of perceptions and interpretations. Supposedly we try to perceive reality, but there is no definite reality, so it all depends on what story we tell about it. I think that misses the fact that we live in situations to begin with. We are in interaction with our mothers in the womb. We exist interactionally in situations. Perception is a later and less basic process. Plants don't perceive, and they live all the time. They consist of interactions, they make themselves of soil and air and light. Our bodies are at least as complex as the plant's. Our bodies make our situations and our interactions. Situations do not consist of the five senses. In fact, one cannot imagine how even a simple situation could be made of bits of color and smell. (Gendlin 1970, 1980, 1981, 1987, 1992a, 1992b, 1996b.)

THE BODY

We are alive with each other in a bodily way before and without perception and interpretation. Those only modify and elaborate our bodily interactions. We elaborate our bodies also with further training. For example, when you drive a car, it is your body that deals with the clutch and the brake. You need only attend to special events outside the windshield. Sometimes your body drives all the way home without your help. Similarly, you walk into a room with your body, and you move and even greet people appropriately without having to talk to yourself about who is there and whether you will smile, and how broadly. You have to talk to yourself about very few things. Your body handles most of your situations all day long.

Your body creates your situations. That is why you never know all that went into what you said and did. In the traditional, disembodied way of talking, this is called the unconscious, but that is only a puzzling concept for the most ordinary activity. The unconscious is the body. And it is not really *un*conscious, as you can verify if you pay attention to it. It is sentient; it will be there if you allow it to speak to you. And it is already living your life. That is why, if you have a discomfort, that discomfort knows why it is uncomfortable. If you are scared of a situation, I say that the scared in there knows why it is scared. You may have very good hypotheses about it. After all, you have lived with yourself all these years, so you can make a pretty good guess. But if you come down to your center, not only will you find the information directly, it will be different, and differently organized, than you expected. And

it will imply and generate steps forward to change and release itself.

The physical relief of a step forward is distinctly different from a mere absence, for example, when the body sense-of has merely lessened or disappeared. These discriminations become very obvious to clients after a while.

CONTACT

I work with a person's body, but I do not do it in a way that bypasses the person. I ask the person to ask the body. I don't work with the person's body without the person.

For example, I ask the client a question. If the client answers immediately, I say, "No, wait. I didn't meant to ask you; I was giving you this question to take downstairs, to ask your body. Ask your body this question." I may also say, "Let the question change as you go along until it gets to be just the right question." I work with the person who came to me, the one who looks out at me through the eyes. If you come, I would work with you. You know who I mean. I mean *you*. I would also work with your organism, your body, but through you. In a way I would be training you, giving you all my tricks one by one, asking you to try them out. You would keep those that work for you.

I would often ask you to check with your body, whether it is ready for this or that. I would not go around you and ask your body myself. I would rather take longer and strengthen people in their ownership of their bodies.

There are times when I relate directly to someone's body after all. For example, when I try to bring home to an audience that I am really talking about the concrete physical body, I may make a sudden startling motion and thump on the stage. Then I apologize to the audience for what I know is an unpleasant thud. Everyone who laughs knows where I mean, when I say "in the body." A body sense-of comes in there, where I make the audience uncomfortable when I startle them. It may be in your chest, stomach, or abdomen. It may be in your throat where we cry. Somewhere in the middle of the body you can get a distinct physical sense-*of* any problem, anything large or small, painful or joyous, and especially anything that needs working on.

DEALING WITH THE BODY SENSE

Sometimes it can be hard to stay with a body sense-of when it comes. In this regard I must tell you a new and important discovery: There are *three* alternatives, when something is too tough to feel. Most people only know two: They know to run away, or to be stubborn and push in. Running away is sometimes called stress reduction, or desensitization, getting away from it. This seems to me similar to alcohol; it works only halfway, only sort of. The tension and the problem are left in the body.

The other well-known alternative is to push in. That may cause resistance, sometimes also dissociation, spacing out. More commonly it makes everything freeze and get stuck. Of course, if you bull your way in there and you have some success, then don't let me discourage you. But there is a third alternative.

One doesn't have to push in or run away; one can also stay close to the painful place, but not *so* close that one becomes overwhelmed. This is a third way that most people have to be shown. We can stay close to something without going further into it, and without running away from it.

If a client tells me that something is "too scary," I say: "Don't go into it, but don't run away either. Back up for a minute, back up until you can breathe. Then stay there."

There is a "just right" distance, different for each problem. It is where you can feel the problem, but you can still breathe.

If a problem is so touchy that you hardly can stand even to think about it, then go further away from it, just as far as you need, but don't turn your back on it. Let's put it far over there, in Canada, but don't turn your back on it. Or it might be something that you need to keep close to you. Then keep it right here, on your lap.

There is a way of not being in something and yet not running away from it either, a third way that *creates a space next to something*. If it is too hard to work with, there is at first no space, no place to be, from which to relate to it. With this way one suddenly finds there is such a spot, where one can be and breathe and still sense the problem. Even if we have done no more than to find such a spot, it is a lot because the body can go on working there, underneath. Just to be at such a spot is a step forward on the problem.

Knowing this third way has another advantage: Once you know it, you need never worry that anything inside could overwhelm you. If it becomes too tough, you make a space next to it. Then you can stay there for a little while.

Therapists should not avoid anything that arises in clients of its own accord. Anything that is already there is less worrisome in company than if I avoid it and leave the client to deal with it autistically alone.

There may be a spot where the client gets foggy and dissociative. This is not worrisome. Just backing up and making a space near the spot is best. A few minutes or a few weeks later a path will be there.

A great deal of change can happen in a little while. Time inside is not mathematical, as you probably already know. Time inside does not consist of always equal units. A bit of clock time can be very long inside. A lot of change may happen when nothing seems to be going on. So it is good when we say, "Right now I can't do this; it's too tough for me. I am going to back up so I can breathe, but I won't run away." Two minutes later I may find that I can now go to it. Or it may take me two hours, or two weeks, or two months. It may seem that I'll never be able even to consider going to it, but a little later it may have become possible.

If the client is in a hard place near the end of the hour, I may say, "Let's make a place here. Let's camp here. Let's pitch a tent and put in firewood, and stay here a while. Here you know where you can touch it. If you move just a little closer, you can feel it too much. So let's stay right here, and wait for steps to come. The next time you check in with it, a step may come—perhaps."

One also can make a good base of operations by asking the person to think of a place they love. But we would not merely substitute this place for the painful experience, because then it remains in the body and hides somewhere. For example, if you think of a beautiful beach you really love, and feel yourself being there, you can for the moment wash out whatever troubles you. That just makes it hard to find again. On the other hand, if you use that same beautiful beach as a kind of base of operations at which to stay, so that *from there* you can approach the problem and also pull back again, then the beach can help a lot.

One therapist (McGuire, 1984) had a client who loved sailing. She asked her client, "Tell me what you love about sailing," until the feelings of sailing had become quite vivid. Then she said: "All right, let's go out on a sailboat together and leave this tough problem on the land there." When they had imagined themselves well out of range, she asked her client to turn toward the problem, and from that distance to feel what it made in her body. At the right distance the felt sense comes very distinctly and at a tolerable intensity. It helps to be in a very positive state, with a whole, sound body, when one wants to process something difficult.

We can let the client own and direct the hour, and also offer many specific ways of bodily processing. Clients learn to use them alone of course, but in relational interaction one can do more than when one is alone. So we can use many of the ways that are being invented by the hypnosis side of therapy, but as instructions for clients to become stronger inside themselves.

PRINCIPLES

My first principle is to stay very present and keep a close connection. For this you need not be concerned with your tone of voice and posture. In fact, while you are concerned with those you cannot be present to the other person. If your attention is on the person, your tone and posture will express your presence quite naturally.

The client can feel my presence in many ways, certainly not only by looking. The gaze may be straight ahead, or down, but the client can nevertheless feel my attention and will miss it if it stays long away in my own thoughts. So it is best to conduct therapy from being *here*. I may think a thousand things, but I do not pursue them for long at a time. I return after moments, and stay here with my attention and presence, so that I am really here.

My second principle is always to take in what the client is trying to convey, and to voice it so that it can be here, within our interaction, and so that the client can re-hear it and go deeper from it if that turns out to be possible.

I can try anything, but if it fails to work I soon drop it and say, "Oh, I see, that didn't fit." Then I usually bring clients back to where they were on their own inner track. I say, "You were just saying . . . "

My third principle is the small bits of instruction for focusing, which are my main topic.

Focusing helps to let a person become continuous inside at that zone between consciousness and the unconscious that is the body; at that edge is where concrete change and novelty arise. And it is at that edge that we can feel what is in the way of being inwardly continuous.

Any method we attempt must quickly become continuous with what arises from inside the client. We may originate it, but if it works, it becomes something that arises truly from inside.

The inner continuity is also a good criterion for what we have to work on. We need not work on every one of our problems and every bad thing, but we do need to sense what is in the way of being continuous inside, so that we can live from far down all the way out into action and speech. In my opinion human nature—what we really *are*—is not any kind of fixed content, not this or that culture or way of living. It is rather a continuity from inside-out into living. As you allow your attention down inside, you may find there a kind of floor, and that you can't get down further. And as you see what is there, you may find that some of that is in the way of your energy. That will probably be where you have to work. What needs work is whatever is still in the way of being whole.

"Integration" was the old concept of being whole. I find it too simple to fit our time. We have to learn to commute between different parts of ourselves. The traditional single-cell person now seems closed and overly simple. But there is a simplicity that does go with wholeness. It is the flowing out from inside. As one client told me: "Now, most of the time, when I do things, *I'm* doing them."

When we live continuously from underneath up into what we say and do, that continuity is precious. Even a tiny thing that interrupts that continuity is worth working on.

If those three things are kept, the relationship, the reception of what the client wants to communicate, and the inner focusing connection, then you can try anything. The more techniques you learn, the better. Each technique sometimes can give you leverage. When there seems to be no way to let a body sense-of come, or when the body sense-of is there but won't budge, it helps to know many helpful things. But the minute they are not helpful, out with them. Try something else. Say, "I can see that didn't work. Is it all right if I ask you another question?"

WORKING WITH THE BODY SENSE-OF

When there is a body sense-of, we ask for a quality word or an image or gesture that fits with it. To convey quality words, I may ask the client, "Is it heavy, or perhaps fluttery?" Notice, such words describe the physical quality of the body sense-of. They are not about the content. Usually it is a unique quality. When the client tries out my quality words, they will not fit. That shows something *is* there for the client that rejects those words. Conversely, if clients do say, "Yes, fluttery" then I am not sure they have a felt sense as yet. I help make sure that one does come. Then I ask: "What is the quality of it?"

If a client says, "I can't find a word for it," I say, "Good, that shows you've got a felt sense there." How would the client know that no word fits? That is possible only when a felt

body sense is there. So I say, "That's all right; you don't have to have a word. You can call it "that one, there."

Although a felt sense clearly rejects words that don't fit, it will accept a label like "that one, there." There is a slight relief, when a handle word works. It is as if the felt sense is a little bit relieved at having a word that speaks for it. So, after a moment, the client usually says: "Oh yeah. That works."

An image can come from a bodily sense-of, and open it further. But when there is no bodily sense-of, some people find it helpful first to let an image come. Then one can ask: "How does this image make your body feel?"

A word, phrase, image, or gesture might fit the felt sense, as might a movement or a color. If the bodily sense-of connects with that name or that picture, one can physically feel that connection, like "Yeah (breath)" or "This speaks for it." Now one feels one has a handle on it. The bodily sense can no longer be lost easily. Such a handle word or image becomes valuable. The person wouldn't give it up and choose another one even if we offered $5 for it. Perhaps for $500, but not for $5.

You see that we spend time attending to the physical quality of the felt sense rather than immediately going for the content. The body quality might be fluttery, sticky, heavy, like glue, or wormy, perhaps. Next we check the word, phrase, image, or gesture; we check it with the felt sense. Does it really fit? Does it speak for the felt sense?

When you check with your felt sense, it seems almost as if this were another person. Just as you would ask another person, you ask the felt sense: "Hmm . . . is that the best word for it?" There is a physical answer: "Ahh hah, (breath) yeah." For the moment this handle works. If not, you might get another word or another image.

We have now gone several steps, letting a felt sense come, sensing its physical quality, getting a handle, and checking the handle. Of course one would not always go exactly through just these steps. Nothing human works always by the same steps. But the steps help a person to stay with the bodily quality, rather than going immediately to the content. Looking for a handle for the bodily quality helps one to concentrate on the physical quality. So does checking. "Does that word really speak for the quality?" "Does that image really connect?" You spend some time with the quality before you ask into the content.

Only then do we ask the felt sense: "What is it?" or "What's in it?" or "What is it about the situation that makes it feel so wormy?" or "What is the wormiest thing about that situation?" or "What is it about that problem that makes this body sense?"

In response to that kind of question, it very often opens. It goes hmmmmmm yeah!! (big breath.) Or, more often, hmm, yeah (little breath.) Then come the little steps of content-mutation.

Another kind of question to ask is, "What does it need? What does it want? What would it take to feel better?"

One must work to put aside the quick answers, so that the question can reach down to the felt sense. With all questions, the client is likely just to answer, even silently. Then the felt sense does not get the chance to do the answering. For example, the client thinks: "What does it need? Oh yeah, I'd feel better if I could do such and so." But let the felt sense answer. Let's ask *it*. What would *it* need, to feel better? What does it want?"

If the client looks blank, I ask:

"Is that body sense still there?"

If not, we have to get it back again, before we can ask it. A quick way to get it back is to ask, "What comes in your body if we try to say that this problem is all solved now? We can celebrate."

"No, it's right there again."

Okay, *now* let's ask it, "What does it need?"

Silence . . . "Hummmmmmm (breath). Oh . . . it's . . . I know . . . just a minute, I haven't got the words yet, uhm . . ."

When a felt sense opens, there is no doubt that it has opened. Conversely, one knows very well when it has not budged. Good hypotheses might have come to mind, but if it has not budged, there it is, still, stubborn and unmoved. The hypotheses might be right in *some* way, but they are not what *this* will say as *its* next step. Let me try to bring home how important this is. We might go through so much that we can think up; we might seem to make a lot of

progress with images, with intense emotions, or we could bring the beautiful beach in here and generate a good feeling, and yet, after all those things, if we let the felt sense of the problem come and attend to it, we may find quite distinctly that it has not budged. Isn't it better, therefore, to employ all those techniques in a direct relationship with the body sense-of, checking constantly at the felt edge of awareness, whether our techniques have connected or not?

Any method, technique, or small intervention can be checked against the bodily sense-of, once we enable the client who has learned how to attend in the body so as to let a felt sense come.

Every technique we know can help sometimes. The more of them we know, the better. We need not decide among techniques. We need not settle the disputes among different methods. We need not choose one orientation over another. What decides is not our preference, but whether this person's unique body sense responds and opens just now, or not. Using only one approach we are soon stuck and without further leverage. The more approaches we know to try, the more likely we are to offer something that lets the felt sense open. The moment it opens, we pursue what arises from it.

ABOUT RELATIONSHIPS

It is both a wonderful fact, and a source of many new problems, that so many millions of people in all the developed countries have become psychologically oriented. This has a very positive meaning for the future, and it also creates an enormous problem in the present. So many of us are living from inside or trying to live from inside, to become continuous from inside, to live from our *uniqueness*, but when two uniquenesses try to live and work together, the connections between us become a problem.

On the one hand, it is possible in this mode to connect much more deeply with another person than was ever possible through the forms of traditional society. You realize the new depths with your clients, perhaps, or in some relationship that is free from the needs of daily love and work. Many therapists connect so deeply with their clients that their other relationships cannot compare with that depth. But that is because the therapist–client relationship is fenced in and limited as to action, so that it *can* be deep and real within its narrow channel. The client nicely goes away and leaves you free after one hour, no matter what happened. Your spouse doesn't do that. And the client comes back nicely next week, and pays you besides. And if you do have a fight, the society says, "You are right because you are the doctor." You don't need the client to understand what you need when you get up in the morning, or what you need to get your job done. So there are far fewer opportunities for you to project and transfer and reinstance your troubles with a client than there are at home, or with your colleagues. Therapy is so well protected. It is so easy!

For this very protected relationship, we give six years of training. For our life relationships of loving or working together we give no training at all. Training is thought to be artificial. It is not yet widely recognized that the more deeply and genuinely we relate from our uniqueness, the more training we are going to need, and what we need is new training that we are just beginning to develop. We need to appreciate how difficult it is for uniquenesses to relate.

It is not yet well recognized that it is not our individual fault that relationships are so bumpy right now. The old cultural routines no longer work. They consisted of certain roles that were common and commonly understood. For two unique systems to find each other is very different. We do not want to go back to the old roles, and even if we should want to we cannot. Long ago the roles did carry life forward at least for many people, but if we try to return to them we try to be cardboard figures. What has since developed and become articulate cannot fit back into those forms.

On the other hand, finding each other's individuality, which is so easy to do in therapy, is hard to do in daily love and work. Of course I know that my wife is the person over there, trying to lead a life, and I do really appreciate that fact, but she is also this person here, making my life difficult. Every person in my life has

to be thought of in these two radically different ways, both of them real. One reality is how that person impinges on me. But the person is also the one over there, and that one's essence does not consist of fitting or not fitting me. That person has her own issues, which can be understood only on a map that remains totally different from mine.

As soon as we see that other person over there struggling to live, we feel a lot of warmth and appreciation. We understand, and we are ready for genuine contact until—the person impinges on us and seems to turn into our trouble. Now it is suddenly difficult to feel the person's uniqueness. Now it does not seem to be uniqueness at all, but rather some annoying trait that we know from its effect on us. But this is not an either/or. The issues the other person creates in my life are real, and it is just as real that that person is not my issue. I have to deal with both.

IN CONCLUSION

It will require some generations to build new patterns of relating. We already know that those patterns will be much more differentiated than the old ones. The distinctions I have just made are only a small sample. But our present troubles actually constitute a very hopeful, very exciting social development. We are trying to relate from inside, as the individuated people we are becoming. It will take time to build new ways of relating. This need not discourage us. We can feel like pioneers.

REFERENCES

Gendlin, E. T. (1970). *Experiencing and the creation of meaning.* New York: Macmillan.

Gendlin, E. T. (1980). *A process model.* Unpublished manuscript.

Gendlin, E. T. (1981). *Focusing* (2nd ed.). New York: Bantam.

Gendlin, E. T. (1987). A philosophical critique of the concept of narcissism. In D. Levin (Ed.), *Pathologies of the modern self*, pp. 251–304. New York: New York University Press.

Gendlin, E. T. (1992a). The primacy of the body, not the primacy of perception. *Man and World, 25* (3–4), 341–353.

Gendlin, E. T. (1992b). Thinking beyond patterns: Body, language and situations. In B. den Ouden & M. Moen

(Eds.), *The presence of feeling in thought* (pp. 25–151). New York: Peter Lang.

Gendlin, E.T. (1996a). *Focusing-oriented psychotherapy* New York: Guilford.

Gendlin, E. T. (1996b). *Language after postmodernism: fourteen commentaries on the philosophy of Eugene*

Gendlin and Gendlin's Replies. D. Levin, Ed. Evanston: Northwestern University Press.

McGuire, M. (1984). Imagery, body, and space. In A. A. Sheikh (Ed.), *Imagination and healing*. New York, Baywood.

Discussion by James Hillman, Ph.D.

We had the privilege of being with a sensitive and intelligent practitioner, who was able to present that sensitivity and disclose how he actually works. Now I want to raise some questions and also make some parallels between your work, Gene, and Jungian work. The first question is in regard to the person who was the central focus of your most important statement at the beginning of your presentation. *Is that person singular?* Is there one person there? Is there anything else beside that person? Is there a soul, a daimon, a genius? Are there other people there? As the newspapers would say, "Is there an inner child there?"

The second part of my question asks: Is it possible to put aside all that which you were doing at the beginning? I raise that question because I feel that all that other stuff in my mind, in my memory, in my habits, is also interwoven with this person. So putting aside is a question I want to ask you about.

The next concern is where we connect with the practice of Jungian therapy (as I understand it). Jungians are very different one from another, and I have sometimes less conviviality with some of my close colleagues than I might have with what you were saying. It's very difficult to say that the Jungians do this or that.

But your sentence, "It knows why it's scared," is absolutely a crucial idea. In Jungian therapy, I always say, "The figures in your dreams know why they are there. You don't know why they are there, and I, the therapist, don't know why they are there. But they come into your dreams and if you want to know why they are there, turn to them. Ask them; begin an imagination with them; begin a dialogue

with them. They know why they are bothering you. You and I don't. We can guess at it—which is an interpretation—but they *know*. They contain an innate sense of their value and their importance." This position is Jung's idea that there is consciousness in the unconscious. So there is a consciousness in the figures that appear.

I am using the word "figures"; Gene was using "sense," the feeling focused inwardly, a bodily sense. I may put my hands on my chest here for it, but it also could be here in my belly. It could also be in my head. But it knows what it is doing and what it wants.

This is another very important notion—*that it wants something*. Translated into Jungian therapy, we could say that the figures in your dreams and your fantasies, particularly those that pursue you, and the ones you don't in some strange way want, want *you* at least they want your attention. I mean, why do they bug you? They want something.

Another observation I'd like to make: Gene made three points about running from it, pushing into it, or staying close with it. It really isn't my place to attack all the other therapies that run from it, but there is an awful lot of that. I think Gene and I agree very much on that. There are all sorts of ways of getting away from the thing that's bugging you. There is also the kind of facing up, heroic encounter, pushing into it. Let's face it together, the therapist will help you do it as if there was a way you could be Hercules and conquer the monster because we can be just as heroic in dominating our unpleasant selves as we can be in dominating the external world.

Colonialism doesn't happen only in Africa. Colonialism happens within the psyche where we are dominating, pushing into and overruling the protests that come as symptoms, the rebellions that don't want to live under the ego's control.

But this third thing about staying close is important—because in another language, staying close means connected. It is also what you do when you love something, you stay close to it, or want to stay close to it. You want it to be around. Instead of talking about love, it's much nicer to talk about staying close, that you want it to stay close, and you want to stay close to it. That's enough, and that's a lot, because if you think of this "other" as the other in Yalom's sense of the existential other, then in German, it is a "Du," it's a "you," a partner, a companion, a friend, a lover, a helper, an angel, a guardian, a daimon, something else that you want to keep close to, something that you don't want to go away. I think that is probably a most important feeling. That is, it's scary; the other may be ugly; it is painful, but for some reason you don't want it to go away because you would feel a loss.

Many people have suffered symptoms—I hope all of us have. I am assuming all of us have symptoms that don't go away, symptoms that don't let you go, symptoms that you can't fix. A time comes when you realize, curiously enough, if it hadn't been for them, I wouldn't be where I am, that they have been doing something for me all this time. They have heightened my sensitivity, or they have been my teachers, or they have been my thermostat—when I get too hot, they click in and pull me down, or whatever. You begin to realize their value in your psychic structure.

So, the staying close is in part an appreciation. I'm trying to bring out the feeling quality of that staying close. I think the most beautiful thing of all psychological work is staying close to the other; that is, the other thing that you don't want. What was originally called the unconscious. Staying at the edge of the place where you are uncertain, at the edge of the place where you are threatened, out on the limb, at the edge. And it isn't pleasant.

But it also is pleasant! That's another part. I think we overemphasize the suffering in all

this. There is something pleasant about being in touch with something that you know is very important, even if it doesn't quite fit in with your pattern, or system, or belief system.

There is a language of quality that Gene mentioned. Language of quality. I was very happy to hear that because I feel that the differentiation of our language is part of making conscious these emotional turmoils, fears, panics, and so on; that it is very important to differentiate language. The philosopher Hegel said that there is not a single state of the soul or of the mind that language cannot express. Poets do it all the time. I think the contemporary poverty of language in psychology makes feelings even more amorphous. I think that it is extremely important to consciousness that we can talk about qualities like "flutteriness," and elaborate them, staying close with them and not elaborating the feelings away, but staying with whatever the quality is. Therapy should not forget the value in the human being of one's unique gift of language. We are the one species that has this kind of language, and that has the physiology, the anatomy for producing speech.

Directly above and connected with—you made this move many times. One of the ways of finding out what it wants is through letting it speak; but there are, I think, other ways of letting it speak, which is through movement. I did some work for about four or five years with a dance and movement therapist. We did workshops together on letting the body make its moves in order to uncover myths and archetypal patterns in movement. There are other ways that this inner body/emotion person can begin to do what it wants and show what it wants through moving.

I want to ask whether the movement into imagery belongs to the work for you as well. In Jungian therapy it is called "active imagination," where you would begin a conversation and enter into an imaginary dialogue with whatever it is on which you are focused.

In my own life, because I spend a lot of time at a table writing, I am unable to deal with focusing and writing at the same time. I can't. I have to go see the chiropractor, and the massage person, and the body worker, and the

Feldenkrais lady, and so on because I have pains in my leg, and pains in my back, or tightness. They want me to notice how I am sitting, what I am doing, when I am working. I can't do it. I cannot focus on the thought and the writing, and the noticing. When I am doing my work at my table, it is extremely difficult to know where my legs are. Or how my weight is distributed in my chair. So, Doctor, I would like to have some help with that.

Coping with Loss in Older Years:
A Personal and Professional Perspective

◆

Mary McClure Goulding, M.S.W.

Mary McClure Goulding, M.S.W.

Mary McClure Goulding is one of the leading exponents of Trans-actional Analysis. Along with her late husband, Robert Goulding, M.D., she developed an approach called Redecision Therapy, which synthe-sizes Transactional Analysis and Gestalt. Together they founded and directed the Western Institute for Group and Family Therapy in Wat-sonville, Calif. The Gouldings wrote two professional books about their approach, and there is an edited volume about the Redecision model. Mary Goulding also wrote two books about Bob, Sweet Love Remem-bered, *and* Time to Say Goodbye: Moving Beyond Loss.

Mary Goulding has served as a member of the Board of Trustees of the International Transactional Analysis Association and is a Teach-ing Member of that organization. She has taught Transactional Analy-sis and Redecision therapy throughout Europe, North America, and South America, and in Japan, New Zealand, and Australia. Her M.S.W. degree was granted in 1960 by the School of Social Welfare, University of California, Berkeley.

INTRODUCTION

In this chapter I will address loss in older years and how therapists can help older cli-ents cope with their losses. I decided to focus on old people, even though what I have to say applies to anyone suffering similar losses. By "old person" I mean someone who is eligible for Social Security or cheaper rides on the buses, although most of us old people prefer to define old as "ten years beyond my present age."

I want to assure you that old people can be interesting, exciting clients. Freed from the necessity to earn a living or raise a family, they can make changes in their lives that would not have been possible in earlier years. If you are willing to discard any prejudices you may have about the elderly, you will be amazed to dis-cover how quickly they take hold of new ideas and how eagerly they strive to enrich their lives. For many, this final stage of living may be the frosting on the cake.

TREATMENT GOALS

With older clients I see three general goals in therapy:

1. To create an active, positive, meaningful life in the present. This may necessitate finding new friends and new interests.

2. To accept help from others and at the same time preserve one's own independence and integrity.
3. To maintain the best possible life, even when the quality of life worsens due to illnesses and additional losses.

Before your older clients have the energy to focus successfully on these goals, they need to deal with the losses they have already suffered.

We old people may have lost our homes, income, jobs, health, mental abilities, and physical attractiveness, and we have lost through death an increasing number of people who were dear to us. Each person reacts idiosyncratically to losses. What may be an insurmountable loss to one person may be a minimal loss or even a gain to another.

ON RETIREMENT

Take for example, retirement: Some people love being retired. In my father's family, retirement was a treasure, eagerly awaited and used mostly joyfully. Finally they were freed from their dull jobs! My father had been a professor at the University of Illinois, others in the family had taught high school, clerked in a bank, worked as accountants, held positions in the state government . . . and finally they could at last do what they wanted to do. They were home free. Some found exciting new hobbies, such as buying and selling antiques, and others sat happily in the shade, visiting with their neighbors.

Because of my family's belief about retirement, I looked forward to it, and since I have stopped working I have been traveling and writing. I love being retired. I love waking up in the morning with the knowledge that I can enjoy the day in whatever manner I choose.

Other oldsters fight furiously to maintain their jobs. In San Francisco, there was a 100-year-old waiter who refused to retire. I believe that he died while still employed. There are lots of old therapists who plan never to stop working. In fact, lots of therapists go on seeing clients almost until the day they die.

Even if they had looked forward to retirement, some old people don't fit smoothly into this next stage of life. They become depressed, withdrawn, apathetic, or quarrelsome. They don't know what to do with their lives, because their creativity for so many years had been utilized only on the job. They define their self-worth by their previous occupations or professions. Also, some have an almost phobic belief that retirement equals incipient death. They need therapy to cope with the loss of the former job and job status, before they can say a healthy hello to a new world ahead.

LOSS OF LIFESTYLE

Another loss that may coincide with retirement is a reduction of income, and therefore the loss of a former lifestyle. Without trying to be a financial consultant, a therapist can help older clients focus on creative priorities, so that they can discover what is most important in their lives. Perhaps it is most important to live prudently with the happy knowledge that their money will make life easier for an offspring or that a favorite charity will receive their money. Perhaps instead a client will decide to take a fantastic trip around the world.

Old people develop serious health problems and disabilities that change and limit their lives. I recommend therapy when old people overestimate the degree of their incapacitation and restrict themselves unnecessarily, when they underestimate and so put themselves in danger, and when depression accompanies health loss. Clients with Parkinson's disease isolate themselves because they are ashamed of their tremors and rigidities, and they do need an understanding therapist. One old man refused to use an electric wheelchair even though he could barely walk and would never walk again, because he insisted he could relearn to walk. Others take to their beds when they could be encouraged to walk. Therapy will include time for mourning the loss of past health before the person can adjust to the new limits that the body imposes.

The United States is said to lead the world in one statistic: Americans who reach age 80 will live longer than their counterparts in Europe and Japan. A longer life is a virtue only if the extra months or years are worth having.

I would like to see comparative statistics that exclude everyone whose mind or body is dead and who nevertheless is kept alive artificially. I believe other nations may be more compassionate in allowing life to end.

Therapists, no matter what their personal beliefs, need to listen without prejudice when a terminally ill patient speaks of wanting to die. I realize that we are not supposed to support a decision to die. Well, beliefs do change. Just 30 years ago, we therapists could be fired from mental health clinics if we discussed contraception with an unmarried woman. Unmarried people were not supposed to have sex, especially if they were poor. At that time, in spite of the rules against it, I showed my clients a list of supposedly reputable abortionists in Mexico, and I was willing to give information about how to obtain contraceptives. Today, the same kind of prejudice exists against the client's right to choose to die. I hope that therapists understand, honor, and help old people who choose to live and also either are helpful to those who choose to die or refer them to therapists who will be helpful. The Hemlock Society has very good literature on the subject of how to die. I'm mentioning this in order to stress that the belief system of the therapist must not overrun the rights of the client to self-determination.

LOSS OF PHYSICAL BEAUTY

Another loss old people face is the loss of youthful physical beauty. Without first-class plastic surgery, and sometimes even with this surgery, we appear old, of course. In fact, I've noticed that a lot of us with sagging chins are looking more and more like iguanas.

I recommend to therapists that they listen understandingly to their clients who are pained by their loss of physical attractiveness. Don't prejudge what is and is not worth mourning about, and don't offer the bromide that society ought to honor the appearance of aging. For some people, this change in their looks is devastating.

In a workshop, a woman mentioned how startled and sad she was to discover that she was losing her pubic hair. Another woman then described the beauty of her firm breasts and her blonde, curly pubic hair when she was a young woman. She said, "Now my breasts are empty bags and I've only got a few scraggly pubic hairs left, and they are straight, not curly." The two women mourned together this perhaps trivial loss.

Your clients may be too ashamed to mention their reactions to such body changes. They tell themselves that they have no right to mourn such things, that they ought to be thankful they are alive, and so on. I think that the accumulation of minor losses can add up to self-depreciation and a very painful depression.

LOSS OF HOMES

Old people lose their homes and neighborhoods. They move or are moved to new apartments, condos, or nursing facilities, or into the homes of their children or other relatives. For some, leaving their own homes is a great loss. Others, like me, are pleased to find new, easier and more exciting places to live.

For those who are not reconciled to the loss of their homes, therapy can help greatly, especially group therapy. In an ideal world some form of group therapy would be available in every group living facility for the aged.

The client who is grieving the loss of a home needs ample time to express sadness and mourning. Then, when the client is ready, the therapist may ask the questions that apply to any person who clings to regrets about the past: (a) "Is there any chance you can get your home (or lover, or eyesight) back?" (b) "If so, what do you have to do to get it back?" (c) "Is it worth doing?" (d) "If you can't get it back or choose not to get it back, are you ready to say goodbye to it?"

A GESTALT APPROACH TO GRIEVING

Saying goodbye to the past frees a client to live more fully in the present. Clients may say goodbye to a job, a home, or a loved person, to whatever or whoever is permanently gone from their lives. I'll review briefly the gestalt format for saying goodbye, which my deceased husband, Bob, and I learned long ago from Fritz Perls. The client recreates in fantasy a real scene from the past, enters the scene, completes whatever had been left unfinished, and says goodbye.

I'll give an example. In a goodbye to a former home, a client may first imagine standing on the front walk, looking at the home, and then enter the home and walk through it, experiencing each room as it used to be, with its decorative scheme, atmosphere, and family history. The client reports thoughts and feelings, while the therapist listens, supports, and asks about anything that isn't expressed. Resentments are reported as well as appreciations and love. During this stage in the goodbye work, the therapist and client may work together on any problems or impasses that the client experiences. For example, a client felt guilty for having sold her property instead of "keeping it in the family." After some two-chair dialogue with various past and present family members, she imagined packaging her guilt in a huge burlap sack, dragging it down the back steps, and leaving it beside the trash cans. Sometimes I encourage a client to express what I call "catch-ups." One way to do this is to tell the home what has happened in the client's life since he or she left it. "After I sold you, I moved in with my daughter. Much as I have missed you, old house, I want you to know that it's been nice watching my granddaughter grow."

At the end of the work, the client walks out of the house and says a personal goodbye. "I've left you and I won't be back. I'll remember you from time to time, but you are no longer a part of my life. Goodbye, old house." The client may imagine walking away, or may watch the scene recede into the distance. This goodbye work can be done with any loss, once a client has mourned and is ready for a goodbye. I remember once helping an arthritic client play one last tennis match in fantasy before saying goodbye to his athletic self. Many return in fantasy to their place of employment in order to say a more meaningful goodbye than they had said in reality.

LOSS OF DREAMS

Another loss suffered by older clients might be described as the loss of ideals, dreams, and hopes for a better world. Arthur Miller expresses this beautifully in his autobiography, *Timebends*. He reflects on his subpoena to appear before the House Un-American Activities Committee: "There was no trace of the American left any more, and nothing in reality to be loyal or unfaithful to. Nothing, that is, except the most generous thoughts of one's youth, which, to be sure, had turned out to be badly mistaken in practical terms, but whose impulse had had some touch of nobility."

All of us like to believe that in our lifetime we helped to make the world better, and it is sad when one step forward seems to be followed by two steps back. For older therapists, for example, it can be traumatic to watch excellent therapy clinics and teaching institutes be dismantled or to see the advances of pharmaceutical knowledge used as an excuse for downgrading psychotherapy.

For those of us who, like Arthur Miller, were proudly and actively liberal or radical and believed we were achieving social reform, the current political scene is very painful. I find it heartbreaking to witness what is being done to the poor, to the children of the poor, and especially to today's African-American young men, who I believe are being crushed quite systematically through lack of opportunity plus very high prison sentences even for nonviolent, victimless crimes.

LOSS OF LOVED ONES

Last, there is the loss we endure with the death of someone we loved. Like members of the gay community, we older people suffer the loss of an ever-increasing number of friends. We attend too many funerals. We become the oldest living generation in our own families, as our parents, aunts, and uncles die. Our brothers and sisters die, and so do some of our children. We lose our spouses, our life companions. Today, I will focus on my own loss in the death of my husband, Bob Goulding, because I live this loss and know it firsthand.

I have found it is important to talk about my loss. As Shakespeare said, "Give sorrow words; the grief that does not speak, whispers the oe'r fraught heart and bids it break." Chekhov wrote, in his short story, "Heartache," about an old taxi driver who was mourning the death of his son. He tried to tell his passengers about this tragedy, and no one listened. The story ends with him telling his horse.

Some people try to suppress their grief. For example, the survivors of Hiroshima did not have cultural permission to express their feelings, to tell of their terrible grief and suffering. In addition to cultural restrictions against displays of emotion, a public blackout was imposed by our Army of Occupation. All art— all poems, novels, drawings, or paintings— about Hiroshima and Nagasaki were forbidden. People were not allowed publicly to mention their suffering. For years the Japanese remained stoically silent. Only recently have they begun to speak out.

The suppression of grieving is learned in childhood. My father explained why he did not weep when his wife, my mother, died by saying, "I didn't cry when I was 12 and my sister died. I didn't cry when I was 13 and my mother died. I'm too old to start crying now." Encouraging but not demanding the open expression of grief is a crucial task for therapists, American as well as Japanese.

I suppose I am ... or was ... a lot like my father. After Bob died, I talked compulsively about him, but I didn't express much grief openly. I read books about grieving, because for me books always have been my support. I cannot not read. However, I found the books on loss and death to be unacceptable to me, including those by Kubler-Ross and others famous in the field of death and dying. I am not a spiritual person. I agree with Simone de Beauvoir, who said, when Sartre died, "His death separates us. My death will not bring us together again. That is how things are."

Since ordinary books about loss weren't helpful, I switched to poetry. I searched for nonreligious and nonspiritual poems, which I read aloud to myself in my apartment. They touched my emotions and gave me permission to grieve intensely. I have made a small collection of this poetry for others who might be helped by it.

During the first year after Bob's death, I wrote and published a book about Bob, *Sweet Love Remembered*, and then wrote a book about my life since his death, *A Time to Say Goodbye*, which will be published in late 1996 by Papier-mache Press. Writing about Bob was an act of love. Writing about my own current experiences was a form of therapy for me. I recommend to others in distress that they keep a daily journal of their current life. It helps people focus on the here and now, and to notice what is going on around them. I'm going to mention briefly some of the issues that I believe are important during the time of mourning.

People who have lost a life partner often are forced to learn new skills. What do we do when a symbiosis is permanently broken? A grieving person who doesn't know how to cook may be infuriated if someone offers a cookbook. Such a person would rather chew crackers than take over the dead lover's role at home.

Bob had always been in charge of our finances. When he became unable to get from the study to his office, I learned to use the computer to keep our financial records. I enjoyed being in charge of my own money for the first time in my long life. Even though Bob had never questioned how I spent money, I felt more free and powerful as my computer and I balanced my accounts each month.

On the other hand, I gave away my automobile after my son phoned to remind me to get the oil changed. I had never been responsible for the upkeep of my car and I wasn't going to start, even though my son explained most patiently that all I had to do was find a garage or gas station somewhere in San Francisco and pay someone to do the job. But how many other jobs would there be from then on? Tires, motors, fan belts, windshield wipers, on and on for the rest of my life. I refused to be responsible.

After Bob's death, I experienced an odd change in myself. I felt more weak physically. Other widows have told me that they too have experienced increased physical weakness, often accompanied by lethargy. I couldn't explain this phenomenon. Perhaps it was a manifestation of the part of me that didn't want to continue living. To counteract this, I swam, took long walks while exploring San Francisco, and, recently, hired a physical trainer. I needed that push toward health as a commitment to myself that I wanted to live. In addition to exercise, I recommend massage for anyone who is grieving. As Eric Berne put it, "Without touch, the spinal cord shrivels."

Another problem. I still have what I call "difficulties with the calendar." I don't know when certain events in my life, including recent events, took place. The past seems to have merged into only two time frames, "before Bob died" and "after Bob died," and often I can't be more specific. I thought this was my own unique thinking disorder, until a friend told me that he still experiences a similar sense of events merging into before and after, even though it has been ten years since his wife died.

I seemed to be more forgetful and sometimes that left me feeling confused. I decided that I was in a not-very-early stage of Alzheimer's disease. I actually needed a personal therapist to remind me that I was writing books and lecturing, both of which require mental ability. I want to add: even if an older person, following a severe loss, seems mentally impaired, give the person time to begin to recover from the loss, before making a diagnosis of Alzheimer's.

In spite of the fact that I lived where I chose, traveled extensively, and handled my own money, my emotional life was chaotic. I veered back and forth between sadness, loneliness, depression, bursts of happiness and laughter, guilt, numbness, vulnerability, and despair. I was bereft. There was no pattern to my grieving, in spite of the patterns that the "how to" books suggest. I lost my heart when I lost Bob.

Bob and I taught the importance of personal autonomy. By this we meant that each person chooses his or her own emotions, beliefs, thoughts, and actions. Although I have felt, since his death, as if I have not been choosing my emotions, I do choose them. I respond emotionally to a song, a memory, a physical sensation, a day with family or friends, an evening alone. My emotions are my own responses to the stimuli I choose to perceive. I choose the stimuli and the responses, and I contaminate both by my constant awareness, my thoughts, of Bob's death.

Some therapists confuse autonomy with self-control. They believe that because people choose and are in charge of their thoughts, emotions, and behavior, people obviously should choose happiness unless there is a rational reason to choose otherwise. A person in mourning should progress from denial to acceptance with appropriate emotions in between. That's idiotic! I hope no therapist tries to get clients to adhere to such an impossible design. It only compounded my misery by telling or when I told myself how I should be reacting. Ultimately, I found it best to listen lovingly to myself and accept without self-criticism whatever was going on inside me. Calling myself names for feeling guilty or angry or sad or bereft didn't make me happy. Accepting what I felt also didn't make me happy, but it was an easier way to exist.

A therapist can offer a real gift to clients by believing that all emotions are natural and acceptable, and that there is no time limit for grief.

Like most grieving widows and widowers, I had a problem with guilt. I am somewhat embarrassed to admit this, as I have told hundreds of clients that guilt is non-productive and irrational. I felt guilty for not having done or said this or that, even though I knew this reaction was bizarre. I was guilty when I was happy. While I was in Costa Rica shortly after Bob died, I took a trip to the jungle. I was enchanted to see and hear a tribe of howler monkeys jumping and playing in a tall tree. They are scrawny little things that sound as loud as lions. In the midst of my excitement, I suddenly felt overpowered by guilt. Later that morning, when I saw a line of tiny, bright red frogs, I was very careful not to enjoy them too much, in spite of the fact that this was a very rare treat that few people get to see even in that jungle.

Another common source of guilt: After the death of a lover, some people feel increased sexual desire. Bereaved clients may need help in accepting that their sexual arousal is healthy and life-affirming. Some clients find a new sexual and/or loving relationship, and may need your help when their sexual behavior clashes with their own internal belief systems.

A problem that distressed me greatly was what I label "psychological vulnerability." In a real sense, Bob had been my back-up, my ballast, and at times I felt powerless without him.

For example, the therapists in our training program were aware that I am an atheist and Bob was a Christian, and we respected each other's positions. Shortly after Bob died, one of these therapists, a physician, invited me to lunch. We were barely seated at a restaurant when he began attempting to convert me to Christianity. Before Bob's death, I would have told him to bug off. I would have had no problem with this. Instead, as this man quoted the Bible and went on about Bob being in Heaven waiting for me, I felt totally helpless. I kept thinking, "If Bob were alive, this man wouldn't dare do this," but I didn't defend myself. Afterwards, I felt emotionally raped and frighteningly vulnerable to anyone who wanted to prey on me. I truly felt like a helpless old lady.

Another time, my hand luggage was stolen from a hotel. As I reported this to the hotel and then to the police, I was sobbing so hard I could barely speak, not because I'd lost anything of value, which I hadn't, but because Bob wasn't alive to take care of me. I don't remember ever before crying in public. While Bob was alive, I traveled all over the world alone, survived an earthquake and major surgery, and I was never helpless. This vulnerability was quite foreign to my personality.

I now understand with much more sympathy the vulnerability of many clients. How terrible it must be to go through a lifetime feeling vulnerable to others. I believe that this sense of vulnerability may be common to old people who have lost too much too quickly.

I hope all of you will treat your vulnerable clients kindly. Be very careful not to push your beliefs, whatever they may be, onto vulnerable people. Instead, with kindness, tact, and gentleness, you can help them be less vulnerable, as you recognize with them their own true strengths. And then you can explore with them the causes of their vulnerability.

I want to conclude by mentioning loneliness. I have felt lonely even in a room filled with friends. Loneliness is an enemy closely tied to depression. It can make clients appear diffident, over-needy, or over-demanding. In therapy loneliness accentuates clients' vulnerability as well as the dependency cravings that a therapist cannot and should not meet. Therapists cannot fill the void that creates loneliness, and they may need to acknowledge this explicitly both to themselves and to their lonely clients. Again, I want to emphasize that all clients are unique. A good therapist learns from each client. The client must be your teacher, as you work together. Therapists have two important tasks: to be caring and to listen well.

Although there are remedies for being alone, I am not sure what remedies to suggest for loneliness after the death of a life companion. Time, with the help of responsive and responsible therapy, is healing.

CONCLUSION

In closing, here are a few lines from a poem written by William Kir-Stimon, Ph.D., who was a poet, a clinical psychologist, and the editor of *Voices* magazine, when he died this year at age 82. He was a much loved and beautiful human being. I read Bill's lines for Bob and for Bill.

Memories do not die a sudden death
nor are they born de novo all at once
but rise and fall a rolling wave of feeling muted
    by time
long long shall I remember you.

Discussion by Joseph Wolpe, M.D.

◆

I found this a most moving paper—truly a beautiful paper, sensitively put together, covering loss as a general concept of which bereavement is an instance—and admirably well-expressed. The paper has two focuses: One is the diminution of strength and power a person suffers in aging, and the other is the effects of specific losses experienced in life both generally and in aging. As time goes on, everybody has to give up on certain things. In my youth and for many years later, I had the fantasy of being a champion runner. When I was young, although I was quite a bit above average, I did not make it to the top; yet I never quite abandoned the idea that one day I would somehow flower into a fine athlete. Sadly, eventually I had to relinquish that fantasy.

Mary dwelt mainly on bereavement—most particularly on the loss of a beloved spouse. The enormity of this experience is impossible to comprehend fully unless one has actually gone through it. Having lost a beloved wife to lymphoma five years ago, after many ups and downs, I am very empathic with Mary in her loss. In addition to the immediate emotionally traumatic consequences of loss, there are long-term feelings of deprivation and sadness.

Mary stated that those who have had a bereavement feel as though they have been through a wringer. I would like to mention some sufferings that I had after emerging from the wringer that I have not heard mentioned elsewhere. I found that I had developed a form of lasting psychophysiological distress, of which the most striking manifestation was a feeling to which I applied the label "unpeace." It was not a depression or an agitation; but a feeling of having lost the normal tranquillity that is a background to ordinary daily functioning. I did not want to go traveling, and felt no desire to attend concerts, plays, or movies, although when I did go I enjoyed them.

The other affliction that arose in me at that time was a hyperacusis, a marked oversensitivity to sounds that were sharp, grating, or disharmonious. For example, if I went into a restaurant, I could not bear the clatter of cutlery against plates. Equally unpleasant were noises and voices at a movie house, if the loudness was even slightly more than average. My discomfort at a movie house was such that I would block my right ear, whose hearing is normal, and receive only the weak input from my left ear, whose acuity is only 25 percent.

After a time, I discovered that these unpleasant reactions were diminished by exposure to pleasurable emotional experiences. About six months after my bereavement, I met a woman who was a very engaging person, even though she was not really suited to me. I formed a relationship with her, which almost immediately began to ameliorate both the unpeace and the hyperacusis. The feeling of unpeace faded away almost completely in about two months; the hyperacusis was more obstinate and took about six months to disappear. I must assume that other people have had similar experiences, although I have not heard tell of them. I wonder what neurological processes are responsible for effects like these.

It is likely that bereavement also sometimes has positive consequences. One that I observed after my wife died was that I became much more emotionally sensitive to slow music, especially many of Mozart's adagios and andantes. An extremely poignant responsiveness continued for several months. When it subsided, I noticed that I had developed a deepened emotional responsiveness to practically all music, even to certain forms of jazz that had previously been peripheral in my life. This new sensitivity has now persisted for several years. One might think of it as a kind of compensation for a terrible loss.

The Therapeutic Power of Attention: Theory and Techniques

Erving Polster, Ph.D.

Erving Polster, Ph.D.

Erving Polster (Ph.D., Western Reserve University, 1950) is co-director of the Gestalt Training Center, San Diego, and is also Clinical Professor at the University of California, San Diego. Dr. Polster is the coauthor, with his wife, Miriam, of the landmark text, Gestalt Therapy Integrated. *He has published two books on his approach,* Every Person's Life is Worth a Novel, *and* A Population of Selves.

INTRODUCTION

Over the years, we therapists have played and replayed theoretical themes. Every time they come out significantly different, with some of the hidden implications of the original themes becoming more apparent. Starting with Freud's early use of hypnosis, the concept of *attention* has been an impelling factor in therapeutic procedure, but it has only rarely been given the acknowledgement it deserves. I want to take a look at this concept again and offer a special slant on it that may help to illuminate attention as an important source of therapeutic impactfulness. After providing some historical background, I will propose three therapeutic vehicles—tight therapeutic sequences, unfolding storyline, and the summoning of self—that can arouse and redirect our patients' attention.

ATTENTION: A PERSONAL EVOLUTION

As background, shifts in attention are crucial for therapists, trying to ready their minds for the complex needs of their patients. In my early years, I was psychoanalytically inclined; my main guides were the concepts of the unconscious, psychosexual stages, the ego, id, and superego triad, insight, transference, free association, and so on. These directed my attention and lit the way every time I sat down to a session. While I thought these principles were largely validated by what actually happened in my sessions, after some years I felt I was missing something. The old principles were almost unrecognizable in the new ones I found. The new language and the expansion of ideas turned my mind around on a number of issues, but earlier concepts bled into the new, blending their colors together.

When I came across gestalt therapy I became more engrossed with the immediacy of experience, raising the sharpness of my focus as well as directly addressing the face value of my patients' words and actions. Instead of orienting primarily to transference, once removed from immediacy, gestalt therapy directed me to the concept of contact, sponsoring a more manifest engagement with my patients and turning up the attention rheostat. Then, instead of prioritizing insight, the concept of awareness helped me to focus more pointedly on the raw materials of the patient's experience; the phenomenology of sorrows, confusions, beatings of the heart, and hungers, which all called for the patient's pointed attention. Further, expanding beyond the techniques of free association and interpretation, the gestalt concept of experiment guided me to create action options. Still further, gestalt therapy helped me to refresh my understanding of personality splits. At first, this new understanding was reserved for the limited split represented by the concept of top dog and underdog. I expanded this recognition of polarities within each person to the recognition of a multilateral composition of many competing aspects of the person (Polster & Polster, 1974). Now, more than ever aware of this multifaceted struggle, I have turned to the recognition of a population of *selves* within, anthropomorphizing and dramatizing the alienations and coordinations among diverse *clusters* of the person's experience (Polster, 1995). More on that later.

A PERSPECTIVE ON FREUD

Gestalt concepts seemed very new to me in the 1950s, but over the years I have become more and more aware that gestalt therapy's concern with immediacy and focus was an extension of Freud's unprecedented sharp attention to details of the life experience of his patients. His transformation of therapeutic focus from the common style of doctor's interviews into psychoanalytic incisiveness constituted the beginnings of a *focus revolution*. As we all know, Freud started his psychoanalytic work by using hypnosis—funneling the patient's focus in order to redirect attention from current suffering back to early events that the patient had disconnected from this suffering. For Freud, the unconscious was the unattended container of experiences, and he hoped for reconnection with it. He wanted to shift a chronic, fixed attention—obsessions and phobias, for example—believing that reconnection with unconscious experiences would establish greater fluidity and broader dimension to the person's current attention options.

But hypnosis didn't satisfy him, even though it restored attention to the early events, because, he believed, it bypassed the patient's *resistance*, crucial to genuine growth. I think he put the blame in the wrong place; not only was the resistance bypassed but, more importantly, Freud's classic way of *inducing* hypnosis caused too drastic a shift in attention away from the patient's ordinary experience. Patients suffered what I would call a "configurational failure" because they could not make the connection between the recovered early experience and their currently real and complex life. That is, the *hypnotic* memories were as dissociated from patients' *everyday* life as they ever were when hidden away in the unconscious. Though the new attention Freud had induced through hypnosis was narrowly focused on the patient's immediate inner experience, which was in itself a momentous innovation, it lacked the *versatility* of attention required in addressing the diverse considerations in anyone's life.

Current hypnosis theory, especially as it comes from Ericksonian circles, contributes mightily to the union between such narrow focus and the ordinary versatility of everyday life. The induction does not require such extreme disconnection as does more classic forms of hypnosis; it may often be indistinguishable from ordinary interpersonal engagement. But Freud was not ready for this. Instead, he went on to free association, a new *induction* of personal absorption, less disconnected from ordinary engagement than his classic form of hypnosis but nevertheless quite disconnected. Still, Freud remained on the trail of a vital factor in therapy—simplified attention. Through free association, he simplified attention by releasing his patients from *interference* from previous values and standards of expression. The patient was still disconnected from everyday life but not so much as under Freud's hypnotism. Through free association he offered patients expressive innocence, unchaining them for a freedom that swept patients into profound concentration and deep inward attention. This level of attention was novel in its day, and prophetically antecedent to current high focus systems such as gestalt therapy, hypnosis, meditation, biofeedback, visualization techniques, and so on. It is difficult for most people to recognize the excitement and sense of emergency that free association can produce in the dedicated person. One is in danger during free association of fracturing one's formed sense of self. This emergency adds to the vibrant attention, quasi-dissociative in its disconnection from familiar morals and grammar.

A corollary reinforcement to this vehicle for concentration was Freud's formulation of the transference phenomenon, which came a step closer still to ordinary engagement than free association and gave great technical primacy to the therapeutic relationship. Because transference was regarded as a microcosmic representation, expressions to the analyst achieved powerful *registration*, creating new *intimacy*, both symbolic and experiential.

So entranced was Freud, however, with the *material* that emerged from free association and transference that, ironically, he did not notice the *trance* he had created in his patients; the new rhythm he had composed between pointed attention and the more versatile attention of everyday life. Then, as the search for understanding dominated the free association and transference processes, the power to induce deeply concentrated attention deteriorated. Instead, too often, therapy became a mind-wandering exercise.

ATTENTION IN GESTALT PRACTICE

A key counterforce came from Frederick Perls. In his 1947 book, *Ego, Hunger and Aggression*, he recognized this deficiency of free association and emphasized the importance of *concentration* as counterforce to avoidance (Perls, 1947, p. 8). Concentration is a form of tuning in sharply to a given stimulus, and with Perls' recognition of its role in therapy, it took its place alongside hypnosis, free association, and transference in enhancing the attention factor. He found concentration to be a lubricant to new experience, as its pointedness reduced the inhibitory intrusions of the ordinary context of a person's life. Here is an example of the simple effects of concentration. In this case, the person had been asked to concentrate on his internal experience and this is part of what he observed: "I was feeling around my insides when I finally got around to the region of my rectum, and there I noticed what seemed to me a silly tension because when I examined myself I found that I did not feel like defecating, but there I sat with the sphincters just about as tense as if I did" (Perls, Hefferline, & Goodman, 1951, p. 91).

This person simply had not noticed what had been there all along, unattended. The attention shift was disarmingly simple, one small palpable representation of an otherwise mystical and elusive unconscious. Because of the greater complexity of most unconscious–conscious interrelationships, it is easy to forget that transforming unconscious phenomena into consciousness is actually achieved by shifting attention. For example, the smiling person who discovers a vein of anger inside has chronically ignored the anger until able or willing to give it the focal attention that would make it a tangible experience. When a wife in couple's therapy complains to her husband but expects a rejection of the complaint, she may not hear him say that she's right. A patient who is a lovable, bright, energetic eccentric gives unremitting attention to himself as a bumbling freak. Nothing I say or lead him into has so far redirected his attention, which remains stuck on the self-image which was embedded in his mind long ago.

DIRECTING ATTENTION

Because examples of the key role of attention are familiar to all therapists, we continually search for new ways to direct the attention of our patients. But we are not alone, and perhaps we can broaden our options if we cull what we need from our fellow explorers. People of religion, politics, advertising, martial arts, and many others are all looking to harness the powers of attention.

From among these, our closest cousins in influencing behavior and feeling are the world's religions, which have directed attention in pointed ways including prayer, meditation, music, and finely honed belief systems. Chanting, rocking the body, and spiritual singing have guided their people into full blown absorption. They have welcomed extravagant phenomena into their process, ranging from miracles and immortality to the induction of devotional, even ecstatic, experience, through practices such as divine healing, laying on of hands, speaking in tongues, and fostering visions. Cult groups sharpen attention by narrowing the complexities of life through minute rules and strictly guided living. Psychological growth and development groups also engage in extravagant sharpening of attention. They have "turned on" their communities through advanced mind control procedures, creating great inspiration and often producing so-called altered states. Perhaps psychotherapists will some day find their own way to such communal escalations of attention.

CONDENSED ATTENTION

But for now, florid, exotic, and phantasmagoric devices used to achieve this concentration are not usually acceptable in therapeutic practice. What is more familiar in the therapeutic setting is a *condensed* attention to all experience, which has an accompanying clarifying and unifying effect. I remember my own astonishment when in my first experience of therapy, this man, my psychoanalyst, actually listened attentively to me for session after session. It seems only logical that he would listen but it was a new experience for me and I was deeply moved by it. The way I knew that he was listening with his full attention was that everything he said was exactly tuned into what I was saying. This resonance itself enhanced my attention.

But, on the whole, though often unwittingly utilizing techniques for enhanced attention, we therapists have been very wary of the sharp induction process, as represented in a number of mind-altering vehicles, of which religion and hypnosis are two examples. Understandably so, because such constriction of the boundaries of attention often narrows people, sometimes for better, often for worse, and may, in the wrong hands, make their individuality and ordinary societal interests inaccessible to them. Whether psychotherapists have been right or wrong to shun these attention sharpeners, it is plain to me that we are in the game already, and that we could extend our influence if we learn to apply the mind-opening powers of enhanced attention in ways that are more compatible with our therapeutic purposes.

FACTORS TO ENHANCE ATTENTION

How then, specifically, may attention be directed and enhanced in therapy, where many of the patients are not geared for the highs that are provided by unfamiliarly dramatic procedures? Can there be a coordination between the casual attention of face-to-face relationships and highly focused attention, providing the benefits of escalated attention while minimizing the risks or requirements that are usually appropriate just for the monks among us? How can we close the gap between a searing attention—fracturing fixed positions or melting them—and a diffuse attention, neutralized by vapid responsiveness and stereotyped positions? We have come to realize that when the therapeutic mission is too abstractly and loosely conceived, it provides poor ground for the full-blooded attention so much more manifest in such phenomena as the trance experience, the religious experience, the brain washing experience, or the meditation experience. Is there a middle ground where we may incorporate the lessons from high-focus systems and produce increased attention in the ordinary therapeutic situation? With these questions in mind, I would like to address three factors that would serve to enhance attention within the parameters of ordinary therapeutic interaction. They are: (1) tight therapeutic sequences, (2) the unfolding storyline, and (3) the summoning of self.

1. TIGHT THERAPEUTIC SEQUENCES

Tight therapeutic sequences (Polster, 1987, 1995) are those experiences—they may be statements or actions or feelings—where the implied consequences are immediately experienced. The creation of tight sequences calls for the restoration of the person's sequential imperative, which moves experience fluidly from one moment to its naturally next moment. I propose that if it is resonantly advanced, this movement builds a momentum that frees people to spontaneously do whatever comes to be naturally next. The result is a heightened absorption—not unlike trance—that helps bypass the distractions created by a lifetime of competing experience.

The key is to tune in resonantly to this natural momentum. Any statement will point ahead, containing a number of intimations (what I call "arrows"), which may point toward what is ahead. For example, while talking about her family playing music together, a patient also may offer snide observations about them. Whether the therapist follows the arrow provided by the snide observations or the family playing music is a choice to be made, and this choice will influence the course of therapy. So will the next choice, and so on. As these next-nesses, sensitively tapped, are successsively navigated by the patient, she is drawn by the momentum of this fluid continuity into a feeling that says "of course" to succeeding experiences. It is as though someone were to say the numbers 9, 8, 7, 6, out loud, then pause. The listener will merely follow the track and say "5." This openness to continuity, with its accompanying absorption, sponsors a confidence in one's direction, much as do hypnosis and meditation.

This should not be surprising. We therapists have always understood *trust* to be an enabling phenomenon. In generating the spontaneous process represented in the of-course mode, we therapists hope to open the person to new experience much as he was introjectively open to it in his formative years. This time around, the hope is that there will be a happier consequence than that created by the original poisonous introjections that bring him to therapy.

CASE EXAMPLE

Here is one example of such tightening of sequences, as it was manifested in a demonstration session with a person at a psychotherapy conference. A young, energetic African-American graduate student in psychology, let's call her Denise, started the session with a lively but abstract account of her frustration, anger, and depression about her development as a professional. Before I could follow the arrow represented in her concern with her professional development, she hurried forward into telling me that she felt guilty about benefitting from the exploitation of people around the world. It was soon plain that she would go on talking at length in a heated but abstract style, expecting nothing consequential to evolve from her valuable feelings.

In trying to honor the neglected consequentiality of her remarks, different therapists would vary on the directions implied. One would guide her to flesh out her guilt, another to explore her professional development, yet another to follow her enthusiasm, still another to tap her courage. For me, what stood out was her grand energy, joined contradictorily with helplessness. In her helter-skelter eagerness she had little sense of the discrepancy between her zest and her helplessness and the resulting stuckness. Therefore, my choice for tightening the sequences was to observe wryly that she had taken on a huge job and to liken it to the work of an aerial acrobat, suggesting that perhaps we could do a few of those flips here on the ground first. She gave a hint of surprise that I took her ambitions with a grain of salt and and that I wanted to help her tame them. Still, she went on almost as though I hadn't said anything, impelled forward by her great cause but still overshadowed by her feelings of helplessness. So, then, with helplessness as my new directional inference, to move this theme forward I asked what aspect of her helplessness we could focus on. She told me how helpless she felt about Mozambique and the fact that the South African army was killing and torturing people. But she still gave me only a misty sense of the problem she wanted to solve. She seemed to be caged in the rageful impotence of it all, wanting to make speeches rather than showing any concern with the actual satisfaction of her needs. Her empathy for the people of Mozambique, obvious to me, was overshadowed by her rage, and I thought her empathy might serve as a deepening element and might make her rage less mechanical. Therefore, I observed how important I thought her empathy to be and this softened her somewhat. She expressed a measure of empathy by saying that she was bothered about the inappropriateness of her anger against people who were inattentive to the world's problems. This made her aware of how impactful she would like to be with these people and took her out of soliloquy, raising her chances for satisfaction. By this time she was getting the feel of continuity from one statement to the next and she said, "Let's say if I am at a particular conference, angry at the profession for not including issues of diversity . . . I want to make everybody else incorporate those issues so that I can learn and know that we as a profession are doing something."

The audience applauded resoundingly. But she was about to go on as though nothing had happened, to make a new impotence-raising speech, eloquent but stuck, like running on a treadmill. When I interrupted by asking her whether she heard the applause, she said, begrudgingly, as though I was interfering with the more important content of the budding speech, "Yeah, I heard a couple of people." Then she began to wonder about *their* neglect of diversity. Wondering led to a proposal of dialogue, empty chair style, between her and the imagined audience. After a further sequence of one thing followed by its consequential next, she wound up in an of-course mode, actually happily passing a pad around to get signatures for advancing the cause of diversity in all future conferences, an action with which she now felt altogether at home.

In what sense does this session compare to mantra meditation and classical hypnosis? It is, after all, a quite familiar clinical interaction, recognizable to every therapist, moving step by step, tracking, with a clear purpose to move from problem to solution. There is also a familiar complexity of ideas and perceptions: Mozambique, helplessness, ambitiousness, diversity, intercommunication, divergence from the therapist's sense of good direction. Yet, in this ordinary interaction, quite distinguishable from classic hypnotic or meditative experiences, there is embedded, nevertheless, an almost unnoticeable element I have been describing, an induction of a sense of natural nextness and a transformation from abstraction and helplessness into a strong focus on actual experience. Though this induction would not be so enabling that a person could lift a car off the ground or have a transcendent experience of unity with the universe, we nevertheless see that through the induction of tightened sequences, there was an increase in palpable and functional engagement and a pointed movement into freely doing what originally would have seemed either impossible or prohibitively forced.

2. THE UNFOLDING STORYLINE

The second vehicle for attention enhancement is the emergence of the patient's storyline (Polster, 1987). By storyline I mean two interrelated things. One is the evocation of particular stories and their role in organizing and animating particular events. Second is that the concept of storyline also includes the succession of such stories that mark the path of a person in his or her lifetime. These stories develop certain thematic qualities, which register the unfolding of a person's life. Both aspects of storyline are key elements in people's fascination with their own lives and the lives of others.

Once the fluidity of experience is released by the tightening of sequences, new stories, spurred by the momentum created, usually will appear. Stories exercise a major hold on the psyche of all people. They enhance attention because they flesh out and organize life's events. They spotlight experience and serve as markers of the person's existence. They open one to the past and stimulate the view into the future with their "and then . . . and then . . . and then" suspense. They animate events and the players within the story. They open people to new empathy with their lives.

Denise, for example, had dimmed her storyline by speaking abstractly and repetitiously about the problems of women and blacks in our society, bypassing events that are the crux of her storyline. In this short session, she came to deal with actual and imagined people, with the live tension of real purpose and its struggles, and the climax created by the actual clash of forces within her world and within herself. The realization of the relationship between her and her audience of potential collaborators helped to animate her ideas and to join her with other people. The players, activities, and conflicts are the elements of storyline that must be restored to help amplify attention.

The therapy office is a hothouse for the remembrance of storyline. One patient, an 18-year-old college student, told me in passing that she was going to traffic school after her session. Always fishing for stories, even though she was about to go on to other matters, I asked her what had happened. She had gotten a traffic ticket when driving a group of friends to a fast food restaurant in the middle of the night. What came out in this otherwise tangential story was the key fact that although she had been plagued by a drinking problem, she was the only one in the car who was not drunk. She would have slid right past this achievement without marking it. Then she went further, inspired by the excitement she now felt, to tell about an earlier traumatic experience, giving it a high sense of reality with a new feeling of acceptance of the person she actually is.

It must be recognized that neither the telling nor the creating of stories assures their attention-enhancing effect, because patients often are inured to their own stories. They have either told them over and over without personal effect, or they leave out key details that would help to spin their minds around, thus squandering their fertility as the stories become limp fragments of a lifetime. The events need the energy that the therapist's technique contributes in order to transform the story from an obsessive commentary on a stuck or painful existence into the palpable experience of a life lived.

3. THE SUMMONING OF SELF

The third source of enhanced attention is the concept of the self and the particular application of it that I have proposed in my recent book, *A Population of Selves* (Polster, 1995), the crux of which I will briefly outline here. This conceptualization does not limit a view of selves to misty classes of a unitary self, such as real self, true self, false self, actual self, or other predesignated classes of self, such as grandiose self, nuclear self, or narcissistic self. Rather, I have accented how selves are individually tailored and how they animate the range of each person's life experiences. What I accentuate is that the self is a *personification* of characteristics and experiences, which are organized into person-like entities. Each self has a name and a role to play within a person's total function. Thus, a person who characteristically comments on everything that happens among his family and friends may be said to "house" a commentator self. To point out that he seems very often to comment on other people's behavior may be a perfectly valid observation for the therapist to make, often sufficient unto itself. But to add life to this observation, the therapist may refer, instead, to his commentator self. When rightly selected, this attribution of self to a cluster of experiences often will give it a brighter reality, and one with which the patient may more strongly empathize.

Is this transformation from experiences or characteristics to self no more than linguistic cosmetics, dressing up an interpretation so as to force added attention where the person might otherwise slide by? I think it is more than cosmetic because of its congruence with two human reflexes: configuration and anthropomorphism.

THE CONFIGURATION REFLEX

First is the configurational reflex, which is a gestalt fundamental. The configurational reflex creates an organized pattern of related experiences. Without this integrative force, usually exercised without awareness, nothing in life would make sense. The naming of self serves to highlight and simplify this complex configurational process, which is always taxed by the prodigious range of anyone's experiences. This generic and often overburdened function is perhaps the reason that people are so compelled to find out who they are and to try to achieve dependable personal identity. How can they put everything they do and feel together so that this infinity of experience may be composed into a good fit? They go to great lengths to discover and then to defend the selves they are, at times carving out the strangest affiliations and the most destructive fights to accomplish this—especially at a time in history where the flux and complexity of experience have risen, and where a summary of one's nature is all the more urgent. Failures in the immensely challenging exercise of the configurational reflex result in the isolation of experiences at all levels, creating the dissociation of certain personal characteristics when they cannot be fit into the total of what people already experience as themselves. A child, believing that he is generous, for example, may not know how to fit his stinginess into the picture, and he may dissociate either his generosity or his stinginess. This struggle creates a large stake for many people, and addressing self-designation will usually draw highly focused attention.

A case example is a patient whose immigrant father spurred her relentlessly to be a person of accomplishment. He loved her deeply, but instead of expressing it he blamed her for every imperfection he could find, as though focusing on her imperfections would inspire her to perfection. She seethed and hissed but went with his game by succeeding

in everything she did. But she became rigidly vigilant about any blame, and would go into rages with her lover when there was any implication of his pressuring her or not accepting her. She also had many other selves, beautiful ones, but when faced with flaws she disconnected from them; her vigilant and angry selves took over. To revisit this internal struggle increased her attention level, with the consequent drama produced by differentiation, conflict, and coordination.

THE ANTHROPOMORPHIC REFLEX

In addition to satisfying the configurational reflex, the naming of selves also satisfies the anthropomorphic reflex, transforming characteristics into person-like entities. We do this all the time, as naturally as we breathe. Among our well-known precedents, love, war, and beauty became manifest in the human-like gods Cupid, Mars, and Venus. Closer to home, an office machine not doing what we want it to do may be seen as stubborn. Similar animation is created by composing selves out of recognized configurations of a person's experience. This anthropomorphic designation often creates a greater understanding and empathy within the person for his own clusters of experiences and characteristics. We accentuate the commentator quality of a person, or her vigilance or generosity or gullibility, by translating these directly describable *characteristics* into the more tangibly accentuated language of *internal characters*. The conflicts, changes, and purposes of these internal characters give a heightened level of realization to what her nonpersonified characteristics might only have registered less brightly.

The criteria for the satisfactory inference of selves are similar to the requirements of good fiction. The images must be faithful to the raw materials one is animating. That is, the attribution of selves must indeed represent the patient. As with all human translations, congruence is vital. One may either enhance a person's sense of self by accurately naming the selves, or violate the sense of self with wrongful understanding and summation. When it is done well, the realization of these selves will saturate the patient with personal identity, creating an absorption that is similar to a reader's relationship to fictional characters with whom she identifies. This empathy is a strong warming factor, loosening the old images, and it increases the acceptability of a changing sense of self.

CONCLUSION

In conclusion, the three factors I have proposed for enhancing attention—tight therapeutic sequences, unfolding storyline, and summoning of self—address a generalized need for people to reexperience qualities of their lives that they would otherwise squander through the reduced or diverted attention that neurosis creates. Furthermore, such amplification

and redirection of attention may be induced through specific techniques. The techniques described can create heightened focus during ordinary therapeutic engagement, not as pointedly as in the classic versions of hypnosis and meditation, but with enough impact to create comparable absorption in the ordinary world of diverse stimulations.

REFERENCES

Perls, F. (1947). *Ego, hunger and aggression.* London: George Allen and Unwin.

Perls, F., Hefferline, R., & Goodman, P. (1951). *Gestalt therapy.* New York: Julian Press.

Polster, E. (1987). *Every person's life is worth a novel.* New York: Norton.

Polster, E. (1995). *A population of selves.* San Francisco: Jossey-Bass.

Polster, E., & Polster, M. (1974). *Gestalt therapy integrated.* New York: Vintage.

Discussion by Ernest L. Rossi, Ph.D.

I feel almost overwhelmed by the embarrassment of riches in Dr. Polster's presentation.

The most urgent question in my mind is what Dr. Polster can tell us about how he optimizes *his* attention. He's given us some wonderful clinical case histories that can guide us in our work with our clients, but who helps us to guide our own development? I'd like to pose this question to Dr. Polster: Any hints you can give us on how you continually optimize your own attention and creativity?

I would like to briefly comment on and amplify the main theme that Dr. Polster presents to us. An enlightening feature of his presentation was that we could rewrite the entire history of psychotherapy from Mesmer to Freud as a history of different methods of facilitating attention. Like Dr. Polster, I've been fascinated with exploring the history of the transition between the early mesmerists and

the hypnotists who tried to focus attention with fascination. One of the earliest books on hypnosis by James Braid, written about 150 years ago, was *Fascination*—an early name for what we now call hypnosis. There was an interesting transition when Freud gave up hypnosis and invented what he called "free association." Many therapists became dissatisfied with that method because free association often falls into mind-wandering and getting lost. I know personally: For at least four years, when I was in my early twenties, I was on the psychoanalytic couch four days a week. I would go on and on, day after day after day, getting lost.

One of the first people to recognize this problem was Carl Jung. Jung felt that free association often led us astray. Jung invented what he called "active imagination;" that is, taking an image that's fascinating, what Jung called "numinous," and having a private dialogue with it. Jung taught that from such an inner dialogue new dimensions of one's consciousness could emerge.

Fritz Perls then came along and made public what for Jung was a very private activity. With Jung, you didn't do "active imagination" in the therapy session—it was something private that you did at home alone. It had a kind of spiritual as well as deeply moral connotation. Fritz Perls brought this process out into the public arena. When I worked with Perls as a young postdoctoral fellow, I sat in a "hot seat" in a circle of colleagues. Having had some of these personal experiences, I can attest to the profound heightening of attention that took place. You had to be really involved with a problem—pretty deeply involved with a desperate inner struggle—to be willing to sit on a hot seat in front of all your colleagues.

We used to sweat! We used to cry! And shout! We always experienced profound states of emotional arousal on the hot seat. There's an activation–arousal aspect to the inner creative work of both Jung and Perls. This is something that I missed in Dr. Polster's paper. Does Dr. Polster feel that this heightening of attention and fascination in classical hypnosis and psychoanalysis also has a *psychobiological* component?

When I began my work with Erickson, I struggled to understand the basic mechanism of healing, and we settled on the idea of indirect suggestion. What is the essence of indirect suggestion? Well, for Erickson it wasn't what the therapist said. It wasn't the therapist's words that were the healing factor. It wasn't a matter of suggestion or programming. Rather, it was what Erickson called the "implication" of the therapist's words: What did the patient do with the therapist's words inside the patient's own head? In other words, how did the therapist's words trip off the creatively important associations, the emotional arousal, and the focusing of the patient's attention? This activity of focusing inner attention on the problem is the main dynamic of all forms of indirect suggestion: *Creative implication* that leads to problem solving is the essence of the inner hypnotherapeutic work

that the patient does with the help of the therapist's words.

It's not suggestion that heals. It's not even so much the focusing of attention, although the focusing of attention brings us to the source of the problem and the inner work that needs to be done. Attention is like a main line, like an energy circuit, pouring energy into the machine of associations. Every psychotherapeutic school seems to have its own method to facilitate the inner work of psychobiological arousal transformation that the patient needs to undergo.

In my view, it's not the therapist's words that are healing, but rather the creative implications they evoke within the client. What is the most powerful grabber of our patient's attention? I'm talking about symptoms, pain. What are symptoms? What is pain if it is not the body's way of shouting, "Emergency, attention, I need some attention, I need some help!"?

Because of Dr. Polster's lecture, I'm going to rewrite some portions of my forthcoming book, *The Symptom Path to Enlightenment.* The symptom path is a focusing of attention on the need to find our own unique path to healing. I really want to thank Dr. Polster for his heightening of *my* attention to the nuances of healing in his work with attention.

I'm particularly intrigued with the evolution of the new approaches that Dr. Polster is bringing us, particularly his idea of the "tightening of sequences." This seems similar to what Erickson called the "implied directive." But in Polster's work it takes another step in its evolution. Tightening sequences helps us move closer to normal patterns of attention, the give-and-take in everyday life.

I'm particularly impressed with the idea of focusing on those aspects of the evolving self in the client. As Dr. Polster talks about poignantly in his early analytic work, simply giving attention to relevant aspects of the client's newly emerging self is to validate, to reify, to help that new reality come into existence.

Perhaps this is one of our highest, most delicate functions: How do we sidestep the old false selves that claim too much of our client's attention, and how do we tune in with that sensitive third ear to the new that's evolving in the client?

Response by Dr. Polster

How does a therapist remain in full attention? Well, I don't know. There's an attention triad of concentration, fascination, and curiosity, if one can allow those to operate and really focus on what's happening.

One time a strange thing happened to me. I see patients one after the other without a break in between, so somebody walks right in after someone leaves. One man came in and said to me, "When do you rest?" And I said, "I rest when I'm working with you."

So I don't know whether or not that answers the question.

(Editor note: After a few questions from the audience, the following exchange ensued:)

Rossi: Did you refer to therapists as monks?

Polster: There are monks among us, yes. Like me, for example. We spend years of life practicing with free association and offering workshops and, writing, and practicing certain kinds of behaviors. I would call that being a monk.

Do you mind my telling a short story?

The story is about a person who is really very taken with being a monk. He went to a monastery and said he wanted to be a monk. They sent him off to a room. He stayed in that room meditating, pondering, and focusing. Whatever you do as a monk, he did it, for six months. All they brought him three times a day was a wafer and shot full of water. And after six months they called him into the office and asked, "Tell us the real truth of life." All he could possibly get out of his mouth was, "More food."

They sent him back again. In another six months they came back and inquired, "Well, what did you learn this time?" And, he said, "More water."

He went back again. The third time they came back, and he said, after they asked him about the real truth of life, "I quit." And they said, "Thank God, we're tired of your complaining all the time."

Beyond One-to-One

Miriam Polster, Ph.D.

Miriam Polster, Ph.D.

Miriam Polster earned her Ph.D. degree in Clinical Psychology from Case Western Reserve University in 1967. She is codirector of the Gestalt Training Center in San Diego, Calif., and Assistant Clinical Professor in the Department of Psychiatry, School of Medicine, at the University of California, San Diego. Dr. Polster is author of Eve's Daughters: The Forbidden Heroism of Women *and along with her husband, Erving Polster, is a coauthor of* Gestalt Therapy Integrated.

INTRODUCTION

Ever since Freud began his lonely explorations and investigations into the psychological mysteries of human nature and experience, the classic atmosphere of the therapist's office has offered an undisturbed focus on the problems of the individual.

But ghosts from the past and troublesome people from the present keep intruding into this supposedly private setting. It became clear to Freud's therapeutic heirs that it might be therapeutically fruitful to invite these influential but absent presences into the actual therapeutic meeting. So we began dealing with numbers larger than the original one-to-one. We invited the spouse into the office and began doing couples therapy. We invited different members of the household and began doing family therapy. We invited other troubled individuals into the office and began doing group therapy. And once we began doing that, we let the whole cat out of the bag and began working with organizations, classrooms, and large groups, teaching them to acquire one desirable trait or to dissolve another destructive one (Wuthnow, 1994).

Gestalt therapy also had its origins, classically enough, in individual work. Frederick Perls was, after all, a product of the psychoanalytic tradition of Germany in the twenties and thirties. But Perls also was influenced by other theorists of that time and place. They were trying to understand individual behavior as embedded in and reactive to the behavioral field in which it occurred; they did not see it as drawing its energy from purely instinctual and internal struggles. Field theorists, including Kurt Goldstein and Kurt Lewin, who also were influential in Germany at that time, inspired Perls to propose the therapeutic necessity of understanding the behavior of any individual as a response to, or interaction with, the environment in which that person functioned. This interaction, which could be rich and fruitful or awkward and unsatisfying, he called "contact."

Interestingly enough, Perls himself was not particularly interested in or adept at working with groups. Although he is known for his teaching demonstrations of therapeutic work with individuals within a large group, he only rarely recognized the group as a presence in his work. He might sometimes ask the person he was working with to address the group or an individual as representing specific outside influences in that person's life or perhaps representing a general public presence. He might (much more rarely) permit someone in the group to respond or offer a personal perspective. Perls' work, even in this setting, was clearly that of the one-to-one therapist–patient interaction, in front of a group but not *within* it. Even so, the public nature of such work was in itself a profound influence. It emerged from the privacy of the original therapeutic scene and increased the range of public responses to personal issues.

GESTALT THERAPY IN GROUPS

Obviously, the possibilities for contact are to be enhanced in any therapy group: There are many people present, each of them with a particular history and set of needs, each with a personal style of response, communication, and presence. Therefore, it is not surprising that several gestalt therapists have described how attention to some basic gestalt therapy principles, such as contact, awareness, and experiment, is central when working with groups (Polster & Polster, 1974; Rosenblatt, 1989; and Feder & Ronall, 1994; to list only a few).

The purpose of any theory of therapy, whether the focus is on the individual or the group, is to define the data and the desired outcome of therapeutic work. As is to be expected, gestalt group therapy views the quality of the contact between the individual and the group as a major criterion. Good contact in turn rests on the individual's "supported awareness" of herself, of the other people who may be present, and of the relevant environmental conditions. Awareness is arousing and can move into fulfilling contact, or it can be inaccurate or disruptive and unwelcome.

The individual's awareness must include the other people in her group and by implication the other people in her life. What is she aware of in observing or interacting with them? Is she flexible and versatile enough to alter the interaction with the other person so as to enrich the interaction between them—to do this without losing what it is she wants to say or do, but tailoring it to connect more sensitively with the other person? Does he expect to be listened to or does his manner tell you that he has already decided that nobody will take him seriously, or that people are only pretending to be interested as a matter of form? And so does he restrict his speech to a superficial, proforma delivery?

One man had a habit of letting the end of his sentences just trail off, as if even he had lost interest in what he was saying. I asked him to continue talking, but to add the phrase "and I *really* mean that!" at the end of his sentences. He began to enjoy what he was doing, putting more animation into his speech. His sentences ended energetically, keeping the rest of the group fully interested until he finished talking.

Contrary to its reputation as a simple here-and-now therapy, the goals in a gestalt group, as in other therapy groups, involve an equal respect for process and content. The group members talk about aspects of their lives that concern, disturb, or baffle them and leave them feeling perplexed and uneasy. So, although we honor the importance of the individual's contact and relationship to her present environment (in this case, the group), we also remember that her environment is composed of both her personal history and her current experience.

A group member's contactful style within the group is influenced not only by the actual events in that particular group but also by the events that have preceded the group meetings and the events that continue to happen in between group sessions. There is much important experience there. We cannot know her well until we hear her story, but the story itself is not enough. It is not only whether or not she tells us the story but also *how* she tells it—and how we listen. The corollary of how compellingly the individual group member speaks is how the group members look, listen, and take seriously what other group members do or say. Their awareness of her as well as their awareness of their reaction are the other half of the person's story.

One woman in an ongoing therapy group was asked, in a perfunctory show of politeness, how she had enjoyed the weekend conference she had just returned from. Her response matched the question; it was a bright, chipper answer. But another woman in the group was listening sharply and didn't buy it. She observed that the answer felt "gift-wrapped," like a bright package, revealing nothing. The first woman, responding to this new tone, wryly told a different tale. She brushed aside the bangs that covered her forehead and revealed a neat bandage. She then told how she had bumped her head on the sharp corner of a table at the first session and had had to go to an emergency room to have it stitched up. It had hurt her for the rest of the weekend. Quite a different story. All this because the other woman in the group had been listening and looking—and was unwilling to settle for the pretty answer.

The leader in a gestalt group is alert to these contradictions. She aims at heightening both the individual's experience and the poignancy and directness of the interaction between members. The quality of the contact between gestalt group members rests on their willingness and ability to see and comment on what they see. Differences or similarities between individual group members and others can be noted and discussed: How do they deal with similarity or difference once it is observed? Are they alienated by difference or interested in it? How might the differences between members offer a sense of options? Does a perceived similarity become too much like a big cloak

that assumes a confluent identity beyond what may actually be justified?

All of these complexities occur within a group—as they do outside the group—and the hope is that experience within the group will have relevance beyond the walls of the office. There are limits, however. Interactions and experiments within the group setting are not to be taken as scripts or dress rehearsals to be put to use indiscriminately. Within the gestalt group there are options that a person might *not* have available in everyday circumstances or might not think of—or dare—to do. There is time and opportunity for a level of individual exploration and group participation that is possible precisely because of the special circumstances.

An important group contribution is its resonance to an individual's work. His story, simply listened to attentively, acquires a weight and dignity that he may not have experienced before. The range of responses moves beyond a single perspective and provides a sense of diversity and option. One man, saddened but determined to leave his marriage and an unfruitful job after a number of painful years in both relationships, was asked by another man what he had learned in that time. As he answered, he was able to list several bits of wisdom, even though painfully acquired. The man who had asked him the question observed, "It sounds like you're not just leaving with empty hands." The other man nodded, touched and enriched.

The gestalt experiment, the "safe emergency," offers the individual the opportunity to explore beyond the personal contact boundaries that have become restrictive and habitual. The person learns the difference between feeling *exposed* and the developing sense of the possibilities in simply being *visible*. The internal struggle between personal polarities, or characters in a life situation, or in a dream, can be brought into the open by having the individual carry on a dialogue between them, with himself playing both parts. Or this struggle may take the form of enacting a metaphor the person has used in describing himself or some person in his life, or a personal predicament, or a circumstance or relationship that plagues him. Using other group members like this loosens his control and risks having other people play their roles in a style that may not be exactly as he conceived them. But it adds an element of surprise that provides a juicy energy to the individual work.

One woman, for example, who was just beginning to be politically active, was feeling uncertain about how to arrange the seating at a table for eight prospective volunteers whom she was sponsoring (as an unpracticed but idealistic novice) in support of a political candidate. So she cast seven group members as these particular people and told them what kind of personalities they had, and what some of their interests would be. She then seated herself in the circle with them and listened to the conversation, exercising her options to reseat them when it became apparent that she had formed an unsuitable pairing. She discovered that she actually had a better sense of how to do it, and furthermore that she *liked* being influential.

Even when it is silent, the group is there. In addition to the sense that they might participate in the drama of another member's life, the group *witnesses* what happens and provides a sense of continuity and breadth. It is a microcosm of possibilities, with a tacit sense of goodwill. This goodwill is not cheaply or casually given. Some of it is accorded simply through the acknowledgment that the group members all want to do something better. Some of it comes from the assurance of continuity and the accumulation of joint experience.

Some of the goodwill also comes from simply learning how other people may work through to resolution. This can encourage another person to create his own way of confronting his dilemma, emulating not the particular solution but the courage and inventiveness that it took to *find* that solution. Even so, much of the goodwill comes from the engagement with struggle, with confusion, and with not being intimidated by uncertainty.

As with all good experiences, the benefits of these therapy groups were clearly too good to remain limited to the private therapeutic setting—more and more people sought ways to extend the relevance of what they had learned.

SUPPORT GROUPS

An issue of a bimonthly referral directory of groups meeting in San Diego listed psychotherapy groups for men and/or women dealing with bereavement, sexuality, overeating, sexual or substance abuse, and other themes of human dissatisfaction (Group Network, 1995). Common issues concerned communication, intimacy, assertiveness, and power, as well as specific diseases or caretaking roles in dealing with disease or disability in relatives. These groups are meeting a widespread need: Recent research reveals that "At present, four out of every ten Americans belong to a small group that meets regularly . . ." (Wuthnow, 1994).

Support groups are communities in miniature, formed to meet individual need in the company of fellows. For a person who is intimidated by the larger scene, they reduce communal interaction into smaller numbers and encourage people to speak of their personal concerns, sometimes in a group identified by a shared problem. Although there is a danger that a theme-oriented group may move too quickly into a sense of intimacy and identity, reducing people to their common symptom, nevertheless theme-oriented groups have proved highly effective in battling a variety of debilitating physical and emotional problems including insomnia, breast cancer, and learning disabilities. There may be some evidence that the *lack* of an identified group also may be injurious. Jonathan Shay, for example, argues that the unavailability of the opportunity to mourn *communally* in the Vietnam war may well have been an important causal factor in the development of Post Traumatic Stress Disorder (Shay, 1994).

Many of us have had the experience of seeing someone who had a shameful secret that he had concealed for years, dealing in isolation with the fear that he alone was crazy, realize that when he finally spoke of it in a group of attentive listeners, it all disappeared. I remember the response of a group of veterans in a VA hospital when one profoundly depressed man revealed, after weeks of silence, that his suicide attempt was a reaction to being rejected by a woman he was in love with. They understood how he felt and they sympathized with him, but they also could keep alive a sense of his eventually being able to find the courage to love again.

Most importantly, groups can provide a transitional setting where their members learn how they might participate in the community that bustles outside the therapeutic meeting room. Satisfying engagement in the larger, more impersonal community calls for a personal balance between commonality and uniqueness. Many people are in support groups because they find this balance difficult to achieve and need the intermediacy of a support group. A good group, like a good community, offers a mixture of support and independence.

The problem is not new. More than 40 years ago Erich Fromm (1955) described the personality packaging some people go through in order to fit into their societies. All too often in a larger society an individual makes an uneasy bargain where one characteristic predominates and another is cast into the shadows. So this individual blends in, like a social chameleon, but finds that any sense of her individual difference is unwelcome and perhaps even frightening. Others may feel uneasy in groups; they see themselves as "loners" who risk their singular integrity when they become group members.

Many of the groups that "four out of ten" people belong to are perfectly in sync with our mobile society. The continuity they promise is the continuity of a negotiable relationship, not unlike a premarital contract that spells out the conditions for ending the relationship, *right from the beginning*. The underlying agreement is that the group is important but *temporary*; any member may quit as long as he or she gives a week's notice in order to "reach closure" properly. Just what a mobile society needs—disposable relationships.

Even so, these groups offer at least a partial solution to a feeling of social isolation in the light of American society's increasing reliance on technological contact. The group is *there*, physically present instead of on the other end of the Internet or a flickering message on the screen of someone's computer.

The remnants of an original community rest like artifacts just below the surface of every-day life. Fewer and fewer of us live in the city where we were born. We raise our children in circumstances where their intimates are friends, and family is too often a group of people you meet after a long trip and on special occasions. Sometimes family is the other half of the original parental scene with whom contact has been regulated in a courtroom. Comic movies adore these situations and send them to us around holiday time so that we can laugh at ourselves for a change. Our old folk seldom live nearby and the richness of personal history as described in the tales of our elders is frequently relegated to a few impatient moments at a family gathering, or the taped reminiscences of an arranged interview. Some of us have closet shelves stacked with boxes of photographs of family members—many of whom we cannot identify.

These historical communities hover on the fringes of individual work and exert their influence from the distance of time and geography. Their customs may sometimes hinder the ability to find a contemporary community. For example, take a child who has been raised by a harsh and begrudging parent, perfectionistic and critical. He learns as an adult in therapy how to resolve the destructive introjects and construct a more accurate self-portrait. The appropriate therapeutic question is, "What next"? How does this person, who in therapy has finally reduced the allegiance to a toxic community, identify where to go and how to find and recognize companions and associates who fit his present sense of self?

There are two forms of group experience that can be useful at this stage. One is the familiar group therapy setting that we have already referred to, where the protocol is expanded beyond the one-to-one interaction of individual therapy but the emphasis still remains primarily therapeutic. In these settings, the purpose is to come up with the resolution of personal difficulties.

The second form of group is predicated upon an identified commonality. Such groups can be designed to deal with specific situational needs, like a large group designed for the entire incoming freshman class of a school, or an introductory session integrating new church members within an established religious congregation. The group forms temporarily to incorporate individuals into an ongoing system—to provide entry and companionship for people coming into a strange new experience.

Other group possibilities come from common causes or activities. Many communal efforts rely on and encourage affiliation; they welcome members because they need impressive numbers in order to speak with a weightier voice. These groups are likely to be focused on issues of political governance and community self-regulation. They may have a temporary focus on a particular issue, but often they have a renewable sense of concern that gives the group a sense of history of past accomplishments and a sense of a future as it continues to focus on recurring issues.

It is not outside the proper sphere of psychotherapy to explore what personal talents and interests a patient has that might lead her into connections with like-minded people. Such abilities may lead into a fresh sense of engagement with her environment. They may lead to membership on voluntary citizen committees. Many such groups offer the promise of continuity and shared experience because they continue to identify new endeavors that engage them beyond the original purpose.

In social action groups that are formed to reach certain social or political aims, there is much to learn and practice in the give-and-take that persuasion and advocacy require. Argument must always leave room for further talk and eventual resolution. Eshtain (1995) calls this the basic "civility" that is an essential component of a "democratic disposition."

Other groups coalesce around a common stage of life or a shared interest. Some of these groups are formed out of a deep-felt need to obtain and share information that pertains to a very specific aspect of their lives. They may be physically close, like the Texas group of 125 laid-off employees of a downsizing move at IBM. They meet regularly at a local church and discuss their individual reactions to their dismissal, which have ranged from depression over the loss to pride in their newly discovered sense of self-reliance. One man observed that he had discovered that he had more time

to volunteer and to "give back to the community" (New York Times, 1995).

The need for community can sometimes transcend physical distance, or even psychological substance. *Smithsonian Magazine* devoted an article to some of the off-beat societies that actually get together only rarely but still provide a sort of sense of community (Watson, 1995). The author, Bruce Watson, introduces the topic by observing, "It's not what you do that counts, it's what you *belong* to." Members keep in touch through correspondence or periodic conventions. Eligibility for membership is simple, ranging all the way from having the same name (the Jim Smith Society), to the same activity (National Organization of Mall Walkers) or the same predicament (Edsel owners). We all know people who belong to a bird-watchers group, a photography association, a race-walking group, or a biking or hiking group.

BEYOND ONE-TO-ONE

Many of the television programs we watch reflect societal trends. We can almost trace our society's values and experiences through the way these shows change. Some of the early programs celebrated the centrality of family connections, like *Father Knows Best, Ozzie and Harriet,* or the *Beverly Hillbillies.* Even explorations of prejudice were peopled by relatives and neighbors—remember *All in the Family*?

Even so, there were notable exceptions that leaned into the future. The opening shot of the old *Mary Tyler Moore* program showed her at the wheel of her car, driving into her newly adopted city. Her parents almost never made an appearance—they were rarely even mentioned. The program centered around the comedic value of colleagues and friends. The popularity of her show may well have recognized the growing concerns of an audience of working women, no longer connected with family and belonging to a group consisting of coworkers and friends. It spawned *Lou Grant,* where a previously comedic character became a serious big-city journalist with professional associates. These settings are now commonplace as sit-coms deal with how people associate with coworkers (*Murphy Brown, ER, LA Law, Designing Women*) or with friends (*Ellen, Friends, Seinfeld*).

To be sure, many TV programs are still the same-old same-old. But there is a refreshing influence in some of the new programming. *ER* and *LA Law*, for example, take seriously the complexities of relationships when both people work hard at what they do and pay for it in exhaustion and disillusionment. *Frasier* strikes a little closer to home for some of us. It deals, comedically of course, with the anonymous distress that seeks advice via the telephone and also with troublesome but vital family relationships. *Mad About You* takes a two-career marriage, adds some troublesome siblings and in-laws, a dog, difficult neighbors, and a temperamental janitor.

We have a lot to learn from comedy. *Seinfeld* has a cast of eccentric friends. These people are all portrayed as having troublesome, outrageous characteristics. They lie, they do disgraceful things, and then they compound the situation by offering incredible justifications for their misdeeds. Obviously, these traits support the comedic intent—we would hardly tolerate them in real life. But here's the point: despite these shenanigans, these people, wonder of wonders, *continue* the relationship. Even the most egregious interactions do not seriously disrupt the friendship. They don't expect perfection from their friends or from themselves. We could learn something from them.

In 1938, not too distant in time from Perls' formulations of gestalt therapy, Henry Murray was formulating his theory of "personology" with an intense focus on individual motivation. He listed 20 needs that he felt motivated and organized individual behavior (Hall & Lindzey, 1978). Here is how Murray describes four of them:

1. *Affiliation:* To draw near and enjoyably cooperate or reciprocate with an allied other (an other who resembles the subject or who likes the subject). To please and win the affection of a cathected object. To adhere and remain loyal to a friend.

2. *Nurturance:* To give sympathy and gratify the needs of a helpless object: an infant or any object who is weak, disabled, tired, inexperienced, infirm, defeated, humiliated, lonely, dejected, sick, mentally confused. To assist an object in danger. To feed, help, support, console, protect, comfort, nurse, heal.

3. *Exhibition:* To make an impression. To be seen and heard, to excite, amaze, fascinate, entertain, shock, intrigue, amuse, or entice others.

4. *Succorance:* To have one's needs gratified by the sympathetic aid of an allied object. To be nursed, supported, sustained, surrounded, protected, loved, advised, guided, indulged, forgiven, consoled. To remain close to a devoted protector. To always have a supporter.

These are needs that can be met only in community. They represent the behaviors that reveal the individual's need for a personal, interactive sense of community. It is important to notice that they are *reciprocal* needs—not only to receive but also to give.

Daniel Goleman (1995) has recently introduced a human capacity that he calls "emotional intelligence." He observes (and we have all noticed at one time or another) that a high IQ alone cannot explain why some individuals prosper and others bungle. He proposes two behaviors, physiologically based but still amenable to change, that comprise emotional intelligence. They are the ability to control impulse, and empathy. To these abilities he links two moral attitudes: self-restraint and compassion. Goleman also talks about the centrality of self-awareness, of managing one's emotions and of handling difficult relationships.

He offers some recommendations for teaching these behaviors to our children and shows how groups that sound like a combination between teaching and psychotherapy can ameliorate destructive behavior in children who may otherwise be headed for trouble. What do these programs teach? Through class discussion and specific exercises, these children learn (among other things) to recognize their own and another's feelings; to cooperate in a group solution; to resolve conflict; and to think of alternate solutions to a disagreement.

Here, I propose, is where group therapy and our current batch of sit-coms meet. An improbable development, but stay with me a moment. Seinfeld's friends are clearly an exasperating bunch. They come up with a series of improbable explanations and convoluted interpretations that get them into more trouble than the original dilemma they were invented to resolve. But these behaviors are absorbed into the basic premise that the relationship is never seriously ruptured. It may flounder, they may holler at each other, but the continuity of their friendship is never in doubt. There is an underlying attitude of hopeful persistence and a willingness to deal with interpersonal troubles that prevents rupture.

The steadfast assurance of a reliable source of community support that was previously based on family and neighborhood took on new forms as a consequence of our love affair with individualism. We have gone through the invulnerability of the rugged loner who rides into town, eliminates the villain and his threats, and then rides out again, like a *deus ex machina* on horseback. Many people are becoming aware of the consequences of this kind of solitary function and saying it won't do. The recent trend of successful career people opting out of the rat-race and either simplifying their lives or becoming their own bosses and being in charge of their own schedules is too broad a trend to overlook.

The skills that Goleman describes are very similar to the behaviors we emphasize in groups. But these skills have a value beyond enabling a person to deal with his or her individual environment. These skills are important in *building* a particular personal community. They are central in learning how to enter the already existing communities that our mobility may plunk us into. These abilities must be transferable beyond therapy and support groups into the communities where people spend the hours and minutes of their lives, living with the people who are important to them and who will be there for a predictable time to come.

Individual therapy is invaluable. It helps us achieve a perspective on troublesome aspects of our lives. But it risks maintaining too narrow a focus compared to the wide-angle life we live with our daily companions and co-workers. Group therapy is an intermediate step between close attention to exclusively individual concerns and finding one's place in the traffic jams of a broader community.

The one-to-one therapeutic style emphasizes the importance of attention to individual needs for resolution, expression, and self-sufficiency. Transposing this attitude to group work—and further understanding its relevance to the larger community—can release some important societal implications that the individual members of the group can apply to their lives outside the therapy group.

CONCLUSION

Most of what we are as individuals is defined and shaped by our encounters with otherness. How we relate to all the similar and dissimilar others who intersect our daily life greatly influences how appetitive and comfortable we feel in these incessant interactions. The sense of uniqueness that challenges and defines every individual requires a personal and communal etiquette of participation and interaction.

One of the most basic sources of interpersonal difficulty is how communities deal with individual difference. The attempt to muzzle disagreement, whether by shouting down a speaker in a public forum, blocking a person's access to medical treatment, threatening a filibuster in a legislative chamber, or assassinating a politician, is not only hateful but does not work. Objection and difference exist, whether we like it or not.

The opposite, dealing with similarity, also is worth examining. Friendship and affiliation cannot require absolute agreement; they cannot depend on an uneasily imposed sense of shared identity. People must learn how to remain in the same group while tolerating variation, perhaps even finding difference a fertile ground for creativity. When a person feels alienated or angry does he become more articulate or less, louder or quieter? How well does he listen to another's response and find ways for clarification or a useful combination of shared purpose?

How can we teach patience, in a harried world where the tempo feels always like a fast march? Patience is when a person listens carefully to what another is saying rather than simply waiting impatiently for him to finish so that she can have her say again. We need to teach how to distinguish between the persistence that moves toward resolution and the fixity that prevents progress.

We must learn, as professionals who deal with difference and conflict, that it is important to work against an indiscriminate sanctification of individuality that allows one individual to label as an enemy a person with whom she differs or whose behavior she disapproves of. This kind of linguistic escalation begins with words but all too often ends in violence. We must learn how to argue with mutual respect. We must learn to persist, not merely by repeating the same old arguments but by restating them, incorporating some suggestions from the other side.

Remember, some of the skills that are learned and practiced in a group may be even more useful as we move beyond one-to-one into the casual encounters where the rules of communication are not always spelled out. Contact under these less structured conditions must be durable enough to be maintained through episodes of poor or frustrating interaction with other people.

It is easy for us to feel the common purpose of a community under special circumstances, when we are engaged in a war or in launching a national space program; these are vast events and we respond with a kind of almost reflexive enthusiasm that we may have thought we lost. With on-the-spot media coverage of these events we can feel a whole nation collectively hold its breath until an endangered space mission returns to earth.

These moments are compelling, but we cannot hang a life on such incidents. Most of our lives are spent in simple communal interactions with other ordinary people. Nothing special. That's the point. We have to learn how to interact in the "not special" moments. We have so many of them.

REFERENCES

Eshtain, J. B. (1995). *Democracy on trial*. New York: Basic Books.

Feder, B., & Ronall, R. (1994). *Beyond the hot seat*. Highland, NY: Gestalt Journal Press.

Fromm, E. (1955). *The same society*. New York: Holt, Rinehart, & Winston.

Goleman, D. (1995). *Emotional intelligence*. New York: Bantam.

Hall, C. S., & Lindzey, G. (1978). *Theories of personality* (2nd ed.) New York: Wiley.

Polster, E., & Polster, M. (1974). *Gestalt therapy integrated*. New York: Vintage.

Rosenblatt, D. (1989). Highland, NY: Center for Gestalt Development.

Shay, J. (1994). *Achilles in Vietnam*. New York: Touchstone.

Watson, B. (1995). *Smithsonian Magazine, 26*(1).

Wuthnow, R. (1994). *Sharing the journey*. New York: Free Press.

Discussion by Alexander Lowen, M.D.

◆

I have to say that I am not nearly half as optimistic about the future, about how we can deal with these problems, as Dr. Polster is. I don't think that you can teach people very much. Or, if you're going to teach them, it will be by the way you behave, not by the ideals and the theories that you set forth.

After all, we learn from our parents not by what they say but from who they are. Not even by what they do, but from who they are. Behavior communicates itself to children. And, as much as we need to really function on a community level, it becomes increasingly difficult in this culture to do so—in fact, I would venture that it's almost impossible.

This is not to say that you mustn't try. I think that to be a good member of a community, you must have a sense of your own personality, your own selfhood. On the other hand, if you belong to a community that is a real community, it increases your selfhood. These two are complementary things, they don't exclude each other.

But where do you start? Do you start with a good community? Or do you start with an individual who has a strong sense of self?

Well, let's say that individual therapy basically aims at helping you achieve a sense of self that enables you to function in a healthy way in relation to others in the community, and a good community furthers that sense of self. Let's hope we can somehow get there.

SECTION VI

Family Therapists

Changes in Therapy

◆

Jay Haley, M.A.

Jay Haley, M.A.

Jay Haley (M.A., 1953, Stanford University) founded the Family Therapy Institute of Washington, DC. He is the chief architect of the strategic approach to psychotherapy. Haley served as Director of the Family Experiment Project at the Mental Research Institute and as Director of Family Therapy Research at the Philadelphia Child Guidance Clinic. He has written eight books, is coauthor of two, and has edited five. Additionally, he has made more than 50 contributions to professional journals and books. Haley is the Founding Editor of Family Process *and the first recipient of the Lifetime Achievement Award of The Milton H. Erickson Foundation.*

INTRODUCTION

I will present a personal view of some of the changes I have observed in therapy over the years, changes that have had consequences to therapists and their teachers. I will not be scientific but reminiscent, and I will confine myself to therapy in the Western world and not discuss the Baleans, or healers, worldwide, who also are changing.

I will use cases to illustrate changes, some of them previously published. I think case summaries are the metaphors that express the underlying ideas of the clinical field.

CLINICAL CHOICES

As ideas about therapy change, all of us must accept the new ways of thinking, or modify them, or deny them and continue with the old views. This is an exciting time in therapy because there is no orthodoxy. Therefore one cannot be a deviant. If one offers a different technique of doing therapy, it is not condemned as heretical, as happened in the 1950s, but it becomes a new school of therapy, particularly if it is given a name. Therapists today must each make choices about how to do therapy. There is now a feast of different ways of doing therapy, most of them contradictory with each other. One might expect that after 100 years there would be consensus in the therapy field on how to formulate a problem, how to make an intervention, and how to follow up a case to make sure success is continued. But there isn't agreement that a therapist should formulate a problem. Nor is there agreement that a therapist should deliberately make an intervention. Many schools recommend merely reflecting with the client on his or her life. With managed care there is some consensus developing, because the business-people in charge want a problem defined and therapy brief and cheap.

Another complication for choosing a therapy approach is the mass of new immigrants arriving in the offices. Therapy was constructed on the unconscious of Europeans, and now a mass of Asians and Central and South Americans have descended upon the field.

FREUD'S CHOICES AND THEIR CONSEQUENCES

I will talk about other changes in therapy to which we all must adapt and begin with what is considered the beginning, Sigmund Freud, even though a number of competent therapists were there before him. I think it was a major event when Freud announced the cause of hysteria in a paper published in 1896. It was entitled "Heredity and the Aetiology of the Neurosis" and it was the first publication where he used the term "psychoanalysis." (Freud, 1896/1959). He proposed that the cause of hysteria was childhood sex abuse that, as he put it, actually involved the genitalia. He reported that 13 out of 13 of his cases of hysteria experienced sexual relations as a child with a brother or an adult male. His findings posed several choices for therapists then and therapists must still react today.

One choice Freud's colleagues and followers could make was to accept his findings and explore their own patients' sexual past. If the patient denied sex abuse had actually ocurred, "energetic pressure" would be exerted to persuade them, because it must have happened if Freud said it had. One might also expect Freud and his colleagues to report brothers and other adult males to the police of Vienna to be arrested for practicing incest with children. Guilty fathers and sons might be removed from the home. In family interviews mothers would be confronted for not protecting their daughters.

There was a more important consequence if Freud's findings were accepted. It would mean accepting the idea that symptoms are caused by the actions of family members in real life, not

by fantasies or misperceptions or unconscious notions. If Freud and the field had held to that position, family therapy would have been born 100, rather than 40 years ago. How we would have progressed by now. Or would we?

Another choice a colleague might have made could have been to call Freud wrong. The argument would be that he was too fixated on sex and was duped by the untrue reports of the patients, all 13 of them. Freud anticipated this objection and defended his therapy, saying that his patients were telling the truth even when they denied that they had childhood sexual experiences. He said, "Why should patients assure me so emphatically of their unbelief if . . . they had invented the very charge that they wished to discredit?" He added, "The mental image of the premature sexual experience is recalled only when most energetic pressure is exerted by the analytic procedure, against strong resistances; so that the recollection has to be extracted bit by bit from the patients, and while it comes back into consciousness they fall prey to emotions difficult to simulate" (Freud, 1896/1959).

What to do with these findings of Freud became academic, as we all know, because he reversed himself on this issue, for mysterious reasons. He announced that childhood sex abuse did not happen but was a product of false memories. Reviewing his ideas in 1904, he said, "I overestimated the frequency of these occurrences, which were otherwise quite authentic, and all the more so since I was not at this period able to to discriminate between the deceptive memories of hysterics concerning their childhood and the memory traces of actual happenings" (Freud, 1905/1959).

This minimizing of sexual childhood experiences, and finding memories to be deceptive, posed a new set of difficult decisions then and today. What actually happened in childhood might or might not have happened depending on whether false memories happen.

Even more important, therapy changed its focus from the behavior of real people to interior ideas as causes of symptoms. This shift led therapists to focus on the fantasies and narratives and perceptions and secret wishes of clients, not on real-life family members actually exploiting children.

Therapists had a dilemma, no matter which premise they accepted. If they said childhood sexual relations happened, action had to be taken with the patriarchal male, which would cause indignation or worse. Yet there was a more severe consequence if therapists did not believe their clients who remembered untrue memories. Because psychopathology is said to be caused by the past, and all else is merely secondary, how could therapists accept the past if false memories made them doubt their truth? The next step could be to believe that therapists influence their data, including the memories of the past. Possibly his clients' memories were created in collaboration with Freud. For example, we now find that therapists can be absolutely sure that a person has multiple personalities. They also can be absolutely sure that the cause is sexual abuse in childhood and so they can persuade their clients, sometimes using hypnosis, to believe that past even when it was not true. Indignant parents are taking therapists to court over these created memories. It is reminiscent of Freud saying "The mental image of the premature sexual experience is recalled only when most energetic pressure is exerted by the analytic procedure against strong resistance" (Freud, 1905/1959).

If there are false memories, how can a therapist believe any memories of a client? Apparently memories can be influenced, even produced, by the social situation, composed of therapist and client or family member and client. Memories change when a client deals with someone with strong beliefs to impose, like a psychoanalyst. It is interesting that back in the 1940s and 1950s Milton Erickson did experiments using hypnosis to build false memories. He wanted to determine if the false memories could be accepted as real by the subject. (Erickson, 1967)

Descriptions of the past can be thought of as metaphors about the present. As an example, I once interviewed a number of mothers of young people diagnosed as schizophrenic. The mothers would describe their history with the child, and I could see them rewriting that history because they had to change the past to make sense of how it led to the present crisis.

There are clients who tell lies about their past and lie deliberately, which is different from memories that clients believe are true when they are not. If false memories exist, one must doubt the reports of clients in therapy. For example, one must question whether specific traumas in the past cause present symptoms. Or one can doubt that symptoms are caused by childhood developmental processes, or that dysfunctional families in the past cause a drinking problem in the present. Our theories are dependent upon our data, which are now questionable. What of the social workers who dutifully take their clients' histories. Are they actually writing fiction?

There are also less abstract consequences if one denies that sexual abuse happened in childhood when a client says it happened. A generation of women was persuaded by therapists that the family sexual behavior they experienced did not actually occur. So they were forced to deny an accurate perception. Instead of analysts using energetic pressure against strong resistance to persuade patients that they had been sexually abused, therapists used that approach to get patients to realize it had not happened. I recall Don D. Jackson, an authority on schizophrenia, saying that forcing people to deny what they know to be true is a potent way to drive people crazy.

Another problem in the real world was that there were many women who experienced incest with a father and were hospitalized as delusional. People sympathized with the father for having a daughter who had fantasies and false memories.

In the 1960s, a time of transition in therapy, I visited a clinical team whose task was to keep people out of the hospital by active therapeutic interventions. A young woman had been making wild scenes and accusing her father of having incest with her. She was brought in to be hospitalized and the task of the team was to see if the problem could be dealt with without hospitalization. The parents and daughter were brought together, and the daughter made her accusations. The mother denied it. The daughter began to yell that it happened, the mother yelled that it did not, The father said he didn't know, he was drunk at the time. (The audiotape of that session is so loud it hurts the ears.)

When the team saw the girl alone, she said that she had been put in a mental hospital twice when she made this accusation. The team faced a difficult problem. They believed the young woman. Yet they knew they could not persuade the hospital staff not to hospitalize her because the staff would be compelled to diagnose her as delusional with false memories. What could be done? The team pointed out to her that if she stopped making the accusation she would not be hospitalized. She was only harming herself. She said, "I want that man to admit he did it." Ultimately, as a way of staying out of the hospital, she agreed to drop the accusation. Was that a correct decision? Because Freud decided to ignore real-life happenings between people, many young women were put in hospitals when they were telling the truth. Today their fathers would be put in jail instead, because the belief now is that the actions *did* happen—they were not fantasies.

The premises that Freud taught led to rules to be followed in therapy. He took the position that the past should be the focus, that false memories should be accepted, that the therapist should be neutral and not impose an idea on the client, and that the therapist should avoid all relatives and so avoid what really happened. Directives should never be given: instead, interpretations should be made. The interpretations should help the client become conscious of the awful ideas in his or her unconscious that were carried over from the past. No symptom would be focused upon, and no deliberate attempt made to cause a change. If someone were to ask an analyst if it was his job to change people, he would say that it was not. He would help people understand themselves but whether they changed was up to them.

These rules, or parts of them, are still present among the teachers trained in the psychodynamic ideology, and there have been several generations of them, including those now teaching supposedly quite different schools of therapy.

POSTANALYTIC PERSPECTIVES

In the 1950s not only did a variety of new premises develop, but the opposite of every one of Freud's procedures was recommended for therapists. As orthodoxy unraveled, everyone was forced to take a position on how therapy should be done. The teachers of therapy faced the worst problem, because they had such an investment in their past training. As therapy changed they had to scramble to catch up.

I was influenced in accepting the idea that analytic therapy took too long by a woman who was in analysis for 18 years. She had begun it when she married. Eighteen years later she divorced her husband and quit her analyst. She was becoming involved with another man, considering marriage, and thinking about going back into analysis again. There was an analyst ready to receive her.

Besides its interminable length, another consequence of "intensive" therapy usually is not mentioned. In psychodynamic and related therapies, including most educational or cognative therapies, people are systematically taught to observe themselves and to wonder why they do what they do. This way of thinking continues after therapy. There are ex-patients who, when they feel sexual pleasure, wonder why. This is a philosophical issue about the goals of therapy and what sort of people it creates. Should one spends one's life monitoring oneself? Or should one just live.

A Zen story influenced me on this point. Two Zen monks, let us call them A and B, were walking into town. There was a pretty young woman who had stopped by a muddy road because she did not want to dirty her clothes. Monk A picked the woman up and carried her across the road. He set her down and the two monks walked on in silence. After a long walk they arrived at their destination, and Monk B said, "A monk should not pick up and carry a pretty young woman." The other monk said, "I left the woman by the road. Are you still carrying her?"

THE ACTIVE THERAPIES

In the 1950s I worked on a research program with Gregory Bateson. We investigated various phenomena, including Zen and therapy. We shared a research building with two young men who were developing behavior therapy. They were to present their research at a staff lunch. Attending were the psychiatric staff of the hospital, all of them psychoanalytically oriented. The training director was an elderly psychoanalyst. The young men said that they would like to introduce a new therapy approach. It had been shown that animal behavior could be influenced with positive reinforcement. The next step had been the finding that human beings could be influenced in the same way. Finally, it was realized that the therapist could be a stimulus who provided positive reinforcement. The young men said that if a therapist wanted a patient to behave in a certain way, he or she could arrange that. If you want a patient to express more emotion, then whenever he expresses an emotion you nod and smile. If he does not express an emotion, you don't respond. If you do that, at the end of an hour you'll have a very emotional patient

The Director of Training became angry. He said that only a cad would treat a patient like that. He said it is not only wrong to try to change patients deliberately, but doing it outside their awareness was absolutely wrong. One of the young men pointed out that therapists do this anyway. If clients do what we like, we respond positively, and if they do what we don't like we don't respond. The training director said, "If you do it and you don't know you're doing it, that's all right!"

In that period premises were changing, forcing therapists to take a position on whether they should just reflect with a client or deliberately set out to change them, even outside their awareness. Therapists also had to decide what behavior they wanted to encourage, which meant that therapists were threatened with having to set goals for therapy. This could mean that outcome could be defined as achieving that goal, and so make outcome research more precise.

There were new theories of why people do what they do as well as how to change them. Listing a few of the premises of behavior therapy means reporting the opposite of the psychodynamic rules:

Therapists did not leave it up to the client to change but were expected to deliberately cause change.

There was no assumption of repressed unconscious ideas. A variety of learning theories were applied instead. The theory of change did not assume that interpretations about unconscious dynamics were relevant.

Therapists gave directives to clients, changing their reinforcements deliberately.

Relatives were spoken to and even interviewed—for example, a mother could be programmed to deal with her child differently. It was not necessary to see only the child in individual therapy.

Of special importance was the abandonment of the medical framework. Symptoms were not medical but behavioral problems, so medical diagnosis was not relevant.

The psychodynamicists and the behaviorists lived side by side in the therapy field, occasionally speaking to each other. Teachers had difficulties. Trained psychodynamically, it was difficult for them to shift and supervise young therapists in the behavioral approaches. They did not know how, and if they tried they were called heretics by their former teachers and colleagues.

When we think of the life of a teacher it is clear that psychodynamic teachers had it best in terms of any demands upon them. They trained by having the student go through personal therapy, and they offered an occasional seminar. They did not have to teach interview skills but only reflected with the student, just as they did with clients. They could not be expected to teach skills when they could never observe the student doing therapy. The therapy process took so long that no one knew if the supervisor's guidance had caused success or failure in the case. Actually, the teacher could not fail because he or she was not considered to be responsible for the outcome of the case. If the student failed with a client, it was not his or her teacher at fault but his or her emotional problems. Only one method need be taught for all clients of whatever kind. A successful training analysis meant that the therapist was trained to do therapy with *anyone* of any background.

FAMILY THERAPY

As if these conflicting views were not enough for therapists to choose among, the family therapies came in at the same time or just before the behavioral therapies in the 1950s. They raised an entirely new set of premises. Not only did the therapy change, but the theories of why people do what they do changed as well. Family therapists differed with individual therapists and with each other. In the 1960s I recall counting a dozen different schools of family therapy. In 1968 I organized a memorial meeting for Don Jackson, and we had 45 family therapists, just about all the family therapists in the country, and they discussed their differing views. The recordings show that the discussions were profound and scientific and systemic, at least sometimes.

Let me deal with the profundity of cybernetics and family systems theory by offering a personal example. For several years at the end of the 1950s I was testing and doing experiments with families. We were trying to determine whether families with an abnormal member, such as a person diagnosed as schizophrenic, delinquent, or psychosomatic, were different from each other and from families with all normal members. For outcome studies we wished to measure the systematic changes in sequences between family members before and after therapy, not the opinions of the family. Our problem was that no test had yet been devised that could measure the sequence of interchanges between family members. We had tests of the perception of the family members about their families by using as stimuli Rorschachs, TATs, or the various individual tests available. These were relevant to individual perception, the inside of people, but they were not relevant to the types of family interchanges which actually happened.

One day I was watching a family behind a mirror as they waited for me to come in and test them. There was a mother, a father and a young boy. The boy began to fool with the microphone. The father said, "Don't fool with the microphone." The mother said, "Don't pick on the boy." The father said, "He shouldn't fool with the microphone." A few minutes later the boy began to look under the table. The father said, "Don't look under the table." The mother said, "Don't pick on the boy." The father said, "He shouldn't look under the table." As I watched this sequence repeat, I realized that what I was trying to make measurements of was that kind of sequence. I was not measuring the perception of the family members about the family but their actions in sequence. It seemed evident they all had to respond in order. The boy had to do something wrong, the father had to comment, the mother had to correct father. This was the kind of sequence that family therapy was trying to change. Changing it was not easy. For example, one might privately ask the boy to be good and to do nothing wrong. If he behaved that way, the father would say, "How come you're so quiet?" The mother would say, "Don't pick on the boy." The father would say, "He shouldn't be so quiet."

Family therapy was born with the idea that people respond to each other in a sequence, and a symptomatic person cannot change unless someone else changes. Focusing on an individual's interior will not change a system. At least two people, if not more, were necessary to affect change, according to systems theory. So now another set of premises arrived for therapists to choose among. Family systems theory offered at least the following premises:

> The motivation of a person's behavior, and the cause of a problem, was not in the past but in the current sequence in which the person was enmeshed.

> The symptom was not irrational, carried over from the past. Rather, it had a current function and so was appropriate behavior in the system. The system had to change for the individual to change.

> The minimum unit of a symptom was two people, and therefore individual theory of why people did what they did, such as the theory of repression or emotional states, was not relevant.

To many of us, these were new and exciting ideas that had not been explored in the centuries of observation and research on human beings as individuals. Certainly they had not been explored in therapy. We became irritated when colleagues tried to drag us back to the individual tradition.

A different theory of motivation was proposed, the idea that a person's problem behavior could stabilize a family system. Therefore, it had a positive function. The adolescent who harms herself is being helpful to someone. The roots of such an idea for therapy came, I think, from the hypnotists at the turn of the century who defined the unconscious as a positive force rather than a hostile environment.

Milton Erickson once told me that if he mislaid a manuscript he did not hunt for it. He assumed that his unconscious would find it when appropriate. You should trust your unconscious and let it lead you. What a contrast this view is to the psychodynamic unconscious, which is full of awful ideas. Apparently the definition of the unconscious divided hypnotists at the turn of the century. Some hypnotists, like Freud, chose to believe in a negative unconscious, and some hypnotists believed in a positive unconscious. Erickson represented the positive view and in the 1950s that was heretical. Twenty years later it was becoming mainstream. A first interview became accepted as an exploration of capabilities and solutions rather than of unfortunate thoughts and impulses.

The 1950s was a social period. Scientists began to study animals in their natural groups, not in zoos. Therapists began to study the individual in his or her family environment, not in hospitals. When therapists began to see actual family behavior in front of a one-way mirror, their ideas of family and symptoms changed, and the reports of individual patients, too, seemed quite different. Often the family view came about because it was simply common sense, which was not too common in therapy previously. The family ideology seemed to have its origins in the American midwest rather than in Europe, the birthplace of earlier therapy ideology. For example, one cannot imagine Freud giving an example of how to get a cow out of a barn when discussing therapy. It seemed quite reasonable when Milton Erickson did that.

I'll report an incident where I was forced to think in a family perspective. When I was in practice, I was referred a young woman who had a shaking right hand. It was an involuntary shaking for which no neurological cause had been found. It was assumed to be based upon some inner anxiety carried over from her childhood. This young woman went into therapy with a psychiatrist friend of mine, and after a few months of exploring her childhood developmental processes he sent her to me. She was about to lose her job over this shaking and he wanted me to use hypnosis to cure the symptom while he continued therapy with her, an arrangement thought reasonable at that time. I hypnotized her and she was a very good subject, able to have amnesia for a trance. I suggested that she cause her left instead of her right hand to shake. That happened, and as her left hand shook her problem right hand stopped shaking. I awakened her and she said, "My left hand is shaking now." "Isn't that better?" I asked. "You don't write with your left hand." She said she didn't want either hand to shake. I gave her suggestions about the hand shaking only when needed and awakened her. Talking with her, I asked a question I had found was helpful in learning the destiny of a symptom. "What if this shaking hand gets worse?" She said, "I'll lose my job." I said, "And what will happen if you lose your job?" She said, "My husband will have to go to work." In a flash of insight I saw the symptom as having a current social function. I could interpret it not as irrational anxiety carried over from childhood, but as having a current purpose.

Her husband had come out of the navy and could not make up his mind whether to go to college or go to work, and he was vacillating while she supported him. She did not like this situation. Thinking in terms of common sense, I asked her how her parents felt about this arrangement. She said they didn't like it at all and wanted her to divorce her husband. Her mother would call her every day and say, "Are you coming home today?" She would say, "Mother, I'm married now. I have my own apartment." The mother would say, "That won't last."

The husband had the dilemma that if he went to college his wife would have to support him, and her parents would not like that. If he took a job it wouldn't be good enough for her parents. He couldn't think of what to do without thinking of their opinions.

In another flash of insight I could see that this could be seen as an individual anxiety problem, or a dyadic problem with the husband, but there was a triangle. The young woman was caught between her parents and her husband and was unable to deal with it.

There was another family view forced upon me by this case. I dealt with the wife and husband and I even taught the husband to hypnotize his wife when she was nervous, which he did. In a few weeks the shaking was gone, the husband went to work, and the parents began to support the marriage. I took the credit for this success. However, I could not avoid the idea that the theory of the family life cycle could explain this change better than my therapeutic skills.

What happened was that the young woman got pregnant. With that, she could legitimately quit her job. Her husband had to go to work. Her parents, who wanted her back home, did not want her back with a baby, and so they shifted and supported the marriage.

This case expressed a new theory imposed on therapists as an explanation of symptoms and what to do with them. That is the family life cycle theory, which assumes that psychological problems do not occur randomly in the life of a family. They cluster at certain points, such as right after marriage, as in this case. Then there is the birth of a child, starting school, adolescence, leaving home, and retirement and old age. This way of thinking about symptoms developed for me when I was writing *Uncommon Therapy* and trying to make sense of Milton Erickson's work. I realized Erikson often talked about the success of a case as indicated by the family shifting to the next stage, such as having a child. He also emphasized parents shifting to the next stage of becoming grandparents—when a daughter has a baby. A therapeutic strategy becomes helping the family shift from being stuck in a problem stage to moving on to the next problem stage. When that is done, the psychodynamics and other phenomena change.

At one time outcome research was finding that 40 to 60 percent of people on a waiting list recovered without therapy. The possibility that people change as their life situation changes makes more sense than believing that waiting lists are curative.

When I look back over the changes in therapy, one problem I see was learning how to give directives. As nondirective therapy died, therapists were untrained in giving directives and persuading people to do what might bring about change. I was fortunate in having access to Milton Erickson for many years and hearing about many of his cases. There was one step I took that I think others did too. I began practice in a period when it was not proper to give directives. A therapist who used them was thought to be strange and shallow. However, if the therapist hypnotized a client, then it was all right to direct him or her to do something. In time I realized that you could tell people what to do without hypnotizing them, and so I became a directive therapist.

Another important matter is therapists' determination to educate. Obviously therapy was born in the universities, and educated people believe that salvation comes through knowledge, particularly self-knowledge. Therefore therapy concentrated on teaching people something. This could be teaching them the ideas in their unconscious, or teaching them how they should live, or teaching people to recognize what in the past caused their problems in the present.

Psychodynamic therapy is obviously a teaching enterprise, but behavior therapists also found themselves teaching learning theory to clients. Some schools of family therapy taught families how they ought to be, hoping that teaching would change them. The cognitivists teach a rational view to their clients. Even when people change without learning, still it is thought that learning somehow must have occurred. I have tried to arrange that therapy trainees not teach but simply arrange a change. They find themselves compulsively explaining to the client what they did that caused the change. I am not suggesting that therapists should be ignorant or should not teach. I am suggesting that thinking that teaching is the cause of change is an error. So let us continue to believe that teaching is necessary and try not to let it interfere with the therapy.

It is in relation to teaching clients about themselves that I discovered the most important question about therapy that is asked by beginning trainees. They may be exposed to psychodynamics, or behavior therapy, or family therapy, or directive therapy, but one question they ask is at the heart of these choices and determines their therapeutic careers. What is that question? It is so obvious that it is difficult to recognize. In fact it is so elementary that I am tempted to drop the matter and not present it here because it is something all of you know. Most beginning therapists have either asked this one question or thought of it but were afraid to ask because they would seem such a beginner. The question every trainee must ask is, "When I see a client or a family, what can I talk about for a whole hour? What do I say to them?"

Different schools of therapy stand or fall on how this question is answered. What can we give trainee therapists to talk about? The winning answer, I believe, is psychodynamic therapy. That is why the ideas have stayed with us so long despite the outcome of the therapy. As soon as trainees discover that they will not have to talk much in an interview, they find that the psychodynamic ideology is the best one. The therapist has the privilege of saying nothing, or very little, and the client does the talking. A therapist need say only hello and goodbye and "Can you tell me more about that?" and "I wonder why you're so quiet today." The patient knows that he or she is supposed to do a monologue on the past in all its detail.

In contrast, behavior therapy is less popular because the trainees find that they must say something to the client. They have to learn the different learning theory ideas and explain them. "You must be consistent and back each other up," they say, as if the client doesn't know that. Most therapist education of clients is about what they already know.

Family therapy offers much to talk about, and it is surpassing the popularity of the psychodynamic monologues. Everyone has been

in a family, and trainees see that one cannot only educate clients about families but they can turn family members upon each other. Then they will do all the talking. The problem can be to shut them up.

A more important challenge is directive therapy. What can a therapist talk about there? Actually the reason a therapist gives directives is not only so they will be followed and cause change, but so that there is something to talk about. The directive becomes the content of the therapeutic conversation. The therapist can discuss whether clients did as they were directed, how they did it, what they discovered from doing it, and so on. Therapists and clients need not talk about the past, or about dreams, or about any of that fantasy sort of thing. The directive and its consequences are present activities to talk about.

Let me cite a case by Milton Erickson that many of you have heard before. I repeat it because I like it, and it illustrates my point so well. A woman came to Erikson with her 50-year-old son who, she said, constantly hung on her and would never leave her alone. She couldn't even read a book because he kept bothering her. Erickson did not choose to explore their history together, or to educate them on how the son should not be so dependent upon her, or how he was helping her by being a problem. Instead he offered a directive. He told her to drive out into the desert with her son. Then she was to stop the car and push him out of it. She was stronger than he was. Then she was to drive the car one mile further out into the desert and park there. Then she should sit in the air-conditioned car and read her book. Her son would curse her and complain, but he would know that he had to walk to the car. "It's hot out there in the desert and he will walk," said Erickson. The woman liked this idea. The son did not, even though Erickson assured him that it would be good exercise for him. The woman did this trip several times and came to Erickson to report on its success. The son asked if they couldn't arrange some other form of exercise besides walking out in that hot desert. Erickson asked what he had in mind. He said, "How about bowling?" The son said that they could go to an air-conditioned bowling alley and his mother could sit in the stands and read her book while he bowled. Erickson agreed to that new plan.

What is evident is that Erickson used directives not only to achieve their ends but to have something productive to talk about. The dependency of the man on his mother, or their past history, did not have to be discussed. The focus was on achieving the goals of the therapy, not educating the person about his deficiencies.

CONCLUSIONS

As I think over the changes in therapy, some of them are puzzling. Clearly we cannot and need not explain everything about therapy. It should have its mysteries and leave room for strange cases and unexplainable therapy techniques, and for intuition. We can get so caught up in a particular method or in the content of the dialogue between therapist and client that we forget that it takes more than conversation to change people. Something else is required for change. That is where the mystery of therapy is hidden. I teach students that symptoms have a function, and dealing with that function is the most efficient way to change the client. However, I also point out that the function need not be a true one but one that guides the therapist to doing something. As trainees grasp the functional notions, I like to introduce some therapy cases where there was a symptom without a function yet the symptom was banished. In fact, I have seen changes when there was no education about anything and when the therapist did not know what the cause of the symptom might be. Because therapists gain power when they are trained, they must also be taught humility. One way is to discuss cases that have been successful despite the lack of any explanation for that success.

Once upon a time a man moved from New York to Philadelphia. He was a complex, important person, who had been through five years of analysis in New York without a change in his symptom. His symptom was odd—every time he went to the bathroom he had to masturbate. Obviously this happened a number of times a day. When he moved to Philadelphia he was referred to an analyst to continue his treatment. This analyst, let us call him A, was wor-

ried about taking this man on because he had already undergone excellent analytic treatment without change. Analyst A asked Analyst B if he would share the therapy in this case. Would he make it a co-therapy and see the patient for alternate sessions? Analyst B agreed. These were adventurous analysts to try such an arrangement. Analyst A interviewed the man again and the following week Analyst B interviewed him for the first time. When the man reported the symptom of masturbating each time he went to the toilet, Analyst B said to him. "Why don't you cut that out? Don't do it anymore." The client stopped that behavior and did not ever do it again.

Analyst A became angry with Analyst B. He said, "How could you do that? The man did not work through the problem." B said, "He had five years in analysis to work through the problem."

Which one was correct? Was the intervention correct? What caused the change in this mysterious case? How could teachers of therapy train therapists in this approach?

Each of us who represents a school of therapy insists there are certain functions or some method that must be followed if change is to take place. That is what most therapy supervisors teach. I think it is better to teach that a therapist should design a therapy for each case, but most students don't care for such complications.

Let me close with a curious case that is more extreme and that raises questions about the very essence of therapy.

When I was in practice a man came to me and said that he had a serious symptom and he would like me to cure him. However, he did not want to tell me what the symptom was. I pointed out that he was posing me quite a difficult problem. He said that he couldn't help it, he could never tell me what the symptom was, but he was desperate to get over it. I agreed to take him on, and I said that because he was posing me such a challenge he would have to cooperate fully in whatever I asked him to do. He agreed as long as it did not require revealing the symptom. I said I needed certain information. Was the symptom there all the time, or was it intermittent? He said it was intermittent. I asked if he knew quite clearly each time the symptom occurred. He said he certainly did know. I chatted with him about other aspects of his life, carefully not inquiring into the symptom. He was an intellectual young man, but rather lazy. He felt he was in good shape but needed more exercise, and he hated exercise. At the end of the interview I said I was ready to give him a task. Was he ready to receive it? Yes, he said. I told him that every time the symptom occurred (and he would have to determine that for himself), he would have to set his alarm for two in the morning and get up and do one hundred and fifty deep knee bends. He was then to go back to sleep. He wasn't to stay up to do the exercise, he was to go to sleep, wake up and do it, and go back to sleep. It should be like a nightmare in the middle of the night.

The man looked pale, but he said, "I'll do it."

I set an appointment for two days later, because I wanted to follow him rather closely. I did not know what I was tampering with and I was concerned about the ethics of changing an unknown problem. He came in and said that he was determinedly doing the task, which took him as long as an hour and a half. He found it upsetting, but he would continue it.

The next week he reported that the symptom was less frequent. I continued to see him irregularly, and apparently he continued to improve. A few weeks later he surprised me when he came in for an interview. He was cheerful and self-assertive, and he told me the symptom was gone. I congratulated him, and I believed him.

It is a case I like to recall when I become too intellectual with a client or too confident about what is necessary for therapy to succeed.

REFERENCES

Erickson, M.H. (1967). Experimental demonstrations of the psychopathology of everyday life. In J. Haley, *Advanced techniques of hypnosis and therapy*, New York: Grune and Stratton.

Freud, S. (1959). Heredity and the aetiology of the neuroses. In S. Freud, *Collected papers* (Vol. 1, pp. 148–150.) New York: Basic Books. (Original work published 1896.)

Freud, S. (1959). My views on the part played by sexuality in the aetiology of the neuroses. In S. Freud, *Collected papers* (Vol. 1, p. 276). New York: Basic Books. (Original work published 1905.)

Discussion by Mary McClure Goulding, M.S.W.

It is an honor to be on the same platform with Jay Haley. Jay, you've done so much for all of us with your emphasis on the family and on family systems. You taught the therapy world to look at the family system behind symptoms. You gave us something very new, after the stultifying years spent trying to be a pseudoanalyst, Freudian version. Your method of family therapy works for families and is extremely valuable.

I am a group and individual therapist, and I do cure individual clients without changing the family system. When one family member makes personal changes, other members may then change, with or without therapy, or the family system may remain untouched while the individual continues to grow.

Our major difference can be summed up in the title of Bob's and my book, *The Power Is in the Patient.* I want the client rather than the therapist to set treatment goals. I say, "What do you want to change about yourself today?" and work quickly with early or current memories to effect these changes. Our entire process differs from Haley's work.

As to what is and is not true in this life: At 5:02 P.M., October 12, 1989, an earthquake struck Watsonville, California. That is reality. The "true" story each of us tells about that earthquake will be unique and idiosyncratic.

We therapists work with such stories because they are the client's reality, whether or not they are real. Cure comes from the client rewriting personal stories and accepting the rewrites. We do not rewrite them. The client does. Clients see new aspects of their stories, look at their histories from different perspectives, and look at themselves differently. They also look differently at their world and their responsibility within it.

The monk story is one of my favorites because most people insist on carrying something that we should have put down long ago. "Yes, you lived in Dachau," or "Yes, you were an abused child," "But how long do you plan to carry that abuse before you are willing to put it down?" Most of my work with clients could be summed up as helping clients put down whatever loads they carry from their pasts.

From my point of view as a redecision therapist and transactional analyst, when father says to son, "Don't do that," and mother says, "You're always attacking him," and everyone ends up unhappy, that is a family game as originally described by Eric Berne. I believe that such games cause family distress and that each individual child learns (decides) his or her part in it. A child may decide from such parental interactions, "I am no good because I caused this quarrel," "My parents are nuts so I won't listen to them," "I better not do anything without checking with my father," "My mother loves me best when I'm bad," and so on.

Although family dysfunction causes great pain for all, I am appalled at the idea that dysfunctional communication causes the psychoses of childhood or adolescence. It may even be that extreme pathology in a child causes the noted dysfunction of the adults. It is unbelievably sad and terrible to be a parent of a very sick child, and these parents need comfort rather than cruel diagnoses. Remember that until recently all asthma was considered to be caused by the "over-possessiveness" of mothers. People are still taught to believe that their bad thoughts or actions caused their cancers. And that they can't lead happy, productive lives today, because somebody did a bad thing to them 30 years ago. The beliefs of therapists prolong the misery and pathology of patients.

Jay Haley and I work differently. Jay wrote that with his system, "You don't have to fool around with the past, with fantasies, with dreams." For me, that's the joy of therapy! I chose my method because I love fantasy and setting up dramas in which a client can imagine new endings. That's why I chose to be a redecision therapist.

Each of you therapists has made or will make your own choices about your work. I hope that your choice is a therapy that "sings to you." This book discusses many different methods and beliefs. Choose your favorites, the therapy that fits you, the therapy you most enjoy. It won't be "the truth" or "the best." It will be yours.

Shame: How to Bring a Sense of Right and Wrong into the Family

Cloé Madanes

Cloé Madanes

Cloé Madanes is Director of the Family Therapy Institute of Washington, DC. in Rockville, MD. She is the author of five books on family therapy and is renowned for her innovative directive approaches to psychotherapy and supervision.

INTRODUCTION

I think I can speak for all of us when I say that we are tired of the absence of a sense of right and wrong at every level of society. It's time for the return of shame. Shame is the emotion that helps us distinguish between right and wrong, that keeps us from harming one another, and that makes it possible to live in an organized group.

In our families and in society, shame is a strong weapon in restraining the abuse of power and the expression of violence. Yet there are various sides to shame. It can be experienced by victims instead of victimizers, and it can bring about compassionate deeds or lead to guilt and failure. Feelings of shame often conceal deep, hidden issues inside a family, an organization, or a nation.

Everyone has something to feel ashamed about. Some of life's dilemmas are unsolvable and always come together with a sense of shame. There are those who feel ashamed for expressing their anger and those who are ashamed of the fear or shyness that prevents them from doing so. Most of us are also ashamed of our desires, be they for food, alcohol, drugs, sex, or other pleasures. No one escapes a feeling of shame about relationships, anger, and desire.

SHAME IN MYTHS

Shame is at the basis of all negative emotions. When Adam and Eve ate of the tree of knowledge, they saw that they were naked and they experienced shame. This first negative emotion—shame—was associated with knowledge, which led to the expulsion from paradise. In the Greek tragedy, Oedipus is overwhelmed with shame and punishes himself, not for having sexual relations with his mother and killing his father, but for knowing that he had done so. In the origin of Buddhism, a sense of shame is implied when the young Prince Siddharta wanders away from the palace and discovers that there is poverty and suffering in the world.

The stories at the beginning of the Judeo-Christian and the Buddhist traditions take us from shame to the guilt associated with knowledge, to a sense of responsibility and compassion. The stories express the path that must be followed in dealing with wrongdoing: to experience the feeling of shame, to suffer appropriate guilt, to take responsibility for one's actions, and to do reparation to those who were harmed. Shame is the gut feeling; guilt is the sense of responsibility; repentance is the recognition of shame and guilt; reparation is the action to recover from shame and guilt.

ASPECTS OF SHAME

Shame is an instrument of justice, yet it can also lead us to despair and suicide. Shame can be experienced in relation to feeling unworthy, yet it can also be experienced in relation to having too much.

Depending on who experiences the shame, it can be an instrument of justice or of oppression. Everyone will agree that it's right for the criminal to feel shame. Yet too often, in certain crimes, it's the victim who feels the shame. The victim may feel violated, diminished, and somehow responsible for having brought about the victimization. When the victim is ashamed, shame has become an instrument of injustice and oppression.

A complication is that we often feel ashamed for others. When observing an injustice or an act of abuse, we feel shame for the abuser. The greater the sense of oneness with humanity, the stronger the sense of shame at what human beings are capable of doing. When we decide that an act is shameful, we decide

that it's shameful not only for us but for every human being.

The dilemma is further complicated because there seems to be three kinds of people in the world. There are the ones who always consider themselves to be right, like the religious fundamentalists who have a direct line to God; those who are always considered to be wrong, like the chronic patient in the mental hospital; and those who have doubts and are often uncertain about who is responsible for what. Most of us fall into this third category. Yet thinking in polarities will help us clarify who should feel shame and what to do about it.

All major religions share the belief that actions have consequences for which shame can and must be acknowledged. When evil is knowingly willed and done, the appropriate emotion is shame and the recognition of guilt leading to repentance and reparation. Without a strong sense of shame, there can be no guilt—and little cause for repentance. But shame and guilt are stigmatized words in our pop psychology culture. Many people see guilt as the root of many emotional problems (low self-esteem, marital problems, difficulties at work, and so on). In our feel-good society, who wants to espouse the value of uncomfortable emotions? Yet is it right for us, as therapists, to help people feel good when they do bad?

Guilt is a stigmatized word in our therapeutic culture. Psychoanalysts long ago mislabeled guilt as a disabling emotion. The fact that some people suffer from inappropriate feelings of guilt should not be used to dismiss the need for a realistic, educated conscience. Strict standards of morality are disqualified as "Jewish guilt" or "Catholic guilt." Yet the only characters we know with no sense of guilt are mass murderers. To eliminate a sense of shame and guilt from the culture is to run the risk of creating monsters.

THE TASKS OF THE FAMILY

How is shame linked to life in a family? Every family has to face and solve three basic kinds of problems: (1) the task of survival; (2) the task of maintaining the structure and normative order of the group; (3) the task of making possible for individual members a tolerable degree of personal fulfillment and happiness (Rajan, 1991).

Survival has to do with finding a place in society and making a living, with parents being able to provide for themselves and for their children. But survival is not enough for a family to exist as a social unit. A pattern of interactions must be maintained over time. There has to be an organizational hierarchy ensuring continuity. The first task has to do with *efficiency*.

The second task deals with the issue of *justice*. For parents to protect and nurture their children, for children to obey and respect their parents, has to do with justice in the family system.

But a family also has to provide self-fulfillment and happiness to its individual members. This may be called the problem of *happiness*—that is, whether the pursuit of individual happiness is possible within the context of the family. It is the issue of whether the family system provides the individual with outlets of gratification, social acceptance, and the recognition of the need to fulfill personal desires.

Every family has to come to terms with the three problems of efficiency, justice, and happiness. If a family succeeds in solving only one, there will be an imbalance leading to disintegration. No family can choose among the three, accepting only one and rejecting the others. But while an absolute choice is not a possibility, the pattern of the relationship between efficiency, justice, and happiness can be a matter of differential choice. Families—because of their own past histories and because of the influence of society and culture—confront the problems of efficiency, justice, and happiness in different ways and with different degrees of intensity and commitment. The three tasks are not perceived as having equal importance and urgency. How tasks are prioritized forms a pattern that structures the perceptions, emotions, and efforts of individual family members.

How the three tasks are prioritized in a particular family is an indication of the predominance of different age groups. In families with young parents or with a prevalence of adolescents or young adults, the themes that prevail are personal fulfillment and expression. The theme of vitality is emphasized through sport, music, and other youthful activities. The task that prevails is happiness. When the emphasis is on the adults of the family, the accent falls on productivity, foresight, and the ability to provide for unforeseen future contingencies. The task is efficiency. When the presence of elders carries weight and importance, the emphasis falls on themes of continuity with the past, tradition, and Justice. As therapists, if we are trying to bring more happiness into a family, we need to rely on the young; for security and efficiency we must rely on the adults; and for justice and continuity we must rely on the elders.

SHAME AND THE FAMILY

The attitudes, motivations, and efforts that are consistent with the family's belief system are held in check by feelings of shame and guilt elicited whenever an individual member fails to comply with the family's priorities. A violation in regard to any of the three tasks will bring on feelings of shame that will reorient the individual toward family goals. In this sense, there is a social coercion to fulfill the family's tasks and shame is the instrument of this coercion. Shame is the glue that holds the family together. Parents feel shame when they cannot support their children. Children are shamed when they do not obey or respect their parents. The whole family suffers from shame when interactions are contradictory to each individual's pursuit of happiness. Shame is inextricably linked with the very existence of the family. A moral sense does not originate within the individual; it arises within the family.

Yet shame can also cause the disintegration of the family. The father who feels shame for not being able to provide for his children may pull away and abandon them. Children may be shamed to the point that they run away from home. The shame of a spouse's sexual infidelity may lead to divorce. Some shame is necessary to hold the family together, yet too much shame destroys it.

APOLOGY

The expression of shame is the apology. A genuine apology admits responsibility and expresses sorrow, remorse, and repentance. It has the power to restore damaged relationships, be they on a small scale, within the family, or on a grand scale, between groups of people, even nations. The apology secures a common moral ground, whether between two people or within a nation. It is a statement that the harmony of the group is more important than the victory of an individual.

As the world becomes a global village, the recognition of shame and apologies are growing increasingly important on both national and international levels. They may become vital to peaceful resolution of conflicts. Within the last few years alone, former South African President J. P. de Klerk expressed "deep regret" that apartheid led to forced removals of people from their homes, restrictions on their freedom, and attacks on their dignity; Exxon apologized for the Valdez oil spill; Pope John Paul II "for abuses committed by Christian colonizers against Indian peoples"; former Japanese Prime Minister Morihiro Hosokawa for Japanese aggression before and during World War II; Russian President Boris Yeltsin for the massacre of 15,000 Polish army officers by Soviet forces during the same war; and the Southern Baptist Church for the abuses committed against African Americans throughout U.S. history.

The question remains whether these apologies mean anything. Do they express true regret? Is it possible for a whole people to repent for atrocities committed by their leaders? Is there any guarantee that the crimes would not be repeated? Does the apology actually trivialize the damage incurred by the wrongdoing?

On the other hand, what are the social and political consequences of not feeling shame and not apologizing? Marion Barry, convicted former crack addict, runs for mayor of Washington, D.C., and wins. Richard Nixon refused to show any shame after Watergate and was buried a hero. Do these events demoralize a nation?

What about our criminal justice system? Is there a place for shame in a system rooted in imposing punishment? More and more judges are proving that shame is effective. A Memphis, Tennessee, judge sometimes sentences thieves to probation with the condition that they permit their victims to come into the thieves' homes, in front of all the neighbors, and take something they want. Agencies that help people collect child support say that one of the most effective techniques available is for the wife to carry a sign outside her ex-husband's office denouncing him. The criminal justice system is in crisis and it may be that it will move toward the creative use of repentance and reparation rather than the customary use of jail time alone to punish criminals.

Apologies are becoming vital to peaceful resolution of conflicts at many different levels of society. But apologies are useful only if done right. There is a method for apologizing correctly, one in which individuals, groups, or nations become responsible for their actions and express their regrets in such a way that relationships can be restored.

The apology is a powerful message. It is not a sign of weakness; it requires empathy and the strength to admit fault. I discovered the healing power of the apology as a therapist working with family violence. I realized that so many people go through life feeling shame, humiliation, and hatred that could have been avoided with a genuine apology.

The apology must be an exchange of shame and power. Typically, the victim carries the shame while the offender has the power. In a successful apology, the offender feels the shame and power is transferred to the victim. A new way of looking at certain criminals is one in which the justice system collaborates with therapists, becoming responsible for eliciting feelings of shame, and consequently remorse and reparation, in the criminal.

CONSCIENCE

Most people would agree that evil acts, knowingly willed and done, should be followed by feelings of shame and guilt. Yet it is often those who commit the lesser evil who feel the stronger guilt. Even worse, those who never feel guilty often enlist the complicity in anti-social behavior of those who can truly repent.

The guiltless are usually great seducers, capable of lying, cheating, and corrupting in such a way that their victims are even grateful for the pain they are made to suffer. Every period in time and every society has had its examples. Caligula seems an out-of-fashion caricature of evil, but we forget that he was beautiful, intelligent, and charming. The twentieth century has many followers of Caligulas who do not fall behind in their contempt for others. The emperor Jean-Bedel Bokassa and president Idi Amin are two of those monsters. Dictators who oppress whole nations, torture, rob and murder, are acclaimed and admired, their followers oblivious to the terror.

For centuries sexual misconduct in the family was seen as off limits to outside judgment. Yet the social consequences of sexual abuse are higher than for most other types of crimes. One sex offender can have dozens of victims who will in turn become victimizers or whose shame may lead them to be victimized over and over again.

CLINICAL WORK

I have developed a successful method for the rehabilitation of the sexual criminal and the victim of incest (Madanes, 1990). In a project involving 72 juvenile sex offenders who were followed independently for at least two years after termination of therapy, there were only three repeat offenses. This is a success rate of 96 percent (Madanes, Keim, & Smelser, 1995).

These results are particularly interesting in light of the fact that more than 50 percent of the offenders suffered from poverty, family violence, substance abuse by themselves or other family members, learning disabilities, and serious health problems. Also, the results are interesting considering that during the initial assessment, 73 percent of the offenders refused to take responsibility for their offenses, and 83 percent showed no signs of remorse for their crimes. All the victims who were blood-related children participated in the therapy. None of these children became sex offenders and all of them were integrated with their families.

The method of therapy consists of a series of steps that I will summarize briefly. The method varies slightly depending on whether or not the victim is part of the family. For the sake of brevity I will present the steps in relation to a situation where the victim is a younger sibling of the offender and is present in the sessions.

First, the therapist gathers the family and asks each one what they know about the sexual crime. The therapist questions the offender and the adults in the family, pointing out that the offender's actions were solely his responsibility. Neither the victim nor anyone else is to blame.

Then the therapist asks the parents and the offender why what he did was wrong, and discusses the various reasons that they bring up. After everyone has spoken, the therapist explains that the sexual crime caused a spiritual pain in the victim. Sexuality and spirituality are related in human beings, so a sexual attack is an attack on the spirit of the person. This is what makes it specially painful and a different kind of pain.

Then the therapist acknowledges the spiritual pain of the offender for having inflicted this pain on another human being, and the pain of every family member because of the hurt inflicted on the child. The offender is asked to get on the floor on his knees in front of the victim and express his sorrow and repentance for what he did. The family and the therapist must judge that he is sincere. If he is hypocritical, he must do it over and over again until everyone decides that he is sincere. The next step is to ask the whole family to kneel in front of the victim and for each to express their sorrow for not having protected the victim and prevented the abuse.

In subsequent sessions, the adults discuss future consequences should the offender commit another sexual crime and agree on the harshest punishment. They agree on what acts of reparation toward the victim will be required from the offender. The therapist enlists from the extended family a protector who will be a sort of godparent, making sure that the victim is not hurt again. The therapist discusses sexuality with the offender, encouraging repression and establishing certain steps for the offender to follow should the wrong sexual impulse arise.

With the victim, the therapist encourages the perspective that the victimization, although traumatic, will not be the major event in her life, that it has not transformed her into a different kind of person. This establishes that the offender, not the child, should carry the shame.

The essential aspects of the method are to make sure that the juvenile takes full responsibility for his crime, that he understands the spiritual pain that he inflicted, that he is truly repentant, that he apologizes in public, and that he does reparation. It is essential for the offender to feel shame, admit his crime, and apologize to the victim, which means literally getting down on his knees. Sexuality is identified with the soul of a person and a sexual injury is consequently a spiritual attack. The offender must show that he understands the spiritual pain that he caused and must humble himself in the apology.

CASE EXAMPLE

I will give you an example. Paul, a pastor, and his wife, Mary, had been foster parents for many years. Despite their wish to have their own children, Mary could not become pregnant. Therefore, eventually they adopted Bill. Bill had been removed from his mother, who was a drug addict and a prostitute, when he was 18 months old. He had lived with a foster mother to whom he became very attached and whom he could still remember when he was 16 years old. When he was about three and a half, he was adopted by the pastor and his wife. At that time, his biological mother's parental rights were finally terminated. Two years later, a little girl was born to Paul and Mary.

When Bill was 14 years old, a cousin on Mary's side of the family, a four-year-old boy, revealed to his mother that he had been sexually abused by Bill for about a year. The abuse had occurred during family vacations when the four-year-old would visit Paul and Mary and stay with them for one or two weeks. The abuse consisted of oral and anal sexual acts performed by Bill on the little boy.

Paul and Mary were shocked. They never had suspected that Bill could be capable of such acts. They consulted a private counselor, and Bill was in individual therapy for a year, but there was no family therapy. During this time, Paul was concerned because Bill continued to be upset and appeared withdrawn and isolated. Finally, one evening he went into his son's room and said, "I know that you have done this to another child."

He really didn't know that, but he felt that more had to be disclosed. Bill then revealed that he had also molested his parents' best friends' child, another four-year-old boy with whom the family would frequently visit. This family was part of the congregation that Paul and Mary ministered to. Bill said that he had stopped this abuse when the other abuse was discovered.

With this revelation, Paul realized that he had to call the police again. After the first case of abuse, the court had allowed him to seek private counseling for Bill, so the abuse had been kept secret within the family. Now the parents of this child had to be notified and they insisted that the abuse should be revealed to the whole congregation. This was done immediately.

When Bill and his family were referred to our program by the court, our therapist, Dinah Smelser, had to deal not only with the abuse of the two young children but also with the fact that the congregation was up in arms because the first abuse had not been revealed to them a year earlier.

Bill is a gifted musician who was the church's organist and pianist. He had been working in Sunday school, and the congregation felt that he could have abused other children. They were furious at the pastor and his wife for not alerting them after the first abuse was discovered. Paul and Mary had not revealed the first abuse because they believed that they had Bill under strict supervision, and they didn't think he would molest another child.

So in this case, the therapist had to plan apologies not only to the two victims and their families but also to the whole congregation. Three months after the initiation of therapy with Dinah, a congregational meeting was called. It was a process nomination because the parishioners believed that there should be an open forum for people's concerns. The pastor would probably lose his position if this meeting were not handled correctly.

By the time the meeting was called, Bill and his parents had already apologized to the cousin's family for the first abuse. Bill was extremely remorseful, which is very common with sex offenders, particularly juveniles, as soon as they understand the spiritual pain they caused in their victims. He said that he had not disclosed the second abuse for fear that his parents would break down. Mary had, in fact, almost collapsed physically and emotionally when the first abuse was discovered, and as a consequence of this initial abuse she had been ostracized by her family.

The estrangement between Mary and her family had been going on for a year by the time the family therapy with Dinah began. Therefore, Bill felt that his mother would go absolutely crazy if she learned of another abuse. He said that was why he had kept the secret, even though he had stopped the abuse of the second child when the first abuse was discovered. The second child's family did not believe this, however, and thought that the abuse had continued until Bill had confessed to his father. Bill was very remorseful and apologized most sincerely to his parents and to his little sister for the pain he had caused them.

When the therapy was beginning to focus on the step of reparation, the father told Dinah about the congregational meeting that was being planned to expel him. He had asked for a leave of absence for six weeks because there was so much anger directed at him that he felt he couldn't do his ministerial work. Another minister had come in to take on his duties.

In discussing the congregational meeting in therapy, the parents said that they would be present to answer to the congregation. Bill insisted that he also wanted to be present and to publicly apologize to everyone for the pain he had caused them.

The congregational meeting went on for three hours, during which everyone who had concerns was allowed to speak. Bill and his parents listened. The second victim's father was there, and at the end of the meeting he stood up and directly accused Bill of not being remorseful, of not being sorry for what he had done. Dinah had not been able to arrange an apology session with this victim's family because of orders for no contact from the court. So the victim's father had never heard what Bill had to say.

Dinah had prepared Bill, helping him express what he wanted to say. He had carefully written it down. This was a very emotional situation for him, and he wanted to be careful about how he expressed himself.

He stood up in front of 100 people and poured out his heart directly to the victim's father, expressing his sorrow for all the pain he had caused the child and the family, and his sorrow to the congregation, who had always been loving and accepting of him. Bill's words were deeply moving to most of the people present, yet it was decided that the congregation would have to take a vote of confidence in the minister and decide whether they wanted him to continue. It took a year for that vote of confidence to take place, for the healing to occur in that congregation, even though Paul had been a minister in the church for 15 years. Until the father was accepted back as minister to the congregation, Bill did not return to the church.

After two years of therapy, Dinah obtained permission from the court to have an apology session with the second child who was molested and his family. They were only ready to listen to Bill after he had written several letters to the parents and to the child expressing his remorse. Both victims' parents did not want Bill to do reparation to their children, so he decided to work on Saturdays for a computer company and to donate the money from this job to sponsor a child through the Save the Children Foundation of the United Nations.

The method of working with juvenile sex offenders can be adapted to situations where the victim is outside the family, to adult offenders such as fathers, and to sexual crimes that happened a long time ago in families where the victims were silenced.

These ideas can be applied to the prevention of social violence on a larger scale. Given the mounting antigovernment feeling prevailing in the country, it's conceivable that had

Attorney General Janet Reno apologized publicly for mistakes the government made handling the tragedy at the Branch Davidian compound in Waco, Texas, where many people died during an FBI raid in 1993, deranged militiamen seeking revenge might not have attacked the federal building in Oklahoma City in April 1995.

For an expression of shame and an apology to be effective, they have to be public. Feeling ashamed in the privacy of one's room does nothing to restore family relationships, nor does apologizing in private to the offended. The remorse and the apology must be expressed in public. In cases of family misconduct, public means in the presence of the whole family. For political misconduct, this means in front of large social groups or the whole nation.

SHAME AND POWER

Yet expressing shame and apologizing are not enough to do away with resentment and vengeance. There must be an exchange of shame and power, with the offended transferring their shame to the offenders, and the offenders restoring power to the offended.

I will give you three examples—two where this exchange took place successfully in the context of the family, and one of a failed attempt in the larger social context.

EXAMPLE ONE

Amy said she had a problem of violence in her marriage and had recently moved in with her mother and stepfather. She came to the first session alone with her three-month-old baby—a beautiful young woman with long, straight, blonde hair and a look of devotion for her baby, whom she nursed almost continuously. She said there had been tension in the marriage because her husband, Jacques, was physically abusive of her. She said it wasn't very bad; he just punched her in the arm or slapped her on the face. I decided to invite the whole family to the next session.

Present at the second session were Jacques and Amy, her mother and stepfather, her father and stepmother, two brothers and a sister. I asked each person in the family to tell me everything they knew about the violence, and, as the mother and stepmother talked, I realized that it was much more serious than what Amy had described. The mother had taken Amy to the hospital for loss of hearing in one ear as a consequence of being hit on the head. Jacques had locked her up in their apartment on numerous occasions and hit her for hours at a time. The brothers and sister and the father were shocked and furious to hear all this.

I turned to Jacques, who sat very formally dressed in a suit, lovingly holding the baby on his lap, tall, gaunt, and dark—totally in contrast to Amy, who sat beside him. He said he missed his wife and his baby and wanted them to come home. I asked him why his violence was wrong. With a heavy accent and great difficulty, he answered that violence is bad, it hurts, but I should understand that Amy had a terrible personality and provoked him to violence.

I explained how provocation was not an excuse and asked the family to support my view. We went around the circle again, and once more I asked Jacques why his violence was wrong. He said he had had meningitis as a child and believed that, as a consequence, he had some brain damage that caused him to lose control. The stepfather supported this view, saying that perhaps Jacques should be on medication. I asked Jacques how many people he had beaten up. He said he had never hit anyone.

I asked again if he had hit a former girlfriend, perhaps someone at work, or someone in his family. He said he had never been violent with anyone except Amy. I said that was very interesting. I had never heard of brain damage that is specific to abusing your wife and your wife alone. Everyone saw my point and agreed that the violence could not be the result of a neurological problem.

So I asked him once more why it was wrong to hit his wife. He said it was wrong because he loved her and she was the mother of his child, but she did provoke him. I explained the spiritual pain that his abuse had caused in Amy: to be attacked by her husband whom she loved and trusted, the father of her child; to be nursing the baby to whom her chemical reaction of fear was being transmitted; to be not just hit but tortured systematically for long periods of time. Jacques said he understood.

So I asked him to get on his knees in front of Amy and express his sorrow and repentance for having abused her. He said he wanted to apologize, but he wouldn't get on his knees.

I asked the family's help and one by one they talked to him. The brothers said they wanted to kill him. The father talked about his own pain at being betrayed by Jacques whom he had trusted and helped. Several times Jacques turned to Amy and said that he was sorry. He cried so much that one could see the tears falling on the carpet, but he did not get on his knees.

After more than half an hour like this, I asked the women to leave the room. I said that wife abuse is a problem of men, and I wanted the men in the family to talk to Jacques. We went around the circle again, and the men talked about taking responsibility for one's actions, about not thinking of a woman as property, about the love for one's child. The brothers, who were big and strong, explained what they did to control their temper. It was to no avail. Jacques wouldn't get on his knees. I asked the men what they would do if Jacques ever hit Amy again, and they said they would report him to the police and he would be immediately deported.

Finally, I ended the session. Jacques had not apologized appropriately. The next week, however, without further pressure, Jacques got on his knees and apologized. He cried profusely and expressed his sorrow and repentance sincerely, to the family's satisfaction. He promised he would never hit Amy again. He wanted her to come home.

I felt that after the apology in front of the family, plus the threat of the brothers' violence and the threat of deportation, Jacques would not hit Amy again. But the family thought differently. They didn't want Amy to go back to the home she shared with Jacques. I respected their view. It was decided that the brothers would be Amy's special protectors. Another month went by before Amy and the baby went back to the apartment with Jacques. The therapy continued for more than a year.

Betrayal of trust in a marriage can be direct as in violence, or indirect as when a spouse sides with a parent against the other spouse. A spouse who feels lonely and unappreciated will eventually feel ashamed—not worthy of love. In extreme situations, symptoms will develop that are self-destructive: physical illness, severe depression, suicidal thoughts.

EXAMPLE TWO

Jill and Harry came to see me because Harry was depressed, and he certainly appeared sad. He spoke little, seemed to lack energy, and looked dejected—his big, dark, droopy moustache gave him a somber look. Pretty soon, however, I discovered that Jill was even more depressed than Harry. She had suffered from postpartum depression after the birth of each of their children.

Jill felt that the responsibility for the whole family was on her shoulders and that Harry didn't help or support her. She had good reason to feel that way. After failing in several businesses, Harry was unable to continue to pay their home mortgage, so the bank foreclosed on their house. Jill had to negotiate with the bank to keep their home by herself, because each time there was a meeting, Harry disappeared. He had been unavailable to Jill in many other difficult situations. His avoidance was so extreme that when Jill had given birth to their first child, he was visiting his mother instead of being with her at the hospital.

Jill felt deeply shamed and thought that Harry's mother was a big part of the problem. He was very close to her and had been working for her until recently, when his parents moved to California. Jill felt that Harry always preferred his mother to her. Even before they were married, Harry had led his mother to believe that they had to get married because Jill had become pregnant instead of explaining the truth, which was that they had planned together to first get pregnant and then get married. In spite of all these difficulties, Jill and Harry wanted to stay together, but they didn't know how to overcome their old resentments and how to change their relationship.

Looking at Harry, I realized that when he married Jill, he had made a choice between two women he loved: his mother and his wife. He had chosen his wife, married her, and had children with her. But he never completed the actions that are necessary to convey to everyone that the choice had been made. He needed now to carry out some action so he would know and feel that he had actually made that choice, and so that his wife would know and feel that he had chosen her.

It was clear to me that the issue for this couple was justice. Jill was being treated unfairly. When justice is the problem, one must look to the elders of the family to correct it—in this case, to Harry's mother.

I looked at Harry in the second session and said: "I have a phone here and I'd like you to get on this phone, right now, while we sit here together. I'd like you to let your mother know that Jill is your wife, that she comes first, that she is a good mother, and she is the first priority for you, and that you hold her dear. In your own words I'd like you to do this right now."

There was a pause and then Harry said that he didn't know his mother's phone number in California.

I suggested he call information or a friend, and after a few minutes we had the number. The first thing Harry said to her was: "Sit down, mom, I need to talk to you." Then he proceeded to explain that he loved his wife even though he had failed her many times, that he had truly wanted to marry her and to have a child with her, and that Jill's postpartum depressions wouldn't have been so serious if he had been more supportive. He said that he alone was totally responsible for all the problems of the marriage and that now he was going to change.

This session was the turning point for Jill and Harry's marriage. Finally the cloud of shame hanging over Jill because of Harry's conflicting loyalties had been lifted.

On a small scale, a confusion of loyalty can destroy a family. Harry's family was almost destroyed because his first loyalty was to his mother, not to his wife. On a grander scale, between groups of people and in international relations, a confusion of loyalty can cause great

damage. When the harmony of a whole group is sacrificed in favor of loyalty to an individual, moral ground is lost and the ensuing demoralization may take years to heal. The problems of loyalty in the government of a nation are not so different from the problems of loyalty in a family.

EXAMPLE THREE

During the Kennedy and Johnson years, Secretary of Defense Robert S. McNamara was in charge of managing America's expanding involvement in Vietnam. In his memoir, *In Retrospect: The Tragedy and Lessons of Vietnam*, he concedes his errors and recognizes that although he had known early on that the war was not winnable, he had refused to act on this knowledge. He doesn't give dates but some believe that he knew as early as 1965, even though he continued proposals for escalation until 1967. He put loyalty to his president above what he had come to see as the unpleasant truth, and he didn't realize that the conflict was about his loyalty to the people of the United States versus his loyalty to the president. He finally left office in 1968, declining to express his doubts publicly.

McNamara's loyalty appears admirable, except that it was to the wrong cause. He wasn't loyal to the truth or to the nation. Loyalty to the Constitution would have entailed confronting the president with the truth he didn't want to hear. Even as he concedes his errors, he still misses the moral point. His greatest shame is in not having acknowledged the suffering his decisions inflicted on hundreds of thousands of human beings.

One might think that Vietnam went wrong because of a whole generation of policy makers, yet McNamara was indeed individually responsible because he could have changed the course of events. He could have stood up for the truth. Responsibility always must be taken individually, and he failed to do so, by his own admission, because of a warped sense of loyalty. This is true for all the policy makers involved in Vietnam. Had any of them taken responsibility to recognize their mistakes and say the truth publicly, great tragedy and the demoralization of the nation might have been avoided. With the sacrifice of so many lives, our sense of justice was shaken. Had our leaders expressed remorse, perhaps a common moral ground could have restored a sense of justice for all of us.

Just like juvenile sex offenders and abusive husbands, political leaders need to express their regrets in such a way that healing can take place and relationships can be restored. On our small planet we are all in the same boat. Relationships between nations and between ethnic groups cannot be destroyed any more than family relationships can be ter-minated. As therapists we know that family ties cannot be broken, and that the connection between offender and victim must be rebuilt, not eliminated. The same applies to all levels of society—terminal separation is impossible.

REFERENCES

Madanes, C. (1990). *Sex, Love, and Violence*. N.Y.: Norton.
Madanes, C., Keim, J., & Smelser, D. (1995). *The Violence of Men*. San Francisco: Jossey-Bass.
Rajan, R.S. (1991). *The Privacy of the Political*. N.Y.: Oxford University Press.

Discussion by James F. T. Bugental, Ph.D.

◆

At one point in her chapter, Cloé Madanes asked, "Is it right for us, as therapists, to help people feel good when they do bad?"

She poses an exceedingly tough question, a question that psychotherapy and psychotherapists have seldom chosen to address. Yet most of us have at times, I imagine, paused to consider at least momentarily the issue implicit in this query. Indeed, speaking personally, I have sometimes recognized that the resistance that needed to be addressed was how the client dodged guilt or shame. When that occurred, I felt inept and unwilling to adopt what might seem a moralistic stance.

But there were the other times, the times when other intrapsychic stresses claimed more attention. Later I might realize that issues of shame and guilt for hurt done others or for failures of social responsibility never received direct attention.

Should they have had such direct attention? Am I . . . Is our profession . . . guilty? Should *we* feel shame?

As I read Madanes, I think that her answer is an implicit "yes." And I think she feels that as a profession and as a society we have become too heedless of moral and ethical issues. I agree.

Yet I do not agree with all that Madanes has said; therefore let me sketch my chief difficulty with the view she has presented. By doing so, I hope to distinguish our two positions so that further discussion can be more focused.

My main problem is the lack of an adequate definition of *shame* and, accordingly, with the lavishing of that term on such a wide range of experiences as to make it hard to follow her logic. It seems that she most frequently uses "shame" as a name for the emotional experience of feeling oneself to be bad or wrong. Yet if we assume that, we are confronted with such statements as the following:

In our families and in society, shame is a secret weapon restraining the abuse of power and the expression of violence.

Everyone has something to be ashamed about.

Some of life's dilemmas are unsolvable and always come together with a sense of shame.

Most of us are also ashamed of our desires, be they for food, alcohol, drugs, sex, or other pleasures.

I suggest that distinctions need to be made among some of the implied meanings for the concept of shame. Social attitudes, guilt for deception and trickery, embarrassment before others, unease with one's own actions, feelings of disloyalty to important others, and probably other meanings can be discerned. Here is a way of thinking about shame that I find useful:

Shame is a subjective response when one (or someone with whom one is closely identified) is discovered to be or to have been morally, ethically, or socially wrong or offensive. It is experienced as acute discomfort at being so seen by others and often, implicitly, by one's self. It is "face work" and has much to do with one's image to others and to one's self.

Shame may be associated with guilt, but that is not always the case. Shame may be occasioned by actual misdeeds, by spoken words, or by private experiences in which the "others" are projected rather than actual.

The contrast in definitions is apparent, and the parting of our ways is sharp. In Ms. Madanes's third sentence she says, "Shame is the emotion that helps us distinguish between right and wrong."

In my clinical experience the self- or other-judgment that one is "wrong" triggers the experience of shame, rather than the reverse as she posits. Our prior values about what is right and what is wrong are the preconditions for the shame experience.

A related issue is her remarkable use of humiliation in having offenders literally go down onto their knees to apologize to their victims. Whether such apologies would lead to reform and restitution or to fury and revenge is an open question.

However, a success rate of 96 percent has no precedent in our field.

I am not a family therapist, but I do want to call attention to what seems to me to be an ingenious and very productive schema that Madanes offers for thinking about the three ages of the family—young, adult, and elder—and the issues typical of each.

"Every family," she says, "has to come to terms with the three problems of efficiency, justice, and happiness." She goes on to say that the *young* family focuses on *happiness* through sports, music, and youthful activities. Next she sees the *adult* family focusing on *efficiency*, emphasizing productivity and foresight, and providing for unforeseen contingencies. Finally, an *elder*-centered family will focus on *justice*, maintaining continuity with the past and tradition.

She then comments that "the attitudes, motivations and efforts that are consistent with the family's belief system are held in check by feelings of shame and guilt elicited whenever an individual member fails to comply with the family's priorities."

This is a confusing statement. It is unclear whether all in the family carry this shame or how it comes to be shared and acted upon to accomplish this "holding in check." It is difficult to attain a clear understanding of what is meant by shame in this context when it is contrasted with her earlier statement that "feelings of shame often conceal deep, hidden issues inside a family. . . ."

I have been critical about this wide ranging use of the concept of shame, I know. My intent is to support and advance the effort to call on our professions to give greater attention to the societal implications of our work.

Now I want to return our attention to that question of Ms. Madanes that I quoted earlier, "Is it right for us, as therapists, to help people feel good when they do bad?"

My own answer is: No, it is not right to help people feel good about doing bad, but it is not our job to make them feel bad about doing so either.

What is our job, then? The answer is that we must work in back of particular feelings and help the client recover or attain a sense of communal identity and responsibility. For too long, psychotherapy has worked with clients as though they existed in isolation. Ultimately that has been neither good therapy nor good psychology. Human beings are in their deepest nature related to all other human beings, and any thorough-going therapy experience must help the client to recognize and act with respect towards that part of her or his nature.

Refining our understanding of such concepts as shame, guilt, blame, and regret is an important step. We have tended to avoid such matters. They smack of the religionists and self-righteous moralists who have so often burdened our clients with destructive feelings. Moreover, the issues are so subjective that we recognize that our own projections heavily influence our views, and that we find ourselves uncomfortable.

At another point Madanes asks, "Should we encourage shame for an extramarital affair? For tax evasion? For not paying child support?" Well, we say, "It all depends." But it depends not only on the circumstances in which each of these "misdeeds"—to give them a somewhat cautious title—occurs; it also depends on who is making the judgment. That's the inescapable subjective part.

I do not have a solution for this situation. Indeed, I would be suspicious of anyone who proposed one out of hand. Yet I feel we need to be addressing these issues much more than we have to this time.

Ms. Madanes opened her address by saying, "I think I can speak for all of us when I say that we are tired of the absence of a sense of right and wrong at every level of society." Indeed, she can speak for me in that statement. The absence of a moral or ethical sense in our culture as a whole is not only a disgrace, but it is a part of the decay of our society. The psychotherapeutic disciplines must take their share of responsibility for bringing this state of affairs into being and must address the problem in fresh ways.

And I salute Cloé Madanes for beginning to bring it before us.

Response by Cloé Madanes

◆

I agree with the difficulty in defining shame. Sometimes people feel an unappreciated emotion of shame and it's not focused; it's a vague feeling. If shame is then followed by guilt, which has to do with taking responsibility, then the unappreciated feeling of shame turns into repentance, which is a focused shame. That's what a therapist has to do: Move the person from the unappreciated sense of shame to a sense of guilt that needs responsibility and then to repentance. People don't change in one step; they go from one bad emotion to one that's a little less bad, and so on.

Also, the step of apologizing on the knees for the sex offenders is one of 15 steps in a long, complicated therapy.

The Leap to Complexity: Supervision in Family Therapy

Salvador Minuchin, M.D.

Salvador Minuchin, M.D.

Salvador Minuchin received his M.D. degree from the University of Cordoba in Argentina in 1947. For ten years, he served as Director of the Philadelphia Child Guidance Clinic. Currently, he is Clinical Professor of Child Psychiatry at the University of Pennsylvania School of Medicine and Research Professor of Psychiatry at New York University.

Dr. Minuchin developed the structural approach to family therapy. He has authored or coauthored seven books. A recipient of the Distinguished Family Therapy Award of the American Association for Marriage and Family Therapy, Minuchin also received the Distinguished Achievement in Family Therapy Award from the American Family Therapy Association.

INTRODUCTION

Contrary to the mythmakers, family theory and therapy did not spring forth, full blown, from the head of Bateson. A number of serious theoretical challenges had made cracks in the monolithic edifice of Freudian psychoanalysis during the 1940s and 1950s. Many of these attacks anticipated the revolution systemic thinking brought to therapy.

EARLY CHALLENGES TO FREUD

I want to focus on two of these challenges to Freud. The first was brought forth by Harry

Stack Sullivan, in his interpersonal focus in psychoanalysis. In Freudian orthodoxy, the analyst, a nonparticipant, a mirror, is supposed to reflect the individual patient's transferential fantasies. She views her countertransference responses as problematic. She is supposed to control them, and be wary of imposing her own intrapsychic fantasies on the patient's intrapsychic processes.

Sullivan moved the focus to the interpersonal relationship between therapist and patient. The Sullivanian psychoanalyst focuses on in-session events in the social field of patient and therapist. Transference and countertransference phenomena are both significant parts of the process. The therapist's responses to the patient are seen as a tool for understanding both patient and analyst.

Much of the material in this chapter is to appear, in different form, in a book whose working title is "Mastering Family Therapy."

Similarly, in the cultural school of psycho-analysis, Eric Erikson, Abraham Kardiner, and Karen Horney emphasized the influence of the social context. Including the context in their understanding of personal responses shook up the narrow concept of the isolated individual.

The second challenge I want to address is the work of Milton Erickson. He carried an optimistic view of the unconscious. To him it was a kind of black box, full of resources that could become accessible to the patient. The therapist paid attention to the here and now, and the small details of the encounter between himself and the patient, to design strategic maneuvers to change the patient's ways. He used his authority and his understanding of the patient to heal her. She needed to trust that the therapist's impositions of new ways was directed by his concern for her.

As you see, both of these challenges to Freud-ianism focus on the way the therapist and his task in the therapeutic process are conceptu-alized.

PIONEERS IN FAMILY THERAPY

It is not happenstance that three of family therapy's pioneers sprang from these new perspectives.

Don Jackson, a psychoanalyst of the Wash-ington school, expanded Sullivan's thinking to produce what I think may be the first paper on the theory of the family that is consistent with interpersonal theory, even though he still focused on the individual patient. The work of another family therapy pioneer, Nathan Ack-erman, came from the Columbia psychoana-lytic school but was also influenced by the sociological perspective of Marie Jahoda, with whom he wrote a book on anti-Semitism. Ack-erman still had no coherent theory about fami-lies; his clinical work preceded those concep-tualizations.

Jay Haley, one of the members of Bateson's research team on the double bind, was heavily influenced by Milton Erickson. Even though Erickson was essentially working with indi-viduals, Jay, in his *Uncommon Therapy* (Haley, 1986), organized Erickson's strategies in a way

that highlighted Erickson's concern for the family.

From the beginning, then, family therapy was sharply divided on the function of the therapist. As I see it, this concern coalesced around three foci, which I will call the inter-ventive, the minimalist, and the self-restrained.

THE FUNCTION OF THE THERAPIST

THE INTERVENTIVE APPROACH

Many of the family therapy pioneers devel-oped a practice that included the therapist as a full participant. Without using the term "coun-tertransference," we incorporated the concept by simply accepting the therapist's response to the family as an essential and necessary part of the process. Of major importance in this direction was the work of Carl Whitaker, who in his early book with Malone, *The Roots of Psychotherapy* (Whitaker & Malone, 1980), had shown the participation and experience of the therapist to be the most important phe-nomenon of the process. In one of his epigram-matic shortcuts, Carl said, "I would never take a patient in therapy who could not change me."

Virginia Satir was also in this group, with her extremely proximal style and her empha-sis on creating positive experience. So was I. I was trained as an analyst at the William Alan-son White school of psychoanalysis and was strongly influenced by the work of Harry Stack Sullivan. From the beginning I recognized the therapist's participation, from the enactment of family conflicts to the search for novelty.

While different in many ways, this group today is represented by many others—by the work of Aponte, with his emphasis on spiritu-ality, by Andolfi in Italy, who focuses on provo-cation, and by Alan Cooklin and Gil Gorrell Barnes in Britain, who focus on children.

THE MINIMALISTS

The second group, the minimalists, includes Haley, Weakland, and Watzlawick. Watzlawick followed Bateson thinking directly, develop-ing a strategic approach that later evolved into the minimalist brief therapy of the MRI, which in its turn influenced the deShazer solution approach.

The strategic school of Jay Haley and Cloé Madanes is in this tradition, though later they were influenced by the structural approach.

THE RESTRAINED

The third group, the restrained, starts with Bateson. I want to read you the metalogue he wrote for his daughter (Bateson, 1972).

Daughter: Daddy, why do things get in a muddle?

Father: What do you mean? Things? Muddle?

Daughter: Well, people spend a lot of time tidying things, but they never seem to spend time muddling them. Things just seem to get in a muddle by themselves. And then people have to tidy them up again.

Father: But do your things get in a muddle if you don't touch them?

Daughter: No—not if nobody touches them. But if you touch them—or if anybody touches them—they get in a muddle and it's a worse muddle if it isn't me.

Father: Yes—that's why I try to keep you from touching the things on my desk. Because my things get in a worse muddle if they are touched by somebody who isn't me.

Daughter: But do people always muddle other people's things? Why do they, Daddy?

Bateson's wariness of imposing the therapist and his fantasies on the patient is strikingly reminiscent of Freud's. Of course, Bateson's concern had other roots, probably the anthropologist's aversion to tinkering with a culture, knowing that one cannot predict the direction of change. But be that as it may, Bateson introduced the conservative focus of orthodox Freudianism—the therapist's neutral, reflective stance—into family therapy. This posed an instant conundrum for the restrained family therapist. How could the influence of the therapist in the session be controlled?

For the psychoanalyst, the tool for developing a self-awareness that served to control countertransferential responses was the training analysis. This could not serve the family therapist. So the field had no solution other than to create external controls on the therapist's interventions. In this, the most ingenious group was the Milan school. They changed the "I" of the therapist to the "we" of the team. An observing team controlled the therapist in the session. Circular questions replaced interpretations and directions. Sessions were held only once a month, and finished with a prescription that included a positively connoted understanding of each family member, so that in its totality the prescription was neutral. The goal of these maneuvers was to ensure the objectivity of the therapist and to activate a process that occurred in family members away from the session and the therapist's influence. The therapists saw themselves as objective interveners, at a distance, tossing psychological pebbles that would create ripples in the family.

Maintaining this separation between therapists and patients in the face of feedback from clinical practice required continuous infusions of theory. I think that is why the restrained schools of therapy so fervently embraced the ideas of a biologist. Maturana argued that organisms respond only to their internal biological stimulation. Thus there is no possibility of instructive interaction. The result, strangely resembling the Freudian focus on the isolated intrapsyche, called for a therapy of distant entities.

When vanFoerster, with his second order cybernetics, showed that no therapist can be objective, or an observer for that matter, because he or she is always part of the system, the field had the opportunity to recapture the essence of systemic therapy. But the result was an increasing politically correct separation between therapist and patient.

A number of technical innovations sprang up to maintain this theoretical separation. These included:

The reflective team of Thom Anderson, in which a change in the direction of light makes the family an observer of the therapists' conversations about their process.

The change of name from therapy to conversation, by which Goolishian and Anderson attempted to level the hierarchies of the therapeutic field.

The position of "not knowing" adopted by Lynn Hoffman and Carol Anderson.

The abandonment of norms in favor of cultural diversity. And so on.

Embracing the work of the French philosopher Foucault, with his sociology of liberation, the Australian family therapists Michael White and David Epston developed a therapy in which patients are encouraged to search for moments of successful challenge to the oppression of the symptom. They have articulated the most coherent theory of the postmodernist group and derived a therapeutic approach based on a complex set of questions that is clearly teachable.

These therapeutic approaches, which are loosely labeled postmodernist or constructivist, have a theoretical appeal given their connections with significant sociological and philosophical theories. But they are reductionist. They have moved family therapy to a solely cognitive orientation, frequently focusing on individuals in the family and excluding their interactions.

CLINICAL EXAMPLE

How does a therapist match the complexity of a family with sensitivity to the nuances of family members' transactions? Searching for an answer, I look back at my professional life. I started as a child psychiatrist, and was trained as a group therapist and an analyst before I became a family therapist. I consider myself a competent and for the most part a successful family therapist, and I have enough anecdotal and research data to substantiate that claim. How do I transform my own experience into a teaching tool that shapes effective therapists

who are self-aware and know how to use themselves in the therapeutic process? I will try to illustrate by summarizing a two-day consultation with a South American family. I will then describe to you what I thought about while I was doing the consultation. Then I will describe the way I use these concepts to help my supervisees to become more effective and complex therapists, and more like themselves.

The Ramos family was in therapy because of Mrs. Ramos' severe obsessive-compulsive behavior, which completely structured the life of the family. Mrs. Ramos described her life as controlled by *asco* (revulsion). Whenever she touched something dirty she had nausea, palpitations, and sweating until she could wash her hands.

I asked her to show me her hands. They were red and raw from washing. I examined them carefully without touching her.

The children—Sara, 11, Tomas, 13, and Juan, 9—and Mr. Ramos listened as Mrs. Ramos vividly described her anxiety attacks when she or somebody in the family touched something dirty.

I expressed surprise when she said that if one of the children or her husband touched their shoes, she could not remain calm until they washed their hands under her supervision. "This is very interesting," I said. "I have seen many people with similar problems. But you are the first I have seen in which anxiety is reduced if family members clean themselves. This is quite interesting," I repeated for emphasis. I then talked with Sara, who told me how her mother asked her to wash and how sometimes she had to wash her hands two or three times before her mother was satisfied. I asked her to stand up and come to me. Without touching her I made a careful observation of both her hands. I explored how each hand and finger felt, repeating frequently, "And this happens to *your* hands."

I stated my amazement at the way Mrs. Ramos' revulsion could be calmed by *other* people's washing. Mr. Ramos then said that they couldn't eat eggs anymore because they were dirty. I looked baffled. Mrs. Ramos explained to me that it was because of where they came from. I asked what would happen if somebody took the shell off. "Ah," she replied, "then they would be clean."

"Do you buy your chickens without their behinds?" I asked.

"Yes," she replied. "I buy only chicken parts."

My attitude in the first 30 minutes of the interview was one of clinical detachment. I felt I was impersonating some of the great French clinicians of the 19th century who could see, smell, hear, and taste an illness. At the same time I was amused by the power of the narrative. How was it possible that the family did not see through the absurdity of my questions? How was it that the symptom expanded to include each and every one of them, so that in the end the entire life of the family was regulated by handwashing?

I asked the children to leave the room and asked the couple about their sexual life. I assumed that sexuality would somehow be dirty and wanted to know how. Mrs. Ramos said that her husband liked to have sex "too much" and that she took pity on him and allowed it every Saturday. He could touch her all over as long as he didn't touch her hands. "My hands are sacred," she said.

We had already spent 40 minutes on the consultation and I was as ignorant about the Ramos family as when we started. Everything had been absorbed in the narration of the symptom.

From some Whitaker memory came a non sequitur: a crazy thought. I asked, "Why don't you trust your husband? Why do you think he lies to you?" It was a long reach, and the result was surprising and satisfactory.

"I frequently dream that I wake up and find him gone." It was as if a faucet had been turned on. She abandoned the symptom and began to describe how critical her husband was, how she tried to please him. But whatever she said was wrong. How she cried when he yelled at her, and how the children would come to console her.

I asked her if Sara protected her, and called Sara back to the room. She described how she felt sorry for her mother and would stroke her hair when she cried, and kiss her forehead until she calmed. The other two children joined the session to tell similar stories of protecting their mother from their father's criticism. But they said at the same time that their father had never been violent with anybody in the family, and that he was very loving.

At this point the symptom had receded from center stage, and we were in a simple familial drama of children participating in a parental conflict. This drama was familiar to me. I have been there many times. I blocked the children, saying that their protection of their mother was not helpful to either of their parents. I encouraged Mrs. Ramos to challenge her husband's lack of understanding. As she did, I supported and amplified her request for fairness.

I asked Mrs. Ramos to tell me about her parents, and which was more critical. She told me that she always had been considered the least pretty and intelligent of her family. As a child she had always worked harder than her sisters to earn her parents' love, but she had always felt second best.

I finished the session inviting the spouses to a second consultation in three days, but I instructed the husband to find new ways of being supportive of his wife. I wanted him to remember earlier times, when he had courted her. He was to buy her a present. I told Mrs. Ramos that she needed to let go of the children's hands so that they could own their own bodies. I asked the children to tell their mother that their hands belonged to *them*, and they would wash them when they thought it was necessary.

As the session finished I shook everybody's hand. Only after they left did I remember that Mrs. Ramos' hands were sacred, and that she didn't touch other people's hands. Both Mrs. Ramos and I had forgotten her symptoms.

At the end of the session I was feeling excited by the changes and decided to have the next session with the couple alone. I also prepared the stage for a romantic ending. I ordered a dozen red roses to give to Mr. Ramos for his wife. I didn't have any idea of how or if I would use these roses.

Three days later the couple returned. Mrs. Ramos had clearly dressed in her Sunday best. She started talking, describing how she had realized that she was damaging the children, and had decided to free them from her demands. During these three days, she said, she had at moments felt anxious when she felt they were dirty, but knew she needed to control herself, and she had.

Her husband said that he had been attentive to her and stopped his criticizing. Mrs. Ramos agreed. As the couple seemed now more emotionally connected I asked Mrs. Ramos to tell me about her family, stating that maybe we could discover together the reason for her symptoms. She told of a difficult childhood on her parents' farm. They were poor and had to work hard. She had developed into the child who worked the hardest just to be as good as the rest. The husband joined in, describing how she always needed to please everybody, and how she was always available to respond to the needs of her parents and sisters. They talked then about how, when Mrs. Ramos' mother was dying, she spent three weeks nursing her mother day and night. At this point Mrs. Ramos began to cry, and described how her mother would become agitated at night and thrash in her bed. To protect her she tied her hands as they had in the hospital. This had been very traumatic for her, she said. She felt guilty for hurting her mother's hands.

At this point, 40 minutes into the session, I was called out to get the roses I had ordered. I returned with the flowers, and gave them to Mr. Ramos, saying I had bought them for him. He could give them to his wife when he felt loving. He took the flowers and began to give them to her. I stopped him, saying it was for later, when they were alone and in the proper mood. The session finished with a discussion about Cinderella. I suggested to Mrs. Ramos that she had been controlled by her need to work harder just to be accepted. I used the word *fregona* (charwoman) to emphasize my point, and said that maybe like Cinderella she could relax and accept her prince.

I really don't know how the session finished as a fairy tale. Something about this family moved me in simple ways. I felt caught in their drama, and in their language. Clearly the Ramoses also felt touched. They were grateful, and Mrs. Ramos didn't hesitate to shake my hand. This time both she and I knew that it was a new step—a shrinking of the tyranny of the symptom.

COMMENT

I have attempted to communicate the process by which a very bizarre symptom began to change in a two-session consult. The family was unique. So was the therapy. I had never before bought roses for clients, and I have never done it since. How can I extract a teaching map from the seemingly spontaneous transaction between the particular me and this particular family? Are there moments in this consultation that transcend the idiosyncrasy of this process? Let me try to generalize.

I think first of my attention to the symptom. The power of a symptom seems to depend on the unvarying rendition of the story. It is like children's stories, told always in the same ways. If a therapist expands the story, includes other people, introduces novelty in any way, the automaticity of the symptom is challenged. Mrs. Ramos' symptom had been strengthened by years of daily repetition and I felt impelled to a detailed exploration of minutiae to give validity to my challenge.

Second, from the beginning I challenged the validity of the story as all-encompassing. My challenges were invisible at first: "I have seen many cases that are similar but this is the first time I've seen. . . ." When I asked each of the children to show me their hands I emphasized that they were *their* hands. I explored details: "Are eggs dirty? Is sex clean?" I accompanied my questions with exclamations of amazement that in repetition challenged the reality of the symptom. These challenges were accompanied by statements of acceptance of the symptom's reality. This is a two-pronged strategy.

Third, I worked with subsystems. I started with the whole family, but when I wanted to challenge the children's intrusion in spousal conflict I asked the children to leave, then asked them to come back when the session again required their participation.

Fourth, I believe that people construct each other. Therefore, Mrs. Ramos' symptoms had to be part of the transactions between her and her husband. My question "Why do you think your husband lies?" was triggered by this concept.

Fifth, once the couple was engaged in therapy, I encouraged conflict and participated to amplify it. Hence, I joined Mrs. Ramos to help her challenge her husband.

Sixth, I believe that parents almost always want to help their children. Therefore, I assigned Mrs. Ramos the task of controlling her anxiety on her children's behalf, expecting that she would control her symptom, and she did.

Seventh, the exploration of history came after we had explored the present, and was a way of exploring the distortions of the present. The second session was dedicated almost entirely to the exploration of the historical development of Mrs. Ramos' devalued sense of self in her family of origin, and to the possibilities of introducing changes in her current view of herself by mobilizing supportive, positive responses from her husband. This was a family session focused on an individual.

In all, the session showed a therapist as part of the therapeutic system, guided in his understanding of the family by his emotional and cognitive responses to them, and triggered to intervene by the pulls of the family. But I questioned whether my definition of the therapist as part of the process was a new interpretation of my practice or was already present in my early thinking. I searched back and found this paragraph in *Families of the Slums* (Minuchin, Montalvo, Guerney, Rosman, & Schumer, 1967, p. 295):

> The therapist's choices of intervention are decidedly limited because he must operate under the organizational demands of the family system. But this has the advantage that awareness of himself in the midst of these "system pulls" allows him to identify the areas of interaction which require modification and the ways in which he may participate in them to change their outcome. . . .
>
> The therapist loses distance and is fully "in" when he enters the role of complementing the family members with counter-responses which tend to duplicate those that they usually elicit from each other. Our orientation encourages the assumption of this role.

I don't think I have ever since described the use of countertransference better.

I turned then to *Families and Family Therapy* (Minuchin, 1974) to revisit this thinking:

> In joining operations the therapist becomes an actor in the family play . . . he functions like the director as well as an actor . . . he also uses himself, entering into alliances and coalition . . . [using] his position . . . within the therapeutic system to pose challenges to which the family has to accommodate. (p. 138)

Half a page later comes a word of caution:

> [The therapist] must resist being sucked into the family system. He must adapt himself sufficiently to the family organization to be able to enter it, but he must also maintain the freedom to make interventions that challenge the family organization, forcing its members to accommodate to him in ways that will facilitate movement toward the therapeutic goals. (p. 139)

Today I sense a change in the tenor of the two writings. In *Families and Family Therapy* I put more emphasis on the therapist as the leader of the system, and cautioned against the power of the family suction to limit the therapist's freedom.

But in *Family Therapy Techniques* (Minuchin & Fishman, 1981) I moved back, and wrote:

> Family therapy requires the use of self. A family therapist cannot observe and probe from without. He must be part of a system of interdependent people. In order to be effective as a member of the system, he must respond to circumstances according to the system's rules while maintaining the widest possible use of self. This is what is meant by therapeutic spontaneity. . . . In this sense, a spontaneous therapist is a therapist who has been trained to use different aspects of self in response to different social contexts. The therapist can react, move and probe with freedom, but only within the range that is tolerable in a given context. (Minuchin & Fishman, 1981, p. 2)

Clearly, since the 1960s my descriptions of therapy have emphasized the therapist. I do not think this is the way structural family therapy is generally thought of in the field, but I think the general perception is a distortion, which I hope to address in what follows.

SUPERVISION

What kind of therapist do I aim to co-create in supervision? Clearly one who has the capacities I described earlier. This therapist has an hypothesis about the best way to help this family. She knows that any hypothesis is only tentative, a map to be changed whenever new information makes a better fit possible. That means a therapist who can take possession of many partial truths and use them as probes, until the family responds and a better fit can be calibrated. She needs to know herself sufficiently well to access the parts of herself that are useful for the therapeutic goal. She needs to have a map of final goals, along with the ability to zigzag in whatever way the process requires, while keeping the goals in mind. This is very much Haley's strategic teaching. Such a therapist would need, like Carl Whitaker, to be comfortable with discontinuity, to possess her irrationality and her reasoning, and be able to be spontaneously out of kilter, knowing that her responses are stimuli for both universal and idiosyncratic reactions.

How do we develop such a sophisticated human instrument?

The psychoanalysts thought that it would require each analyst to undergo his or her own training analysis. Haley objected to that, saying that he knew many well-analyzed people who were lousy therapists. To be a good therapist one must be trained in the art of therapy. But I want a supervisee who knows herself as a therapeutic instrument without necessarily needing to undergo therapy herself.

As I have pointed out, I think that I have always held these ideas. But it may be that my supervision, in earlier days, did not adequately address my goals. As I think about the ways I used to supervise trainees, I see that while I was *writing* about the use of self in therapy, I was engaged in *teaching* techniques. I never thought that techniques and the use of self can be separated. They are the two sides of the coin of clinical practice. But as I remember that early in the seventies Braulio Montalvo and I were trying to develop an "alphabet" of skills, as I read *Families and Family Therapy* and especially as I read *Family Therapy Techniques*, I see that technique was on the front

burner. "Joining," "reframing," "enactment," "focus," "intensity," "restructuring," "unbalancing," and "constructing," each had a chapter. In the last chapter, called "Beyond Techniques," I wrote "Close the book now. This is a book on techniques. Beyond technique, there is wisdom, which is the knowledge of the interconnectedness of things." But by then, I think, the damage had been done. Technique had overshadowed both therapy and therapist.

How do I supervise today? To reach the goal of a therapist who is both strategic and self-aware, I have learned in my supervision to focus on the therapist's style—that is, on his or her use of a preferred, narrow set of predictable responses under a variety of diverse circumstances.

We start by working on understanding students' therapeutic style. What are the responses in their repertory that they utilize most frequently? We accept them. They are okay. Then we declare them wanting. The therapist's style is all right as far as it goes, but it can be enlarged.

One therapist may be very involved in content. Perhaps he holds an ideology, such as feminism or cultural diversity. Then we look at how an ideological perspective dominates what the therapist sees. Sometimes style relates to basic characterological responses in the therapist, like conflict avoidance, a hierarchical stance, fear of confrontation, focusing exclusively on emotions or on logic, or a preference for happy endings.

But for the most part the elements of the style are less visible, including focusing on small details, remaining aloof, being indirect, talking too much, lecturing, or not owning his own ideas. Whatever we identify in the beginning becomes the point of departure. From this base the goal is to challenge the style of the therapist, to expand his repertory. The goal is a therapist who is able to respond from a variety of perspectives in ways that are complementary to the family's needs. A clinician who can manipulate herself on behalf of therapeutic change, and nonetheless be spontaneous.

As I start the training year, during the first supervisory session I develop a gross diagnostic assessment of the therapist's style. I often ask my students, tongue in cheek, to devise a front page headline in the National Enquirer about their style. Andy Schauer wrote, "Human therapist declares himself empty vessel." Others are less poetic and more descriptive.

I accept these headlines, and declare them partial. "There are other things you do that you don't know. You are richer than you realize. You are ignorant about your own ways."

The rest of the year each supervisee is subjected to an inquiry on what she did, what she thought she did, and how this was or was not useful for the family, every time she presents a tape or a live interview. She is also invited to listen to other students' opinions and incorporate voices that are different from hers. This process is interesting, exciting, and painful. An experiential dialogue develops between therapist and supervisor that demands the evolvement in the supervisee of a monitoring of herself as a therapeutic tool. When she is successful, she becomes sensitive to the pulls and pushes of the family, to her emotional response to their demands. She develops pauses, measures alternatives, and accepts the freedom of being absurd and the responsibility of leadership that includes not knowing.

SUPERVISION CASE EXAMPLE

Let me tell you a story. I have selected some excerpts of a draft that one of my supervisees, Dorothy Leicht, wrote about my supervision of her work (Leicht, in press). Dorothy was an individual therapist with 15 years' experience who was studying to become a family therapist. Therefore, she had one of the more common problems—trying to move her focus from the inside of the individual to the relationships between people. What became the focus of our supervision was her style. She was always driven by the events of the session. She intensively tracked whatever detail the family brought, with the result that she focused on small matters with little overview of the larger picture. So supervision focused on her lack of commitment to her own therapeutic goals.

Let me read you part of her draft, which shows her presenting a tape. She is working with a stepparent family, and her goal is to encourage the stepfather, Joe, to take more of a parental role toward his wife Helen's children. Dorothy is presenting a segment that shows, for the third time, how in joining this family she sabotages her own goal.

Helen: We almost didn't find a coat to fit Phil.

Joe: I thought. . . .

Phil: That's what I said, Ma!

Joe: I thought—that's why I suggested we go to a mall.

On the tape we could see Dorothy look at the boy, tense her body as though to stop him from interrupting, then sit back in her chair. I stopped the tape and said, "You were doing something you wanted to do, Dorothy, and the boy interrupted you. What stopped you from going ahead with what you wanted to do?" My voice was low and intense. I avoided looking at her, to convey my deep disappointment at her performance. I had decided that only high emotional intensity between us could stop her automatic responses.

"Well," Dorothy said, "when I reviewed the tape I could see . . ."

"No," I interrupted. "Don't tell me you didn't see it at the time. You did see it. It's in your body language. Why didn't you defend what you wanted to do?"

"I wanted to get them to talk, and to work together," she said.

"No," I contradicted. "Something happened that disrupted you, and you know it. What stopped you from maintaining your focus?"

"I don't know. Maybe I didn't have a focus," she said.

"Isn't that strange?" I marveled. I wasn't about to let her get away with that. "We all know the direction you had chosen. You told us, and we agreed with you. Why didn't you stay the course?"

"I guess this is the point I get pulled into the details of what's going on."

Dorothy was angry at me, and wanted to escape from our stressful transaction. But I felt that to lower the intensity of the encounter would be isomorphic with her way of doing therapy. It would have left her where she was, and that would have been a betrayal. So I was relentless. "The question is, what handicaps you in using your own authority? What handicaps you from saying to the boy, 'Hey, wait a minute, that is between your dad and your mother.'"

Dorothy was upset. "I don't know . . . Maybe I am not strongly enough committed to what I am doing . . . I don't know because it starts all over again and I lose it."

I didn't allow Dorothy this escape hatch. My goal was to make it impossible for Dorothy to meet with this family again without feeling my presence in the room. "It's clear that you do know. Besides, it's not even a question of knowing. It is a question of commitment to your position in the process."

I flicked on the videotape again.

Helen: Phil doesn't know what he wants.

Dorothy: Could Phil and Joe have gone to buy a coat?

Helen: I don't think so.

Joe: That's why we all went to the mall. I thought we'd have a better chance of finding something at the mall.

Dorothy: Helen, what would happen if Joe and Phil went shopping?

I stopped the tape. "Dorothy," I reproved, "to whom did you ask that question?"

"To the mother."

"Why?"

"I wanted to see what's possible in terms of her not being so central and controlling everything."

"So what you did is the opposite of what you wanted to do. You interrupted the father while he was talking, and activated the mother. Why do you want to activate her? I thought you wanted him to talk."

My language was repetitive. What do you want? Why don't you do what you want? She needed to see herself as a framer of the therapeutic process.

"That is interesting," she said. "I guess I am thinking it is only going to happen with her permission.

"No," I said, "it happened with your permission. You are permitting her to be central. That is not what you want."

"But Joe is only going to be able to have a role if she permits it," Dorothy objected.

"No, it's if you permit it." I turned to the class. "I think that Dorothy needs to be respectful of herself. I think if she doesn't respect herself she will not commit herself to the way in which she wants to work."

Here Dorothy wrote:

He was like a gorilla in my path, I couldn't cajole or distract him. He was becoming more and more impatient and I was becoming more and more discouraged. Each time I had to present a session, it was an ordeal. I was proving difficult to teach, maybe impossible. It was a predicament, I couldn't go back . . . I couldn't go forward. This was the moment when I had to let go of the handrail of content, jump into uncertainty, and trust that something would come if I knew where I wanted to go, believed in myself, and was willing to take a stand.

At her next supervisory session, Dorothy presented a segment which clearly showed her following a therapeutic goal in a family session.

Two years later, Dorothy wrote:

I am still trying to distill what it was that created the change. Was it that not changing had become impossible? Was it a coming together of learning, and then the courage to trust myself and travel into uncharted territory? I don't know, but I know that there was a great sigh, from me, from Sal, and from my fellow supervisees who had been my greatest support.

I do therapy differently now. When I feel that I'm being drawn into the content, I go to the top corner of the room because that is where I'm free to use what's inside of me. When I'm fearful of confronting, I remember the gorilla.

In the last decade my supervision has become an imprecise pas de deux. It is specifically tailored to each supervisee. Sometimes it fails to evolve into anything meaningful, but frequently it is an experience in which, at the end, both the student and I have the sense of growth.

REFERENCES

Bateson, G. (Ed.) (1972). Metalogue: Why do things get in a muddle?" In *Steps to an ecology of the mind*. New York: Ballentine, pp. 3–13.

Haley, J. (1986). *Uncommon therapy: The psychiatric techniques of Milton H. Erickson, M.D.* New York: W. W. Norton.

Leicht, D. O., Untitled. In S. Minuchin, G. M. Simon, & W-Y. Lee. (Eds.). *Mastering family therapy*. (In press). New York: Wiley.

Minuchin, S. (1974). *Families and family therapy*. Cambridge, MA: Harvard University Press.

Minuchin, S., & Fishman, H.C. (1981). *Family therapy techniques*. Cambridge, MA: Harvard University Press.

Minuchin, S., Montalvo, B., Guerney, Jr., B. G., Rosman, B., & Schumer, F. (1967). *Families of the slums: An exploration of their structure and treatment*. New York: Basic Books.

Whitaker, C. A., & Malone, T. P. (1980). *The Roots of Psychotherapy*. New York: Brunner/Mazel.

Discussion by Jeffrey K. Zeig, Ph.D.

◆

THE LEAP TO COMPLEXITY: SUPERVISION IN FAMILY THERAPY

Sal Minuchin is easy to categorize; he is a cybernetician, a Zen rabbi, a sociodramatist, a humorist, and a strategist. To describe Minuchin we need metaphors. Literal interpretations will not suffice because he deals in a world of systems, experiential learning, Talmudic wisdom, social institutions, theater, constructive bemusement, and military precision. Curiously, he is accomplished in each of these arenas.

Sal speaks with peerless authority from diverse perspectives. Moreover, he is not one to mince words. That is, Sal will not cloak himself in collectively acceptable generalities. In this chapter, for example, he has performed an intellectual striptease and we are wise to be avid voyeurs. There is much to be learned on many levels.

I had two self-serving reasons in assigning myself to discuss Sal's work. First, I wanted to revisit his contributions from my current level of knowledge. Prior to the conference, I read three of Sal's books. He is a marvelous writer, and no therapist can consider himself complete until he or she has studied Sal's work. The other reason that I assigned myself to serve as the discussant was as follows: Each

of the faculty fills out forms from which I compose the schedule. On the forms, faculty indicate whom they prefer as a discussant. Among others, Sal listed my name as a possible commentator. Being a good hypnotic subject, I responded.

I first met Minuchin in about 1973 when I served as a student volunteer at one of the workshops he offered in California. I still remember how much he scared me. He was very confrontive, and I worried that I would be the target of some of that intensity. To me, he rampaged through families and among students wielding a potent club.

More than 20 years later, having shared the podium with him on a number of occasions, I still find him scary, but it is more of a feeling of awe and appreciation. However, there is also an admixture of frustration and depression generated by the difficulty in mastering the melding of the profound simplicity of his interventions with the depth and complexity of his analysis.

I first got to know Sal personally at the 1985 Evolution of Psychotherapy Conference. He offered one of the most stunning and insightful of all of the addresses. It was entitled, "My Many Voices."

I had asked the faculty at that conference to present essentials of their respective approaches in their speeches. Instead, Sal surveyed and appraised the field of family therapy. He spoke about such luminaries as Satir, Whitaker, and Haley, and indicated how they spoke through him. However, rather than extolling his own approach, he talked about seminal influences. I was so inspired that I read the chapter four or five times to be sure that I could grasp the process underlying Sal's 1985 address, as well as the content.

In studying Sal's contribution here, I think that Satir may have had more of an influence on him than even Sal acknowledges. In the present chapter—which is just as profound as his 1985 presentation—Sal allows us to be privy to aspects of his evolving self. However, rather than addressing voices, he now presents parts. Effectively, he has invited us to be spectators at an internal parts party.

Three parts are revealed in this chapter. They comprise Sal's own internal family. We see Sal-the-Godfather, Sal-the-Father, and Sal-the-Grandfather.

Parenthetically speaking, I suspect that Sal's overall design is a metaphorical ruse to engage us in the systemic world of process rather than with linear content. An alternate formulation is that he grew up in a family of all brothers. There is a conspicuous absence of "mother" nature. I will return to this topic later.

Let's examine Sal's three manifestations: First, we encounter Sal-the-Godfather, who surveys the field of family therapy and describes seminal contributions. Sal credits Erickson's influence on the field of family therapy in print. I don't know that he has done so before. Shortly before Erickson died, they had their first and only meeting. Perhaps Sal is a good hypnotic subject.

In his rendering of streams and developments in family therapy, Sal does himself a disservice by minimizing his pivotal contributions. Clearly, he has been one of family therapy's primary architects.

In the second manifestation, we encounter Sal-the-Father, the name I have given to his role as a clinician. According to his own definition, Minuchin is a transparent therapist. That is, he increases complexity and choice in the family. Sal assumes that families perceive themselves inaccurately and in limited ways.

He begins with the assumption that there are resources behind the current limitations that can be stimulated. He especially values when people speak for themselves and maintain personal autonomy; they should not overprotect or underinvolve. The case that he presents is a marvelous example of his masterful use of linguistic subtlety and therapeutic finesse. It demonstrates that he is especially adept with issues of differentiation and integration. To Sal, therapy is a drama, and I see him as the consummate dramatist.

Through my study of Sal's work, I have found that there are features of his therapy that are similar to my approach: I find it necessary to bring therapy into the session as much as possible. For example, Sal's use of flowers and fairy tales fits with my metaphoric predilection. Moreover, I often use the technique of pattern disruption by which one introduces novelty. We know that therapy happens whenever a systemic change is made in chronic and ineffective structures. Sometimes changing a symbolic aspect of the problem provides constructive and enduring systemic reverberations. I also subscribe to the notion that insight is the dessert and not the main course of therapy. Similarly, Sal waits to understand history until significant changes have been accomplished by the patient.

I am especially in awe of Sal's ability to understand and intervene with boundary issues. His certainty is admirable. I'm not so certain. Individual issues and interpersonal issues are like strong and weak forces in physics, except that in physics strong and weak forces are static. In therapy, strong forces flip-flop with weak forces. Consequently, I'm not so certain which predominates at any given time.

In the third manifestation, Sal-the-Grandfather, he takes on the role of supervisor. Curiously, I find myself at a similar point in development to the one Sal described. For example, earlier in my career I exclusively taught techniques rather than clinician self-development. My recent orientation has taken a turn similar to Sal's in that I now emphasize the development of the self of the therapist, at least as much if not more than technique.

Sal indicates that a goal of supervision is to "challenge the style of the therapist to expand his repertoire." I like that sentence. However, I don't know that I would say it that way. One reason for differing has to do with archetypes that have influenced us. He is from the John Wayne generation. I am from the John Lennon generation. Sal deals in a world of challenges and sharp lines. I live in a world of more ambiguity and less clarity. Moreover, in my family of origin, there were three powerful women. As a result, I learned "mother nature" from an early age.

There is one theme that connects all three manifestations. In each we find one constant: Sal-the-Warrior. He defines, sharpens, and clarifies boundaries. I am much more *sleepy* in my approach; consequently, Sal would place me in the minimalist camp.

There is another aspect I would like to address that is common to all of Sal's manifestations—his interest in contaminating dubious thinking. In my Ericksonian mentality, I describe it as eliciting associations. Adler called a related technique "spitting in the patient's soup." Sometimes a therapist can intervene in such a way that he contaminates the associative net. For example, his supervisee is visited by hallucinations of gorillas every time she goes into a therapy room. Similarly, I work to modify the associative net in my patients and students. However, I tend to challenge more by implication.

In conclusion, an anecdote:

There is the story about Herman Melville, who visited Nathaniel Hawthorne and his wife one evening and told them about a fight that he had witnessed on a South Sea island in which one of the Polynesian warriors had fiercely and heroically wielded a club. Melville danced around the room demonstrating the battle.

After Melville's departure, Mrs. Hawthorne remembered that he left empty-handed and questioned Hawthorne as to whether or not Melville took his club with him. Hawthorne agreed that he had. Besides, when they looked through the room they couldn't find it.

On the next visit between the Melvilles and Hawthornes, an inquiry was made about the club. At it turned out, there was no club. It only existed in the minds of the Hawthornes, who were so entranced by the vividness of Melville's story.

Editor's Note: At the conclusion of the discussion, I presented Sal with a gift—a styrofoam club. I told him that I didn't know what he would do with it. Sal's response was immediate. He took the club and "knighted" me.

SECTION VII

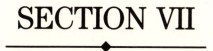

Philosophical Approaches

Case History: Evolution or Revelation?

James Hillman, Ph.D.

James Hillman, Ph.D.
James Hillman received his Ph.D. degree from the University of Zurich. He has served as honorary secretary of the International Association for Analytical Psychology and for ten years was Director of Studies at the C.G. Jung Institute in Zurich. Dr. Hillman has written twenty books and was nominated for a Pulitzer Prize.

I

The question I now posit is quite small and quite simple, although basic to all therapy—and basic to adult life itself: What is the nature of a case history? How do we tell our life story? What is an autobiography? And—how do we therapists hear the story told us, by means of what constructs, what frame?

I shall be contending—and I do like to be contentious—that how we hear the patients depends very much on how we have formed our own biography. Therefore, I think it very important, if we want to listen consciously, to be conscious about the narrative, the kind of story we put ourselves in.

Because this entire book here has a major theme—the evolution of the therapist—I am obliged to tell stories of my therapeutic training and my thinking about therapy. So, I am obliged to be somewhat personal and bio-graphical, much as I dislike this mode of discourse. The self-importance, the narcissism of personal stories—*my* experience, *my* journey, *my* therapy—afflicts the age. I do dislike contributing more such egocentric tales; but I shall try to do it in a classical style; that is, by making some sort of point out of the stories, using them, as the rabbis did and the Catholic fathers and the Eastern sages and monks. When they told stories about what happened, it was a form of teaching, a lesson, making a moral, drawing some kind of consequence. A story then is not literal event that "happened to me," but an anecdote of a wider truth, an emblem of an idea useful to other lives.

The first story goes back to my training in the 1950s at the Jung Institute in Zurich, Switzerland. We had supervision colloquia where we candidates presented our cases—about ten of us, weekly, with an old-hand supervisor.

I disliked these sessions. I disliked the kibbitzing. I disliked the presumption of knowledge on the part of everyone about what to do, what not to do, what was going on in the patient, between me and the patient, and their suppositions about what was going on in me. Of course I felt exposed and inadequate. But especially, I felt something fundamentally wrong about one person reporting on the soul life of another. One time, when my turn was coming up, I proposed bringing the case itself to the session, that is, inviting the patient to present his own case. In the back of my mind was T. S. Eliot's line "You are not here to report."

I felt that my presentation would be a fiction, a take, a spin, on the patient, and that what other people said to what I reported was another fiction piled on top of the first one. I had not yet begun to doubt the patient's story as a fiction too. But then, I thought, why not get it straight from the horse's mouth, the patient being the horse.

My proposal was turned down. I believe, however, that the proposal revealed an essential of my view of therapy. The "talking cure," as Freud called it at the beginning, is really a cure of talk, of story. We are working on the life story, the narrative, that the patient presents, and we are elaborating a new narrative in the therapy, the therapeutic fiction: "I went into therapy, this happened, then this, then I discovered this, and I got clearer, or better, or fell in love, or something else happened, and then, it ended—or I went elsewhere . . ."

Later this seed doubt about case history as a fictional form became an essay, and appears in my book *Healing Fiction*, which caused quite a stir. The idea itself is widespread today as part of postmodern deconstructionism: Case histories are not truths as facts, as objectively verifiable reports. They are constructs for romancing your life.

A second place where I was troubled by case history: This appears in my first therapeutic book, *Suicide and the Soul* (Hillman, 1993). There I tried to distinguish all the data that go into a case history from something else, something interior, something mysterious, maybe destinal or fateful, that I called then "soul history." Following is a short seg-ment from that book. (This was 30 years ago, by the way, before Soul got on TV, when it was still a word used only in churches, revival meetings, and at funerals, or on the street: soul brother, soul food, soul music.)

Outside and inside, life and soul, appear as parallels in "soul history." A case history is a biography of historical events in which one took part: family, school, work, illness, war, love. The soul history often neglects entirely some or many of these events, and spontaneously invents fictions and "inscapes" without major outer correlations. The biography of the soul concerns experience. It seems not to follow the one-way direction of the flow of time, and it is reported best by emotions, dreams, and fantasies. Gulfs of years and events are dispensed with out of hand, while the dreams circle around and around certain aspects of the case history as symbols of meaning that carry the experience of the soul.

Case history reports on the achievements and failures of life with the world of facts. But the soul has neither achieved nor failed in the same way because the soul has not worked in the same way. Its material is experience and its realisations are accomplished not just by efforts of will. The soul imagines and plays—and play is not chronicled by report. What remains of the years of our childhood play that could be set down in a case history? Children, and so-called "primitive peoples," have no history; they have instead the residue of their play crystallized in myth and symbol, language and art, and in a style of life. Taking a soul history means capturing emotions, fantasies, and images by entering the game and dreaming the myth along with the patient. *Taking a soul history means becoming part of the other person's fate.* Where a case history presents a sequence of facts leading to diagnosis, soul history shows rather a concentric helter-skelter pointing always beyond itself. (Hillman, 1964, pp. 77–78)

Well, I finished my training and finished my time in the *Burghölzli* asylum in Zurich, where the term *schizophrenia* was invented and Jung did his word association experiments—a very historical place—and I gathered material from patients in folders—material consisting of notes, addenda, and case reports; and at the asylum I watched the psychiatric residents write up their case histories by hand, sometimes going on for 30 pages. A tremendous labor, and I had to submit a long detailed case report plus a bunch of shorter ones for my finals.

All along I was wondering about this proliferation of written material. All this stuff filed away, going back to Freud and Charcot and Bernheim, the thousands, probably millions, of pages of case write-ups, and dreams, and interpretations of dreams. Why and what is this written material stored away in analysts' offices and attics and hospital archives?

What is this genre of writing? What kind of writing is this? What are these accounts of the most intimate aspects of life? Not quite medical reports, not quite recounting of dreams, not quite memoirs, not quite confessions—yet a bit of all this. Is it autobiography? Who is the story about? Is that person the same person who is telling/writing the story? (Here I am not casting doubt on the veracity of memory. I am not coming down on either side of the early abuse question and the false memory syndrome issue.)

I am, rather, contending that every case history is first of all a *story* that places the teller in a privileged position as the central figure in the story. I am contending that the major result of all case history writing, and autobiography itself, reinforces the centrality of the *I*, that first person singular. *I* as subject of the plot becomes the victim of events and the agent of events—a forward motion through time, with all other people, animals, objects, and institutions only accessories to the main plot of the developmental journey of the *I*.

Is this what case history then really is for? Is it really a therapeutic technique for strengthening and centralizing that fictional figure that therapy has named *Ego*?

No wonder I was doubting it—because therapy, as I conceive it, following Jung and most philosophical and spiritual disciplines, aims to relativize the "I," to place it as a lesser light among the many other psychic figures, such as those who inhabit our dreams.

You see that by discounting case reports, I was removing the patient from the center and replacing the patient with the wider psyche—all the "little people" as Jung has called the

complexes, phantoms, and fantasies that inhabit the soul and appear in a life as symptoms, desires, wishes, regrets, and so on. I was moving from an ego-centered therapy to a soul-centered therapy. I was forming my version of psychotherapy—strengthening the wider psyche's imaginative and recuperative powers, the psyche as a field in which the ego complex was only one player among many.

All this is rather *dis*integrative, which reveals another essential notion of my therapeutic theory. I call it *dehumanizing*—moving the anthropocentric vision of therapy, with its too-narrow focus only on humans, to a psyche felt in the world, not merely in "me" and "my" relations.

II

You can well grasp that the developmental model of human life does not suit my understanding of case history or of biography. Yet the developmental model that we all learned in college Psychology 101 informs all psychotherapy regardless of school or system. Can we, however, look at life less as a developmental journey than as a revelation of essence? We are each different, even one-egg twins are different, and therapy for me is the study of this uniqueness and how it tries to come to terms with all the "sames" required by the world of common life. Can we look at our cases less as a result of history than as an expression of essence? Rather than the development story, I prefer one I call "Growing Down."

This model is Platonic, perhaps Buddhist, too. It says the soul chooses exactly the life you are born into. You enter the world with a *daimon*, a guiding spirit, a *genius*, angel, acorn, nucleus, soul code, a *paradeigma*, that already wanted just what you got. According to Plato and Plotinus, your soul chose these four crucial factors: your parents, your place, your body, and your circumstances. These are what your daimon requires, and it leads you down into these realities.

So, everything reverses. Not your parents made you; your soul chose them. They are the only possible people who could mess your life in just the right way for your soul's destiny.

Same for your body in which your soul resides and the place and circumstances of your situation on earth.

Your job is simply growing down into these realities—not growing up out of them!

The Kabbala image in Jewish mysticism provides a parallel: The tree of life has its roots not in the earth but invisibly in the heavens. Your life tree is rooted in high and mighty visions, principles, and longings. Slowly the tree descends through stages down into this world. As a baby begins with a big head, and normally dives into the world head first, so it takes a very long time to get your feet on the ground. An idea or image of our lives comes before the life can be lived.

My standing here this morning and stating these things is a late piece of my soul's growing down. It is putting high and mighty ideas of the soul down into the public arena of practical therapy.

Revelation of essential character seems to work in several ways. First, as a clear annunciation. For instance, Yehudi Menuhin. Just three years old, he went to a concert with his parents. During the concert, he pointed to the first violinist and said he wanted a violin and *that* man to teach him to play it. Just like that. Simple. So a friend of the family gave him a toy violin with metal strings on his fourth birthday. Little Yehudi burst into tears, threw it away, left the room. Was he an ungrateful little prince? No, he was Yehudi Menuhin, and for Yehudi Menuhin the violin is no toy with metal strings. From the usual perspective, the little boy was defending the acorn from this insulting toy. That tantrum came from a daimon that the boy must carry and try to bring down into life.

Ella Fitzgerald wanted to dance. She prepared and practiced on skinny legs in Harlem. At 16 she showed up for amateur night, went on stage, and was announced by the MC as this little lady here, who is going to dance for you. Ella Fitzgerald stopped him, interrupted, and said, no, I'm going to sing. The sudden switch came out of nowhere. She won the prize, and never stopped singing.

Ambivalent. Irresponsible. Hysterical—or did the acorn seize upon the right moment—an audience awaiting, a stage and lights—to reveal her calling.

The philosopher R. G. Collingwood, when he was eight years old, one day in his father's professorial library took down a little leather covered book from a higher shelf. It was Kant's *Theory of Ethics*. In his biography, Collingwood writes: "As I began reading it, my small form wedged between the bookcase and the table, I was attacked by a strange succession of emotions. First came an intense excitement. I felt that things of the highest importance were being said about matters of the utmost urgency; things which at all costs I must understand." Although written in English using words he could grasp, the "meaning baffled" him. Strangest of all, he felt that "the contents of this book were somehow my business, a matter personal to myself, or rather to some future self of my own. . . ."

Collingwood was called to philosophize. Already present in his eight-year-old heart was a destiny given by his daimon, which took a long career to grow down into.

The task of growing down shows differently in the cases of Judy Garland and Josephine Baker. By the time she was two-and-a-half, Judy Garland performed on stage, and knocked the audience dead and to such an extent that they wouldn't let her go, encore after encore, just as the audiences everywhere in her adult years wouldn't let her go. She had immediate magical rapport, a touch that never deserted her even during her descent into messy drunken doped appearances toward the end of her horrendous star-struck life. For Judy Garland could not find a way down from "Over The Rainbow." It is as if she had to fall down to get down, dying in the middle of the night on a toilet in a London flat.

Josephine Baker in contrast lived in her youth as extravagantly as Garland. The rage of Paris, the most beautiful body in the world, the lover of kings and tycoons, a star beyond the world with hundreds of pieces of baggage, pet animals, cosmetics by the pounds, followers, fans . . . until slowly she grew down into clandestine spy work for the Free French against the Germans, took part in the racial struggles of the sixties, adopted eleven stray children and raised them in a country retreat to which she gave all her money, until she was thrown out, broke, aged, but recognized—not only for her stage glory, but for her contributions to freedom, justice, and charity.

These stories of Menuhin and Garland and Baker, and many, many more, I have told in more detail in my new Random House book *The Soul's Code*. I have only abbreviated them here to illustrate my thesis: As the body comes with its genes, so the soul comes with its code, which it is the job of the therapist to watch out for, and perhaps watch over. And to examine all symptoms not only in terms of ego adaptation and societal norms, but as expressions of something else which may belong to calling, character, and fate. Taking a case history then becomes a task of deciphering the soul's code in which all the peculiarities, maladaptations, and idiosyncrasies become clues to the soul's attempts to grow down into life. I see our task as one that looks at an adult not in terms of the vicissitudes of childhood, but at childhood in terms of the full configuration of an adult.

III

For these 'called' children the developmental model makes less sense than my so-called acorn theory—that you come into the world with an innate image, with intimations of a destiny, a daimon who calls the soul and gives it directions that are perilous to deny.

Moreover, for these famous children, and I suspect for *all* children, else I would not be speaking now as a therapist to therapists, the developmental model may do damage. It sees symptoms instead of revelations, fixations instead of fidelity—Menuhin's temper tantrum as a statement of faith—or maladaptive dysfunctionings when what might also be going on are alternative routes to the realization of a person's essential nature.

School is often the place where the claims of the daimon and the demands of society most forcibly clash. Sigrid Undset, the Norwegian novelist, declared: "I hated school so intensely. I avoided the discipline by an elaborate technique of being absent-minded during classes." Nobel physicist Richard Feynman called his early school "an intellectual desert." Kenneth

Branagh, the actor, so feared school when he was about 11 that he tried throwing himself downstairs to break a leg rather than go. Later he withdrew into his room and read and read. The German film-maker Werner Fassbinder simply "could not remain in the company of normal children" and eventually was put in a Rudolf Steiner school. Jackson Pollock, "who flouted . . . school requirements as blithely as he ignored its dress code" was expelled from Los Angeles High School. John Lennon was expelled from kindergarten.

The imaginative, existentialist author Paul Bowles

did not get along with his new teacher, Miss Crane. He resented her authoritative style and . . . he adamantly refused to take part in class singing and as a method of revenge devised a system to do what to him were meaningless assignments without really doing them: he simply wrote everything perfectly, but backwards (Sawyer-Laucanno, 1989).

For Bowles, it was singing, for others it will be Latin, or algebra, or sports, or English composition. The acorn draws the line, and no one can force it to cross into the territory of its incompetence.

Edvard Grieg, the composer, said: "School developed in me nothing but what was evil and left the good untouched." Thomas Edison said, "I was always at the foot of the class." Stephen Crane, Eugene O'Neill, William Faulkner, and F. Scott Fitzgerald all failed courses in college. For Ellen Glasgow, a Pulitzer-award writer, school was "intolerable." Willa Cather, Pearl Buck, Isadora Duncan, and Susan B. Anthony also disliked school. Cezanne was rejected by the Beaux Arts Academy in Paris. Proust's teacher considered his compositions disorganized and Zola got a zero in literature, also failing in German language and in rhetoric. Einstein wrote of his middle school (from age 9½): "I preferred to endure all sorts of punishments rather than to learn gabble by rote." Earlier at primary school he was not especially noticeable and was called "Biedermeier," meaning a little dull, a little simple, a little "unclever." His sister wrote that "he wasn't even good at arithmetic in the sense of being quick and accurate." Some of these characteristics were due to his slowness of speech.

General George S. Patton was dyslexic and was kept back; Winston Churchill, at Harrow, "refused to study mathematics, Greek or Latin and was placed in the lowest form"—in what today would be termed the remedial reading class, where slow boys were taught English. His English was not poor; his knowledge of Shakespeare was unusual and self-motivated.

Examination especially can be a trial. The master bacteriologist Paul Ehrlich had to be excused from compositions because of his "complete ineptness." Puccini consistently failed exams. Gertrude Stein would not take her final in a class at Harvard. Chekhov refused to study classics, and failed his school exams twice. These failures at school gave him nightmares. "All his life he was to be haunted by dreams of teachers trying to 'catch him out'." Picasso, who could never remember the sequence of the alphabet left school at ten "because he stubbornly refused to do anything but paint." Even his private tutor gave up on him because Pablo could not learn arithmetic.

Maybe we should read the data of learning disorders and the cases of school problems differently. Instead of failed at school, saved from school—not that this is my personal recommendation. I ask only that the sadnesses of children in school be imagined not merely as examples of failure but as exemplars of the acorn. The daimon's intuition often cannot submit to the normalcy of schooling and becomes even more demonic. We need to read life backwards, we need to look at the gestures of the acorn from the taller perspective of the full tree.

But what parent and what counselor can perch so high and see so well, and what child—even a "genius"—can stick stubbornly enough to its intuitions, unless driven there by complete misunderstanding or by incapacitating symptoms like dyslexia, attention deficit, allergies and asthma, hyperactivity—all of which can keep a child from school. From school, yes, but not from learning. For those of us who watch over children and supposedly guide them, a door to the invisible factors at work in their disorders must be kept open, just in case it is an angel knocking and not merely a malady.

Remember Jung's phrase, "The Gods have become diseases." Seeing the angel in the malady takes an eye for the invisible, a certain blinding of one eye and another open to elsewhere. It is impossible to see the angel unless you first have a notion of it; otherwise the child is simply stupid, willful, or pathological.

IV

Let us imagine another way of posing our opening question: Evolution or Revelation—growing up or growing down. Let us imagine them not opposed.

Let us imagine evolution *toward* revelation, or increasing revelation. Of course, as with Judy Garland and Josephine Baker, with Menuhin and Collingwood, revelation was sharp and clear and never got sharper or clearer than when it first broke forth.

Generally, for most, it is not so much that we develop into something, but that as we age, our character and our calling stand out more clearly. The oak is an articulated displayed acorn. Age makes essence more transparent, the skeleton shows through the confusions of flesh.

I use again my story as example in keeping again with the theme of the evolution of the therapist.

I was a sophomore year high school student, age 14, after class, questioning the teacher: Why do the theorems always come out? Why do the angles have numbers like 30 and 60 so that they come out to 90? What if it were different? What was the underlying reason? The teacher was tolerant, but she had no answer. This was the way it was: Geometry was perfect since Euclid.

In other words, I was seeing through the given and asking for the archetypal ground, the myth behind the logic. I have never stopped doing that.

My problem was not geometry, but received ideas that were merely passed on and not rethought. This, I have since learned, is Vaclav Havel's definition of stupidity—ideas you simply mouth without thinking them through. My question, too, could be called stupid, but I suppose I was driven by fear of becoming yet more dumb, by not asking the question.

This story, from when I was 14, also reveals an intellectual passion. And, besides, important to note, it did not disturb my relation with the teacher—I did not regard her inadequate reply as a sign of her stupidity or anything like it. No one was put down, not she, not me. We got on well, I got decent marks. Not great, but decent.

In other words, feeling was not disturbed by thinking. Please—the "head" is not antihuman, or against feeling, heart, body, soul, and so on. In fact, I have come to believe that headless feeling is usually indiscriminate, and feeling-less head is without value, accuracy, or relevance.

Another story that reveals essence. At four, I put jigsaw maps together—cut-out wood images of the different states, and one of the world, a globe with ceramic cut-outs that fit into the continents. From the time I was eight or nine I had maps thumbtacked onto the walls and even on the ceiling of my small room on the top floor of an old house. I could lie in bed and look at all these places. They were maps of places: abstractions, of course, but they allowed imagination of travel, discovery, exploration. I was a geography nut.

What bit of acorn was that? It did not develop into my becoming a foreign correspondent, a traveling diplomat, an international businessman, an importer of foreign goods, a surveyor, a cartographer, a teacher of displaced children. . . No logical development in a literal sense. But the imagination of unknown places, of visiting actualities that begin as abstractions—this belongs to my ventures to the interior of psychology of the unconscious. I have done lots of traveling, lived in foreign countries, taught in many parts of the world and most every state of the union, and have translations into lots of languages, some of which I speak . . . but that is not the developmental consequent of the geography nerd in the upstairs room.

It was a primary display, then, of worldliness, of differentiation of the world into many shapes and sizes and colors, of the wonders of abstraction itself—all of which shows up not only in my worldly concerns about the soul, but in the essential of my polytheistic psychology—that there are an immense number of different shapes and configurations. As they compose this planet, so they also compose the psyche's world. Unity is less interesting than variety and multiplicity.

There are two points to make from these two stories of geometry and geography.

First: A *literal* understanding of revelation—that is, taking the developmental model as your guide, leads to false conclusions. My geometry question did not develop into my becoming a mathematician or architect, or even an engineer or an abstract thinker. There was no evolution of my question, no linear development from an early seed.

Rather it was a revelation of the way my mind works, of its need to challenge assumptions.

So too the maps. My cartographic obsessions did not lead to that profession. In fact, when I was inducted into the Navy when I was 18 I tried to get into that mapping branch of the service. I was not accepted. No development, but instead a revelation of essence: the connection between imagination aids, maps as images, for fantasies connected to the world. My way of growing down into the world was and is via images and abstractions.

So the two points: reading a young person's interests and hang-ups literally leads you wrong. And second, as Picasso said, "I don't develop. I am." Time may be far less important than we like to believe.

I shall bore you with yet one more of these tales. This has to do with writing and the way I write. I have been writing since my teen years, and now have some 20 books, almost all of them still in print, and mobs of papers, and so on. However, I never could put "writer" down on a form asking "profession." I always put "psychologist," though now I've escaped that term too, and put "housekeeper," for that's how I seem to spend most of my time.

Anyway: again boyhood. Around 12 I began cutting up and gluing balsawood to make miniature ships for a large naval game. I made gunboats and aircraft carriers and cruisers and so on, with pins for guns, and so on. Not the models you buy in boxes and assemble, but my own crude designs inspired by *Jane's Navies of the World.*

I obsessively worked late at a table with razor blade and glue. I did not develop into a ship builder or a craftsperson. In fact I make nothing, do nothing with my hands, never did, but housekeeping, bandaging and nursing, cooking and gardening. No repairs. No carpentry. No wiring. There was no development of this manual cutting and gluing: My skill is as primitive today as it was then.

But that's how I write, even to this day. I use no computer, but I sit obsessively at a table, with scissors and rubber cement, and put all my books together. All the rewrites, the changes, the paragraphs, the editings, are a cut-and-paste job. My handwork remains just as it was when I was a boy. No development. Revelation.

This idiosyncratic style of writing reveals something else: Cut and paste is also an art form called collage. You assemble pieces into images. Now, images are the bread and butter of my therapy and thoughts about therapy. I follow Jung in saying "psyche is image." For me the word "unconscious" translates rather congruently into the word "imagination," a body, a place, a faculty, a realm of images.

Is my cut-and-paste method basically an imagistic way of thinking rather than a linear, developmental, or logical one? I believe it is, and maybe my emphasis again and again on therapy as an art, not a science, on the rhetoric and style of therapy rather than its empirical evidence, are all part and parcel of the very way my hands work.

Maybe too, I can account for why my writings have never caught on in German and in French. Germany and France: too rational and conceptual—while nearly everything I have ever written appears at once in Italian, and much of it also in Brazil and Japan—all three, Italy, Brazil, and Japan, places where style and language and traditions are more imagistic, aesthetic, and rhetorical. Also I can better understand why my work finds its way into drama and film departments, into art and poetry magazines, religion and literature, even architecture schools, but hardly ever into the kingdoms and queendoms of psychology departments or therapy training institutes.

V

I am still struggling with descent, still looking for the right pair of shoes that keep the feet down on the ground. Which reminds me—after my first face-to-face, knee-to-knee session with old Jung, I came home and told my wife what huge shoes he had. With fifty years between us and all the difference in body and soul that that implies, I suppose it was easier to stare at Jung's feet than to look him in the eyes.

A last phase of this growing down is being here with you this morning. I am bearing witness as I stand here to what I am contending. The more I reveal, the more I get down.

For many people, the last stages of growing down are exemplified by Josephine Baker, extending into the world through her eleven children, or "grandchildren." We need however to deliteralize children and grandchildren, and to displace the subject of "family values" altogether from its identity with literal families.

Children and grandchildren are also those produced from the mind—the ideas, the spirits, the thoughts that have been fathered and require attentive child support. Remember, there are various kinds of sperm. The Greek Stoics spoke of the *logos spermatikos*, the spermatic seed-word that inseminates, strikes sparks, generates. I must care for the ideas that come forth from me, not merely let them sprout untended, wild oats, abortions, bastards.

Especially those ideas that bear upon my psychological family, the therapeutic community: You who are in this room with me today. Care for this community becomes a late task of this growing down: protecting it, warning it, finding ways to father it.

For our family's values are endangered. We are increasing in numbers all the while becoming an endangered species. Railroaded by managed care, debased and ridiculed by pop TV, reduced by post-modern irony, menaced by right-wing literalists, attacked by pharmaceutical profiteers, and infantalized by our own weak thinking with its clinging dependence on genetics, on salvational religions, on techniques, gimmicks, masters, and cults.

Care for our community is also care for the body politic that is in desperate need of our care. Not only hungry children and bad old-age asylums and prisons filled with injustice and abuse, but the plants and animals, the rivers and soils, the cities, especially the cities. The sensitization resulting from therapy forces us to be activists of one sort or another.

We know how to be activists politically—to march, to contribute to causes, to attend meetings and volunteer. And we know how to be therapists—to bring psychological awareness to the knots and painful tangles of the day. But do we know yet what therapeutic activism is? I mean, do we yet know what *psychological* activism is? How to be psychological and also active—not by interpreting the world's dilemmas, internalizing its problems as patriarchal, or penis envy, or homophobia, or shadow projection, or acting out of envy and rage, but rather a kind of psychology focused on what Robert J. Lifton calls "imagining the real." Our psychology is still stuck in people and has not gone far enough with the great task of imagining technology, economics and capitalism, ethnicity, geography, the city. This for me is the late stage of growing down—trying to bring psychology downwards and outwards from the personal and private sphere into the actual day and its dilemmas.

Finally a word, about the word "care." It has taken on a very sweet tone. It tends now to mean comforting, supporting, tending. It brings to mind nursing and helping.

But caring is also passion, fighting for something, protecting values, standing firm against damage and wrongs. Compassion is too wobbly by itself—what do they call us liberals,

"bleeding hearts." Compassion with passion. Compassion has passion in it; as Michael Meade wrote: passion first then compassion. And a piece of passion is *outrage*.

Care as passion reveals what you care about. and there are things to care about—despite irony and deconstruction and postmodern wise-ass virtual realities, despite militant fundamentalists, their meanness and murderous Puritanism. There is honor and dignity and courage. There are ideals; there is social justice, there is friendship and frankness and decency—and the willingness to stand for these.

Care does not merely nurse the wounded; care stands at the cave's mouth looking outward watching the dark with a fierce eye, keeping a smudge stick smoldering to ward off false comfort and vain hopes and corporate snake-oil.

Care takes us into strife. Let us remember the great Greek psychologist even before Sophocles and Socrates, I mean Heraclitus, who said one thing we probably all recall: "You will not measure the boundaries of the soul; so deep is its measure." But I wish to leave you with what he also said in different ways and several times: "Strife [sometimes called *polemos*, *eris*, war, fighting] is the father of all things." "Strife is justice; and all things come into being and pass away through strife."

REFERENCES

Hillman, J. (1964). *Suicide and the Soul.* New York: Harper & Row.
Hillman, J. (183). *Healing Fiction* Woodstock, CT: Spring.
Sawyer-Laucanno, C. (1989). *An invisible spectator.* London: Bloomsbury.

Discussion by Irvin Yalom, M.D.

◆

I feel very privileged to have just heard this address, as I am sure all of you do. Though we may not be able to repeat the words precisely, we know that something very important has

come our way in the last hour. I tried to free associate to it—to write down a few comments as I was listening. The first thing to come to mind is an incident that I heard described just a few weeks ago at a birthday party for Jim Bugental. A friend of his was speaking about a conference he had been to quite some time ago. Such arcane and abstruse constructs were expressed that he turned to a friend of his, Gregory Bateson, the great anthropologist, with some puzzlement about what was being said. Bateson, as enigmatic and elusive as ever, drew a picture of someone holding up his hands and looking in the mirror. The man didn't understand Bateson's point and then Bateson whispered to him, "Satan is left-handed." For the moment he felt satisfied. He wasn't sure what it meant, but it seemed, momentarily, to explain much. The effect soon faded and after the conference he desired more clarity and followed Bateson out to question him. Bateson's response was "truth lurks in metaphors."

When Jim Hillman started to speak, he indicated that he was going to tell us stories, metaphors and I've think we've all experienced that truth does lurk in metaphors—the metaphors we've heard today.

I learned from Jim Hillman just a few days ago about the topics he would be addressing today, and I was hoping that some incident might happen in my clinical practice that I could speak about in my discussion. About a hundred years ago at the weekly Viennese psychoanalytic meetings, one of Freud's real irritants was a man named Wilhelm Steckel who in rejoinder to some point Freud made would invariably rise and say, "Well, only this morning I had a patient who disproved what you were saying." Wilhelm Steckel's famous Wednesday-morning patient was always there and always convenient.

But I *did* have an illustrative clinical session this Wednesday. I listened to a patient, whom I shall call Matthew, with Jim Hillman's constructs in mind, and also Jim's recent book, *We Had a Hundred Years of Psychotherapy and the World is Getting Worse*; it's a wonderful book.

Matthew was a businessman who had some extraordinary success quite recently; so much that a well-known magazine sent two reporters to write a feature story on him. The reporters were permitted to spend an entire day with him, from the moment he woke up to the moment he went to sleep. This is one method

of writing a feature story. He came to see me the day following that surveillance and he was very upset; he's always had a defense of feeling fraudulent underneath, and his fear was that as a result of the feature story, his entire shadow would be revealed; he was going to be exposed to all the world.

I said, "Well, what is it they will find out?"

He replied, "Well, to take only one example—I talked about my education, about dropping out of school when I was 19. I told them I had to drop out of school because I had to work, but I didn't tell them the truth: They will find out that I dropped out of school because of pure laziness."

So I inquired, "What did you do when you dropped out of school?"

He said, "Well, I was married. I did have to work. I had three jobs and I was selling door to door—all sorts of objects—and learning something about sales, and learning something about the sales world."

"And what else did you do?"

"I figured out a reasonably good system for parimutuel betting, but it didn't quite work out."

"What else did you do in your laziness? Plunk yourself in front of the TV?"

"No, no, no, I'd never do that. I was constantly reading. I can't tell you how many books I read during that time."

I scratched my head and thought that I didn't see a lot of laziness here. Then, informed and inspired by many of the metaphors that Jim has given us today, I said to him, "You know, you've had such a remarkable success. You are such a maverick in your field. You have such a creative imagination. You've been able to pull together so much information. Can't you see that when you dropped out of school you were really preparing yourself for the person that you are today—you needed that experience in sales, that immersion in so many fields of knowledge—you were becoming you. You were fulfilling your destiny. There was something in you that knew—something you had to do to prepare yourself, to groom yourself for the very career into which you ventured."

My words were so meaningful and so relieving to him that he wept. It was so moving I almost feel tearful talking about it now. He then talked about his mother. When he was an adolescent, he had chosen to leave his mother and go with his father when his parents divorced. He always maintained that he went with his father because that was where the money was, but now as he looked back on it as we talked this week, he said he now knew, applying the same reasoning—the idea of the destiny that was built into him—that he *had* to go with his father. If he had stayed with his mother, she would have been so intrusive that he would have become only an empty shell and he could never have done what he had done with his life. The wrong choice would have been destructive for him and he must have had some awareness of that at an earlier time.

So my patient, Matthew, and I both thank you, Jim, for this advice. It was a very useful hour.

The concept of what-one-must-become is, I think, a very powerful concept in therapy. Nietzsche's first granite sentence of self-perfection is "become who you are." He used that throughout his life as he talked about self-perfection and self-overcoming—become who you are destined to be.

There is another point which Jim raised that I think is powerful. In his book *A Hundred Years of Psychotherapy*, he said, "It means that our history is secondary or contingent and that the image in the heart is primary and essential. If our history is contingent, and not the primary determinant, then the things that befall us in the course of time, which we call development, are various actualizations of the image, manifestations of it, and not causes of who we are. I'm not caused by my history. My parents, my childhood, and development—these are mirrors. These are mirrors in which

I may catch glimpses of my image." Those are very beautiful and powerful statements.

During my training I had a wonderful professor named John Whitehorn. He didn't write very much, but he did write one very important article. In its collection of the most important 50 articles in the last 50 years, the *American Journal of Psychiatry* included his paper, "Cause and Manifestation in Psychotherapy." He was making a similar point to Jim. So often what we think of as historical causes, are, as Jim puts it, not causes but *manifestations* of the same image, of the same temperament, of the same person who is present now or was present then. What goes before is not necessarily cause, but merely an earlier manifestation.

This idea of destiny is very useful in therapy. This thinking leads us to a certain type of therapeutic strategy, which is that clinicians primarily are here to remove obstacles to the patient becoming who he or she is. We are not here to instill or inspirit someone. If someone has difficulty in loving, we can't instill the ability to love. We can't instill "love-ability."

I like that term "love-ability." If someone is lovable, it means that we can love him or her. But we can love him or her because he or she has the *ability* to love others. So what do we do? We don't create: we remove the obstacles that prevent that person from exercising that love-ability on his or her own.

I've know Jim Hillman only a couple of years—not long enough, not nearly—but I've never had a trivial conversation with him. I've never heard him speak in any way that has been trivial. He has always made me think in new ways, in new directions, even reversing, as he has today, our views of what is up, what is down. Thank you, Jim.

The Healing Word:
Its Past, Present, and Future

Thomas Szasz, M.D.

Thomas Szasz, M.D.
Thomas Szasz (M.D., University of Cincinnati, 1944) is Professor of Psychiatry Emeritus at the State University of New York Upstate Medical Center in Syracuse. He has received numerous awards, including the Humanist of the Year Award from the American Humanist Association and the Distinguished Service Award from the American Institute for Public Service. He has received a number of honorary doctorates and lectureships, and he serves on the editorial board of many journals.
Dr. Szasz has written more than 400 articles, book chapters, reviews, letters to the editor, and columns. He also has more than 20 books to his credit.

Though it is absolutely required of a man that he should intend to help others, the power to do so is outside his control. . . . [T]he final aim of every critic and teacher must be to persuade others to do without him, to realize that the gifts of the spirit are never to be had at second hand.

(Auden, 1948)

A BRIEF HISTORY OF HEALING

In the *Apology*, Socrates articulated his vocation as philosopher, by which he meant a person who cares for the human *psyche* or soul. Because only people have souls, this view stamped him as an ally of the individual and an adversary of the *polis*, a role he made no effort to conceal. Addressing the Athenian authorities, he pledged: "Gentlemen, I owe a greater obedience to God than to you." He then defined his role, as physician of the soul, as follows:

[I]t is my belief that no greater good has befallen you in this city than my service to my God. For I spend all my time going about trying to persuade you, young and old, to make your chief concern not for your bodies nor for your possessions, but for the highest welfare of your souls. (Hamilton & Cairns, 1961, p. 15)

For the post-Socratic philosophers, especially the Stoics, the philosopher was a physician of the soul who, employing the healing word (*iatroi logoi*), offered counsel to those perplexed by problems in living. Seneca, for example, advised his mother, grieving over his exile to Corsica, to give herself up to "the study of philosophy, sovereign remedy for sadness" (McNeil, 1951).

After the triumph of Christianity, the priest as confessor-counselor replaced the philosopher as rhetorician of consolation. For most of the next nearly two thousand years, doctors of divinity (and parish priests) served as the curers of the Western soul. The cure of bodies, at the same time, became the domain of doctors of medicine (and barber surgeons).[1] The ensuing distinction between the cure of souls and the cure of bodies was recognized as early as the fourteenth century. Petrarch (Francesco Petrarca, 1304–1374)—the great Renaissance poet-philosopher, often called "the first humanist"—warned against the literal interpretation of the medical metaphor of rhetorical healing. Declaring that "The care of the mind calls for the philosopher," he urged that doctors should use "herbs not words" and "leave the cure or moving of minds to the true philosophers and orators" (McClure, 1991, p. 20, 51).

A CRITIQUE OF PSYCHOANALYSIS

I should now like to summarize how I see the birth, growth, and death of psychotherapy, epitomized by psychoanalysis.

The real name of "Anna O."—the patient who, according to Freud, "discovered" catharsis and psychoanalysis—was Bertha Pappenheim. In 1880, when Pappenheim became Joseph Breuer's patient, she was a 21-year-old woman, living the existentially stifled life of an intelligent, overprotected daughter of wealthy Viennese-Jewish parents. In an effort to escape from the meaningless existence to which her family and social station condemned her, she pretended to be ill and was duly diagnosed as suffering from hysteria.[2] Aided by the affection and sympathy of an exceptionally humane physician, who lavished vast amounts of time on her, Pappenheim rediscovered the ancient power of the healing word, or, more precisely,

of the healing dialogue. The patient named the therapy—in English—the "talking cure" and "chimney sweeping." Her physician named it—in Greek—*catharsis* (Breuer & Freud, 1893/1961). It was unthinkable, for patient as well as doctor, to call a spade by its proper German name, that is, to call the Healing Word *das heilende Wort*, or its use *Heilung durch dein Geist* ("spiritual healing"). Using ordinary German words to describe these phenomena would have exposed the patient as a malingerer, and the physician as a quack.

It is important to note here that many of the "symptoms" Pappenheim exhibited were not only plainly self-created but involved the use of language. For example, she had mysterious "spells," during which she was mute in German, her mother tongue, but could speak in English. Not surprisingly, Breuer—an astute and scientifically trained physician—realized that the "talking cure" was not a genuine medical treatment, quickly abandoned its use, and actively opposed psychoanalysis.[3]

As fate had it, one of Breuer's protégés was a young physician, named Sigmund Freud, to whom Breuer related his misadventure with Pappenheim. Thereupon Freud decided to make listening and talking to patients his life's work—not like other physicians, as an incidental part of the therapeutic effort, but as an integral part of it, indeed its sole ingredient. In the sophisticated intellectual climate of pre-World War I Vienna, it did not take long before Freud's sweeping claims about the efficacy of the treatment he called psychoanalysis were challenged and exposed as "the disease of which it claims to be the cure" (Szasz, 1990).[4]

[1.] Freud acknowledged that the roots of catharsis and psychoanalysis lie in the Socratic dialogue and the Catholic confessional.

[2.] I will use the words "illness," "treatment," and so on with the understanding that we are not dealing with real diseases or real treatments.

[3.] Like the word "disease," the word "treat" has a wide range of meanings. For example, we say that a man treats his dog badly, call seeing a good play "a treat," and denote as treatments certain interventions defined as "medical treatments" by the state (the use of which by persons not licensed to practice medicine constitutes a crime). I do not wish to quibble about the meaning of words or limit their colloquial use. I wish here only to draw a clear distinction between the physical cure of bodily diseases (exemplified by surgical operations and blood transfusions), and the nonphysical cure of souls in distress (exemplified by the Catholic confessional and psychotherapy). I regard the former as literal treatments, the latter as metaphorical treatments.

[4.] "Die Psychoanalyse ist jene Krankheit, fur deren Behandlung sie sicht halt."

Karl Kraus, the author of that aphorism, objected to the talking cure not because it consisted of talking, but because it was miscast as a treatment (Szasz, 1990).[5]

Psychoanalysis thus began modestly, as the private medical practice of an obscure *Nervenarzt* ("nerve doctor") (Zweig, 1932). However, thanks to Freud's genius as a merchandiser—illustrated by his cleverly deceptive choice for the name of his particular style of rhetorical healing—the enterprise he founded soon grew into an international franchise that proceeded to erase all traces of its historical and intellectual origins. With its lineage forgotten and its true nature repudiated, psychoanalysis was recast as a science of the "unconscious mind" as well as an effective method for treating mental diseases.

PSYCHIATRY VERSUS PSYCHOANALYSIS

Because Freud was a practicing physician who treated people officially denominated as patients, and because he defined psychoanalysis as a treatment of mental diseases, we must now situate psychoanalysis—as the paradigm of modern psychotherapy—in the context of the history of psychiatry.

For centuries, madmen and mad-doctors alike were banished to madhouses, located on the outskirts of towns or in the countryside. Alienists—renamed psychiatrists in the nineteenth century—worked, and often lived, in insane asylums, where they oversaw desolate scenes of human misery. When Freud came on this scene, insane people were considered to be legally incompetent, insanity was considered to be an incurable illness, and individuals denominated as insane were incarcerated in insane asylums, usually for life. Because Freud's work appeared to have little relevance to the work of professionals engaged in caring for the insane (many of whom suffered from the neurological ravages of syphilis), European psychiatrists first ignored psychoanaly-

sis and then rejected it as unsuitable for "serious" cases of mental illness. In contrast, American psychiatrists, imbued with characteristically American therapeutic optimism, considered no disease indefeasible and embraced psychoanalysis as an ally in the war on mental illness. *Pari passu*, American psychoanalysts—ostensibly to protect the public from psychoanalytic quackery—defined psychoanalysis as a medical activity and excluded nonmedical analysts from among their ranks. This marriage between psychiatry and psychoanalysis was a catastrophe for both parties, but more so for psychoanalysis and, ultimately, for psychotherapy. It is important that we understand the nature and consequences of this fateful misalliance.

In the eighteenth century, Western societies began to delegate to mad-doctors—subsequently called alienists, psychiatrists, mental health professionals, and therapists—the task of separating insane people from sane people and incarcerating the former in madhouses (see footnote p. 302). To justify this enterprise, psychiatrists fabricated appropriate pseudomedical explanations about why some people display certain kinds of unwanted behaviors, about the dangers they pose to themselves and society as a result, and about the interventions mental healers must use to protect patients from themselves and the public from the patients.

At the beginning of this century, psychoanalysts appeared on the scene and claimed to be especially adept at explaining why people behave the way they do. American psychiatrists seized on these explanations as useful addenda to their own mystifications. The amalgamation of psychiatric and psychoanalytic theories received further impetus during World War II. Many of the analysts were recent refugees from Nazism who felt it was their patriotic duty to respond to the needs of the military. In the service, they were happy to do the bidding of their superiors, finding men fit or unfit for duty as the military authorities decreed. This use of psychoanalytic concepts was phony, but expedient, for the military as well as psychoanalysis. The result was that psychoanalysis and psychiatry were joined, much as a veneer of mahogany may be bonded

---

[5.]Similarly, Kraus objected to psychoanalytic explanations not only because they were often used to discredit opponents, but mainly because Freud claimed that psychoanalysis was a science.

to a piece of pine furniture. For a brief period, the prestige of this superficially psychoanalyticized psychiatry carried over into civilian life.

But it was all show. Psychiatrists in public mental hospitals, privately practicing psychiatrists who treated their patients with electric shock, and psychiatrists accredited as analysts all pretended that the similarities far outweighed the differences among them. In the process, the core elements of curing souls with healing words (individualism and noncoercion) were replaced by the core elements of treating mad minds (statism and coercion).[6]

The aims and values of these two conflicting undertakings may be summarized as follows:

- To effect a cure, the psychiatrist coerces and controls his "patient": He incarcerates the (involuntary) victim and imposes various unwanted chemical and physical interventions on him.
- To conduct a dialogue, the psychoanalyst contracts and cooperates with his "patient": He listens and talks to his (voluntary) interlocutor, who pays for the services he receives (Szasz, 1988).

The differences between the psychiatric and psychoanalytic relationships replicate the differences between two familiar types of political relationships, namely, paternalistic absolutism (unlimited government) and classical liberalism (limited government and the rule of law). The essence of individual liberty is the absence of capricious, unlawful coercions (traditionally present) in relations between rulers and ruled. Failure by the state to respect private property and its interference in voluntary acts between consenting adults destroy individual liberty. *Mutatis mutandis*, the essence of psychoanalysis is the absence of coercions (traditionally present) in relations between psychiatrists and mental patients. The analyst's failure to respect the analysand's personal autonomy (paternalism) and his interference in the client's life (betrayal

of confidentiality and coercion) destroy the psychoanalytic relationship.

In its initial stages, psychoanalysis represented a genuinely new social development, a noncoercive, secular help ("therapy") for problems in living (called "neuroses"). The term "psychoanalysis" was then used to denote a confidential dialogue between an expert and a client, the former rejecting the role of custodial psychiatrist, the latter assuming the role of responsible, voluntary patient. Recast in such light, it is hardly surprising that psychiatry acquired neither the aims nor the practices of psychoanalysis. It could not have done so and fulfilled its social mandate. The two enterprises rest on totally different premises and entail mutually incompatible practices:

- The traditional psychiatrist was a salaried physician who worked in a mental institution; his source of income was the state; he functioned as an agent of his bureaucratic superiors and the patient's relatives. The typical mental hospital inmate was a poor person, cast in the patient role against his will, housed in a public mental hospital.
- The classical psychoanalyst was a self-employed professional who worked in his private office; his source of income was his patient; he functioned as his patient's agent. The (typical) analytic patient was a rich person (usually wealthier than his analyst), cast in the patient role by himself, living in his own home or wherever he pleased.

The basic differences between psychiatry and psychoanalysis are dramatically captured in the following statements by, respectively, Benjamin Rush, the father of American psychiatry,[7] and Sigmund Freud, the father of psychoanalysis:

- Rush: "Let our pupil be taught that he does not belong to himself, but that he is public property" (Richman, 1994).

---

[6] I refer here to mad-doctoring/psychiatry as it developed in Europe from the eighteenth century on, characterized primarily by the involuntary confinement of (innocent) people in insane asylums.

[7] Benjamin Rush was a physician, a signer of the Declaration of Independence, and the author of the first American text on mental diseases. He is the undisputed father of American psychiatry: His portrait adorns the official seal of the American Psychiatric Association.

"Let us view them [mankind] as patients in a hospital. The more they resist our efforts to serve them, the more they have need of our services" (Szasz, 1988).

- Freud: "Nothing takes place in a psychoanalytic treatment but an interchange of words between the patient and the analyst" (Freud, 1905/1961).

"[T]he patient should be educated to liberate and fulfill his own nature, not to resemble ourselves" (Freud, 1917/1961).

The merger between psychiatry and psychoanalysis was a hopeless match, a marriage of convenience in which each party proceeded to rob his partner of whatever seemed of value to him. Psychiatry acquired the worst features of psychoanalysis, its pseudo-explanations and vocabulary of stigmatizations; psychoanalysis acquired the worst features of psychiatry, disloyalty to the patient's self-defined interests and coercion. In short, psychoanalysts (and psychotherapists along with them) sold their noble, but financially unprofitable, birthright for a mess of pottage, the fakery of psychodiagnostics and psychotherapy. The result is an ignoble—and, for the time being, financially profitable—"mental health" profession, masquerading as biological science and medical treatment.[8]

A CRITIQUE OF FREUD

How did psychotherapy get itself into this mess, if a mess it be?[9] Ironically, it was Freud himself who insisted on the self-contradictory proposition that psychoanalysis is both a *dialogue* and a *treatment*.[10] "Words," he wrote, "are the essential tool of mental treatment. . . .

As a method of treatment it [psychoanalysis] is one among many, though, to be sure, *primus inter pares* [first among equals] (Freud, 1905)." Finally, Freud predicted and welcomed the embrace of a medicalized psychoanalysis by the modern welfare state:

[I]t is possible to foresee that at some time or other the conscience of society will awake and remind it that the poor man should have as much right to assistance for his mind as he now has to the life-saving help offered by surgery; and that the neuroses threaten public health no less than tuberculosis, and can be left as little as the latter to the impotent care of the individual members of the community. . . . Such treatments will be free. It may be a long time before the State comes to see these duties as urgent. . . . Some time or other, however, it must come to this. (Freud, 1919/1961).

This passage appears only two pages after Freud's claim that the aim of psychoanalysis is to "liberate" the patient, a proposition that formed an integral part of Freud's thesis that psychoanalysis is *not* a treatment. Instead of curing the patient, the analyst's task, he declared, is "to bring to the patient's knowledge the unconscious repressed impulses existing in him" (Freud, 1919/1961). Finally, in *An Outline of Psychoanalysis*—the summation of his life's work—he wrote: "We [psychoanalysts] serve the patient in various functions, as an authority and a substitute for his parents, as a teacher and educator" (Freud, 1938/1961).

Freud's dexterity as a high-wire artist—balancing himself between his roles as personal counselor and as medical doctor—never deserted him. After identifying the therapist as parent, teacher, and educator, Freud quickly reasserted his lifelong commitment to a materialist-medical treatment for personal problems as mental diseases. "But here we are concerned," he wrote, "with therapy only in so far as it works by psychological means; and for the time being we have no other. The future may teach us to exercise a direct influence, by means of particular chemical substances, on the amounts of energy and their distribution in the mental apparatus" (Freud, 1919/1961).

As a result of Freud's labors, it is now a part of received wisdom that psychoanalysis

---

[8.]In the third edition of the *Psychiatric Dictionary*, the word *psychotherapy* is defined as "The art of treating mental diseases . . . with the object of removing, modifying, or retarding existing systems . . ." (Hinsie & Campbell, 1960).

[9.]I realize that many psychotherapists believe that their profession is now in the best condition it has ever been in and that it is steadily improving ("evolving").

[10.]In my opinion, the assertion that talk is treatment is as self-contradictory as the assertion that science rests on faith.

is a method for "analyzing" human behavior; that it is a valid "theory" for explaining the behavior not only of living people but also of dead people and of people who never existed—that is, of myth, religion, legend, and literature; and that listening and talking to a person—called "talk therapy"—is a *bona fide* medical treatment.

The degeneration of psychoanalysis—and of psychotherapy in general—is an inexorable consequence of the medicalization of life, that is, of the tendency to regard despair and deviance as diseases, and talking as a treatment. Viewing a person's complaints about his life as if they were the symptoms of a mental illness *defines* the complaint as a disease and the effort to ameliorate it as a treatment. However, ideas have consequences that have a habit of coming back to haunt us. If we view diabetes as a disease, we rightly consider it a serious error—*prima facie* medical negligence—to treat a diabetic person solely by listening and talking to him. The same goes for viewing mental illnesses—whose disease status is established as legal "fact" by the DSM-IV diagnoses attached to them—as chemical disturbances in the brain treatable with drugs. The upshot is that practicing the "talking cure" (especially by a physician) has been rendered *de jure* malpractice, and hence *de facto* impractical and irrelevant.[11] But that is not all. With the liquidation of the most essential prerequisite of psychotherapy—that the relationship between therapist and client be based on a free contract between them—the nature of the "correct therapy" is no longer defined jointly by the two parties to the agreement; instead, henceforth the scientifically correct diagnosis of the patient's disease determines the scientifically correct treatment he needs and that the therapist must provide.

ABOUT PSYCHOTHERAPY

The psychoanalyst's assertion that his method was a genuine treatment for genuine diseases, superior to all other treatments, natu-

rally provoked a torrent of controversy and criticism that is still continuing. Eager to eclipse Freud, his competitors typically gave faint praise to psychoanalysis as an early form of psychotherapy, the better to claim superiority for their brand of mental healing. Eager to execrate Freud, his critics typically claimed that psychoanalysis is no more effective than no treatment at all (Eysenck, 1952; Rosenhan & Seligman, 1984). Recasting psychotherapy as dialogue transcends this futile controversy and dispels the mystery that continues to envelope mental healing, especially the question of its so-called effectiveness.

Since ancient times, people have recognized that words powerfully affect the listener, and that like double-edged swords they cut both ways. Indeed, our vocabulary possesses numerous adjectives for characterizing both types of speech acts, such as: blasphemous, impious, obscene, perjurious, pornographic, profane, and sacrilegious for words deemed to be harmful; and calming, cheering, comforting, consoling, encouraging, heartening, inspiring, motivating, and reassuring for words deemed to be helpful.

Dreading the effects of harming words and desiring the effects of healing words, every society prohibits speech acts it considers deleterious and encourages those it considers beneficial. It seems to me that the fact of censorship is proof enough that words can heal. My point here is simply to show that it is absurd to contend—as many people have contended and continue to contend—that psychotherapy is (inherently) ineffective. The truth is far simpler: The benefit or detriment of a particular discourse depends on the subject's susceptibility to the speaker's message. In the final analysis, just as the beauty or ugliness of a face lies in the eyes of the beholder, so the benefit or detriment of a speech act lies in the ears of the hearer. It is *a priori* impossible to marshall objective evidence to support or refute claims about the effectiveness or ineffectiveness of psychotherapy. The validity of this assertion is intrinsic to the ontological character of psychotherapy-as-discourse.[12]

[11.]Despite this political-economic climate, or more likely because of it, many American psychologists are now clamoring for prescription privileges.

[12.]Not surprisingly, as soon as private and public health insurance plans started to pay for certain "talk therapies"

Let me now briefly restate my concept of psychotherapy, as the name of a class of interactions in which two (or more) people voluntarily listen and talk to one another. In this view, psychotherapists dispensing diverse therapies resemble clerks in a department store, each selling a different merchandise under the same roof. To be sure, psychotherapists differ from clerks: Selling merchandise (or performing a standardized medical procedure) is an impersonal act that a person does in his persona as the purveyor of goods (or services); whereas healing with words is a personal activity, not just a job a person does but something that he *is*. It is morally fitting that it should be so. The person who seeks help through the healing word suffers not from an impersonal illness, such as an inflamed appendix, but from a distinctively personal perplexity. It follows that just as it would demean both marital partners to speak of a "method" a husband uses to relate to his wife or vice versa,[13] so it demeans both therapist and client to speak of a method of psychotherapy (Szasz, 1988).

Mental illness and psychotherapy are fictions. Neither exists. Only the patient, the therapist, and a particular relationship between them exist. Both participants are responsible moral agents. Each is existentially equal to the other, each influences the other, and each is responsible for his behavior. The therapist can neither cure the patient nor make him sick. However, the patient can do both of these things—for or to himself—by making use of the therapist's healing or harming words. These simple insights—commonplaces to the early religious and rhetorical curers of souls and their clients—have disappeared into the mystifications of the mental health professions and the gulag of the Therapeutic State.

Clearly, there are as many authentic types of psychotherapies as there are authentic

people using words to heal. I respect every one of these "methods," provided their practitioners eschew force and fraud. My own work as therapist was based on the premise that the focus of the therapeutic relationship can only be how the patient lives, how he might live, and how he ought to live (Szasz, 1988). The expert's role is to engage the client in a process of searching self-examination, with the aim of enabling him, if he so chooses, to become more free and more responsible. To accomplish this task, the therapist must eschew interfering, in any way whatever, in his client's life outside the walls of the consulting room (including receiving information from, or giving information to, anyone other than the client). Such a curer of souls must reject playing doctor or therapist. Instead of promising relief from suffering—or promising any particular outcome—his duty is to fulfill his promise to the client, that is, to respect his autonomy and confidences and engage him in a searching, open-ended dialogue. The outcome of the interaction must be left in the client's hands, because he has more control over it than the expert and, more importantly, because that is where it rightly belongs.[14]

IN CONCLUSION

To paraphrase Shakespeare, I have come to praise the healing word, not to bury it. But I must report to you that the healing word is no more: It has committed suicide by overdosing on therapy.[15]

The modern soul-doctors succumbed to the temptation to treat human beings as material susceptible to improvement by experts, ceased to respect the Other as a moral agent, and renamed discourse "treatment." They are the sinners whose offense W. H. Auden satirized thus: "We are all here on earth to help others; what on earth the others are here for, I don't know" (Auden, 1968).

---

as *bona fide* medical treatments, mental health professionals began to produce an avalanche of "studies," some demonstrating the effectiveness, others the ineffectiveness, of every conceivable "method" of psychotherapy. This has enabled experts on psychotherapy to cite "scientific evidence" to support virtually any claim, pro or con, about any therapy.

[13.]Using a method in such a situation is what we mean by "manipulation."

[14.]As I noted already, in the United States today practicing mental health in accordance with these principles is synonymous with professional negligence (malpractice).

[15.]Because hearing and speaking the Healing Word are needs intrinsic to human nature, its use will surely return in a fresh incarnation.

REFERENCES

Auden, W. H. (1948). Criticism in a mass society. *The Mint, 1*, 13.

Auden, W. H. (1968). *The dyer's hand, and other essays.* New York: Vintage.

Breuer, J., & Freud, S., (1893/1961). Studies on hysteria. In J. Strachey (Ed. and Trans.), *The standard edition of the complete psychological works of Sigmund Freud* (Vol. 2, pp. 8, 30). London: Hogarth Press.

Clark, R. W. (1980). *Freud: The man and the cause.* London: Cape.

Eysenck, H. (1952). The effects of psychotherapy: An evaluation. *Journal of Consulting Psychology, 16*, 319–324.

Freeman, L. (1972). *The story of Anna O.* New York: Walker.

Freud, S. (1905/1961). Psychical (or mental) treatment. In J. Strachey (Ed. and Trans.), *The standard edition of the complete psychological works of Sigmund Freud* (Vol. 7, p. 283). London: Hogarth Press.

Freud, S. (1917/1961). Lines of advance in psychoanalytic therapy. In J. Strachey (Ed. and Trans.), *The standard edition of the complete psychological works of Sigmund Freud* (Vol. 17, p. 165). London: Hogarth Press.

Freud, S. (1919/1961). Lines of advance in psychoanalytic therapy. In J. Strachey (Ed. and Trans.), *The standard edition of the complete psychological works of Sigmund Freud* (Vol. 17, p. 167). London: Hogarth Press.

Freud, S. (1938/1961). An outline of psychoanalysis. In J. Strachey (Ed. and Trans.), *The standard edition of the complete psychological works of Sigmund Freud* (Vol. 23, p. 181). London: Hogarth Press.

Freud, S. (1933/1961). New introductory lectures. In J. Strachey (Ed. and Trans.), *The standard edition of the complete psychological works of Sigmund Freud* (Vol. 22, p. 157). London: Hogarth Press.

Hamilton, E., & Cairns, H. (Eds.). (1961). *The complete dialogues of Plato.* Princeton, NJ: Princeton University Press.

Hinsie, L. E., & Campbell, R. J. (1960). *Psychiatric dictionary* (3rd ed.). New York: Oxford University Press.

McClure, G. W. (1991). Sorrow and consolation in Italian humanism. Princeton, NJ: Princeton University Press.

McNeil, J. T. (1951). *A history of the cure of souls.* New York: Harper & Row.

Richman, S. (1994). *Separating school and state.* Fairfax, VA: Future of Freedom Foundation.

Rosenhan, D. L., & Seligman, M. E. P. (1984). *Abnormal psychology.* New York: Norton.

Szasz, T. S. (1977). *The theology of medicine.* Syracuse, NY: Syracuse University Press.

Szasz, T. S. (1988). *The ethics of psychoanalysis.* Syracuse, NY: Syracuse University Press.

Szasz, T. S. (1990). *Anti-Freud: Karl Kraus's criticism of psychoanalysis and psychiatry.* Syracuse, NY: Syracuse University Press.

Woods, J. A. (Ed.). (1967). The correspondence of Benjamin Rush and Granville Sharp, 1773–1809. *Journal of American Studies, 1*, 8.

Zweig, S. (1932). *Mental healers: Franz Anton Mesmer, Mary Baker Eddy, Sigmund Freud* (Eden Paul & Cedar Paul, Trans.). New York: Viking.

Discussion by Paul Watzlawick, Ph.D.

◆

It is a great honor for me to make a commentary on Dr. Szasz' presentation. His *Myth of Mental Illness* was one of the most powerful single factors in my own professional development. It has helped me to do that 180-degree turn from being a Jungian analyst—a training analyst even—to a totally new perspective.

When I began to work as a Jungian analyst, I knew almost everything, for instance, about Siberian creation myths, but I didn't know what to do with a person who chewed his fingernails. That bothered me.

Above all, what Dr. Szasz' book helped me to understand was the fallacy of the belief that mentally normal people see the world as it "really" is, while so-called mental patients have a distorted view of it. This myth of a real reality has maintained itself almost exclusively in our field. In a conversation with Heisenberg, back in 1926 in Copenhagen, Einstein already is supposed to have said, "It is wrong to assume that theories are based on observation. The opposite is the case. The theory determines what we can observe." And in philosophy since Kant and Schopenhauer, the same issues have been questioned.

In his 1985 presentation in Phoenix, Dr. Szasz already warned about the dogma perceived as truth. For me and my professional development, it was very important to learn from Dr. Szasz that all psychiatric concepts are *mythologemes*—"monstrous distempers." This is the term he uses. Proofs of this assumption reach into antiquity. For me, it is particularly interesting what Plutarch wrote in his *Miscellanies and Essays* about an incident that happened in the city of Milesia, in Asia Minor. He says: "A certain dreadful and monstrous distemper did seize the Milesian maids, arising from some hidden cause. It is most likely the air had acquired some infatuating and venomous quality that did influence them to this change and alienation of mind. For all of a sudden, an earnest longing for death, with furious attempts to hang themselves, did attack them, and many did accomplish it. The arguments and tears of parents and the persuasion of friends availed nothing, but they circumvented their keepers and all their contrivances and industry to prevent them, still murdering themselves. And the calamity seemed to be an extraordinary divine stroke and beyond human help, until by the counsel of a wise man a decree of the Senate was passed, enacting that those maids who hanged themselves should be carried naked through the market place. The passage of this law not only inhibited, but quashed their desire of slaying themselves." You see, brief therapy existed already in those days.

So it is really a nice example of the difference between a mythologeme and the simplicity of what nowadays would be called a direct intervention. Epictetus already knew about the underlying structure of our experience of the world when he said: "It is not the things that concern us, but the opinions that we have about the things."

And Paracelsus, in the 16th century, in making a step away from the idea that religious or other assumptions have to be the basis of our understanding of mental illness, talked about "invisible illnesses," and wrote a book about this subject.

Another very interesting reference is found in the work of two French psychiatrists, Lasègue and Falret, who wrote an important paper called "La folie à deux ou folie communiquée" in the 1880s. In it they describe the patient and then continue, "The above description belongs to the insane person, the agent who provokes the situation in a *délire à deux*. His associate is a much more complicated person to define and yet careful research will

teach one to recognize the laws which are obeyed by this second party in communicated insanity.... Once the tacit contract that ties both lunatics is almost settled, the problem is not only to examine the influence of the insane on the supposedly sane man, but also the opposite, the influence of the rational on the deluded one and to show how through mutual compromise the differences are eliminated."

Gregory Bateson wrote several "metalogues"—fictitious conversations with his little daughter—and in one of those metalogues the daughter asks, "Daddy, what is an instinct?" And Gregory Bateson precisely does not commit the traditional mistake of saying something like: "An instinct is a genetically transmitted behavior pattern." No, he says, "An instinct is an explanatory principle." That's all.

You are all aware of the enormous power that our explanatory principles have. I am reminded of a conversation that I had with a capable lay hypnotist who was hired by doctors to help them in their work. One day they invited him to come to a reception and to talk more about his approach and his work. As he arrived at the doctor's house, he saw, in his own words, that "Every horizontal surface in the meeting room was covered by vases of freshly cut flowers." He had an allergy to freshly cut flowers, and soon he began to feel it. His eyes burned, his nose dripped, his eyes itched and ran, and he said to his host: "Listen, I don't think I will be able to give my presentation. I have this horrible allergy to fresh flowers."

And the doctor said, "Oh, that's strange. These flowers are plastic." So the hypnotist went to touch them, and saw that indeed they were artificial, and within three minutes the allergic reaction was gone.

So you see the power of the meaning that we give to the objects of our so-called reality.

The assumption, for instance, that the exploration of the past is a precondition for a change in the present has been neatly demolished by the philosopher Karl Popper. He called such assumptions "self-sealing propositions." A self-sealing proposition, according to Popper, is a proposition whose validity is proven by both the success and the failure of its practical application. For instance, if a patient's condition improves as a result of insight-oriented therapy—of trying to find the causes in the past—this clearly proves the correctness of this approach and its usefulness. If, on the other hand, the patient's condition does not improve, it proves merely that the search for the causes in the past has not yet been driven far and deep enough into the unconscious. The proposition wins either way.

What Dr. Szasz warns against continues to repeat itself invariably. The philosopher Santayana already said, "There is nothing new under the sun except the forgotten." Take the recent epistemological tendencies in our field. The pendulum swings from an unlimited belief in the definitive correctness of the psychoanalytic approach to the pharmaceutical approach, the belief in a purely biochemical therapy. Colleagues of mine at Stanford some years ago said, "Not only will we have the healing medications for every mental and emotional illness, but we shall also understand the bio-chemical basis of love and creativity." I hope I shall not be around anymore when that happens!

Nowadays, as you all know, a new epistemology, a new basic idea, is becoming powerful, and that is the discovery of repressed childhood memories as the true cause of emotional problems. I know of no other authority who has made us as aware of these problems as Dr. Szasz. Small wonder that as early as the publication of the first edition of his book, *The Myth of Mental Illness*, the commissioner of the New York State Department of Mental Hygiene demanded that Dr. Szasz be dismissed from his university position because he did not believe in mental illness. I wonder if the same had already happened to the counselor of the Senate of the city of Milesia, who had managed to stop that suicide epidemic among young women because he obviously did not see it as a "monstrous distemper arising from some hidden causes."

"Insight" May Cause Blindness

◆

Paul Watzlawick, Ph.D.

Paul Watzlawick, Ph.D.
Paul Watzlawick received his Ph.D. degree from the University of Venice in 1949. He has an Analyst's Diploma from the C.G. Jung Institute for Analytic Psychology in Zurich. Dr. Watzlawick has practiced psychotherapy for more than 40 years. Currently, he is Research Associate at the Mental Research Institute and Clinical Professor Emeritus in the Department of Psychiatry and Behavioral Sciences, Stanford University Medical Center.
Dr. Watzlawick received the Distinguished Achievement Award from the American Family Therapy Association, the Distinguished Professional Contributions to Family Therapy Award from the American Association for Marriage and Family Therapy, the Lifetime Achievement Award from The Milton H. Erickson Foundation and the Gold Medal for Meritorious Service from the City of Vienna. He is the recipient of three honorary doctorates. Watzlawick is author, coauthor, or editor of 15 books in 74 foreign language editions and more than 130 book chapters or articles in professional journals.

INTRODUCTION

Consider the case of a man who claps his hands every 20 seconds. When asked for the reason of this strange behavior, he replies: "To chase away the elephants." "Elephants? But there aren't any elephants around here," marvels the other person. "See," he replies, "it works."

How can he be helped? My colleague, Fritz Simon, envisages four possible therapeutic strategies (personal communication):

1. To gradually establish a relationship of trust with this man, until he believes that there really are no elephants around. Needless to say, this may take a long time.

2. To analyze the man's past, find the unconscious reasons for his strange behavior, interpret them, and thus make them accessible to his mind through insight. This process, too, is known to take a long time.

3. Introduce elephants into the therapy sessions, so that the man will realize that his clapping does not scare them away. This will have little practical result because it will not alleviate his fear of the animals.

4. This fourth possibility has nothing to do with therapy: The man has a traffic accident, breaks one of his wrists, and now has it encased in a plaster cast. Owing to the plaster cast, he cannot clap his hands, and thus notices that no elephants appear.

Of these four "strategies," the second and fourth are of importance to my subject. They represent two different and mutually exclusive approaches to the solution of the problem. (As it should become clear in a few minutes, I do not recommend breaking people's wrists as a therapeutic intervention.)

ON INSIGHT

Let us first examine the concept of *insight* in its classical sense. Different and often contradictory as the classical schools of therapy are among themselves, they have *one* assumption in common—that problems can be resolved only by the discovery of their causes. This dogma is based on the belief in a linear, unidirectional causality, running from the past to the present, which in turn generates the seemingly obvious need to gain insight into these causes before a change can take place. Permit me to make a somewhat heretical remark: Neither in my own life (in spite of 3½ years of training analysis), nor in my subsequent work as Jungian analyst, nor in the lives of my clients have I ever come across this magical effect of insight.

But never mind my personal blindness. Of real importance—or so at least it seems to me—is that insight (in its classical, psychodynamic sense) is what the philosopher Karl Popper would have considered "nonfalsifiable"; that is, an assumption whose correctness is proved both by the success as well as by the failure of its practical application. If the patient's problems improve (or disappear altogether) as a result of insight into the causes, this proves the correctness and efficacy of this approach. If, on the other hand, there is no improvement, this proves that the search for the causes in the past has not yet been pushed deep and far enough into history. The assumption wins either way.

In recent years the unquestioned belief in the absolute necessity of insight has become even more pervasive since the replacement of the concept of the Oedipus complex as the cause of most human problems by the discovery of the unique consequences of repressed childhood memories of physical or sexual abuse. Patients who cannot remember any abuse are obviously in need of help to gain access to the recall of these nightmares. Especially in the treatment of smaller children, occasionally this search seems to create a situation that for the child has a totally different meaning: It is an examination that they can pass only if they manage to discover which answer will be considered the right one by the "teacher." In her very interesting (and, of course, heretical) article "Remembering Dangerously," Elizabeth Loftus (1995, p.20) refers to these recalls as "memories that did not exist until a person wandered into therapy."

THE CORRECTIVE EXPERIENCE

In total contradiction to insight is the only seemingly facetious solution of the above-mentioned hand-clapping problem. There we are up against what Alexander and French called the phenomenon of a *corrective emotional experience*:

It is not necessary—nor is it possible—during the course of treatment to recall *every* feeling that has been repressed. Therapeutic results can be achieved without the patient's recalling all important details of his past history; indeed, good therapeutic results have come in cases in which not a single forgotten memory has been brought to the surface.... This new corrective experience may be supplied by the transference relationship, by new experiences in life, or by both (1964, p.22).

A classical example of such a solution can be found in Balint's book *The Basic Fault*, in what he calls the somersault incident. He was working with "an attractive, vivacious, rather flirtatious girl in her late twenties, whose main complaint was her inability to achieve anything." This was due, in part, to her "crippling fear of uncertainty whenever she had to take any risk, that is, take a decision." Balint describes how after two years of psychoanalytic treatment:

She was given the interpretation that apparently the most important thing for her was to keep her head safely up, with both feet firmly planted on the ground. In response, she mentioned that ever since her earliest childhood she could never do a somersault, although at various periods she tried desperately to do one. I then said: 'What about it now?'—whereupon she got up from the couch and, to her great amazement, did a perfect somersault without any difficulty. (1968, pp.128–29)

Balint described this as a real breakthrough, followed by many changes in her life; for instance, "She managed to get permission to sit for, and passed, a most difficult postgraduate professional examination, became engaged, and was married."

An analogous example, taken from a totally different field, is the decision the Hungarian government made in 1989 to tear down some sixty miles of rusty barbed wire along its border with Austria. This seemingly totally insignificant action triggered off an avalanche of historic events—from the fall of the Berlin wall to the collapse of the Soviet empire and the end of the Cold War—whose achievement had been attempted with no success by the Western powers for many decades.

There are countless stories of Milton H. Erickson's use of what might be called "planned chance events." The case of a young man who wanted hypnotherapy for his phobia to cross streets comes to mind. When he came for his first appointment, Erickson had prepared an addressed and stamped envelope that, he explained to the young man, contained a very urgent letter. Erickson asked his patient to do him the favor of taking it downstairs and throwing it in the mail box in front of Erickson's house. Only after having followed this request and mailed the letter did it dawn on the client that he had just crossed the street twice without any discomfort.

THE THERAPY OF AS IF

One of the most important events in my evolution as a therapist was my discovery of a book by the philosopher Hans Vaihinger called *The Philosophy of 'As If'* (1924), a work that is almost forgotten today. Originally published in 1911, it had the effect of a scientific bomb, and greatly influenced, for instance, Alfred Adler's and, to a lesser degree, Freud's thinking.

In a mere 800 pages Vaihinger gives a plethora of examples, taken from all walks of life, showing that we always and inevitably work with unproven and unprovable assumptions regarding the nature of reality, and yet we arrive at concrete results. One of these assumptions, for instance, is the conviction that human beings are endowed with free will. There is not and never will be any proof that this is the case. Yet there never has been and never will be, or can be, a society whose members do not behave *as if* this were the case; for if we did not all believe in free will, human interaction would be total chaos, with people deprived of responsibility and, therefore, of order. Vaihinger's book culminates in the assertion—shocking for many people—that truth is only the most useful error.

I first became aware of the as-if nature of certain therapeutic interventions during my training in hypnosis. If the hypnotist achieves a hand levitation, the hand has not, of course, become lighter than air, but the subject is behaving *as if* this were the case and experiences it as *being* the case. If a socially inhibited and frightened person can be motivated to behave *as if* other people were frightened and in need of reassurance, this almost immediately can bring about a change in the nature of that person's interaction with others, regardless of whether the others "really" were frightened. This as-if assumption has served its purpose and, in Vaihinger's words, now "drops out," regardless of whether the others were "really" frightened, and without the need of any insight.

THE INTERACTIONAL VIEW

Such therapeutic interventions also opened my eyes to the ever-present feedback processes of human interaction, a phenomenon that in my training had been strictly limited to the phenomena of transference and countertransference; that is, to *individual* behaviors. When Gregory Bateson taught me to look at interaction rather than at linear cause-effect processes, I began to see that, yes, cause produces effect, but this effect then feeds back on its cause, thereby creating what since the beginning of cybernetic epistemology has been known as a self-maintaining, self-reinforcing feedback loop. The nature, the qualities, and, therefore, also the pathologies of this loop no longer can be attributed to just one of its single components. It is an *emergent quality*, something more than, and different from, the sum total of its single constituents. In the interactional view of therapy, the "patient" is the relationship pattern, and no longer a single individual.

But how can I get acquainted with this patient? After having had the privilege of watching the work of Gregory Bateson, Don D. Jackson (the founder and first director of our institute), Milton H. Erickson, and others, it occurred to me that in a very real sense we may compare ourselves to a man who does not know the rules of chess and travels to a foreign country, the language of which he does not speak. In that country he comes across two people, sitting opposite each other at a table and moving figures on a board. They are obviously engaged in playing a game. Our man would like to learn that game, but because he does not speak the players' language he cannot ask them for an explanation. What he can do, however, is to watch their behavior for repetitions, for redundancies that in turn will enable him to draw tentative conclusions regarding the rules underlying their behavior. The first such redundancy that he will be able to identify is that they behave *as if* they had a rule that a move by player *A* is always followed by a move by player *B*, whereupon it seems to be player A's turn again. In a similar, but increasingly complex way, he will gradually arrive at similar assumptions regarding the apparent rules governing the moves of every single piece, and finally at an understanding of the endpoint of the game, the checkmate.

What to me seems important about this analogy are three points:

1. The observer arrived at an understanding of the rules of the game without being able to ask direct questions. As therapists we could, of course, ask the members of a family or of any other human interaction system "What are your rules of interaction?" but it

is unlikely that we would get a meaningful answer to this ununderstandable question.

2. In terms of the mathematical game theory, chess is a game with "complete information"—all the necessary information is present on the board at any given moment. *How* this situation arose in the course of the game is completely irrelevant: What matters is the position of the figures in relation to each other *here* and *now*.

3. Even though there exist beautiful stories regarding the "meaning" of chess (for example, it has been described as a fight between the forces of good and evil), such an interpretation would add as little to the understanding of the game as astrology adds to astronomy.

To summarize: The observer arrived at an understanding of the "patient" (the system) by the observation of behavioral redundancies in the here and now, without searching for their causes or trying to interpret them in terms of some epistemological mythology.

However, there is an important issue that the chess observer does not have to deal with—the mind-boggling complexity of any human relationship system. How to deal with this complexity? There are two main strategies about how *not* to deal with it:

DEALING WITH COMPLEXITY

One way not to deal with complexity is the classic approach that consists in breaking the whole down into its single parts, studying each part separately, and thereby expecting to arrive at an understanding of the whole. But, as already mentioned twice, the whole is more and different than the sum of its parts.

The other approach is the attempt to introduce change into the system by devising a change strategy equally complex as the system itself. In most cases this turns out to be impossible, because the complexity is likely to be way beyond our capability to match it.

Long before the beginning of our work at the Mental Research Institute, of course, this problem had already been the subject of intensive research in the fields of systems theory, cybernetics, and others. Although using different terms, researchers in these fields had postulated interventions that help to reduce systemic complexity *without destroying it.* In his book *Cybernetics and Management*, for instance, Stafford Beer (1967, p.54) points out that simple traffic rules make vehicle circulation possible even at rush hour, when a busy town is teeming with vehicles, all following different routes at different speeds, independent of each other and subject to innumerable random variations.

Another (admittedly less scientific) example of this kind of complexity (or variety) reduction is that story of the mathematician Carl Friedrich Gauss, who, like many famous scientists, first showed signs of genius in his childhood. According to this story, Gauss's elementary school teacher wanted to procure himself half an hour of silence, and so he gave the class the task of adding all the numbers from one to hundred. Had I been there, of course I would have begun: $1 + 2 = 3, + 3 = 6, + 4 = 10, + 5 = 15,$ and so on, and probably it would have taken me more than half an hour to arrive at 100. After two minutes, little Gauss stood before the teacher with the result: 5050. Being a genius, he had found a *variety reducer* by realizing that he was faced with a string of numbers, the first of which (one) and the last (hundred) added up to 101. The second (two) and the next-to-last (ninety-nine) again added up to 101; the third (three) and ninety-eight also amounted to 101. He thus found himself faced with 50 pairs of numbers, each adding up to 101. 50 times 101 equals 5050. Easy, isn't it?

ATTEMPTED SOLUTIONS

In our work at MRI we gradually arrived at a complexity reducer that to us seems the most practical and therefore the most useful when we are faced with the complexity of human interaction: the *attempted solution.* After having obtained what appears to be a sufficiently clear definition of the problem, we ask our clients what they have so far done to solve it and what advice they have received from others. This information is relatively easy to obtain and enables us to identify the very mecha-

nisms by which the system maintains its *homeostasis.* Freud already was aware of the fact that many of his patients tended to commit the same mistake over and over again. He called it the repetition compulsion. But Darwin had already pointed out that the survival of a species may be threatened by its inability to abandon what at one time amounted to an optimal (and thus absolutely nonpathological) adaptation, but whose stubborn maintenance in the face of the constantly changing environmental conditions eventually may threaten its survival. The conviction of having found the optimal solution (coupled with the attempt to "perfect" this solution strategy in the face of increasing difficulties) renders people blind to those change strategies that may be present and available at any time. A human system caught in this vicious cycle is likely to expect from therapy one and only one form of help: Change us without changing us . . . It is caught in what may be called a *game without end,* recurrent behavior patterns strictly governed by rules but lacking any rule for the change of their rules. The early cyberneticians pointed to the important difference between *first-order* change (a change from one of the system's rules to another) and *second-order* change (a change of the system's rules themselves). As the following example shows, the inability to effect a second-order change may be fatal.

There is a type of ant, called the *army ant* (or *eciton*), whose habitat stretches over almost the entire tropical area of South America. These ants are known to have an almost unbelievably complex and purposeful social order; they march in columns of thousands, and because of their highly organized and extremely aggressive behavior they are known as the "huns and tartars of the insect world." However, there is, write Schneirla and Piel (1955), the possibility of

an ironic catastrophe which occasionally overtakes a troop of army ants. It can happen only under certain very special conditions. But when these are present, army ants are literally fated to organize themselves in a circular column and march themselves to death. . . . The ants, numbering about 1,000, were discovered at 7:30 a.m. on a broad concrete sidewalk. . . . They had apparently been caught by a cloudburst which washed away all traces of their colony trail. When first observed, most of the ants were gathered in a central cluster, with only a company or two plodding, counterclockwise, in a circle around the periphery. By noon all of the ants had joined the mill, which had now attained the diameter of a phonograph record and was rotating somewhat eccentrically at fair speed. . . . At dawn the next day the scene of action was strewn with dead and dying Ecitons. A scant three dozen survivors were still trekking in a ragged circle. . . . This peculiar calamity may be described as tragic in the classic meaning of the Greek drama. It arises, like Nemesis, out of the very aspects of the ant's nature which most plainly characterize its otherwise successful behavior.

PROMOTING SECOND-ORDER CHANGE

The story of the ants is an example of a social system that cannot generate from within itself the rules that would ensure its survival under special circumstances. It is obvious that in cases like this, the premises under which the system is functioning here and now require a change that the system is unable to generate by itself and, therefore, needs to be introduced from outside. As already mentioned, such an eye-opening outside factor may be a corrective emotional experience of a totally fortuitous nature. Alternatively, it may be a "planned chance event" introduced into the system by someone standing outside it. It also may be the result of what in our field has come to be known as *reframing*—the attribution of a different meaning to the same situation. Wittgenstein already refers to this form of intervention in his *Remarks on the Foundations of Mathematics*. If somebody draws our attention to a particular aspect of a game, it stops being that game. "He taught us a different game in place of our own. But how can the new game have made the old one obsolete? We now see something different and can no longer naively go on playing" (1956, p. 100).

Reframing is a therapeutic technique, based on the induction of change into what we call reality—the structure of meaning, significance, value, and so on that we ascribe to the world but which is projected by us into that outside world. We are usually quite unaware of this process. The total relativity of our world view is the gist of the well-known saying: "What is the difference between an optimist and a pessimist? The optimist says of a bottle of wine that it is half full; the pessimist says of the same bottle that it is half empty." Both are probably convinced that they are right and the other "therefore" wrong. Hence the stubbornness of our world views, as well as the ever-present potential of change from a painful world view to a less painful one—through the process of putting the same situation (the so-called reality of the first order) into a different frame, thereby creating a second-order reality of a different kind, or, in Wittgenstein's terms, teaching somebody a different game.

CONSTRUCTIVISM

Needless to say, for many of our colleagues the idea that reality may be an invention rather than an objective fact is totally unacceptable. And indeed, as long as we are convinced that mental health or illness can be measured by the degree of a person's "reality adaptation" we shall remain blind to the constructivist alternative (itself, of course, a mere construction). In just about all other fields of science, including physics and even mathematics, the idea of an objective reality, existing out there and accessible to our minds, has been abandoned. "It is the theory that decides what we can observe," said Einstein to Heisenberg. And 19 centuries before him, the stoic philosopher Epictetus already had arrived at the similar conclusion: "It is not the *things* that worry us, but the *opinions* that we have about the things." One is also reminded of Marcus Aurelius' dictum: "If you are distressed by anything external, the pain is not due to the thing itself but to your own estimate of it. This you have the power to revise at any moment."

Thus also the conviction of having discovered (or, at least, having to discover) the ultimate truth produces blindness for specific solutions that may be available at all times. This blindness is thus self-induced and it is essentially identical with the refusal of Copernicus' contemporaries to look through his telescope, because what he claimed to have discovered simply *could not* be the case.

There exists, then, an intimate relationship between certain actions and realizations that are inaccessible to our minds before we take that action. Heinz von Foerster, the internationally known biocybernetician and one of our great mentors, has succinctly expressed this in what he calls his *aesthetic imperative*: "If you desire to see, learn how to act."

In a similar vein, in his book *Laws of Form* (1973) George Spencer-Brown states:

The professional initiation of the man of science consists not so much in reading the proper textbooks, as in obeying injunctions such as 'look down that microscope.' But it is not out of order for men of science, having looked down the microscope, now to describe to each other, and to discuss amongst themselves, what they have seen, and to write papers and textbooks describing it. Similarly, it is not out of order for mathematicians, each having obeyed a given set of injunctions to describe to each other, and to discuss amongst themselves, what they have seen. . . . But in each case, the description is dependent upon, and secondary to, the set of injunctions having been obeyed first. . . .

It may be helpful at this stage to realize that the primary form of mathematical communication is not description, but injunction. In this respect it is comparable with practical art forms like cookery, in which the taste of a cake, although literally indescribable, can be conveyed to a reader in the form of a set of injunctions called a recipe.

INJUNCTIONS

But how can we, as therapists, motivate people to carry out injunctions—to take actions that in their view of reality make no sense, even though they are at all times possible? It is again at this point in my evolution as a therapist that training in hypnosis was of decisive importance. Of particular importance was Erickson's rule: "Learn and speak the client's language." This, of course, is by no means limited to hypnosis. In his *Retorica ad Alexandrum*, Aristotle already suggested: "If you want to convince somebody, use his own arguments." In our work, this form of convincing

often may take the form of prescribing (rather than opposing) resistance. A prescribed resistance ceases to be resistance. It becomes compliance; for even if the clients want to continue to resist, they must therefore abandon their particular form of resistance. Of course, this does not mean that they will cease to resist, but any different form of resistance in which they now engage may very well produce a basic change in their interactions, with the therapist, with members of their relationship system, or with both. The spouses who are caught in endless arguments and who have been told by everybody that they should fight less, may find it very difficult to follow their therapist's prescription to have an additional, intentional argument every evening exactly from 8 o'clock to 8:20.

ACTIVE INTERVENTIONS

In the course of our work at the Brief Therapy Center of our institute, we have seen three types of active interventions gradually emerge, each based on what seems to be the clients' resistance to change. Needless to say, this "degree" is not an objective measurement, but our impression of their openness to engage in new problem-solving behaviors.

The first are *direct behavior prescriptions*, or, as mentioned already, the introduction of planned chance events by the therapist. This intervention is indicated with clients who appear to be willing to accept the prescription even if they may not see its point. Needless to say, the acceptance will be made easier—and thus more likely to be successful—if the prescription is utterly simple, not embarrassing, not dangerous, not expensive, and, therefore, will not harm if it does not help.

The second category are the so-called *paradoxical prescriptions*. (Paradox is used according to its classical definition, and does not, as many colleagues appear to think, mean something that is simply weird, unexpected, or surprising.) This type of intervention is based on the classical paradoxes that have been known since antiquity. In his work with schizophrenic patients and their families, Bateson noticed the frequent presence of paradoxical communication patterns that he called double binds (Bateson, Jackson, Haley, & Weakland, 1956). They create a situation that gives the recipient of this communication only two possible reactions, both of which are mad, bad, or helpless. This can even happen to God: According to a story that apparently created a crisis in medieval Christian theology, the devil proved to God, in one of their then apparently frequent conversations, that God was not omnipotent. The devil achieved this by asking God to create a rock of such enormous size that not even God himself could lift it. Obviously, if God cannot lift the rock, he is for that reason not omnipotent. If, however, he *can* lift it, he is not omnipotent because he could not make it big enough. Unfortunately, God's answer remained unknown.

A less historic example of a double bind is Dan Greenburg's (1964) advice to a Jewish mother: "Give your son Marvin two sport shirts as a present. The first time he wears one of them, look at him sadly and say in your Basic Tone of Voice: 'The other you didn't like?' " The son is thus left with only two possibilities: To wear the one or to wear the other. This means if he did *A* he should have done *B*; if he did *B* he should have done *A*, and he is therefore bad. If, to avoid this trap, he would have worn both shirts at the same time, he would have been mad.

Similia similibus curantur (likes can be cured by likes), our Roman ancestors already claimed: This means that paradoxical communication can also be therapeutic; it need not only be pathogenic. Viktor Frankl's concept of the *paradoxical intention* is probably the first modern application of paradox to therapy, preceding the work of the Bateson group. It is in essence a prescription of the very symptomatic behavior that the clients would like to overcome. Because the symptom is experienced as something spontaneous and uncontrollable, its prescription creates what may be called a "be spontaneous" paradox. When clients are motivated to increase their symptoms intentionally instead of trying to repress them, they arrive at totally new and unexpected solutions. *How* to motivate them to behave in this way—in their view quite an absurd and counterproductive way to act— is, of course, largely

determined by the therapist's ability to enter into their reality by finding the linguistic and semantic formulations that are acceptable to the clients' language.

The essence of a paradoxical injunction can be found in the Zen story of a young wife who, on her death bed, demands of her husband a promise that he will never get involved with another woman. If he were to break this promise, she would return as a ghost and cause him endless trouble. The husband very willingly promises this, but after several months he meets another woman and falls in love. Soon afterwards a female ghost begins to haunt him every night, accusing him of having broken his solemn promise. She not only knows exactly everything that goes on between him and his beloved, but also his feelings, hopes, and innermost thoughts. As the situation becomes unbearable and produces serious problems in his new relationship, the man decides to consult a Zen master. This expert realizes that there is no point in trying to convince the man that it is all in his head, that there are no ghosts, and so on. Rather, he instructs him to wait for the ghost's next appearance, then take a handful of soy beans and ask her how many beans he holds in his hand. He accepts the prescription and as the ghost appears, as she always does, he asks: "Since you know everything, tell me how many beans I am holding in my hand."—There was no longer any ghost to answer that question (P. Reps, 1961).

The third category of interventions are the so-called *positive* connotations. They appear indicated when we are working with clients who—for whatever obscure reasons—are playing the game of "defeating the expert." In very general terms, their reaction to any suggestion or advice is "anything—except *that*." In more specific terms they may be saying something like: "No, no—that does not work; Dr. So-and-so [their previous therapist, whom they left after three sessions] already thought of that. Give us better help." If we let them impose on us the same zero-sum game (as this kind of interaction is called in the mathematical theory of games), the treatment is likely to last (again) two or three sessions. The positive connotation strategy regretfully defines the present situation—unpleasant and difficult as it may be—as the best one possible (hence the term "positive connotation"), and insists that *any* change would only make things worse. If they now want to continue their game of "defeating the expert," they will have to prove to him that he is wrong and that a change for the better *is* possible. To this the therapist reacts with increased skepticism and worry.

CONCLUSION

And now, to terminate, a prescription to an imaginary colleague who expresses his shock at the techniques defined in this paper. He can (perhaps) be helped by pointing out that he is right, that this approach is unethically manipulative (even he may begin to wonder if there is *any* form of help that is not manipulative), and that the results of this treatment (if any) must be short-lived, superficial and cosmetic, because the deep, underlying causes have not been lifted into consciousness through insight, but that you somehow know that the author wrote this paper as a loyal sacrifice to his colleagues who, he

hopes, will find it unscientific and scandalous and, therefore, will be confirmed in their (perhaps sometimes shaky) conviction of having found the definitive truth.

REFERENCES

Alexander, F., & French, T. (1964). *Psychoanalytic therapy.* New York: Ronald Press.
Balint, M. (1968). *The basic fault.* London: Tavistock.
Bateson, G., Jackson D.D., Haley, J., & Weakland, J. (1956). Towards a theory of schizophrenia. *Behavioral Science, 1,* 251–264.
Beer, S. (1967). *Cybernetics and management.* London: English Universities Press.
Foerster, H. von. (1981). On constructing a reality. *Observing systems.* Seaside, CA: System Enquiry Series.
Greenburg, D. (1964). *How to be a Jewish mother.* Los Angeles: Price/Stern/Sloane.
Loftus, E.F. (1995). Remembering dangerously. *Skeptical Enquirer,* March/April 1995, 20–29.
Reps, P. (1961). *Zen flesh zen bones.* New York: Doubleday.
Schneirla, T.C., & Piel, G. (1955). The army ant. *Twentieth century bestiary.* By the editors of Scientific American: New York.
Spencer-Brown, G. (1973). *Laws of form.* New York: Bantam Books.
Vaihinger, H. (1924). *The philosophy of 'as if'.* (C.K. Ogden, Trans.). New York: Harcourt Brace.
Wittgenstein, L. (1956). *Remarks on the foundation of mathematics.* Oxford: Basil Blackwell.

Discussion by James Masterson, M.D.

◆

Dr. Watzlawick has presented a thoughtful, well-organized, well-written, half-philosophical and half-clinical presentation of his theoretical point of view. It stimulates, it challenges, it stakes out his territory in a compelling and articulate manner. It deserves to be taken seriously.

One of the objectives of this volume is to bring together therapists from different theoretical persuasions to compare and contrast and learn from each other. However, such a dialogue requires a degree of openness and reasonableness on the part of both parties. What is one to do when one's point of view is under such a scathing attack? Confess the error

of one's ways and try to amend them? I guess so, if you conclude that your perspective is invalid. However, of course, if you think that it is not, if you believe in it, you must defend it. And, unfortunately, what tends to result when you are required to do this is more of a battle than a dialogue.

Let us make no mistake about Dr. Watzlawick's paper. Underneath a philosophic umbrella that, incidentally, I found by itself quite interesting, although I am not philosophically inclined, he has launched an all-out attack on what he calls "the linear cause–effect," I assume, "analytic perspective." I think it is important to keep in mind here that we are not just talking about abstract theory, but about perspectives around which both of us have organized our lives.

Dr. Watzlawick states that insight never helped him, nor did it help any of his patients. In terms of philosophy, I'm wondering if it's a solid premise to generalize from the particular: If it doesn't work with one, it doesn't work with all. I will leave to readers' speculation the possible causes of why it did not work, but whatever those causes are, they must, it seems to me, be relevant to the attack he feels the need to take in this chapter.

In contrast to his view and his own experience, in my own experience insight has been and continues to be extremely helpful to my patients, producing enormous changes in their lives.

What I would like to do in the discussion is first to respond to some degree to this attack, and then to make some other comments about the rest of the paper and about Dr. Watzlawick's point of view about treatment. Before I get into that, I would like to make this point: It seems to me that if you set out your principles of what you think the problem is and how you wish to treat it, within the parameters of your theory you have a more-or-less valid proposition that holds water of its own accord.

I don't see why it's necessary to knock other theories in order to support your own theory. In essence, Dr. Watzlawick accuses the analytic perspective of being not a scientific search for the truth, but a religion or a dogma that must be blindly followed. In so doing, it seems to me he creates a straw man to attack. That view is so distorted that it has no relevance to my work; for example, of course I have seen rigid, dogmatic analysts. We all have seen them. Does that mean that all analysts are rigid? Does that mean that even Dr. Watzlawick's perspective doesn't have a few rigid dogmatic adherents? For example, let me illustrate what he says: The linear perspective is "a dogma to be blindly followed without questioning." His remarks about insight, from his view, are considered "heretical." Also, he explains: "Insight is magical."

These words, "dogma," "heresy," and "magical," are more suited to talking about religion than about science. Furthermore, he goes on to state that the Oedipal complex, as a source of etiology, has been replaced by memories of sexual abuse. I don't think that this is literally true. The way I would frame it is as follows: The Oedipal complex is not the only etiology. In personality disorders alone, the principal etiology is pre-Oedipal, not Oedipal.

About the notion that insight is the only agent for change: I think a little history might be helpful here. Freud and the early analysts worked mostly with psychoneurotic patients—in discussing them, for want of a better description I can say those patients dealt with a conflict between two agencies, the *id* and the *superego*, which unavailable to the ego. The nature and structure of neuroses indicated to Freud and others that the change agent to be used was insight—bringing to the awareness of the ego these unrecognized forces so they could be redistributed.

We have long recognized that there are other possibilities for change. For example, in my own field it is my impression that insight follows rather than produces change, although it can produce change somewhat.

Dr. Watzlawick calls the linear cause–effect approach an "epistemologic mythology." Well, as I mentioned, I don't have a philosophic bent. Of course, I remember that word, but I had to go back to the dictionary to look it up. It's a branch of philosophy that studies the contents and boundaries of human knowledge. So the linear perspective is an "epistemologic mythology," it produces a feeling of having discovered the ultimate truth, thus creating a blindness toward specific solutions that may be available at all times.

In my view, Dr. Watzlawick is hoisted on his own petard with this argument. I think his paper is a beautiful example of his thesis that insight causes blindness. He seems convinced that his system approach is the way and therefore he is unable to see the analytic perspective for what it is, a constantly changing, questioning, growing scientific inquiry into the truth of the human psyche. This blindness leads him, like the army ants he described in his paper, to cogitate in ever-narrowing philosophic and cybernetic circles that block the possibility of change.

I would like to cite just one change that the analytic perspective is undergoing in recent years, one that is related to my own life. For many years, analysts attempted to treat personality disorders as if they were Oedipal conflicts, but without success. Through the follow-up study of analytic patients in treatment and through the child observation studies of analytic observers of children going through the early stages of development, the theory evolved that their problem was pre-Oedipal. A whole new treatment perspective has emerged and has been quite successful.

There are a few other issues I would like to take up, one by one. I couldn't agree more with him on his view, as he describes it, about the child who has to produce abuse memories that satisfy the teacher. I think it's sad to say that too much of this goes on in our country. There are therapists who seem to produce abusive memories. There is a False Memory Syndrome and I agree with what he cited.

In my own experience and my own approach, the therapist has no business getting into the patient's memories. If the therapist deals with the defenses against those memories, it will not require the therapist (or the teacher) to acknowledge their validity. As the patient spontaneously gets access to them, the patient—the only one for whom it's meaningful—will establish their validity.

I was a bit perturbed by the notion that—no matter what one's theory is, whether it is Dr. Watzlawick's approach or the theory that I use—the patient's improvement is scientific proof of the theoretical approach. I wish that this were true, but it is not.

There are so many other variables that are not controlled for, and perhaps are not even considered. It's really impossible to say that just because a patient gets better, it's your theory that's responsible for it. This doesn't prove that it's not true, but it doesn't prove that it is true either. That's why we have so many different theories and all of them seem to work.

I certainly agree with the idea that if you're going to work with patients, the way to do it is to learn to understand and work with their language. I must say that I loved the chess analogy. As I was reading it, it made me think

of the way I work with a patient and it is quite similar.

As to Dr. Watzlawick's description of his systems perspective and approach to treatment, I found it difficult to comment on that because in my perspective the most important issue in trying to determine what interventions to use is the patient's diagnosis. Therefore, I have to know what kind of patients he's talking about when he talks about these prescriptions. Are they schizophrenic? Are they psychoneurotic? I found, in general, the discussion of his approach to treatment interesting, and perhaps with some types of patients yet to be described possibly valid. My understanding is that Bateson's work was done mostly with schizophrenic patients and I'm not certain whether or not what Dr. Watzlawick is referring to is work with schizophrenic patients.

In other words, I would have to know the diagnosis of the patients and the kind of change that is sought. I think one of the key issues between us is the kind of change that is sought. I don't have any doubt that Dr. Watzlawick and his group are getting change from what they do. The question in my mind would be whether this change is in behavior or in character and intrapsychic structure. There are many approaches that can produce changes in behavior. However, change in behavior, while important in itself, does not offer as much as enduring change in intrapsychic structure.

I will give two examples from my own work: A young man who came to us was a computer expert and now is a nationally famous novelist. I saw an adolescent whose psychiatrist told his parents that he should be put in a state hospital for the rest of his life. He's now a famous radiologist. I'm sure Dr. Watzlawick has similar examples.

Dr. Watzlawick implies that if you change the system, you change the patient in the system. I submit that what changes is the behavior, not the intrapsychic structure. I believe that if you change the intrapsychic structure or character of the patient, this will be reflected in changes in behavior that also will change the system.

As to Dr. Watzlawick's three therapeutic prescriptions, again, I would have to think about them from my point of view on personality disorders. For example, if your objective was behavioral change with a personality disorder, some of these prescriptions might be of value. On the other hand if your objective was intrapsychic change, I would see them as perhaps being too directive and further traumatizing the patient's fragile self by taking over responsibility for it by use of these prescriptions.

I also was concerned about his notion that what the prescription does is change resistance to compliance. In my view, the objective of our treatment is not compliance, but freeing the sense of self from its emotional burdens.

Dr. Watzlawick's paper intrigued me and forced me to go back and review issues that I had not thought about in many years. It brought back all the anxieties, doubts, and conflicts that I had as a young person about psychotherapy in general and what kind of psychotherapy to use when entering this field.

I'm sure Dr. Watzlawick had similar doubts and conflicts as a young man when he entered the field. I resolved them in one way, or at least I thought I did. He chose to resolve them in another way. These resolutions seem to have worked for both of us as well as for our patients.

Perhaps out of this encounter I can learn to give more emphasis than I have to the relational perspective. Perhaps Dr. Watzlawick might learn to give more emphasis to individual aspects. In any event, it's important that we keep up the dialogue, learn to disagree without being disagreeable, and thereby keep ourselves from the insight that blinds us and thereby keeps us clapping our hands to keep the elephants away.

Response by Dr. Watzlawick

◆

Ladies and gentlemen, you may have the impression that this here was a well-planned and executed role play. No, it is not, but I am very grateful to Dr. Masterson that he took seriously the last paragraph of my paper and did me the favor of following my behavior prescription and proving that at least certain aspects of my approach are, of course, unacceptable from a different approach. So thank you very much for doing this.

MASTERSON: I'll tell you something: When I read your last paragraph I knew you had this up your sleeve. Therefore, I had to think that matter through and I decided that whether or not I was complying with your prescription depends on my motivation. I thought my motivation was more from my sense of self rather than from trying to comply with your description.

WATZLAWICK: So I was more right than I thought.

Let me briefly mention something that I found very useful in my approach to abandon totally; namely, diagnostic terms. Of course, there are fantastically complex scientific explanations and descriptions of what schizophrenia is, for instance. But I am far too impressed by what Korzybski, the founder of General Semantics, said: "The name is not the thing; the map is not the territory." We commit the mistake of believing that if there is a name, then the *thing* thus named must also exist. This is, to my mind, responsible for this multitude of different and largely contradicting views about the nature of the human being. I think we ought to abandon this practice. We ought not to say, "This is a schizophrenic." We ought to say, "This is a person who suffers: Let's see how we can alleviate his suffering."

Otherwise we get caught precisely in an idea that ultimately leads to the assumption that there is a real reality out there that is accessible to our minds—that in fact the definition of normalcy is to be aware, to see this reality as it really is, that the concept of reality adaptation is the measure of mental health or illness.

Philosophers and theoretical physicists have totally abandoned the idea of a real reality existing out there. I think that gradually we ought to follow them.

SECTION VIII

State of the Art

The Temperament Program

◆

Stella Chess, M.D.

Stella Chess, M.D.

Stella Chess is a Full Professor in Child Psychiatry at the Department of Psychiatry, New York University Medical Center. She received her M.D. in 1939 from the New York University College of Medicine. Dr. Chess is a Fellow of the American Psychiatric Association and a Life Fellow of the American Orthopsychiatric Association. She has served on a number of editorial boards of prestigious journals; has received a number of research grants; and has been awarded distinguished honors from professional organizations and governmental agencies. Dr. Chess has authored, edited, or co-authored 16 professional books and 150 articles and chapters. She is renowned for her contributions to child psychiatry, especially in the study of temperament.

INTRODUCTION

I wish to thank the organizers of this conference for their invitation to me. You are giving me the opportunity to review, for a most appropriate audience, the contribution of the study of temperament that my colleagues and I have made to the understanding of normal and abnormal behavioral development. The theory and practice of temperament in its contemporary meaning is now largely an accepted component of psychologic thought. It is a rare book on theories of human development or one on training in the helping professions that now fails to include a discussion of temperament theory and some consideration of its clinical applications. So accepted is temperament theory that it may have been forgotten, or perhaps has not been known by many in this audience, that the modern study of tem-

perament is only four decades old. Leon Eisenberg, M.D., Professor Emeritus of Social Medicine and Psychiatry at Harvard Medical School, has said, regarding the New York Longitudinal Study and the concept of temperament, "Today, their insights have been so thoroughly incorporated into the mainstream of theory and clinical practice in psychiatry and pediatrics that it may be difficult for students to recognize how revolutionary they were 36 years ago" (Eisenberg, 1994). The awareness of the importance of those individual differences in human behavior that are contained in the concept of "temperamental style" arose in its embryonic form in personal discussions between my husband, Dr. Alexander Thomas, and me in the 1940s, as a function of our interest in becoming better clinical psychiatrists and psychotherapists. The longitudinal study that we initiated in 1956 has succeeded in defining temperamental styles and in providing evidence of immensely important interaction between the human organism and the environment.

The nature of our inquiry required that we start our study with our subjects at or shortly after birth and follow them over years, if possible through a lifetime. We have now succeeded in tracing them through their fourth decade and the beginning of the fifth (age 40+). The length of this longitudinal study, it now appears, may be defined by our own life spans rather than that of our cohort, because we are now in our 82nd year. When our subjects were in their late 20s and early 30s in the 1980s, we reported our findings to that date in the book: *Origins and Evolution of Behavior Disorders from Infancy to Early Adult Life.* (Chess & Thomas, 1984)

Our writings on the impact of temperament on behavioral development are largely associated with the childhood years and to a lesser degree with adolescence. This has been determined by the nature of such a prospective study in which the childhood years have been searched for the predictive insights that only become evident when later decades are studied. I shall try, in this presentation, to describe temperament as an evolving concept and to clarify the implications of its clinical applications to individuals of all ages.

First, I shall place the concept of temperament within the framework of psychological theories at the time of our first stirrings of awareness. Then I will define the scope of temperament and explain how these definitions and parameters were reached. Next, I shall review very briefly the research of others, both in this country and elsewhere, with populations of varied cultures. The concept of goodness of fit and poorness of fit, our important organizing principle of diagnosis and intervention with behavior problems, will then be presented and its implications explored within person–environment interactions. And, finally, I shall summarize the current numerous clinical applications of temperament theory in such areas as pediatrics, nursing, education, psychology, the teaching of parenting skills, and psychotherapy.

PSYCHOLOGIC ATMOSPHERE

At the time of our medical and psychiatric training, western society had freed itself from the dominant 19th century unidimensional constitutional concept of a predetermined familial origin of morality and character. Phrases such as "the apple doesn't fall far from the tree" and such endeavors as seeking a criminal bent from such bodily features as the shape of the ears, or the linking of body build to personality type, had previously been largely accepted as scientific. Even Charles Dickens reminds us that Oliver Twist, although born in a workhouse and brought up in squalid circumstances, speaks from the beginning as the little gentleman he is explained to be by birth. Dickens also anticipated the wave of the future in *Great Expectations*, in which both the daughter of two murderers and a son of the lower classes are turned, by their upbringing, into a lady and a gentleman with sensibilities to fit their new station.

In the behavioral field, the constitutional-heredity view was discredited by the work of Freud and Pavlov, each of whose theories focused on the powerful influence of the environment. Pavlov's theory of conditional reflexes was better known in the United States through the work of John Watson, the behaviorist. In psychoanalytic theory the individual's future harmonious or problem-laden mind and behavior are determined by environmental events occurring at predetermined developmental stages. This was presented as a message of hope. An environmentally caused neurosis could, it was presumed, be undone by recollection and understanding. It was, in fact, an era of social hope, as the movement of community organizations that attempted to provide some degree of benign influence in the lives of the poor will attest.

Freud did recognize individuality. He stated that "each individual ego is endowed from the beginning with its own peculiar dispositions and tendencies" (1950). Beyond this mention, this individuality, however, had no part in psychoanalytic psychotherapy. Its focus was on the predetermined states—oral, anal, and so on—during which specific traumata and conflicts laid the groundwork for specific neuroses or types of personalities.

Watson, the American spokesman for conditioning theory, is often quoted as saying that given a dozen healthy infants and his own planned environment for each, he would be able to create doctor, lawyer, Indian chief, rich man, poor man, beggar man, or thief. Such enormous environmental power had no place for the infants' individualities (1928).

If you are interested in more detailed comments on a host of observations on individual differences reported in many behavioral, physiological and biochemical areas from the 1930s through the 1950s, I refer you to our book: *Temperament and Development* (1977). While these reports helped lay the basis for our thinking, no systematic investigations had followed these interesting findings at that time.

THE CHESS AND THOMAS
DEFINITION OF TEMPERAMENT

The initial observations that piqued our interest in behavioral individuality as an essential element in human development came from several sources. As parents of our four children, we found ourselves reacting very differently to each. Our squeaky wheel did not always need the attention she demanded: The scraped knee evoked anguish as loud and long as did a deep gash. In contrast, if our little stoic dashed silently to his room to hide, thumb in mouth, the chances were that he had just been exposed to some deeply upsetting inequity that deserved redress and an immediate inquiry was warranted. And when the third member of the quartet pursued his elaborate erector set without letup until completion, we approved this persistence. However, when the same degree of persistence was applied to a repeated request that had already been refused numerous times, we tended to use the word nagging. Our highly active child needed close watching lest he run into dangerous situations out of sheer ebullience. And he could equally cheerfully carry out assigned tasks, provided they required continuous motion at high speed with much opportunity to chatter. Simultaneously, we reviewed the children we had

watched grow up and those of our friends and neighbors. The rich variety of styles of behavior became evident; we also had the impression that at least in the early years, these behavioral styles were enduring personal signatures.

As we discussed these insights, we began to review our adult patients, who, after all, were individuals too, along with their fears, phobias, anxieties, aggressions, submissiveness, and a host of other maladaptive attitudes and actions. An adult example was a couple trying to work out their marital conflicts. A frequent event was the beginning of a vituperative quarrel with the wife ventilating her anger in extreme denunciations, leaving the room in a fury, only to return a half hour later in good humor, apologizing for her words, and continuing with a cheerful conversation. Her husband, fuming with resentment, stated that she must be repressing hidden resentment, and insisted that they must immediately examine the quarrel. They then proceeded to quarrel just as furiously about whether the wife did or did not have within her a simmering resentment, ending in much the same scenario. It was not until their differing styles of reactivity had been clarified, a task of some difficulty, that they began to accept that their differing reactions and behavior were genuine. Once they had achieved a respect for each other's individuality, then they could address themselves to the basic genuine psychological issues between them.

As I rethought the children under my psychiatric care, I gained an insight into a child–parent conflict that had been baffling me. Six-year-old Charlotte's parents characterized her as "oppositional." There were battles over choice of clothing, choice of food, bath temperature, indeed over most routines of daily living. With inquiry, it did seem that a number of areas of pleasant interaction also existed, but these were poisoned by the frequent conflicts. Charlotte agreed with the description of the conflicts. But, she insisted, the pants *were* tight, she always *hated* eggs, and she could not understand why her parents didn't believe her. As we reviewed her life history, Charlotte's parents did recall that when she was an infant, she had always been sensitive to rough fabrics, certain tastes, odors, bright lights, and loud noises. But now, at school age, they had expected her to be "reasonable." With an understanding that her refusals might be due to low sensory threshold, not malevolence, a parent–child partnership could be forged to eliminate the difficulties that were now seen as legitimate. With this area of conflict out of the way, it was now possible to see that there was no oppositionality and no need for further psychiatric treatment. She was, in fact, a reasonable child.

From such anecdotal insights it became clear that our next task was to put our hypothesis of behavioral individuality to the test. As clinicians, we had had no training in researching such hypotheses. We turned to our friends and colleagues who were career researchers. We had long and earnest consultations with them. Their unanimous conclusion was that they themselves could not devise a research design to fit this question, and they were glad that this was our problem and not theirs. Emboldened by the awareness that we had no precedent to break, we thought for ourselves. Ignorant of the perils of research, we designed our own.

SOURCES OF DATA

The research design and our analyses were initiated with the New York Longitudinal Study (NYLS), which consisted of 133 subjects from child-oriented middle and upper middle class families. The sample was collected through personal contact during pregnancy or shortly after birth with parents who were willing to cooperate in a long-term study of normal child development.

The cumulative collection of subjects was started in March 1956. Eighty-seven families were enrolled and all children born to these families during a six-year period were included in the study.

In order to minimize the influence of sociocultural variability, we started with this middle class group homogeneous as to value systems. At a later date we did study the influence of some environmental factors by means of different homogeneous sociocultural groups.

RESEARCH DESIGN

Our researcher friends failed to give us one invaluable insight, namely, that the elegant research designs reported in scientific journals were rarely a first selection. It is often through the analyses of the first inadequate designs that a workable method was finally devised—and this was the case with us. Our first strategy was Pavlovian, an attempt to capture the individual patterns of conditionability among infants. However, it was in the course of exploring this failed attempt during nightly phone conversations that we realized the wealth of information parents were capable of giving. And in order to be sure that I was obtaining a clear picture, I was becoming better and better at turning generalities, opinions, and interpretations into reports of actions and interactions and documenting the variability between different infants and different parents. One of the earliest criticisms of our work was that we had used such biased informants as our primary source. However, in our training in the medical model, we had learned to use such subjective informants as people in pain, to form a pattern as to the timing, place, and intensity of this pain as our initial step in diagnosis. Our task then was to learn how to devise the kind of questions and to obtain the examples that would give clear pictures of interactions with timing, intensity, emotionality, and other features of the individuality we were seeking to define.

From this initial work, a protocol began to emerge from which an organized body of data was to be obtained. The babies' actions were divided into functional units such as hunger, sleeping and waking, being bathed, and so on, and specific questions were to be answered with specific facts. These data were to be obtained in the course of open-ended conversations, punctuated by requests for clarification and examples. Any interaction flowing between parent and child was to be described from its initiation to its completion. As these newborns became more mature, additional areas of functioning were added. I have given these details of the initiation of our temperament investigations for one important reason. As clinicians our purpose was, and continues to be, the delineation of this additional tool for prevention and intervention directed toward behavior disorders and problems of interpersonal and work functioning of people as individuals.

It was clear that these items of information must be able to be transformed into quantifiable data and that their reliability and replicability be tested. To do this, we, Dr. Thomas and I, formalized our protocol (Thomas & Chess, 1977). In our "free" time we made home visits, where we conducted interviews in the manner described. We selected three-month intervals, starting at age 2 to 3 months. This decision was to ensure that the data would be prospective, descriptive of the moment, and not tainted by a lengthy period of retrospective recall that might produce faulty and selective reports. In these visits it was often possible to observe the infants and ask parents such questions as, "Is this the behavior you meant?" After a year we had accumulated four interviews each on 22 children, the last interview at 12 months of age.

We reviewed all of this, and once again called for help. We now appealed to our friend, the late Herbert Birch, at that time a prominent animal behavior researcher. Our fellow clinicians, whatever their professional identities, were united in their doubts that prelingual children could be properly understood behaviorally. Dr. Birch, accustomed to understanding animal behavior through observation and interactive sequences, saw no such difficulty. He took our interviews for study and using induction analysis he was able to isolate ten general stylistic behavioral characteristics. Then, out of our series of animated and argumentative sessions, we three carved out the working of the individual behavioral styles as the "how" of behavior as opposed to the "why" or motivation, or the "what" or abilities. We agreed on the criteria of: (a) being present in all interview protocols, (b) being definable and consequently able to be rated, and (c) being meaningful in the child's interaction with the environment. With these judgments, we retained and defined the following nine traits: (a) activity level, (b) regularity or rhythmicity, (c) approach versus withdrawal, (d) adaptability, (e) threshold of response or sensitivity, (f)

intensity of reaction, (g) mood (positive versus negative), (h) distractibility, and (i) attention span and persistence.

We found that certain traits tended to cluster together. One such grouping was biologic regularity, interest in and approach toward new events and new people, speedy adaptation, predominance of positive mood, and moderate or low levels of intensity. We named this group "the easy child." Children with this cluster were in fact easy to care for, and during childhood they tended not to develop behavior problems. They were the largest group, making up 40 percent of the total.

The opposite cluster we named "the difficult child." These youngsters were biologically irregular, moved warily away from new people and places, adapted slowly, were more often unhappy than happy, and were intense in their emotional expressiveness. Although representing only 10 percent of the total, in early childhood most of the behavior problem children had this temperament constellation. Problems were able to be solved as easily as with other children and in adolescence and adulthood they did not predominate in behavioral disturbances.

The cluster of high withdrawal, slow adaptation, negative mood, and slow or moderate intensity we called the slow-to-warm-up child. These are the very shy children who quietly stand on the edges while getting their bearings before testing the waters. They make up about 15 percent of the group and have a mild risk of behavior disorder.

The rest, about 35 percent, have a variety of combinations of traits. All children have all temperamental traits to a high, low, or moderate degree. Detailed explanations of each of these characteristics and clusters with examples are to be found in Appendix A of our book, *Temperament in Clinical Practice*, published by the Guilford Press in 1986 and reissued in 1995.

From this time until his death in 1973, Dr. Birch remained one of the three principal investigators of the New York Longitudinal Study. We three together argued theory, conceptualization, methods of rating and of data analysis. And for the sensible suggestion that we replace the cumbersome phrase "individual differences in early childhood" by the single word "temperament" we are indebted to Michael Rutter, M.D., now Sir Michael Rutter. We were further helped in our strategies for data analyses by Dr. Sam Korn, and especially by Dr. Jacob Cohen.

To flesh out our information, we added I.Q. testing, independent home observations, and maternal and paternal separate interviews, during which we obtained parents' opinions of their own parenting styles. We made ourselves available for advice, parent guidance, psychiatric consultation, and arrangements for psychotherapy as requested or needed. Thus we laid the basis not only for our original question as to the reality of temperament and its role in healthy or problem development, but also the relationship between temperament at early ages and its relationship to later functioning, on into adult life. Also, because our data related to one middle class group, eight years later we added a second study with identical methodology, using a population of stable, child-oriented families of Puerto Rican origin.

As our work began to be known, it came to the attention of development psychologists, bringing broadening vistas. Then we were consulted by Dr. William Carey, a pediatrician, who found the concept valuable for clinical practice but was hindered by the cumbersomeness of our lengthy interview. He was able to enhance the practicality of the study of temperament by producing the first temperament questionnaire in 1970, starting our long and valuable collaboration. His data and experiences have just appeared in the book he wrote with S. McDevitt, *Coping with Children's Temperament* (1995).

RESEARCH

I shall review only those researches that relate to the origin of temperament—an essential question. In our study we could find no evidence that children's temperamental characteristics were derivative of their parents' attitudes and child care practices. While, at that time, we had no evidence as to origin, our speculation was that temperamental characteristics were biologic.

In recent years, evidence for biologic origin has been mounting through an expanding number of increasingly sophisticated studies. These inquiries have found correlations between both genetic and other biologic factors and temperamentally determined behaviors.

A traditional approach to questions of genetic relationship has been twin studies, which compare monozygotic and same-sex dizygotic twin pairs. Two twin studies in the 1970s investigated this question. In 1975, Buss and Plomin had reported finding greater temperamental similarities in identical compared with fraternal twins. In 1978 a Norwegian study by Torgersen and Kringlen of same-sex twin pairs indicated a greater similarity in temperamental characteristics in the monozygotic twins in infancy. Thus, evidence developed that pointed toward a partial genetic basis for temperament.

Further biologic correlates were first reported in 1984 by Kagan and his group. They compared a group of children who were socially inhibited with a group of socially uninhibited children. The inhibited group corresponded closely to our classification of the cluster we termed "slow-to-warm-up." In the laboratory, Kagan and his associates observed these children carrying out age-appropriate simple tasks while electrodes simultaneously recorded heart rate. They reported that the inhibited children had higher and more stable heart rates while performing these tasks than did the uninhibited children (Kagan, Resnick, Clarke, Snidman, & Garcia-Coll, 1984). Pursuing this direction with further studies they have since found evidence that in the inhibited children, during cognitive stress, there is also pupillary dilatation, norepinephrine activity, and higher cortisol level in the saliva (Kagan, Resnick, & Snidman, 1988).

Since this time there has been an explosion of studies examining the relationship of physiologic, neurohormonal, neurochemical, and other similar factors with temperamental traits.

The 1992 temperament conference was focused on a wide variety of such studies and has been reported in the proceedings edited by Bates and Wachs (1994). One can, at this time, talk only of correlations—it is too soon for judging cause and effect. But one can now say with authority that temperament has a biologic source. This statement does not change the fact that biologic features are susceptible to environmental influences. Height is a commonly used example. While height has a genetic basis, it is profoundly influenced by nutrition and other environmental features. And nutrition in its turn is influenced by geography, by cataclysms, by cultures, and by parental attitudes and child care practices. Similarly, the shaping of temperament from infancy through adulthood is determined by a constant interplay of biology and environment.

GOODNESS OF FIT

While a linear theory of adaptation and maladaptation would be convenient, our data consistently pointed toward the necessity of examining a multiplicity of factors to determine what interactions are important with a specific person at a specific time and place and toward particular goals. This is quite a mouthful and it seemed important to find parsimonious and elegant phrases that fit this principle. In 1983, Dr. Judd Marmor enumerated the types of variables that have to be considered in the systems approach to the study of personality: faulty parenting; temperament; the diverse personality patterns and culturally acquired value systems and expectations of the parents; economic, racial, and ethnic realities; dietary adequacy or inadequacy; the nature of relationships with sibs, extended family members, peers, teachers, and other influential individuals. He concludes, "We begin to get a glimpse of how difficult it is to accurately trace the origins of specific personality patterns at all, let alone to try to derive them from one or two variables" (Marmor, 1983, p. 836).

Such complex interactions have also been thoroughly discussed with regard to health by the biologist Rene Dubos in his 1965 book, *Man Adapting*. His principle was equally applicable to the complexities of human behavior. "Health can be regarded as an expression of fitness to the environment, as a state of adaptedness . . . the words 'health' and 'disease' are meaningful only when defined in terms of a given person functioning in a given physical and social environment" (pp. 350–351). This organizing principle of goodness or poorness of fit of the individual to the demands and expectations of the environment can embrace either a very simple imbalance or one with enormous complexity. Let me give some illustrations.

CHILDHOOD

Three-year-old Elaine awoke at night and demanded help, although heretofore she had been proud of her independence. Requests were for services such as being escorted to the bathroom in the middle of the night. Neither parent was alarmed, but by the end of two weeks of this, her mother was exhausted.

Three weeks earlier, Elaine's mother had a baby. Previously an only child, Elaine had been well prepared for her brother's coming, and while she was in the hospital recovering from a normal delivery, her mother had made nightly phone calls. Her mother had repeatedly reassured Elaine that when she came home, Elaine and brother Greg would have equal attention. If her mother got up during the night to feed Greg, Elaine might call her and be taken care of also. After two weeks of this, when I arrived for a regularly scheduled interview I found a thoroughly exhausted and short-tempered mother who was in tears over how she had presumably laid the groundwork for a destructive sibling rivalry. I found that during her mother's hospitalization Elaine stayed at home under the daytime care of their familiar housekeeper and nothing seemed amiss. She had not shown any signs of distress, did not cling, visited her friends' homes happily, had shown no change in sleep pattern, and had no nightmares. During the day she happily assisted in Greg's care and diapered and fed her dolls. Temperamentally, Elaine was an easy child. She had an approaching style with speedy adaptations. New situations were approached with pleasure, new people welcomed. Her mood was and remained predominantly positive and her intensity was moderate. After some thought, I suggested that with her three-year-old cognitive level, she had misunderstood her mother's reassurance as a request to call on her at night, particularly when Greg was being cared for, and she had obliged. I suspected that not only her mother, but also Elaine might welcome an uninterrupted night's sleep. I suggested that her mother tell Elaine that she could go back to being a big girl and take care of her own toileting as before. From this time on, Elaine slept through the night. A follow-up discussion again showed neither aberrant behavior, nor any unusual sibling fighting then or a year later. This had been a situation in which Elaine's temperamental traits in response to misreading of signals had been the source of problem. The advice, therefore, also was temperamentally based. Two guidance sessions sufficed.

A second example of turning a poorness-of-fit into goodness-of-fit is more complicated. Eight-year-old Nicky, a tall, well-developed, articulate, and intelligent boy, was constantly belittling himself. Although he had many friends, was an excellent athlete, and a good and thoughtful student, with his first error he gave up. If he missed an early question on an examination, the remainder of his answers showed little thought. After an argument with friends, he frequently dropped out of a planned expedition. His parents and teachers became increasingly distressed at the boy's failing self-confidence, growing self-depreciation, and declining performance. The data that emerged in the diagnostic workup became illuminating in the goodness-of-fit context. A tall infant of tall parents, Nicky had been advanced in all developmental milestones except emotional maturity, where he was age appropriate. At 18 months he was frequently taken for a three-year-old, not only because of his height but also due to his physical coordination, sophisticated language, and inquiring mind. But emotionally he behaved like the 18-month-old that he was. At home, for the most part, there was a good fit as the parents generally respected both his advanced abilities and his social level. Thinking back, however, the parents recalled numerous scenes in which Nicky had been scolded by outraged parents, "Give that toy back to the baby. You should be ashamed of yourself!" Yet when Nicky's parents asked the age of the "baby," it usually turned out that he or she was in fact older than Nicky. And age or no age, other parents saw him as aggressive and made him an outcast. He was, in fact, temperamentally gentle and easy, adaptable, and gregarious, but bewildered. Once school age was reached and the environment became more formalized, his functioning was at first excellent and he was accelerated in school. Then gradually his sensitivities re-emerged. Nicky's complaints, checked by his parents, showed that he was being held to higher standards in school than was appropriate. It was now teachers who were surprised to be reminded that Nicky was a year younger than his classmates. Because of his outward maturity, he was often expected to show more restraint and social understanding than children who were well ahead in emotional development. In self-protection, Nicky began to withdraw at the first adverse comment and began now to show increasing self-dissatisfaction. Clearly this was a poor fit. Although Nicky could not articulate his feelings in our diagnostic meeting, he turned to my play materials; while we talked of neutral topics, an interesting scenario developed. A play character, Joe, was driving a car that began to careen wildly on the play table. He passed a red light and a police car pulled alongside to give him a ticket. Joe sped up and there was a wild chase, ending when he hit and injured a pedestrian. I asked why Joe had not simply accepted his ticket—after all, it was not such a great crime. Joe, Nicky explained, was always being blamed for things he didn't do and he just didn't want to go home and say he got a ticket.

I worked with Nicky for about a year and a half. He never discussed his problems or feelings directly. But Joe was always present, and we could talk freely about Joe's behavior and the reasons for his actions. And as Joe gradually became more ready to take chances and to feel good about himself, I received parallel reports from Nicky's parents. In my strategy, I had decided that while Nicky's accommodating temperament played its part in imposing his style on his responses, of greater importance was the poor fit determined by the discrepancy between his capabilities and the environmental expectations. In our favor were several features. A supportive family was one essential element. Nicky's superior qualities, once relieved of excessive stress, were able to be appreciated by others, and then by himself. With time, other boys' physical growth made him less deviant: His tallness now was an asset. And the older he grew, the more emotional maturity evened out. And, through the device of Joe, he had announced his unwillingness to confront (be blamed for) his problems directly, but Joe gave him just enough protection to allow introspection. Little by little, Joe would talk about his escapades, acknowledge that they were, after all, not really blameworthy, just misfortunes. Joe's adventures became smaller, fewer ended in disaster, and he became rather boring. Finally, I asked 9-year-old Nicky whether he had ever noticed that Joe was a bit like himself. He gave this some thought, said, "Maybe so, but Joe was really a dope and not very interesting anymore."

ADOLESCENCE

The case of Danielle illustrates the application of a goodness-of-fit model to the problems of an adolescent. Danielle, age 15, had been reported by the school to have been responsible for setting a fire, cutting school, and failing in her classwork.

Until Mrs. L.'s appeal for help, Danielle, a member of our New York Longitudinal Study, had presented no special problems. A mother of five children, coming from a large family herself, Mrs. L. had been a competent mother. In contrast to her other children, Danielle needed time to familiarize herself in new situations and with new people although she did adapt at moderate speed. Her mood was evenly divided between positive and negative and her intensity tended to be high. In a busy household, her childhood tantrums tended to be ignored and unimportant, while her positive enthusiasms added zest to the family atmosphere. The greatest problem was the periodic family moves, which were taken in stride by the other children but were difficult for Danielle.

Mr. L., a business executive, was reassigned to a new location about every four years, necessitating family upheaval and changes of school and friends for the children. Although Danielle was always shy at the beginning of a new school and family location, with maternal support she had always before seemed to adapt well after several months. She had always been a satisfactory student. Up to this point, there had been a good fit.

The latest family move had occurred during the previous summer. In November, to her parents' shock, Danielle was accused of setting the school lavatory on fire, smoking, cutting school, and failing subjects. It seemed that she and two other girls had been smoking in the girls' lavatory. When a teacher entered unexpectedly, they attempted to flush the lit cigarettes down the toilet but the lid caught on fire, acrid smoke billowed through the school, and the fire department was called. Further inquiry showed that the three girls had been cutting school to hang out at the neighborhood mall and all had failing grades in most subjects. The youngsters were interrogated separately, and the other two stated that Danielle was the ringleader and denied having smoked with her. Danielle, in contrast, had owned up to everything she had done. Mrs. L. was shocked at her daughter's actions, yet also fiercely defended her, finding this behavior out of keeping with her usual actions. Her mother believed Danielle, pointing out to the school authorities that the other two girls had been friends for several years and had previously been in trouble, had cut classes the previous year, and were known to be poor students; she felt that Danielle, as a new girl in the school, was being scapegoated. At the same time, she felt that something was seriously amiss with Danielle and called upon me for help. This was consonant with our promise to give assistance whenever needed. In the meanwhile, the school had given all the girls psychological tests and stated that Danielle showed deep conflicts that required lengthy psychotherapy.

My review of the data on Danielle from early childhood on indicated that she fell into the slow-to-warm-up group. Despite her vulnerability to changes, because of the support of her family through her early and middle childhood, especially during her adaptations to the moves, the child–environment interactions had been a good fit. Our psychological tests at ages three and six had both shown normal psychological profiles and above-average intelligence.

Having obtained details of the episodes from school and a copy of their test, I did a full diagnostic interview. Danielle had known about the Longitudinal Study, and with her parents' confidence in me she accepted me as an advocate. During several discussions, she told of the pain of leaving her friends. She had made several good friends in her four years at her previous home, with whom, in adolescent fashion, she had exchanged secrets and advice. While she continued to correspond with her old friends, it was clear that they were moving away from her. Assuming that inevitably there would be another family move, she could not bear to make, and then be parted from, good friends once again. Besides, it was hard for her to make new friendships. She shared her mother's low opinion of her new friends. In fact, she had moved into their orbit largely because she would not be hurt by parting from them. Her movement into class cutting, then school absences, had been gradual, and she did not know how to extricate herself. By now, the nice girls avoided her, her school work was slipping, and she had begun protective lying. She had been relieved to have the situation come to a head, was overjoyed by her parents' trust in her, and was now determined to restore her self-esteem and her self-image.

Being led into temptation by bad companions is ordinarily a poor excuse and denial. But in Danielle's case, this judgment had merit. Vulnerable temperamentally to multiple new demands, needful in adolescence of lasting and close friendships, she had found a pseudo solution. She could not blame her father for uprooting her: As she saw it, her father had little choice. There was no indication that Danielle's delinquent actions were consciously or unconsciously her real desires. Optimum treatment required both parent guidance and direct therapy. After giving the situation some thought, both parents came for guidance sessions. After my discussion describing Danielle's temperamental qualities, their strengths and vulnerabilities, and the link between the periodic uprooting and her defensive reaction, Mr. L. stated that he had now decided not to accept

any future reassignments, at least for the foreseeable future. In his scale of values, Danielle's personal needs came before economic gain. By the end of three sessions, they were oriented to her needs and had communicated to her their trust in her. For Danielle, therapy was quite brief—six sessions in all. She had put our early discussions to good use, now realized her need for slow acclimatization, and was reassured that she would make close friendships without fear of separation. Since she did not have unconscious conflicts, this discussion sufficed.

As a follow-up, when she was interviewed on schedule at early adulthood, she was functioning well in college.

GOODNESS OF FIT IN YOUNG ADULTHOOD

Carl, at age 28, had developed a set of annoying tics. Involuntarily he found himself blinking and squeezing his eyelids, and his cheek would go into minute muscle contractions. He stretched his fingers, shrugged his shoulders, cleared his throat. All in all there were at least a dozen of these tics, which plagued him from morning to night. They had started gradually and he had thought they were due to fatigue. But once it was clear that they would not go away, he sought a consultation with me, as he had done once before. Because he was a member of our New York Longitudinal Study, I was able to review his temperamental style and his prior adaptations before meeting with him.

Although temperamentally Carl had fit into the difficult child classification to an extreme degree, he had never presented a behavior disorder. The parents were pleased with their "lusty" (their word) infant. As an infant and toddler he had been biologically irregular, withdrew from new situations, and was slow to adapt. Negative moods were frequent and they were expressed in high intensity, so that during periods of rapid change he spent much time crying loudly or having tantrums. When each new demand had been mastered, however, he typically was equally lusty in his infectious laughter and robust good humor. In addition, Carl was a highly persistent child with a high activity level. Carl's parents learned to introduce him to new situations and expectations in a gradual manner, and because he maintained well what he had mastered, by middle childhood he had acquired a small but close group of friends, enjoyed school, and was an excellent student. He had few negative reactions and was popular because of the zest and excitement he brought to endeavors. Between parental management, the appropriateness of developmental demands, and the positive nature of the environmental response, his functioning expressed a good fit. Because the family did not need to move its domicile, he moved together with his friends to junior and then senior high school, which limited the unfamiliarity of these changes. His occasional quarrelsome outbursts were accepted as minor events and untypical.

The prior consultation had occurred when Carl went to a residential college that none of his friends had selected. To his dismay and surprise, he found himself miserable, isolated socially, and floundering academically. Because things were no better when Carl came home for the Thanksgiving holiday, a consultation with me was arranged. His repeated phrase was "This isn't me!" Sure of his academic capabilities, he had arranged a more-than-full class schedule but could not keep up in most subjects. The demands, both in amount of work and depth of comprehension, were beyond him; he had made no friends, and he was determined to overcome this, because he couldn't believe himself incapable of college. As I listened to the details, it became clear that for the first time since early childhood, he had been faced with a multiplicity of new expectations simultaneously. While he was intellectually capable of meeting the challenge, temperamentally he needed to impose a timing on himself that would permit familiarization to occur. To make clear what I meant, I showed him his nursery school records. With amusement he read of his initial withdrawal and isolation. With the understanding of teachers, he was given time to become used to the routine, the rules, the activities, the new building, the teachers, and the other children. By winter, he had been described as lively, popular, boisterous, helpful, and delightful. His recollection

was only of enjoying nursery school, but he realized that the description of his initial reactions had its parallels to those of the present, and that his identity had not been lost. In essence, he had one repertoire of reactions when faced with massive unfamiliarity, and another when he had adapted to the challenges facing him. On his own, Carl instituted several well-thought-out rules. He moved into an apartment that was shared with a group of students, and he accompanied them to all social events no matter how shy he felt. He studied in the library, where he scheduled himself a minimum of two hours at a time with each subject (a timing well within his prior attention span). Carl thought that things were just beginning to be better. I encouraged his plans, and went into detail on his temperamental style and what he must do to work in consonance with his own style to reach his high goals, basically a matter of achieving familiarization as an initial goal. This program proved successful, and when Carl decided to transfer to another college, he was prepared for an initial several weeks of discomfort while he was working on attaining the familiarization that was essential to his optimum functioning and a good fit.

Why then, a decade later, was Carl blinking, twitching, and feeling harassed? A recital of Carl's schedule made me feel harassed, although he appeared pleased with his many interests, which he was pursuing with high intensity. He was engaged to be married, and professed a deep commitment to his fiancée although she complained, with reason, that he spent little time with her. After several changes of jobs in the computer field, each with a substantial raise in salary, he was now thinking of establishing his own software company. On the other hand, he might want to take a year off to see whether his talent was enough to establish himself on the concert stage. He had long been an excellent pianist and harpsichordist. Because athletics were necessary for his sense of well being, he tried to work out daily. He listed also five or six hobbies, each of which he would like to find time to pursue. On inquiry, each of these accomplishments had been acquired slowly in the initial stages, and then with giant leaps once familiarization had occurred. Now this slow-to-adapt individual was overwhelmed with interests with which he could have filled not one but two or more life spans. I assured Carl that if he did not do some selecting, not only would his tics continue, but he might lose his fiancée. And clearly he could not simultaneously become a concert artist and run a creative and successful business. In the course of his report, apparently Carl had heard himself, and realized the accuracy of what I had said. I now discussed with him the necessity for taking into account the side of his temperament mix that made him vulnerable for insatiability of persistent activities. This new self-awareness was as important to his successful functioning as had been the need to learn how to begin new ventures. He was fortunate that his need for muscular movement had provided an early warning system. If his large muscles failed to obtain regular use, his small muscles would express his tensions with tics. In this case, the one discussion was enough. Follow-up showed that Carl had placed musical performance in the category of personal pleasure. He had found the time to spend with his fiancée and for athletic activity, and became more selective with his hobbies. Offered a new and higher paying job, he decided against starting his own business and his tics were gone.

PREVENTION AND
EARLY INTERVENTION

By now, we know that the concept of temperament is useful in such diverse areas as education, nursing, pediatrics, psychology, social work, and parent education, among others. Parenting centers are a widespread phenomenon and temperament programs increasingly have become their focus. Examples of this include programs in La Grande, Oregon; Vancouver, Canada; and Minneapolis, Minnesota. Books for parents on child care increasingly include references to temperament, and some are entirely focused on temperament. The same is true about professional books on pediatric and psychologic issues.

The most substantial and longstanding clinical application of temperament is done at the Kaiser Permanente Health Maintenance Organization's Temperament Program. It was first introduced in the Kaiser Permanente San Rafaele facility ten years ago. David Rosen, M.D., a child psychiatrist who is chief psychiatrist of this facility, together with James Cameron, Ph.D., the executive director of The Preventive Ounce, a nonprofit preventive mental health organization in Oakland, were the architects of the program, and Dr. Thomas and I served as consultants. An essential component of the program was a temperament counselor. This program uses infant and preschool temperament questionnaires and a computer software program as preliminary steps for the clinician's use. At the request of several of the other northern California K-P facilities, the program was extended and set up as a controlled study. Ten years later the data were presented to the K-P administration, which is dedicated to preventive medical programs. With a database of 1000 infants, comparisons were made between those infants in Temperament Programs and the control group. The Temperament Program infants, followed to later childhood, showed fewer behavior disorders, fewer pediatric visits, fewer extended parental phone calls, and fewer specialty examination requests. The pediatricians welcomed the program, the parents found it useful, and it was cost effective. In other words, it was an effective preventive program, saving referrals to child psychiatry and saving expense. On this basis, Kaiser Permanente, which has more than six million subscribers, decided to hold a conference to introduce the Temperament Program to all its regions, and made four training videotapes for that purpose. A number of regions, including Hawaii, have already voted to include the program and have had training sessions. A second conference for training purposes was held in November, 1995. In Phoenix, Arizona, where there is no Kaiser Permanente HMO, The Temperament Program and the services of The Preventive Ounce have been extended to the CIGNA HMO at their request. Dr. Rosen is now in the process of introducing the Temperament Program to psychiatrists. In a personal communication he reports his own experience. Approximately 25 percent of the parents who came to him with behavioral concerns about their children did not require further visits after receiving temperament information and related advice.

CONCLUSION

This discussion is a summation of 40 years of work. I have focused on the clinical, preventive, and psychotherapeutic aspects of temperament theory and practice. Questions central to temperament concepts still remain and our own research still actively continues. For example: Is temperament immutable or is it capable of changing? Is temperament destiny or does self-awareness provide power over life's direction?

In the event I have not made myself sufficiently clear, I have compiled a short list of what temperament is *not*. *All of the following are incorrect.*

1. "It is only temperament." The implication is that the behavioral reaction is not a real problem; that this declaration is the end of the matter; that the making of the temperament statement obviates the need for further action. *False.*
2. Goodness of fit between a child and a parent means that both have identical or highly similar temperamental identities. For example, that both parent and child be of low activity or high intensity. *False.*
3. To state that temperament is a predominant or important aspect of the psychological problem is to believe that no other dynamic or organic explanations are pertinent to the problem. *False.*
4. To state that some other factor or factors are involved rules out the possibility that temperamental factors may play a part in the dynamic interplay. *False.*
5. That implicating temperament as an important factor in a child's psychological problems is equivalent to exonerating parents from the responsibility to examine and alter their parenting practices. Essentially this inaccurate idea confuses the elimination of false guilt with the removal of parental responsibility. *False.*

6. Having identified temperament and poorness of fit as the areas of importance in a particular psychological problem, the therapeutic task has been completed. *False.*
7. There are good temperaments and bad temperaments. *False.*
8. Only someone with educational sophistication can understand the concept of temperament. *False.*
9. Understanding temperament is merely common sense and requires no realization that it is essentially an interactive concept. *False.*
10. Temperament theory and practice apply only to infants and young children and is of minor significance in the functioning of adults and adolescents. *False.*
11. Temperament counseling is bandaid therapy. *False.*

REFERENCES

Bates, J.E., & Wachs, T. (Eds.) (1994). *Temperament: Individual differences at the interface of biology and behavior.* Washington, D.C.: American Psychological Association.

Buss, A.H., & Plomin, R. (1975). *A temperamental theory of personality.* New York: Wiley.

Carey, W.B., & McDevitt, S. (1995). *Coping with children's temperaments.* New York: Basic Books.

Chess, S., & Thomas, A. (1984). *Origins and evolution of behavior disorders from infancy to early adult life.* New York: Brunner/Mazel.

Chess, S., & Thomas, A. (1986). *Temperament in clinical practice.* New York: Guilford Press.

Dubos, R. (1955). *Man adapting.* New Haven, CT: Yale University Press.

Eisenberg, L. (1994). "Advocacy for the health of the Public." In W. B. Carey & Sean C. McDevitt (Eds.), *Prevention and early intervention: Individual differences as risk factors for the mental health of children.* New York: Brunner/Mazel.

Freud, S. (1950). "Analysis terminable and interminable." In *Collected Papers,* 5, 316. London: Hogarth Press.

Kagan, J., Resnick, J.S., Clarke, C., Snidman, N., & Garcia-Coll, C. (1984). "Behavioral inhibition to the unfamiliar." *Child Development,* 55, 2212–2225.

Kagan, J., Resnick, J.S. & Snidman, N. (1988). Biological bases of childhood shyness. *Science, 240,* 167–171.

Marmor, J. (1983) Systems thinking in psychiatry: Some theoretical and clinical implications. *American Journal of Psychiatry, 140,* 833–838.

Thomas, A., & Chess, S. (1977). *Temperament and development.* New York: Brunner/Mazel.

Torgersen, A.M., & Kringlen, E. (1978). Genetic aspects of temperamental differences in twins. *Journal of the American Academy of Child Psychiatry, 17,* 433–444.

Watson, J.B. (1928). *Psychological care of infant and child.* New York: W.W. Norton.

Postmodernism and Family Therapy

Lynn Hoffman, A.C.S.W.

Lynn Hoffman, A.C.S.W.

Lynn Hoffman is an internationally renowned theorist and lecturer on family therapy who has written many books and articles including Techniques of Family Therapy, Foundations of Family Therapy, Milan Systemic Family Therapy, *and* Exchanging Voices. *She is currently Consultant to the Center for Collaborative Studies at North Central Human Services in Gardner, Mass., and serves on the faculty of the doctoral program at Smith School of Social Work. She is an emeritus faculty member of the Ackerman Institute for Family Therapy in New York. In 1988, Hoffman was awarded the Life Achievement Award for Distinguished Contribution to the Field of Family Therapy by the American Association for Marriage and Family Therapy. She is an advisory editor of* Family Process. *She received her M.S.W. in 1971 from the Adelphi School of Social Work.*

INTRODUCTION

I have noticed that due to health care reform, the mental health field is moving in an increasingly biological and behavioral direction. For instance the lesser orders of the spectrum are being asked to dress up in medical clothes in order to be presentable to managed care. I recently got a form from the Massachusetts Blue Cross telling me the amount they would pay for a family therapy session, which they are now calling a "family medical interview." I said to myself: "What next, white coats?"

At the same time, there is a growing subgroup of family therapists who see their work differently. They believe that emotional difficulties, whatever their physical aspects, are socially constructed and collectively construed. For them, stories determine the meaning of facts. This group looks at the way people are positioned in their relational and cultural fields and offers therapies that derive from a postmodern point of view.

As a result, the field is on the cusp of a philosophical divide. On the one hand you have the traditional or "modern" stance, which is based on the claims to objectivity of modern science. On the other, you have a "postmodern" stance, which is that reality in any complex human sense is never immutably out there, independent of our languaged ways of knowing it. Social psychologist Kenneth Gergen (1994) describes the postmodern position as (a) challenging the supremacy of science in studying human affairs; (b) questioning the correspondence theory of language, that words mirror items in the external world, and (c) believing that "reality" is a matter of storied social agreement.

In investigating this position, I became very intrigued with it and began to search for an approach to therapy that would express its values. I was particularly struck by the idea that language is the lattice upon which we build our lives. Since language arts were my first love, and family therapy a much later interest, I feel that at this point in my life I have come back home. Let me tell my story.

I was an English Literature major in the 40s at Radcliffe, by then part of Harvard, and studied with some renowned New Critics as we called literary critics then. Unfortunately, the only teacher I had who took any notice of me was a poet named Ted Spencer. As he was not a New Critic and only a fair poet, I confess that I underestimated him. However, he remains gratefully in my memory for having told someone that I reminded him of a clear door with fog in front.

He got it perfectly. I graduated first in my class but was cut out of the graduation ceremony because I carelessly had not attended graduation practice. The dean got cross and told me, "You have a certain 'Je m'en fiche' about you, Lynn Baker." So I watched myself not receive my diploma from the balcony of the auditorium (I got it later), and I never went back to academia. But what my college years left me with was an enduring idea from the New Criticism that a poem—or any literary work—was a verbal icon, built around a free-standing structure of symbols that only a New Critic could discern.

In 1963, one marriage and three children later, I stumbled onto the work of the Mental Research Institute in Palo Alto. This organization succeeded Gregory Bateson's ten-year research project on communication and employed many of the same people. I had been asked to edit Virginia Satir's *Conjoint Family Therapy* (1964), a book that located the origins of so-called mental problems in family communication. Twelve years earlier, Bateson (1951) had co-authored a book with psychiatrist Juergen Ruesch called *Communication: The Social Matrix of Psychiatry* Psychiatric symptoms were defined as disturbances of communication and the psychiatrist became a "communications engineer." This was the language that ten years later Satir too was using.

The work of the MRI reminded me of the analysis of texts I was familiar with from the New Criticism. Members of the group were busy analyzing the conversation of families with a child who had come to community attention. They believed that you could tell from an unrelated conversation between the child's parents whether the child was "abnormal" and in what way. I remember hearing with fascination someone wonder whether a small baby in a research family might twenty years later surface as a schizophrenic.

In 1964, Jay Haley presented a paper linking pathology with family organization. I remember being at a research meeting in which he first shared his essay "Toward a Theory of Pathological Systems" (1997) and saying to myself, "This will make history." Unfortunately it did. Haley's theory was the first to spell out an easily apprehended structure of relationships that could account for emotional and behavioral distress. From then on, the concept of the dysfunctional family was on its way to its present status as an icon of popular psychology and the bane of parents everywhere.

At the same time, Haley's colleagues at the MRI, Paul Watzlawick, John Weakland, and Richard Fisch (1974), basing their ideas on the work of Milton Erickson, were proposing an approach that asked not so much about the origin of problems as what to do about them. Instead of thinking of themselves as changing pathogenic family structures, they interfered with the behaviors that maintained the problem. If their strategies were working, the problem would drop away without the people involved having to know why. This position went more or less against the psychoanalytic belief that insight causes change.

And so a new industry was launched. Family therapy gained a reputation for a behavioral emphasis, and for discounting psychodynamic or humanistic models as "do-nothing" approaches. It emphasized change in the present rather than exploration of the past. And here was the difference from all previous approaches to therapy: Direct observation was possible, not only of the family but of the practitioners themselves.

In this way, the field not only prospered but studied itself, going from model to model in a search for a family therapy holy grail. But whatever the model, the work remained highly instrumental, deficit oriented, and what we would now call modernist in spirit. It wasn't until the mid-eighties that hints of an oncoming shift began to disturb us. Instead of talking about changing systems, we began to talk about interpreting beliefs. The interventionist stamp that had characterized family therapy from the beginning began to break down. I began to think we were approaching a continental divide and looked for a signpost.

I found my signpost in the social constructionist views of Kenneth Gergen (1994). In emphasizing the social basis of knowing, Gergen challenges the Enlightment position that consciousness resides in the mind of the individual knower. For him, it is a product of the web of language and communication that weaves us in from birth. He also states that we are moving from a cognitive to a linguistic lens in describing what we call reality. The truth-bearing function of language, he says, loses ground as the objects of accounts lose their ontological status. Since the so-called treatment of psychiatrically defined problems is highly dependent on this truth-bearing function, Gergen's is a discomfiting point of view. It seems that as soon as you move away from the limited aspect of human difficulties covered by the laws of matter, you find yourself in a Pirandello play.

For a while I thought that a social constructionist position was the same as a theory of cognitive development called *constructivism*. This latter position holds that the nervous system builds up "constructs" about the world through which it apprehends "reality." Strategic therapists, many of whom subscribe to constructivism, attempt to change peoples' perceptions of the situation they complain of through embedded suggestions and ingenious tasks. They present their work as more or less neutral, like engineering.

Eventually, I began to realize that constructionists subscribe to a different set of beliefs. They believe that our understandings about the world are communally constructed and socially maintained. The idea of the freestanding knower is replaced by the idea that self, identity, and personhood are the product of rich social weavings created by many hands. In other words, minds are on the boundaries between people, not inside their heads. I agreed with this view but I was puzzled about how it would be applied to therapy, which resonates to concepts of individual responsibility and blame.

THE DIFFERENT VOICE

Then I read a small book by Carol Gilligan called *In a Different Voice* (1982). Gilligan's research focused on stages of moral reasoning. Finding that studies of moral choice were based on research done on men, she did similar research including women and found that women seemed to have what she called a "different voice." Where men subscribed to abstract standards of truth and justice, women would stretch the rules to preserve relationships. Their principles seemed to be based on what Gilligan called "an ethic of care." I wasn't sure about women owning care, but agreed with Gilligan that even if there were only one different voice, it should be honored.

This point of view led me to look for formats that would reflect a more horizontal and connecting stance. As if I had ordered it, one came up: the "reflecting team," proposed in the mid eighties by Norwegian psychiatrist Tom Andersen (1987). Andersen would ask a family to listen in as a group of clinicians discussed their situation and then would ask the family to comment in turn. Interventions were replaced by a potentially infinite succession of folds, as one group commented on the ideas of another. This format seemed to tap unexpected depths of imagination and felt not only more democratic but immensely freeing to the therapist.

Another contribution came from two Texas psychologists, Harlene Anderson and the late Harry Goolishian (1988). Their collaborative language systems approach dictated that the therapist come from a position of "not knowing." This stance was congruent with the postmodern stricture against foundational truth, but to someone used to family therapy's authoritative style it seemed radical. Harlene and Harry would sit in a family interview and listen to an individual speak at length, apparently doing little to influence the course of the conversation. I called this "imperceptible therapy." Then I began doing something like it myself and realized that it was just as influential as perceptible therapy, but in a different way. As the professional renounced authority, the capability of the customer seemed to increase.

I should mention here the solution-focused model of the Milwaukee group headed by Steve de Shazer and Insoo Berg because although it is not exactly postmodern, it seems to be a bridging approach. It is modern in that it offers a clear formula for producing change, and emphasizes therapist expertise. At the same time, therapists are asked to abandon the usual concern with problems, looking instead for exceptions to the complaint or solutions. In this sense, it moves with the postmodern distrust of concepts of pathology.

An aversion to the idea of deficits is particularly evident in the work of narrative therapists Michael White and David Epston (1990). Drawing inspiration from the writings of the French social philosopher Michel Foucault (Rabinow, 1984), these practitioners see therapy as a work of personal and cultural liberation. Their methods for "re-authoring lives" (White, 1995) are supported by a strong pull for agency. Most importantly, through their use of a storying metaphor they have severed the tie to family systems modernism.

These innovations became a primary source of influence on my own work. I began to put together pieces of an approach I called in a general sense "collaborative." Picking and choosing, I linked the reflecting team, with its democratizing format, to Goolishian and Anderson's not-knowing stance and to elements of White and Epston's critical practice. The result was a core of beliefs that modified the distance the medical model created between practitioner and customer and seemed to establish a more level playing field. The move away from a framework of pathology was particularly important. From a purely personal point of view, I wanted to naturalize a process that I had always experienced as an abasing ritual from a very formal world. My idea of the "different voice" was one way to suggest an alternative.

However, I did not believe this different voice belonged to women. My colleague Mary Olson (1994) has suggested that women as a class might have a different epistemology from men for historical rather than psychological reasons. Using linguist Walter Ong's (1982) distinction between an oral and a literate consciousness, Olson surmises that women may feel at home with an oral style because until recently they were excluded from the conversation of literacy (especially philosophy and psychology) that for centuries was the private property of men.

Another point is that many of the world's countries are steeped in an oral consciousness. This may account for some of the resistance people from non-Western cultures and less-educated classes have in encountering the Anglo-European therapy ritual. An oral style has not been deliberately represented in therapy except perhaps for the work of Carl Rogers. Such home-grown therapists as bartenders and beauticians are naturals who know how to listen and when to talk, but we are lucky when such a person happens to become a family therapist. I can think specifically of only two cases—Carl Whitaker and Harry Goolishian—and now neither of these people is with us.

In experimenting with this orally based collaborative style, I was struck by the degree to which it "sheds power." As it is said of the Tao Master: "When his work is done, the people say, 'Amazing, we did it all by ourselves.' " Social psychologist John Shotter (1993) talks of "knowing of the third kind," which he says is not internal knowing, as in the concept of the individual mind, nor outside knowing, as in knowing about the world. What he means is knowing that takes the form of joint action, as with a Ouija board. No one person controls the process; the outcome is the result of many hands pushing the counter about the board. Putting this line of thought into practice, I added the concept of "collaborative knowing" to my lexicon.

As an example, a year ago I was watching Harlene Anderson speak with a teenage daughter in the presence of her family. Harlene sat quietly while the daughter told her story at some length. According to my previous training, giving the floor to one person like that was almost illegal. I later asked Harlene what effect she thought this had on the family. She said she felt that her style of listening was contagious, and that everyone else in the group listened more attentively as a result. It occurred to me at that point that she was less interested in changing the person than the community.

However, this community was not the aggregate we think of as the neighborhood but the collection of sensibilities that always surround human events like a school of fish. I called it a "perceiving community." Perhaps, I thought, we have all been mistaken in trying so hard to discover the problem—or the solution either, for that matter. Perhaps when therapy works it is because of a change in attitudes within this community, this manifestation of the collective mind, rather than anything more specific. Therapy may be closer in this sense to dialysis than to a surgical intervention.

However, we are still talking about a therapy based on ideas about change. I favor dropping this word, associated as it is with modernist approaches, and replacing it with the idea of critical practice as Michael White (1995), Marcelo Pakman (1996) and others have been using it. This concept, derived from postmodern deconstructionism, offers the missing piece, the edge that comes with the idea of revising the very ground and identity of the therapy process as one is engaged in it. I will elaborate below.

DECONSTRUCTION THEORY

At the same time that I was experimenting with a different voice for therapy, I was very conscious of the effects of postmodernism's wild child, deconstructionism. This stance, based on ideas from French social thinkers Michel Foucault and Jacques Derrida, has been used to expose hidden power relations in the discourse of governing institutions and in canonical texts. The idea of deconstruction was first proposed by Derrida (1988), who analyzed the writings of giants like Freud and Nietzche as if they were rhetorical works like any other. He subjected these texts to literary criticism of a most peculiar kind. As if researching the negative space of the painter, Derrida looked for what was not said or what was opposed to what was said. He claimed that only then could the "ruling illusions" of Western thought—the claims to knowlege of the dominant texts of our culture—be unmasked.

Derrida also gave a definitional character to the term "postmodernism." With his insistence that knowlege consists of texts conversing with other texts, he shook loose the tie between language and the natural world. References only led to other references in infinite succession. This position, when applied to intellectual discourse, had the same effect as abandoning the gold standard.

Derrida's compatriot, Foucault (1986), was also abandoning the gold standard, though in a different way. By tracing the "genealogy," as he called it, of modern institutions of surveillance and correction, he pierced through the fog of impenetrable authority that surrounded them. In former times, Foucault explained, this authority could be clearly traced to kings and rulers; now it emanated from faceless bureaucracies. Foucault's writing gave visibility to the hidden ways in which modern societies control their subjects' lives. Although he was not a political radical, he gave us tools to counteract what has been called "the micro-fascism of everyday life."

Deconstructionism has become immensely popular with two groups in the United States: postmodern academic thinkers and critical feminists. I will describe a few examples of this research to give a general idea of its import. Let me start with the first group, which consists of a small band of revisionist social theorists. Unlike pure feminists, who are mainly concerned with exposing and correcting forms of gender oppression, they have used their deconstructionist ideas as a way to revise the underlying assumptions of their disciplines. They are academic rather than social radicals, but they nevertheless have made a signal contribution in challenging the modernist paradigm on which contemporary psychology and social psychology are based.

It is Gergen (1995) who has argued most persuasively that postmodernism is a new paradigm. He states that a true paradigm exists on three levels: It must allow each discipline to offer a theory at the level of the field, an overarching metatheory, and an application linking it to daily life. In his view, twentieth century psychology had put together a template that contained all three. Its discipline was behaviorism, its metatheory was based on behavioral research, and it included behavior therapies of different kinds. A successor paradigm was suggested by the cognitive movement that accompanied the computer revolution, but this approach had no metatheory, unless you count the ideas swirling around cybernetics.

At present, a paradigm for psychology based on language and communication, for which social constructionism has become the metatheory, is making its claim. In describing this development, Gergen says:

It is a revolution that extends across the disciplines and which replaces the dualist epistemology of a knowing mind confronting a material world with a *social epistemology*. The locus of knowledge is no longer taken to be the individual mind but rather patterns of social relatedness. (p. 129)

Agreeing with Gergen, social psychologist Rom Harre (1984) replaces the word "self" with "personal being," which he likens to a gravitational field in physics. He states that selfhood is not an internal property but only achieved through "public and collective activities that are located in talk." Cultural psychologist J. S. Bruner (1990) comes to the same conclusion, saying that we must stop thinking of the self as "one enduring nucleus" and see it instead as scattered about in books and conversations and "situated" in a community of learning.

These positions supported my own discomfort with notions of the self. My particular quarrel has been with the concept of the "psyche" on which the field of psychology and most psychotherapy is based. The psyche has been presented as a unit that develops according to the same sort of genetic blueprint as a simple organism or plant. It is as if the fetus, when it is born, has another little fetus inside it that has to grow up. Problems are said to arise when its growth is truncated, and this belief is presented as the rationale for many treatments for emotional distress. The psyche thus becomes an object about which truth claims can be made. This is a modernist position *par excellence* and suffers from the usual fallacy of confusing a poetic construct with a material body.

The idea of the "family system" is flawed for the same reason. Harvard sociologist Talcott Parsons (1951), who was the first person to use the phrase, talked of social life in terms of nested systems, with the larger ones regulating the smaller. Harlene Anderson and the late Harry Goolishian (1988) were the first family therapists to complain about this "onion theory," as they called it, because it reifies social structure. My own view is that once you link pathology to any unit at all, individual or family or whatever, it is an easy step to defining it as functional or dysfunctional. Then you can create tests to determine where on the continuum the unit goes. This is the slippery path to deficit ideas of human functioning.

Another important idea that social psychologists are tearing down is the life span trajectory, with its thesis that the early years of life determine the adult personality. Gergen (1982) rejects the dictum that psychological maturation takes place according to a predetermined set of stages, as psychodynamic and developmental theories would have it, saying that outcomes depend on a host of factors such as temperament, environment, and luck. An aleatory or chance-determined view, he says, would explain the vicissitudes of human experience much better.

It occurred to me that this scepticism could also be applied to the family life cycle. This sequence has also been described as following normative stages: the couple, the young family, the adolescent launching phase, the empty nest. Just as symptoms in an individual are thought to indicate delayed or stunted psychic growth, so problems in a family have been linked to the "stuckness" of the family life cycle. However, this cycle is hitched to the vanishing ideal of the American nuclear family and current theories on the subject are undergoing intense revision.

But enough on the academic revisionists. Let me cover briefly the contribution of critical feminists to this subject.

CRITICAL FEMINISM

A complaint common to this movement is that feminist research and opinions are ignored by the male-dominated intellectual establishment. Another is that a male style of academic discourse prevails. Morawski (1990) states that "what is reflected in the structure of science are social relations that are fitted to the experiences of men and a hierarchical social world" (pp. 000). This male discourse, she says, is highly adversarial. Academic achievement, for instance, is attained by promoting one's own framework and denigrating everyone else's. Thus feminists have the job not only of exposing gender bias, but of dealing with the competitive and hierarchical style in which this bias is encoded.

In the pursuit of this enterprise, feminist research in psychology is beginning to rack up some telling points. After her "different voice" work, Carol Gilligan, with Lyn Mikel Brown (1992), did a longitudinal study of young women as they went into adolescence. They found that these girls, although forthright as children, became uncertain and confused around age 12, almost as if they were having a culture-wide nervous breakdown. This finding bypassed the usual obsession with interior and individual factors to focus on pressures from the cultural and social environment.

Another milestone is Erica Burman's *Deconstructing Developmental Psychology* (1994), which exposes the sexist assumptions built into the field as well as its regressive social agenda. Burman remarks on the myopia of such early childhood theories as attachment theory, which describes defective mothers as the primary source of toxic influence. Bonding theory offers another trap: If the mother bonds insufficiently, the child will not grow; if she bonds too much, the child can't leave. Berman also points out that the narrow dyadic focus of infant studies screens out other relational influences.

Mary Crawford is another bright spirit in the area of gender and language. In *Talking Difference* (1995) she describes the enterprise known as assertiveness training as just another sexist pursuit pretending to be help. Where is it written, she asks, that women's deferential speaking style is the problem? What about the oppressive speaking style of men? Crawford also critiques the "two cultures" view of gender roles (Tannen, 1990), which defines difficulties between the sexes as miscommunication. Crawford objects to placing aggressions like rape in this category. Again, she asks, why are women the ones who have to correct the situation by making meanings clear?

I would like to include many other contributions of critical feminism to this subject, like Lenore Tiefer's *Sex Is Not a Natural Act* (1995) and Elaine Showalter's *The Female Malady* (1985), but that is for another paper. For now I will go on to the challenges to psychotherapy in recent years

THERAPY UNDER FIRE

If the field of psychology has been under small-arms fire, one could say that psychotherapy has been lobbed by grenades. A correction is undoubtedly overdue. Most therapies have little in common with hard-nosed science but are really small cultures of faith; mini-religions if you will. Their adherents are correspondingly passionate, and even the most indefensible of these ideologies can have enormous persistence and staying power, despite paucity of proof.

What has surprised me is the relative immunity the practice rationales of therapy have had to scholarly examination. What there is of critical scrutiny represents a grab bag of polemicists from different contexts. Research psychologist Robin Dawes' *House of Cards* (1994) with its provocative subtitle, *Psychology and Psychotherapy Built On Myth*, surveys outcome studies for all kinds of therapy, and comes up with a sobering conclusion. Even though most researchers agree that therapy "works," neither professional status, nor experience, nor training, nor model, seems to make a discernable difference. Dawes also takes the opportunity to blast some common myths of therapeutic practice. Examples are the "self-esteem obsession," the belief in the "tyranny of childhood," and the uncritical acceptance of the accuracy of retrospective memory.

An even more unforgiving position is represented in *Against Therapy* by Jeffrey Masson (1988), the former *enfant terrible* of the Freudian Archives. In this persuasive polemic, Masson starts by describing the early treatment of disobedient women who were classified as hysterics and consigned by their families to rest cures in Switzerland. These stories, like the case histories of women treated by Freud and his colleagues, are quite disturbing, and would probably invite malpractice suits if they occurred today.

Masson scrutinizes a variety of more recent therapeutic approaches, objecting to the abusive treatment of patients by the psychiatrist John Rosen; the fascist sympathies of Carl Jung; the self-aggrandizement of gurus of the Human Potential movement; and the authoritarian stance of many family therapists. He appreciates the benevolent style of Carl Rogers, but asks why Rogers condoned inhumane practices in the hospitals where he worked. Only the psychiatrist Sandor Ferenczi, who suggested that his patients ought to analyze him in turn, comes off well.

Masson has been joined by another obstreperous voice, that of Frederick Crewes (1995), whose conversations with Freudians in *The New York Review of Books* have been published in one volume. Linking the repression theory of psychoanalysis to the therapeutic beliefs of the recovered memory movement, Crews calls both to task for shaky causal connections between early trauma and symptoms later on. His chief objection is to the renewal of psychoanalysis by means of a "revived seduction theory." I found his arguments compelling, and began to wonder about the many traces of repression theory in the family therapy repertoire (that's another paper).

But the views that influenced me most profoundly were those coming from critical feminist literature. In *The Family Interpreted* (1988), Deborah Luepnitz attacks the family

therapy pioneers, who were almost all male, for their sexist and modernist theories, as if she were some light-winged spirit toppling down the Easter Island heads. When I read her book, I realized for the first time that systems therapists had intelligent enemies. I had a similar reaction to Gerald Erickson's (1988) scathing indictment of family systems theory. Erickson accuses it of an almost fascist exaltation of the system over the individual, and recommends a social network approach within a humanizing political and cultural frame. I was among those whose ideas were criticized by both authors, and I had to admit the truth of many of their charges. I date my own discomfort with the family systems viewpoint from that time.

Finally, I must mention my admiration for the work of psychologists Janet Surrey, Jean Baker Miller, Judith Jordan, and Irene Stiver at the Stone Center in Wellesley (1992). These women, among others, have pioneered a radical departure from the authoritarian treatment practiced in most mental hospitals. In view of research that shows that the majority of mental patients are women with a history of trauma and abuse, they have moved away from explanations that blame the person. And because they believe with Gilligan that women's developmental pathways predispose them to interdependence rather than autonomy, they have reshaped their clinical work to suit. They call their approach simply "relational."

ALTERNATIVE PRACTICES

These ideas are catching therapists in a pincer movement. Managed care dictates an ever-increasing reliance on diagnoses and treatment plans, but these requirements lock people into straitjackets of deficit just as crippling as chemical ones. Relieving emotional distress also involves freeing people from these insidious and stigmatizing bonds. The problem is how to do so without becoming Joan of Arc. In the past, the radical therapist has presented herself as the savior of a downtrodden client against an injurious establishment, but establishments hate being put in the wrong. The deconstructive formats I am talking about are less foolhardy in that they offer an option of alternative practices rather than a set of more correct beliefs. If the experience is successful, the reward is built in. If not, we keep on trying.

I have already mentioned some of these formats. Tom Andersen's reflecting team embodies an implicitly radical experience. The reflecting team puts the family in a "last shall be first" position by asking family members to be consultants to their own case. In addition, the folding over and over of commenting groups contradicts the hierarchy of therapy and its orientation toward a "goal." Andersen's practice of letting the family have the last word interferes with the usual prescription at the end and as a result, the closing intervention that was such a trademark of family therapy has begun to fade.

Also in this category is the powerful revision that Harlene Anderson and the late Harry Goolishian introduced with their concept of "not knowing." This stand hits hard at the assumptions of authority built into the therapist role and supports a style that seems to many people absurdly nondirective and laissez-faire. Experimenters like me, who have tried to leach attributes of knowingness out of their work, get displeased reactions from workshop audiences. However, the people we see seem to appreciate being treated as partners, and invest themselves all the more willingly in the work.

Of all the voices contributing to a "counter-conversation" for therapists, Michael White's is to my mind the most brilliant and original. Some truly wonderful examples of therapeutic partnership can be found in his work. I also believe that his approach offers a huge lift of morale to our beleaguered field. Stating boldly what many of us believe, that the use of pathologizing discourses is responsible for "one of the great marginalizations of our time," he has offered a number of ideas for creating an alternative practice. For instance, by asking therapists to "historicize" their ideas and positions—to give a personal or contextual backdrop for them—he gives us a way to demystify the therapeutic process without denying our experience or training.

A newer voice adding to this lexicon comes from Argentinian psychiatrist Marcelo Pakman. Pakman (1996) speaks up for therapeutic work based on "critical social practice." What he means is any conversation that is organized reflexively, so that different stories about accepted ideas might implicitly challenge those ideas just by being passed back and forth. For instance, a North American back pain might not be a Puerto Rican back pain. Pakman sees therapy as an opportunity to deconstruct our ideas of what is normal. As such, he says, it has a decolonizing role to play, not only for the people we see but for us as professionals too.

COLLABORATIVE KNOWING

The contributions I have mentioned above have given body and dimension to my search for a practice of collaborative knowing. I should also mention some contributions from outside the field. For instance, postmodern researcher Elliot Mishler (1986) calls attention to the methods used by researcher Marianne Paget in interviewing women artists on their creativity. Instead of following an interview schedule, she used open-ended questions, deliberately held herself back, and created space for her respondents by her silences. If she herself spoke, it was in a hesitant and halting style. As a result, her respondents were emboldened to work out their thoughts in front of her.

Crawford (1995) offers another example when she says that if women compete with men for talk time, this simply reconstructs dominance as a conversational form. Instead, she suggests that women try to establish "a more inclusive dynamic," and presents an anecdote from another researcher about a situation where women in a graduate seminar dominated by males turned the tables:

The professor and most of the male students monopolized talk, controlling the floor through eye contact, interruption, and throwing the floor to one another. Those who were squeezed out analyzed these patterns and set out to change them, not by adopting the dominant discourse, but by empowering one another. They arrived early and sat in a way that diffused eye contact around the group; they built on one another's comments in the discussion, giving the mutual gift of interaction work; they invited the silent to speak. Rather than overvaluing and imitating the dominant style . . . they used collaborative patterns to draw in, and empower, more participants. (quoted from Thorne et. al., 1983).

One concern for postmodernist therapists is how to deconstruct their own authority. Michael White, following Foucault (1973), has pointed to the "clinical gaze" as part of the intimidating repertory male professionals historically have drawn upon. One virtue of the reflecting team is that it places people in an overhearing position. Not having to look people in the eye, and not being looked at in turn, is often experienced as a great freedom. Another deconstructive practice would be the habit of "situating" one's professional knowledge. I will sometimes pull a suggestion or interpretation out of the bag I have labeled "Biggest Hits of Family Therapy," but I try to include the story of how I came by it and how it is supposed to work.

I also try to practice "imperceptible therapy." This means knowing how to wait for an answer longer than is comfortable, how to listen as if one were deaf, how to shut up when one is about to be brilliant, and how to grope openly when one is confused. We do this all the time, but are trained to cover it up. A related notion is to stop having conversations in our heads with the field (supervisors, mentors, colleagues, students, books), as in "What is the right question to ask here?" or "What would X say about that?" because this can cut into what I think of as the proprioceptive flow. Research psychologist Jan Beavin (personal communication, 1994) has devised some striking experiments that show the paralyzing effect on a conversation of stopping this flow. Dogmatic therapies with tightly designed procedures often have this effect and dogmatic methods of supervision always do.

In teaching, I will often use reflecting formats because they create instant neighborhoods. For instance, I might ask smaller units or "pods" to talk among themselves while the rest listen in. In a large group, this allows every-

one a voice, while creating a sense of safety for the large number of people, often women, who hesitate to speak up when the circle is larger than four.

Another example of "affirmative action for shy people," as one graduate student put it, is to ask everyone to share thoughts around the room. If I use that American art form, the open and honest discussion, the more forceful people in the group will dominate it. These people sound, and probably feel, smarter and smarter, while the others look as if they were about to get a booby prize. A reflecting format, where everyone gets to talk before any discussion begins, seems to cut into these escalations and metaphorically allows everyone to breathe.

There is one huge pitfall in asking trained clinicians to join a reflecting team: They will use objectifying descriptions. When this happens during a seminar or workshop, I always feel that I have set innocent offenders up to be wrong and so I am reluctant to criticize them. But if you "historicize" a comment, as White recommends, you can release it from its negative valence. For instance, someone else on the team might ask how what the person is talking about relates to their own experience. Explaining the genealogy of a view cuts into the Moses' Tablets effect from which the utterances of professionals too often draw their strength.

I also ask reflecting people to refrain from suggestions or advice and instead offer associations—to books, movies, images, stories, or songs. These, being many-sided and ambiguous, usually do not have pejorative implications. They can also be personal. A story from one's own experience that fits the occasion can be particularly powerful. This sounds like self-disclosure and challenges the sacred icon of the therapeutic boundary, but I think this is one icon that has become a fetish in recent years.

Finally, words are important. Michael White has been getting rid of pejorative terms that go with the territory, like calling people "patients" or "clients," referring instead to "persons." This may sound like political correctness, but I think that many of the clinical words we are expected to use are a form of hate speech. The word "clinical" is itself suspect. So is "case," for which I substitute "situation." Stopping oneself from using these phrases, or putting mental quotes about them if one has no choice, is important, even when not one "person" is in sight.

ENDING

Family therapy in its first stage distanced us from theories that defined emotional problems as disorders of the mind, seeing them instead as adaptive responses to human predicaments. More recently, the social constructionists among us have come to the conviction that all we have are stories, accounts by ancient mariners or blessed damozels. Traditional psychological approaches are increasingly buying into scientific modes: biological assessments, behavioral treatments, and cognitive tests. Psychodynamic and humanistic models, like traditional family therapies, are facing extinction. But the family field has a record of resistance to its own establishments. As I have been telling myself, "The midnight rebels are once more on the march."

As a result, the story about family therapy is itself changing. I am wary of the idea of a paradigm shift because it has been used so often to herald a false dawn. Never expect a Messiah, because you may get one—every year. Nevertheless, I am convinced that the move from a natural science framework to a sociolinguistic framework offers something truly revolutionary: the first new philosophical base for human studies since Descartes. As Harry Goolishian used to say, "It is no longer "*I think* therefore I am," but "*We speak* therefore I am." If one really internalized this change, one would never again be the same kind of therapist. Perhaps, in the accepted sense, one would not be a therapist at all.

REFERENCES

Andersen, T. (Ed.). (1990). *The reflecting team*. New York: W.W. Norton.

Anderson, H. & Goolishian, H. (1988). "Human systems as linguistic systems." *Family Process, 27*; 371–393.

Berman, A. (1988). *From the new criticism to deconstruction*. Chicago: University of Chicago Press.

Brown, L. M., & Gilligan, C. (1992). *Meeting at the crossroads*. New York: Ballantine.

Bruner, J. (1990). *Acts of meaning*. Cambridge, MA: Harvard University Press.

Burman, E. (1994). *Deconstructing developmental psychology*. London: Routledge.

Crawford, M. (1995). *Talking difference*. Thousand Oaks, CA: Sage.

Crewes, F. (1995). *The memory wars*. New York: New York Review of Books.

Dawes, R. (1994). *House of cards: Psychology and psychotherapy built on myth*. New York: The Free Press.

Derrida, J. (1988).

Erickson, G. (1988). "Against the grain: Decentering family therapy." *Journal of Marital and Family Therapy, 14,* 225–236.

Foucault, M. (1973). *The birth of the clinic*. (A. Smith, Trans.). New York: Random House.

Gergen, K. (1982). *Toward transformation in social knowledge*. Thousand Oaks, CA: Sage.

Gergen, K. (1994). *Realities and relationships*. Cambridge, MA: Harvard University Press.

Gilligan, C. (1982). *In a different voice*. Cambridge. MA: Harvard University Press.

Haley, J. (1997). "Toward a theory of pathological systems." in P. Watzlawick and J. Weakland, (Eds.), *The interactional view*. New York: W.W. Norton.

Harre, R. (1984). *Personal being*. Cambridge, MA: Harvard University Press.

Luepnitz, D. (1988). *The family interpreted*. New York: Basic Books.

Masson, J. (1988). *Against therapy*. London: Fontana Paperbacks.

Miller, J. & Stiver, I. (1991). "A relational reframing of therapy." Work in Progress, No. 52. Wellesley, MA: Stone Center Working Paper Series

Mishler, E. (1986). *Research interviewing: Context and narrative*. Cambridge, MA: Harvard U. Press.

Morawski, J. (1990). "Toward the unimagined." In R. Hare-Mustin and J. Marecek (Eds.), *Making a difference*. New Haven: Yale University Press.

Olson, M. (1995). "Conversation and writing: A collaborative approach to bulimia," *Journal of Feminist Family Therapy, 6,* 21–44.

Ong, W. (1992). *Orality and Literacy*. New York: Routledge.

Pakman, M. (1996). "Therapy in contexts of poverty and ethnic dissonance," *Journal of systemic therapies, 14,* 64–71.

Parsons, T. (1951). *The social system*. Glencoe, IL: The Free Press.

Rabinow, P. (1984). *The foucault reader*. New York: Pantheon.

Ruesch, J. & Bateson, G. (1951). *Communication: the social matrix of psychiatry*. New York: W.W. Norton.

Satir, V. (1964). *Conjoint family therapy*. Palo Alto, CA: Science and Behavior Books.

Shotter, J. (1993). *Cultural politics of everyday life*. Toronto, Canada: University of Toronto Press.

Showalter, E. (1985). *The female malady*. New York: Random House.

Spence, D. (1984). "Narrative Smoothing and Clinical Wisdom." In T.R Sarbin (Ed.), *Narrative Psychology*. New York: Praeger.

Tannen, D. (1990). *You just don't understand*. New York: Ballantine.

Tiefer, L. (1995). *Sex is not a natural act.* Boulder, CO: Westview Press.

Watzlawick, P., Weakland, J., & Fisch, R. (1974). *Change; Principles of problem formation and problem resolution.* New York: W.W. Norton.

White, M. & Epston, D. (1990). *Narrative means to therapeutic ends.* New York: W.W. Norton.

White, M. (1995). *Re-authoring lives.* Adelaide, Australia: Dulwich Centre Publications.

From Rehabilitation to Etiology: Progress and Pitfalls

◆

Margaret Thaler Singer, Ph.D.

Margaret Thaler Singer, Ph.D.

Margaret Singer received her Ph.D. degree in 1952 from the University of Denver. She has held a number of academic appointments, including serving as a Professor Emeritus in the Department of Psychology at the University of California, Berkeley. She has received numerous honors including the American Association for Marriage and Family Therapy Award for Cumulative Contributions to Research in Family Therapy. Dr. Singer has served on a number of editorial boards and has been the recipient of numerous grants. She is past president of the American Psychosomatic Association. Dr. Singer has made more than 100 contributions to professional journals and books. She has authored Cults in our Midst *and* "Crazy" Therapies.

INTRODUCTION

Therapists fall prey to fads, pseudoscience, politics, and cultural trends. During the five decades that I have been a psychologist, fads and fringe psychotherapy practices have come and gone. Some of these will be described briefly ending with the current vogue—"repressed memory" therapy. Assumptions underlying various bursts of therapist zeal will be explored, and some links to cultural and social forces considered.

Paul McHugh (1992, pp. 498, 509) has called some of these practices "psychiatric misadventures." He noted that certain cultural fashions have led the theory and practice of psychotherapy off in false, even disastrous directions. "Psychiatric practice has con-

doned some bizarre misdirections, proving how all too often the discipline has been the captive of the culture ... [engaging in] the intimidating mixture of medical mistake lashed to a trendy idea."

The entire field of psychotherapy, not just psychiatry, has had some fads and "misadventures" over the past few decades. I am not condemning psychotherapy, but directing attention to that segment within the mental health professions who have at times been caught up in fads, trends, and misadventures. I also want to look at some of the unspoken assumptions inherent in a number of therapists' practices, with the hope of causing some thoughtful reassessment of certain practices and trends.

REHABILITATIVE PSYCHOTHERAPY

Fifty years ago psychological and psychiatric treatment focused on rehabilitation, much of it based on the psychobiology of Adolf Meyer (1948). It was a forerunner of today's biopsychosocial models of behavior. Meyer urged practitioners to study a patient's medical history, life events, and responses to learn how each patient's "reactions," habits, and coping methods evolved. Meyer's approach was optimistic, supplanting an earlier pessimistic period in psychiatry in which mental disorders were seen as reflections of immutable biological abberations.

Psychologists, psychiatrists, and psychiatric social workers of the era worked within medical and educational frameworks to rehabilitate clients and patients. Meyerian and other rehabilitative therapy was designed to help the patient change ineffective, disorganized, and deteriorated habits and reactions to his or her inner self and outer environments, and to learn more functional ones.

At that time, therapy had to be educational and supportive, because there was no lithium, antidepressants, or neuroleptics; the few methods there were included cold wet packs, continuous tubs, insulin, and electroconvulsive therapy. Talk therapy focused on the alleviation of symptoms and the presenting distress. At least since Freud, who began with a focus on symptom relief, there has been a gradual shift away from symptom reduction toward therapists minimizing the alleviation of presenting problems and instead convincing patients that they need the particular type of therapy the therapist knows and believes in.

Martin Williams succinctly outlined the changes from Freud's early use of hypnosis to produce symptom relief, to the use of free association and interpretations that held that correct interpretations bring repressed material to consciousness and eliminate the need for symptomatic expression of various impulses. Only when treatment began to focus on transference issues did the switch away from dealing with presenting problems change to the application by the therapist of his or her preferred long-term therapy. Williams (1985) labels this the "bait and switch" maneuver. The patient seeks what she expects will be a short-term symptom-relief therapy, only to be led by the therapist to accept and enter into long-term etiologically based therapy that is the therapist's preferred or often only mode of treatment. How and why this shift came about, and the contents of the therapist's theories and their impact on patients, is one of the central currently debated topics in psychotherapy.

Symptom alleviation was especially clear during World War II, when hypnosis and sodium amytal interviews were used to treat conversion symptoms in both military and civilian patients. These methods rapidly eliminated symptoms, while subsequent talk therapy assisted patients to understand their pseudo-neurological and other conversion disorders as reactions to trauma. These patients learned that talking about the trauma and stress was useful. These techniques are still used with a highly selected group of patients. However, the success of this application of hypnosis to a special subgroup may be part of the cause for the generalized and often indiscriminate use of hypnosis with almost any patient in a number of current therapies, and for the use of amytol to search out the forgotten.

ETIOLOGICAL THEORIES OF PSYCHOTHERAPY

After World War II, interest in psychoanalysis and the psychodynamics of mental disorders burgeoned. This opened a floodgate of therapeutic fads based on two yet to be proven assumptions: that first discovering the etiology of a person's distress (recalling and reporting traumatic events) and then abreacting (reliving in the therapy session the emotions associated with the traumatic event) would relieve the person's psychological distress.

Implicit in the above notions are that parental figures are the prime traumatizers, and that the mind is conceptualized in a mechanical 19th-century model as akin to a vessel. Thus, if a person emptied out the bad memories through discovering their etiology and abreacting the associated emotions, the person would be, so to speak, cleansed psychically. It also falsely assumes a videotape model of human memory, rather than the reconstructive process that it is.

Controversy over rehabilitative versus etiologically based therapies has brewed for decades. Guze (1992) states that therapists adhere to either the rehabilitative or the etiological paradigm. The goals, methods, and expectations of each type rest on quite different assumptions.

The etiological model is inherently dramatic and appealing, and is predicated on the assumption that the psychotherapeutic process will lay bare the psychological forces or events that are etiologically responsible for the patient's behavior and problems. The etiological therapist assumes psychic determinism, and hopes to locate dynamic factors. It is assumed that these factors explain the patient's problems and once they are discovered they will release the patient. There is an implicit assumption that cure rests on catharsis: The patient will be reborn, free at last, and will not have to work on changing habits and attitudes. The only effort to be exerted will be to locate causality, unlike rehabilitative therapy, where the client or patient is expected to *work* on changing habits and attitudes.

The rehabilitative therapist uses the same raw materials—interviews, observations, data from others—as the bases of therapy but requires no assumptions about the etiology of the disorders being treated. "Attitudes, emotions, perceptions, strengths, weaknesses, expectations, and relationships are explored, characterized and discussed. The aim is to help the patient understand himself or herself better and function more effectively with less discomfort and less disability, even when little is known about the reasons for the patient's illness or how the patient's personality developed" (Guze, 1992, p. 72). The patient may have to be confronted by the therapist, who will help him or her learn more autonomous, comfortable, productive, responsible styles of reacting.

The etiologies of schizophrenia and bipolar disorders are still unknown, but medications and rehabilitative therapies help people so diagnosed lead more effective lives. Nor is the etiology of the lesser personality disorders known, yet rehabilitative therapies have been

of great help to people with these disorders as well.

Therapists of a few decades past who were trained in the etiological model were cautioned against unduly influencing patients. Their work was monitored to avoid the pitfalls of "wild analysis" and therapists imposing their value systems on patients. There was training in a number of therapy modalities ranging from supportive interpretations, to hypnosis, psychoanalysis, behavior modification, and other techniques. The therapist was expected to treat a wide range of behavior with appropriate and patient-specific methods. The rehabilitative therapist was expected to be able to treat a wide range of patients with an equally broad range of techniques. The therapist was akin to a custom tailor. However, currently, many therapists are fitting patients into a Procrustean bed—patients are being led to accept the therapist's favorite mode of treatment, which may not necessarily be the one most needed by the patient, but is the one the therapist most prizes (Singer, 1977; Singer & Lalich, 1996: Williams, 1985).

Recently there has been a proliferation of therapists, many with abbreviated training, limited supervision, rare consultations, and limited experience with a narrow range of techniques with which to help patients. Many seem unaware or unconcerned about the authority and power that their roles and titles convey. Patients and clients see therapists as supposed authorities with superior knowledge, training, and skills. The society supports placing trust in experts and cloaks them with credibility. Additionally, certification and licensing add to the aura of expertise.

Thus, therapists' words, attitudes, values, and beliefs can wield remarkable influence over patients. The well-trained ethical therapist remains aware of the dependency and suggestibility of patients, which causes them to tend to endow therapists' words and suggestions with great weight and to be compliant in relation to the therapist's direct and implicit suggestions. There is an extensive literature in psychodynamic psychology and hypnosis that, along with professional ethics and legal codes, warns therapists of the highly suggestible, dependent roles of patients and the need for therapists to remain aware of the power imbalance between them and their patients.

Many therapists pay little heed to how guided imagery, hypnosis, and leading questions can increase suggestibility and induce compliance in patients who are dependent on their therapists' care. Hypnotically refreshed testimony is barred from most courts in the United States (Orne, Whitehouse, Dinges, & Orne, 1988; Orne & Dinges, 1989), unless the testimony was developed under fairly stringent conditions and the court has the ability to oversee the hypnotic session through videotaped records to check for the presence of leading and suggestive behavior. Yet certain current therapies rely heavily on guided imagery, hypnosis, suggestive and leading questioning to produce recovered memories and so-called narrative rather than factual historical material.

Yapko (1990, p.256) points out that "the use of leading questions can create a false memory that can become a pathological frame of reference for the client that will last a lifetime. Formal trance is not necessary for this to occur." He further warns (p. 2) of "the possibility of hypnotically implanting false memories—vivid memories of things that never actually happened that the client comes to believe as true recollections. "Yapko pointed out the risks of suggestive procedures and urged caution in suggesting memories of any sort. "In some cases it is all too easy for therapists to unintentionally create the very problems they must then treat."

THE MYSTIQUE OF PSYCHOLOGICAL IMPROVEMENT

This sequence of developments since World War II popularized the use of individual therapy. From that emerged the use of group therapy, followed by the popularization of "psychological fitness" for the general population, not just those people who usually sought psychotherapy. Training or T-groups, sensitivity training, and encounter groups spread and were followed by commercially sold large group awareness training programs, such as est, Lifespring and other programs (Finkelstein, Wenergrat, & Yalom, 1982).

Simultaneously with the popularization of cathartic group experiences, there was a proliferation of pop psychology books. Nationally readers were propagandized that they could improve their personalities and become popular, outgoing, and successful through "psychological awareness." Self-help psychology volumes now fill bookstore shelves across America. About 2000 are published every year (Doheny, 1988). Self-help books are seen to be taking the place of the legendary oracle at Delphi and replacing older sources of guidance, including religion (Starker, 1989). One researcher furthered this idea by explaining that across time the term *soul* changed into *mind*, which eventually became *self*, making the self almost a reverential concept (Gambrill, 1990, 1992). Today, as a populace we tend to place faith and reliance on self-help and pop psychology movements much in the way we would have trusted in oracles centuries ago.

A GROWTH INDUSTRY

In an early article of mine written with Dr. L.J. West (1980) describing cults, quacks, and the nonprofessional psychotherapies, we noted that quackery exists not only in physical treatments but in psychological treatments as well. We noticed a "personal growth" industry that was combining intense social influence tactics with psychological techniques, sometimes occurring in cults, sometimes in wildcat psychotherapies that use either individual or group methods (Yalom, 1986).

In the 1970s, the United States moved into an era in which it became easy to fall prey to accepting all sorts of "alternative therapies." Many were West Coast phenomena that soon spread across the nation. Bizarreness and irrational assumptions underlying the therapies did not and still do not slow sales or popularity. Often it is only when legal redress for damages is sought that some of the therapies fade from the scene. Some therapists appear to disregard the potential dangers to patients and families involved in trendy therapies.

A form of group fight therapy was briefly popular. Group members were encouraged to hit fellow participants both for their own and the target's good. Several legal suits for physical damages incurred followed, and this cooled the ardor of the psychologists promoting that therapy. In another instance a therapist was sued for allegedly instructing a 200-pound mother to sit on her son to control him. The mother alleged that the therapist told her that one of the elder statesmen of psychiatry had once given another woman similar instructions and the method was effective. The mother who sued followed the therapist's advice and sat on her child for two hours. The child died.

The oddness of the source of the therapy often is not challenged. A businessman claimed to have received psychically a new form of therapy from a psychiatrist who had died six months earlier (Hoffman, 1976). Former patients of this therapy report procedures in which they "prosecuted" their parents, and performed mock burial ceremonies on their mothers, fathers or selves, lying in a coffin. Sessions run three to five hours and clients often spend 20 hours a week on therapy homework. "Spiritual guides" made through visual imagery are created early in therapy and later used to replace the therapist. The group claims that it uses professional and "noncredentialed" personnel to conduct intensive psychotherapy (Zweben, 1980, p. 230). Relatives of the dead psychiatrist eventually sued to have his name removed from the therapy. This therapy, with a new name, is in its second decade.

Some therapists reasoned that once a therapist accepts the etiological model and begins the search for the causes of a person's behavior, why not regress the patient back to infancy and then bottlefeed, diaper, and reparent the patient? Thus emerged a series of regressive-reconstruction therapies primarily growing out of Sechehaye's (1951) book and later taken up as "reparenting" therapies in which "parentectomies" were accomplished (Schiff, 1970). Families turned over teenage and young adult schizophrenic offspring; later nonschizophrenics were included, placed by the therapist in foster homes where they lived when not in long therapy sessions in which they were regressed to bottle feeding and diaper stages. The therapy reportedly was moved overseas after the scalding death of a young patient.

A variety of rebirthing therapies have been offered, ranging from those given in blue bubble-bath solutions in ordinary tubs to those done in redwood hot tubs, to dry-rebirthing done by rolling people in carpets. Purportedly the founder of the rebirthing idea received significant revelations while spending long periods of time in the bathtub, and later concluded that children panic at birth when they draw their first breath and then retain a nameless fear (Orr & Ray, 1977). Rebirthing therapy is supposed to free the person from that first shock of breathing on his or her own, and thus allow an expanded awareness of his or her capabilities.

Pure catharsis underlies some therapies. Three schools of scream therapy evolved in the 1970s. Janov's (1970) primal scream therapy assumes a person has early Primal Pain, and that an adult can learn to release by reexperiencing the pain before a primal therapist through emitting agonizing screams that are said to "dissolve neurosis." Casriel (1963; 1980, p.430) introduced his New Identity Process (NIP) scream therapy in 1963 in a "Synanon-styled, hostile-provocative encounter group" as a way of producing abreactions in the total range of patients, excepting only the organically damaged. Saltzman's (1980) bio-scream psychotherapy grew out of NIP scream therapy and the creator sought to add more warmth to the process. It was applied individually or in group settings.

MEMORY ENHANCEMENT ISSUES

Two recent types of therapy are causing intense reactions in both professional and popular literature because of the zeal with which certain therapists are promoting their use and because of the repercussions on the families of patients. These are recovered memory therapy and facilitated communication therapy. They share many common features. *Recovered memory therapy* is done through ordinary oral conversation between therapist and patient. In *facilitated communi-*

cation (FC) therapy, the therapist guides a nonspeaking patient to spell out answers. Both of these therapies are the subject of considerable scrutiny and debate currently because of two primary criticisms: (a) the therapist takes on the role of suggesting and leading the patient, and (b) many reportedly false accusations against parents and others of alleged molestation have been elicited from patients.

In facilitated communication or assisted communication therapy, which is applied especially to handicapped and autistic children and adults, the therapist has a board with letters and numbers that resembles an old-fashioned ouija board. The patient closes his or her fist with the index finger pointing out. The therapist's hand is placed on top of the patient's, grasping the closed fist. The therapist then guides the patient to spell out answers to questions (Dillon, 1993; Myers, 1993; Rimland, 1992). The letters and numbers can be on any smooth surface. Even a typewriter or electronic keyboard can be used. The general method has been used since the early 1970s to work with cerebral palsy cases, but in 1991 it was introduced into the United States to use with autistic patients. Early and continuing criticism of the method is that the products spelled out by the facilitator–subject interaction are purely the suggested products of the facilitator.

Rimland (1992) writes of cases in the United States and Australia: "In case after case, poorly trained, overzealous facilitators have uncovered, they believe, evidence of child molestation by family members. They report the parents to the authorities and then the nightmare begins." Some cases, according to Dillon (1993), have been dropped at pretrial stages, some have gone on to lengthy trials, and some are still in courts.

Cummins and Prior (1992, pp. 239–240) concluded: "On not one single occasion has a systematic investigation of assisted communication revealed consistent and valid evidence that such communication emanates from the client. Rather, all relevant investigations have revealed that, in each instance studied, the assistant has, wittingly or unwittingly, been responsible for the recorded response. . . . It is evident that some assistants, through the use

either of tactile/visual cues or through the actual imposition of movement, manipulate their client's responses." Myers (1993, p. 3) presents a summary of the current status of FC, especially from a legal standpoint, and notes the heated debate among adherents and critics, warning that "caution is warranted in using facilitated disclosures of abuse in court."

These cases are similar to those of the alleged false memories cases growing out of recovered memory therapy. In the latter, families allege that therapists lead and suggest to patients molestation scenes that the patients are encouraged to use to confront their families, to sue them in civil suits, or to press criminal charges (Loftus, 1994; Ofshe & Singer, 1994; Ofshe & Watters, 1993, 1994; Pendergrast, 1994; Yapko, 1994).

Critics are noting that in many recovered memory procedures, therapists, in both individual and group sessions, act as powerful social influence forces. Patients report that they responded to leading suggestions because they saw the therapist as an expert, and that failure to recall and embellish memories was seen as "resistance to wanting to get well" and being "in denial." In some groups, participants report being aggressively urged to conform to group expectations by both therapist and other members to produce "acceptable" memories—acceptability being judged by how closely the response met the therapist's theory of causality, or the personal prejudices or biases of the group or the therapist.

A group of therapists has developed a theory that sexual abuse lies beneath all or almost all psychological disorders. The patient is led to see herself as the victim of an abusive, dysfunctional family (a few clients are men, who are also reporting their experiences in recovered memory therapy). Thus patients are being taught a victim role. Therapy becomes a period of historical revisionism.

Many writers, both professional and in the media, while emphasizing that child sexual abuse occurs and is reprehensible, are likening the current spate of allegations growing out of recovered memory therapy practices to today's version of the Salem witch trials (Mulhern, 1991; Ofshe & Watters, 1993). The recovered memories are not only about alleged sexual abuses by family; certain therapists specialize in space alien abuse, in satanic cult abuse, and in past-lives abuse (Baker, 1988, 1991; *Common Ground*, 1993; Hammond, 1992; Mack, 1992, 1994; Mulhern, 1992; Scheafer, 1993; Spanos, 1986, 1987).

Recently, through its House of Delegates the American Medical Association (*Clinical Psychiatry News*, 1993) went on record stating that the use of memory enhancement techniques in eliciting accounts of childhood sexual abuse "to be fraught with problems of potential misapplication" and directed its Council of Scientific Affairs to evaluate "the validity of techniques used to help patients recall childhood experiences." The California Board of Behavioral Science Examiners (Okerblom & Sauer, 1993, p. B4) commissioned a psychologist to study the status of ritual abuse therapy. The state boards normally do not regulate particular types of therapy, but in his report the evaluator recommended that the two state boards that license psychologists and social workers examine whether ritual abuse therapy violates ethical standards of the profession, or if it constitutes gross negligence because it is "an extreme departure from normal standards of care. If you are creating mythical memories in children and adults which are damaging their families and other people, then that is gross negligence under the law."

BAIT AND SWITCH, BLAME AND CHANGE

The increasing popularity of etiologically based therapy has led therapists and the public to expect a search for the cause of a patient's distress, poor attitudes, depression, eating problems, marital difficulty, and the myriad of human discomforts that are presented to therapists.

Mental health professionals for some time have been commenting on the trends in psychotherapy. Rehabilitative therapy gives credence to and accepts the contributions of the environment, the family, the patient's genetic makeup, and so forth to that person's distress. But at the same time, rehabilitative therapy has always assisted patients to see that learned

attitudes and habits, over which they had some control, appeared to instigate and perpetuate a certain portion of the distressful interactions they were experiencing. Patient acceptance and understanding was provided, but patient responsibility for change and self-control and the learning of new ways was a central part of the therapeutic work.

Psychologists who have critiqued the underpinnings of many current psychotherapies have noted the limited range of most therapists' skills, the unspoken assumptions underlying their practices, and the potentially unethical behaviors involved in certain practices. Williams (1985) has bluntly labeled the practice of "bait and switch" carried out by all too many therapists. He compared the therapies to the unethical retail sales practice of baiting customers with advertisements for a low-price item and then switching them to a higher priced item. He showed that psychotherapy can bait clients to think that they will get symptom reduction and emotional relief in a brief time. But once they are hooked into treatment, clients are led to believe that their problems are complex and they are switched to long-term therapy. Williams (1985, p.111) writes: "The form of treatment, then, is determined by the therapist's habitual approach and not by the nature of the problem that the patient brings in."

Moving on from the bait-and-switch method, Campbell (1992) explicates the "blame and change" philosophy underlying much therapy. He credits M. Duncan Stanton for originating the term blame and change. Campbell (1992, p. 474) writes: "When therapists assume that clients have endured a history of betrayal by significant others, their assumptions can substantially influence a course of treatment." He draws upon the rather extensive psychotherapy research literature in which researchers have noted that therapists' assumptions color and mold what transpires in therapy.

Many writers have noted that it has become almost a culturally approved politically correct stance for therapists to assume patients have been betrayed, abused, emotionally deprived, and variously harmed by family and environments. Again, no thinking person is saying that families and circumstances are always wholesome, loving, and ideal. But the critics of biased therapists' negative attitudes toward patients' relatives note that such therapists subsequently may make mostly or only pejorative interpretations about family, and in the end patients are led to feel that if they blame the past, especially their parents, that will change them. Campbell (p. 475) writes, "In their effects, these kinds of accusatory interpretations suggest to clients that therapy must blame them (significant others) in order to change you." Campbell notes that "blame-and-change maneuvers are diverse enough to serve as an organizing theme for an entire course of treatment . . . therapists can encourage them [clients] to recall events supposedly verifying a history of betrayal by significant others. Obviously, however, any client's recollection of such events is influenced significantly by the therapist's a priori assumptions. Those assumptions are conveyed to clients, sometimes subtly and sometimes not, by the questions their therapists ask them (for example, 'Do you realize that you grew up in a severely dysfunctional family?')."

Thus clients are eventually led to create "narrative truths" rather than "historical truths" when they recount their histories. Just as there are "historical revisionists" who claim that Hitler did not create Auschwitz and that there was no Holocaust, we have therapists who have little or no commitment to learn about the actual histories of their clients in an unbiased way. Therapists' a priori assumptions lead clients to fill in the blanks, so to speak, in response to promptings that assume betrayal, sexual abuse, and whatever the therapist may have personal or political leanings to include as the "causes" of their client's presenting symptoms.

One of the current points of scrutiny of recovered memory therapy is that observers and critics are asking, What are the motivations of these therapists? Families are being destroyed, reputations ruined, and finances depleted in legal defenses. Accusations have sent parents and others to prison on the basis of therapy-derived recountings. Furthermore, patients are not being cured or made more content and functional.

Not only are recovered memories alleging family abuse, but four other types of searching for so-called recovered memories are being offered in psychotherapy today—space alien abuse, satanic cult abuse, entitites abuse, and past-lives abuse.

John Mack (1992, p.7), a Harvard psychiatrist, avers that "hundreds of thousands, if not millions, of American men, women and children may have experienced UFO abductions or abduction-related phenomena." He lists some "common symptoms" including "the appearance for no apparent reason of small cuts, scars or odd red spots . . . a history of small beings or a presence around the patient's bed. . . ." Other UFOlogists (Hopkins, Jacobs & Westrum, 1992, p.9) allege that at least 2 percent of the population present "the UFO abduction syndrome"—which includes partial or total repression of the UFO experiences that can be recalled with the aid of hypnosis or other relaxation techniques, and may include scars on the legs or upper body as a result of quasimedical examinations at the hands of UFO personnel. A Southern California psychotherapist who counsels UFO "abductees" reports that he has discovered a new stigmata of alien abduction: a hole in the palate of the mouth (not withstanding *Gray's Anatomy*, which notes that "occasionally there may be a hole in the middle line of the hard palate" (Scheaffer, 1993, p.21).

Thus there are growing numbers of people who are seeking counsel with mainstream therapists, and occasionally with lawyers, as they begin to question the veracity of various "recovered memories." These people report that they have been treated by therapists with credentials ranging from doctoral degrees in medicine and psychology, master's degrees in marriage, family and child therapy, or in social work, to "alchemical hypnotherapists." Many therapists advertise in California publications pronouncing that through trance states a patient can experience past lives and be transformed. The recovered memory therapists are involved in recovering memories from one's family, the family's satanic cult, past lives, UFO abductions, and entities' possession. History revisions and the creation of narratives are being reported based on these influenced experiences. Again let it be noted that there are a myriad of ethical, conscientious psychotherapists who are not being spoken of here, for this presentation is about therapists' fads and foibles.

WHY NOW?

The past five decades have seen the rise of etiologically based theories of psychotherapy. At the same time, there have been advances in rehabilitative therapy and undreamed-of progress in medication for certain mental–emotional conditions. Also there has been a proliferation of therapists in the United States—the American Psychological Association with 130,000 members, the American Psychiatric Association with 34,000 members. California's Board of Behavioral Science Examiners reports that as of July 1993, in that state licenses were held by approximately 36,000 marriage, family, and child counselors (a master's level requirement); 16,000 clinical social workers (a master's level requirement); and approximately 11,000 psychologists (a doctoral level requirement). There are approximately 3000 psychiatrists in the state. These figures do not include psychological assistants or licensed hypnotists.

Add to this the number who are licensed or who belong to professional organizations, the countless nonprofessional counselors, psychological assistants, and graduate students in training placements across the United States, and you will see that the number dispensing "psychotherapy" becomes awesome. Some states have license and credential criteria; others do not. Even with licensing, particular types of psychotherapy are not regulated. Thus, it is easy to see that quality control in therapy is not easy. There are diverse theories of personality development, and even more theories of therapy. The science of psychotherapy is primitive compared to the offerings of surgeons, orthopedists, veterinarians, optometrists, dentists, and so forth, whose practices are built upon far more standard, scientifically based theories.

For some time the extensive number of therapies a consumer can purchase has been noted. Herink's (1980) guide listed over 250 different psychotherapies. Rudestam (1982) limited his book to experiential group therapies, classifying dozens of variants into eleven categories. O'Brien and Woody (1989, p. 1568), referring to "talking treatment in which a trained person deliberately establishes a professional relationship with a patient for the purpose of relieving symptoms," estimated that over 100 different types of this talking treatment exist.

Goleman (1980) summarized the status of psychotherapy in a way that seems applicable now: "Since there is no quality control built into the therapeutic process, the best advice is that the buyer beware, or at least be informed." However, to become informed is a formidable task.

REFERENCES

Baker, R.A. (1988). The aliens among us: Hypnotic regression revisited. *Skeptical Inquirer, 12,*(2) 147–162.

Baker, R.A. (1991). The current status of psychotherapy. *Skeptical Inquirer, 15,*(4), 407–412.

Campbell, T.W. (1992). Therapeutic relationships and iatrogenic outcomes: The blame-and-change maneuver in psychotherapy. *Psychotherapy, 29,* 474–480.

Casriel, D. (1963). *So fair a house: The story of Synanon.* Englewood Cliffs, NJ: Prentice-Hall.

Casriel, D. (1980). New identity process. In R. Herink (Ed.), *The psychotherapy handbook.* New York: New American Library.

Clinical Psychiatry News. (1993). American Medical Association House of Delegates.

Common Ground. (1993). Resources for personal transformation. San Anselmo, California.

Cummins, R.A., & Prior, M.P. (1992). Autism and assisted communication: A response to Biklen. *Harvard Education Review, 62,* 228–241.

Dillon, K.M. (1993). Facilitated communication, autism and ouija. *Skeptical Inquirer, 17,* 281–287.

Doheny, K. (1988). Self help. *Los Angeles Times,* October 2, Part VI, 1.

Finkelstein, P., Wenergrat, B., & Yalom, I. (1982). Large group awareness training. *Annual Review of Psychology, 33.*

Gambrill, E. (1990). *Critical thinking in clinical practice: Improving the accuracy of judgments and decisions about clients.* San Francisco: Jossey-Bass.

Gambrill, E. (1992). Self-help books: Pseudoscience in the guise of science? *Skeptical Inquirer, 16,* 389–399.

Goleman, D. (1980). Forward. In R. Herink (Ed.), *The psychotherapy handbook.* New York: New American Library.

Guze, S. B. (1992). *Why psychiatry is a branch of medicine.* New York: Oxford University Press.

Hammond, C. (1992). *Satanic ritual abuse.* Taped lecture, June, 1992, Arlington, VA: Audio Transcripts.

Herink, R. (1980). *The psychotherapy handbook.* New York: New American Library.

Hoffman, R. (1976). *Getting divorced from mom and dad.* New York: E.P. Dutton.

Hopkins, B., Jacobs, D.M., & Westrum, R. (1992). *The UFO syndrome report*. Las Vegas, NV: Bigelow Holding Corporation.

Janov, A. (1970). *The primal scream*. New York: G.P. Putnam's Sons.

Loftus, E. and Ketcham, K. (1994). *The myth of repressed memory*. New York: St. Martins Press.

McHugh, P.R. (1992). Psychiatric misadventures. *American Scholar*, Autumn, 497–510.

Mack, J.E. (1992). *Unusual personal experiences*. Las Vegas, NV: Roper/Bigelow.

Meyer, A. (1948–1952). *Collected papers of Adolf Meyer*. Baltimore: Johns Hopkins Press.

Mulhern, S. (1991). Satanism and psychotherapy: A rumor in search of an inquisition. In J.T. Richardson, J.M. Best, & D.G. Bromley (Eds.), *The satanism scare*, pp. 145–172. San Francisco: Aldine DeGruyter.

Myers, J.E.B. (1993). Facilitated communication discussion continues. *National Resource Center on Child Sexual Abuse News*, 2, 1, 3.

O'Brien, C.P., & Woody, G.E. (1989). Evaluation of psychotherapy. In H.I. Kaplan and B.J. Sadock (Eds.), *Comprehensive textbook of psychiatry*, pp. 1568–1573. Baltimore: Williams and Wilkins.

Ockerblom, J., & Sauer, M. (1993). Probe of 'ritual-abuse' therapy urged. *San Diego Union-Tribune*, January 18, pp. B4,10.

Ofshe, R., & Singer, M.T. (1994). Recovered memory therapies and robust repression: A collective error. *International Journal of Clinical and Experimental Hypnosis*.

Ofshe, R. and Watters, E. (1994). *Making monsters*. New York: Charles Scribner.

Orne, M.T., & Dinges, D.F. (1989). Hypnosis. In H.I. Kaplan & B.J. Sadock, (Eds.), *Comprehensive textbook of psychiatry* (5th ed.). Baltimore: Williams and Wilkens.

Orne, M.T., Whitehouse, W.G., Dinges, D.F., & Orne, E.C. (1988). Reconstructing memory through hypnosis: forensic and clinical implications. In H.M. Pettinati (Ed.), *Hypnosis and memory*, pp. 21–63. New York: Guilford Press.

Orr, L., & Ray, S. (1977). *Rebirthing in the New Age*. Millbrae, CA: Celestial Arts.

Pendergrast, M. (1996). *Victims of memory*, 2nd Ed. Hinesburg, VT: Upper Access, Inc.

Rimland, B. (1992). Facilitated communication: Now the bad news. *Autism Research Review International*, 6, 3.

Rudestam, K.E. (1982). *Experiential groups*. Monterey, CA: Brooks/Cole Publishing.

Saltzman, N. (1980). *How to do bio-scream psychotherapy*. (Audio casettes and booklet.) Saltzman: 25 East 86th St, Suite 13F, New York, NY, 10028.

Scheafer, R. (1993). Alien stigmata, sky craft and a UFO conference. *Skeptical Inquirer*, *18*(1), 21–23.

Schiff, J. (1970). *All my children*. New York: M. Evans.

Sechehaye, M. (1951). *The autobiography of a schizophrenic girl*. New York: Grune.

Singer, M. T. (1977) *Granny psychology or the Procrustean bed?* Unpublished address given to graduating class, California School of Professional Psychology, June 1977.

Singer, M.T., Lalich, J. (1996). *"Crazy" Therapies*. San Francisco: Jossey-Bass.

Spanos, N.P. Past-life hypnotic regression: A critical view. *Skeptical Inquirer*, *12*, 174–180.

Starker, S. (1988). Do-it-yourself therapy: The prescription of self-help books by psychologists. *Psychotherapy*, *25*, 142–146.

Starker, S. (1989). *Oracle at the supermarket: The American preoccupation with self-help books*. New Brunswick, NJ: Transactions.

West, L.J., Singer, M.T. (1980). Cults, quacks and non-professional psychotherapies. In H.I. Kaplan, A.M. Freedman, & B.J. Sadock (Eds.), *Comprehensive textbook of psychiatry III*, pp. 3245–3257. Baltimore: Williams and Wilkins.

Williams, M.H. (1985). The bait-and-switch tactic in psychotherapy. *Psychotherapy*, *22*, 110–113.

Yalom, I. (1985). Group psychotherapy. *Annual Review, Psychiatry Update, Vol 5*, A. Francis & R. Hales (Eds.) Washington, D.C.: American Psychiatric Association.

Yapko, M.D. (1990). *Trancework: An introduction to the practice of clinical hypnosis* (2nd ed.). New York: Brunner/Mazel.

Yapko, M.D. (1992). Editor's viewpoint. *Milton H. Erickson Foundation Newsletter*, Autumn, p. 2.

Zweben, J.E. (1980). Fischer-Hoffman process. In R. Herink (Ed.), *The psychotherapy handbook*. New York: New American Library.

Yapko, M.D. (1994). *Suggestions of abuse*. New York: Simon & Shuster.